IN FOCUS

BRAZIL

A Guide to the People, Politics and Culture

Jan Rocha

LATIN AMERICA BUREAU

INTERLINK BOOKS
NEW YORK

© 1997   Jan Rocha.   All rights reserved.
First published in 1997

In the U.S.:

Interlink Books
An imprint of Interlink Publishing Group, Inc.
99 Seventh Avenue, Brooklyn, New York 11215

Library of Congress Cataloging-in-Publication Data

Rocha, Jan.
  Brazil in focus: a guide to the people, politics and culture /
by Jan Rocha
    p. cm. (The in focus guides)
    Includes bibliographical references and index.
    ISBN 1-56656-261-9 (pbk.)
    1. Brazil - Guidebooks. 2. Brazil - Civilization. I. Title
II. Series: In focus (New York, N.Y.)
F2509.5.R63   1997
918.104'64-dc21   97-9939
                                              CIP

In the U.K.:

Latin America Bureau (Research and Action) Ltd,
1 Amwell Street, London EC1R 1UL

The Latin America Bureau is an independent research and publishing
organization. It works to broaden public understanding of issues of
human rights and social and economic justice in Latin America and the
Caribbean.

A CIP catalogue record for this book is available from the British Library

ISBN: 1 899365 00 1

Editing: Duncan Green
Cover photograph: Tony Morrison/South American Pictures
Cover design: Andy Dark
Design: Liz Morrell
Cartography: Royal Tropical Institute, The Netherlands and the Drawing
Office, Department of Geography, University of London

Already published in the *In Focus* series: Argentina, Bolivia, Colombia, Cuba, Eastern Caribbean, Ecuador, Jamaica, Mexico, Venezuela

Printed and bound in Korea

CONTENTS

INTRODUCTION

"Next stop, Paradise", barks a matter-of-fact voice over the intercom of the train on the São Paulo Underground. Nowadays Paradise is just a rather dingy district of downtown São Paulo, a station on the North-South Metro line, but when the first explorers reached Brazil five hundred years ago, they thought it was the real thing. They found friendly, beautiful natives, an abundance of fruit and fertile soil. Travelers ever since have marveled at the beauty of Rio de Janeiro, gazed in awe at the vastness of the Amazon river and delighted in the palm-fringed beaches of the Northeast.

Few other countries are as close to being an earthly paradise, yet for millions of Brazilians life in the land of plenty means a struggle for survival. One of the six largest countries in the world, Brazil is blessed with millions of acres of fertile land, hundreds of rushing rivers, minerals of every sort, and is free of natural disasters like earthquakes or hurricanes. Yet millions live in overcrowded fetid slums, squeezed into the unwanted spaces of the big cities – under bridges, clinging to steep hillsides, on the banks of sewage-choked streams, next to rubbish dumps, or in daily fear of floods and mud-slides.

The gap between rich and poor is the widest on earth, with the wealthiest one per cent earning more than the poorest fifty per cent. Brazil is a land of baffling paradoxes. It is free of the religious, racial, or ethnic divisions that have brought civil war to other countries, yet violence is the major cause of death among young males. In the last twenty years, over a thousand trade unionists, religious workers, rights activists, and indigenous leaders have been assassinated for political reasons. It is a major world food producer, but millions of its own people go hungry. It covers an area of 3.3 million square miles, yet two-thirds of the population of 156 million live in towns and cities. It has the tenth largest economy but social indicators comparable with some of the poorest countries in the world. Economically dynamic, socially Brazil stagnates.

The explanation for these riddles lies in Brazil's history. Slavery lasted longer and was more widespread than in any other country of the Western Hemisphere. It was only abolished just over 100 years ago. The attitudes that went with slavery grew so deeply entrenched that they still influence the mentality of today's Brazilians. Brazil never had a political or cultural revolution, or any violent rupture of the status quo. Slavery was abolished, but what took its place was not equality and fraternity, but an unofficial system of first- and second-class citizenship, a social apartheid more difficult to fight than any official system of discrimination. Parts of Brazil are as modern as anywhere in the industrialized world, but life for many Brazilians is still rooted in the past.

1   HISTORY

Exploring the unknown world in their cramped craft, the Portuguese navigators were the astronauts of the fifteenth century. At Sagres, a medieval NASA built on the westernmost tip of Portugal, they perfected new navigation instruments, developed modern map-making, and calculated the circumference of the world, when officially it was still flat. In the medieval spice race, Portugal and Spain competed to find new, faster routes to the Indies, pushing back the frontiers of the known world. The monotonous European diet craved spices – pepper, nutmeg, cloves, and cinnamon – not only for their flavor, but because they were invaluable for preserving meat during the winter. Tea, sugar, chocolate, potatoes, and coffee were still unknown.

In 1500 a fleet of Portuguese ships on its way to the East round the Cape of Good Hope, commanded by Pedro Alvares Cabral, was blown off course and sighted land: by accident, Europe had "discovered" Brazil. Baptized the "Land of the True Cross" (Terra da Vera Cruz), the new land at first seemed disappointing: no gold or silver in sight, just lots of friendly natives, fruit, and forests. The only commercially viable product was a reddish wood. Because of its color they called it cinderwood, *pau brasa*, and so the new land became Brasil (in Portuguese), or Brazil (in English). A few trading posts were set up, but it was an inauspicious beginning to a country which would eventually supply the gold to finance Britain's Industrial Revolution, the rubber that made possible the motorcar, and which would feed the world with sugar and coffee. Brazilwood quickly gave way to sugar. Sugar plantations needed labor but the Indians who had welcomed the white man to their land were hunters and gatherers and resisted recruitment. Peaceful co-existence was over.

Indians and Slaves

Slaving expeditions were organized, and the hunters became the hunted. Nobody really knows how many million Indians there were when the Europeans arrived, but today there are just over 300,000 left. The Catholic missionaries who had come with the Portuguese explorers and settlers had a problem. Could the Indians be enslaved if they had souls? Did they have souls if they worshiped pagan gods and lived as primitives? The Jesuits decided that Indians did have souls and set about converting them, gathering thousands of Guarani Indians into fortified settlements known as "reductions." The Indians worked the land, became literate, studied music and learnt crafts. But the plantation owners needed slaves, not musicians, and the reductions were regularly raided and destroyed.

By claiming that Indians had souls, the Jesuits became an embarrassment, standing in the way of development. Accused of setting up a state within the state, in 1759 they were expelled from Brazil by the Portuguese Crown, as they had been from the Spanish-speaking colonies. Priests in chains were shipped back to Europe and the first of Latin America's many attempts at building Utopia ended in flames. The slavers became Brazil's first explorers, sailing thousands of miles upriver in search of Indians and gold. They became known as *bandeirantes,* because they carried the flags (*bandeiras*) of their patrons on their expeditions. They were a bloodthirsty lot, killing and enslaving wherever they went – one boasted of possessing 30,000 dried human ears. Nevertheless, the word "bandeirante" has heroic associations today, especially in São Paulo, whose early development was based on their activities.

By the seventeenth century, Brazil was Europe's leading sugar supplier and Portugal's most important colony. To meet the need for labor, slave ships brought Africans in ever increasing numbers. One historian calculates that forty per cent of the estimated 9,500,000 slaves transported to the New World went to Brazil. Others believe that up to 13 million men, women, and children were imported during slavery's 350-year reign in Brazil, before abolition in 1888. They were counted not as individuals, but as merchandise, by weight, and referred to as *"peças,"* pieces. Many years later the Nazis also referred to their Jewish prisoners loaded into cattle wagons for transport to the death camps as *stucken,* pieces.

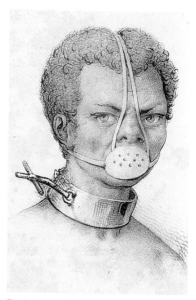

Brazil imported six times more Africans than the United States, double the number that went to the Spanish colonies or the British West Indies. Originally intended for the sugar plantations, they ended up wherever there was economic activity. For four centuries, Brazil's immense wealth was accumulated by the work of slaves. They cut cane, panned for gold, and picked cotton and coffee. They were porters for the bandeirantes and tilled fields for priests and monks. In the towns, they worked as cooks, house servants, nursemaids, street sellers, sedan chair carriers, water carriers, and laborers. Slaves were the hands and the feet of their masters. With Indians, they made up the bulk of the army in Brazil's war against Paraguay in 1865.

On arrival from Africa, people from the same tribe were separated to make rebellion difficult. They spoke different languages, they came from

Punishment of a slave

Slaves on a coffee-plantation

different regions, they had different customs, but they were united by their suffering and in their revolt at the inhuman conditions to which they were subjected. The average life span of a plantation slave was between seven and eight years. Many came with trades: they were artisans, goldsmiths, silversmiths, blacksmiths. In the gold region of Minas Gerais, they built the baroque churches that still stand today. "The Brazilian dream was to have one or two slaves whose labor could be hired out for a price high enough to free the dreamer from ever having to work. Begging was preferable to work. Even beggars had slaves," wrote Pedro I, Brazil's first post-independence ruler.

Clovis Moura, a black sociologist, believes that slavery became the blueprint for Brazilian society. It provided the dominant ethos, laid the foundations for economic inequality and exploitation, and influenced the way institutions, groups, and classes developed after abolition.

Slave Rebellion

Generations of Brazilian schoolchildren studied history books that omitted a whole side of slavery – the many revolts, rebellions and uprisings and the existence of the *quilombos*. Free territories set up by groups of runaway slaves, the quilombos took root all over Brazil. Their direct descendants can still be found in remote villages today, using the odd word of Bantu or Nagô. The runaways defended themselves from attacks and raided plantations, stealing food and killing the owners.

Zumbi and Palmares

The most famous and longest surviving quilombo was the Republic of Palmares, which lasted from 1630-1695, with up to 30,000 people in dozens of villages scattered over an area of 17,000 square miles in what is now the state of Alagoas. Even Indians and poor whites came to join the runaway slaves. Plantations and villages were raided for women, but the sexual imbalance was so great that polyandry became the custom, each woman having up to five husbands. Palmares developed its own language, a mixture of Bantu and Portuguese. The ex-slaves fed themselves by hunting, fishing, and farming, made pottery and baskets, wove clothes and forged iron. They made musical instruments and weapons with which to defend themselves. For a few years, solidarity, equality, and cooperation replaced the degradation and exploitation of the plantations.

But for Brazil's rulers, Palmares was diabolical and dangerous, a permanent incentive to revolt which had to be destroyed and its memory erased. Supported by the Church and the plantation owners, they organized armies of bandeirantes, mercenaries, and criminals to do the job. In 1695, after several expeditions, Palmares was finally overrun. All the inhabitants were killed or enslaved, and the severed head of Zumbi, its legendary leader, was put on display to terrorize black Brazilians, who had come to believe that he was immortal.

In a way he was. Three hundred years later, Zumbi is officially a national hero and Brazil's rulers make pilgrimages to the site of Palmares. Even after the most famous quilombo was destroyed, slaves continued to escape. In 1741 the King of Portugal ordered all runaways to be branded with the letter F for *Fujão* (runaway). Nineteenth century newspapers carried columns of "wanted" advertisements for runaway slaves which convey an idea of the treatment they were fleeing from. The *Diário de Pernambuco* of May 23, 1839 offered a reward for a runaway called Joana, who had "burn marks on her breasts and few front teeth." In 1870 the same paper was looking for a slave called Germano, aged 17 or 18, "with a sad look, big feet, long legs and marks of recent punishment on his buttocks."

Abolition

In 1850 the British banned the international slave trade and blockaded Brazilian ports, but slaves continued to be smuggled in. Inside Brazil, the abolition campaign was gathering momentum, but slaves were not finally freed until 1888. By then only five per cent of the 14 million Brazilians were slaves, down from a third in 1850, due to European immigration and the release of slaves prior to abolition.

Slave owners had predicted disaster when the traffic ended, but instead the end of investment in human suffering freed capital for investment in infrastructure and encouraged the immigration of free workers. While slaves had been captive, land was free to anyone who occupied it; once they were free, land had to be paid for. After abolition, some slaves were kept on by their former masters as employees, but many were abandoned, without money, jobs, land, or homes. A new vagrancy law was enacted, making anyone without a fixed address and work liable to arrest. The law is still on the statute books.

Independence

One of the reasons slavery lasted longer in Brazil than anywhere else in the Americas was the survival of the monarchy. Long after all the other colonies of Latin America had become republics, Brazil was ruled by an Emperor. The American War of Independence and the French Revolution had been over for a century when Brazil finally became a republic in 1889. The delay was not for want of trying. Like the Americans, Brazilians objected to the taxes imposed by Lisbon and resented the ban on any industry or indeed learning in Portugal's richest colony. Printing presses, bookstores, universities, and foreign newspapers were all forbidden.

Tiradentes

In 1792 the small town of Vila Rica, now known as Ouro Preto, was the center of Brazil's lucrative gold industry. There, a group of prominent citizens, including lawyers, a priest, and landowners, began plotting for independence. They rejected Portuguese taxes and demanded the right to build factories, universities, and steel mills. The rebels even sent emissaries to ask the newly independent USA's Thomas Jefferson for military aid in exchange for future trade preferences.

The conspiracy foundered when they were betrayed and arrested, and the Crown decided to make an example of one of them. A young military officer called Joaquim José da Silva Xavier, better known as Tiradentes, the Toothpuller, was hung, drawn, and quartered and his descendants officially cursed (only recently was the curse withdrawn). While his fellow conspirators are forgotten, Tiradentes is now Brazil's national hero. He was also the only one of the rebel band who thought that independence should also mean an end to slavery. Six years after his death, inspired by the successful slave rebellion in Haiti as well as the French Revolution, slaves in Salvador staged an uprising which failed. After that, none of the many rebellions against the Portuguese and the Brazilian monarchy ever seriously threatened royal rule.

Dom Pedro I, the first emperor
of independent Brazil

*Courtesy of South
American Pictures*

Royal Independence

Instead it fell to Napoleon to consolidate Brazil's unique variety of royal independence. To escape from his triumphant advance through the Iberian Peninsula in 1808, the entire Royal Portuguese Court of 15,000 people fled to Brazil aboard a fleet of ships, led by King João VI. Suddenly Brazil was no longer a distant colony, but the center of the Portuguese empire. All around Brazil, the Spanish colonies were fighting for independence, but the presence of the monarchy gave Brazil metropolitan status, allowing it to trade directly with other countries.

When the Napoleonic Wars were over and the King returned to Lisbon in 1821, the Portuguese tried unsuccessfully to turn the clock back and return their richest possession to colonial status. Left behind as regent, the King's son, Pedro, soon realized that his best move was to lead the burgeoning movement for independence, rather than oppose it. Instead of the bloody warfare that ravaged the other Latin American countries, Brazil, so the story goes, became independent in 1822 with a single shout – the *Grito do Ipiranga*, the river where Pedro allegedly yelled his melodramatic "Independence or Death."

The monarchy lasted another 67 years. Acting as a focus for loyalty and political unity, it prevented the vast country, which shared borders with ten other colonies, ex-colonies, and independent states, from breaking up. It also enabled an aristocratic white class to prolong its rule over a slave society. Brazil was free from Portugal, but most Brazilians had yet to become free citizens. Pedro I's son, Pedro II, did not see why slavery should be abolished, even though he championed the latest technological inventions. Under his rule, Brazil became the second country after England to introduce postage stamps. The Emperor was the first Brazilian to have a telephone installed, and encouraged the spread of the railways. Brazil was modernizing, but slavery continued.

The Republic

By the 1880s, coffee had long surpassed sugar and gold as Brazil's most important product, and the São Paulo coffee planters had become the most powerful political and economic group in the country. They wanted a republic, and once slavery was gone, pressure grew to abolish another anachronism (the monarchy). The Republican movement found allies among military officers who had served in the war against Paraguay and were discontent with government policy. On November 15, 1889 "in the name of the people, the army, and the navy," Emperor Pedro II was deposed and given 24 hours to leave the country, and a provisional republic, headed by Marshal Deodoro da Fonseca, a war hero, was installed. Church and state were separated and the Republic of Brazil was formally created in February 1891 with a constitution drawn up by a Constituent Assembly. With the monarchy went the Catholic Church's status as the official religion. The republicans turned instead to positivism, preferring scientific rationalism to religious belief. The country's new flag, with its motto "Order and Progress," was inspired by the new thinking.

Antônio the Counselor

The monarchy had gone, southern cities now had gas lighting, telephones, and electric trams, but in the Northeast, the home of Brazil's first cycle of sugar wealth, little had changed. Landowners were authoritarian patriarchs, some of them despots, and most of the population lived in extreme poverty, worsened by a devastating drought in 1877. Thousands emigrated to the Amazon, where the rubber boom was in full swing, or to the south. Those who stayed, starved.

Without help from the government, the landowners, or the Church, people turned to mysticism. They began to follow a man with a flowing beard and rough robes who roamed the *sertão* (drylands) preaching that the end of the world would come in the year 1900. Hundreds, then thousands, flocked to hear the charismatic Antônio Maciel, who became known as the *Conselheiro* (Counselor). What began as a religious movement developed into a challenge to the existing social and political system of the Northeast.

The Conselheiro talked about the need for a better life in the here and now. He protested by tearing down the public notices announcing tax increases. The Church declared him a subversive, while the state governor wanted him locked up in a mental asylum. As thousands abandoned their homes to follow the preacher, landowners feared a labor shortage. In 1893 the band was attacked by soldiers and the Counselor realized he must find a sanctuary. Like an Old Testament prophet, he led his followers on a five-week march into the sertão until they came to an isolated valley surrounded by five mountain ranges. Within two years, the city of Canudos founded by the Counselor and his followers had become one of the largest towns in Bahia, boasting 20,000 inhabitants, two churches, and a thriving economy which even exported goatskins to Europe.

Visitors reported in wonder, "there are neither rich or poor, the land belongs to all, there is no hunger or misery, no money, no police or thieves, no locks on doors, no brothels, no alcohol, everyone is happy in a big brotherhood." A five-hour working day left time for prayers and leisure. There were schools for the children. The Counselor had modeled Canudos on Thomas More's *Utopia*, which he had read.

But there was no place for Utopia in the Brazilian Northeast. By offering the example of a successful but egalitarian society, Canudos threatened the existing system of exploitation, hunger, ignorance, and wealth for the few. Like Palmares before it, Canudos had to be destroyed, before the example could spread. In Rio de Janeiro, the capital, Canudos was used as an excuse by the military to attack the remaining monarchists. The Counselor and his followers were portrayed as a bunch of dangerous fanatics, plotting to overthrow the republic and restore the monarchy, helped by foreign military advisers.

Yet the apparently easy task of wiping out a backlands rebellion turned instead into the Brazilian army's biggest and bloodiest campaign since the war against Paraguay, twenty years earlier. The men and women of Canudos resisted with improvised guerrilla tactics and rustic weapons, harassing the soldiers as they approached the town through the canyons and hills. It took four military expeditions over a year to overrun Utopia, costing the lives of nearly ten thousand men.

The End of Canudos

The final, victorious expedition in 1897 brought together ten thousand soldiers drawn from eleven different states, and 19 heavy cannon. As they advanced through the dry inhospitable *sertão*, they passed the skeletons of soldiers from the previous expeditions. Twelve days before the final attack, the Counselor died. Once the government troops had taken the city, after fierce hand-to-hand fighting, they set fire to it, killed most of the survivors, and handed out the children as booty. Many ended up as prostitutes. For the Counselor's followers, the end of the world had come three years early. The Counselor's body was disinterred and his head cut off and examined unsuccessfully for signs of madness.

The battle for Canudos was reported in Europe, where *The Times* of London named him "the Backlands Messiah," and criticized the manipulation of the uprising to attack monarchists. Official Brazilian history labeled

Canudos a story of religious fanaticism, and in his book *Os Sertões,* which became a classic, journalist Euclides da Cunha attributed the movement to madness brought on by racial mixing. A twelve mile-long dam now covers the ruins of the town. Beside it is a new town, Nova Canudos, which exhibits the same misery, backwardness, and ignorance that led to the founding of Canudos a hundred years ago. Today the Northeast still has the worst inequality, illiteracy, and hunger in Brazil.

The Rubber Boom

Thousands of miles west of Canudos, the need for rubber to make pneumatic tires for Europe and America's newly invented motorcars was making fortunes in the Amazon rainforest. English and American companies set up trading posts along the rivers, enlisting Indians to collect the rubber in a system of virtual slavery. The Amazon capital Manaus, a small settlement on the edge of the river, flourished. Solid European-style buildings and an extravagantly beautiful opera house appeared among the huts and boats. Famous opera stars traveled across the Atlantic and a thousand miles upriver to sing there. The sidewalk around the opera house was paved with rubber tiles to muffle the sound of the horses' hooves as the carriages drew up. The rich sent their laundry to Paris, while ships brought back German sausages, hats from Paris, and Polish prostitutes.

The boom lasted until 1912, when cheaper rubber grown from thousands of saplings smuggled out of the Amazon to Kew Gardens by an Englishman called Wickham Steed began to inundate the market. Malaya, where the saplings had flourished, soon dominated the world market and Manaus sank back into torpor. Millions of dollars had been earned by the rubber barons at the cost of thousands of Indian lives, but little had changed.

Supplying rubber for the West's vehicles was not Brazil's only contribution to advancing technology. Competing with the Wright brothers, Alberto Santos Dumont made the first registered flight in a heavier-than-air machine in Paris in 1906. He also invented the wristwatch to keep his hands free for flying. Years later he committed suicide, grieved by the use of his invention for making war.

Traditional rubber processing in the Amazon
Mary Evans Picture Library

European Immigration

Exports of coffee and other agricultural products still dominated the Brazilian economy in the first few decades of the twentieth century, but coffee wealth had stimulated industry and thousands of factories were opening, attracting a flood of immigrants. Between 1888, when slaves were freed, and 1928, 3.5 million people arrived in Brazil, principally Italians, Portuguese, Spanish, Germans, and Japanese. The new expanding urban classes had more in common with their counterparts in Europe and North America than with the landowners and the dirt-poor peasantry of the countryside. Italian and Spanish anarchists soon dominated the factories and led the first strikes for better conditions, but failed to threaten the rural elites who still controlled political power.

The Prestes Column

After overthrowing the monarchy, the military was impatient for change. In 1924 an army officer named Luis Carlos Prestes led a rebellion against the federal government, demanding social and economic reforms. The rebels marched through the backlands of Brazil, attacking and occupying towns, traveling over 15,000 miles in three years. The 1500 men who began the march were devastated by cholera and eventually sought exile in Bolivia. Prestes later became Secretary General of the Brazilian Communist Party (PCB), after spending three years in Moscow. In the 1930s he was imprisoned for nine years while his wife, Olga Benário, a German Jew, was deported back to die in Ravensbruck concentration camp.

Getúlio Vargas

The unbroken rule of the rural oligarchies of São Paulo and Minas Gerais, known as the coffee-with-milk alliance because of their respective products, was finally overthrown by a man from the southern state of Rio Grande do Sul in 1930. When Getúlio Vargas' troops tethered their horses to the monuments of São Paulo and Rio, they opened a new chapter in Brazilian history.

A former deputy, minister, and governor, in Rio Grande do Sul, Vargas ruled for fifteen years, first as constitutional president, then as dictator, following a failed Communist uprising by military officers in 1937. His "New State," inspired by Italian Fascism, lasted until the end of the Second World War. Vargas reorganized the trade unions along corporatist lines, run by men hand-picked to collaborate with the government. Strikes were banned but working conditions were improved, and labor rights introduced, including the minimum wage.

The Fascist influence of the time is still visible in Brazil, not only in the structure of the trade unions, but in some of its public buildings. In the Governor's Palace in João Pessoa, capital of Paraíba state, the ornamental tiled floor incorporates a swastika design.

Getúlio Vargas   *AP*

The Second World War

After 1937 Vargas stamped out opposition, closed Congress, and political prisoners were routinely tortured by his dreaded head of secret police, Filinto Muller. For the first three years of the Second World War Brazil maintained relations with the Axis powers, but in 1942 U.S. economic pressure forced Vargas to allow Allied air bases on the northeast coast, the nearest point to Africa. In retaliation, German submarines attacked Brazilian merchant ships off the coast, killing over 600 people. Brazil declared war on Germany and sent a contingent of 25,000 men to fight with the Allies in the invasion of Italy in 1944, the only Latin American country to do so.

In the Amazon, 30,000 tappers recruited in the Northeast temporarily revived the dying rubber industry to supply the Allies, cut off from their Asian plantations by the Japanese invasion of Malaya. Dumped in the rainforest, thousands of the northeasterners died from malaria, attacks by wild animals, and hunger. In exchange for Brazilian collaboration and raw materials, the U.S. financed the infant steel industry and by the 1950s industry had overtaken agriculture in economic importance.

Vargas invested in infrastructure and accelerated Brazil's industrialization by establishing powerful state companies. Brazil soon ceased to be a predominantly rural country, as a massive migration began from the countryside to the cities. By the 1980s, three-quarters of the population was living in urban areas.

The post-war clamor for democracy reached Brazil and Vargas had to resign, only to return as elected president in 1950. In his second term in office, Vargas continued to invest in infrastructure and industrialization and widened workers" benefits. In response to nationalist demands, he created the state oil company Petrobras, earning the hostility of the conservative establishment and the Americans. Under political and economic pressure and facing a hostile press and Congress, Vargas, once the all-powerful dictator, felt isolated.

Putting Brazil on the Map

In 1954 he committed suicide, setting off a turbulent period of forty years during which only one elected president, Juscelino Kubitschek, elected to succeed Vargas in 1955, completed his term of office. Kubitschek, whose slogan was "fifty years in five," was an optimistic expansionist who believed in Brazil's destiny as a great country. In three years he built Brasília, a brand new capital set down in the flat empty plains of central Brazil, 700 miles inland from Rio and São Paulo. To finish it on time, bricks were flown in by the plane-load. Construction workers flocked to build Brasília from all over the country and stayed on to become the first inhabitants of the city, living in dormitory suburbs well out of sight of the impressive planned center.

Kubitschek also built the first road link to the Amazon, running from Brasília to Belém, and encouraged the multinational car industry to open factories in São Paulo. He put Brazil on the world map, at the cost of accelerating inflation. Kubitschek was succeeded in 1961 by Jânio Quadros, a charismatic but eccentric populist who mixed campaigns against bikinis and horse racing with a non-aligned foreign policy, decorating Che Guevara, then Cuban Minister of Industry, and supporting Fidel Castro when the U.S. launched the Bay of Pigs invasion in the same year.

Goulart Government

By now inflation was accelerating fast and, accused of planning a coup d'état against a hostile Congress, Quadros surprised everyone by resigning after only eight months in power, blaming "hidden forces" for his downfall. Conservative military officers tried to stop vice-president João Goulart, regarded as a leftist, from taking office, but Goulart's brother-in-law, Leonel Brizola, governor of the state of Rio Grande do Sul, led pressure for the constitution to be respected.

During Goulart's three-year government, Brazil became increasingly polarized between those who wanted radical reforms and those who wanted to uphold the status quo, rejecting reforms as communist-inspired. The Catholic Church was alarmed by what it perceived as the communist threat in the Northeast, where peasant leagues were demanding land reform. Washington shared its suspicions.

Role of the United States

The U.S. government had always reserved for itself the right to determine economic and political policy in its "backyard," Latin America, using a mixture of carrot and stick. After 1945 American policies in the hemisphere were dominated by the Cold War, and above all, after the Cuban Revolution of 1959, by the need to prevent "another Cuba." In 1961 President Kennedy launched the Alliance for Progress, an aid and development program designed to bind Latin American countries into an anti-communist chorus. Peace Corps volunteers were poured into Latin America – Brazil alone received over 600.

The U.S. also tried to stop the threatened nationalization of foreign companies, using a combination of open economic pressure (cutting credits and refusing to renegotiate foreign debt) and covert methods, such as financing local right-wing organizations. Washington wanted Brazil's agricultural policy to provide a market for U.S. farm equipment and U.S. exports like wheat and dairy products. Secretary of State John Foster Dulles is alleged to have once said, "Brazilian desires are secondary, though it is useful to pat them a bit and make them think that you are fond of them." When U.S. interests were threatened by a left-wing government and peasants began calling for land reform, the U.S. backed a military coup.

Military Dictatorship

The coup eventually came in 1964, when the army high command, supported by the conservative classes and backed by the U.S., overthrew Goulart. Once the generals were in command of the economy, they promoted the development of Brazilian industry behind high protectionist barriers, creating the so-called "tripod" of state, national and multinational companies which became the basis for Brazil's much-vaunted "economic miracle." To help the miracle along, unions were stifled, strikes banned, and wages reduced, while censorship banned any but favorable economic news.

For the U.S., Brazil under military rule became an important regional leader and ally in the Cold War. Relations later turned sour when President Jimmy Carter made human rights an issue, and Brazil began to seek a more independent trade policy, looking not only to Europe and Japan, but to the Third World for markets.

The avowed aim of what the generals christened the "Glorious Revolution" was to "restore democracy, reduce inflation, and end corruption." Instead, the long-lasting military regime shattered democratic organizations, fed corruption by introducing press censorship, and left behind, 21 years later, a huge, unpayable foreign debt. Unlike other military dictators, such as Chile's General Pinochet, or Paraguay's Alfredo Stroessner, the Brazilian generals stuck to four-year terms of office, succeeding each other in power.

During the dictatorship, over 20,000 Brazilians were imprisoned, most of them tortured, some were killed, and at least 150 prisoners "disappeared."

Military ceremony during the inauguration of a civilian president in 1985, ending twenty years of military rule

Julio Etchart/Reportage

Thousands more went into exile, including the current president, Fernando Henrique Cardoso, and several of his ministers.

Urban guerrilla groups appeared after Congress, unions, and every available democratic forum had been closed down by repression and censorship. After making an initial impact by hijacking planes, raiding banks, and kidnapping the American, German, and Swiss ambassadors and exchanging them for political prisoners, the groups were implacably hunted down and eliminated. When eighty guerrillas moved from the cities to the Araguaia region of the Amazon basin in 1972 to begin a Maoist-inspired revolution deep in the forest, they were soon discovered. Fifteen thousand soldiers were deployed in the region, peasant farmers were intimidated and tortured for information, and all the group was killed or captured.

Economic Miracle

Politically pacified, Brazil became the darling of foreign investors because of its "economic miracle," averaging over ten per cent growth rates every year between 1968 and 1973. The middle classes, beneficiaries of growing income inequality, had never had it so good, while the U.S. recognized Brazil as an emerging world power. "Where Brazil goes, there goes the rest of the hemisphere," President Nixon told one of the general-presidents,

Emilio Medici, in 1973. Between 1973 and 1980, Chile, Uruguay, Argentina, and Bolivia all suffered bloody military coups.

Brazil's military had a clear geopolitical plan to turn it into a world power, dominating Latin America and controlling the South Atlantic. The generals also intended to make Brazil a nuclear power, concluding a $10 billion nuclear cooperation agreement with West Germany in preference to signing the Nuclear Non-Proliferation Treaty.

The military planned massive relocations of the population to secure "empty" areas and to ease pressure for land reform. Displaced by dam-building and mechanization for export crops in the south and drought in the Northeast, hundreds of thousands of peasant farmers were encouraged to occupy the Amazon region or cross the border into the fertile lands of Paraguay. Armies of migrant laborers hired to build dams in the Amazon were subsequently left to become itinerant gold prospectors, polluting the rivers and invading Indian reserves.

By the time the military handed power back to a civilian government in 1985, the economy had grown to rank tenth in the world, but wages, health, and education levels had failed to keep up. The military regime left behind a more unequal, more corrupt society with weakened political institutions. A decade-long "safe, gradual" transition from military to civilian rule averted political upheaval or the trial of military personnel for human rights violations. Instead, many of the civilians who had served the regime without opposing its use of torture and repression remained in power.

2 SOCIETY

One hundred years after the end of slavery, Brazilian society is multiracial and complex, but remains hugely unequal. While some young Brazilians are at ease with cellphones and the Internet, others are being shot dead because they want land reform or because they live on the city streets. Most of the population live in towns and cities, but small groups of isolated Indians still wander in the Amazon rainforest.

Indians

Place names like Guanabara, Curitiba, and Cuiabá are a perpetual reminder of Brazil's original inhabitants. Brazilians with not a drop of indigenous blood boast Indian names like Iracema and Moacyr. Manioc flour and the guaraná drink are part of the national diet, and most fish, fruit, and fauna are known by their Indian names. Most people in the North and Northeast still sleep more comfortably in a hammock than a bed.

The Indians now number little more than 300,000, only 0.2 per cent of the total Brazilian population, divided into 200 different groups speaking 170 languages. Relations between the surviving indigenous groups and white society have fluctuated. During nationalist periods they have been romanticized as the most genuine of all Brazilians. In the nineteenth century this produced Brazil's only famous opera, *O Guarani*, by Carlos Gomes, and *Iracema*, a novel by José de Alencar that became a classic. More recently it led to a short-lived attempt to substitute Santa Claus with a home-grown alternative, "Papai Índio."

But in recent years the tide has turned against the Indians. Once the military regime began the drive to conquer the Amazon in the 1970s, Indian communities again came to be seen as obstacles to progress, development, and wealth. Roads were deliberately driven through reserves, spreading disease and introducing alcohol and prostitution. In 1974 the Indians began to fight back. Despite speaking different languages and coming from villages all over Brazil, they found they had something in common: the need to stop their land being invaded by whites.

Land Conflicts

Demarcation was the answer. If indigenous areas were clearly marked out and their boundaries officially recognized, then it would be easier to defend them. But the process has been slow and invasions have continued. In the Greater Amazon region, the Xavantes lost their land to the Italian company

Yanomami Indian family with malaria, being flown to a mission hospital. The disease was introduced by gold prospectors, who invaded their lands

Julio Etchart/ Reportage

Liquigas; the Waimiri Atroari saw part of their reserve flooded by the Balbina dam and now a road is being driven through it by the army, and the Parakanâ were first moved to make way for the Transamazon Highway and then for the Tucuruí dam. The Nambiquara were displaced by ranches and then by the Cuiabá to Santarém highway, the uru-Weu-Wau-Wau and the Zorro were in the way of the World Bank-funded Polonoroeste road and development project.

Invasion and land feuds have brought violence in their wake. In 1988, fourteen Ticuna were murdered by loggers; in 1993, sixteen Yanomami were shot dead by gold prospectors. Individual Indian leaders and several missionaries who worked with Indians have been murdered.

Yanomami

Most of Brazil's indigenous groups have had contact with surrounding society, sometimes over centuries, but there are still small groups of "isolated Indians," glimpsed in remote corners of the Amazon rainforest. In the Northern Amazon live the Yanomami, numbering about 9,000, the last large group of relatively isolated Indians in the Americas. Another 12,000 live over the border in Venezuela. In their communal huts deep in the forest, most Yanomami still live a nomadic, stone age existence, but in 1990 thousands of *garimpeiros* (wildcat gold prospectors), supplied and supported by local businessmen and politicians, began invading their gold-rich territory.

Periodically, when international pressure from environmentalists and development agencies becomes intense, the federal government intervenes to expel the gold miners, but they always return, with devastating results. Over the years at least 1500 Yanomami have succumbed to malaria, TB, influenza, and other diseases to which they have no resistance. Some have been shot dead during clashes. Unable to find fish and game because of the noise and pollution of the rivers, many Yanomami have also died from malnutrition.

Government Policy

In 1996 a change in Indian land rights legislation permitted any person, company, or local authority to lay claim to part of a reserve, if they could come up with documents proving it was theirs. A government memo admitted that the aim was to open the way for economic development "in the areas where most indigenous peoples live" – the Amazon basin.

The change was condemned by everyone from the European Parliament to the Indians themselves, who said it would endanger their lives. An eloquent example of what happens to tribes crowded into smaller and smaller reserves and forced to work in hostile surroundings comes from the Kaiowa Indians in Mato Grosso do Sul. Over the last five years, 250 have committed suicide, most of them teenagers who worked in the local sugar-cane alcohol distilleries.

The National Indian Foundation, FUNAI, the government agency responsible for Brazil's Indians, has a checkered history. Many FUNAI workers have been brave, dedicated people, some giving their lives to protect the Indians. But the agency has become associated with corruption, inefficiency, and a chronic lack of funds. Set up as a guardian of Indian interests, FUNAI officials have all too often conspired against them, in return for bribes from the loggers, ranchers, and garimpeiros. Some Indian groups, too, have allowed loggers and garimpeiros onto their reserves in exchange for pitiable rewards of food, vehicles, or money.

Brazilian law, based on the positivist idea that one nation corresponds to one territory ruled by a single, monolithic state, does not accept the idea of a pluri-ethnic or multi-nation state. Successive governments have tried to integrate Indians into Brazilian society as individuals, effectively denying them any right to communal land or reserves.

The Indians are fighting for their right to be different with growing sophistication. Their organizations, both national and regional, hold regular assemblies, organize protests and demonstrations, and increasingly collabo-

Luiza Erundina, former
mayor of São Paulo

*Julio Etchart/
Reportage*

rate with other popular movements like the *sem terra* (landless peasants) who fight for land.

Women

The only women mentioned in Brazilian history books are queens, princesses, or mistresses. *Machismo* is still enshrined in Brazilian law: whereas a woman can be sent to prison for three years for having an abortion, and adultery is still a crime, rape is treated, not as an act of violence, but as a "crime against custom." Betrayed husbands still use "honor" as a defense for murdering their wives. But in other ways women's rights have advanced in the last ten years, since the 1988 constitution introduced equal rights and obligations for men and women, bringing Brazil into line with the most advanced European countries.

Women and Power

Twenty per cent of households are now headed by women, and more women have paid jobs than in any other Latin American country. In the professions, Brazilian women are everywhere. More women than men graduate from university; two-thirds of medical graduates and nearly half the law graduates are women. Even in engineering, a traditionally male career, a fifth of the graduates are now women. Pay has yet to catch up, however. Women still earn, on average, only just over half as much as men for doing the same job.

The Supreme Court is still all-male, but lower down the judicial pecking order, women judges have made most of the courageous decisions in recent legal history. Judge Denise Frossard became famous overnight for taking on the previously untouchable Rio gambling mafia and sentencing fourteen of their most notorious leaders to six years in jail. In politics, power remains firmly in male hands, with only a handful of women ministers, senators, and national deputies.

Outside Congress, 171 of Brazil's 5,000 towns and cities are now run by women. Between 1988 and 1992 the mayor of São Paulo, South America's largest city, was the Workers Party (PT)'s Luiza Erundina de Souza. Brazil's first-ever woman governor, the Liberal Front (PFL)'s Roseana Sarney, was elected for Maranhão in 1994. Two of the current five women senators overcame immense handicaps to get there. The triumphant progress of Benedita da Silva, a black Rio shanty-town dweller and former maid, has been an inspiration to many other black women. From the opposite end of the country 37-year-old Marina da Silva, a rubber-tapper's daughter who learnt to read and write when she was 14, and now has a university degree, provides another example of amazing perseverance. Both women belong to the PT.

Contraception and Fertility

Although women's groups have mushroomed, issues like contraception, abortion, and sterilization remain almost taboo in the press, largely thanks to the continuing influence of the conservative sector of the Catholic Church. The tradition of not allowing women to decide their own affairs goes back a long way. In the 1600s, convents were forbidden in Brazil because women were needed to increase the population, not shut themselves away and pray. At the end of the twentieth century, most Brazilian women still have no access to reliable information on contraception. Political parties of all persuasions wash their hands of responsibility, denying women's right to knowledge and access to safer alternatives.

Yet despite official inaction, the last fifty years have witnessed one of the world's most dramatic falls in the population growth rate. In 1940 a woman of childbearing age typically had over six children – by 1990 that figure had fallen to less than three. Resorting to mass sterilization, illegal abortion, and the pill sold over the counter without a prescription, Brazilian women have carried out, on their own, one of the most drastic population control programs in modern times. An estimated six to eight million women have been sterilized, fifteen per cent of them young girls aged between 15 and 24 years old. In contrast, only one per cent of Brazilian men have had vasectomies. Sterilization has also become popular because politicians offer it as a vote catcher during election campaigns, and some employers illegally demand proof of it to avoid the risk of having to pay maternity leave.

Women's Police Stations

A Brazilian invention, run entirely by and for women, the first women's police station opened in 1985 in São Paulo. The first day, three hundred women, many with visible cuts and bruises from their latest battering, queued up outside to register complaints. The policewomen had expected to deal with cases of rape by strangers, as well as domestic violence, but they found that most sexual abuse was committed inside the family by fathers, stepfathers, uncles, and brothers. Now there are 150 of the stations all over Brazil, and the idea has been adopted in other countries.

Children

Brazilians believe that children should be seen and heard, even in restaurants late at night. Children from wealthier families are often pampered, waited on by maids, chauffeured by mothers to and from after-school activities. Children tend to grow up less inhibited in a society where touch is not taboo and affection is openly expressed. Brazilians like children, except when they live on the street. Then they are perceived as a threat.

Films like *Pixote*, TV documentaries, and numerous books have told the world about Brazil's street children. Street children are not unique to Brazil. What is unique is that most of them expect to be killed before they are eighteen. Many of the killers are off-duty policemen involved in protection rackets and drug trafficking. Children are eliminated because they know too much or even if not already involved in crime, are seen as potential bandits. "I killed you because you didn't go to school and had no future," read a note left beside the body of nine-year-old Patricio Hilario, found in a Rio street in 1989. The National Movement of Street Children (MNMMR) says that ninety per cent of the murderers are never brought to justice. Ironi-

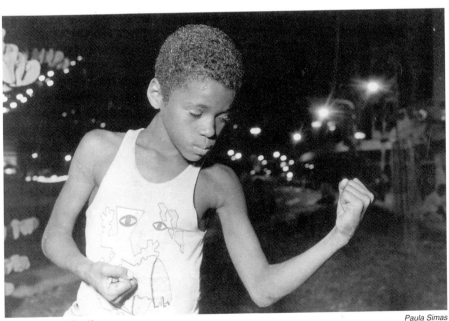

Street child in Recife

Paula Simas

Selling sugar cane,
Rio de Janeiro

*Julio Etchart/
Reportage*

cally, a progressive Children's Act introduced in 1990 enshrined children's rights in law and introduced an innovative system of local children's councils. In Brazil, theory and practice are often distant relatives.

In 1993 eight children and adolescents were shot dead near the Candelaria church in the center of Rio. Juvenile court statistics show that in the three years since, over 3000 children aged eleven to seventeen died violent deaths in Rio, and the vast majority of them were murdered, by death squads, police, or other gangs. Because the Candelaria killings caused an international outcry, several policemen went on trial, creating a crack in the edifice of impunity which protects most killers.

Working Children

Children are driven onto the streets by the need to earn money as soon as they can beg or carry a tray of chewing gum around the cars at traffic lights. Now, in an attempt to prevent children taking to the streets, some local authorities have begun offering poor parents monthly payments for each child going regularly to school, to compensate for the income they would otherwise bring home.

Three and a half million Brazilian children work. In rural areas, poverty drives children into the cane fields and the charcoal ovens. In Pernambuco 60,000 children work as cane cutters. Ninety per cent start work between seven and thirteen, earning up to half their family's income. Obliged to use the same large machetes as the adults, over half have suffered accidents while cutting cane.

In Minas Gerais and Mato Grosso do Sul up to 6,500 children work with their families in primitive camps in the eucalyptus forests, producing charcoal for the giant steel companies in Belo Horizonte. Most have never been to school. The children feed the ovens with logs and later remove the red-hot charcoal, working in dense smoke and violent temperature changes. Their feet get burnt by the hot coals, their hands get splinters from the logs, their eyes are red from the smoke.

Four million children of school age are not in school. The current government of Fernando Henrique Cardoso has promised to outlaw child labor and make primary education a priority, raising the abysmally low wages of teachers. Some local authorities in the charcoal-producing areas and elsewhere have followed Brasília's example in paying low-income families a wage in exchange for them keeping their children at school.

Race

Brazil's patron saint, Nossa Senhora da Aparecida, is a black madonna and half of Brazil's 150 million people are black or mixed race, but official Brazil is white and TV commercials are positively Scandinavian. "Blacks only appear on TV as soccer players, suspects, or stiffs," complains one black activist. President Cardoso appointed the first ever black minister, footballer player Pelé. His soccer artistry dazzled the world but Pelé has always avoided the racial issue and never uses his prestige to attack prejudice.

Racism

Racial discrimination is illegal and offenders can be prosecuted, but few cases ever get to court. Discrimination is often too subtle, like the job adverts which ask for a "good appearance." Many blacks themselves are still ashamed of their color. When asked to describe themselves in the 1980 census, people came up with all sorts of euphemisms: "very sunburnt," "coffee-colored," "the color of caramel." Immigrants, adventurers, ex-Nazis, and runaway bank robbers have found more tolerance in Brazil than its own black citizens.

European and Japanese Immigration

People of European descent form the second-largest contingent. After the Portuguese, hundreds of thousands of Germans and Italian immigrants settled in the South. In Santa Catarina there are still German-speaking towns and villages. Blumenau's beer festival rivals Munich's, while São Paulo's pizzas owe nothing to those of Rome. Dutch, Poles, Swiss, Finns, and American Confederates have all created their own enclaves. In Espirito Santo, there is a higher than average incidence of skin cancer among the farmer descendants of Pomeranian immigrants who have intermarried and kept their very white skins.

Japanese immigration began in 1906, when the first boatload of second sons arrived, unable to inherit land in their own overcrowded country. Many soon fled the harsh conditions of the coffee estates and headed for the cities, especially São Paulo, which now has three-quarters of a million first, second, and third generation Japanese, making it the largest community outside Japan. They not only dominate the market gardening sector but have moved steadily up the social ladder. Yakotas, Uekis, Hanishoros, and Matsudas can be found in every area of business and politics. Wandering through São Paulo's Liberdade district, you might forget you are in South

America. All the shop signs are in Japanese (except for the occasional Chinese or Korean restaurant) and there are stores crammed with Japanese foodstuffs and locally-produced Japanese newspapers.

In the 1980s, Japanese immigration went into reverse as several hundred thousand children and grandchildren of Japanese immigrants left for Japan in search of a better life. They were disappointed to find that, although they looked Japanese and might even speak it, they were still treated as foreigners – their Brazilian lack of formality instantly gave them away.

Brazil has also seen an influx of Lebanese and Palestinians in the last twenty years, adding to its older Arab colony of Egyptians and Syrians. In the interior, where many Arabs used to work as traveling salesmen, they are confusingly called "*Turcos,*" Turks. Like the Jewish community, the Arabs have founded hospitals and clubs, and in Brazil, the two have been able to work together. Not so long ago, the president of the São Paulo stock market was an Arab, his vice-president a Jew.

The ease with which someone can disappear into the vast interior or the chaos of the huge cities has also encouraged less desirable immigrants. The infamous Nazi war criminal, Dr. Josef Mengele, spent twelve years in Brazil before he died, sheltered by Austrian sympathizers. Ronald Biggs, the English train robber, has lived peacefully in Rio for 21 years, exempt from deportation because he fathered a Brazilian child. Italian Mafiosi and Belgian mercenaries have all found it easy to blend into the cosmopolitan population.

Religion

The name of God is on everyone's lips in Brazil because of the ubiquitous catch-phrase "*Se Deus quiser,*" "God willing." "Inflation will be lower this month, God willing," says every Minister of Finance. "*Se Deus quiser,* I will get that bandit," swears the policeman, cradling his machine-gun. Few Brazilians would admit to being atheist, but their relations with God tend to be practical, rather than spiritual. Long-distance trucks sport hand-painted slogans invoking divine protection.

Churches like the Basilica of Brazil's patron saint, Aparecida, near São Paulo, are crammed with ex-votos, plaster casts of legs, hands, torsos, heads, whichever bit of the body was cured by divine intervention. On saints' days the roads are clogged with buses and trucks full of pilgrims going to "pay their promises" – give thanks for mercies received.

Once a year, hundreds of thousands of pilgrims crowd into the small Northeast town of Juazeiro, to give thanks for blessings received from Padre Cicero, a local priest and political leader excommunicated by the Church for performing miracles. Padre Cicero died many years ago, but remains far more popular than any saint canonized by the Vatican.

Statue of Christ, Rio de Janeiro   *Paul Smith*

Rio's most famous landmark is the statue of Christ looking down over the city from Corcovado Mountain with his arms outstretched. Even the twentieth century concrete and glass palaces of Brasília have attracted their own brand of worshipers. Widely believed to be a city of cosmic forces due to its supposed location at the center of a magnetic field, in the nearby Valley of Dawn a mystic sect draws thousands of followers. The "Legion of Goodwill" has erected a pyramid there. Being a planned city, Brasília even has a special religious quarter, where temples, churches, and chapels of the different faiths co-exist side by side.

Rise of the Pentecostals

Brazil's 150 million people make it numerically the world's largest Catholic country, but the 500-year rule of the Roman Catholic Church is coming to an end, as Pentecostal Protestant churches spring up in converted cinemas and bingo halls across the country. Between 1990 and 1992, 710 new churches, five a week, were opening in Rio, ninety per cent of them Pentecostal. During the same period only one new Catholic church was consecrated.

The fastest-growing Pentecostal sect is the Universal Church of the Kingdom of God, led by self-styled Bishop Edir Macedo, a former lottery clerk.

In the days of high inflation, smartly dressed ushers raced up and down the aisles collecting sack-loads of money as worshipers dutifully paid their tithes and gave to special causes. Preachers told them that giving was the way to godliness. At the end of 1995, the Church was being investigated for fraud and charlatanism after a former preacher revealed the dubious methods used to extract more money from worshipers. Macedo has become a wealthy man, owning a fast-growing TV network and scores of radio stations. He is spreading his empire to many other countries in Latin America, Africa, Europe, and the U.S..

Catholic bishops recognize that the Pentecostals offer an attractive mix of emotion, participation, and faith healing. Some see them as something more sinister – a covert U.S. strategy to weaken the progressive Catholic Church and ease the way for neoliberal economic policies. But to people lost in the chaos and pressures of big city life the new churches seem to offer above all a moral code and a sense of self respect. Most of their preachers come from the same class and culture as their congregations, unlike the priests of the Catholic Church, many of whom, especially in the Amazon region, are foreigners.

Radical Catholicism

The spread of the evangelical Protestant Churches marks the end of Catholicism's monopoly and means that Brazil is becoming religiously pluralistic for the first time. It also means that the heyday of the Catholic Church's grassroots movement, the Comunidades Eclesiais de Base (CEBs), is over.

In the 1970s and 1980s, the CEBs were seen by some as the launchpad for a social revolution. They formed a key part of the reform movement that began within the Church in 1962 and deepened at the Bishops conference of 1968 in Medellín, Colombia, when the Latin American Church made an "option for the poor," based on the theories of liberation theology. Rejected by the conservative Church because it drew on Marxism, liberation theology inspired the practices of the CEBs.

The CEBs began as small neighborhood groups in rural areas or city slums who met to read the Bible, and discovered that what they read could be applied directly to their own lives. They spread rapidly all over Brazil, aided by the shortage of priests, which made the idea of laity-led groups more attractive to the Church. At their peak, they numbered 80,000 separate groups. During the military dictatorship (1964-85), the Catholic Church provided a sanctuary for the opposition movement – the only voice left for those without a voice and often the only place where trade unionists and human rights activists could meet in safety.

Base Christian Community, São Paulo   *Paul Smith*

It did not begin like that. On the day of the coup, the bishops' conference gave thanks for Brazil's delivery from communism. But as the repressive nature of the regime became apparent, the bishops issued ever-stronger statements, criticizing torture, censorship, social injustice, and the lack of land reform, and calling for a return to Christianity.

As a result, churchmen and women became targets themselves. By 1979, 122 religious and 273 lay workers had been imprisoned, many of them tortured, and four priests had been murdered. The name of the outspoken Archbishop of Recife, Helder Câmara, was banned from mention in the press. In the Amazon, the bishop of São Félix do Araguaia, Pedro Casaldaliga, narrowly missed assassination because of his firm defense of the land rights of Indians and peasants. In Rio, the late Bishop of Nova Iguaçu, Adriano Hipólito, was kidnapped, stripped naked, and covered in red paint because of his "communism."

In São Paulo, Archbishop Paulo Evaristo Arns made his church a center of resistance to the military regime. There, he received and comforted the mothers of disappeared prisoners, wives of imprisoned strikers, tortured peasants, and refugees from other Latin American regimes. He was also sought out by multinational executives, military emissaries, and even, once or twice, by repentant torturers. When Jewish journalist Vladimir Herzog died as a result of torture, announced as suicide, Arns organized an ecumenical service which became an act of defiance towards the regime and the police and troops who had encircled the Cathedral.

The Church has also created new organizations to fight for social justice. CIMI, the Indian Missionary Council set up in 1972, and CPT, the Pastoral Land Commission founded in 1975, support and campaign for the Indians and landless peasants threatened by invasions, evictions, and violence. The various Justice and Peace Commissions defend human rights, and the Centro Santo Dias in São Paulo helps victims of police violence.

Decline of the CEBs

In 1985 the last military president, General João Figueiredo, handed over to a civilian president, José Sarney. The return of political parties, unions, and popular movements to center-stage left the Church without a clear political and social role.

In Rome, the new Pope, John Paul II, a conservative, had embarked on a campaign to tame the Brazilian Church, appointing conservative bishops to replace progressives and closing down seminaries that taught liberation theology. Cardinal Arns could not be removed, but the São Paulo archdiocese was divided up into five separate dioceses to reduce his power. In 1984 Brazil's leading liberation theologian, Franciscan friar Leonardo Boff, was summoned to Rome for an inquisition on his writing and banned from teaching or publishing for a year. He later gave up the priesthood.

African Religions

The African slaves brought their own gods with them, but since open worship was banned, they disguised them with Catholic names. So Ogum became St. George, Iansã became St. Barbara. The hybrid religions thrive today under their own names, candomblé, macumba, and umbanda. Candles burning at a crossroads or the headless body of a black hen are signs of a *trabalho*, an offering to the gods for something desired, or a curse on somebody. Whatever their religion, most Brazilians will treat such signs with respect.

In Bahia, which has Brazil's largest black population, candomblé priestesses have become well-known personalities, respected by political leaders. Syncretic practices, like the ceremony of washing the steps of the church of Nosso Senhor do Bonfim by candomblé followers, have become a regular tradition. On New Year's Eve, a million people of all religions pack the beaches of Rio to throw offerings into the sea for the goddess Iemanjá. Brazilians find no problem in keeping a foot in more than one church, selecting what they like from each different religion.

CANDOMBLE: RELIGION OF BLACK BRAZIL

Candomblé, the religion of the Yoruba nation of West Africa, arrived in Brazil aboard the slave ships. Banned from worshiping their own gods in a Catholic land, the slaves disguised them with Catholic identities: Ogum, the god of war, became St. George; Omolú, the god of healing, became St. Lazarus, and Iansã, goddess of winds and storms, became St. Barbara. The religious syncretism which resulted, also includes elements from indigenous beliefs. The cults involve animal sacrifices and offerings to the gods, accompanied by singing and drumming. In Bahia where candomblé is strongest, some priestesses (mães-de-santo) have become well-known public figures and candomblé ceremonies like the washing of the steps of the Bonfim church are part of the religious calendar.

Originally found only in the state of Bahia, Candomblé has spread throughout Brazil. Two believers, just initiated, enter the temple.
(Margreet Willemier Westra-Karten)

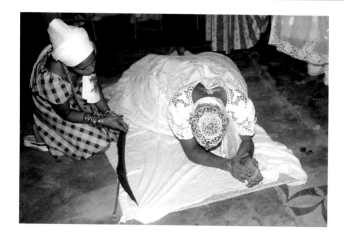

During the dance believers are possessed by Yoruba gods. A god greets believers in the temple by possessing and speaking through a spiritual medium.
(Margreet Willemier Westra-Karten)

As soon as the intermediary is possessed, he or she is dressed in the clothes of the appropriate Candomblé deity (orixá). This man is the chanel for Oxum, goddess of fountains and beauty.
(Margreet Willemier Westra-Karten)

Oxóssi, the god of hunting, is also the commander of an army of Indians and is many times portrayed as a soldier. On the altar lie offerings of food, made to him by his disciples.
(Margreet Willemier Westra-Karten)

An Indian Orixá, Caipó, is seen here consuming a sacrificial bird. Caipó was already worshiped before the Portuguese arrived in Brazil.
(Margreet Willemier Westra-Karten)

This altar is devoted to the Exus, messengers of the gods associated with evil, who when bribed with food and drink, can be persuaded to answer requests for help.
(Margreet Willemier Westra-Karten)

The ghosts of dead children provide comic relief during the ceremonies. Possessing adults and children alike, they make jokes, jump around, eat sweets and drink lemonade, and scrounge money.
(Margreet Willemier Westra-Karten)

3   POLITICS

In just over a hundred years Brazil has been a monarchy, a republic, and a federation. It has been ruled by parliament, civilian presidents, military juntas, general-presidents, and by a civilian dictator. Being president of Brazil involves a certain degree of occupational hazard. In the last fifty years, one president has committed suicide, one resigned, one was impeached, another was overthrown by a coup, and one was taken fatally ill on the eve of taking office. Since 1955 only one elected president has completed his term of office.

Besides the plethora of presidents, there has been a surfeit of legislation. Since independence, seven constitutions have been approved or imposed. The latest, approved in 1988, is already being revised.

Two Brazils

Yet such constant changes only mask an unchanging, unwritten political system based on patronage and privilege. Through them all, the unofficial division of Brazilians into first- and second-class citizens has remained intact, leaving the ruling classes more secure and more economically successful than anywhere else in Latin America.

The huge gap between rich and poor has made the emergence of solid democratic institutions more difficult. Congress remains unrepresentative, with few members to defend the interests of the rural and the urban poor, black Brazilians, or indigenous communities, while hundreds of senators and deputies protect the property and purses of the wealthy. Brazil has never had a socialist or left-wing government, although members of left-wing parties have been ministers in coalition governments.

Weak Parties

Without strong parties, interest groups have taken precedence over ideologies, clientelism over the public interest. In Europe, class and religious conflicts gave rise to the first party systems, in the U.S. the presidential election system consolidated the American parties, but in Brazil, under the monarchy the small ruling elite stifled the formation of political parties which might escape its control. When the republic came, the executive joined forces with local oligarchies to maintain power by preventing the rise of independent parties. Fraud was easier without strong opposition.

So while other Latin American countries have for generations had their *Blancos* and *Colorados*, their *Liberales* and *Conservadores*, in Brazil parties appear and disappear overnight. In the last Congress, members changed parties 200 times during its four-year term. In 1995 eighteen parties were represented in Congress, out of thirty which fought the last elections.

This fragmentation of the parties has slowed the work of Congress, as each bill has to be painstakingly negotiated not only with each party, but with each of its separate factions. Instead of representing an ideological position, most parties have become agglomerations of politicians representing regional, class, corporate, business, or individual interests. The *ruralistas*, representing farming and agribusiness, are one of the most powerful lobbies, with over 120 votes. The Amazon Bloc brings together 90 mostly conservative, anti-environmental, anti-Indian congressmen and women from the nine Amazon states.

The over-representation of conservative interests was increased and made permanent in a piece of gerrymandering by General-President Ernesto Geisel in 1977, after a vote had failed to go his way. As a result, each congressperson from São Paulo currently represents 467,000 inhabitants, while one from the small northern state of Roraima represents only 30,000, skewing power in favor of the right-wing representatives from the interior.

Political Parties

PMDB: The Brazilian Democratic Movement was set up during the military regime to be the official opposition party and maintain the fiction of a democracy. It evolved into a real opposition and in 1985 formed the government under the first civilian president, President José Sarney. It still commands many votes, but ideologically it is a rainbow coalition which can vote in any way.

PSDB: The Brazilian Social Democrat Party, also called the Tucano party after its symbol, a toucan, was created in 1989 by center-left dissidents from the PMDB, including current President Fernando Henrique Cardoso. Like the toucan, the PSDB is top-heavy. It has big names but lacks votes and so ended up adopting a neoliberal economic program and allying with the conservative PFL in order to win the 1994 presidential election.

PFL: The Liberal Front Party, launched in 1984 by a group of dissidents who wanted to distance themselves from the unpopular pro-military PDS party, has managed to stay in power by offering votes and financial support to more charismatic candidates from other parties. Strongest in the more backward northeast states, it now forms part of the ruling coalition with the PSDB.

PT: The Workers Party, founded in 1979 by a group of trade union leaders and intellectuals, is the only ideological political party. After two defeats in presidential elections, in 1995 its charismatic president Luis Inácio Lula da Silva stood down as leader. The party is split internally between a hard-line left-wing and a more social democrat faction. It has slowly increased its congressional representation, and has elected two state governors and several city mayors.

The Return to Democracy

Brazil moved from authoritarian regime to a politically free society without rupture, bloodshed, show trials, or purges, but it has paid the price. The extraordinarily drawn-out transition period gave time for numerous politicians to abandon ship, disengaging themselves from the unpopular military and presenting themselves instead as the opposition, where they vigorously resisted pressure for more radical reforms.

In 1984 a Congress still intimidated by the generals voted to maintain the indirect system of presidential elections, despite a campaign that had brought unprecedented millions on to the streets clamoring for the right to choose their own president.

Playboy President

When they at last regained that right in 1989, Brazilians voted for Fernando Collor, an arrogant young outsider whose glamorous image dazzled much of the electorate, tired of dour generals and elderly politicos. Supported by the powerful TV Globo network, Collor used an array of dirty tricks to overtake the PT's Luis Inácio Lula da Silva at the last moment. Collor wowed the population with his playboy lifestyle, his mastery of the sound-bite ("*I'll kill inflation with one karate chop*") and his ambitious promises to modernize Brazil, bring it into the First World, smash corruption and streamline the government.

His first drastic anti-inflation measure, the confiscation of almost all of the nation's savings for eighteen months, brought ruin to many people and plunged the economy into recession. Fidel Castro, in Brazil for Collor's inauguration, commented, "Even I wouldn't have dared do that." Collor reduced import barriers and opened up the economy, but inflation surfaced again and in 1992 his own brother, Pedro Collor, accused him of corruption. A congressional inquiry decided he had misused his public office and after mass demonstrations, Collor resigned, as Congress was about to vote for his impeachment.

Fernando Henrique Cardoso

Collor was succeeded by Itamar Franco, a mediocre politician chosen as vice-president exactly because he would never overshadow his charismatic boss. Franco

Fernando Collor, disgraced former president

Julio Etchart/ Reportage

Fernando Henrique Cardoso   *AP*

was honest but unpredictable. Although something of a populist, he chose as his Finance Minister the former sociologist Fernando Henrique Cardoso, who was determined to introduce a market economy. Cardoso became in effect Franco's prime minister, running the economy and the government, but by now he had his own political ambitions.

After the high drama of Collor's presidency, Franco provided an easy-going interregnum in which the economy grew and Brazil won the 1994 World Cup. But inflation began to spiral, reaching nearly fifty per cent a month in May 1994. Four months before the presidential elections, the Real Plan was introduced, choking off inflation and successfully stabilizing the economy, but with a much higher cost of living.

After years of grappling with bundles of banknotes and calculating in thousands and millions and seeing prices rise every day, suddenly life became much simpler. Prices stayed the same and Brazilians had more money in their pockets. The PT's Lula had been leading all the way in the election campaign, but the Real Plan's rush of feel-good factor won the day for Cardoso.

The Plan sparked a consumer boom, as the return of hire purchase enabled people to buy consumer durables on credit. To keep prices down, the government reduced import duties and Brazilian streets crowded for decades with locally-built Fords, GMs, and Volkswagens were suddenly full of imported BMWs, Mercedes, and Hondas.

Cardoso was popular with many different groups. An intelligent, cosmopolitan man who looked and sounded good, his promises of constitutional reforms to denationalize state sectors and deregulate the economy were welcomed by foreign investors, bankers, and governments as a return to sensible government after ten years of roller-coasting. In Brazil, the establishment felt safe because of his alliance with the PFL, while progressives felt that he would honor his intellectual past and his campaign pledges by introducing social reforms.

However, Cardoso failed to capitalize on this goodwill and after a year in government had achieved little in the way of lasting reform. His hopes of rising above the old habit of exchanging favors for votes had proved misplaced. With so many parties to deal with, confusion reigned and important votes went the wrong way. "The government needs a leader just to deal with the fifteen party leaders it has to negotiate with," joked José Genuíno Neto, a PT deputy.

On the social front, the government was slow to act. In an unguarded moment Communications Minister Sérgio Motta complained that "sociological masturbation" was delaying action. The only new social initiative was the *"Comunidade Solidária,"* modeled on Mexico's Solidarity program. Run by Cardoso's anthropologist wife, Ruth, it directed government grants and food to needy communities.

Record interest rates were introduced to kill off the consumer boom and damp down the risk of inflation, but only at the cost of rising unemployment. A million people in São Paulo alone were jobless at the end of the year.

Grassroots Movements

Modeled on the state-controlled unions of Italian Fascism in the 1930s, emasculated into welfare centers by the military in the l960s, only in the l980s did the trade unions begin to recover their independence and combativity. The new phase began in l978, when 120,000 workers in the car industry in São Paulo's industrial zone defied the ban on strikes, downed tools, and packed the small football stadium at Vila Euclides to listen to the fiery oratory of an unknown young union leader, Luis Inácio da Silva, known simply as Lula. Despite police harassment and tear-gas attacks, the strike was victorious, turning Lula into a national figure and establishing the São Bernardo Metalworkers Union as the heart of the new union movement.

In 1983, defying the government ban on union organizations that included different trades, the Central Unica dos Trabalhadores, CUT, was created. It included both urban and rural workers from all over Brazil. CUT soon became Latin America's largest trade union organization with 15 million affiliated members, although millions of Brazilians in unregistered jobs continue to be unrepresented by any union. To weaken the influence of the left-wing CUT, the government encouraged the creation of a rival organization, the Força Sindical, led by a former communist, Luis Antonio Medeiros.

Lula, the PT's charismatic leader

Julio Etchart/ Reportage

At the same time that the unions were beginning to flex their muscles, other popular movements began to appear. In 1977 church groups began a protest at the cost of living and persuaded a million people to sign a petition. The cost of living movement subsequently evolved into numerous local organizations, such as the *favelados* (shanty-town dwellers) and the *sem teto* (homeless). Many maintained close links with the progressive Catholic Church, drawing members from radical Base Christian Communities and support from radical priests and nuns. Their meetings were often held in church halls. In the 1980s, national movements of street children and the *sem terra* (landless) also grew up.

With their promise of empowerment and change and the threat they pose to the status quo, the popular movements are looked on with mistrust and suspicion by many of Brazil's more affluent citizens. They are routinely branded as violent and criminal whenever they show signs of being well organized or successful. In the mid-1980s, over 200 plots of waste land in São Paulo's East Zone were invaded by groups of "sem teto" unable to afford rising rents. Some of the squatters' camps were destroyed after battles with the police in which one man was killed and many injured, but others won the right to stay. The Workers Party mayor, Luiza Erundina de Souza, who was elected in 1988, began a self-help building scheme with the "sem teto." Over 10,000 families benefited but her successor, right winger Paulo Maluf, suspended the scheme, claiming financial irregularities.

A Land Occupation

April 1, 1995: Under the cover of darkness over a hundred buses and coaches approach the Arco Iris cattle ranch in the Pontal do Paranapanema, 500 miles west of São Paulo. The vehicles are packed with landless peasant families and their household belongings. Soon black-plastic-roofed shacks are dotted over the empty fields, stoves and beds are quickly installed inside, and committees are set up to organize water, food, sports, and schools.

The squatters cut the wire fences and the next day, tractors are plowing up the fields for planting. With military precision, the Sem Terra Movement (MST) has organized another land invasion. Eighteen hundred families are now camped there, hoping that soon a piece of these empty pastures will be theirs. Then they will plant food and feed their families instead of living in favelas, where they must get up at three or four in the morning to travel out to the big farms to cut cane or pick fruit for starvation wages.

Landless Movement

The Sem Terra Movement (MST) began in 1984 when, tired of official promises, a group of rural activists decided that land reform for Brazil's 4.5 million landless families would only come through direct action. With the slogan "Occupy, resist, and produce" they began seizing large estates all

MST members blessing each other with soil from
newly occupied land during a religious service

Paul Smith

over Brazil. Each target was carefully studied beforehand to make sure it would fit the legal definition of unproductive and so be eligible for expropriation by the government under Brazil's land legislation.

Since then, more than 22 million acres have been expropriated by the government, the owners compensated, and 131,000 families settled. At the beginning of 1995, a further 17,000 families were squatting in 45 camps all over Brazil, some at the roadside, some inside invaded areas, all waiting for official expropriation. Some squatters have occupied the same patch of land ten or twenty times, each time being evicted by police, before the government has finally agreed to expropriate the land and hand it over.

Not all the newly-settled areas have succeeded. Denied technical assistance or credit, some have failed, forcing new settlers to abandoned their hard-won land. But thousands of former sharecroppers, tenant farmers, and migrant workers have been transformed into productive small farmers, often working their land cooperatively. A 1991 survey by the UN's Food and Agriculture Organization (FAO) showed that average incomes in these settlements were three times higher than the minimum wage and productivity was above average. Some even export their produce.

Unlike other popular movements, the MST has deliberately chosen a collective form of leadership to avoid providing targets for assassination. New generations of leaders are constantly being trained. The movement's success has prompted accusations that it is running secret training camps where guerrilla tactics are taught. In fact, while the MST's broader aim is to create a socialist state, and Che and Mao posters can be seen in MST offices, its heroes include national historical figures such as Zumbi and Antonio Conselheiro. In São Paulo's Pontal region, leaders have been arrested on charges of forming a criminal gang.

At a national level, genuine land reform has been promised by every president since 1964, but the powerful landowners" lobby has always blocked any serious attempt, either in Congress or through bloodshed. In the first two years of the Cardoso government there were two massacres of "sem terra."

In 1995 in Corumbiara, in the Amazon state of Rondônia, police surrounded 600 families who had occupied a ranch before dawn and ten people, including a seven-year-old child, were shot dead. Two policemen also died. In April 1996 in Eldorado do Carajás, Pará state, police fired on a group who were on a protest march to the city of Belém, killing nineteem men. In both cases the police were accused of executing men who had already been detained, local ranchers were alleged to have paid off the police and in spite of the outcry, police destroyed evidence to hamper investigations.

Campaign Against Hunger

In recent years, one of the most prominent grassroots movements has been the Campaign Against Hunger, launched by one man in 1993 and spreading rapidly to create over 5000 committees at its high point, spread across Brazil. The original idea was simply to bring food to as many as possible of the 32 million Brazilian families officially classified as poor. Since then it has moved on to creating jobs, training, and campaigning for land reform.

The Campaign's founder and inspiration is a man sometimes compared to Gandhi. Herbert de Souza, universally known as Betinho, is thin and fragile, an HIV-positive hemophiliac whose amazing drive and energy enable him to cut through red tape and recruit the rich and famous to the socially acceptable cause of feeding the hungry and providing jobs. Campaign committees, set up in schools, churches, neighborhoods, and banks, have provided the impetus for hundreds of self-help projects in shanty-towns and poor communities, from vegetable gardens to computer classes and waste recycling.

4   THE ECONOMY

As the plane flies into São Paulo, first-time visitors to Brazil cannot believe their eyes. Stretching away to the horizon is the biggest concentration of skyscrapers on the planet. Overshadowed by the more glamorous Rio, São Paulo's sheer size is breathtaking. With 17 million people, (second only to Mexico City in world terms), São Paulo is the locomotive that drives Brazil, accounting for half of its economic output. São Paulo is the industrial and banking center; it is where the PT and the CUT began; it is the part of Brazil that reminds you that the country is the world's tenth largest industrial economy, a major supplier of food to the world and one of the top ten arms manufacturers.

At night the city's cosmopolitan heart pulsates with a hundred different rhythms from tango to techno, and the aromas of thousands of *cantinas*, *churrascarias*, pizza palaces, Chinese restaurants, bars, and bakeries mingle in the air. But at every traffic light there is a reminder of how Brazil's wealth is built on poverty, as hordes of adults and children descend on waiting cars to sell chewing gum, flowers, biscuits, or fruit. Over a million people in São Paulo live in favelas, over three million live in *cortiços*, the overcrowded tenements where ten or more families share a single bathroom.

Boom and Bust

"Everything that is planted here, grows," Pedro Alvares Cabral wrote home ecstatically in 1500. Like the other European colonies, Brazil's role was to be plundered for the enrichment of the mother country. At different times in the ensuing 500 years, Brazilian products have dominated world trade, providing raw materials such as sugar, coffee, rubber, and gold that became essential to the way of life of the developed world.

During the gold boom in the seventeenth century, Brazilians (excluding the slaves) had the highest per capita income in the world. Brazil has always been a rich country, but its wealth has remained in the hands of the few. Little has been shared with those who helped to create it.

The first Brazilian export, the redwood used to make a dye much in demand in Europe, set the pattern. For 30 years after discovery, 300 tons a year were exported until the accessible wood was exhausted and trade declined. Today mahogany is being furiously logged to supply the world's demand and by the year 2000 there will be little left.

Sugar and Gold

For 400 years the Brazilian economy was dominated by successive single product cycles of boom and bust. After redwood came sugar, its master and slave system leaving a legacy that still shapes Brazilian society today. "King Sugar" produced over half of all export earnings during the entire colonial period. Then came gold. Brazil's gold rush lasted only a hundred years, but during that time Brazilian gold accounted for half the total production of all the Spanish and Portuguese colonies.

In the seventeenth century, Brazil was the world's greatest gold producer and the capital city symbolically moved south from Salvador, near the sugarcane fields of the Northeast, to Rio, close to the gold mines of Minas Gerais. Brazil became the engine of Portugal's economy, its gold paying for imports of British manufactured goods. In this way, Brazilian gold helped finance England's Industrial Revolution, but in Brazil itself the Portuguese monarchy banned industrial development, so that all available manpower would be available for agriculture and mining.

Coffee

After sugar and gold came coffee. Coffee may seem as Brazilian as football and Carnival, but it is an imported plant, first brought to Brazil from French Guiana in 1727 by a certain Sergeant Palheta. The climate and soil in the South around Rio, São Paulo, and much later, Paraná, proved ideal for coffee. By the 1900s, Brazil was the world's major producer and coffee remained its leading export from 1831 to 1973. Immigrants rapidly replaced slaves on the coffee plantations – in one twenty-year period from 1879 to 1899, nearly one million immigrants settled in São Paulo state.

Whereas sugar had concentrated wealth in a few hands, coffee helped to spread it. Coffee, unlike sugar, did not need plantations but could be grown by smallholders. Neither was it a monopoly crop: beans and cereals could be grown between the rows of trees. Coffee brought development: railroads and ports had to be built to transport it overseas to the consumer markets of the North. Santos, on the São Paulo coast, is still Brazil's biggest port, though now it exports cars and machinery as well as coffee and fruit. Coffee wealth paid for elegant country houses furnished with the best that Europe had to offer, and large mansions began to appear in the small provincial town of São Paulo, turning it into Brazil's main financial center. Money brought industry and political power in its wake.

At the end of the nineteenth century came the shortest of all Brazil's commodity cycles, rubber. The bicycle and the motorcar had appeared and the U.S.A and Europe clamored for rubber to make pneumatic tires. Manaus, the Amazon capital, briefly became the wealthiest city in Brazil as fortunes

Coffee harvest in Minas Gerais
Tony Morrison/
South American Pictures

were made from the latex collected by enslaved Indians. The rubber boom was cut short when plantation rubber from Malaya and Ceylon began to swamp the market, grown from saplings smuggled out of the Amazon by an Englishman. Wild Brazilian rubber's share of the world trade fell from 90 per cent in 1910 to two per cent in 1937.

Before and after independence, the British had dominated Brazil and the other Latin American economies, finding them doubly useful as suppliers of essential raw materials and markets for the products of the mills and factories that mushroomed with Britain's industrial revolution. But by the Second World War, the U.S. had replaced Britain as its dominant trading partner, supplying half of Brazil's imports and taking 40 per cent of its exports.

Industrialization

In the 1940s, President Getúlio Vargas laid the foundations of Brazil's post-war industrial boom by creating giant state steel and oil companies and nationalizing Brazil's twenty private railways.

Between 1950 and 1980, first under elected governments and then under military rule, Brazil's economy enjoyed an average growth rate of seven per cent, one of the longest periods of sustained high growth in world history. In a far cry from today's free market fashions, the government subsidized and directed private sector activity, whether local or foreign.

State-led industrialization and import substitution led to rapid urbanization. Within 30 years Brazil was transformed from a largely rural society into a country where three-quarters of the population lived in towns and cities. A large workforce was needed for the new factories being set up by companies from Europe and the U.S. to produce cars, TV sets, and domestic appliances, attracted by tax incentives of all sorts. Even so, the job supply failed to keep up with demand, as millions of impoverished peasants flocked to the cities in search of the new jobs.

The corporations dominated the private sector, producing consumer goods, while the military concentrated on developing their own missiles, planes, armored cars, and weapons, swiftly turning Brazil into a major arms exporter. The middle classes soon developed the same consumer expectations as their peers in the U.S. and Europe, because economic policies, especially under the military, increased income concentration at the expense of the poor.

Rising Debts

Foreign loans poured into Brazil, as Western bankers rushed to offload their surplus dollars regardless of the long-term viability of the projects they were financing. Whether going to state or private companies, the repayment of these loans, at floating interest rates, was guaranteed by the government. Foreign debt was nothing new. On independence in 1822, Brazil already owed over £3 million to the London banks. The Brazilian economic miracle was loquaciously admired by First World bankers and politicians, who preferred to remain silent about the embarrassing underbelly of the regime – the torture, censorship, and repression being exposed by human rights organizations.

Brazil's "miracle" was finally destroyed by the military's disastrous response to the oil shocks of the 1970s. The steep rise in oil prices meant that Brazil, an oil importer, was suddenly faced with a greatly increased oil bill and a resulting trade deficit. Unwilling to admit the country's difficulties because they would reflect on the success of military rule, President Ernesto Geisel, the fourth general to rule the country since the coup in 1964, reacted with imperial disdain. Brazil, he declared, was an island of tranquillity and recession was unnecessary. Instead Brazil simply borrowed more dollars to cover the trade deficit, adding to the debt being run up by Eletrobras, the state energy utility, and the other state companies involved in the military's ambitious infrastructure program of nuclear power stations, giant dams, roads, railroads and a petrochemical complex.

Enter the IMF

Crisis turned into disaster when the second oil shock of 1979 was followed by a dramatic rise in U.S. interest rates. The military and government technocrats refused to seek rescheduling of the snowballing foreign debt, which had grown from $12.6 billion in 1973 at the beginning of the oil crisis to $64.2 billion by 1980. They delayed because rescheduling would involve accepting an International Monetary Fund (IMF) austerity package, and this might affect government candidates' chances in the November 1982 governorship elections.

In the event, they lost out on both counts. The opposition won in all the major states and Brazil was virtually bankrupt, having used up all its foreign reserves. The government had no choice but to go, cap in hand, to the IMF. Between 1983 and 1985 Brazil submitted seven letters of intent to the IMF, promising free market reforms in return for a partial debt bail-out. Brazil had the economic clout to impose more reasonable terms and even set up a debtors cartel to negotiate jointly with the banks, a prospect much feared in Washington and Frankfurt, but the generals and technocrats buckled under and paid up, despite the cost to Brazilians in the shape of recession and savage cuts in social programs.

Economic Stagnation

The government failed to meet its IMF targets on spending cuts and other measures, but kept up its debt repayments. Economic stagnation followed as Brazil added dollars to its long list of exports to the First World. By 1985, when the 21-year-old military regime finally handed over power to a civilian government, inflation was on the rise and the country was in the worst recession since the Depression of the 1920s.

Free of the generals, wage strikes took off and inflation spiraled to nearly twenty per cent a month. President José Sarney responded by introducing the Cruzado Plan, freezing wages and prices and changing the currency, the first of many attempts over the next ten years to stabilize the economy.

Brazil began a ten-year cycle of rising inflation, change of finance minister, wage and price freeze, new currency, a brief respite, then back to rising inflation. Between 1986 and 1994, the government got through eight finance ministers, seven stability plans, and six currencies. In 1987, a moratorium on foreign debt payments was belatedly declared, supported with nationalist fervor by the president of Congress, Ulisses Guimarães, an outspoken opponent of the military regime, who declared, "The debt is a hemorrhage, bleeding the country to death."

But Finance Minister Dilson Funaro's pilgrimage to Western capitals to plead for a debt reduction was met with scorn by hard-faced bankers, indifferent both to the human cost of the capital outflow and to the individual tragedy of Funaro, a man whose missionary zeal was inspired by the knowledge that he did not have long to live because of cancer. Despite the repayments, Brazil's total debt rose relentlessly, almost doubling to reach $123.4 billion by 1990.

Brazil remains the Third World's largest debtor, second only to the United States in world terms. In 1994, with the debt standing at nearly $150 billion, Finance Minister Fernando Henrique Cardoso finally reached agree-

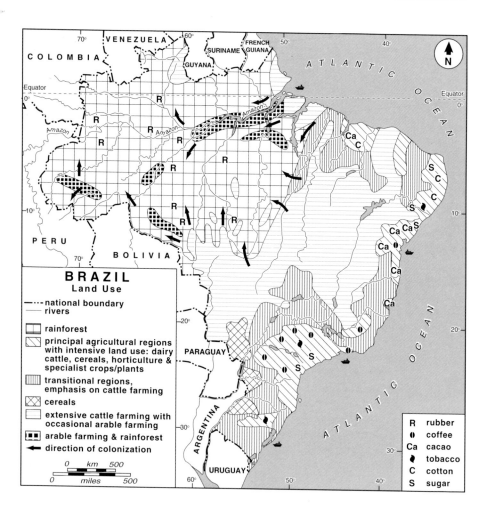

BRAZIL
Land Use

- – · · · national boundary
- —— rivers
- rainforest
- principal agricultural regions with intensive land use: dairy cattle, cereals, horticulture & specialist crops/plants
- transitional regions, emphasis on cattle farming
- cereals
- extensive cattle farming with occasional arable farming
- arable farming & rainforest
- direction of colonization

R	rubber
0	coffee
Ca	cacao
♪	tobacco
C	cotton
S	sugar

ment with the banks. Repayments reached $21.7 billion in 1995, $20 billion in 1996. With a gross domestic product close to $700 billion, the payments do not represent the huge burden they do in some smaller countries. Nevertheless, they mean billions of dollars less for social programs, which is where cuts are inevitably made.

Unleashing the Market

The election of the inexperienced Fernando Collor in 1989 began a new phase in Brazilian economic policy. Collor wanted to drag Brazil helter-skelter into the First World by liberalizing the economy and shrinking the state sector. "Better to be the last country in the industrialized world than the first of the developing countries," he claimed. On his first day in office, Collor froze private assets and savings, plunging the economy into chaos. Thousands were ruined overnight; some committed suicide.

In the rush to deregulate, efficient and essential government agencies were abolished along with the inefficient and unnecessary, aggravating the chaos. In 1992 Collor resigned just as Congress approved his impeachment for corruption and was succeeded by vice president Itamar Franco who continued to privatize and open up the economy.

Brazil's extremely high interest rates and low priced utility shares soon had it classified as an attractive "emerging market." The projected privatization of giant state companies like Petrobras (oil), Telebras (telecommunications), Eletrobras (electricity), and the São Paulo state gas, water, and energy companies had investors rubbing their hands. But after a year of the Cardoso government, the necessary constitutional reforms were still held up by a Congress determined to wring every possible concession in exchange for their votes. Investor enthusiasm began to wane.

Real Plan

In 1994 Cardoso was elected on the back of the success of the Real Plan, an economic stabilization program which he had introduced as Itamar Franco's Finance Minister. Introduced on July 1, when inflation was nearing 50 per cent a month, the plan's success depended on freezing wages and ending indexation, once prices had been allowed to rise to a peak. The plan also involved the biggest currency switch ever carried out in any country, as the new *Real* replaced the *cruzeiro* and billions of banknotes and coins had to be distributed throughout the vast country.

Brazil then enjoyed an unprecedented period of low inflation, down to single figures throughout 1995 and into 1996, boosting Cardoso's popularity. But in 1996 concern began to grown about soaring unemployment figures of over fifteen per cent in São Paulo and over 30 per cent in Recife. Industry was undercut by cheap imports and being battered by some of the highest interest rates in the world, as the government sought to keep inflation down and attract foreign capital into the country.

Inequality

Brazil is now the world's tenth largest industrial economy, with a gross domestic product of almost $700 billion, far ahead of every other developing country except China, yet the income gap within its borders is widening. Not only have the rich increased their share of the national income, but a World Bank study has shown that the rich even receive a larger slice of government social spending. The top twenty per cent of the population

A *favela* in Vila Prudente, eastern São Paulo
Paul Smith

receive the benefits of 21 per cent of government spending, while the poorest twenty per cent get only fifteen per cent.

Private hospitals, for example, most of them profit-making, were allocated 62 per cent of the Ministry of Health's budget for hospital care in 1995, while public hospitals received only 38 per cent. At the same time, the funds for preventive medicine were cut back, including nutritional programs which help the poor most. Experts say that Brazil's spending on social programs would be adequate if it were targeted specifically at the 24 million people who live below the poverty line.

It has been left to local governments to show that important improvements can be achieved at little cost. When Brasília's governor, Cristóvam Buarque, decided to pay out a monthly allowance of $100 to nearly 15,000 low-income families, in return for them keeping their children at school instead of sending them out to work, the measure took just 0.6 per cent of the capital's budget. By attending school more regularly, the children perform better, and subsequently have a chance of getting better jobs than their parents, breaking the cycle of poverty that traps future generations.

5   AMAZON AND ENVIRONMENT

For those used to the Thames or the Potomac, the vastness of the Amazon is difficult to grasp. Rising in the Andes, flowing into the Atlantic, the 3,800 mile-long Amazon is the longest river in the world. The river basin, two-thirds of it in Brazil, drains an area as big as the United States, excluding Alaska. Seventeen of its tributaries are over 1,000 miles long. Five hundred miles upriver from the sea, the mouth of one of these tributaries, the Tapajós, is twelve miles across. Marajó, the island that lies in the mouth of the Amazon, is larger than Denmark. Two thousand different species of fish live in the Amazon basin, which covers one twentieth of the world's surface and contains a fifth of its fresh water.

The rainforest proper covers 1.5 million square miles, and just one acre may contain up to 179 species of tree. The average for temperate forests is six. The Amazon rainforest contains the planet's largest gene reserve, its greatest store of biodiversity, a pharmaceutical cornucopia. Gold, uranium, bauxite, manganese, cassiterite, oil, and gas have been found in the subsoil. The rainforest does not cover all the Amazon basin: there are also savan-nah, valleys, and mountains, in-cluding Brazil's highest moun-tain, the Pico da Neblina. As de-struction advances at the fringes, there are now millions of acres of cleared forest used for cattle pasture and farming.

Utopian myths: a "tiger hunt" in the rainforest

Myths and Legends

A fertile source of myths and legends of lost explorers, giant sloths, and amorous dolphins, the Amazon has always attracted explorers, adventurers, and eccentrics. Its fantastic size has inspired equally fantastic plans to dominate it, all of them eventually defeated by the conditions that have also earned it the title "Green Hell." Henry Ford tried to tame the wild rubber tree into growing in plantations: he planted three million neat rows of trees at Fordlandia on the edge of the Tapajós river, only to see them wiped out by a fungus. In the 1960s, the Hudson Institute in the U.S. proposed damming the Amazon to turn it into a series of great lakes.

In 1967 American billionaire Daniel Ludwig bought 4 million acres of rainforest at less than $1 an acre in the state of Amapá. He cleared the forest and planted imported species such as the fast-growing *gmelina* and California pine to provide wood for a pulp factory, which he had towed across the world from Japan. Many of the trees died. He brought Dutch engineers to build polders for rice paddies, but the rice did not flourish. He built a railroad, hundreds of miles of roads, and a model company town, while across the river 15,000 laborers and prostitutes squeezed into the Beiradão, a waterside favela. After spending an estimated $3 billion, Ludwig gave up and pulled out. Only the wood-pulp factory remains in business.

Conquering the Amazon

The idea of penetrating the forest with railways or roads has always appealed. At the end of the nineteenth century, when the rubber boom was at its peak, first the British, then the Americans, planned a railroad to bring Bolivian rubber through Brazil to Belém on the Atlantic coast. The British gave up, the Americans succeeded. Twentey-two thousand men, recruited from all over the world, worked on the 200 mile-long track connecting the Mamoré and Madeira Rivers, which finally opened in 1912, just as the rubber boom was collapsing. Over 6,000 men died from malaria, yellow fever, dysentery, and other diseases during the five years it took to build the aptly-named Devil's Railway. In 1971, after years of decline, the railway was finally closed and the engines sold off as scrap.

The dream of conquering the Amazon remained. In 1972, sixty years after the ill-fated Madeira-Mamoré was opened, the Brazilian military decided it was time to link the Atlantic and Pacific Oceans, via the Amazon. The generals wanted to integrate the "empty" Amazon region with the rest of the country, easing social tensions in other regions by shipping off landless farmers to occupy its empty lands. The "wilderness" would then become a profitable productive area of export agriculture.

Finance Minister Delfim Neto talked of conquering a new country within the Brazilian nation and called on businessmen to carry out the definitive conquest of the Amazon. The Transamazon Highway was presented as the solution to the drought that was devastating the Northeast. The "people without land," the drought victims, would be transferred to the "land without people" and installed in agrovilas, purpose-built settlements strung out along the new road.

Manaus harbor on the Amazon

Julio Etchart/Reportage

Critics feared it would merely be linking a dry desert to a humid wilderness, but machines began bulldozing the red earth road through the dense trees. Families were airlifted to their new homes in the forest. Today much of the road has been washed away by the heavy rains, and most of the families have abandoned the land where they were dumped and then forgotten.

The state of Rondônia was set aside as a solution for the small farmers of the south, driven off their land by hydroelectric dams and soybean farms. In a modern-day equivalent of America's nineteenth-century wagon trails, hundreds of thousands of families set out on buses and trucks to travel two thousand miles north, and settle on the subsidized plots supplied by the government. Between 1970 and 1980, Rondônia's population multiplied tenfold. The military regime also offered tax incentives to big companies, multinational corporations, and banks to set up cattle ranches.

By 1977, 336 agricultural projects in the Amazon basin region had been approved for funding by SUDAM, the government development agency. Seventy per cent of their investments was covered by the public purse. A network of over a hundred hydroelectric dams was planned to provide energy: heavily subsidized electricity was offered to giant aluminum projects set up on the coast.

A sharecropper clears a patch of Amazon rainforest

Julio Etchart/Reportage

In 1980 another ambitious development project, Greater Carajás, was launched. An 18 billion-ton iron ore mountain had been discovered in the Eastern Amazon. Delfim Neto said the iron ore would be enough to "pay off the foreign debt," which then stood at $60 billion. By 1995, not only was it not paid off, it had doubled to $160 billion.

Infrastructure for the project included a 550 mile-long railroad to carry the ore to the port in São Luis. When it was announced, the heavily subsidized Greater Carajás project promised jobs and prosperity to a region where thousands of rural workers and landless peasants lived in poverty. Yet outside the model company town which houses the employees of the state-owned Vale do Rio Doce Company, ragged families of charcoal-burners still live in miserable huts at the side of the road, and the forest has been razed and burnt to make way for cattle.

In 1994 the military unveiled a new megaproject for the Amazon. The Air Force wanted to buy a $1.4 billion U.S.-manufactured radar system to monitor air traffic in a region which has become a drug-traffickers paradise. Defenders of the project suggested it could also be used to detect invasions of indigenous and ecological reserves. President Cardoso was a keen supporter of the project, known as Sivam, although a police bug on a diplomat's phone revealed a tangled web of corruption, influence peddling, and CIA involvement in the scheme.

The latest plans to develop the Amazon region put the emphasis on eco-tourism, including a jungle monorail, floating hotels for 30,000 visitors and a 100-feet-high statue in the middle of the river at Manaus, proposed by the flamboyant governor of Amazonas state, Amazonino Mendes, who has a reputation for outlandish ideas. The Manaus Opera House has been lovingly restored to all its former splendor for the 1996 centenary.

Environment

In 1972 the Brazilian delegation famously informed the Stockholm Environment Conference that development was more important than pollution. Twenty years later, Brazil hosted the 1992 Earth Summit and was able to show off a whole infrastructure of specialized agencies for protecting the environment, from a special ministry down to state and municipal secretariats. There is even a new breed of "environmental prosecutors" who take both state and private companies to court for crimes of pollution and contamination, while the 1988 constitution introduced a five-year deadline for the demarcation of indigenous reserves and the need for environmental impact reports before new development or industrial projects could go ahead.

Theory and Practice

But good legislation is little use when political will is lacking. The environment secretary of the Amazon state of Roraima in 1994 was a well-known mining entrepreneur; in the town of Itaituba, at the heart of the Tapajós gold-mining area, the municipal environment secretary in 1993 was the owner of a clandestine mining camp; a recent environment minister, Henrique Brandao Cavalcanti, included two loggers in Brazil's delegation to an international congress on protected species to lobby against the inclusion of mahogany.

In the run-up to the Earth Summit, the G-7 group of developed industrial countries came up with a Pilot Plan for Tropical Forests. They promised $1.5 billion for environmental protection, including the demarcation of Indian reserves and conservation parks. Compared with other Latin American and European countries, Brazil has few protected areas: only 1.8 per cent of its total area, compared with 15 per cent in Venezuela, 8 per cent in Colombia or 5.5 per cent in Holland.

Not only the Amazon is at risk. According to the World Wide Fund for Nature, "the rapid occupation of territory and the absence of a policy of creating conservation areas makes the protection of important ecosystems like the Atlantic Forest and the Cerrados doubtful." Less than one per cent

Pollution at a gold mine in the Amazon state of Pará

Julio Etchart/Reportage

of the Atlantic Forest's area is protected, while 80 per cent is in private hands. The Cerrados – the vast plateau of central Brazil – loses eight million acres of open land to agriculture each year.

Mining and Logging
In the Amazon region itself, the invasion of Indian and ecological reserves continues by loggers and garimpeiros who contaminate Amazon rivers with the mercury illegally used in gold-panning. Studies show mercury contamination of riverside and Indian populations, who eat the fish from rivers used by the garimpeiros. Almost all the mercury is imported from Europe for other purposes and smuggled up to the Amazon where it is freely sold in pharmacies and stores.

Logging is now probably the greatest threat to the rainforest. To reach the scattered mahogany trees, hundreds of miles of dirt tracks are illegally cut through the forest. Trucks loaded with giant tree trunks lurch down them on their way to the sawmills, now scattered in thousands throughout the Amazon region. Floating carpets of trunks destined eventually for the furniture shops of London, Tokyo, and New York cover stretches of river.

Under pressure from boycott campaigns, British timber importers have tried to ensure they buy only legally-logged wood, but face a whole system of falsified documents and fraudulent certificates issued by corrupt officials at IBAMA, the government's environmental agency. As a result, illegal logging of mahogany from Indian and ecological reserves continues apace. A proposed road to give Brazil a Pacific outlet through Peru, via the state of Acre, is condemned by environmentalists because it will bring the diminishing mahogany stands much nearer to the Japanese market. Asian loggers, having exhausted their own forests, have moved into Brazil's northern neighbors, Guyana and Surinam, and have begun to buy up logging companies in Brazil.

The huge forest fires of the late 1980s, when tracts of rainforest were burnt for cattle pasture, covering the region in a heavy pall of smoke and ash, slowed in the early 1990s, but the government's space research institute, INPE, has recorded a substantial rise in the burning since 1994. The amount of rainforest already destroyed is nearly twelve per cent.

Defending the Forest

The environmental cost of Amazon dams like Tucuruí, Brazil's largest national dam, and Balbina, built in the early 1980s, was initially ignored, but in 1989 protests by the well-organized Kayapó Indians forced the suspension of the proposed Monte Belo dam on the Xingu river. The dam-building program was then largely shelved for lack of funds.

In the 1980s, Chico Mendes, a trade union organizer in Acre, led rubber tappers in collective actions known as *empates* to stop cattle ranchers felling the forest which contained their livelihood. In December 1988 he was shot dead by a cattle-rancher's son. His murder made him an international environmental "eco-martyr" and the government felt obliged to implement Mendes' proposals for environmentally sustainable "extractive reserves" for the rubber tappers. Unfortunately, the abysmally low price of wild rubber has since forced many tappers to leave for the towns.

Concrete Jungles

For most Brazilians, the Amazon is as remote as Siberia and urban pollution is their main environmental concern. Since the Real Plan was introduced in 1994, and gas became relatively cheap, traffic on the streets of Rio and São Paulo has increased by over twenty per cent. So far, city authorities have failed to come up with any solution, except to build more tunnels and bridges.

Success in Curitiba

Yet Brazil has one city, Curitiba, which has become a byword for environmental innovation. The city's fame began with Jaime Lerner, an architect who served three terms as Curitiba's mayor. The secrets of the city's success are ingredients rarely found elsewhere in Brazil today – long-term planning, administrative continuity, and a belief that rich and poor are entitled to the same high standard of public service.

Instead of expressways for private motorcars, Curitiba has created a fast-moving and cheap public transportation system, which has attracted nearly a third of the city's rush-hour motorists, so reducing air pollution levels. The city has doubled in size since the 1970s, but most favelas have basic infrastructure, and recyclable waste can be exchanged for fresh food, school books, and even Easter eggs. Neighborhood centers, open 24 hours, have brought government departments nearer to people, while new parks, cultural centers, and pedestrian precincts mean that the city now has 50 square yards of green space per inhabitant compared to São Paulo's 12 square yards.

While the quality of life has been improving in Curitiba, it has steadily deteriorated in most of Brazil's cities. The Tietê and the Pinheiros rivers that divide São Paulo are narrow and unglamorous, unlike the breathtaking Bay of Guanabara which encircles Rio de Janeiro. Yet both are heavily polluted – the rivers with industrial sewage, the bay with oil and detritus from the ships in Rio's port. Internationally-financed projects to clean up the waters are now under way.

Struggles in Cubatão

Some hope is offered by the experience of Cubatão, the industrial complex near Santos which belched out so many tons of polluting particles from its petrochemical and steel plants that the region became known as the Valley of Death. In Cubatão, pollution got so bad that some doctors claimed that babies were being born without brains in the nearby town of Vila Parisi. In 1983, after an emergency shut-down when levels got dangerously high, Governor Franco Montoro invested in a pollution control program which successfully reduced particle emissions.

The environmental prosecutors of Cubatão also won a victory in court, obliging the French multinational Rhône Poulenc, which for years had dumped toxic waste in the region, to pay compensation. In 1995, in an effort to reduce air pollution from the city's three million vehicles, the state environmental secretary, Fabio Feldman, proposed that motorists should only use their cars on alternate days, but the mayor, Paulo Maluf, refused to cooperate. "Traffic jams mean progress," he explained without conscious irony.

6   CULTURE

Carnival

The Rio Carnival is the biggest song and dance spectacle in the world, with a strong element of Roman circus as the rich and the famous, ministers, presidents, sports stars, film idols, tycoons, bankers, and playboys banquet and booze the night away in luxurious boxes overlooking the *Sambodromo*, the purpose-built parade ground where the samba schools perform.

Down below, hour after hour, to the hypnotic and deafening beat of hundreds of drummers and percussion players, thousands of exuberantly dressed dancers twirl, gyrate, leap, and sway. The TV cameras focus on the near-naked women, but each school has up to 3000 sambistas dressed in rich costumes of plumes, sequins, and satins. It is hard to believe that once Carnival is over, the eighteenth century courtiers, Amazon Indians, African warriors, and Egyptian pharaohs will metamorphose back into maids, bus drivers, laborers, shop assistants and garbage collectors.

The samba schools began in the favelas and still draw most of their members from one locality. Celebrities, TV stars, models or soccer players are invited to "appear" with the school, and increasingly middle-class Brazilians and even tourists buy themselves a Carnival experience, their less-than-expert samba steps mercifully hidden in the general melee.

Behind the four-day parade lie months of rehearsals and an extraordinary amount of research into each school's theme, often used to satirize historical or current events. The 1994 winner, Imperatriz Leopoldinense, dug up a little known century-old episode, when Pedro II decided to import camels to cope with the drought in the Northeast. The camels succumbed, while the local donkeys survived, allowing an ironic reflection on the superiority of the underrated homegrown product.

The satire sometimes becomes surreal – where else would torture become a Carnival theme? Yet a few years ago the Santa Cruz school, celebrating the 25th anniversary of the satirical newspaper *Pasquim*, a fervent critic of the military regime, produced a float with gigantic torture instruments. Around the float danced 25 dwarfs dressed as generals.

The conservative archbishop of Rio, Dom Eugenio Sales, has frequently criticized the excesses of Carnival. On one occasion, he took out a court injunction to stop a replica of the Corcovado Christ being put on a float. The answer of Joãosinho Trinta, one of Rio's most famous and creative *carnavalescos*, was to wrap it up in black plastic so that nobody could see it, although everyone knew what it was. It was Trinta who coined a phrase that became famous in answer to criticisms of the extravagant luxury of his floats and costumes: "Intellectuals like poverty, the people want luxury."

Capoeira, a combination of dance and martial art born out of slavery *Julio Etchart/Reportage*

As Carnival has grown and attracted live coverage by the major TV channels, so commercial interests have become more intrusive. Advertising by Brazil's two major beer companies is everywhere. For all that, one of the great delights of the Rio Carnival is still the juxtaposition of the ordinary and the fantastic, the sight of a group of Roman legionnaires going home by bus, or a couple of the older women clambering into a car in their vast crinolines.

Music

Brazilian music is much more than samba. In the 1960s, Tom Jobim's hit tune *The Girl from Ipanema* turned bossa nova into a global sensation; in the 1980s it was the turn of the sensual lambada to storm clubs around the world. Bahia, home of Brazil's largest black population, has thrown up generations of creative singers, composers and musicians, including singer-composers like Caetano Veloso, his sister Maria Betania, Gilberto Gil, and Gal Costa, with their warm, melodious voices singing of love, poverty and protest.

Today they are joined by all-black bands such as Olodum and Timbalada and composers like Carlinhos Brown. In a country where so few people read, music is an important form of communication; most of Brazil's radio and TV commercials are sung, each political party has a theme tune at election time, and in the Northeast, *repentistas* make up instant ballads about current events, full of innuendo and irony.

During the dictatorship, the military insisted that the lyrics of all new songs had to be submitted to the censors and some were banned from performance. Nevertheless, *Caminhando* (Walking), by Geraldo Vandré became the anthem of the resistance movement, while everyone realized that Chico Buarque's apparently innocent *Apesar de Você (In spite of you, there must be another day)* referred to the military. Elis Regina's *O Bebado e o Equilibrista (The Drunk and the Tightrope Walker)*, which referred to well-known exiles, became another opposition favorite.

In Rio Grande do Sul, the revival of regional pride in the 1980s led to a spurt of music festivals where singers and musicians abandoned rock and pop and began singing forgotten gaúcho songs and composing new ones.

Literature

Brazil cannot claim any writer with the universal prestige of Colombia's Gabriel García Márquez. The book that has sold best abroad, *Beyond All Pity*, is not the work of a famous writer, but the diary of a black woman, Carolina Maria de Jesus, describing her tough daily life in a São Paulo favela. She died a few years ago, ignored and penniless.

The literary prestige of at least one nineteenth century writer, however, is growing fast. Joaquim Maria Machado de Assis (1839-1908) is now hailed as one of the most important contributors to Portuguese literature. Setting his novels in the Rio of the mid-1800s, he described the intimate details of daily life, class conflict, and the corrosion of institutions in a decaying, slave-owning, patriarchal society.

Of mixed blood and humble background, Machado de Assis has been described as the most profound interpreter of the dying days of Brazil's Empire. His best known works are *Memórias Póstumas de Bras Cubas, (Epitaph of a Small Winner), Dom Casmurro* and *Quincas Borba (Philosopher or Dog)*. Another classic of the nineteenth century was Euclides da Cunha's *Os Sertões (Rebellion in the Backlands)*, describing the war to destroy Canudos. Sent to cover the military campaign against the rebels by a Rio newspaper, da Cunha shared the prejudice of the time against the rebels, who he portrayed as ignorant religious fanatics, but also revealed the brutality of the upholders of law and order.

Search for Identity

In 1922 a Week of Modern Art held to commemorate 100 years of independence became a landmark event, launching a search for a distinctive

Brazilian identity to replace the prevailing Eurocentrism of art and politics. Indian and black culture were rediscovered and the dehumanization of the modern industrial world rejected. Out went waltzes and polkas, in came the samba. Erudite composer Heitor Villa-Lobos wove Brazilian rhythms into his music and created the famous *Bacchianas Brasílianas*. Candido Portinari painted scenes from the plantations, the docks, and the drought. Jorge Amado, a communist whose books became popular on both sides of the Iron Curtain, described the harsh life of the cacao plantations of Bahia, while Érico Veríssimo portrayed the cruelty and bloodshed of the separatist wars in Rio Grande do Sul.

Sociologist Gilberto Freyre wrote *Casa Grande e Senzala* (*The Masters and the Slaves*). Although Freyre's theory of benevolent master-slave relations has been widely rejected, he helped to make the idea of miscegenation (racial mixing) more acceptable by extolling its advantages. In 1928 Mario de Andrade wrote *Macunaíma*, the story of an anti-hero. Based on a legend of the Makuxi Indians, *Macunaíma* is an outrageous, amoral survivor who lives on his wits and so was seen as a fitting hero for modern Brazilians. For some, the book was also the first example of what was to become Latin America's most successful literary export, magical realism.

Cinema

Although it has one of the largest cinema audiences in the world, Brazil's own film industry has struggled to establish itself, winning just 50 international awards in nearly 100 years of film-making. In the 1960s, the *Cinema Nôvo* (New Cinema) directors Glauber Rocha and Ruy Guerra won acclaim with films that mixed religious fervor and social realism like *O Pagador de Promessas* and *Deus e o Diabo na Terra do Sol*, but they then fell victim to censorship under the military regime.

During the 1970s and 1980s, when political films were banned, the state film agency Embrafilme ended up funding mostly soft porn and children's films. In 1990 President Collor closed down Embrafilme and the film industry collapsed, but in 1995 with the introduction of tax breaks for companies who backed films, a revival began.

Architecture

Past, present, and future are all to be found within a few hours of each other in Brazil. The city of today is São Paulo, incessantly tearing down the past and building yet more sophisticated skyscrapers, road tunnels and shopping malls, while the tenacious favela dwellers cling to every bit of empty land, no matter how steep, risky, or cramped.

Only ten hours away by road is Ouro Preto, a hillside town of steep, cobbled streets and baroque churches built of soapstone, still essentially the

The Prophet Oseas, by
Aleijadinho, Congonhas

*Tony Morrison/
South American
Pictures*

same as in its heyday during the eighteenth century gold rush. Here, Tiradentes and the other rebels conspired against the Portuguese monarchy, while Aleijadinho, the half-caste son of a slave, left his inspired mark on hundreds of church carvings and statues in and around Ouro Preto. Crippled by leprosy, his tools had to be tied to his mutilated hands.

Brasília

Another six hours by road from Ouro Preto is the city of the future, Brasília, Brazil's third capital, a brand new city built in empty scrubland which now has well over a million inhabitants. The brainchild of President Juscelino Kubitschek, the city was planned by Lúcio Costa in the shape of an airplane fuselage.

But the man most associated with Brasília is architect Oscar Niemeyer, universally recognized as one of the great names of modern architecture. Born in 1907 and a life-long communist, Niemeyer designed many well-known buildings abroad, but it was the innovative architecture of Brasília, with its curves, ramps, and columns that made his international reputation. For André Malraux "the only columns comparable in beauty to the Greek columns are those of the [presidential palace of the] Palace of Alvorada."

Niemeyer wanted the new capital to be "the act of affirmation of an entire people." This philosophical concept took priority over the functional aspects of the buildings, to the future discomfort of its eventual more prosaic users – diplomats, civil servants, and congressmen and women. He wanted Brasília to be a democratic city where rich and poor would share the advantages of a planned, healthy environment. "Brasília was the proposal for a country which never was, created during the only moment of faith in itself which we've experienced in recent years," observed the poet Ferreira Gullar.

Instead, Brasília repeated the pattern of Brazil's older cities. The poor were expelled from the center to the periphery, in this case satellite towns, some of them 30 miles away. When the military took power, the Three Powers Square, where Executive, Congress, and Judiciary faced each other on equal terms, was disfigured by the erection of a giant flagstaff, a symbolic reminder of where power really lay.

Football

Every sort of sport is practiced in Brazil. If you look hard enough you can find old Italians playing *boche* (bowls), third generation Japanese playing baseball, and even the odd game of cricket at the British clubs in São Paulo and Rio. But there is only one game that counts: soccer, as essential a part of the Brazilian identity as samba and black beans.

It is hard to believe that when soccer was first played in Brazil it was derided as "the funny English game," a foreign transplant that would never catch on, more suitable for the well-nourished Anglo-Saxons than the less athletic Brazilians. One short-sighted commentator wrote, "It is like borrowed clothes that do not fit. For a foreign custom to establish itself in another country it must be in harmony with the people's way of life and fill a gap, and we already have the corn straw ball game...."

Soccer first came to Brazil in 1894, when Charles Miller, the Brazilian-born son of British parents, returned from school in England with a couple of footballs and a set of rules in his steamer trunk. It went on to become the national passion. Miller's daughter, still alive, says proudly "My father brought joy to Brazil." Intense joy, on the four times when Brazil won the World Cup, the last in 1994, but also intense anguish, when it failed. In 1950 the World Cup final was being played in Rio's famous Maracanã stadium before a capacity 150,000 crowd. An easy victory for Brazil against tiny Uruguay was a foregone conclusion, so when Uruguay unexpectedly scored to win, a deathly silence fell on the giant stadium. People wept with disbelief, men had heart attacks, and some committed suicide. Forty years later the unfortunate Brazilian goalkeeper is still haunted by that terrible moment.

The King

There have been generations of brilliant players. Pelé, real name Edson Arantes do Nascimento, is probably the best-known soccer player of all time, scoring over a thousand goals during his professional career. In 1995 President Fernando Henrique Cardoso chose Pelé, who has often admitted to cherishing political ambitions but always avoided the race issue, as Minister of Sport. Known as *O Rei* (The King), Pelé visited South Africa at the same time as Britain's Queen Elizabeth. When President Nelson Mandela reportedly rescheduled the Queen's program to fit in a meeting with Pelé, Brazilian papers had their headline ready: "The King overshadows Queen's visit."

The passion for football has made fortunes and political careers. During the military regime, giant stadiums were built in many cities. The national championship grew bloated as second-rate clubs were promoted to favor

Passion of the people: fans at the Flamengo v.
Fluminense soccer derby in Rio's Maracanã stadium

Julio Etchart/Reportage

local political supporters. Election candidates still donate club gear to local teams in exchange for votes.

But using soccer as an opium for the people has sometimes backfired. During an international match in Paris in 1978, TV cameras could not help showing the giant banners unfurled by Brazilians in the crowd calling for an amnesty for political prisoners, while famous soccer players, like Socrates, have campaigned for the Workers Party. Corruption scandals are frequent, involving rigged games and bribed referees. Many of the clubs and federations have been run by the same officials for decades. Known as *"cartolas"* – literally "top hats" – these officials enjoy immense power and prestige and have become wealthy men.

The national passion has also claimed its share of victims. In 1989 the pilot of a commercial airliner on a routine flight in the Amazon was so engrossed in listening to the Brazil v. Chile match in Rio that he failed to notice he was flying south instead of north. When the plane ran out of fuel it crashed in dense rainforest and was only found three days later. Luckily, most of the passengers survived.

Motor racing

Only motor racing has come anywhere near the popularity of soccer, but interest has waned since Ayrton Senna's tragic death on the Imola track in 1994. In the last twenty years, Brazil has produced two other Formula One champions, Emerson Fittipaldi and Nelson Piquet. Three times Grand Prix champion Senna was mourned like a national hero. On the day of his funeral, São Paulo came to a standstill as over two million people turned out to line the route and say farewell to their idol, buried with all the honors of a head of state.

Gambling

On almost every street corner, a man sits at a small table, or leans against the wall of a bar. He merges in with the other sidewalk habitués: the fruit-seller, the popcorn man, the lame beggar, the car-washer, the lottery ticket seller. During the day a steady stream of people come up to him, and he writes numbers down on slips of paper. Money discreetly changes hands. If you get close enough, you might hear the words "butterfly" or "lion." For this is Brazil's mysterious, clandestine *jogo do bicho*, the animal game.

It all began a hundred years ago, when the owner of the Rio Zoo ran out of money to feed the animals and started a raffle to raise funds. The winner had to choose the right animal. It soon became a craze and the Zoo was packed out, not with animal lovers, but with gamblers. The game grew so popular that it spread to the streets and all over the country. The authorities attempted without success to ban the new national obsession. It is said that 60,000 people work for the jogo do bicho in Rio alone and the annual turnover is put at $2 billion.

The game is now more sophisticated but is still based on 25 animals and the total honesty of the bookies, as no receipts are given. The jogo do bicho has become part of Brazilian culture – anyone who dreams about snakes or monkeys knows they must bet on that particular animal.

Mafia Connections

What for millions is just an innocent flutter also has its more sinister side. Jogo de bicho is run by a mafia and the bosses, known as *bicheiros*, have become powerful men accused of involvement in crime and drugs. Being patrons of the popular jogo do bicho means they can present themselves as benevolent members of society, masking their criminal activities by sponsoring samba schools and local soccer teams.

The law has traditionally been unable or unwilling to tackle them, but in 1994 a judge broke through their protective shield of bribery and corruption and sentenced fourteen of the bosses to six year sentences for forming an armed gang. Even so, the press soon reported that their cells were equipped with color TVs and hi-fis, they received visitors for barbecues and birthday parties, and continued to conduct their deals on mobile phones.

Media

Illiteracy is dropping, but twenty per cent of adult Brazilians are still unable to read and write, and up to 60 per cent can do little more than write their own name. As a result, newspapers are read by a tiny minority and most people get their news, opinions, ideas, and prejudices from commercial television and radio.

One network, Globo TV, has dominated the airwaves for decades and been the mouthpiece of every government, military or civilian. Presidential pronouncements are always timed to precede the main evening Globo news – even its competitors arrange their schedules around it. The Globo TV network covers 99 per cent of Brazilian territory, and until recently claimed audiences of nearly 80 per cent. Seventy-five per cent of Brazilian TV's media advertising budget goes to Globo, while TV's total share of the national advertising budget is 50 per cent (compared to about twenty per cent in the U.S.).

Internationally, TV Globo ranks fourth amongst the world's television networks, with almost as many employees as the BBC. But alongside its size and sophistication are the idiosyncrasies of a family firm. Like Alfred Hitchcock appearing in his own films, Globo's aging president, Roberto Marinho, likes to feature in his own newscasts, receiving awards or decorations, and writes moralistic editorials to be read at the end of the news.

Marinho has been a power behind the throne of every recent president, and has been accused innumerable times of slanting the news to favor the government. But during the worst excesses of the military regime, even TV Globo had to obey the yard-long official telexes, listing all the subjects that must not be mentioned to avoid jeopardizing national security.

TV Globo has sold its fast-moving, often humorous, sometimes satirical, but always sexy soap operas around the world. Its costume soaps top the ratings in China and Cuba with the story of Isaura, a white girl brought up as a slave, transforming actress Lucélia Santos into a star better known in those countries than in Brazil. After 30 years of dominating audience ratings, Globo's stranglehold is now under threat from other commercial channels such as SBT, Manchete, Record and Bandeirantes.

Although TV and radio concessions are free, they carry no public service obligations. That is left to the impoverished state TV channels. Globo does, however, transmit supplementary school courses for young adults and used to have an excellent children's program. The Cardoso government plans to tap the huge potential of TV and video for educational purposes.

Traditionally, governments have awarded TV and radio concessions in reward for political services. In 1988 President José Sarney bought himself

Bahiana woman selling
snacks, Salvador

*Tony Morrison/South
American Pictures*

an extra year in office by distributing hundreds of new TV and radio concessions. Virtual licenses to print money because of the advertising revenue, they are also invaluable aids to winning elections.

Food and Drink

Centuries of growing sugar-cane has given Brazilians a sweet tooth. The ubiquitous *cafezinho* – small black coffee – invariably comes steeped in sugar. Sugar-cane rum, or *pinga,* is drunk neat but the delicious *caipirinha*, an aperitif, adds sugar, lemon, and ice to the rum. The result is widespread tooth decay and millions of people who have lost all their teeth before they are middle aged.

Brazilian cuisine is rich, varied, and tasty. The national dish, *feijoada*, a black bean stew, was invented by slaves who had to make do with the left-over bits of pig, the trotters, tail, and ears, while their masters feasted off the prime cuts. The result is a tasty, if heavy, dish eaten with manioc flour, a slice of orange, and rice. Restaurants serve feijoada only on Wednesdays and Saturdays. Manioc (cassava) flour is a staple all over the North, where it accompanies freshwater fish, and in the Northeast, where it is eaten with *carne do sol*, dried meat.

In Bahia, where the slave population outnumbered the white, regional dishes are heavily influenced by African traditions and dendê palm oil is widely used. In Rio Grande do Sul, the eating habits of the original Indian population have been preserved, but made sophisticated. The *churrasco*, barbecued meat, is no longer cooked on spits stuck in a hole in the ground but roasted on electrically rotated spits. Up-market apartments include their own barbecue room. The *chimarrão* (mate tea) is still drunk from a gourd through a silver-plated siphon, but these days the boiling water comes from a thermos flask.

Guaraná, an Amazon fruit used as a stimulant, can now be found in pills and capsules in health shops all over the world. In the Amazon it is sold in a hard stick which should then be grated with the dried tongue of the *pirarucu* fish and mixed with water.

CONCLUSION

"If we wished to, we could make of this country a great nation," said Brazil's national hero, Tiradentes. Two hundred years on, Brazil has become an economic power with enormous potential, but it remains trapped in an archaic political system of privilege and shocking social inequality. Throughout history the economy has endlessly adapted to new cycles, new products, new demands with dynamism and versatility. Yet the mental legacy of the slave system prevents the same dynamism being applied to social change, preserving instead a two-tier system of citizenship – the included and the excluded.

The ruling classes' excuses have always been the same: wealth must trickle down, the cake must be allowed to grow before it can be divided. History shows that Brazil has always produced immense wealth and that it has always been cornered by a minority and used for consumption, not investment. Gigantic funds are not needed to change Brazil. What is needed is the will to change. Brazil needs a mental revolution, a reversal of priorities, so that its social development can catch up with its economic development. Otherwise, the currency can change, the president can change, even the capital city changes place every now and again, but Brazil risks entering the third millennium still labeled the land of the future.

WHERE TO GO, WHAT TO SEE

Wherever you go in Brazil, the language is Portuguese and the passion football, but each region has a very distinctive flavor. The distances are huge, so it makes sense to get an air pass when you arrive. The welcome end to hyperinflation brought with it an overvalued *Real*, so Brazil is no longer a cheap country and internal airfares are expensive.

Rail Travel

Railroads are rare, run-down, and slow. The exceptions are the breathtakingly beautiful line that runs past waterfalls and across gorges from Curitiba down to the port of Paranaguá on the Paraná coast. Or in the North, the thrice-weekly, sisteen-hour trip which takes you 550 miles southwest from São Luis to the iron ore mine at Carajás in the Eastern Amazon. The nightly train that runs between Rio and São Paulo has been privatized, modernized, and renamed the Silver Train. You can now wine and dine aboard but a sleeping cabin will cost you $100.

Buses

Hitchhiking is not much practiced and anyway buses are plentiful and cheap. Half of Brazil always seems to be traveling: buses and bus terminals are always crowded. Slightly more expensive are the *onibus leito* (literally, bed-buses), which offer you a fully reclining seat and unlimited coffee and mineral water as they roll through the night or day.

Rio de Janeiro

Rio's reputation as one of the most beautiful cities in the world has been tarnished by its more recent fame as a violent, dangerous place to walk around. Behave as you would in any big city – leave your valuables and passport in the hotel, take nothing to the beach, and keep your eyes open.

Ouro Preto

Eight hours from Rio, ten hours from São Paulo, Ouro Preto, recognized by UNESCO as the most complete eighteenth century colonial town in the world, is a tightly-packed mass of cobbled streets, houses, and richly decorated churches, built with the gold of the local mines. Look for Aleijadinho's work, scattered in different places. Semi-precious stones and soapstone artifacts are on sale everywhere.

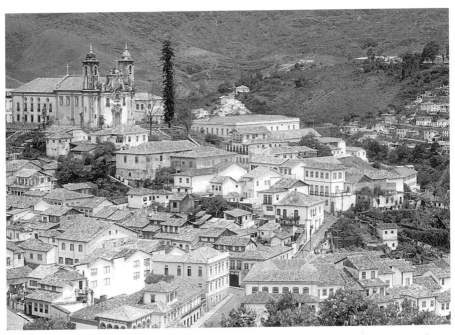

Ouro Preto

Tony Morrison/South American Pictures

Salvador

Brazil's capital when the slave trade was at its height, it still has the highest proportion of black people. Syncretism has produced a unique mix of Catholic and African candomblé religions. Musical creativity is at its height in Salvador, with the powerful drumbeat of Olodum and other mass percussion bands echoing round the cobbled streets, the annual invention of new Carnival rhythms blaring out to the massed crowds that dance behind the *trios elétricos* (mobile band platforms) and the gentle twang of the *berimbau* player. South or north of Salvador is lotus-eater's paradise – soft sandy beaches where you can lie under palm trees sipping from a fresh coconut and snacking on freshly-caught seafood. Brazil's Atlantic coastline offers hundreds of beaches, some exploited, many unspoiled.

Belém

Built round an old fort on the mouth of the Amazon, the streets are lined with ancient mango trees. Ver o Peso is an open air waterfront market selling charms, herbs, and essences guaranteed to cure every conceivable physical and emotional problem, from cancer to unfaithfulness.

Marajó

A boat or plane ride takes you from Belém to the world's biggest river island, home to herds of wild and domesticated buffalo. Even the police ride buffalo instead of horses.

The Amazon

To get a feeling of the real width of the mighty Amazon, travel upriver to Santarém, where the Tapajós river flows into it. Buy a hammock and a length of rope and go down to the quayside where the riverboats wait for the evening tide to sail to Oriximina or Obidos. Join the other passengers in the forest of gently swaying hammocks, fall asleep to the throbbing of the engine as the boat chugs across the river, with the moon shining on the water. Wake at dawn and discover you have exchanged the open sea of the Amazon for the confines of a river. A slug of coffee from the communal thermos flask, a quick wash, and you can stand at the rail and watch life on the riverbank, children splashing and swimming, women washing clothes, men silently paddling canoes.

Manaus

A thousand miles upriver from the sea is the Amazon capital, where the few reminders of the rubber boom include the beautiful 100-year-old Opera House, and the floating dock built to accommodate an annual tidal rise and fall of up to 50 feet. Manaus is now reachable by road from the south but the main highway into the depths of the Amazon remains the river, with boats of all sizes carrying cargo and passengers.

Pantanal

One of the world's largest wildlife areas, these vast wetlands lie in the west of Brazil, spilling over into Bolivia and Paraguay. There are over 600 bird species and river banks lined with sunbathing caiman alligators and herds of capivara (the world's largest rodent). You can take boat trips from Corumbá, a sleepy, baking-hot waterfront town on the Paraguai river, while from Campo Grande and Cuiabá, you can join safaris or reach ranch-hotels.

Rio Grande do Sul

Along with Santa Catarina, Brazil's most southern states offer a temperate climate and a strong German and Italian influence, present in food, architecture, and last names. But the characteristic barbecue (*churrasco*) and mate tea (*chimarrão*) are customs inherited from the original inhabitants of the rolling pampas and valleys, the Indians.

TIPS FOR TRAVELLERS

People

Brazilians respond much better to a smile than a shout, to a joke rather than an insult. Don't be afraid of physical contact: Brazilians, like other Latins, do not have the same horror of touching each other that most Anglo-Saxons have. Everyone shakes hands all the time, friends and often mere acquaintances kiss once, twice, or even three times on the cheek, men pat or thump each other on the back. When they are talking to each other Brazilians not only wave their hands around but feel the need to touch the person they are talking to.

Safety

Brazil has a reputation for petty crime, especially in the big cities like Rio, São Paulo, and Recife, where muggers and bag snatchers are common and tourists are fair game. However, you can reduce the risks by taking a few basic precautions.

Be streetwise – leave passports, travelers checks and money in the hotel safe and carry only small amounts of cash when you go out. Take your camera in an ordinary plastic bag, not around your neck. Don't wear expensive jewelry or watches. In Rio and other seaside resorts, take as little as possible to the beach. Even clothes get stolen while you are swimming! Don't walk on Rio's Copacabana beach at night, it's a notorious mugging spot. Don't visit shanty-towns unless accompanied by somebody who knows the residents.

Health

Taking a few precautions can also avert health problems which can spoil your trip, or worse. Don't drink tap water – mineral water is generally available; don't eat unwashed lettuce or fruit – market gardeners use liberal amounts of pesticide; and don't overdo the sunbathing, especially around midday.

You only have to worry about malaria if you are going away from the main tourist centers into certain areas of the Amazon. It is more prevalent during the rainy season, which runs from October to April. Mosquito nets can be purchased at any Amazon town.

If you pick up some form of bug or parasite, go to an English-speaking Brazilian doctor because he will be more familiar with the symptoms.

Pharmacies sell over the counter many medicines and drugs that would be available on prescription only in UK and the U.S.. Tampons and similar items are sold everywhere in pharmacies and supermarkets, as are condoms.

Women Travelers

It is becoming more and more common to see women traveling on their own, eating on their own. Except in the more remote places, lone women should not encounter any problems.

Changing Money

Dollars and travelers checks can now be changed at many banks, travel agencies, and exchange (Cambio) shops. Hotels also exchange money, but give a lower rate. Don't be confused by the existence of three different rates – commercial, tourist and "parallel," the Brazilian euphemism for black market. There is almost no difference between them, so it is best to change at a bank, agency, or shop. Outside the main cities, changing money is much more difficult, and international credit cards are not always acceptable, so it is best to change sufficient before you travel to the interior.

Souvenirs

The best places to buy souvenirs are in the open air markets. Never accept the first price, always haggle.
São Paulo: Praça da Republica and Praça de Liberdade (oriental fair). Markets are held on Saturdays and Sundays.
Rio: Praça General Osorio and along the beaches.
Belém: Ver o Peso market, renowned for charms and potions of all sorts.
The government's Indian affairs agency, FUNAI, runs shops at the major airports which offer indigenous artifacts at reasonable prices.

Children

Because of baby trafficking and pedophile scandals, foreigners taking small children or babies out of Brazil may be required to prove their relationship with them. If traveling with children, be prepared for this by taking their birth certificates with you.

Drugs

Brazilian prisons are crowded with foreigners caught attempting to smuggle out drugs, sometimes just a few grams. Brazil is a major corridor for cocaine produced in Bolivia, Colombia, and Peru: the police are very alert; the sentences are long, and prison conditions are harsh. Don't risk it.

ADDRESSES AND CONTACTS

BRAZIL

Brasília

British Embassy, Setor de Embaixadas Sul, Quadra 801, Conjunto K. Tel: 225 2710

Canadian Embassy, Av. das Nacões, Q803, lote 16, sl. 130 Tel: 321 2171

U.S. Embassy, Av. das Nacões, lote 3. Tel: 321 7272 or 224 9344 (after hours)

Curitiba

British Trade Office, Rua Presidente Faria 51, 7 andar, Tel: 322 1202

Porto Alegre

British Commercial Office Rua Antenor Lemos 57 Conjunto 403 Tel: 249 1060; 249 6688

U.S. Consulate, Rua Cel. Genuino 421. Tel: 226 4177

Recife

British Consulate, Av. Marques de Olinda 200, room 410, 4th floor. Tel: 2214 0650

U.S. Consulate, Rua Gonçalves Maia 163, Boa Vista. Tel: 221 1412/1413, 222 6577/6612

Rio de Janeiro

British Consulate-General Praia do Flamengo, 284/2 andar Tel: 553 3223

Canadian Consulate, Rua Lauro Müller 116, Room 1104, Torre Rio Sul, Botofago. Tel: 275 2137

U.S. Consulate, Av. Presidente Wilson 147, Centro. Tel: 292 7117

São Paulo

British Consulate-General Av. Paulista 37, 17 andar. Tel: 287 7722

Canadian Consulate, Av. Paulista 854, Bela Vista Tel: 285 5099

USA AND CANADA

Amaaka'a Amazon Network, 339 Lafayette St., New York, NY 10003

Global Exchange, 2017 Mission St., Rm. 303, San Francisco, CA 94110. Tel: (415) 255 7296, organizes "Reality Tours" to a number of countries, including Brazil. These provide participants with a chance to meet local people and learn about the most pressing issues facing the country. Also Women-to-Women Exchanges, which sets up internships with Brazilian women's organizations.

News from Brazil, PO Box 42536, Los Angeles, CA 90050-0536, monthly magazine with 60 pages on politics, culture, soccer news, etc.

Rainforest Action Network, 450 Sansome St., Suite 700, San Francisco, CA 94111. Tel: (415) 398 4404.

Rising Youth for Social Equity (RYSE), 2017 Mission St., 3rd floor, San Francisco, CA 94110. Tel: (415) 863 1100. Fax: (415) 863 9798. Email: kidryse@aol.com, builds links between U.S. and Brazilian youth to organize for positive social change.

50 Years Is Enough Coalition, 1025 Vermont Ave, NW, Suite 300, Washington DC 20005. Tel: (202) 879 3197. Works on World Bank and structural adjustment issues.

BRITAIN

Action Brazil, 26A Chatsworth Road, London NW2 4BS, promotes "Campaign Against Hunger in Brazil", raising funds and sending second-hand clothes to Brazil.

Brazil Network, PO Box 1325, London SW9 0RA, links individuals and organizations working on Brazil and interested in keeping up to date on events. Publishes a quarterly newsletter.

Brazilian Arts and Community Centre, 1 Elgin Avenue, London W9, provides a range of services for the Brazilian community.

Brazilian Contemporary Arts, Palingswick House, 241 King St., London W6 9LP, organizes cultural events and publishes a regular newsletter.

Brazilian Embassy, 32 Green St., London W1Y 4AT, the embassy has an Internet site on http://www.demon.co.uk/Itamaraty/, with a range of economic, political and other information on Brazil.

Leros, 25A Collingbourne Rd., London W12 0SG.
Free Portuguese-language magazine for the Brazilian community in Britain.

Workers Party (PT), PO Box 3698, London SW2 1XB.
Contact for its London branch. Organizes events, fund-raising.

Task Brasil, 140 Bermondsey St., London SE1 3TX.
New organization, planning to set up a network of shelters for street children in Brazil.

FURTHER READING AND BOOKSTORES

Fiction

Amado J., *Dona Flor and Her Two Husbands*, New York, 1969
Amado J., *The War of the Saints*, New York, 1993
de Andrade M., *Macunaíma*, New York, 1984
Dourado A., *A Hidden Life*, New York, 1969
Lispector C., *Family Ties*, Austin, Texas, 1972
Lispector C., *The Hour of the Star*, Manchester, 1986
Machado de Assis, J.M., *Epitaph of a Small Winner*, New York, 1952
Machado de Assis, J.M., *Dom Casmurro*, New York, 1953
Machado de Assis, J.M., *Philosopher or Dog*, New York, 1954
de Queirós R., *The Three Marias*, Austin, Texas, 1963
Ramos G., *Childhood*, London, 1979
Ribeiro D., *Maíra*, New York, 1984
Ribeiro J.U., *An Invincible Memory*, New York, 1988
Souza M., *The Emperor of the Amazon*, New York, 1977
Torres A., *The Land*, London, 1987

Non Fiction: Politics and Society

Branford, S. and Kucinski, B., *Brazil, Carnival of the Oppressed: Lula and the Brazilian Workers' Party*, London, 1995
Caipora, *Women in Brazil*, London, 1993
de Castro, J., *Death in the Northeast: Poverty and Revolution in the Northeast of Brazil*, New York, 1966
da Cunha, E., *Rebellion in the Backlands*, Chicago, 1957
Dannaher, K. and Shellenberger, M. (eds), *Fighting for the Soul of Brazil*, New York, 1995
Dimenstein, G., *Brazil: War on Children*, London, 1991
Freyre, G., *The Masters and The Slaves*, New York, 1964
Guillermoprieto, A., *Samba*, London, 1990
Keck, M., *The Workers' Party and Democratization in Brazil*, New Haven, 1992
de Jesus, C.M., *Beyond All Pity: The Diary of Carolina Maria de Jesus*, London, 1990
Macauley, N., *Dom Pedro: The Struggle for Liberty In Brazil and Portugal*, Durham NC, 1986
Scheper-Hughes, N., *Death Without Weeping: The Violence of Everyday Life in Brazil*, Berkeley, 1992
Sutton, A., *Slavery in Brazil*, London, 1995

Non Fiction: Amazon and the Environment

Branford, S. and Glock,O., *The Last Frontier: Fighting Over Land in the Amazon*, London, 1985

Cummings, B., *Dam the Rivers, Damn the People: Development and Resistance in Amazonian Brazil*, London, 1990

Hecht, S. and Cockburn, A., *The Fate of the Forest*, London, 1990

Hemming, J., *Red Gold: The Conquest of the Brazilian Indians*, London, 1995

Hemming, J., *Amazon Frontier: The Defeat of the Brazilian Indians*, London, 1995

Macmillan, G., *At the End of the Rainbow? Gold, Land and People in the Brazilian Amazon*, London, 1995

Mendes, C. and Gross, T., *Fight for the Forest: Chico Mendes in his Own Words*, London, 1992

Fr. Ricardo Rezende, *Rio Maria: Song of the Earth*, London, 1994

Bookstores in Brazil

São Paulo

Cultura, Conjunto Nacional, Avenida Paulista 2073, Cerqueira César, has a big selection of English-language books, as do *Bestseller*, Av. Tietê 184, Cerqueira César and *Kosmos*, Av. São Luis 162, Centro. More English-language books, along with a wide selection of Portuguese-language work, can be found at *Brasiliense*, Rua Barão de Ipateninga 99, Seridó.

Recife

Livro 7, Rua Sete de Setembro 329, in the city center, has foreign-language books.

Rio de Janeiro

For English language books, try the various branches of *Unilivros*, scattered all over Rio, e.g. at the Largo do Machado (Flamengo) and at Av. Ataúlfo de Paiva 686 (Leblon).

FACTS AND FIGURES

GEOGRAPHY

Official Name: República Federativa do Brasil

Situation: Between 5° 16" N and 33° 45" South, and between 35° and 74° West. Occupies most of eastern-central part of South America, with 92% of the country located between the Equator and the Tropic of Capricorn. Four different time zones. Maximum north-south distance 2678 m.; east-west 2683 m.

Surface Area: 3,282,226 sq.m., (approx same size as USA, 35 times the size of the United Kingdom). Covers 21% of the Americas and 47% of South America. The Amazon region (Amazonia Legal) covers 1.9 million sq.m., 60% of Brazil's total area.

Frontiers: 9,746 m. of land frontiers with nine other countries: Argentina, Uruguay, Paraguay, Bolivia, Peru, Colombia, Surinam, Guyana, and French Guyane.

Administrative division: Brazil is a federal republic with 26 states and 1 federal district (Brasília).

Capital: Brasília, 1.3 million inhabitants

Other Cities: There are 9 metropolitan areas with over 1 million inhabitants, the largest being São Paulo with 17 million and Rio de Janeiro with 10 million. Belo Horizonte and Salvador have over 2 million, and Salvador, Belém, Fortaleza, Curitiba, and Porto Alegre over 1 million (1991 census).

Infrastructure and travel: 990,000 m. of roads, but only 9% paved (1993). Uruguay, Paraguay, Argentina, Bolivia, Peru, Venezuela, and Guyana can be reached by road. Some excellent expressways in the São Paulo area.

Air travel: excellent network connects Brazil with Europe, North and South America, Africa, and Asia. All major Brazilian cities and many smaller ones reachable by air: three national private airlines (Varig, Vasp, Transbrasil) plus several regional carriers.

Railroads: 13,600 m. of track, divided into six regional networks. Passenger services Rio-São Paulo, Curitiba-Paranagua (most scenic), São Paulo-Santos, São Paulo-Brasília, São Luis-Carajás. Commuter networks in Rio, São Paulo, and other large cities very overcrowded, ancient rolling stock, badly maintained. São Paulo and Rio have very modern, efficient but limited metro systems.

Waterways: the Amazon region has 50,000m. of navigable waterways: passenger boats and cargo boats taking passengers ply all the main rivers (cabins and hammocks).

Ports: South Atlantic ports: Santos, Rio de Janeiro, Rio Grande, Tubarão, Paranaguá. North Atlantic: Belém and São Luis

Relief and landscape: Brazil's vast areas offers great variety, from the rainforest in the north to the *caatinga* drylands in the Northeast. North of the Amazon the rainforest changes to savannah before reaching the Surinamese and Guyanese borders. The Pantanal wetlands in the west cover 58,000 sq.m., extending into Bolivia and Paraguay, and are home to thousands of species of birds, reptiles and mammals. Between the Amazon region and the caatinga region there is a fertile transition zone of undulating hills covered in palm trees. Central Brazil is a plateau of open plains with twisted trees and acid soils (*cerrados*). In the South little is left of the once extensive pine (araucaria) forests and only 8% remains of the Atlantic Forest which once covered the entire Atlantic seaboard. Brazil's 4,500 m. of sea-coast include thousands of attractive palm-fringed beaches. Brazil's most mountainous regions are the central state of Minas Gerais and the southern state of Santa Catarina. The highest peak is the 9886ft. Pico da Neblina on the Amazon border with Venezuela.

Temperature and rainfall: in most of Brazil the climate is tropical with temperatures rarely under 65°F. In Rio summer temperatures can reach the 100s. In São Paulo winter (July-August) temperatures can fall to under 50°F. Snow occasionally falls in the southern states of Santa Catarina and Rio Grande do Sul, when below freezing temperatures are recorded. In São Paulo and Rio summer (December-March) rainstorms often lead to extensive flooding.

Fauna: there are no large wild animals in Brazil but many smaller ones and thousands of bird, fish, and insect species. 36 species, including jaguars, monkeys, and anteaters are considered to be in danger of extinction.

POPULATION

Population (1995): 155.8 million. Sixth largest in world.

Population growth (cumulative): 1980-1991: 23.3% (urban 37.9%, rural -7.0%)

Population density: 45.8 inhabitants per sq.m. (world average 98 per sq.m.)

Urbanization: 75% live in cities and towns, most of them on or near the coast.

Age structure: rapid changes due to the fall in family size: percentage of under 15s will fall from 35% to 24% by the year 2020, while over 65s rise to 8% of population.

Fertility rate: 2.7 children per woman of reproductive age in 1990, compared to 6.1 in 1940

Birth rate: 1.7% (1990-95), 3% (1960-69)

Infant mortality rate (1994): 56/1000; 156/1,000 (1950s)

Average life expectancy (1993): women: 68.9 years, men: 64.1

Adult illiteracy (1993): 17.6% (10% in São Paulo, 40% in Piauí)

Education: primary education is free between 7 and 14 (8 years), secondary education is free 14-18 (4 years). Only 50% of school-age children are in school.

UNDP Human Development Index (1995): 63rd out of 174

Language: Portuguese, and 170 indigenous languages spoken by Brazil's 320,000 Indians.

Ethnic composition (1991 census): Whites 54%, blacks 6%, mestiços (mixed race) 39%. The proportion of whites and blacks if falling, while that of mestiços is rising.

Religion: Roman Catholicism

BRAZIL
Population Density
by State 1995

—·—·— national boundary
— — — regional/state boundaries
——— rivers

Density per square mile
- under 8
- 8 - 25
- 25 - 100
- 100 - 200
- 200 - 260
- 350 São Paulo
- 775 Brasília (Federal District)
- 780 Rio de Janeiro

remains the majority religion, but the numbers are falling steadily. An estimated 15% (and rising) belongs to Protestant, including Pentecostal Churches. 3.5 million belong to the fastest growing Pentecostal Church, the Universal Church of the Kingdom of God.

The national statistical institute (IBGE) estimates that up to 1.5% of heads of families follows Afro-Brazilian religions such as candomblé and umbanda, while the Afro-Brazilian Federation says 70 million Brazilians have links with them.

Sources: Instituto Brasileiro de Geografia e Estadística (IBGE); UNDP; World Bank, Europa Yearbook of South America, Central America and the Caribbean

HISTORY AND POLITICS

Some key dates.
1500 Pedro Alvares Cabral sights land and names it "Land of the True Cross"* 1530 first African slaves arrive in Brazil * 1630-1695 Palmares Quilombo* 1789 Conspiracy discovered to overthrow Portuguese rule and declare republic * 1792 Tiradentes, one of plotters, hung, drawn, and quartered * 1808 Portuguese court moves to Brazil * 1822 Independence of Brazil declared. Pedro I becomes emperor * 1865 Brazil, Argentina, and Uruguay form Triple Alliance and declare war on Paraguay * 1888 Slavery abolished * 1889 Republic declared * 1924 Prestes column begins march * 1930 Getúlio Vargas leads a revolution, President Washington Luis deposed * 1932 São Paulo oligarchy declares constitutional revolution against Vargas * 1937 Getúlio Vargas creates Estado Nôvo, a populist dictatorship * 1942 Brazil enters Second World War in support of the Allies * 1954 Vargas commits suicide * 1960 Brasilia, Brazil's new capital, inaugurated * 1961 President Jânio Quadros resigns, setting off political crisis that leads to military coup three years later * 1964 Military overthrow President João Goulart * 1968 President Costa e Silva closes Congress and introduces repression with Decree AI-5 * 1979 Amnesty introduced by military *

1985 Tancredo Neves, first civilian president after 21 year military regime, dies before taking office. Vice-president José Sarney becomes president * 1986 President Sarney introduces Cruzado Plan, the first of series of unsuccessful economic plans designed to tame inflation * 1987 Brazil declares moratorium on foreign debt repayments * 1989 First direct presidential elections since 1960. Fernando Collor elected after using dirty tricks to defeat left-wing trade unionist Luis Inácio Lula da Silva * 1992 President Collor resigns to avoid impeachment * 1994 President Itamar Franco introduces Real Plan to curb inflation * 1994 Fernando Henrique Cardoso elected President
Constitution: presidential republic: election for 5-year term by universal suffrage (over 16 years). Legislative power is exercised by the 81-seat senate and the 513-seat chamber of deputies, elected for 4-year terms by universal suffrage. The size of legislative assemblies in each state varies according to its population.
Head of state: Fernando Henrique Cardoso (term began Jan. 1995)
Congress: main parties (numbers fluctuate) are Partido da Social-Democracia Brasileira (PSDB, Party of Brazilian Social Democracy); the right-wing Partido da Frente Liberal (PFL, Party of the

Liberal Front; the centrist Partido do Movimento Democrático Brasileiro (PMDB, Party of the Brazilian Democratic Movement); the right-wing Partido Progressista Brasileiro, (PPB, Brazilian Progressive Party), former pro-military Arena); the left-wing Partido dos Trabalhadores (PT, Workers Party), and the center-left Partido Democrático Trabalhista (PDT, Democratic Labor).
Armed Forces: Total armed forces in 1994 comprised 336,800. Of these, 219,000 were in the army (including 126,500 conscripts); 58,400 in the navy (2,000 conscripts) and 59,400 in the air force (5,000 conscripts).
Membership of international organizations: UN and UN agencies, Organization of American States, Rio Group (with other South American states, plus Mexico), Mercosul (with Argentina, Uruguay, and Paraguay), G77, Latin American Integration Association, International Monetary Fund
Media/communications: There are 15.5 million telephones, including 1.6 million mobiles (1995). Daily newspapers with national distribution are *Folha de S.Paulo*, *O Globo*, *O Estado de São Paulo*, *Jornal do Brasil*, and *Gazeta Mercantil*. The main weekly news magazines are *Veja*, and *Isto É*. There are 257 TV Stations. The largest commercial networks are

GERMANY by Felix Bucher

Above: *Metropolis*

in the same

SCREEN SERIES

edited by Peter Cowie

produced by The Tantivy Press

EASTERN EUROPE
by Nina Hibbin

SWEDEN 1 & 2
by Peter Cowie

JAPAN
by Arne Svensson

THE AMERICAN MUSICAL
by Tom Vallance

THE GANGSTER FILM
by John Baxter

Forthcoming

FRANCE
by Marcel Martin

ITALY 1
by Ken Wlaschin

ITALY 2
by Felix Bucher

THE WESTERN
by Allen Eyles

A CONCISE HISTORY OF THE CINEMA
2 vols, edited by Peter Cowie

screen SERIES

GERMANY

in collaboration with Leonhard H. Gmür

by Felix Bucher

A. ZWEMMER LIMITED, LONDON
A.S. BARNES & CO., NEW YORK

Acknowledgements

THIS BOOK could not have been completed without the aid of the following publications: *Deutsche Stummfilme 1923-1926, 1927-1931*, both volumes by Gerhard Lamprecht; *Deutscher Spielfilm-Almanach 1929-50*, by Dr. A. Bauer; *Lexicon degli autori e dei film; Prominenten Filmlexicon*, by Glenzdorf; *Wir vom Film*, by Charles Reinert; *Expressionismus und Film*, by Rudolf Kurtz, *From Caligari to Hitler*, by Siegfried Kracauer; *Kleines Filmlexikon*, by Charles Reinert; *Die Verfilmung literarischer Werke*, by Alfred Estermann; *Filmgegner von heute – Filmfreunde von morgen*, by Hans Richter (re-issue 1968); *Der Weg des Films*, by Friedrich von Zglinicki; the catalogues of the Export Union of the German Film Industry; the publications of the Austrian Film Institute, the Austrian Film Archive and the Austrian Society for Film Science, as well as a number of standard books written by or about film-makers (Lotte Eisner, *The Haunted Screen;* Erwin Leiser, *Germany Awake!)*, various catalogues and retrospectives, and pamphlets issued by the Deutsche Kinemathek, Berlin.

The author also wishes to extend personal thanks to the following individuals: – Elisabeth and Peter Cowie, Werner Zurbuch and D.I.F.F. (Munich), Ursula Hafemann and the Press Service of DEFA, Hanspeter Manz and Buchhandlung Rohr Zürich, the staff of the Information Department of the British Film Institute, Anthony Slide, Max Mack, Hermann Warm, and Erika Gregor.

This dictionary has been compiled with the indispensable help and knowledge of Leonhard H. Gmür, especially where the silent period and *Junger deutscher film* are concerned.

Cover Stills

Front: DAS WACHSFIGURENKABINETT. *Back:* DIE ABENTEUER DES WERNER HOLT (left); Gert Fröbe in DIE TAUSEND AUGEN DES DR. MABUSE (Centre); Lilli Palmer with Romy Schneider in MÄDCHEN IN UNIFORM (right); and Alexander Kluge in ABSCHIED VON GESTERN (bottom)

Library of Congress Catalogue Card No. 69-14899
SBN 498 07517 6 (U.S.A.)
SBN 302 02007 1 (U.K.)

Printed in Holland by Drukkerijen De Bussy Ellerman Harms nv,
Amsterdam

Introduction

THE DATE with each film refers nearly always to the year in which it was released (and not to the production year). In doubtful cases, or when there is a considerable time lapse between the production and release dates, the production year as well as the date of the release are stated (e.g. 1927/28). **For reasons of time and space, films released after approximately November 1969 have been omitted.**

If the director is not mentioned in the book, he is stated after the *première* date in brackets. When two directors are given (and not connected by &), the first directed the German version and the second one the foreign version (e.g. *Dämon des Meeres/Moby Dick,* 1931, Michael Kertesz/Lloyd Bacon, G/USA. Michael Kertesz [i.e. Michael Curtiz] directed the German version, whereas Lloyd Bacon the one in Hollywood). The question of artistic supervision is answered only in those cases where the director or the artistic supervisor is mentioned in the book. In special cases of interesting or important silent films, the number of parts (I, II, I-IV, etc.) is given.

When a film has been released, or is well known, in Britain and the U.S.A., it is cross-referenced under its English title.

As most of the significant films were made prior to 1945 there is a preponderance of material about the earlier period. This explains the absence of many figures in the entertainment film, mainly after 1945. Preference has been given to the people really responsible for the creation of those vintage German films between 1919 and 1933 – the set designers, cameramen, writers, and of course directors.

The most important set designers created a vital link between film and the other arts (esp. painting and architecture), e.g. Poelzig, Warm and Reimann. Because so many German film personalities have a theatre background, details have been given of their stage work. The Guide is intended primarily as a textbook and the specialist may well notice that certain names have been omitted. This is mainly due to a shortage of space. Within the range of 415 filmographies, every effort has been made to include the vast majority of films. There is still a largely uncharted area of the German cinema before 1920, in which personalities like Messter, Froelich and Oswald flourished. Instead of devoting space to men like Heinrich Gärtner, Erich Waschneck, Hochbaum, Junghans, Robert Liebmann, and others, I have included, for instance, Carl Boese, whose career spanned practically the whole field of German film-making, so that one has a cross-section sometimes more revealing than any number of individual entries. Austrian film-makers have only been included when they were actually involved in the German cinema proper (therefore Paul Henreid and Oskar Werner for example have been omitted). On the other hand I have noted Austrian films with which German *cinéastes* were connected (titles of Austrian features are not necessarily those given to them on their German release). Switzerland has been ignored entirely.

Whenever the director of a film does not have an entry in the text, his name appears in brackets after the film's title in the Index Section. In principle, the date given is that of the film's release in Germany.

ABBREVIATIONS

A : Austria
B : Bulgaria
Cz : Czechoslovakia
D : Denmark
F : France
Fi : Finland
G : Germany
GB : Great Britain
H : Hungary
I : Italy
J : Japan
M : Mexico
N : Netherlands
P : Poland
Port : Portugal
R : Rumania
Sp : Spain
Sw : Sweden
Switz : Switzerland
USA : United States of America
USSR : Soviet Russia
Yug : Yugoslavia

No films made outside Germany and Austria, and/or foreign films made without German financial participation, are included in the filmographies. Thus, for example, Louise Brooks's American work is not listed.

Note: Frankfurt means Frankfurt-am-Main unless otherwise stated. Freiburg means Freiburg im Breisgau (not in Switzerland).

When a filmography starts with the remark "incomplete" it means that there must be more films to be listed but that they could not be traced within the limits of the research made for this dictionary. From 1923 onwards, the filmographies are mostly complete.

The date after a title indicates in every case that the film was directed by the individual.

Main Entries

1 ABEL, ALFRED (1880-1937). B: Leipzig. D: Berlin. Actor. At first forester, gardener, merchant and bank clerk. Sees Asta Nielsen (q.v.) on screen and decides to take up acting, sponsored by Nielsen. In films since 1913.

Films (incomplete): *Der niegeküsste Mund, Sodoms Ende, Venetianische Nacht, Weisse Rosen, Die Geschichte der stillen Mühle, Es werde Licht (iv), Kameraden, Lache Bajazzo, Das Laster, Rausch, Sündige Eltern, Das Tagebuch meiner Frau, Die im Schatten gehen, Die Frau ohne Seele, Grausige Nächte, Die rote Mühle, Sappho, Irrende Seelen, Der Streik der Diebe 21* (also actor), *Bigamie, Der brennende Acker, Dr. Mabuse der Spieler, Der falsche Dimitri, Die Flamme, Fra Diavolo, Die Intriguen der Madame de la Pommeraye, Menschenopfer, Die Nacht der Medici, Phantom, Arme Sünderin, Die Buddenbrooks, Im Rausche der Leidenschaft, Die Prinzessin Suwarin, Das Spiel der Liebe; Dudu, ein Menschenschicksal; Die Finanzen des Grossherzogs, Die Frau im Feuer, Versuchung, Mensch gegen Mensch, Das Spiel mit dem Schicksal, Der Bankraub Unter den Linden, Die Feuertänzerin, Der Herr Generaldirektor, Eine Dubarry von heute, Der Gardeoffizier, Die lachende Grille, Menschen untereinander, Metropolis, Tragödie einer Ehe, Die Tragödie eines Verlorenen, Das Geheimnis von Genf, Jahrmarkt des Lebens, Laster der Menschheit, Ein Tag der Rosen im August ... da hat die Garde fortgemusst, Das tanzende Wien, Ariadne im Hoppegarten, Heut' spielt der Strauss, Mein Herz ist eine Jazzband, Eine Nacht in Yoshiwara, Rasputins Liebesabenteuer, Wer das Scheiden hat erfunden, Ehe in Not, Die Flucht vor der Liebe* (only script), *Giftgas, Narkose 29* (also acting), *Die Schmugglerbraut von Malorca* (only script in collab. with Katscher). Then sound: *Sei gegrüsst, Du mein schönes Sorrent, Dolly macht Karriere; Meine Frau, die Hochstaplerin; 1914, die letzten Tage vor dem Weltbrand; Mary, Das Ekel, Der Herzog von Reichstadt, Das Schicksal der Renate Langen, Der Herr Bürovorsteher, Die Koffer des Herrn O.F., Der Kongress tanzt, Das Mädel vom Montparnasse, Spione im Savoy-Hotel, Jonny stiehlt Europa, Der weisse Dämon, Kampf, Das schöne Abenteuer, Mansolescu, der Fürst der Diebe, Salon Dora Green, Wege zur guten Ehe, Die kleine Schwindlerin, Brennendes Geheimnis, Glückliche Reise 33* (only dir.), *Eine Siebzehnjährige, Die Liebe siegt, Viktoria, Alles um eine Frau 35* (only dir.), *Das Hofkonzert; Und Du, mein Schatz, fährst mit; Spiel an Bord, Ein seltsamer Gast, Skandal um die Fledermaus, Maria, die Magd; Kater Lampe, Unter Ausschluss der Oeffentlichkeit, Millionenerbschaft, Ich möcht' so gern mit Dir allein sein, Sieben Ohrfeigen, Frau Sylvelin.*

2 ADALBERT, MAX (1874-1933). B: Danzig. D: Munich. RN: Max Krampf Actor Theatre work in Lübeck, St. Gallen (Switz.), Vienna, Berlin (Kleines Theater, Reinhardt-Bühnen). At the beginning of sound period Adalbert created one of his best parts in *Der Hauptmann von Köpenick* (31).

Films (incomplete): *Der Schirm mit dem Schwan, König Nicolo oder So ist das Leben, Die Verführten, Der Dummkopf, Der müde Tod, Dr. Mabuse der Spieler, Die Flamme, Lebenshunger, Sein ist das Gericht, So und die Drei, Vorderhaus und Hinterhaus.* Then sound: *Das gestohlene Gesicht, Hans in allen Gassen, Drei Tage Mittelarrest, Der Herr Finanzdirektor, Das Ekel, Der Hauptmann von Köpenick, So'n Windhund, Hurrah – ein Junge, Die Nacht ohne Pause, Die Schlacht von Bademünde, Kyritz – Pyritz, Mein Leopold, Mein Herz sehnt sich nach Liebe, Spione im Savoy-Hotel, Der Schützenkönig, Ein toller Einfall, Husarenliebe, Lachende Erben, Hände aus dem Dunkel.*

3 ADORF, MARIO (1930-   ). B: Zürich. Actor. 1953-1955: trained at Falckenberg School, Munich. 1955-1960: Kammerspiele Munich, then guest appearances. 1954: enters films, playing mainly heavy

roles. Has lived in Rome since 1960. National film award 1958.

Films: *08/15 I, 08/15 II, 08/15 in der Heimat, Harte Männer – heisse Liebe; Nachts, wenn der Teufel kam; Kirschen in Nachbars Garten, Der Arzt von Stalingrad, Vater unser bestes Stück, Robinson soll nicht sterben, Das Mädchen Rosemarie, Das Totenschiff, Bumerang; Am Tag, als der Regen kam; Haut für Haut, Schachnovelle, Mein Schulfreund, Lulu, Endstation 13 Sahara, Die Strasse der Verheissung, Moral 63, Winnetou I, Die Goldsucher von Arkansas, Der letzte Ritt nach Santa Cruz; Vorsicht, Mr. Dodd; Die Herren, Spione unter sich, Vergeltung in Catano, Ganovenehre, Ich habe sie gut gekannt, Unser Boss ist eine Dame, Zärtliche Haie; Engelchen macht weiter, hoppe, hoppe Reiter; Der Bettenstudent oder: Was mach' ich mit den Mädchen.*

4 ALBERS, HANS (1892-1960). B: Hamburg. D: Tutzing. Actor. Appeared first in circus and variety, then to Berlin in operettas, later in plays. At first comic parts, then into character acting. Blond, ardent, adventurous type on the screen (e.g. as Mazeppa

in *The Blue Angel*), but later assumed more serious roles.

Films (incomplete): *Die Jahreszeiten des Lebens* (date for this film unobtainable, but it was certainly made prior to 1923), *Im grossen Augenblick, Der Mut zur Sünde, Baronchen auf Urlaub, Die Sünden der Väter, Zigeunerblut, Komödianten, Die Macht des Geldes, Der Totentanz, Wenn die Maske fällt, Zu Tode gehetzt, Ich hatt' einen Kameraden, Die Marquise von O., Der Falschspieler, Madeleine, Die Geliebte des Königs, Der böse Geist Lumpazivagabundus, Der falsche Dimitri, Söhne der Nacht, Menschenopfer, Der Tiger des Zirkus Farius, Versunkene Welten, Fräulein Raffke, Lydia Sanin, Das Testament des Joe Sievers, Auf Befehl der Pompadour, Gehetzte Menschen, Guillotine, Das schöne Abenteuer, Taumel, Ein Sommernachtstraum, Athleten, Der Bankraub Unter den Linden, Die Gesunkenen, Küssen ist keine Sünde, Halbseide, Der König und das kleine Mädchen, Luxusweibchen; Mein Freund, der Chauffeur; Die Venus von Montmartre, Vorderhaus und Hinterhaus, An der schönen blauen Donau, Deutsche Herzen am deutschen Rhein, Die drei Mannequins, Eine Dubarry von heute; Die Frau, die nicht "nein" sagen kann; Husarenliebe, Ich hatt' einen Kameraden, Jagd auf Menschen, Der lachende Eheman, Der Mann aus dem Jenseits, Seeschlacht beim Skagerrak, Drei Seelen – ein Gedanke, Nixchen, Nur eine Tänzerin, Der Prinz und die Tänzerin; Schatz, mach Kasse; Der Soldat der Marie, Die Villa im Tiergarten, Die Warenhausprinzessin, Wir sind vom k. und k. Infanterie-Regiment, Die Dollarprinzessin und ihre sechs Freier, Eine kleine Freundin braucht jeder Mann, Es zogen drei Burschen, Die glühende Gasse, Der goldene Abgrund, Der grösste Gauner des Jahrhunderts, Primanerliebe, Rinaldo Rinaldini, Dornenweg einer Fürstin, Frauenarzt Dr. Schäfer, Herr Meister und Frau Meisterin, Prinzessin Olala, Rasputins Liebesabenteuer, Der rote Kreis, Saxophon-Susi, Weib in Flammen, Wer das Scheiden hat erfunden, Asphalt; Ja, ja die Frauen sind meine schwache Seite; Mascottchen, Möblierte Zimmer, Drei machen ihr Glück, Vererbte Triebe.* Then sound: *Die Nacht gehört uns, Der Greifer* (30), *Der blaue Engel, Hans in allen Gassen,*

Drei Tage Liebe, Der Draufgänger, Bomben auf Monte Carlo, Quick, Der Sieger, F.P. 1 antwortet nicht, Der weisse Dämon, Flüchtlinge, Ein gewisser Herr Gran, Heut' kommt's drauf an, Peer Gynt, Gold; Henker, Frauen und Soldaten; Varieté (35), Unter heissem Himmel, Savoy-Hotel 217; Der Mann, der Sherlock Holmes war; Die gelbe Flagge, Fahrendes Volk, Sergeant Berry, Wasser für Canitoga; Trenck, der Pandur; Ein Mann auf Abwegen, Carl Peters, Münchhausen, Grosse Freiheit Nr. 7, Shiwa und die Galgenblume, ... und über uns der Himmel, Föhn, Vom Teufel gejagt, Blaubart, Nachts auf den Strassen, Käpt'n Bay-Bay, Jonny rettet Nebrador, An jedem Finger zehn, Auf der Reeperbahn nachts um halb eins, Der letzte Mann (55), Vor Sonnenuntergang, Der tolle Bomberg, Das Herz von St. Pauli, Das gab's nur einmal, Der Greifer (58), Der Mann im Strom, 13 kleine Esel und der Sonnenhof. Kein Engel ist so rein.

5 **ALEXANDER, GEORG** (1889 or 1892 or 1895-1945). B: Hannover. D: Berlin. Actor. RN: Werner Louis Georg Lüddeckens. Well-known for his elegant, comic roles.

Theatre *début* in Halberstadt, then Magdeburg, Aussig, Hamburg, Hannover, Berlin. 1919: enters films.

Films (incomplete): *Der Schwiegervater seines Leutnants, Die Dollarprinzessin und ihre sechs Freier, Fahrt ins Blaue, Die platonische Ehe, Falscher Start, Der Mann ohne Namen, Das Mädchen aus der Fremde, Der Film ohne Namen, Lady Hamilton, Das Mädchen aus dem goldenen Westen, Das Spiel mit dem Weibe; Stubbs, der Detektiv; Die Tänzerin der Königs, Vanina oder die Galgenhochzeit, Der Frauenkönig, Die Frau mit den Millionen, Das Milliardensouper, Das Paradies im Schnee, Die grosse Unbekannte, Komödianten des Lebens, Mein Leopold, Das schöne Abenteuer, Die schönste Frau der Welt, Eifersucht, Herrn Filip Collins Abenteuer, Der Herr ohne Wohnung, Husarenfieber, Liebe macht blind, Gasthaus zur Ehe, Die Insel der verbotenen Küsse, Die Kleine vom Varieté, Die Mühle von Sanssouci, Nanette macht alles, Die Welt will belogen sein, Colonialskandal, Die Dame mit dem Tigerfell, Die Dollarprinzessin und ihre sechs Freier, Eins plus Eins gleich Drei, Flucht vor blond, Die Frau ohne Namen, Die indiskrete Frau, Die Jagd nach der Braut, Der Kampf um den Mann, Der Orlow, Venus im Frack, Dyckerpott's Erben, Er geht rechts – sie geht links, Die grosse Abenteurerin, Leontines Ehemänner, Liebe im Schnee, Die lustigen Vagabunden, Mikosch rückt ein, Prinzessin Olala, Sechs Männer suchen Nachtquartier, Unmoral, Was ist los mit Nanette, Autobus Nr. 2, Die Garde-Diva, Der Leutnant ihrer Majestät, Das Recht auf Liebe, Schwarzwaldmädel, Ehestreik.* Then sound: *Die singende Stadt, Liebeswalzer, Zärtlichkeit, Leutnant warst Du einst bei den Husaren, Geld auf der Strasse, Die Bräutigamswitwe, Der Liebesexpress, Wiener Liebschaften, Trara um Liebe, Opernredoute, Der verjüngte Adolar, Die Fledermaus 31, Hurra – ein Junge!, Mamsell Nitouche, Ehe m.b.H., Das Testament des Cornelius Gulden, Wie sag' ich's meinem Mann, Durchlaucht amüsiert sich, Ein bisschen Liebe für Dich, Flucht nach Nizza, Wenn die Liebe Mode macht, Moderne Mitgift; Liebe, Scherz und Ernst; Und wer küsst mich?, Mein Liebster ist ein Jägersmann, Madame wünscht keine Kinder, Eine Frau wie Du, Der Zarewitsch, Ist mein*

Mann nicht fabelhaft?, Liebe muss verstanden sein, Das Blumenmädchen vom Grand-Hotel, Zigeunerblut, Der Doppelgänger, G'schichten aus dem Wienerwald, Die englische Heirat, Alles hört auf mein Kommando, Tanzmusik, Der alte und der junge König, Ein falscher Fuffziger, Ein idealer Gatte, Der Schlafwagenkontrolleur, Ein Mädel aus guter Familie, Ein Teufelskerl, Der Vogelhändler, Rendezvous am Rhein, Martha, Das Frauenparadies, Das Schloss in Flandern, Donaumelodien, Mädchen in Weiss, Eskapade, Abenteuer in Warschau, Eine Nacht mit Hindernissen, Die Fledermaus 37, Krach und Glück bei Künnemann, Hahn im Korb, Karussell, Zwei mal zwei im Himmelbett, Verliebtes Abenteuer, Das Mädchen von gestern Nacht, Der Fall Deruga, Geld fällt vom Himmel, Heimat, Die Frau am Scheidewege; Kleiner Mann, ganz gross; Unsere kleine Frau, Gastspiel im Paradies, Wenn Männer verreisen, Leinen aus Irland, Frau am Steuer, Der arme Millionär, Die kluge Schwiegermutter, Was will Brigitte?, Der Kleinstadtpoet, Das himmelblaue Abendkleid, Oh diese Männer, Frau Luna, Frauen sind doch bessere Diplomaten, Ein Zug fährt ab, Abenteuer im Grandhotel, Die beiden Schwestern, ... und die Musik spielt dazu, Die Frau meiner Träume, Der Meisterdetektiv.

6 ALLGEIER, SEPP (1895-1968). B and D: Freiburg. Director of photography. Trained at first as textile designer. Enters cinema as cameraman for newsreels, then films on sport, documentaries and records of expeditions to Greece and Spitzbergen. During Second World War reporter for newsreels. Allgeier was also cameraman for television in later years. With Hans Schneeberger and Richard Angst (both q.v.) specialist in *"mountain" films* (q.v.) in collaboration with G. W. Pabst and mainly Arnold Fanck (both q.v.)
Films: *Jiu-Jitsu, die unsichtbare Waffe; Das Wunder des Schneeschuhs, Pömperly's Kampf mit dem Schneeschuh* (co-phot. with Günther Krampf), *Zehntausend Mark Belohnung, Der Berg des Schicksals* (co-phot. with Fanck, Schneeberger, Eugen Hamm and Herbert Oettel), *Der heilige Berg* (co-phot. with Helmar Lerski, Kurt Neubert, Benitz and Schneeberger), *Alpentragödie*

(co-phot. with Willy Goldberger), *Der grosse Sprung* (co-phot. with Angst, Benitz, Neubert, Schneeberger and Charles Métain); *Milak, der Grönlandjäger* (co-phot.), *Frau Sorge* (co-phot. with Martinelli), *Der Kampf ums Matterhorn* (co-phot.), *Tagebuch einer Verlorenen.* Then sound: *Die weisse Hölle vom Piz Palü* (co-phot.), *Stürme über dem Montblanc* (co-phot.), *Berge in Flammen* (co-phot. with Benitz and Giovanni Vitrotti), *Der Rebell* (co-phot. Benitz, Kuntze and Willy Goldberger), *Der Kampf ums Matterhorn* (co-phot.), *Wilhelm Tell* (co-phot.), *Der Springer von Pontresina, Friessennot, Ewiger Wald* (co-phot. with Werner Bohne, Seeber etc.), *Standschütze Bruggler* (co-phot. with Karl Attenberger and Alexander von Lagorio), *Der Berg ruft* (co-phot. with Bennitz, Walter Riml, Otto Martini and von Rautenfeld), *Das sündige Dorf, Ein Robinson* (co-phot. with Benitz and Hans Ertl), *Wetterleuchten um Barbara, Grenzstation 58.*

7 AMBESSER, AXEL VON (1910-   ). B: Hamburg. Actor and director. RN: Axel Eugen Alexander von Oesterreich. Stage début in Hamburg, later Kammerspiele Hamburg and Kammerspiele Munich, Deutsches Theater and Staatstheater Berlin, Theater in der Josefstadt and Burgtheater Vienna, Staatsoper Vienna. Salzburg Festival. Also writer of comedies. 1935: enters cinema. Ambesser directed some of his films.*
Films: *Der Gefangene des Königs, Salonwagen E 417, Die kleine Nachtmusik, Ein hoffnungsloser Fall, Die unheimlichen Wünsche, Traummusik, Das Herz der Königin, Tanz mit dem Kaiser, Annelie, Frauen sind keine Engel, Karneval der Liebe, Die kluge Marianne, Verlobte Leute, Frau über Bord; Der Mann, dem man den Namen stahl; Die seltsamen Abenteuer des Herrn Fridolin B., Verspieltes Leben, Drei Mädchen spinnen, Komplott auf Erlenhof, Kommen Sie am Ersten* (only commentary), *Verträumte Tage, Der Mann in der Wanne, Tanzende Sterne, Glück muss man haben 53* (also * and script), *Und der Himmel lacht dazu 54* (only *), *Columbus entdeckt Krähwinkel* (only script), *Ihr erstes Rendezvous 55* (only * and co-script), *Die Freundin meines Mannes 57* (only *), *Der Pauker 58* (only *), *Bezaubernde Arabella 59* (also *), *Frau im*

besten Mannesalter 59 (only *), Die schöne Lügnerin 59 (only *), Der brave Soldat Schweik 60 (only *), Der Gauner und der liebe Gott 60 (only *), Gustav Adolfs Page, Eine hübscher als die andere 61 (only *), Er kann's nicht lassen 62 (only *), Kohlhiesels Töchter 62 (only *), Es war mir ein Vergnügen, Frühstück im Doppelbett 63 (only *), Das hab' ich von Papa gelernt 64 (also *), Die fromme Helene 65 (also * and script), Das Liebeskarussel 65 (also *, part iv).

8 ANDERGAST, MARIA (1912-   ). B: Brunnthal (Bavaria). Actress. Trained at Vienna Conservatory. Theatre appearances in Aussig, Prague and Berlin. Brought to cinema by Luis Trenker (q.v.), mainly in bucolic parts.

Films: Der verlorene Sohn, Abenteuer eines jungen Herrn in Polen, Der Vogelhändler, Mein Leben für Maria Isabell, Endstation, Der Kurier des Zaren, Skandal um die Fledermaus, Seine Tochter ist der Peter, Die Drei um Christine, Donaumelodien, Manja Valewska, Drei Mäderl um Schubert, Monika, Die glücklichste Ehe der Welt, Husaren heraus, Das Geheimnis um Betty Bonn, Das grosse Abenteuer, Schüsse in Kabine 7, Die Pfingstorgel, Hochzeitreise zu Dritt, Unsterblicher Walzer, Roman eines Arztes, Das Glück wohnt nebenan, Der Herr im Haus, Polterabend, Ein Leben lang, Der liebe Augustin, Ihr Privatsekretär, Der laufende Berg, Sechs Tage Heimaturlaub, So ein Früchtchen, Das grosse Spiel, . . . und die Musik spielt dazu, Ein Mann gehört ins Haus, Der Hofrat Geiger, Zyankali, Kleine Melodie aus Wien, Schicksal in Ketten; Auf der Alm, da gibt's ka Sünd, Der alte Sünder, Die Mitternachts-Venus, Eva erbt das Paradies, Hallo Dienstmann, Die Wirtin vom Wörthersee, Der Mann in der Wanne, Der Verschwender, Junggesellenfalle, Sanatorium total verrückt, Wenn die Alpenrosen blühen, Verlobung am Wolfgangsee, Kaiserball, Die fröhliche Wallfahrt, Das Schloss in Tirol, Almenrausch und Edelweiss.

9 ANDERS, GÜNTHER (1909-   ). B: Berlin. Director of photography. Trained at Staatliche Hochschule für Phototechnik in Munich. From 1922: at Ufa, assistant on Die Nibelungen, Metropolis, Variété.

Films: Viktoria, Das Einmaleins der Liebe, Die lustigen Weiber, Der mutige Seefahrer, Verräter (co-phot. with Heinz von Jaworsky), Im Trommelfeuer der Westfront, Susanne im Bade, Der Herrscher (co-phot.), Brillanten, Urlaub auf Ehrenwort, Unternehmen Michael; Mein Sohn, der Herr Minister; Patrioten, Sein bester Freund (co-phot.), Pour le mérite (co-phot. Heinz von Jarowsky), Capriccio, Legion Condor, Ins blaue Leben (co-phot.), Die Hochzeitsreise, Bal paré, Wunschkonzert (co-phot.), Kadetten, Heimkehr, Hochzeit auf Bärenhof, Am Ende der Welt, Das Ferienkind (co-phot. with Herbert Thalmayer), Das Herz muss schweigen, Ulli und Marei (co-phot. with E. W. Fiedler and Angst), Das Leben geht weiter, Zwischen Gestern und Morgen, Fregola (co-phot. with Hans Staudinger), Der Engel mit der Posaune, Das Kuckucksei (co-phot. with Staudinger), Eroica (co-phot. with Staudinger), Erzherzog Johanns grosse Liebe, Prämien auf den Tod (co-phot. Staudinger), Wiener Walzer, Der blaue Stern des Südens, Der Weibsteufel, Das Tor zum Frieden (co-phot. Willi H. Somh), Ich hab' mich so an Dich gewöhnt, Bis wir uns wiederseh'n, Im weissen Rössl, Liebeskrieg nach Noten (co-phot.), Ich und meine Frau (co-phot. with Staudinger), Meines Vaters Pferde I & II (co-dir.), Dieses Lied bleibt bei Dir, Feuerwerk, Das Bekenntnis der Ina Kahr, Der letzte Akt, Ein Herz voll Musik (co-phot. with Franz Koch), Die Toteninsel, Die Barrings (co-phot. with Staudinger), Dunja, Kaiserjäger, Fuhrmann Henschel, Heute heiratet mein Mann, Kronprinz Rudolfs letzte Liebe, Lügen haben hübsche Beine, Robinson soll nicht sterben; Wien, Du Stadt meiner Träume; Die Heilige und ihr Narr, Die unentschuldigte Stunde, Man müsste noch mal zwanzig sein, Herz ohne Gnade, Stefanie, Der Priester und das Mädchen, Geliebte Bestie, Das schöne Abenteuer, Faust, Gustav Adolfs Page, Frau Cheney's Ende, Geliebte Hochstaplerin, Der Lügner, Ein fast anständiges Mädchen, Der Alpenkönig und der Menschenfeind 65 (dir. and phot.), Lumpazivagabundus, Schwanensee.

10 ANDERS, HELGA (1948-   ). B: Innsbruck. RN: Helga Scherz. Actress. Child parts in Bielefeld theatre. Later Bauernbühne am Tegernsee. Since 1962: many roles in television and films. Well-known teenage star of television serial *Forellenhof* with Helmuth Förnbacher (q.v.). Main film parts in *Mädchen, Mädchen* and *Tätowierung*. National film award 1967. Star of *Junger deutscher Film* (q.v.).

Films: *Max, der Taschendieb; Der Kongress amüsiert sich, 00-Sex am Wolfgangsee, Bel Ami 2000 – oder wie verführt man einen Playboy; Mädchen, Mädchen, Der Mörderclub von Brooklyn, Das Rasthaus der grausamen Puppen, Tätowierung, Zuckerbrot und Peitsche, Sommersprossen, Erotik auf der Schulbank (i), Häschen in der Grube, Schreie in der Nacht, Unser Doktor ist der beste.*

11 **ANDRA, FERN** (1895-   ). B: Natzeka (Illinois). Actress. In early films (directed by Charles Decroix) used name *Andrée* and *André*. After making some films in U.S.A., comes to Austria where she joins Max Reinhardt's (q.v.) theatre classes. Films with Reinhardt, goes to Germany. 1917-1927: works for Ufa (where she helps to produce some of her own films), then returns to U.S.A., where she appears in two more films. 1933: star of some productions in American provincial theatres. Finally turns to politics.

Films: *Es fiel ein Reif in der Frühlingsnacht* (dir., acting and script), *Der Stern, Todessprung* (dir., acting and script), *Wenn Menschen reif zur Liebe werden* (dir., acting and script) – (dates for these films unobtainable, but all were made certainly prior to 1923). Films (incomplete): *Eine Motte flog zum Licht* 15 (prod., dir., script and acting), *Zwei Freunde, Ernst ist das Leben* 16 (prod., dir., script and acting), *Des Lebens ungemischte Freude, Um Krone und Peitsche, Gebannt und erlöst* (co-prod. with Georg Bluen, script and acting), *Genuine, Madame Recamier, Die Nacht der Königin Isabeau, Die treibende Kraft, Der rote Reiter* (also prod.), *Zalamort* (also prod.), *Die Liebe ist der Frauen Macht* (also prod.), *... und es lockt ein Ruf aus sündiger Welt, Frauen der Leidenschaft, Funkzauber.*

12 **ANDREE, INGRID** (1931-   ). B: Hamburg. Actress. RN: Ingrid Tilly Unverhau. Trained at High School for Music and

Theatre in Hamburg, *début* at Thalia-Theater, later Schauspielhaus Hamburg, Schlosspark- and Schiller-Theater Berlin. At her best in petite, charming, poetic roles.

Films: *Primanerinnen, Oh, Du lieber Fridolin; Liebeserwachen, Sanatorium total verrückt, ... und ewig bleibt die Liebe, Drei vom Varieté, Die Frau des Botschafters, Oberwachtmeister Borck, Du darfst nicht länger schweigen, Ihr Leibregiment, Roman einer Siebzehnjährigen, Verlobung am Wolfgangsee, Der Bauer vom Brucknerhof, Bekenntnisse des Hochstaplers Felix Krull, Die liebe Familie, Ein Stück vom Himmel; Wie schön, dass es Dich gibt; Wiener Luft, ... und nichts als die Wahrheit; Peter Voss, der Millionendieb; Auch Männer sind keine Engel, Schlag auf Schlag, Der Rest ist Schweigen, Rosen für den Staatsanwalt, Sturm im Wasserglas, Treibjagd auf ein Leben, Nachts ging das Telephon.*

13 **ANGST, RICHARD** (1905-   ). B: Zürich. Director of photography. Worked in photo laboratory, then became asst. cameraman to Arnold Fanck (q.v.). Belongs to famous trio Allgeier/Schneeberger/Angst (both q.v.) well known for their *"mountain" films* (q.v.). Made films in U.S.A. and Netherlands.

Films: *Der grosse Sprung* (co-phot. with Allgeier, Bennitz, Schneeberger, Kurt Neubert and Charles Métain), *Milak, der Grönlandjäger* (co-phot.). Then sound: *Stürme über dem Montblanc* (co-phot.), *Zwei Menschen* (co-phot. with Mutz Greenbaum and Giovanni Vitrotti), *Die heiligen drei Brunnen* (co-phot. with Viktor Gluck and Winterstein), *Der weisse Rausch* (co-phot. with Kurt Neubert and Hans Gottschalk), *Die Wasserteufel von Hieflau* (co-phot. with Herbert Körner and Ernst Kunstmann), *Abenteuer im Engadin* (co-phot. with Schneeberger and Heinrich Gärtner), *S.O.S. Eisberg* (co-phot. with Schneeberger, Ernst Udet and Franz Schrieck), *Brennendes Geheimnis* (co-phot.), *Nordpol – ahoi!, Der weisse Traum* (co-phot. with Kurt Neubert), *Die weisse Hölle vom Piz Palü* (co-phot.), *Der Dämon des Himalaya* (co-phot. with Hans Ertl and Fritz von Friedl), *Die Kopfjäger von Borneo* (co-phot. with Walter Traut and Hans Staudinger), *Kleine Scheidegg, Die Tochter des Samurai* (co-phot.

with Walter Riml), *Eine kleine Nachtmusik, Die unheimlichen Wünsche, Die Geierwally, Mein Leben für Irland, Rembrandt, Der Strom, Das heilige Ziel, Der grosse Schatten, Gabriele Dambrone, Ein schöner Tag, Melusine, Ulli und Marei* (co-phot. with Anders and E. W. Fiedler), *Erde, Föhn, Der fallende Stern, Fanfaren der Liebe* (co-phot. with Alfred Westphal), *Herz der Welt, Vater braucht eine Frau, Cuba Cubana, Hokuspokus, Schlagerparade, Der erste Kuss, Ingrid, Geschichte eines Photomodells; Drei Männer im Schnee, Der letzte Mann* (55), *Ich denke oft an Piroschka, Ich suche Dich, Die Lindenwirtin vom Donaustrand, Das heilige Erbe* (co-phot. with Albert Höcht, Fritz Olesko, Hans Gessl, Alfred Westphal, Lothar Kern, Karl Rauscher, Heinz Auer, Alexander Posch), *Meine schöne Mama, Petersburger Nächte, Wir Wunderkinder, Der Tiger von Eschnapur, Das indische Grabmal, Das Wirtshaus im Spessart, Peter schiesst den Vogel ab, La Paloma, Bilderbuch Gottes* (co-phot. with Bertl Höchst and Fritz Oleska), *Ramona, Die seltsame Gräfin, . . . und so was nennt sich Leben, Via Mala; Axel Munthe, der Arzt von San Michele; Das Geheimnis der schwarzen Koffer, Sherlock Holmes und das Halsband des Todes, Frühstück im Doppelbett, Der Henker von London, Der schwarze Abt, Das Phantom von Soho, Das siebente Opfer, Dr. med. Hiob Prätorius, Ferien mit Piroschka, Heidi, Spione unter sich* (co-phot. with Pierre Petit), *Hokuspokus – oder wie lasse ich meinen Mann verschwinden, Liselotte von der Pfalz, Herrliche Zeiten im Spessart, Rheinsberg, Kampf um Rom I & II.*

14 ANSCHÜTZ, OTTOMAR (1846-1907). B: Lissa (Poland). D: Berlin. Pioneer of German cinematography. Inventor of the instantaneous shutter and other devices for still photography. Also invented the Tachyscope and the Electro-Tachyscope, improved devices for animating cartoon pictures and photographs. His work is in some ways similar to that of Muybridge.

15 ASHLEY, HELMUT (1919-). B: Vienna. Director of photography and director. RN: Helmut Fischer-Ashley. Trained at Graphische Staatslehr- und Versuchsanstalt (photographic dept.) in Vienna. From 1943:

Assistant to Oskar Schnirch. 1947: becomes cinematographer. Later also director *, abandoning camerawork.

Films: *Der Prozess, Schuss durchs Fenster, Duell mit dem Tod, Jetzt schlägt's 13, Dämonische Liebe, Geheimnisvolle Tiefe* (co-phot.), *Weisse Schatten, Gefangene Seele, Verlorene Melodie, Gefährliches Abenteuer, Die Spur führt nach Berlin, Ein Herz spielt falsch, Solange Du da bist, Muss man sich gleich scheiden lassen?, Wenn Du noch eine Mutter hast . . ., Sauerbruch – Das war mein Leben, Geständnis unter vier Augen, Zwischenlandung in Paris, Du darfst nicht länger schweigen, Hanussen, Regine, Alibi, Nina* (also co-scripted), *Kitty und die grosse Welt, Der Stern von Afrika* (co-phot. with Robert Hofer and Jost Graf von Hardenberg), *Banktresor 713, Endstation Liebe, Nasser Asphalt, Hunde wollt ihr ewig leben, Das schwarze Schaf* 60 *, *Mörderspiel* 61 *, *Das Rätsel der roten Orchidee* 61 *, *Weisse Fracht für Hongkong* 64 *, *Rechnung – eiskalt serviert* 66 *.

16 AVANT-GARDE: this movement grew up during the mid-Twenties, quite independent of the commercial cinema. German *avant-garde* emphasised the filmic form as opposed to the content. The main features of the abstract film were montage of shifting spatial and area forms with no logical links within either the spoken text or the line of thought; the sound or music was not accompaniment, but a "new dimension." Later the movement became more figurative, pure film and documentary.

The key figures of the German *avant-garde* were: Viking Eggeling (1880-1925), founder and leading representative of abstract films (among others *Diagonalsymphonie*, 1925), Walter Ruttmann and Hans Richter (both q.v.), Oskar Fischinger (b. 1900, pupil of Ruttmann), who made abstract cartoons as a mixture of movements in sound, form and colours, and experimented with painting directly on the soundtrack (*Studien 1 – 12* [among them Hungarian Dances by Brahms], *Komposition in Blau* 1933) and Ernö Metzner (q.v.).

The *avant-garde* exerted a strong influence on Dziga Vertov and English documentary, as well as on Norman MacLaren, etc. During the Nazi period most of the representatives of German *avant-garde* emigrated and the only field in which the movement continued to play a part was the documentary, which was much used by the Nazis (main representative of this kind of filmmaking: Leni Riefenstahl, q.v.).

17 **BAAL, KARIN** (1940-ʼ). B: Berlin. Actress. RN: Karin Blauermel. Brought to films in 1956 by Georg Tressler (q.v.), later trains as actress. 1961: she wins German film critics' award as most promising actress. Guest appearances at various theatres.

Films: *Die Halbstarken, Jede Nacht in einem andern Bett, Das Herz von St. Pauli, Der müde Theodor, Das Mädchen Rosemarie, Der eiserne Gustav, So angelt man keinen Mann, Jons und Erdme, Boddy Todd greift ein, Der Jugendrichter, Arzt ohne Gewissen, Wir Kellerkinder, Die junge Sünderin, Vertauschtes Leben, Die toten Augen von London, Blond muss man sein auf Capri, Das letzte Kapitel, Und so was nennt sich Leben, Zwischen Shanghai und St. Pauli, Strasse der Verheissung, So toll wie anno dazumal, Ganovenehre, Mord am Canale Grande, Der Hund von Blackwood Castle.*

18 **BABERSKE, ROBERT** (1900-1958). B: Berlin. D: East Berlin. Director of photography. Worked with Karl Freund (q.v.) a great deal in the Twenties; and with Wagner (q.v.) and also Angst (q.v.) at the start of the sound period. The directors he mostly worked for are: Erich Waschneck, Lamprecht and Froelich (both q.v.), later also K. Georg Külb and Harald Braun (q.v.). After 1945: in G.D.R., with DEFA (q.v.). State award 1950.

Films: *Der letzte Mann* (asst. to Freund), *Die Abenteuer eines Zehnmarkscheines* (co-phot. with Helmar Lerski), *Madame wünscht keine Kinder* (co-phot.), *Berlin – Die Symphonie einer Grosstadt* (co-phot. with Kuntze and Laszlo Schäffer), *Dona Juana* (co-phot. with Freund and Adolf Schlasy), *Der Sohn der Hagar* (co-phot. with Günther Krampf and Sparkuhl), *Eine Nacht in London* (co-phot.), *Fräulein Else* (co-phot. with Schlasy and Freund), *Napoleon auf St. Helena* (co-phot. with Wagner, Lippert and Weinmann), *Lohnbuchhalter Kremke* (co-

phot. with Franz Koch). Then sound: *Dolly macht Karriere* (co-phot.), *Kameradschaft* (co-phot.), *Nie wieder Liebe* (co-phot.), *Ronny* (co-phot.), *Gassenhauer* (co-phot.), *Das schöne Abenteuer* (co-phot.), *Das Abenteuer der Thea Roland* (co-phot.), *So ein Mädel vergisst man nicht, Das Lied einer Nacht* (co-phot.), *Es wird schon wieder besser* (co-phot.), *Das hässliche Mädchen, Keine Angst vor Liebe, Johannisnacht, Kleines Mädel – grosses Glück* (co-phot. with Bruckbauer and Walter Pindter), *Brennendes Geheimnis* (co.-phot.), *Schön ist jeder Tag, den Du mir schenkst, Marie Luise, Spione am Werk* (co-phot. with Wagner and Robert Weichsel), *Besuch am Abend, Hanneles Himmelfahrt, Ich heirate meine Frau, Jede Frau hat ein Geheimnis, Glückspilze, Die törichte Jungfrau, Mach' mich glücklich, Der höhere Befehl, Einer zuviel an Bord, Das Mädchen Irene, Schlussakkord, Inkognito, Gewitterflug zu Claudia* (co-phot. with Heinz von Jaworsky), *Karussell, Die Kronzeugin, Streit um den Knaben Jo, Das Verlegenheitskind, Eine Nacht im Mai, Preussische Liebesgeschichte, Das Mädchen von gestern Nacht; Kleiner Mann, ganz gross; Was tun, Sybille?, Ihr erstes Erlebnis* (co-phot. with Werner Bohne), *Der Stammbaum des Dr. Pistorius, Fräulein, Ich bin gleich wieder da, Mann für Mann, Zwischen Hamburg und Haiti, Liebesschule, Die Rothschilds, Jungens, Der Seniorchef, Anschlag auf Baku* (co-phot. with von Rautenfeld, Herbert Körner and H. O. Schulze), *Sommerliebe, Zwischen Himmel und Erde, Kohlhiesels Töchter, Träumerei, Neigungsehe, Familie Buchholz, Wie sagen wir es unsern Kindern?, Der stumme Gast, Herz könig, Eins – zwei – drei Corona, Unser täglich Brot, Die Kuckucks, Bürgermeister Anna* (co-phot. with Walter Rosskopf), *Familie Benthin* (co-phot. with Karl Plintzner and Walter Rosskopf), *Der Untertan, Das Beil von Wandsbek, Frauenschicksale* (co-phot. with Hans Hauptmann), *Die Geschichte vom kleinen Muck, Leuchtfeuer, Ein Polterabend, Robert Mayer, der Arzt aus Heilbronn, Abenteuer des kleinen Muck.*

19 **BAKY, JOSEF VON** (1902-1966). B. Zombor (Hungary). D: Munich. Director. Trained at Technical School, Budapest. At first film distributor, later assistant to Geza

von Bolvary. Since 1936: director.

Films: *Intermezzo* 36, *Die Frau am Scheidewege* 38, *Die kleine und die grosse Liebe* 38, *Menschen vom Varieté* 39, *Ihr erstes Erlebnis* 39, *Der Kleinstadtpoet* 40, *Annelie* 41, *Münchhausen* 43, *Via Mala* 45, . . . *und über uns der Himmel* 47, *Der Ruf* 49, *Die seltsame Geschichte des Brandner Kaspar* 49, *Das doppelte Lottchen* 50, *Der träumende Mund* 52, *Tagebuch einer Verliebten* 53, *Hotel Adlon* 55, *Dunja* 55, *Fuhrmann Henschel* 56, *Robinson soll nicht sterben* 57, *Die Frühreifen* 58, *Gestehen Sie, Dr. Corda!* 58, *Stefanie* 58, *Der Mann, der sich verkaufte* 59, *Die ideale Frau* 59, *Marili* 59, *Sturm im Wasserglas* 60, *Die seltsame Gräfin* 61.

20 **BALÁZS, BÉLA** (1884-1949). B: Szeged (Hungary). D: Prague. RN: Herbert Bauer. Writer, author, director, and theoretician. One of the leaders of the German *avant-garde* (q.v.). Wrote the three influential books *Der sichtbare Mensch* 1924, *Der Geist des Films* 1930 and *Film: Werden und Wesen einer neuen Kunst* 1948. Also co-scripted films in Hungary, e.g. *Somewhere in Europe* and *Enek a buzamezökröl (Song of the Cornfields)*.

Films: *Die Abenteuer eines Zehnmarkscheines, Madame wünscht keine Kinder, Dona Juana* (in collab.), *Eins plus Eins gleich Drei* (in collab.), *Grand Hotel . . .!, Das Mädchen mit den fünf Nullen, Narkose.* Then sound: *Sonntag des Lebens* (co-scripted with Edmund Goulding), *Die Dreigroschenoper* (co-scripted with Leo Lania and Vajda), *Das blaue Licht, Chemie und Liebe* (idea).

21 **BALSER, EWALD** (1898-   ). B: Elberfeld. Actor. Stage training and *début* in Barmen-Elberfeld. Theatre work in Basle, Düsseldorf, Kammerspiele Munich, Burgtheater Vienna, Deutsches Theater Berlin, and Volksbühne Berlin. Also appears at the Salzburg Festival. Later Vienna.

Films: *Jana, das Mädchen aus dem Böhmerwald; Die Frau am Scheidewege, Die unheimlichen Wünsche, Der Weg zu Isabell, Befreite Hände, Umwege zum Glück, Das Fräulein von Barnhelm, Ehe man Ehemann wird, Rembrandt, Ein glücklicher Mensch, Schule des Lebens, Das heilige Feuer, Der dunkle Tag, Gabriele Dambrone, Der Scheiterhaufen, Glaube an mich, Der Prozess, Die Lüge, Welttheater – Salzburg zur Festspielzeit, Eroica, Opfer des Herzens, Das Jahr des Herrn, Das gestohlene Jahr, Sensation in San Remo, Mein Herz darfst Du nicht fragen, Sauerbruch – Das war mein Leben, Kinder, Mütter und ein General, Spionage, Geheimnis einer Aerztin, Versuchung, Sarajevo, Wilhelm Tell, Vater unser bestes Stück, Die grünen Teufel von Monte Cassino, Nachtschwester Ingeborg, Es geschah am hellichten Tage, Man müsste nochmal zwanzig sein, Der Priester und das Mädchen, Ohne Mutter geht es nicht, Arzt ohne Gewissen, Don Carlos, Glocken läuten überall, Jedermann, Der Ruf der Wildgänse.*

22 **BASSERMANN, ALBERT** (1867-1952). B: Mannheim. D: Zurich. Actor. One of the most prominent actors on stage and in films in his time. At first chemist, then amateur actor in Mannheim. Worked in the cinema from an early stage, more in supporting than in leading parts. Before

Albert Bassermann with Asta Nielsen in ERDGEIST

15

1939: to Switzerland, France and then U.S.A. From 1945: occasional stage appearances in Germany. Films: *Der letzte Tag* (date unobtainable, but made certainly prior to 1923). Films (incomplete): *Der Andere, Der König, Eine schwache Stunde, Das Weib des Pharao, Christoph Columbus, Frauenopfer, Lukrezia Borgia, Erdgeist, Helena; Briefe, die ihn nicht erreichten; Der Herr Generaldirektor, Wenn das Herz der Jugend spricht, Fräulein Else, Napoleon auf St. Helena.* Then sound: *Dreyfus, Alraune, Kadetten; 1914, die letzten Tage vor dem Weltbrand; Voruntersuchung, Zum goldenen Anker, Gefahren der Liebe, Ein gewisser Herr Gran.*

23 BECCE, GIUSEPPE (1887-   ). B: Padua. Composer. Ph. D. Professor. Since 1906: in Berlin. From 1913: works for cinema, at first mainly Oskar Messter (q.v.). Accompaniments for many silent films. Wrote *Handbuch der Filmmusik*, composed operettas, suites for orchestra and symphonies. Also worked in Italy. Famous for his scores for Fanck and Trenker (both q.v.). Played title role in *Richard Wagner* 1913.

Acted in: *Richard Wagner*. Films: *Der Günstling von Schönbrunn, Das alte Lied, Zweierlei Moral, Fra Diavolo, Berge in Flammen, Zwischen Nacht und Morgen, Unter falscher Flagge, Razzia in St. Pauli* (in collab. with Kurt Levaal), *Das blaue Licht, Der Rebell, Die Vier vom Bob 13* (in collab. with Will Meisel), *Der Läufer von Marathon, Spione am Werk, Hans Westmar* (in collab. with Ernst Hanfstaengel), *Gipfelstürmer, Das Lied der Sonne, Der verlorene Sohn, Ich heirate meine Frau, Symphonie der Liebe, Der ewige Traum, Polarstürme, Peer Gynt, Die weisse Hölle vom Piz Palü, Wunder des Fliegens, Hundert Tage, Künstlerliebe, Die Stunde der Versuchung, Der Kaiser von Kalifornien, Nanga Parbat* (in collab. with Bernd Scholz), *Ein seltsamer Gast, Du bist mein Glück, Manja Valewska, Der Berg ruft, Die gelbe Flagge, Madame Bovary, Condottieri, Die Stimme des Herzens, Der Spieler, Liebesbriefe aus dem Engadin, Salonwagen E 417, Frau im Strom, Der Feuerteufel, Ein Abenteuer am Thunersee, Krischna, Clarissa, Viel Lärm um Nixi, Mit den Augen einer Frau, Fahrt ins Abenteuer, Tiefland, Im Banne des Monte*

Miracolo, Bergkristall, Gesetz ohne Gnade, Was das Herz befiehlt, Hinter Klostermauern, Strasse zur Heimat, Karneval in Weiss, Der Herrgottschnitzer von Ammergau (in collab. with Fred Rauch), *Der Ehestreik, Junges Herz voll Liebe, Ruf der Berge, Das Schweigen im Walde, Der Jäger von Fall, Der Edelweisskönig, Der Schäfer vom Trutzberg.*

24 BEHN-GRUND, FRIEDL (1906-   ). B: Bad Polzin (Pommerania). Director of photography. Studied languages, literature and art. Started as asst. cameraman to Erich Waschneck. From 1945: at DEFA (q.v.), twice winner of state award. From 1950: free-lance cameraman in West Germany.

Films: *Der gestohlene Professor* (co-phot. with Erich Waschneck), *Der Kampf um die Scholle; Mein Freund, der Chauffeur; Die Strasse des Vergessens, Brennende Grenze, Der Mann im Feuer* (co-phot.), *Die Warenhausprinzessin, Die Frau mit dem Weltrekord, Die geheime Macht; Regine, die Tragödie einer Frau; Der Sprung ins Glück* (co-phot. with Victor Armenise), *Die blaue Maus, Die Carmen von St. Pauli, Schiff in Not SOS* (co-phot. with Armenise and Willi Teske), *Skandal in Baden-Baden, Vom Täter fehlt jede Spur, Diane, Die Drei um Edith, Ehe in Not, Die Herrin und ihr Knecht, Jenseits der Strasse, Die Schmugglerbraut von Malorca, Der Detektiv des Kaisers; O Mädchen, mein Mädchen, wie lieb' ich Dich!, Der Witwenball.* Then sound: *Der Günstling von Schönbrunn, Der Hampelmann* (co-phot.); *Wien, Du Stadt der Lieder* (co-phot. with Paul Holzki); *Das alte Lied, Die zärtlichen Verwandten, Dreyfus* (co-phot. with Heinrich Balasch), *Zapfenstreich am Rhein* (co-phot.), *24 Stunden im Leben einer Frau, Salto Mortale* (co-phot. with Akos Farkas), *Der Liebesarzt* (co-phot. with Winterstein and Hermann Böttcher); *Luise, Königin von Preussen; Der Mörder Dimitri Karamasoff, Der Stolz der 3. Kompanie, Jeder fragt nach Erika, Die Faschingsfee, Die Tänzerin von Sanssouci; Peter Voss, der Millionendieb; Melodie der Liebe* (co-phot.), *Ich bei Tag und Du bei Nacht, Acht Mädels im Boot, Ich und die Kaiserin, Des jungen Dessauers grosse Liebe, Hände im Dunkel, Die schönen Tage von Aranjuez, Musik im Blut, Der Polizei-*

bericht meldet, Mein Herz ruft nach Dir, Die englische Heirat, Der junge Baron Neuhaus, Petersburger Nächte, Ich liebe alle Frauen, Liebesleute, Barcarole, Truxa, Flitterwochen, Eskapade, Donogoo Tonka, Ein Hochzeitstraum, Sein bester Freund (co-phot.), *Manege, Alarm in Peking, Die göttliche Jette, Versprich mir nichts, Napoleon ist an allem schuld, Der Tag nach der Scheidung, Ich liebe Dich, Die kleine und die grosse Liebe, Die goldene Maske, Silvesternacht am Alexanderplatz, Robert und Bertram, Schneider Wibbel, Traummusik, Casanova heiratet, Die 3 Codonas, Was wird hier gespielt?, Das andere Ich; Kopf hoch, Johannes; Ich klage an* (co-phot. with Franz von Klepacki), *Ohm Krüger* (co-phot. with Wagner and Karl Puth), *Die Nacht in Venedig, Titanic, Fritze Bollmann wollte angeln* (co-phot. with Walter Rosskopf), *Ich hab' von Dir geträumt, Die Jahre vergehen, Jugendliebe, Philharmoniker, Wir seh'n uns wieder* (co-phot. with Walter Rosskopf), *Die Kreuzlschreiber, Dr. phil Döderlein, Frau über Bord, Die Mörder sind unter uns* (co-phot.), *Razzia* (co-phot.), *Ehe im Schatten* (co-phot.), *Affaire Blum* (co-phot. with Karl Plintzner), *Die seltsamen Abenteuer des Herrn Fridolin B.* (co-phot. with Karl Plintzner), *Begegnung mit Werther* (co-phot. Ernst W. Kalinke), *Die Buntkarierten* co-phot. with Karl Plintzner), *Nächte am Nil, Der Rat der Götter, Skandal in der Botschaft, Was das Herz befielt, Rausch einer Nacht, Maria Theresia, Die Perlenkette, Die Försterchristl, Alraune, Karneval in Weiss* (co-phot. with Walter Riml and Kurt Neubert), *Käpt'n Bay-Bay, Die grosse Versuchung* (co-phot.), *Einmal keine Sorgen haben, Der letzte Walzer, Meines Vaters Pferde* I & II (co-phot.), *Das fliegende Klassenzimmer, Morgengrauen, Der Engel mit dem Flammenschwert, Geliebte Feindin, Der Himmel ist nie ausverkauft, Vor Gott und den Menschen, Ein Mädchen aus Flandern* (co-phot. with Dieter Wedekind), *Griff nach den Sternen, Nacht der Entscheidung; Anastasia, die letzte Zarentochter; Liebe, die den Kopf verliert; Ohne Dich wird es Nacht, Stresemann, Wie ein Sturmwind, Bekenntnisse des Hochstaplers Felix Krull, Der gläserne Turm, Das einfache Mädchen, Der Graf von Luxemburg, . . . und abends in die Scala, Nachtschwester Ingeborg, Unruhige*

Nacht, Ihr 106. Geburtstag, Polikuschka, Frau im besten Mannesalter, Der Mann, der sich verkaufte; Die unvollkommene Ehe, Die Buddenbrooks, Mit Himbeergeist geht alles besser, Es muss nicht immer Kaviar sein, Diesmal muss es Kaviar sein, Das Riesenrad, Unter Ausschluss der Oeffentlichkeit, Auf Wiedersehn, Eheinstitut Aurora, Finden Sie, dass Constanze sich richtig verhält?, Hochzeitsnacht im Paradies, Die lustige Witwe, Das schwarz-weiss-rote Himmelbett (co-phot. with Heinz Schnackertz), *Ein Alibi zerbricht, Heirate mich, Chéri, Schwejks Flegeljahre, Die fromme Helene, Ganovenehre.*

25 BENITZ, ALBERT (1904-   ). B: Freiburg. Director of photography. Technical and artistic training for six years under Arnold Fanck (q.v.) in Freiburg. Also worked for Luis Trenker (q.v.).

Films: *Der heilige Berg* (co-phot. with Allgeier, Schneeberger, Helmar Lerski and Kurt Neubert), *Der grosse Sprung* (co-phot. with Allgeier, Angst, Schneeberger, Neubert and Charles Métain), *Milak, der Grönlandjäger* (co-phot.). Then sound: *Der Sohn der weissen Berge* (co-phot. with Planer and Kurt Neubert), *Berge in Flammen* (co-phot. with Allgeier and Giovanni Vitrotti), *Der Rebell* (co-phot. with Kuntze, Allgeier and Willy Goldberger), *Abenteuer eines jungen Herrn in Polen* (co-phot.), *Der verlorene Sohn* (co-phot.), *Der Kaiser von Kalifornien* (co-phot. with Heinz von Jaworsky), *Der Berg ruft* (co-phot. with Walter Riml, Allgeier, von Rautenfeld and Otto Martini), *Condottieri* (co-phot. with von Rautenfeld and Walter Hege), *Ein Robinson* (co-phot. with Hans Ertl and Allgeier), *Der Feuerteufel, Aufruhr des Herzens* (co-phot.), *Am Abend nach der Oper, Tiefland, Das seltsame Fräulein Sylvia, Im Banne des Monte Miracolo* (co-phot. with Umberto Della Valle and Ernst Elsigan), *Zugvögel, Die Söhne des Herrn Gaspary, Menschen in Gottes Hand, Diese Nacht vergess' ich nie, Martina, Der Fall Rabanser* (co-phot. with Walter Hrich), *13 unter einem Hut, Herzen im Sturm* (co-phot.), *Taxi-Kitty* (co-phot. with Emil Eisenbach), *Lockende Gefahr, Engel im Abendkleid* (co-phot. with Otto Merz), *Kommen Sie am Ersten* (co-phot. with Heinz Pehlke), *Liebe im Finanzamt, Klettermaxe,*

Der Onkel aus Amerika, Rote Rosen, rote Lippen, roter Wein; Mit 17 beginnt das Leben, Keine Angst vor grossen Tieren, Die Privatsekretärin, Der Raub der Sabinerinnen, Meine Schwester und Ich, Grosse Starparade, Die Stadt ist voller Geheimnisse, Flucht in die Dolomiten, Des Teufels General, Der falsche Adam, Banditen der Autobahn, Unternehmen Schlafsack (co-phot. with Jobst Graf Hardenberg), Die Ehe des Dr. med. Danwitz, Ein Herz kehrt heim, Spion für Deutschland (co-phot. with Heinz von Jaworsky), Der Hauptman von Köpenick, Tierarzt Dr. Vlimmen, Wetterleuchten um Maria, Dr. Crippen lebt, Für zwei Groschen Zärtlichkeit, Glücksritter, Das haut einen Seeman doch nicht um, Das Mädchen vom Moorhof; Vater, Mutter und neun Kinder; Natürlich die Autofahrer, Die Bande des Schreckens, Bei Pichler stimmt die Kasse nicht; Mein Mann, das Wirtschaftswunder, Heute kündigt mir mein Mann; Max, der Taschendieb, Das Testament des Dr. Mabuse, Schüsse aus dem Geigenkasten.

26 **BENKHOFF, FITA** (1908-1967). B: Dortmund. D: Munich. Actress. Stage début in Dortmund, then Lübeck, Düsseldorf, Breslau, Vienna and Volksbühne Berlin. Very good in frothy supporting roles.

Films: Mutter und Kind, Schwarzer Jäger Johanna, Was bin ich ohne Dich; Ein Kind, ein Hund, ein Vagabund; Gold, Die beiden Seehunde, Alte Kameraden, Das Erbe von Pretoria, Ein Mädel wirbelt durch die Welt, Der Meisterboxer, Charleys Tante, Krach um Jolanthe, Heinz im Mond, Liebeslied; Henker, Frauen und Soldaten; Die Werft zum grauen Hecht, Amphitryon, Der Ammenkönig, Moral, Diener lassen bitten, Die un-erhörte Frau, Boccaccio, Der schüchterne Casanova, Strassenmusik, Petermann ist dagegen, Capriolen, Manege, Heiratsschwindler, Wenn Frauen schweigen, Diskretion – Ehrensache, Schüsse in Kabine 7, Spassvögel, Lauter Lügen, Schneider Wibbel, Opernball, Drunter und drüber, Die goldene Maske, Casanova heiratet, Ihr Privatsekretär, Was wird hier gespielt?, Das Fräulein von Barnhelm, Was will Brigitte?, Frau Luna, Immer nur Du, So ein Früchtchen, Meine Freundin Josefine; Johan, Ich brauche Dich, Freitag, der 13; Ich hab' von Dir geträumt, Der Scheiterhaufen, Morgen ist alles besser, Die Zeit mit Dir, Der Biberpelz, Krach im Hinterhaus, Kein Engel ist so rein, Melodie des Schicksals, Taxi-Kitty, Das gestohlene Jahr, Die Mitternachtsvenus; Hilfe, ich bin unsichtbar; Die Frauen des Herrn S., Durch Dick und Dünn, In München steht ein Hofbräuhaus, Die Diebin von Bagdad, Pension Schöller, Tanzende Sterne, Wenn abends die Heide träumt, Von Liebe reden wir später, Das singende Hotel, Fanfaren der Ehe, Muss man sich gleich scheiden lassen?, Der Raub der Sabinerinnen, Fräulein vom Amt, Auf der Reeperbahn nachts um halb eins, Maxie, Der Hauptmann und sein Held, Der Himmel ist nie ausverkauft, Ein Herz voll Musik, Wenn der Vater mit dem Sohne, Drei Mädels vom Rhein; Dany, bitte schreiben Sie; Der erste Frühlingstag, Der Bettelstudent, Opernball (56), Wenn wir alle Engel wären, Zwei Herzen voller Seligkeit, Familie Schimek, ... und die Liebe lacht dazu, Wenn Frauen schwindeln, Ist Mama nicht fabelhaft?, Majestät auf Abwegen; Liebe, Luft und lauter Lügen; Immer die Mädchen; Ein Sommer, den man nie vergisst; Ingeborg, Bei Pichler stimmt die Kasse nicht, Liebe will gelernt sein.

27 **BERGER, LUDWIG** (1892-1969). B: Mainz. D: Schlangenbad. Director, writer, scriptwriter. RN: Ludwig G. H. Bamberger. Educated in Munich and Heidelberg. Theses on history of art, Ph.D. Kunstgewerbemuseum Stuttgart, Theatre Mainz, Stadttheater Hamburg, later Volksbühne am Bülowplatz Berlin under Friedrich Kayssler (q.v.). Director of Shakespearian plays for Max Reinhardt (q.v.). Collaborated with his brother (set designer) Rolf Bamberger. 1927: to U.S.A., but comes back to Germany after 1945.

Films: Der Richter von Zalamea 20 (also script), Der Roman der Christine von Herre 21 (also script), Agnes Bernauer (only script), Das Spiel der Königin 23 (also script in collab. with Adolf Lantz), Der verlorene Schuh 23 (also script), Ein Walzertraum 25, Königin Luise (only script), Der Meister von Nürnberg (27 also script in collab. with Robert Liebmann and Rudolf Rittner), Das brennende Herz 29. Then sound: Ich bei Tag und Du bei Nacht 32, Walzerkrieg 33, Stresemann (only co. script).

28 **BERGER, SENTA** (1941-   ). B: Vienna. Actress. At first ballet training, later stage training at the Reinhardt-Seminar in Vienna. Enters cinema through Artur Brauner (q.v.). Also appears in American and international productions. Produced Paarungen together with her husband Michael Verhoeven (son of Paul Verhoeven, q.v.).

Films: *Die Lindenwirtin vom Donaustrand, Der veruntreute Himmel, Der brave Soldat Schwejk, Ich heirate Herrn Direktor, O sole mio; Adieu, lebwohl, good bye; Es muss nicht immer Kaviar sein, Diesmal muss es Kaviar sein, Immer Aerger mit dem Bett, Junge Leute brauchen Liebe, Ramona, Das Wunder des Malachias, Frauenarzt Dr. Sibelius, Das Geheimnis der schwarzen Koffer, Sherlock Holmes und das Halsband des Todes, Das Testament des Dr. Mabuse, Jack und Jenny, Kali Yug I & II, Volles Herz und leere Taschen, Schüsse im 3/4-Takt; Lange Beine, lange Finger; Unser Boss ist eine Dame, Mit teuflischen Grüssen, Paarungen (only prod.), Geier können warten.*

29 **BERGMANN, WERNER** (1921-   ). B: Wendisch Bork. Director of photography.

Trained as photographer and front line reporter during Second World War. At DEFA: at first popular science and documentary films, from 1953 works on feature films, mainly in collaboration with Konrad Wolf (q.v.).

Films: *Aus unseren Tagen* 50 (also dir.), *Die Sonnenbrucks, Das kleine und das grosse Glück, Alarm im Zirkus, Einmal ist keinmal, Genesung, Der Hauptmann von Köln, Lissy, Die Sonnensucher, Sterne, Leute mit Flügeln, Professor Mamlock, Julia lebt* (cophot. with Peter Brand), *Der geteilte Himmel, Mörder auf Urlaub* (co-phot. with Ognjen Milicevic), *DEFA 70* 67 (only dir. and script; short), *Ich war neunzehn.*

30 **BERGNER, ELISABETH** (1897 or 1898 or 1900-   ). B: Drohobycz (Mähren). Actress. RN: Elisabeth Ettel. Konservatorium in Vienna, Municipal Theatre Innsbruck 1916-1917, then Zurich, Barnowsky Theatres Berlin, Neue Wiener Bühne 1919-1920, Kammerspiele and State Theatre Munich, Reinhardt (q.v.) and Barnowsky Theatres Berlin 1922-1927. From 1928: guest appearances. 1932: to England. 1939: to U.S.A. From 1945: guest appearances on Swiss, Austrian and German stage. Enters

cinema 1924. Her performances embody an ideal of tender and almost sublime femininity.

Films: *Der Evangelimann, Nju, Der Geiger von Florenz, Liebe, Dona Juana, Fräulein Else.* Then sound: *Ariane, Der träumende Mund, Die glücklichen Jahre der Thorwalds.*

31 BERNHARDT, KURT (CURTIS) (1899-). B: Worms. Director. Stage training in Frankfurt. Actor and director in Berlin. 1934: to France. 1935: to England, where he founds "British Unity Pictures" in 1937. 1940: to U.S.A.

Films: *Qualen der Nacht* 26 (also script in collab. with Carl Zuckmayer), *Die Waise von Lowood* 26, *Kinderseelen klagen an* 27, *Das Mädchen mit den fünf Nullen* 27, *Schinderhannes* 27 (also script in collab. with Zuckmayer), *Das letzte Fort* 28, *Die Frau nach der man sich sehnt* 29. Then sound: *Die letzte Kompanie* 30, *Der Mann, der den Mord beging* 31, *Der Rebell* 32 (co-dir. with Trenker), *Der Tunnel* 33 (also script with Reinhart Steinbicker).

32 BEYER, FRANK (1932-). B: Nobitz. Director. At first dramaturg, then studies at FAMU (Prague Film School). Assistant to Kurt Maetzig (q.v.). 1966: appointed Director of Staatstheater, Dresden. Since 1957: director of own films for DEFA (q.v.).

Films: *Zwei Mütter* 57 (also script with Jo Tiedemann), *Eine alte Liebe* 58 (also script with Werner Reinowski), *Fünf Patronenhülsen* 60, *Königskinder* 62, *Nackt unter Wölfen* 63, *Karbid und Sauerampfer* 64.

33 BIRGEL, WILLY (1891 or 1892-). B: Cologne. Actor. Goldsmith's son. Theatres: Bonn, Dessau, Aachen, Mannheim, Berlin. 1933: enters cinema. Plays a severe, often cold type of man in his best parts.

Films: *Fürst Woronzeff, Ein Mann will nach Deutschland, Barcarole, Schwarze Rosen, Einer zuviel an Bord, Das Mädchen Johanna, Schlussakkord, Ritt in die Freiheit, Verräter, Zu neuen Ufern, Fanny Eissler, Menschen ohne Vaterland, Unternehmen Michael, Geheimzeichen LB 17, Der Blaufuchs, Der Fall Deruga, Verklungene Melodie, Der Gouverneur, Kongo-Express, Maria-Ilona, Hotel Sacher, Feinde, Das Herz der Königin, ... reitet für Deutschland, Kameraden, Diesel, Du gehörst zu mir, Der dunkle Tag, Ich brauche Dich, Der Majoratsherr, Musik in Salzburg, Mit meinen Augen, Die Brüder Noltenius, Leb' wohl Christina, Zwischen Gestern und Morgen, Vom Teufel gejagt, Das ewige Spiel, Wenn die Abendglocken läuten, Der Kaplan von San Lorenzo, Mein Herz darfst Du nicht fragen, Sterne über Colombo, Die Gefangene des Maharadscha, Konsul Strotthoff, Rittmeister Wronski, Ein Mann vergisst die Liebe, Rosenmontag* 55 (also dir.), *Die Toteninsel, Rosen für Bettina, Ein Herz kehrt heim, Zwischen Zeit und Ewigkeit, Johannisnacht, Die Heilige und ihr Narr, Frauenarzt Dr. Bertram, Liebe kann wie Gift sein, Der Priester und das Mädchen, Geliebte Bestie, Arzt aus Leidenschaft, Wenn die Glocken hell erklingen, Frau Cheney's Ende, Die blonde Frau des Maharadscha, Romanze in Venedig, Ein Sarg aus Hongkong, Agent 505 – Todesfalle Beirut, Schonzeit für Füchse.*

34 BLECH, HANS CHRISTIAN (1925-). B: Darmstadt. Actor. Theatres: Baden-Baden, Kiel, Freiburg, Leipzig (Old The-

Hans Christian Blech with Gisela Trowe in AFFÄRE BLUM

atre), Kammerspiele Munich. Many guest appearances. Has also worked for American companies. Played probably his best part in *L'enclos* (61, Belgium).

Films: *Affäre Blum, Epilog, Lockende Gefahr, 08/15 I, Geständnis unter vier Augen, Sauerbruch – Das war mein Leben, Phantom des grossen Zeltes, 08/15 II, Kinder, Mütter und ein General, Banditen der Autobahn, 08/15 in der Heimat, Weil Du arm bist, musst Du früher sterben, Schwarzer Stern in weisser Nacht, Solange das Herz schlägt, Das Erbe von Björndal, Ich schwöre und gelobe, Der Besuch, Schornstein Nr. 4, Cardillac.*

35 **BLEIBTREU, Hedwig** (1868-1958). B: Linz. D: Vienna. Actress. Begins theatre career as "dialect" actress in a Bavarian folk theatre group. Since 1893: member of Vienna Burgtheater. Several guest appearances in Germany, Switzerland etc., Salzburg Festival. Named Professor for Theatre, Science and Actor's Training. 1923: enters cinema. Grand old lady of the Burgtheater for many years.

Films (incomplete): *Die Kurtisane von Venedig.* Then sound: *Das Lied ist aus, Tänzerinnen für Südamerika gesucht; Scampolo, ein Kind der Strasse; Der Prinz von Arkadien, Pygmalion, Es flüstert die Liebe, Das Mädchen Irene, Die ganz grossen Torheiten, Der Spieler, 13 Stühle, Das Leben kann so schön sein, Waldrausch, Maria Ilona, Hotel Sacher, Wunschkonzert, Alles Schwindel, Meine Tochter lebt in Wien, Wiener G'schichten, Der ungetreue Ekkehart, Herzensfreud – Herzensleid, Fahrt ins*

Leben, Dreimal Hochzeit, Aufruhr im Damenstift, Sommerliebe, Wiener Blut, Frauen sind keine Engel, Ein Mann für meine Frau, Wiener Mädeln, Wiener Melodien, Alles Lüge, Der Engel mit der Posaune, Grosstadtnacht, Gefangene Seele.

36 BOESE, CARL (1887-1958). B and D: Berlin. Director. Polytechnic Leipzig, and later studied philosophy. Introduced to films in 1912 by Paul Wegener (q.v.). 1917: after war service, makes series of films with Grete Weixler. Routine director although some of his silent films are not without artistic interest.

Films (incomplete): *Nocturno der Liebe 18, Die Geisha und der Samurai 19, Drei Nächte 20, Der Golem, wie er in die Welt kam 20* (co-dir.), *Die Herren vom Maxim 20, Das Floss der Toten 21, Die rote Mühle 21, Die Tänzerin Barberina 21, Das Auge der Toten 22, Gespenster 22* (also script in collab. with Bruno H. Bürger), *Die grosse Lüge 22, Landstreicherin Courage 22, Das ungeschriebene Gesetz 22, Graf Cohn 23, Ein Kind – ein Hund 23, Maciste und die chinesische Truhe 23, Die Frau im Feuer 24, Sklaven der Liebe 24* (also script in collab. with Margarete Maria Langen), *Die drei Portiermädel 25, Die eiserne Braut 25, Grüss mir das blonde Kind am Rhein 25, Heiratsschwindler 25, Krieg im Frieden 25, ... und es lockt ein Ruf aus sündiger Welt 25, Wenn Du eine Tante hast 25, Es blasen die Trompeten 26, Kubinke, der Barbier, und die drei Dienstmädchen 26, Ledige Töchter 26, Die letzte Droschke von Berlin 26, Der Mann ohne Schlaf 26, Nanette macht alles 26, Der Seekadett 26, Die Sporckschen Jäger* (prod. and script in collab. with B. E. Lüthge), *Das edle Blut 27, Die elf Teufel 27, Die heilige Lüge* (only prod.), *Die indiskrete Frau 27, Schwere Jungens – leichte Mädchen 27, Die weisse Spinne 27, Eva in Seide 28* (also script in collab. with Luise Heilborn-Körbitz), *Kinder der Strasse 28, Lemkes sel. Witwe 28* (also script in collab. with Heilborn-Körbitz), *Ossi hat die Hosen an 28* (and prod.), *Der Piccolo vom Goldenen Löwen 28* (and prod.), *Wenn die Mutter und die Tochter ... 28* (and prod.), *Alimente 29, Bobby, der Benzinjunge 29, Geschminkte Jugend 29, Der Detektiv des Kaisers 30, Ehestreik 30, O Mädchen, mein Mädchen, wie lieb' ich Dich! 30.* Then sound: *Drei Tage Mittelarrest 30, Komm mit mir zum Rendezvous 30* (also script with Robert Florey and Walter Hasenclever), *Kasernenzauber 30, Bockbierfest 30, Der ungetreue Ekkehart 31, Der Schrecken der Garnison 31, Der schönste Mann im Staate 31, Vater geht auf Reisen 31, Die schwebende Jungfrau 31, Meine Cousine aus Warschau 31, Dienst ist Dienst 31, Grock 31, Man braucht kein Geld 31, Keine Feier ohne Meyer 31, Die Herren vom Maxim 32, Annemarie, die Braut der Kompanie 32, Theodor Körner 32, Der Frechdachs 32* (co-dir. with Heinz Hille), *Drei von der Kavallerie 32, Paprika 32, Lumpenkavaliere 32, Gruss und Kuss, Veronika! 33, Die Unschuld vom Lande 33, Roman einer Nacht 33, Das Lied vom Glück 33, Eine Frau wie Du 33, Heimkehr ins Glück 33, Die kalte Mamsell 33, Drei blaue Jungs – ein blondes Mädel 33, Gretel zieht das grosse Los 33* (also script), *Schützenkönig wird der Felix 34, Liebe dumme Mama 34, Fräulein Frau 34, Wenn ein Mädel Hochzeit macht 34, Das Blumenmädchen vom Grand-Hotel 34, Der Schrecken vom Heidekrug 34, Meine Frau, die Schützenkönigin 34, ... heute Abend bei mir 34, Herz ist Trumpf 34, Eine Nacht an der Donau 35, Der Gefangene des Königs 35, Ein falscher Fuffziger 35, Ein ganzer Kerl 35, Die Fahrt in die Jugend 35, Der verkannte Lebemann 36, Dahinten in der Heide 36, Engel mit kleinen Fehler 36, Männer vor der Ehe 36* (also script with Erwin Kreker), *Mädchen für alles 37, Abenteuer in Warschau 37, Eine Nacht mit Hindernissen 37, Wie der Hase läuft 37, Heiraten – aber wen? 38, Steputat & Co. 38, War es der im 3. Stock? 38, Schüsse in Kabine 7 38, Fünf Millionen suchen einen Erben 38, Schwarzfahrt ins Glück 38, Meine Tante – Deine Tante 39, Drei Väter um Anna 39, Hallo, Janine! 39, Polterabend 40, Hochzeitsnacht 41, Familienanschluss 41, Alles für Gloria 41* (also script with Riemann, Fritz Rau and M. Rau), *Um 9 kommt Harald 42, Leichtes Blut 42, ... und die Musik spielt dazu 43* (also script), *Das Hochzeitshotel 44, Der Posaunist 45* (also script with Gerhard T. Buchholz and Hans Weissbach), *Beate 48* (also script with E. Klein), *Wenn Männer schwindeln 50* (also script with

Curth Flatow), *Das Mädchen aus der Konfektion* 51 (also script with Vineta Bastian-Klinger), *Der keusche Lebemann* 52, *Der Onkel aus Amerika* 52, *Der keusche Josef* 53, *Das Nachtgespenst* 53, *Die spanische Fliege* 55, *Meine Tante – Deine Tante* 56, *Vater macht Karriere* 57.

37 **BÖHM, KARL-HEINZ** (1928-   ). B: Darmstadt. Actor. Son of the conductor, Karl Böhm. Theatre training in Vienna by Albin Skoda and Werner Krauss (q.v.). Stage appearances at the Burgtheater and Theater in der Josefstadt Vienna. Enters cinema as assistant to director Karl Hartl. Became well known as partner of Romy Schneider (q.v.) in the *Sissi* series. Has also worked in France, Italy, U.S.A. and England.

Films: *Haus des Lebens, Alraune, Der Tag vor der Hochzeit, Der Weibertausch, Salto mortale, Arlette erobert Paris, Der unsterbliche Lump, Hochzeit auf Reisen, Die Sonne von St. Moritz, ... und ewig bleibt die Liebe, Die Hexe, Die goldene Pest, Die heilige Lüge, Ich war ein hässliches Mädchen, Unternehmen Schlafsack, Schwedenmädel, Dunja, Sissi, Die Ehe des Dr. med. Danwitz; Sissi, die junge Kaiserin, Nina, Kitty und die grosse Welt, Blaue Jungs, Sissi – Schicksalsjahre einer Kaiserin; Das Schloss in Tirol, Man müsste nochmal zwanzig sein, Das haut einen Seemann doch nicht um, Das Dreimäderlhaus, La Paloma, Der Gauner und der Liebe Gott, Kriegsgericht.*

38 **BOIS, CURT** (1901-   ). B: Berlin. Actor. Child parts in Berlin, then cabaret in Germany, Austria and Switzerland. 1922-1933: on Berlin stage (Theater am Kurfürstendamm, Lessing Theatre). 1933: to U.S.A., with stage appearances and films in New York and Hollywood. Since 1950: back in Germany.

Films: *Klebolin klebt alles, Die Austernprinzessin, Der goldene Schmetterling, Gräfin Plättmamsell, Der Jünglich aus der Konfektion Wehe, wenn sie losgelassen; Dr. Bessels Verwandlung, Der Fürst von Pappenheim, Majestät schneidet Bubiköpfe, Anschluss um Mitternacht.* Then sound: *Der Schlemihl, Ein steinreicher Mann, Herr Puntila und sein Knecht Matti, Ein Polterabend* 55 (only dir. and script with Werner Bern-

hardy), *Das Spukschloss im Spessart, Ganovenehre.*

39 **BORCHERT, WILHELM** (1907-   ). B: Berlin. Actor. Trained at Hochschule für dramatische Kunst Berlin. Stage *début at* Ostpreussenbühne des Bühnenvolksbundes. Theatres: Erfurt, Cologne, Volksbühne Berlin. After 1945: in Berlin (Hebbel-Theater, Deutsches Theater, Schiller- and Schlosspark-Theater). Also worked for radio and well known "voice" on dubbed versions. His best performance is in *Die Mörder sind unter uns.*

Films: *U-Boote westwärts, Mein Leben für Irland, Der Strom, Der ewige Klang, Die Mörder sind unter uns, Und wieder 48!, Schicksal aus zweiter Hand, Sauerbruch – Das war mein Leben, Herr über Leben und Tod, Du darst nicht länger schweigen, Hunde wollt ihr ewig leben.*

40 **BORSCHE, DIETER** (1913-   ). B: Hannover. Actor. At first trained as a dancer by Yvonne Georgi and Harald Kreutzberg. 1928: stage training in Hannover. Stage work: Weimar, Danzig 1939, Breslau 1942, Kiel 1946-1949. Many guest appearances.

Films: *Alles weg'n dem Hund, Wie einst im Mai, Preussische Liebesgeschichte, Die kluge Schwiegermutter, Die Geliebte, Nachtwache, Es kommt ein Tag, Der fallende Stern, Dr. Holl, Fanfaren der Liebe, Sündige Grenze, Herz der Welt, Vater braucht eine Frau, Die grosse Versuchung, Der Kaplan von San Lorenzo, Fanfaren der Ehe, Muss man sich gleich scheiden lassen?, Königliche Hoheit, Zwischenlandung in Paris, Ich war ein hässliches Mädchen, Die Barrings, San Salvatore, Wenn wir alle Engel wären, Rot ist die Liebe, Nachts im grünen Kakadu, Zwei Herzen im Mai, U 47 – Kapitänleutnant Prien, Das hab' ich in Paris gelernt, Sabine und die 100 Männer, Ein Thron für Christine, Die toten Augen von London, Die glücklichen Jahre der Thorwalds, Muss i denn zum Städtele hinaus, Der rote Rausch, Ein Toter sucht seinen Mörder, Das Feuerschiff, Der Henker von London, Der schwarze Abt, Scotland Yard jagt Dr. Mabuse, Ein Frauenarzt klagt an, Die Goldsucher von Arkansas, Das Phantom von Soho, Der Schut, Durchs wilde Kurdistan,*

Der Arzt stellt fest, Wenn Ludwig ins Manöver zieht, Der Arzt von St. Pauli, Lady Hamilton.

41 BRANDES, WERNER (1889-1957). B: Brunswick. Director of photography. Enters cinema thanks to Joe May (q.v.). To England briefly at the end of the silent period. Very busy and efficient cameraman. In Switzerland during the War. See also Hans Richter.

Films: Königin Luise, Die heilige Simplizia (co-phot. with Günther Krampf), Die Herrin der Welt, Der Hund von Baskerville, Das indische Grabmal (co-phot. with Karl Puth), Die grüne Manuela (co-phot. with Puth); Ein Weib, ein Tier, ein Diamont; Mensch gegen Mensch, Der Demütige und die Sängerin, Der Flug um den Erdball, Liebe macht blind, Ein Walzertraum, Der Mann im Feuer (co-phot.), Sein grosser Fall, Die Frau im Schrank, Die selige Exzellenz, Walpurgisnacht (co-phot. with Curt Helling), Die Durchgängerin, Der Bund der Drei. Then sound: Rosenmontag, Der Schuss im Tonfilmatelier, Die blonde Nachtigall, Liebeswalzer (co-phot.), Emil und die Detektive, D-Zug 13 hat Verspätung, Das gelbe Haus des King-Fu, Der kleine Seitensprung, Friederike (co-phot. with Werner Bohne), Das Mädel vom Montparnasse, Wenn die Liebe Mode macht, Goethe (co-phot. with Kurt Stanke), Strich durch die Rechnung (co-phot. with Werner Bohne), Stern von Valencia (co-phot. with Karl Puth), Eine Tür geht auf (co-phot. with Werner Bohne), Heideschulmeister Uwe Karsten, Die Bande von Hoheneck, Abschiedswalzer, Regine, Einmal eine grosse Dame sein, G'schichten aus dem Wienerwald, Die Töchter Ihrer Exzellenz, Die Pompadour, Winternachtstraum, Stradivari, Die ganze Welt dreht sich um Liebe, Das Schloss in Flandern, Wo die Lerche singt (co-phot. with Hans Imber), Die Entführung, Die Leuchter des Kaisers, Das grosse Abenteuer, Musik für Dich, Lumpazivagabundus, Der Unwiderstehliche, Der Herrscher (co-phot.), Spiegel des Lebens, Die unruhigen Mädchen, Zwischen Strom und Steppe (co-phot. with Karl Drömmer), Der singende Tor, Sommerliebe am Bodensee (co-phot. with Wolf Schneider).

42 BRAUN, CURT JOHANNES (1903-). B: Guttstadt. Scriptwriter and author. Studied at University. Ph.D. Braun has written many novels, and also for the stage (e.g. Die Stadt ist voller Geheimnisse) and radio. Especially busy during early Thirties. Films: Thamar, das Kind der Berge (co-scripted with Rolf E. Vanloo), Die Frau ohne Geld, Der Kampf gegen Berlin, Der Turm des Schweigens, Derby, Die Fahrt ins Abenteuer (co-scripted with Robert Liebmann), Harry Hill auf Welle 1000, Jagd auf Menschen, Menschenleben in Gefahr (co-scripted with Wilhelm Stücklen), Das Panzergewölbe (co-scripted), Die Piraten der Ostseebäder, Alpentragödie; Anastasia, die falsche Zarentochter; Fassadengespenst, Gaunerliebchen, Der Gefangene von Shanghai, Ich heirate meine Frau, Manege, Kampa, der Tiermensch, Ariadne im Hoppegarten, Ein Mädchen und drei Clowns (co-scripted with Henry Edwards), Fräulein Chauffeur (co-scripted with Jonas), Frau Sorge, Der geheime Kurier (co-scripted with Jonas), Das Haus ohne Männer, Der Heilige und ihr Narr (co-scripted with Hagenbruch), Der Herzensphotograph, Der Ladenprinz, Das letzte Fort, Das letzte Souper, Mein Herz ist eine Jazzband, Quartier Latin (co-scripted with Fritz Falkenstein), Der Ruf des Nordens (co-scripted with Malasomma), Das grüne Monokel (co-scripted with B. E. Lüthge), Die stärkere Macht (co-scripted with Berthold Seidenstein), stud. chem. Helene Willfüer (co-scripted with Rosenfeld), Der König von Paris (co-scripted with Michael Linsky), Das Land des Lächelns (co-scripted with Anton Kuh and Leo Lasko), Wellen der Leidenschaft (co-scripted with Heinz Fischer), Der Greifer 30 (only dialogue with Max Ehrlich), Ich glaube nie mehr an eine Frau, Der Walzerkönig (co-scripted with B. E. Lüthge), Der unbekannte Gast (co-scripted with Walter Jonas), Vater geht auf Reisen (co-scripted with Fritz Falkenstein), Die grosse Attraktion (co-scripted with Anton Kuh and Richard Schneider-Edenkoben), Schachmatt, Ehe m.b.H. (co-scripted with B. E. Lüthge), Keine Feier ohne Meyer (co-scripted with Fritz Falkenstein), Gesangverein Sorgenfrei (co-scripted with Herbert Rosenfeld), Der tolle Bomberg, Die Vier vom Bob 13, Grün ist die Heide (co-scripted with Lüthge), Der schwarze Hu-

sar (co-scripted with Philipp Lothar May-ring), *Der Frauendiplomat* (co-scripted with Lüthge), *Aus einer kleinen Residenz* (co-scripted with Falkenstein), *Inge und die Millionen* (co-scripted with Emil Burri), *Die kleine Schwindlerin, Gipfelstürmer* (co-scripted with Lüthge), *Zwischen zwei Herzen, Klein-Dorrit, Polarstürme* (co-scripted with Nunzio Malasomma), *Der Doppelgänger* (co-scripted with Peter Ort), *Konjunkturritter* (co-scripted with Lüthge), *Die Liebe und die erste Eisenbahn, Schwarze Rosen* (co-scripted with Walter Supper and Paul Martin), *Grossreinemachen* (co-scripted with Josef Stolzing Czerny), *Stärker als Paragraphen, Waldwinter* (co-scripted with Fritz Peter Buch), *Das Schloss in Flandern, Manege, Der Herrscher* (co-scripted), *Serenade* (co-scripted), *Du und ich* (co-scripted with Eberhard Frowein), *Drei wunderschöne Tage, Die barmherzige Lüge* (co-scripted with Werner Klingler and Günther Kulewayer), *Was wird hier gespielt?*, *Herz modern möbliert, Meine Tochter lebt in Wien* (idea), *Auf Wiedersehen, Franziska* (co-scripted), *Kleine Mädchen – grosse Sorgen* (co-scripted with Gerhard T. Buchholz), *Die Sache mit Styx, Meine Freundin Josefine, Die Entlassung* (co-scripted with Felix von Eckart), *Ein glücklicher Mensch, Kollege kommt gleich, Man rede mir nicht von Liebe, Der Engel mit Saitenspiel* (co-scripted with Helmut Weiss), *Frau über Bord, Wo ist Herr Belling?*, *Das seltsame Fräulein Sylvia* (co-scripted with Just Scheu), *Verlorenes Rennen, Arlberg-Express, Der Fall Rabanser, Eva im Frack, Liebe Freundin, Torreani, Das seltsame Leben des Herrn Bruggs, Der fröhliche Weinberg, Der Vogelhändler, Der letzte Walzer, Der unsterbliche Lump, Die Sonne von St. Moritz, Der Zigeunerbaron, Der Engel mit dem Flammenschwert, Die Stadt ist voller Geheimnisse* (co-scripted), *Auf der Reeperbahn nachts um halb eins* (co-scripted with Gustav Kampendonk), *Geliebte Corinna* (co-scripted with Ernst von Salomon), *Stresemann* (co-scripted), *Viktor und Viktoria, Nachts im grünen Kakadu* (co-scripted with Helmut M. Backhaus), *Franziska* (co-scripted with Käutner and Georg Hurdalek), *Frühling in Berlin, Der Greifer* (58), *Hoppla, jetzt kommt Eddie; Peter Voss, der Millionendieb* (co-scripted Gustav Kampendonk), *Bobby Todd greift ein*.

43 BRAUN, HARALD (1901-1960). B: Berlin. D: Xanten. Director. Ph.D. Radio work (Reichssender Berlin). Director at the Heidelberger Kammerspiele. Asst. director to Carl Froelich (q.v.), later co-scriptwriter. 1945: Co-founder of Neue Deutsche Filmgesellschaft (NDF). Braun later founded Freie Film Produktion GmbH with Staudte and Käutner (both q.v.). His real career started after 1945, when he made certain films with Protestant overtones. Scripted many of his own films *.

Films: *Heimat* (only *), *Die Umwege des schönen Karl* (only * with Jakob Geis and Philipp Lothar Mayring), *Das Herz einer Königin* (only * with Geis and Rolf Reissmann), *Der Weg ins Freie* (only * with Geis and Rolf Hansen), *Zwischen Himmel und Erde* 42 (also * with Geis), *Hab' mich lieb* 42, *Träumerei* 44 (also * with Herbert Witt), *Nora* 44 (also * with Geis), *Der stumme Gast* 45 (also * with Kurt Heynicke), *Zwischen Gestern und Morgen* 47 (also * with Herbert Witt), *Das verlorene Gesicht* (only * with Rolf Reissmann), *Nachtwache* 49 (also * with Paul Alverdes), *Der Mann, der zweimal leben wollte* (only * with Heinz Pauck), *Der fallende Stern* 50 (also * with Witt), *Herz der Welt* 51 (also * with Witt), *Vater braucht eine Frau* 52, *Solange Du da bist* 53, *Königliche Hoheit* 53, *Der letzte Sommer* 54 (also * with Emil Burri and Georg Hurdalek), *Der letzte Mann* 55, *Regine* 55, *Herrscher ohne Krone* 57, *Der gläserne Turm* 57 (also * with Odo Krohmann and Wolfgang Koeppen), *Buddenbrooks* (only * with Erika Mann and Geis), *Die Botschafterin* (only * co-scripted).

44 BRAUNER, ARTUR (1918-   ). B: Lodz (Poland). Studies at Technical High School in Lodz. From 1946: producer in Berlin. Owner of his own studios since 1950. Founder and principal shareholder of CCC-Film GmbH (Central Cinema Company). Co-produced first film which was made after 1945 under British licence, *Sag' die Wahrheit*. One of the most powerful and efficient producers in German postwar cinema, who adapted himself very quickly to the current fashion and public tastes and has managed to survive many crises. Brauner is still a prominent figure. Many co-productions. Also very much involved with television productions.

Films: *Sag' die Wahrheit* (co-prod.), *Herzkönig, Morituri, Man spielt nicht mit der Liebe, Mädchen hinter Gittern, Fünf unter Verdacht, Maharadscha wider Willen, Epilog* (also idea with Fritz Böttger), *Das Mädchen aus der Konfektion, Sündige Grenze* (also idea), *Schwarze Augen, Der keusche Lebemann, Man lebt nur einmal, Die Spur führt nach Berlin, Der Onkel aus Amerika, Die Kaiserin von China, Hollandmädel, Die Privatsekretärin, Der Raub der Sabinerinnen, Meine Schwester und ich, Grosse Starparade, Der Zarewitsch, Roman eines Frauenarztes, Liebe ohne Illusion, Der 20. Juli, Stern von Rio, Die Ratten, Der Hauptmann und sein Held, Du mein stilles Tal, Hotel Adlon; Liebe, Tanz und 1000 Schlager; Das Bad auf der Tenne, Studentin Helen Willfüer, Frucht ohne Liebe, Der erste Frühlingstag, Vor Sonnenuntergang; Mein Vater, der Schauspieler; Du bist Musik, Liebe, Musikparade, Das alte Försterhaus, Ein Mann muss nicht immer schön sein, Wie ein Sturmwind, Die Unschuld vom Lande, Kindermädchen für Papa gesucht, Das einfache Mädchen, Die Letzten werden die Ersten sein, Einmal eine grosse Dame sein, Siebenmal in der Woche, Franziska, Liebe, Jazz und Uebermut, Die Frühreifen, Die grosse Sünde* (co-prod. with Alfu), *... und führe uns nicht in Versuchung, Der Graf von Luxemburg, Italienreise – Liebe inbegriffen, ... und abends in die Scala, Es geschah am hellichten Tag* (co-prod. with Praesens Film), *Gestehen Sie, Herr Dr. Corda; Mädchen in Uniform, Münchhausen in Afrika, Petersburger Nächte, Der Czardas-König, Mann im Strom, Ihr 106. Geburtstag, Polikuschka* (co-prod. with Bavaria), *Der Stern von Santa Clara; Wehe, wenn sie losgelassen; Der achte Wochentag, Scala total verrückt, Ohne Mutter geht es nicht, Der Tiger von Eschnapur, Das indische Grabmal; Hier bin ich, hier bleib' ich, Menschen im Hotel, Du bist wunderbar, Ein Engel auf Erden* (co-prod.), *Abschied von den Wolken, Alt Heidelberg* (co-prod. with Ulrich), *Marili, ... und das am Montagmorgen* (co-prod. with Sokal/Goldbaum), *Was eine Frau im Frühling träumt, Der brave Soldat Schwejk, Herrin der Welt* (co-prod. with Continental Rome & Franco London Paris), *Kein Engel ist so rein, Liebling der Götter, Sabine und die 100 Männer, Scheidungsgrund Liebe, Stefanie in Rio* (co-prod. with Ufa), *Die 1000 Augen des Dr. Mabuse* (co-prod. with Cei-Incom Rome), *Es muss nicht immer Kaviar sein* (co-prod. with CEC Paris), *Diesmal muss es Kaviar sein* (co-prod. with CEC Paris), *Die Ehe des Herrn Mississippi* (co-prod. with Praesens Zurich), *Im Stahlnetz des Dr. Mabuse* (co-prod. with Criterion Paris & Spa Cinemat. Rome), *Das Riesenrad, Unter Ausschluss der Oeffentlichkeit, Via Mala, Endstation 13 Sahara; Axel Munthe, der Arzt von San Michele* (co-prod. with Cine Italia Rome & Criterion Paris), *Das Geheimnis der schwarzen Koffer, Sherlock Holmes und das Halsband des Todes* (co-prod. with Criterion Paris & Incei Rome), *Das Testament des Dr. Mabuse, Ein Toter sucht seinen Mörder* (co-prod. with Raymond Stross), *Die unsichtbaren Krallen des Dr. Mabuse, Der Fluch der gelben Schlange, Die Flucht* (co-prod. with Avala Beograd), *Frühstück im Doppelbett, Der Henker von London, Scotland Yard jagt Dr. Mabuse, Der Würger von Schloss Blackmoor, Fanny Hill* (co-prod. with Famous Players Corp.), *Ein Frauenarzt klagt an, Freddy und das Lied der Prärie* (co-prod. with Avala), *Old Shatterhand* (co-prod. with Criterion Paris, Serena Rome & Avala), *Das Phantom von Soho, Der Schut* (co-prod. with Criterion Paris, Serena Rome & Avala), *Das siebente Opfer, Die Todesstrahlen des Dr. Mabuse* (co-prod. with Franco London Paris & Serena Rome), *Das Ungeheuer von London City, Durchs wilde Kurdistan* (co-prod. with Balcazar Barcelona), *Die Hölle von Manitoba* (co-prod. with Midega Madrid), *Im Reiche des silbernen Löwen* (co-prod. with Balcazar), *Mädchen hinter Gitter, Die Pyramide des Sonnengottes* (co-prod. with Franco London Paris, Serena Rome & Avala), *Der Schatz der Azteken* (co-prod. with Franco London Paris, Serena Rome & Avala), *Der Arzt stellt fest* (co-prod. with Praesens Zurich & Fono Berlin), *5000 Dollar für den Kopf von Jonny R.* (co-prod. with Tilma Films), *Die Hölle von Macao* (co-prod. with Criterion Paris & Senior Rome); *Lange Beine, Lange Finger; Die Zeugin aus der Hölle* (co-prod. with Avala), *Geheimnisse in goldenen Nylons* (co-prod. with SNF & TC Prod. Paris & Metheus Rome), *Die Nibelun-*

gen I & II (co-prod. with Avala), *Rheins-berg* (co-prod. with Independant), *Erotik auf der Schulbank, Kampf um Rom I & II* (co-prod. with Italy and Rumania), *Schreie in der Nacht* (co-prod. with Italy), *Shalako* (co-prod. with Kingston), *Tevye und seine sieben Töchter* (co-prod. with Noah Israel), *Winnetou und Shatterhand im Tal der To-ten* (co-prod. with Italy and Jadran Zagreb), *Vento dell'est* (co-prod. with Italy), *Hoch-zeitsreise, Liebesvögel* (co-prod. with Comp. P. Ass. Rome).

45 BRESSART, FELIX (1892-1949). B: Eythkuhnen (East Prussia). D: Hollywood. Actor. Comic of stage and film. 1938: goes to U.S.A., where Henry Koster (q.v.) offers him his first foreign role. En route makes *Wie d'Warret würkt* in Switzerland.

Films: *Liebe im Kuhstall.* Then sound: *Es gibt eine Frau, die Dich niemals vergisst; Eine Freundin so goldig wie Du, Drei Tage Mittelarrest, Die zärtlichen Verwandten, Die Drei von der Tankstelle, Der Sohn der weis-sen Berge, Das alte Lied, Der keusche Jo-seph, Hirsekorn greift ein, Trara um Liebe, Der Herr Bürovorsteher, Der wahre Jakob, Nie wieder Liebe, Der Schrecken der Gar-nison, Die Privatsekretärin, Holzapfel weiss alles; Goldblondes Mädchen, ich schenk' Dir mein Herz; Und wer küsst mich?*

46 BROOKS, LOUISE (1906-   ). B: Cherryvale (Kansas). Dancer, pupil of Ruth Saint-Denis, then signed up by Ziegfeld. Appeared mainly in American films, worked twice with Pabst (q.v.) in *Pandora's Box* and *Diary of a Lost Girl.* Before returning to U.S.A. (1930), she made one film in France – *Prix de Beauté.* Retired in 1938.

Films: *Die Büchse der Pandora, Das Ta-gebuch einer Verlorenen.*

47 BRUCKBAUER, GEORG (1888-   ). B: Vienna. Director of photography. Franz Planer (q.v.) brought him to Berlin, where Bruckbauer commenced his career in col-laboration with Carl Boese (q.v.). A ver-satile cameraman who has spent many years in the film industry, and is well known for his work on entertainment films.

Films (incomplete): *Die Frau, die nicht "nein" sagen kann* (co-phot. with Willy Goldberger); *Es steht ein Wirtshaus an der*

Above: Louise Brooks in DAS TAGEBUCH EINER VERLORENEN

Lahn, Die leichte Isabell (co-phot. with Goldberger), *Wien, Wien nur Du allein; Ariadne in Hoppegarten* (co-phot.), *An-schluss um Mitternacht* (co-phot. with Gold-berger), *Morgenröte* (co-phot.), *Die Schleier-tänzerin* (co-phot. with Günther Krampf), *Sturm auf drei Herzen, Der Weg durch die Nacht, Die Somme* (co-phot. with Gluck, Sidney Blythe & Frederick A. Young), *Die Sünde der Lissy Krafft.* Then sound: *Ver-klungene Träume* (co-phot. with Laszlo Schäffer), *Walzerparadies* (co-phot.), *Schat-ten der Manege* (co-phot. with Viktor Gluck), *Douaumont* (co-phot. with Gluck), *Einer Frau muss man alles verzeih'n* (co-phot. with Gluck), *Trenck* (co-phot.), *Melo-die der Liebe* (co-phot.), *Tannenberg* (co-phot. with Gluck), *Unsichtbare Gegner* (co-phot.), *Keinen Tag ohne Dich* (co-phot.), *Schwarzwaldmädel* (co-phot. with Ewald Daub), *Kleines Mädchen – grosses Glück* (co-phot. with Baberske and Walter Pindter), *Alte Kameraden, Früchtchen; Meine Frau, die Schützenkönigin; Der Schrecken vom Heidekrug, Wenn ein Mädel Hochzeit macht, Hilde Petersen postlagernd* (co-phot.), *Vergiss mein nicht* (co-phot. with*

Herbert Körner, Bruno Timm and Kurt Neubert), *Schatten der Vergangenheit, Der Dschungel ruft* (co-phot. with Karl Vass and Hans Gottschalk), *Onkel Bräsig, Stärker als Paragraphen, Dahinten in der Heide, Mutterlied, Gauner im Frack, Man spricht über Jacqueline, Meine Freundin Barbara; Nanu, Sie kennen Korff noch nicht?, Konzert in Tirol, Prinzessin Sissy, Verdacht auf Ursula, Irrtum des Herzens, Ich verweigere die Aussage, Meine Tochter tut das nicht, Meine Tochter lebt in Wien, Der Meineidbauer* (co-phot.), *Liebe ist zollfrei, So gefällst Du mir, Die Sache mit Styx, Die grosse Nummer* (co-phot. with Walter Rosskopf), *Akrobat schö-ö-ön, Romanze in Moll, Solistin Anna Alt, Die Degenhardts, Der Verteidiger hat das Wort, Der Scheiterhaufen, Leb'wohl Christina, Eine alltägliche Geschichte, Blockierte Signale, Strassenbekanntschaft, Der Herr vom andern Stern, Eine grosse Liebe; Hallo, Fräulein; Wenn eine Frau liebt, Verführte Jugend, Der bunte Traum, Die verschleierte Maja, Hanna Amon* (co-phot. with Werner Krien and Eugen Schuhmacher), *Professor Nachtfalter, Alle kann ich nicht heiraten* (co-phot.), *Der grosse Zapfenstreich, Tanzende Sterne, Der Kaplan von San Lorenzo, Sterne über Colombo* (co-phot.), *Kaisermanöver, Der Gefangene des Maharadscha* (co-phot.), *Der Zarewitsch, Verrat an Deutschland* (co-phot. with Shizu Fujii), *Liebe ohne Illusion, Rosenmontag* (co-phot. with Bruno Stephan), *Der Kongress tanzt* (55); *Weil Du arm bist, musst du früher sterben; Zwischen Zeit und Ewigkeit, Du bist Musik, . . . und wer küsst mich?, Das Bad auf der Tenne, Der Bauerndoktor von Bayrisch-Zell, Der Fuchs von Paris, Scherben bringen Glück* (co-phot. with Wolfgang Hewecker & Werner Kraft), *Frühling in Berlin, Zwei Herzen im Mai, Die Beine von Dolores, Grabenplatz 17, Schwarzwälder Kirsch, Der Maulkorb, Der eiserne Gustav, Schlag auf Schlag, So angelt man keinen Mann, Alle Tage ist kein Sonntag, Blond muss man sein auf Capri, Die blonde Frau des Maharadscha* (co-phot.), *Das grosse Liebesspiel, Ist Geraldine kein Engel?, Ein Ferienbett mit 100 PS.*

48 BUCHHOLZ, HORST (1932-   ). B: Berlin. Actor. Stage training under Marlise Ludwig in Berlin. Theatre work: Hebbel-theater, Tribüne, Renaissance, Schiller- and Schlosspark-Theater (all Berlin). Dubbed for other actors in several foreign films. Also worked for American companies, in France and Italy.

Films: *Marianne, Himmel ohne Sterne, Regine, Die Halbstarken, Herrscher ohne Krone, Robinson soll nicht sterben, Die Bekenntnisse des Hochstaplers Felix Krull, Monpti, Endstation Liebe, Nasser Asphalt, Auferstehung, Das Totenschiff, Johnny Banco − Geliebter Taugenichts.*

49 BUCHOWETZKI, DIMITRI (1895-1932). B: U.S.S.R. D: U.S.A. Director. Studied law. Then director of Russian films. Goes to Germany after the October Revolution, and proves very successful with costume dramas. 1919: series of films with Max Linder. Later goes to Sweden, and then to Hollywood (in 1924).

Films: Die Brüder Karamasoff 20 (co-dir.), *Das Experiment des Professor Mithrany* 20, *Die letzte Stunde* 20, *Danton* 21 (also script), *Der Galiläer* 21, *Sappho* 21 (also script), *Der Stier von Olivera* 21 (co-dir. with Erich Schönfelder), *Die Gräfin von Paris* 22, *Othello* 22, *Peter der Grosse* 22, *Das Karussell des Lebens* 23 (also script in collab. with Alfred Fekete). Then sound: *Weib im Dschungel* 30, *Die Nacht der Entscheidung* 31.

50 BÜRGER, ANNEKATHRIN (1937-   ). B: Berlin. RN: Annekathrin Rammelt. Actress. Trained as stage designer. 1956: enters cinema through director Gerhard Klein. Film School in East Berlin. Since 1965: member of the Volksbühne Berlin.

Films: *Eine Berliner Romanze, Spur in der Nacht, Tilman Riemenschneider, Reportage 57, Verwirrung der Liebe, Fünf Tage − fünf Nächte, Septemberliebe, Guten Tag, lieber Tag; Königskinder, Das zweite Gleis, Mörder auf Urlaub, Nichts als Sünde, Abschied; Mit mir nicht, Madam.*

51 BUSCH, ERNST (1900-   ). B: Kiel. Actor. Trained as locksmith. 1920: appears at the Union House in Kiel. 1927: member of the "Proletarian Theatre" under Erwin Piscator, and meets Brecht. 1937: to Spain. Spends war in various prisons. After 1945 in G.D.R., mainly at the Berliner Ensemble.

Three times winner of state award, in 1949, 1956, and 1966. Very important actor in the Brecht tradition.

Films: *Katherina Knie*. Then sound: *Gassenhauer, Niemandsland, Die Dreigroschenoper, Die Koffer des Herrn O.F., Kameradschaft, Kuhle Wampe, Razzia in St. Pauli, Strafsache van Geldern, Die Zwei vom Südexpress, Eine von uns, Das Meer ruft, Kämpfer, Mutter Courage und ihre Kinder.*

52 CHARELL, ERIK (18? -19?). B: Pressburg. Director. Well known as a brilliant director of operettas in the Twenties and Thirties, mostly in Berlin. International reputation after his only film in 1931 (as a result he makes one film in Hollywood). After 1945: minor contributions to films of Forst and Hoffmann (both q.v.).

Films: *Der Kongress tanzt 31, Im weissen Rössl* (production manager, co-scripted with Horst Budjuhn and Harry Halm), *Feuerwerk* (idea and choreography).

53 CHRISTIAN, NORBERT (1925-). B: Berlin. Actor. Stage training, then theatrical work in Griefswald and Rostock. Brecht enrolled him in the Berliner Ensemble. Now acting at the Volksbühne Berlin.

Films: *Die Unbesiegbaren, Kein Hüsung, Junges Gemüse, Der junge Engländer, Geschwader Fledermaus, Ware für Katalonien, Leute mit Flügeln, Seilergasse 8, Hochmut kommt vor dem Fall, Einer von uns, Die heute über 40 sind, Italienisches Capriccio, Mutter Courage und ihre Kinder; Mir nach, Canaillen!, Die Abenteuer des Werner Holt, Chronik eines Mordes, Entlassen auf Bewährung, Ohne Pass in fremden Betten, Das Mädchen auf dem Brett; Der Mord, der nie verjährt.*

CHRISTIAN, PAUL see HUBSCHMID, PAUL.

54 CHRISTIANS, MADY (1900-1951). B: Vienna. D: South Norwalk (Connecticut). Actress. When aged twelve came to New York, where her father Rudolf Christians took over the German Irving Place Theatre and she played children's roles. 1917: to Germany, trained at theatre school of Deutsches Theater Berlin; stage experience at Reinhardt-Theatres Berlin (q.v.), later Theater in der Josefstadt and Volkstheater, both Vienna. 1933: emigrates. First film (in U.S.A.): *Adrey.*

Films (incomplete): *Die Krone von Kertzyna, Der Mann ohne Namen, Es leuchtet die Liebe, Das Weib des Pharao, Kinder der Zeit, Malmaison, Die Buddenbrooks, Das Spiel der Königin, Der verlorene Schuh, Der Wetterwart, Die Finanzen des Grossherzogs, Mensch gegen Mensch, Soll und Haben, Der Abenteurer, Die vom Niederrhein, Der Farmer aus Texas, Die Verrufenen, Ein Walzertraum, Die geschiedene Frau, Nanette macht alles, Die Welt will belogen sein; Wien, wie es weint und lacht; Zopf und Schwert, Die Königin vom Moulin-Rouge, Grand Hotel . . .!, Heimweh, Königin Luise, Der Sohn von Hagar, Fräulein Chauffeur, Eine Frau von Format, Priscillas Fahrt ins Glück, Das brennende Herz, Meine Schwester und ich.* Then sound: *Dich hab' ich geliebt, Leutnant warst Du einst bei den Husaren; Die Frau, von der man spricht; Das Schicksal der Renate Langen, Friederike, Der schwarze Husar, Salon Dora Green, Ich und die Kaiserin; Manolescu, der Fürst der Diebe.*

55 CLAUNIGK, ERICH (19? -). B: Grünwald near Munich. Director of photography. Enters film industry in 1936. Modest camerawork with no special qualities. Mostly works on entertainment films.

Films: *Drei tolle Tage, Hilde und die 4 PS* (co-phot. with Hugo von Kaweczynski), *Ein kleiner goldener Ring* (co-phot. with Edgar Ziesemer), *Petermann ist dagegen, Scheidungsreise, Drei wunderschöne Tage, Das Ekel, Fahrt ins Leben, Liebeskomödie, Anuschka, Der dunkle Tag, Johann* (co-phot. with Heinz Schnackertz), *Die unheimliche Wandlung des Axel Roscher, Das Lied der Nachtigall, Es fing so harmlos an, Ein Mann wie Maximilian, Es lebe die Liebe, Philine, Liebesheirat, Die kupferne Heirat, Das Geheimnis der roten Katze, Die drei Dorfheiligen, Ich mach' Dich glücklich, Der Theodor im Fussballtor, Die gestörte Hochzeitsnacht, Die Tat des Andern, Glück aus Ohio, Eine Frau mit Herz; Mein Freund, der Dieb; In München steht ein Hofbräuhaus, Einmal am Rhein, Das Geheimnis einer Ehe, Fanfaren der Ehe, Salto mortale* (co-phot.), *Junggesellenfalle, Strassenserenade, Colum-*

bus entdeckt Krähwinkel, Fräulein vom Amt, Der doppelte Ehemann, Drei Tage Mittelarrest, Meine Kinder und ich, Drei Mädels vom Rhein, Ein Herz schlägt für Erika, Ich und meine Schwiegersöhne, Wo die Lerche singt, Die Stimme der Sehnsucht, Hotel Allotria, Die verpfuschte Hochzeitsnacht, Lemke's sel. Witwe, Zwei Bayern im Harem, Frauenarzt Dr. Bertram, Blitzmädels an die Front, Der Pauker; Hoppla, jetzt kommt Eddie; Liebe auf krummen Beinen, Hula hopp – Conny!, Arzt aus Leidenschaft, Auch Egon, Der Hochtourist, Er kann's nicht lassen, Meine Tochter und ich; Vorsicht, Mister Dodd.

COOK, MARIANNE *see* KOCH, MARIANNE.

56 COURANT, CURT (KURT, CURTIS) (18 -   ). Director of photography. Starts his career in Germany shortly after the First World War, although he had worked previously in Italy (on *Cabiria*, etc.), and was to work there again later in the silent period (on *Quo Vadis* and other epics). 1933: emigrates to France and England, where he gains an international reputation photographing such films as Carné's *Le jour se lève*, Renoir's *La Bête humaine* and Chaplin's *Monsieur Verdoux*. Father of the young director of photography, Willy Kurant, known for his work for directors of the French new wave (including Godard).
Films (incomplete): *Hilde Warren· und der Tod* (co-phot.), *Hamlet* (co-phot. with Axel Graatkjaer, Präsident Barrada, Der Abenteurer, Mädchen aus der Ackerstrasse, Das Mädel vom Piccadilly, Die Sassenkönigin, Der Pantoffelheld, Peter der Grosse* (co-phot.), *Das Paradies im Schnee* (co-phot. with Max Schneider & Robert Freckmann), *Komödianten des Lebens, Zwei Kinder, Ich liebe Dich, Die Insel der Träume, Liebesfeuer, Die Fahrt ins Abenteuer, Der fesche Erzherzog, Die Flucht in die Nacht* (co-phot. with Arpad Viragh), *Gräfin Plättmamsell, Die Kleine vom Varieté; Wehe, wenn sie losgelassen; Die Welt will belogen sein* (co-phot. with Sophus Wangoe), *Die Czardasfürstin, Familientag im Hause Prellstein, Der Kampf des Donald Westhof* (co-phot.), *Schuldig* (co-phot. with Eugen Hrich), *Geheimnisse des Orients* (co-phot. with Nikolai Toporkoff & Burgassoff), *Hurrah! Ich lebe!* (co-phot. with Burgassoff), *Das brennende Herz, Die Frau im Mond* (co-phot. with Tschet, Kanturek & Oskar Fischinger), *Die Frau nach der man sich sehnt*. Then sound: *Der König von Paris* (co-phot. with Max Brink), *Der weisse Teufel* (co-phot. with Nikolai Toporkoff), *Der Hampelmann* (co-phot.), *Die singende Stadt* (co-phot. with Arpad Viragh), *Meine Cousine aus Warschau; Der Mann, der den Mord beging; Wer nimmt die Liebe ernst?, Scampolo, Ein Kind der Strasse; Rasputin, Die – oder keine, Gitta entdeckt ihr Herz, Ich will Dich Liebe lehren* (co-phot.).

57 CZINNER, PAUL (1890-   ). B: Budapest. Director. Married to Elizabeth Bergner (q.v.) and director of most of her films. Doctor of Philosophy and Literature. Started as theatre producer in Budapest prior to 1914, and later went to Vienna where he made his first films (e.g. *Homo immanis* and *Inferno*), then to Germany. Although he made his first English film in 1930, Czinner only emigrated to England in 1933. From 1955 onward his films tend to be reproductions of stage productions. *See also "Kammerspielfilm".*
Films: *Der Unmensch* 19, *Inferno* 20, *Nju* 24⁴ (also script), *Eifersucht* (only script), *Der Geiger von Florenz* 26 (also script), *Liebe* 26 (also script), *Dona Juana* 27 (also co-scripted), *Fräulein Else* 29 (also script). Then sound: *Ariane* 31 (also script with Mayer), *Der träumende Mund* 32 (also script with Mayer), *Der träumende Mund* 53 (only script with Johanna Sibelius, based on Mayer's script from 32).

58 DAGOVER, LIL (1887 or 1897-   ). B: Pati or Madiven on Java. Actress. RN: Marie Antonia Siegelinde Martha Seubert. 1903: to Germany. Enters cinema thanks to her marriage with actor Fritz Daghofer (1872-1936). Discovered and launched by Robert Wiene (q.v.). Works temporarily abroad (1927 in Sweden, 1928-1929 in France, 1932 in U.S.A.). Acted in theatres: Deutsches Theater Berlin, Salzburg Festival. Became very famous for her performances in "expressionist" films (q.v.). Her role was usually that of the frail heroine with the "haunted" look.

Lil Dagover with Conrad Veidt and Werner Krauss in DAS KABINETT DES
DR. CALIGARI

Films: *Harakiri, Das Kabinett des Dr.
Caligari, Die Spinnen, Das Geheimnis von
Bombay, Der Richter von Zalamea, Spiritis-
mus, Die Toteninsel, Die Jagd nach dem
Tode, Das Medium, Der müde Tod, Dr.
Mabuse der Spieler, Luise Millerin, Macht
der Versuchung, Phantom, Tiefland, Die
Prinzessin Sawarin; Seine Frau, die Unbe-
kannte; Komödie des Herzens, Der De-
mütige und die Sängerin, Liebe macht blind,
Tartüff, Zur Chronik von Grieshuus, Die
Brüder Schellenberg, Nur eine Tänzerin,
Der Veilchenfresser, Der Anwalt des Her-
zens, Orientexpress, Der geheime Kurier,
Ungarische Rhapsodie, Die Ehe, Es flüstert
die Nacht . . ., Spielereien einer Kaiserin.*
Then sound: *Der Günstling von Schön-
brunn, Va banque, Das alte Lied, Der weisse
Teufel, Boykott, Es gibt eine Frau, die
Dich niemals vergisst; Die grosse Sehnsucht,*
*Der Kongress tanzt, Der Fall des General-
stabs-Oberst Redl, Die Tänzerin von Sans-
souci, Das Abenteuer der Thea Roland, Jo-
hannisnacht, Ich heirate meine Frau; Eine
Frau, die weiss was sie will; Der Flüchtling
von Chicago, Lady Windermeres Fächer,
Der Vogelhändler, Der höhere Befehl,
Schlussakkord, Fridericus, August der Starke, Das Mädchen Irene, Das Schönheits-
pflästerchen, Streit um den Knaben Jo, Die
Kreutzersonate, Maja zwischen zwei Ehen,
Dreiklang, Rätsel um Beate, Umwege zum
Glück, Friedrich Schiller, Bismarck, Wien
1910, Kleine Residenz, Musik in Salzburg,
Die Söhne des Herrn Gaspary, Man spielt
nicht mit der Liebe, Vom Teufel gejagt, Es
kommt ein Tag; Rote Rosen, rote Lippen,
roter Wein; Königliche Hoheit, Schloss Hubertus; Ich weiss, wofür ich lebe; Die Barrings, Der Fischer vom Heiligensee, Rosen*

im Herbst, Meine 16 Söhne, Kronprinz Rudolfs letzte Liebe, Bekenntnisse des Hochstaplers Felix Krull, Unter Palmen am blauen Meer, Buddenbrooks, Die seltsame Gräfin.

59 **DAHLKE, PAUL** (1904-   ). B: Streitz (Poland). Actor. Trained in the Actors' School of the Deutsches Theater Berlin. Enters cinema thanks to director Karl Ritter (q.v.). A versatile actor in various parts, especially up to 1950.

Films: *Liebe, Tod und Teufel; Lady Windermeres Fächer, Verräter, Fridericus, Der zerbrochene Krug, Patrioten, Daphne und der Diplomat; Mein Sohn, der Herr Minister; War es der im 3. Stock?, Capriccio, Schwarzfahrt ins Glück, Frauen für Golden Hill, Verwehte Spuren, Pour le mérite, Die Hochzeitsreise, Befreite Hände, Die unheimlichen Wünsche, Robert Koch, Morgen werde ich verhaftet, Die barmherzige Lüge, Wer küsst Madeleine?, Kennwort Machin, Es war eine rauschende Ballnacht, Die keusche Geliebte, Das Fräulein von Barnhelm, Friedrich Schiller, Heimaterde, Die Kellnerin Anna, . . . reitet für Deutschland, Kameraden, Venus vor Gericht, Geliebte Welt, 5000 Mark Belohnung, Andreas Schlüter, Dr. Crippen an Bord, Gefährlicher Frühling, Ich vertraue Dir meine Frau an, Seine beste Rolle, Romanze in Moll, Der Täter ist unter uns, Das war mein Leben, Ich brauche Dich, Orientexpress, Ein Mann wie Maximilian, Das Gesetz der Liebe, Dreimal Komödie, Der Posaunist, Frech und verliebt, Und finden dereinst wir uns wieder, Menschen in Gottes Hand, Das verlorene Gesicht, Die Zeit mit Dir, Lang ist der Weg, Der Bagnosträfling, Begegnung mit Werther, Die Reise nach Marrakesch, Krach im Hinterhaus, Falschmünzer am Werk, Der Schatten des Herrn Molitor, Der Fall Rabanser, Kein Engel ist so rein, Der fallende Stern, Die gestörte Hochzeitsnacht, Rausch einer Nacht, Lockende Sterne, Liebe im Finanzamt, Der Tag vor der Hochzeit, Vergiss die Liebe nicht, Arlette erobert Paris, Dalmatinische Hochzeit, Die tolle Lola, . . . und ewig bleibt die Liebe, Clivia, Das fliegende Klassenzimmer, Drei vom Varieté, Ihr erstes Rendezvous, Meine Kinder und ich, Wunschkonzert, Roman einer Siebzehnjährigen, Drei Männer im Schnee, Frucht ohne*

Liebe, Die Ehe des Dr. med. Danwitz, Der erste Frühlingstag, Kitty und die grosse Welt, Liebe – wie die Frau sie wünscht, Anders als Du und ich, Heute blau und morgen blau, Made in Germany, Stresemann, Alle Sünden dieser Erde, Die feuerrote Baronesse, Die Nackte un der Satan, Die Wahrheit über Rosemarie; Liebe, Luft und lauter Lügen; Abschied in den Wolken, Drillinge an Bord, . . . und immer ruft das Herz, Ein Student ging vorbei, Jedermann, Die ihre Haut zu Markte tragen, Das Mädchen und der Staatsanwalt, Das Haus in Montevideo, Mit besten Empfehlungen, Die schwarze Kobra, Begegnung in Salzburg, Das Geheimnis der chinesischen Nelke, Die Heiden von Kummerov und ihre lustigen Streiche; Donnerwetter, Donnerwetter, Bonifatius Kiesewetter.

60 **DEFA:** East German production company *(Deutsche Film Aktien Gesellschaft)*, founded May 17, 1946. At first launches film productions in the Soviet zone of Berlin (first postwar film in Germany: *Die Mörder sind unter uns*). When the G.D.R. was founded in 1949, DEFA became "Company of the State." At first only very few films but these usually more significant than those of West German production companies, because DEFA's films were made more carefully and seriously (e.g. *Ehe im Schatten, Affäre Blum, Wozzeck*). Technical facilities were better than in the West, as DEFA was able to use the old Babelsberg studios. Since 1949 a completely new film industry has been organised, including departments for feature films, documentaries, popular science films, etc., with ample scope for trainee directors and writers. At the beginning of the official DEFA period, Wolfgang Staudte was still the leading figure *(Der Untertan* being his finest film of that period) until he left their studios and moved to the West. Newcomers like Maetzig and Wolf (both q.v.) revealed considerable talent

Opposite: Hildegard Knef and Wilhelm Borchert in the DEFA production DIE MÖRDER SIND UNTER UNS (above); Sabine Thalbach and Werner Peters in DER UNTERTAN (also DEFA, below)

in their early features, but later veered towards the official line.

In 1952 there was a conference on the cinema in the G.D.R., and the Communist partly laid down the "principles" of film-making, urging all directors to stress in their work the growth of the Socialist state and the positive side of life. The result was a series of purely propagandist films (like *Ernst Thälmann I* and *II*), costume dramas, and pictures that contrasted the pristine quality of life in the East with the corruption of society in the West.

Directors like Dudow, Wolf and Maetzig were still able occasionally to produce interesting and even revealing works. Quite a few artists worked in the DEFA studios for a while when they found more satisfying conditions there than in the West *(see* Porten, Staudte, Behn-Grund, etc.).

The artistic level of DEFA production is variable and depends one way or another on the party line. The fact that the process of film-making in the G.D.R. involves the approval of many departments can be regarded as a major handicap.

Key figures of the DEFA: Beyer, Dudow, Hellberg, Kunert, Maetzig, Wolf (for feature films), Heynowski and Thorndike (for documentaries), all q.v.

61 DELSCHAFT, MALY (1900-   ). B: Hamburg, Actress. *Début* in children's parts at the Stadttheater Hamburg. Until 1934 Miss Delschaft was featured in many German theatres (Bremen, Breslau, Berlin). Enters cinema through Murnau (q.v.). Occasional work for DEFA (q.v.).

Films (incomplete): *Danton, Dämon Zirkus; Dudu, ein Menschenschicksal; Der letzte Mann, Lumpen und Seide, Die Anne-Liese von Dessau, Die drei Portiermädel, Die eiserne Braut, Der Hahn im Korb, Der Mann auf dem Kometen, Sündenbabel, Varieté, Wenn Du eine Tante hast, Die Abenteuer eines Zehnmarkscheines, Als ich wiederkam, Die da unten, Die Fahrt ins Grüne, Jagd auf Menschen, Der Kavalier vom Wedding, Die Kleine und ihr Kavalier, Kreuzzug des Weibes, Die letzte Droschke von Berlin, Der Mann ohne Schlaf, Mitgiftjäger, Die Wiskottens, Die Ausgestossenen, Der Fluch der Vererbung, Liebe geht seltsame Wege, Die Lindenwirtin am Rhein,*

Petronella, Das Recht zu leben, Die Strecke, Unter Ausschluss der Oeffentlichkeit, Casanovas Erbe, Herr Meister und Frau Meisterin; Das Lied, das meine Mutter sang; Sechzehn Töchter und kein Papa, Andreas Hofer, Die keusche Kokotte, Das Recht des Ungeborenen, Unschuld, Eros in Ketten, Die Sünde der Lissy Kraft. Then sound: *Dienst ist Dienst, Verklungene Träume, Strohwitwer, Keine Feier ohne Meyer; Meine Frau, die Hochstaplerin; Heimat am Rhein, Kampf um den Bär, K 1 greift ein; Nur nicht weich werden, Susanne; Wilhelm Tell, Liselotte von der Pfalz, Paradies der Junggesellen, Angelika, Hochzeitsnacht, Mit den Augen einer Frau, Die grosse Nummer, Die goldene Spinne, Ein Blick zurück, Affäre Blum, Schuld allein ist der Wein, Familie Benthin, Die Jungen von Kranichsee, Der Kahn der fröhlichen Leute, Die Sonnenbrucks, Das Beil von Wandsbek, Frauenschicksale, Anna Susanna, Der treue Husar, Leuchtfeuer, Star mit fremden Federn, Ich war ein hässliches Mädchen, Vor Gott und den Menschen, Alibi, Studentin Helen Willfüer, Thomas Müntzer, Schlösser und Katen, Witwer mit fünf Töchtern, Nur eine Frau, Emilia Galotti, Meine Frau macht Musik, Der Czardaskönig, Kein Aerger mit Cleopatra.*

62 DELTGEN, RENÉ (1909 or 1912-   ).B: Esch-sur-Alzette (Luxembourg). Actor. Trained at Schauspielhaus Cologne. Theatres: Cologne, Frankfurt, Heidelberg, Berlin.

Films: *Das Mädchen Johanna, Einer zuviel an Bord, Port Arthur, Savoy-Hotel 217, Unter heissem Himmel, Starke Herzen, Urlaub auf Ehrenwort, Schwarzfahrt ins Glück, Geheimzeichen LB 17, Ab Mitternacht, Kautschuk, Nordlicht, Der grüne Kaiser, Kongo-Express, Das leichte Mädchen, Achtung! Feind hört mit!, Die drei Codonas, Mein Leben für Irland, Dr. Crippen an Bord, Fronttheater, Das grosse Spiel, Anschlag auf Baku, Wen die Götter lieben, Spähtrupp Hallgarten, Wenn der junge Wein blüht, Zirkus Renz, Kolberg, Augen der Liebe, Das Hochzeitshotel, Zwischen Nacht und Morgen, Sommernächte, Wir beide liebten Katharina, Der stumme Gast, Nachtwache, Tromba; Tobias Knopp, Abenteuer eines Junggesellen* (speaker), *Export in*

Blond, Torreani, Das letzte Rezept, Unter den tausend Laternen, Weg ohne Umkehr, Sterne über Colombo, Die Gefangene des Maharadscha, Der Mann meines Lebens, Der letzte Sommer, Frühlingslied, Phantom des grossen Zeltes, Vom Himmel gefallen, Hotel Adlon, Ohne Dich wird es Nacht, Königin Luise, Der Tiger von Eschnapur, Das indische Grabmal, Die blonde Frau des Maharadscha, Die goldene Göttin vom Rio Beni, Neues vom Hexer, Der Arzt stellt fest.

63 **DESNEY, IVAN** (1922-   ). B: Peking. Actor. RN: Ivan Desnitzky. Studied in France, and trained as an actor there. Enters cinema as speaker for dubbed versions. Actor in international cinema (e.g. Antonioni's *La Signora senza Camelie* and Ophüls's *Lola Montès),* and known in Germany mainly for his suave, sinister "Casanova" roles.

Films: *Weg ohne Umkehr, Geständnis unter vier Augen, Die goldene Pest, Herr über Leben und Tod, André und Ursula, Mädchen ohne Grenzen, Dunja, Lola Montès, Rosen für Bettina; Anastasia, die letzte Zarentochter; Wie ein Sturmwind, Von allen geliebt, Skandal in Ischl, Alle Sünden dieser Erde, Petersburger Nächte, Frauensee, Polikuschka, Was eine Frau im Frühling träumt; Heisse Ware, Der Satan lockt mit Liebe, Geständnis einer Sechzehnjährigen, Zarte Haut in schwarzer Seide, Sherlock Holmes und das Halsband des Todes, Jack und Jenny, Ist Geraldine ein Engel?, Der Unsichtbare, DM-Killer, Frühstück mit dem Tod, Heisse Spur Kairo-London, Das Geheimnis der Lederschlinge, Das Liebeskarussell (ii), Heisses Pflaster für Spione, Der Tod eines Doppelgängers, Heisses Spiel für harte Männer, Tanker.*

64 **DESSAU, PAUL** (1894-   ). B: Hamburg. Composer. Studies in Berlin. 1933: to Paris. 1940-1943: Music teacher in New York (Settlement House), after 1945 to G.D.R. His works contain political references that are closely linked with those of Brecht's circle. Music for stage and many film scores. Main work: his opera *Das Verhör des Lukullus.*

Films: *Die grosse Sehnsucht* (in collab. with Hollaender, Rudolf Eisner and Karl Brüll), *Ich glaub' nie mehr an eine Frau,*

Das lockende Ziel, Zärtlichkeit (in collab. with Erwin Ludwig), *Stürme über dem Montblanc, Salto mortale* (in collab. with Artur Guttmann and Walter Jurmann), *Die grosse Attraktion* (in collab. with Franz Lehar, Kaper and Grothe), *Der weisse Rausch* (in collab. with Fritz Goldschmidt), *Melodie der Liebe* (in collab. with Kaper and Jurmann), *Abenteuer im Engadin, Anna und Elisabeth, Nordpol – ahoi!, S.O.S. Eisberg, Du und mancher Kamerad* (56, doc. DEFA), *Mutter Courage und ihre Kinder.*

65 **DEUTSCH, ERNST** (1890-1969). B: Prague. D: Berlin. Actor. Educated in Prague. 1914-1915: Volksbühne Vienna. Theatres: Dresden, Berlin, Burgtheater Vienna. 1938: to London, later U.S.A. 1947: back to Austria and Germany, guest appearances at the Burgtheater Vienna and the Schillertheater Berlin among others.

Films (incomplete): *Die Rache der Toten, Der Galeerensträfling, Die Geisha und der Samurai, Gerechtigkeit, Monika Vogelsang, Das Frauenhaus von Brescia; Der Golem, wie er in die Welt kam; Judith Trachtenberg, Die Tochter des Henkers, Von morgens bis Mitternacht, Brennendes Land, Hannerl und ihr Liebhaber, Die Dame und der Landstreicher, Herzog Ferrantes Ende, Der Kampf ums Ich, Sein ist das Gericht, Das alte Gesetz; Mutter, Dein Kind ruft, Die Pagode, Soll und Haben, Dagfin, Artisten, Das Frauenhaus von Rio, Zwei unterm Himmelszelt. Then sound: Der Prozess, K – Das Haus des Schweigens, Wenn abends die Heide träumt, Symphonie Wien, Sebastian Kneipp.*

66 **DIEHL, KARL LUDWIG** (1896-1958). B: Halle. D: Berghof/Obbayern. Actor. Received his training from Reinhardt (q.v.) in Berlin. Stagework: Wiesbaden, Kammerspiele and Staatsstheater Munich, Berlin (various theatres). From 1950: appears at the Deutsches Theater Göttingen.

Films: *Die Tragödie der Enterbten, Masken.* Then sound: *Rosenmontag, Zärtlichkeit, Liebeswalzer, Der Greifer 30, Aschermittwoch, Die Königin einer Nacht, Der Zinker, Täter gesucht, Im Geheimdienst, Schatten der Manege, Scampolo, ein Kind der Strasse, Das Geheimnis um Johann Orth, Rasputin, Die unsichtbare Front, Zwei in*

einem Auto, Schuss im Morgengrauen, Volldampf voraus, Spione am Werk, Die Freundin eines grossen Mannes, Ein Mann will
nach Deutschland, Abenteuer im Südexpress, Episode, Der höhere Befehl, Ein
idealer Gatte, Der grüne Domino, Der
stählerne Strahl, Meine Tochter ist der
Peter, Es geht um mein Leben, Die Leuchter
des Kaisers, Andere Welt, Liebe kann lügen,
Liebe geht seltsame Wege; Der Mann, der
nicht nein sagen konnte; Ein hoffnungsloser
Fall, Der Schritt vom Wege, Der Fuchs von
Glenarvon, Die schwedische Nachtigall, Annelie; Was geschah in dieser Nacht?, Der 5.
Juni, Die Entlassung, Nacht ohne Abschied,
Die Hochstaplerin, Wo ist Herr Belling?,
Ruf an das Gewissen, Die Reise nach Marrakesch, Das seltsame Leben des Herrn
Bruggs, Bis wir uns wiederseh'n, Geliebtes
Leben, Eine Liebesgeschichte, Der Mann
meines Lebens, Die Stadt ist voller Geheimnisse, Des Teufels General, Es geschah am
20. Juli, Banditen der Autobahn, Ein Herz
bleibt allein, Meine 16 Söhne.

67 **DIESSL, GUSTAV** (1899-1948). B and
D: Vienna. Actor. Trained as painter. After
1918: stage appearances in Vienna and Berlin. Diessl also worked in Italian and American cinema. "Mountain" films with Trenker
and Fanck (all q.v.).

Films: Ssanin, Im Banne der Kralle, Die
Rache der Pharaonen, Abwege, Der lebende
Leichnam, Sensations-Prozess, Die Büchse
der Pandora, Die Drei um Edith, Die Ehe,
Frauen am Abgrund; Der Mann, der nicht
liebt; Mutterliebe, Moral um Mitternacht.
Then sound: Die weisse Hölle vom Piz Palü,
Hans in allen Gassen, Die grosse Sehnsucht,
Leutnant warst Du einst bei den Husaren,
Westfront 1918, Das gelbe Haus des King-
Fu, Teilnehmer antwortet nicht, Eine von
uns, Die Nächte von Port Said, Der golde-
ne Gletscher, Die Herrin von Atlantis, Ro-
man einer Nacht, S.O.S. Eisberg, Das Tes-
tament des Dr. Mabuse, Die weisse Majestät,
Der Dämon des Himalaya, Alles um eine
Frau, Moskau – Shanghai, Die Liebe des
Maharadscha, Schatten der Vergangenheit,
Starke Herzen, Das indische Grabmal (38),
Der Tiger von Eschnapur (38), Kautschuk,
Fortsetzung folgt, Ich verweigere die Aus-
sage, Ich bin Sebastian Ott, Der grüne Kai-
ser, Herz ohne Heimat, Stern von Rio,

Komödianten, Menschen im Sturm, Clarissa,
Ein Blick zurück, Nora, Ruf an das Gewissen, Kolberg, Der Prozess.

Wilhelm Dieterle with Lu Deyers in DER
HEILIGE UND IHR NARR

68 **DIETERLE, WILHELM** (William)
(1893-   ). B: Ludwigshafen. Actor and
director. Theatres: Heidelberg, Zurich, Munich. 1918: with Max Reinhardt (q.v.) in
Berlin. Brought to cinema by Dupont (q.v.).
Starts to direct * in early Twenties. 1932:
to U.S.A., 1958: back to Germany. Famous
for his "bio-pics" in the Thirties and Forties such as Juarez and The Life of Emile
Zola.

Films (incomplete): Fiesco, Der Ratten-
fänger von Hameln, Die Geierwally, Die
Hintertreppe, Frauenopfer, Fräulein Julie,
Der Graf von Charolais, Lukrezia Borgia,
Malmaison, Tiefland, Bohème, Die grüne
Manuela, Der Mensch am Wege 23 (also *
and script), Die Pagode, Der zweite Schuss,
Carlos und Elisabeth, Moderne Ehe, Mutter
und Kind, Das Wachsfigurenkabinett, Die
Blumenfrau vom Potsdamer Platz, Die
Dame aus Berlin, Die vom Niederrhein, Die
Gesunkenen, Der Hahn im Korb, Lena
Warnstetten, Der rosa Diamant, Sumpf und

Moral, Wetterleuchten, Die vom Schicksal Verfolgten, Familie Schimeck, Faust, Die Flucht in den Zirkus, Die Försterchristl, Hölle der Liebe, Der Jäger von Fall, Der Pfarrer von Kirchfeld, Qualen der Nacht, Wie bleibe ich jung und schön, Zopf und Schwert, Am Rande der Welt, Heimweh, Ich habe im Mai von der Liebe geträumt, Liebesreigen; Der Mann, der nicht lieben darf 27 (also * and script), *Petronella, Unter Ausschluss der Oeffentlichkeit, Violantha, Die Weber, Der Zigeunerbaron, Frau Sorge, Geschlecht in Fesseln* 28 (also *), *Der Heilige und ihr Narr, Ritter der Nacht, Frühlingsrauschen* 29 (also *), *Ich lebe für Dich* 29 (also *); *Ludwig der Zweite, König von Bayern* 29 (also *), *Das Schweigen im Walde* 29 (also *). Then sound: *Eine Stunde Glück, Der Tanz geht weiter* 30 (also *), *Die Maske fällt, Dämon des Meeres, Die Fastnachtsbeichte* 60 (only *), *Herrin der Welt* 60 (only *).

69 **DIETRICH, MARLENE** (1902 or 1904-   ). B: Berlin. Actress. RN: Maria Magdalena von Losch. Officer's daughter. Music school in Weimar, Konservatorium Berlin (Berthold Held), stage training under Reinhardt (q.v.). Abandoned music on account of a sprained wrist. Theatre appearances and variety work. Enters cinema in 1922. Goes to U.S.A. in 1930 with Josef von Sternberg. 1923: Married Rudolph Sieber, production manager of Joe May Film Company (q.v.). Probably the most internationally famous of all German actresses, known principally for her work with Sternberg.

Films: *So sind die Männer, Tragödie der Liebe, Der Mensch am Wege, Der Sprung ins Leben, Die freudlose Gasse, Eine Dubarry von heute, Der Juxbaron, Manon Lescaut, Café Electric, Sein grösster Bluff, Prinzessin Olala, Die Frau nach der man sich sehnt, Gefahren der Brautzeit, Das Schiff der verlorenen Menschen.* Then sound: *Ich küsse Ihre Hand, Madam; Der blaue Engel.*

70 **DOMNICK, HANS** (1909-   ). B: Greifswald. Director, producer. Studied law. Enters cinema as editor 1937 (Ufa). From 1945 he becomes the head of the film company, Filmaufbau Göttingen. 1949: launches his own production film. Also directed some

films *, mostly documentaries. Brother of Ottomar Domnick (q.v.).

Films: *Amico* (also script with Gerhard T. Buchholz), *Unsterbliche Geliebte, Frauenarzt Dr. Prätorius, Das Haus in Montevideo* (also script with Curt Goetz), *Hokuspokus, Der goldene Garten* 53 (doc., also * and editing), *Meine 16 Söhne* 55 (also script, * and editing), *Traumstrasse der Welt* 58 I & II (doc., also *, phot., commentary with Erwin Kreker, completed version 68, re-edited and new material added), *Das Haus in Montevideo, Hokuspokus – oder wie lasse ich meinen Mann verschwinden* (co-prod. with Independant Munich).

71 **DOMNICK, OTTOMAR** (1907-   ). B: Greifswald. Director, producer. Brother of Hans Domnick (q.v.). Studies medicine in Berlin, Hamburg, Frankfurt. 1938: neurosurgeon in Stuttgart. 1950: own clinic. 1947: publishes book *Die schöpferischen Kräfte der abstrakten Malerei.* 1949: book on Hugo Hartung. Since 1948: publisher of art books. 1950: first films, documentaries on art and appreciation. Experimental features.

Films: *Neue Kunst – Neues Sehen* 50 (short), *Willi Baumeister* 54 (short, doc.),

Jonas 57, *Gino* 60, *Ohne Datum* 62, *N.N.* 68-69 (prod., dir., script., and phot.).

72 DOMRÖSE, ANGELICA (1941-). B: Berlin. Actress. At first secretary. Acted in the amateur-circles of FDJ Berlin. Enters cinema through Slatan Dudow (q.v.); later trains at film school and receives contract offers from DEFA (q.v.). Member of the Berliner Ensemble.

Films: *Verwirrung der Liebe, Die Liebe und der Co-Pilot, Papas neue Freundin, Die aus der 12b, Wenn Du zu mir hälst, An französischen Kaminen, Julia lebt, Sonntagsfahrer, Die Abenteuer des Werner Holt, Chronik eines Mordes, Entlassung auf Bewährung, Ein Lord am Alexanderplatz.*

73 DOR, KARIN (1938-). B: Wiesbaden. Actress. RN: Katherose Derr. Stage and ballet training; enters cinema as an extra in Wiesbaden; becomes well known in films directed by her husband Harald Reinl (q.v.). to whom she was married between 1954 and 1968. Also some parts in international films, such as *Topaz.*

Films: *Rosen-Resli, Der schweigende Engel, Ihre grosse Prüfung, Solange Du lebst, Santa Lucia, Kleiner Mann – ganz gross, Die Zwillinge vom Zillertal, Almenrausch und Edelweiss, 13 alte Esel und der Sonnenhof, Mit Eva fing die Sünde an, Skandal um Dodo, Worüber man nicht spricht, So angelt man keinen Mann, Das blaue Meer und Du; Ein Sommer, den man nicht vergisst; Im weissen Rössl, Die Bande des Schreckens, Bei Pichler stimmt die Kasse nicht, Im schwarzen Rössl, Der grüne Bogenschütze, Der Fälscher von London, Am Sonntag will mein Süsser mit mir Segeln gehn, Ohne Krimi geht die Mimi nie ins Bett, Der Schatz im Silbersee, Teppich des Grauens, Die unsichtbaren Krallen des Dr. Mabuse, Das Geheimnis der schwarzen Witwe, Die weisse Spinne, Der Würger von Schloss Blackmoor, Zimmer 13, Der letzte Mohikaner, Winnetou II, Hotel der toten Gäste, Der Mann mit den tausend Masken, Der unheimliche Mönch, Das Geheimnis der gelben Mönche, Gern hab' ich die Frauen gekillt, Ich habe sie gut gekannt, Caroline Chérie, Die Nibelungen I & II, Die Schlangengrube und das Pendel, Winnetou und Shatterhand im Tal der Toten.*

74 DORSCH, KÄTHE (1889 or 1890-1957). B: Neumarkt (Oberpfalz). D: Vienna. Actress. 1904: joins the theatre in Nuremberg. Played operettas in Mainz and Berlin. 1920: performs at the Lessing-Theatre Berlin. 1936: Staatstheater Berlin. 1939: Burgtheater Vienna. Many guest appearances in Germany and Austria.

Films (incomplete): *Der Blusenkönig, Memoiren des Satans, Die blaue Mauritius, Gefesselte Menschen, Klatsch, Fräulein Julie, Paragraph 144.* Then sound: *Die Lindenwirtin, Drei Tage Liebe, Eine Frau ohne Bedeutung, Savoy-Hotel 217, Yvette, Irrtum des Herzens, Morgen werde ich verhaftet, Mutterliebe; Trenck, der Pandur; Komödianten, Fahrt ins Glück, Singende Engel, Der Bagnosträfling, Das Kuckucks-Ei, Regine.*

75 DRACHE, HEINZ (1924-). B: Essen. Actor. Stage *début* at Schauspielhaus Nuremberg (1942-1945). Then theatres: Deutsches Theater Berlin, Schauspielhaus Düsseldorf (1947-1954), Schlosspark- and Schiller-Theater Berlin.

Films: *Dalmatinische Hochzeit, Bei Dir war es immer so schön, Kein Auskommen mit dem Einkommen, Gefährdete Mädchen, Madeleine – Tel. 13 62 11, Die Strasse, Der Rest ist Schweigen, Eine Frau am dunklen Fenster, Mit 17 weint man nicht, Der Rächer, Die Türe mit den sieben Schlössern, Das indische Tuch, Nur tote Zeugen schweigen, Der schwarze Panther von Ratana, Der Zinker, Der Hexer, Ein Sarg aus Hongkong, Das Wirtshaus von Dartmoor, Neues vom Hexer, Schüsse im 3/4-Takt, Die Zeugin aus der Hölle, Der Hund von Blackwood Castle.*

76 DREWS, CARL (1883-1940). Director of photography. Enters cinema in early Twenties, working usually in collaboration with others. Mainly known for his contributions to musical and entertainment films.

Films (incomplete): *Das Geheimnis der Mumie, Lukrezia Borgia* (co-phot. with Freund & Karl Voss), *Sodoms Ende, Das Spiel mit dem Weibe, Tatjana, Dreiklang der Nacht* (co-phot. with Arkos Farkas), *Gentleman auf Zeit, Der Farmer aus Texas* (co-phot. with Antonio Frenguelli), *Das Haus der Lüge, Zur Chronik von Grieshuus* (co-phot. with Ernst Nitzschmann & Wagner), *Dafgin* (co-phot. with Edgar Zeisener, Hjalmar Lerski & Karl Puth), *Derby* (co-phot. with Ziesener and Albert Schattmann), *Die da unten, Die von der Waterkant, Familie Schimeck, Die geschiedene Frau; Wien, wie es weint und lacht; Zopf und Schwert, Die Hose, Die indiskrete Frau, Das Mädchen aus der Fremde, Pique Dame* (co-phot. with Nitzschmann), *Prinz Louis Ferdinand, Ariadne in Hoppegarten* (co-phot.), *Die Dame mit der Maske, Ihr dunkler Punkt* (co-phot. with Nitzschmann), *Die Jacht der sieben Sünden* (co-phot. with Zeisener), *Moral, Das Erlebnis einer Nacht, Heilige oder Dirne, Der Held aller Mädchenträume* (co-phot. with Gotthard Wolf), *Der lustige Witwer* (co-phot. with Wolf), *Vertauschte Gesichter.* Then sound: *Ich küsse Ihre Hand, Madam* (co-phot. with Gotthard Wolff), *O alte Burschenherrlichkeit, Hilfe! Ueberfall!, Ein süsses Geheimnis, So lang' noch ein Walzer von Strauss erklingt, Chauffeur Antoinette, Der Liebesexpress, Ehe m.b.H., Der grosse Bluff, Die Herren vom Maxim* (co-phot. with Heinz Kluth), *Eine von uns, Der tolle Bomberg, Der Frauendiplomat, Durchlaucht amüsiert sich, Trenck* (co-phot.); *Johann Strauss, k. und k. Hofballmusikdirektor; Traum von Schönbrunn, Kitty schwindelt sich ins Glück, Zwei im Sonnenschein, Die Stimme der Liebe, Der Traum vom Rhein, Glück im Schloss, Keinen Tag ohne Dich* (co-phot.), *Unter der schwarzen Sturmfahne* (co-phot. with Gustav Stiefel), *Die kleine Schwindlerin, Mädels von heute* (co-phot. with Albert Kling), *Charleys Tante, Heinz im Mond, La Paloma, Der letzte Walzer, So ein Flegel, Die Liebe und die erste Eisenbahn, Ein Mädel wirbelt durch die Luft, Abenteuer im Südexpress, Stützen der Gesellschaft, Hilde Petersen postlagernd* (co-phot.), *Ein falscher Fuffziger, Ehestreik, Punks kommt aus Amerika, Männer vor der Ehe, Annemarie, Kater Lampe, Kinderarzt Dr. Engel, Das Herrmännchen, Wenn Du eine Schwiegermutter hast; Husaren, heraus; Mädchen für alles, Schüsse in Kabine 7, Lauter Lügen, Schwarzfahrt ins Glück, Die Stimme aus dem Aether, Der Polizeifunk meldet, Kornblumenblau, Paradies der Junggesellen, Wunschkonzert* (co-phot.).

77 **DUDOW, SLATAN** (1903-1963). B: Zaribrod (Bulgaria). D: Berlin (car accident). Director. 1922: goes to Berlin, studies theatre technique. Assistant to Lang, Pabst, Jessner (all q.v.) and Jürgen Fehling. Study period in U.S.S.R. (where he met Eisenstein). Shoots first film in 1932, emigrates to Switzerland in 1933, and was active as a writer. 1946: to G.D.R. and DEFA (q.v.), three time winner of state award 1950, 1955, 1957, also "patriotic order of merit."

Films: *Kuhle Wampe* 32, *Siefenblasen* 33, *Unser täglich Brot* 49 (also script with Hans Joachim Beyer and Ludwig Turek), *Familie Benthin* 50 (co-dir. with Kurt Maetzig, also script with Johannes R. Becher, Kuba and Ehm Welk), *Frauenschicksale* 52 (also script with Ursula Rumin and Gerhard Bengsch), *Stärker als die Nacht* 54, *Der Hauptmann von Köln* 56 (also script with Michael Tschesno-Hell and Henryk Keisch), *Verwirrung der Liebe* 59 (also script), *Christine* 63 (unfinished).

78 **DUNKELMANN, ERIKA** (1913-   ). B: Rostock. Actress. Theatre in Rostock since 1933, but does not appear as an actress during Nazi period. After 1945: stage and film appearances. Well known for her part in *Ernst Thälmann.* State award 1966.

Films: *Stärker als die Nacht, Ernst Thäl-mann – Sohn seiner Klasse, Gefährliche Fracht, Das geheimnisvolle Wrack, Ernst Thälmann – Führer seiner Klasse, Der Teufelskreis, Besondere Kennzeichen: Keine, Eine Berliner Romanze, Genesung, Schlösser und Katen, Bärenburger Schnurre, Alter Kahn und junge Liebe, Berlin – Ecke Schönhauser, Klotz am Bein, Ein Mädchen von 16½, Maibowle, Schritt für Schritt, Silvesterpunsch, Eine Handvoll Noten, Der Arzt von Bothenow, Das verhexte Fischerdorf, Menschen und Tiere, Die Glatzkopfbande, Die Hochzeit von Länneken, Solange Leben in mir ist, Ein Lord am Alexanderplatz.*

79 **DUPONT, EWALD ANDRÉ** (1891-1956). B: Zeitz (Sachsen). D: Hollywood. Director. Starts as writer, then becomes one of the first German film critics. Enters cinema through Erich Pommer (q.v.), later contracted to Carl Laemmle for Universal. To U.S.A. via Great Britain. 1933: arrives in Hollywood. 1941-1949: talent scout and agent. Returns to film-making in 1951.

Films (incomplete): *Die Buchhalterin* (dir. & script), *Durchlaucht Hypochonder* (dir. & script), *Der ewige Zweifel* (dir. & script), *Ferdinand Lassalle* (only script), *Das Geheimnis des Amerika-Docks* (dir. & script), *Mitternacht* (dir. & script), *Nur um tausend Dollars* (dir. & script), *Der Onyxkopf* (dir. & script), *Das Perlenhalsband* (dir. & script), *Rennfieber* (dir. & script), *Der Saratogakäfer* (dir. & script), *Die sterbenden Perlen* (dir. & script), – dates for these films unobtainable, but all were made certainly prior to 1923.

Films: *Die Japanerin* 17 (also script), *Sturmflut* (only script), *Der Mann aus Neapel* 18, *Die schwarze Schachdame* 18, *Es werde Licht* 18 (co-dir. & co-scripted), *Der lebende Schatten* 18 (also script), *Der Teufel* 18, *Sündige Mütter* (co-scripted), *Mord ohne Täter* 20 (also script), *Der weisse Pfau* 20 (also co-scripted), *Die Geierwally* 21, *Whitechapel* 21, *Kinder der Finsternis* 22, *Sie und die Drei* 22, *Das alte Gesetz* 23, *Die grüne Manuela* 23, *Der Demütige und die Sängerin* 25 (also script in collab. with Max Glass), *Varieté* 25 (also script). Then sound: *Atlantik* 29 (also script), *Menschen im Käfig* 30 (also script with Viktor Kendall), *Peter Voss, der Millionendieb* 32 (also script with

Bruno Frank and Albrecht Joseph), *Der Läufer von Marathon* 33.

80 **DURIEUX, TILLA** (1880-   ). B: Vienna. Actress. RN: Ottilie Godeffroy. Theatre school Arnau in Vienna. Theatres: Stadttheater Olmütz, Breslau, Lessing-Theatre Berlin 1912-1913. Later in Berlin with Otto Brahm, Reinhardt (q.v.) and Barnowsky. Guest appearances (e.g. New York). 1933: emigrates. After 1945: some stage and a few film appearances e.g. Theatre in Bremen, provincial tours as guest performer. Was married to Eugen Spiro, publisher Paul Cassirer and Ludwig Katzenellenbogen.

Films (incomplete): *Mahira, Die Launen einer Weltdame, Prinz Karnival, Die Frau im Mond.* Then sound: *Die Stärkere, Die letzte Brücke; Anastasia, die letzte Zarentochter; Von allen geliebt, Auferstehung, Labyrinth, Morgen wirst Du um mich weinen, Verdammt zur Sünde, Es.*

81 **EGGEBRECHT, AXEL** (1899-   ). B: Leipzig. Scriptwriter. Educated at Leipzig University. 1917-1918: soldier. 1920-1925: Member of the Communist Party. 1925-1930: dramatic adviser for various film companies. 1933: sent to concentration camp and later has to give up writing. Since 1935: screenwriter of entertainment films. 1945-1949: works for NWDR Hamburg (Radio). Later dramaturg, author, scriptwriter and writer for radio (e.g. *Der halbe Weg*, 1950).

Films: *Der Kampf der Tertia* (co-scripted), *Die Republik der Backfische* (co-scripted with David). Then sound: *Fräulein Frau, Der Ammenkönig* (co-scripted with Ernst Hasselbach and Erich Kröhnke), *Der Abenteurer von Paris; Maria, die Magd* (co-scripted), *Wenn der Hahn kräht* (co-scripted with August Hinrichs), *Alles für Veronika, Ihr Leibhusar, Millionenerbschaft* (co-scripted with Hans Neumann), *Steputat & Co.* (co-scripted with Hellmuth Lange), *Musketier Meier III* (co-scripted with Karl Bunje), *Das Mädchen mit dem guten Ruf* (co-scripted with Hasselbach), *Bel ami* (co-scripted), *Ich bin Sebastian Ott* (co-scripted with Eberhard Keindorff), *Gold in New Frisco* (co-scripted with Hasselbach), *Marguerite: 3* (co-scripted), *Operette* (co-scripted), *Komödianten* (co-scripted with Pabst and Walther von Holländer), *Wiener Blut* (co-scripted with Ernst Marischka), *Anuschka* (co-scripted), *Ein Mann wie Maximilian*, *Der Verlorene* (co-scripted with Lorre and Benno Vigny), *Das Land des Lächelns* (co-scripted with Hubert Marischka), *Eine Liebesgeschichte* (co-scripted with Carl Zuckmayer), *Rittmeister Wronski*, *Die Frau des Botschafters* (co-scripted with Ilse Lotz-Dupont), *Stresemann* (co-scripted).

Marta Eggerth with Rolf von Goth in ES WAR EINMAL EIN WALZER

82 EGGERTH, MARTA (1912-). B: Budapest. Actress. At first star of operetta. 1923: Budapest Opera. Theatres: Johann Strauss-Theater Vienna, Hamburg, Berlin. Enters cinema in 1930 through Eichberg (q.v.). Spends war period in U.S.A., later returning to Germany. Films in Italy and America.

Films: *Der Draufgänger*, *Trara um Liebe*, *Eine Nacht im Grandhotel*, *Die Bräutigamswitwe*, *Der Frauendiplomat*, *Kaiserwalzer*, *Das Blaue vom Himmel*, *Es war einmal ein Walzer*; *Ein Lied, ein Kuss, ein Mädel*; *Traum von Schönbrunn*, *Moderne Mitgift*, *Leise flehen feine Lieder*, *Der Zarewitsch*, *Die Blume von Hawaii*, *Mein Herz ruft nach Dir*, *Die Czardasfürstin*, *Ihr grösster Erfolg*.

Die ganze Welt dreht sich um Liebe, *Die blonde Carmen*, *Das Hofkonzert*, *Wo die Lerche singt*, *Das Schloss in Flandern*, *Zauber der Boheme*; *Immer, wenn ich glücklich bin*; *Das Land des Lächelns*, *Frühling in Berlin*.

83 EICHBERG, RICHARD (1888-1952). B: Berlin. D: Munich. Director, producer. One of the first German film directors (with Joe May, Max Mack, Carl Froelich, all q.v.) who in 1914 became also his own producer. At first actor, with well over a hundred film roles during the silent period. From 1938: in U.S.A. Returned to Germany after the War. Discovered Lilian Harvey. (q.v.). First married to Lee Parry, later to Kitty Jantzen, both stars of the silent period. Produced almost all the films he directed as well as other people's films *.

Films (incomplete): *Im Banne der Schuld* (*), *Leben um Leben* (*), *Das Tagebuch Colins* (*), *Todesreigen* (prod. & dir.) – dates for these films unobtainable, but all were made certainly prior to 1923. Films: *Strohfeuer* 14, *Problematische Naturen* (only actor), *Kinder der Landstrasse* 19, *Nonne und Tänzerin* 19, *Sklaven fremden Willens* 19, *Sünde der Eltern* 19, *Jugend* 20, *Der Tanz auf dem Vulkan* 20, *Der lebende Propeller* 21, *Die Liebesabenteuer der schönen Evelyn* (*), *Die Macht des Blutes* (*), *Ihre Hoheit, die Tänzerin* (*), *Monna Vanna* 22, *Das Strassenmädchen von Paris* 22, *Fräulein Raffke* 23, *Die Motorbraut* 24, *Die schönste Frau der Welt* 24, *Die Frau mit dem Etwas* 25 (* and supervision), *Die Kleine vom Bummel* 25, *Leidenschaft* 25, *Der Liebeskäfig* 25 (* and supervision), *Liebes und Trompetenblasen* 25, *Luxusweibchen* 25 (* and supervision), *Durchlaucht Radieschen* 26, *Die keusche Susanne* 26, *Prinzessin Tralala* 26 (* and supervision), *Der Prinz und die Tänzerin* 26, *Der Soldat der Marie* (*), *Das Fräulein von Kasse 12* (*), *Der Fürst von Pappenheim* 27, *Die Leibeigenen* 27, *Die tolle Lola* 27, *Du sollst nicht stehlen* (*), *Das Girl von der Revue* 28, *Rutschbahn* 28, *Song* 28, *Grosstadtschmetterling* 29, *Ein kleiner Vorschuss auf die Seligkeit* (*). Then sound: *Wer wird denn weinen, wenn man auseinandergeht* 29, *Hai-Tang* 30, *Der Greifer* 30, *Der Draufgänger* 31 (also script with Josef Than), *Trara um Liebe* 31, *Die Bräu-*

41

tigamswitwe 31, *Die unsichtbare Front* 32, *Früchtchen* 34 (also script), *Die Katz' im Sack* 35, *Der Schlafwagenkontrolleur* 35, *Der Kurier des Zaren* 36, *Es geht um mein Leben* 36 (also script with Hans Klaehr), *Der Tiger von Eschnapur* 37, *Das indische Grabmal* 37 (for both also script with Arthur Pohl and Hans Klaehr), *Die Reise nach Marrakesch* 49, *Skandal in der Botschaft* 50 (supervision).

84 **EICHHORN, BERNHARD** (1904-). B: Schortewitz (Anhalt). Composer. Studies music at Munich University (under Sandberger and Kutscher). From 1929: conductor Munich, Berlin and Dresden. After 1945: he appears briefly at the Städtische Bühnen in Munich. From 1946: free-lance composer, often for Käutner (q.v.).
Films: *Im Banne der Berge, Kleider machen Leute, Dr. Crippen an Bord, Anuschka, Fritze Bollmann wollte angeln, Reise in die Vergangenheit, Unter den Brücken, Klein Platz für Liebe, In jenen Tagen, Frau Holle, Film ohne Titel, Der Apfel ist ab* (in collab. with Adolf Steimel), *Die Zeit mit Dir, Königskinder, Hans im Glück, Epilog, Der Geigenmacher von Mittelwald, Herbstgedanken, Weisse Schatten, Die Alm an der Grenze, Die Martinsklause, Die schöne Tölzerin, Haus des Lebens, Das Dorf unterm Himmel, Der Klosterjäger, Rosen-Resli, Schloss Hubertus, Der schweigende Engel, Der dunkle Stern, Himmel ohne Sterne, Suchkind 312, Ein Mädchen aus Flandern, Der Hauptmann von Köpenick, Die Geierwally, Monpti, Paradies und Feuerofen, Der eiserne Gustav, Der Schinderhannes, Der Rest ist Schweigen, Die schöne Lügnerin, Jons und Erdme, Die Gans von Sedan, Der brave Soldat Schwejk, Das Glas Wasser, Der Traum von Lieschen Müller, Unter Ausschluss der Oeffentlichkeit.*

85 **EISBRENNER, WERNER** (1908-). B: Berlin. Composer. Studied music in Berlin (under Dahlke, Hernried). Runs academy for church and school music. A very versatile composer with several film scores to his credit.
Films: *Wenn ein Mädel Hochzeit macht* (in collab. with Carl Blume), *Der höhere Befehl, Der blaue Diamant* (in collab. with Adolf Perris), *Donogoo Tonka* (in collab.

with Franz Doelle), *Zwei mal zwei im Himmelbett, Einmal werd' ich Dir gefallen* (in collab.), *Gewitterflug zu Claudia, Frauen für Golden Hill, Grossalarm, Anna Favetti, War es der im 3. Stock?, Zentrale Rio, Kennwort Machin, Ich bin gleich wieder da, Fräulein; Wie konntest Du, Veronika; Zwischen Hamburg und Haiti, Kriminalkommissar Eyck, Oh diese Männer* (in collab. with Friedrich Schröder), *Zwischen Himmel und Erde, Nacht ohne Abschied, Romanze in Moll* (in collab. with Lothar Brühne), *Die goldene Spinne, Die beiden Schwestern, Titanic, Träumerei, Ich hab' von Dir geträumt* (in collab. with Ernst Erich Buder), *Grosse Freiheit Nr. 7, Dr. phil. Döderlein, Der stumme Gast, Shiva und die Galgenblume, Der Fall Molander, Ich glaube an Dich, Eine reizende Familie, Sag' die Wahrheit, Freies Land, Razzia, Zugvögel, Zwischen Gestern und Morgen, Die Söhne des Herrn Gaspary, Berliner Ballad* (in collab.), *Menschen in Gottes Hand, Wege im Zwielicht, Das Fräulein und der Vagabund, Der Bagnosträfling, Diese Nacht vergess' ich nie, Martina, Dieser Mann gehört mir, Herrliche Zeiten* (in collab.), *Der Fall Rabanser, Melodie des Schicksals, Der fallende Stern, Blaubart, Nachts auf den Strassen, Herz der Welt, Ich heisse Niki, Im weissen Rössl, Ein Herz spielt falsch, Solange Du da bist, Jonny reitet Nebrador, Eine Liebesgeschichte, Gefangene der Liebe, Geständnis unter vier Augen, Der letzte Sommer; Kinder, Mütter und ein General; Die Ratten, Griff nach den Sternen, Die Frau des Botschafters, Der letzte Mann* (55), *Der Cornet, Studentin Helen Willfüer, Vor Sonnenuntergang, Spion für Deutschland; Mein Vater, der Schauspieler; Herrscher ohne Krone, Banktresor 713, Der gläserne Turm, . . . und nichts als die Wahrheit, Ich werde Dich auf Händen tragen, Kriegsgericht, Buddenbrooks, Abschied von den Wolken, Die Botschafterin, Der letzte Zeuge, Sturm im Wasserglas, Barbara.*

86 **EISLER, HANNS** (1898-1962). B: Leipzig. D: Berlin. Composer. Studies music in Vienna, pupil of Arnold Schönberg. To Berlin, where from 1925 onwards he was a teacher for composition, working with Brecht and Dudow (q.v.). 1933: leaves Germany and travels through various countries,

arriving in the U.S.A. in 1938. Since 1949: in G.D.R. Member of East German Academy of Arts. Wrote technical work *Composing for the Film*. Twice winner of state award in 1950 and 1958. Composer of film scores for Soviet, French, British and American films.
Scripts: *Fidelio* (co-scripted with Walter Felsenstein), *Gasparone* (co-scripted with Karl Paryla).
Music for films: *Niemandsland* (in collab. with Kurt Schröder), *Kuhle Wampe* (in collab. with Josef Schmid), *Unser täglich Brot, Der Rat der Götter, Wilhelm Pieck* (doc.), *Frauenschicksale, Bel ami, Schicksal am Lenkrad, Herr Puntila und sein Knecht Matti, Gasparone* (in collab. with Oskar Wagner), *Die Hexen von Salem, Aktion J.* (doc.), *Geschwader Fledermaus, Trübe Wasser*.

87 EMIGRANTS. Actors, directors, cameramen, composers and scriptwriters who left Germany either before or even during the Nazi *régime*. The following are all cited elsewhere in this book: Bassermann, Bergner, Berger (Ludwig), Bernhardt, Bois, Bressart, Busch, Charell, Christians, Courant, Czinner, Dessau, Deutsch, Dieterle, Dietrich, Dupont, Durieux, Eggerth, Eisler, Farkas (Nikolaus), Forster, Freund, Gerron, Gert, Granach, Grune, Haas, Heller, Helm, Höllering, Homolka, Jessner, Kaper, Kiepura, Kiesler, Kortner, Kosterlitz, Lang, Lieven, Mannheim, Maté, Joe and Mia May, Mayer, Metzner, Nebenzal, Nielsen (Asta), Ophüls, Oswald (Richard), Palmer, Parlo, Planer, Pommer, Pressburger, Reinhardt, Reisch, Richter, Sagan, Schünzel, Schüfftan, Sierck, Siodmak, Slezak (Walter), Sokoloff, Spira, Steckel, Thiele (Wilhelm), Tourjansky, Twardowski, Ulmer, Veidt, Viertel, Wachsmann, Wangenheim, Wiene, Wilder, Wisbar, Wohlbrück, Wolf.
German film emigrants also include: Felix Basch, Karl Farkas, Friedrich Feher, Jakob Julius and Louise Fleck, Paul Henreid, Anatole Litwak, Gustav Machaty, Rudolf Meinert, Erwin Piscator, Otto Ludwig Preminger *(see* Reinhardt), Fred Zinnemann (all directors); Claude Farell (other names: Monika Burg, Paula Viardi, Paulette Colard), Leopoldine Konstantin, Lotte Lenja, Franz Lederer, Ernst Morgan, Ludwig Stoessel (actors); Hans May (composer), Otto Kan-

turek (cameraman), Ernst Neubach, Curt Siodmak, Carl Zuckmayer (authors, scriptwriters). Some of the artists cited left Germany before, or around, 1933, when they were offered parts in foreign films; not all of them had to escape, but remained abroad for their personal safety.

88 EMIGRANTS' FILMS. It was impossible to make a critical analysis of internal German political and social problems in film terms between 1933 and 1945. Many emigrants (q.v.) formed groups abroad to shoot films that often reflected the solid tradition of the Twenties and early Thirties in German cinema. Within these groups some anti-Nazi and anti-Fascist films were made. They include: *Kämpfer* 35 (U.S.S.R.), *Hitler's Madman* 44 (dir. Sierck/Sirk), *Hangmen also Die* (dir. Lang, scripted by Berthold Brecht), *To Be Or Not To Be* (dir. Lubitsch), *The Seventh Cross* 44 (dir. Zinnemann, based on a novel by Anna Seghers), *Man Hunt* 41 (dir. Lang) – all in U.S.A.

89 ENGEL, ERICH (1891-1966). B: Hamburg. D: Berlin. Director. Important theatre producer, working with Brecht on several *premières* of his plays. At first producer at the Kammerspiele Munich (plays by Toller and Kaiser), then at the Bayrisches Staatstheater Munich, and Deutsches Staatstheater Berlin with Reinhardt (q.v.). 1928: world *première* of Brecht's *Dreigroschenoper* in Theater am Schiffbauerdamm (where the Berliner Ensemble is now located). Enters cinema in 1930. After 1945: works for DEFA (q.v.), although he was director of Städtische Bühnen in Munich for two years until Brecht called him to East Berlin. Twice winner of state award 1949 and 1957, "patriotic order of merit" 1961.
Films: *Wer nimmt die Liebe ernst?* 31, *Fünf von der Jazzband* 32, *Inge und die Millionen* 33, *Pechmarie* 34 (also script with Eva Leidmann), *Hohe Schule* 34, *Pygmalion* 35, *... nur ein Komödiant* 35, *Ein Hochzeitstraum* 36, *Die Nacht mit dem Kaiser* 36, *Mädchenjahre einer Königin* 36, *Gefährliches Spiel* 37, *Der Maulkorb* 38, *Hotel Sacher* 39, *Der Weg zu Isabell* 39, *Ein hoffnungsloser Fall* 39, *Nanette* 39, *Unser Fräulein Doktor* 40, *Viel Lärm um Nixi* 42, *Sommerliebe* 42, *Altes Herz wird wieder*

jung 43, *Man rede mir nicht von Liebe* 43, *Es lebe die Liebe* 44, *Wo ist Herr Belling?* 45, *Fahrt ins Glück* 45, *Affäre Blum* 48, *Der Biberpelz* 48, *Das seltsame Leben des Herrn Bruggs* 51, *Kommen Sie am Ersten* 51, *Die Stimme des Andern* 52 (also script with Stemmle, Kortner and Horst Budjuhn), *Der fröhliche Weinberg* 52, *Der Mann meines Lebens* 53, *Konsul Strotthoff* 54, *Du bist die Richtige* 55, *Liebe ohne Illusion* 55, *Vor Gott und den Menschen* 55, *Geschwader Fledermaus* 59.

90 **ENGELS, ERICH** (1889-   ). B: Remscheid. Director, producer. Enters cinema as distributor and producer. Mainly thrillers. Not to be confused with Erich Engel (q.v.).

Wrote many scripts *. Films: *Das Millionentestament* 32, *Das Geheimnis des blauen Zimmers* 32, *Kriminalreporter Holm* 32, *Die Nacht im Forsthaus* 33, *Das lustige Kleeblatt* 33, *Peter, Paul and Nanette* 34 (also *), *Kirschen in Nachbars Garten* 35 (also * with Reinhold Bernt and Gernot Bock-Stieber), *Donner, Blitz und Sonnenschein* 36 (also * with Max Nekut), *Sherlock Holmes* 37 (also * with Hans Heuer), *Mordsache Holm* 38, *Im Namen des Volkes* 39 (also * with Walter Maisch), *Zentrale Rio* 39, *Das himmelblaue Abendkleid* 41 (also * with Berthold Ebbecke and Ilse Paul-Czech), *Dr. Crippen an Bord* 42 (also * with Kurt E. Walter and Klaren), *Die goldene Spinne* 43 (also * with Wolf Neumeister and Ulrich Vogel), *Freitag, der 13.* 44, *Das Geheimnis der roten Katze* (only idea), *Mordprozess Dr. Jordan* (also * with Neumeister), *Die Dame in Schwarz* 51 (also * with Neumeister), *Die Nacht ohne Moral* (only * with Neumeister), *Keine Angst vor Schwiegermüttern* 54 (also * with Hans Wolff), *Kirschen in Nachbars Garten* 56 (also * with Neumeister), *Dr. Crippen lebt* 57 (also *), *Witwer mit 5 Töchtern* 57 (also * with Rolf and Alexander Becker), *Grabenplatz 17* 58 (also * with Neumeister), *Vater, Mutter und neun Kinder* 58 (also * with Neumeister), *Natürlich die Autofahrer* 59, *Im Namen einer Mutter* 60.

91 **ENGLISCH, LUCIE** (1906-1965). B: Baden, near Vienna. D: Erlangen. Actress. 1920: joins Stadttheater Baden, then Stadt-theater Eger, Theater in der Josefstadt Vienna (1923), Lustspieltheater Vienna (1925), Frankfurt, Berlin. In her best comic parts she was familiar as the naïve country girl.

Films (incomplete): *Alimente, Ruhiges Heim mit Küchenbenutzung, Der Witwenball.* Then sound: *Die Nacht gehört uns, Ein Walzer im Schlafcoupé, Drei Tage Mittelarrest, Das lockende Ziel, Das Rheinlandmädel, Zweimal Hochzeit, Kasernenzauber, Zwei Menschen, Komm' zu mir zum Rendezvous, Keine Feier ohne Meyer, Der Schrecken der Garnison, Dienst ist Dienst, Um eine Nasenlänge, Mein Leopold, Reserve hat Ruh, So'n Windhund!, Schuberts Frühlingstraum, Ballhaus goldener Engel; Annemarie, die Braut der Kompanie; Die Gräfin von Monte Christo, Aus einer kleinen Residenz, Die kalte Mamsell, Heimat am Rhein, Gretel zieht das grosse Los, Die Unschuld vom Lande, Wenn ein Mädel Hochzeit macht; Meine Frau, die Schützenkönigin; Der mutige Seefahrer, Der Kampf mit dem Drachen, Ein falscher Fuffziger, Der ahnungslose Engel, Wo die Lerche singt, Der lachende Dritte, Der Postillon von Lonjumeau, Du kannst nicht treu sein, Die Landstreicher, So weit geht die Liebe nicht, Pat und Patachon im Paradies, Die verschwundene Frau, Ihr Leibhusar, Eine Nacht mit Hindernissen, Dir gehört mein Herz, Die unruhigen Mädchen, Unsere kleine Frau; Immer, wenn ich glücklich bin; Kleines Bezirksgericht, Premiere der Butterfly, Rheinische Brautfahrt, Weltrekord im Seitensprung, Der ungetreue Eckehart, Herzensfreud – Herzensleid, Was geschah in dieser Nacht, Tanz mit dem Kaiser, Ein Zug fährt ab, So ein Früchtchen, Drei tolle Mädels, Fahrt ins Arbenteuer, Ein Walzer mit Dir, Spiel, Die heimlichen Bräute, Philine, Die Kreuzlschreiber, Der Theodor im Fussballtor, Alles für die Firma, Es liegt was in der Luft, So sind die Frauen, Schwarzwaldmädel, Durch Dick und Dünn, Wildwest in Oberbayern, Drei Kavaliere, Das weisse Abenteuer, Der eingebildete Kranke; Mönche, Mädchen und Panduren; Mikosch rückt ein, Karneval in Weiss, Der Mann in der Wanne, Fiakermilli – Liebling von Wien, Der keusche Josef, Tante Jutta aus Kalkutta, Die Nacht ohne Moral, Auf der grünen Wiese, Der treue Husar, Der Engel mit dem Flammenschwert. . . . und* ewig bleibt die Liebe, Die fünf Karnickel, Die heilige Lüge, Oh diese "lieben" Verwandten, Liebe ist ja nur ein Märchen, IA in Oberbayern, Der Jäger vom Roteck, Seine Tochter ist der Peter, Zwei Bayern in St. Pauli, Johannisnacht, Wo der Wildbach rauscht, Der Glockengiesser von Tirol, II A in Berlin, Die Magd von Heiligenblut, Vater macht Karriere, Tante Wanda aus Uganda, Familie Schimek, Ober zahlen!, Hoch droben auf dem Berg, Jungfrauenkrieg, Die fidelen Detektive, Der Wilderer vom Silberwald, Heiratskandidaten, Zwei Bayern im Urwald, Liebe – wie die Frau sie wünscht, Der Pfarrer von St. Michael, Hallo Taxi, Gräfin Mariza, Die singenden Engel von Tirol; Wehe, wenn sie losgelassen; Herrn Josefs letzte Liebe, Hubertus-jagd; Peter Voss, der Held des Tages; Drei weisse Birken; Schwarze Rose, Rosemarie.

92   EXPRESSIONISM: Movement in art, literature and music (among others Schoenberg with "Erwartungen" and "Glückliche Hand") which influenced German cinema and theatre enormously between 1919 and 1923, and rejected the principles of impressionism. Key figure was writer Carl Mayer (q.v.); set designers brought his writings to life in their *décors*. ("A script by Mayer is already a film," said Karl Freund.) First elements of "Expressionism" are to be found in films by Rippert (q.v.), his *Homunculus* serial in 1916. As an art movement, "Expressionism" rejects reality in favour of a more powerful visual form, with religious

Pabst was one of the greatest expressionist directors in the Twenties. Above: DIE BÜCHSE DER PANDORA

and abstract themes. Therefore, no exteriors were used, only studio sets where light, costumes, and *décor* could be manipulated at every level. Social and political problems were ignored. The prime example of the movement was *The Cabinet of Dr. Caligari*, written by Mayer (with former officer, Hans Janowitz), from which came the term "caligarism," which in essence defined an attitude to life at that time ("a ready means of eluding reality" – Kurtz). Another film which combined "Expressionism" of both the theatre and architecture was *Von morgens bis Mitternacht* by Karl Heinz Martin, based on the play by Georg Kaiser (1878-1945); Martin (1886-1948), a prominent personality of the *avant-garde* theatre (mostly in Berlin), made another *expressionist* film *Das Haus zum Mond*, later co-scripted *Berlin-Alexanderplatz* and then evaded the political scene in the Thirties with musical films and thrillers.

Other key figures: cameramen like Freund, Hoffmann, Seeber, and Wagner; set designers Warm, Röhrig, Herlth, Reimann, Poelzig, and Hunte; directors Wiene, Lang, Murnau, Leni, Pick, Dupont, Robison, Grune, Rippert, and von Gerlach (all q.v.). Among scenarists, Thea von Harbou was the most influenced by Mayer.

Other key films: *Genuine, Der Golem* (20), *Der müde Tod, Vanina, Waxworks; Dr. Mabuse, the Gambler; Torgus, Raskolnikov, Orlacs Hände*, and *Die Bergkatze*.

"Expressionism" exerted a great influence on Lang's "monumental" films and "*Kammerspiel*" (q.v.).

93 EYCK, PETER VAN (1913-1969). B: Steinwehr (Pommerania). D: Männedorf (Switzerland). Actor. RN: Götz von Eick, At first in Paris, then to Hollywood, where he makes his film *début* under Billy Wilder (q.v.) in *Five Graves to Cairo*. Actor and asst. director in Hollywood. Between 1945-1948: information officer in Berlin. Long successful career as the blond, rather vain character in international productions like *The Wages of Fear* and *Station Six Sahara*.

Films: *Hallo, Fräulein!; Epilog, Export in Blond, Königskinder, Der Dritte von rechts, Opfer des Herzens, Der Cornet, Der gläserne Turm, Dr. Crippen lebt, Schwarze Nylons – heisse Nächte, Das Mädchen Rosemarie,*

Schmutziger Engel, Du gehörst mir, Rommel ruft Kairo, Verbrechen nach Schulschluss, Der Rest ist Schweigen, Lockvogel der Nacht, Labyrinth, Abschied von den Wolken, Geheimaktion Schwarze Kapelle, Liebling der Götter, Die 1000 Augen des Dr. Mabuse, An einem Freitag um halb zwölf, Kriegsgesetz; Die Stunden, die Du glücklich bist; Unter Ausschluss der Oeffentlichkeit; Finden Sie, dass Constanze sich richtig verhält?, Endstation 13 Sahara, Im Namen des Teufels, Ein Toter sucht seinen Mörder, Ein Alibi zerbricht, Das grosse Liebesspiel, Scotland Yard jagt Dr. Mabuse, Verführung am Meer, Kennwort: Reiher, Die Todesstrahlen des Dr. Mabuse, Duell vor Sonnenuntergang, Das Geheimnis der Lederschlinge, Die Herren, Spione unter sich, Der Chef schickt seinen besten Mann, Karriere, Sechs Pistolen jagen Professor Z., Shalako, Tevye und seine sieben Töchter.

94 FANCK, ARNOLD (1889-   ). B: Frankenthal. Director. Doctor of Geology. Pioneer of "*mountain*" *films* (q.v.). Founder of the Freiburg school of cameramen. His famous cameramen include Schneeberger, Allgeier and Angst (all q.v.). His favourite actress was Leni Riefenstahl (q.v.) who was a dancer and became a director largely thanks to him. 1920: makes his first short documentaries with Dr. Taurn (e.g. *Wunder des Schneeschuhs* and *Im Kampf mit dem Berg*).

Films: *Das Wunder des Schneeschuhs* 21 (also script), *Pomperly's Kampf mit dem Schneeschuh* 22 (co-dir. and scripted in collab. with Holger-Madsen), *Der Berg des Schicksals* 24 (prod., dir., script, phot. in collab. with Allgeier, Schneeberger, Herbert Oettel and Eugen Hamm), *Der heilige Berg* 26 (also script), *Der grosse Sprung* 27 (also script), *Der Kampf ums Matterhorn* (only script). Then sound: *Die weisse Hölle vom Piz Palü* 29 (co-dir. also co-scripted), *Die drei heiligen Brunnen* (only idea), *Stürme über dem Montblanc* 30 (also script), *Der weisse Rausch* 31 (also script), *Abenteuer im Engadin* (only idea), *S.O.S. Eisberg* 33 (also script with Fritz Loewe, Ernst Sorge, Hans Hinrich, Tom Reed, E. Knopf and F. Wolff), *Der ewige Traum* 34 (also script), *Der Kampf ums Matterhorn* (only idea), *Die Tochter des Samurai* 37 (also script), *Ein Robinson* 40 (also script with Rolf Meyer).

95 FARKAS, NIKOLAUS (1891-). B: Hungary. Director of photography. RN: Farkas Miklos. Starts his career in Hungary, then goes to Austria and later to Germany, where he is active mostly on entertainment films (his best work being Jutzi's *Berlin-Alexanderplatz*). 1933: to France (films include Pabst's *Don Quixote*), later to U.S.A.

Films (incomplete): *Samson und Delila* (co-phot. with Josef Zeitlinger and Maurice Armand Mondet), *Zigeunerliebe, Kinder Revolution, Wenn Du noch eine Mutter hast, Der Fluch, Gräfin Mariza, Die Moral der Gasse; Nick, der König der Chauffeure* (co-phot. with Arpad Viragh), *Die Rache der Pharaonen, Der Tänzer meiner Frau, Ein Mädel und drei Clowns, Der Fall des Staatsanwaltes M . . .* (co-phot. with Eduard von Borsody), *Küsse, die man nicht vergisst, Liebe im Mai, Die Sache mit Schorrsiegel, Mädchen am Kreuz, Nachtgestalten, Das Recht auf Liebe, Das Schiff der verlorenen Menschen, Die weissen Rosen von Ravensburg*. Then sound: *Danton, Fra Diavolo, Berlin-Alexanderplatz* (co-phot. with Erich

Giese), *Der Ball, Madame hat Ausgang* (co-phot. with Franz Farkas), *Die Firma heiratet*.

96 FEILER, HERTHA (1916-). B: Vienna. Actress. Stage training in Vienna, then Scala Vienna. 1937: speaker on dubbed versions for Fox in Rome. Makes guest stage appearances after 1945. Enters cinema through husband Heinz Rühmann (q.v.).

Films: *Liebling der Matrosen, Lauter Lügen, Adresse unbekannt, Kleider machen Leute, Flucht ins Dunkel, Männer müssen so sein, Frau im Strom, Lauter Liebe, Hauptsache glücklich, Rembrandt, Der kleine Grenzverkehr, Der Engel mit dem Saitenspiel, Sag' die Wahrheit, Quax in Fahrt, Die kupferne Hochzeit, Heimliches Rendezvous, Ich mach' Dich glücklich, Wenn der weisse Flieder wieder blüht, Pünktchen und Anton, Dein Mund verspricht mir Liebe, Die schöne Müllerin, Lass die Sonne wieder scheinen, Wenn die Alpenrosen blüh'n, Charley's Tante, Solange noch die Rosen blüh'n Opernball, Johannisnacht, Die Heilige und ihr Narr; Wien, du Stadt meiner Träume; Der Maulkorb, Die singende Engel von Tirol, Mein Schulfreund, Die Ente klingelt um* ½8.

97 FELMY, HANSJÖRG (1931-). B: Berlin. Actor. At first locksmith and printer. Stage training in Braunschweig. Theatres: Braunschweig, Aachen, Cologne. Felmy is often seen as a rather misunderstood daredevil *manqué*. In 1966 he appeared in Hitchcock's *Torn Curtain*.

Films: *Der Stern von Afrika, Haie und kleine Fische, Das Herz von St. Pauli, Der Greifer, Herz ohne Gnade, Wir Wunderkinder, Der Maulkorb, Unruhige Nacht, Menschen im Netz, Und ewig singen die Wälder, Buddenbrooks; Ein Tag, der nie zu Ende geht; Der Mann, der sich verkaufte; Die Botschafterin, Schachnovelle, Die zornigen jungen Männer, Endstation 13 Sahara, Die Ehe des Herrn Mississippi, Das letzte Kapitel, Die glücklichen Jahre der Thorwalds, Die Flusspiraten vom Mississippi, Der Henker von London, Nebelmörder, Das siebente Opfer, Das Ungeheuer von London City; An der Donau, wenn der Wein blüht.*

98 FINCK, WERNER (1902-). B: Görlitz. Actor, cabaret artist. Art school Dresden. 1927-1929: Landestheater Darmstadt. 1930-1935: head of the cabaret "Die Katakombe" in Berlin. Works as journalist for *Berliner Tageblatt.* Later prevented by Nazis from performing. Soldier. 1948: head of cabaret "Die Mausefalle" in Stuttgart.

Films: *Die Wasserteufel von Hieflau, Die verliebte Firma; Ein Lied, ein Kuss, ein Mädel; Der Choral von Leuthen, Die Fahrt ins Grüne, Keine Angst vor Liebe, Das Tankmädel, Der Läufer von Marathon, Wenn am Sonntagabend die Dorfmusik spielt, Der Vetter aus Dingsda, Ferien vom Ich, Herr Kobin geht auf Abenteuer, Was bin ich ohne Dich, Jungfrau gegen Mönch, Das Blumenmädchen vom Grand-Hotel, Die Freundin eines grossen Mannes, Die Liebe siegt; Eine Frau, die weiss was sie will; Frischer Wind aus Kanada; April, April; Die Landstreicher, Die unentschuldigte Stunde, Sherlock Holmes, La Habanera, Autobus S, Die glücklichste Ehe der Welt* (also script with Peter Francke and Werner P. Zibaso), *Der Maulkorb, Die Umwege des schönen Karl, Verklungene Melodie; Der Mann, der nicht nein sagen konnte* (also script with Mario Camerini and Karl Lerbs, also dir. of dialogue), *Das Mädchen von gestern Nacht, Film ohne Titel, Kleiner Wagen – grosse Liebe, Meine Nichte Susanne; Tobias Knopp, Abenteuer eines Junggesellen* (speaker), *Es begann um Mitternacht, Es geht nicht ohne Gisela, Die Frauen des Herrn S., Heldentum nach Ladenschluss, Hanussen, Lola Montès, Ich und meine Schwiegersöhne, Heute heiratet meine Frau, Lumpazivagabundus, Viktor und Viktoria, Die Zürcher Verlobung, Tolle Nacht, Heiraten verboten, Die Zwillinge vom Zillertal, Maya, Die liebe Familie, Der müde Theodor, . . . und das am Montagmorgen, Labyrinth, Gangsterjagd in Lederhosen; Mein Schatz, komm mit ans blaue Meer; Rosen für den Staatsanwalt, Im weissen Rössl, Klassenkeile, Der Partyphotograph.*

99 FINKENZELLER, HELI (1914-). B. Munich. Actress. Stage training in Munich (under Otto Falckenberg). Then appears at the Kammerspiele Munich. Enters cinema through director Karl Ritter (q.v.).

Films: *Der höhere Befehl, Ehestreik, Kö-nigswalzer, Boccaccio, Weiberregiment, Gleisdreieck, Der Schimmelkrieg in der Holledau, Spiel in der Tenne, Der Mustergatte, Wie der Hase läuft; Mein Sohn, der Herr Minister; Scheidungsreise, Konzert in Tirol, Diskretion – Ehrensache, Die kleine Nachtmusik, Opernball, Hochzeitsnacht, Alarmstufe V, Ehe man Ehemann wird, Der siebente Junge, Fronttheater, Alles aus Liebe, Kohlhiesels Töchter, Ich werde Dich auf Händen tragen, Das Bad auf der Tenne, Wo ist Herr Belling?, Münchnerinnen, Hallo – Sie haben Ihre Frau vergessen, Zwölf Herzen für Charly, Die Frau von gestern Nacht, Es begann um Mitternacht, Stips, Mikosch rückt ein, Am Brunnen vor dem Tore, So ein Affentheater, Briefträger Müller, Emil und die Detektive, Es geschah am 20. Juli, Der Zigeunerbaron, Suchkind 312, Der erste Frühlingstag, Tausend Melodien, Die wilde Auguste, Ciske – Ein Kind braucht Liebe, Acht Mädels im Boot; Ein Sommer, den man nie vergisst; Wegen Verführung Minderjähriger, . . . und so was nennt sich Leben, Die lustigen Weiber von Tirol.*

FISCHER-ASHLEY, HELMUTH *see* ASHLEY, HELMUT.

100 FISCHER, OTTO WILHELM (1915-). B: Klosterneuberg, near Vienna. Actor. Attends Vienna University (German and English literature and languages, history of art). Studies with Reinhardt (q.v.) in Vienna. 1936: Theater in der Josefstadt, Vienna. 1930-1943: Deutsches Volkstheater, Vienna. 1946-1952: Kammerspiele Munich and Burgtheater Vienna. Since 1960 his stage appearances have been very rare.

Films: *Burgtheater, Anton der Letzte, Meine Tochter lebt in Wien, Der Meineidbauer, Wien 1910, Sommerliebe, Die beiden Schwestern, Sieben Briefe, Spiel, Glück unterwegs, Shiva und die Galgenblume, Triumph der Liebe, Leuchtende Schatten, Sag' endlich ja, Das unsterbliche Antlitz, Verlorenes Rennen, Hin und her, Liebling der Welt, Erzherzog Johanns grosse Liebe, Märchen vom Glück, Verträumte Tage, Heidelberger Romanze, Das letzte Rezept, Tausend rote Rosen blüh'n, Ich hab mich so an Dich gewöhnt, Bis wir uns wiederseh'n, Cuba Cabana, Der träumende Mund, Ein Herz spielt falsch, Solange Du da bist,*

Elisabeth Flickenschildt and Robert Graf in WIR WUNDERKINDER

*Tagebuch einer Verliebten, Eine Liebesge-
schichte, Bildnis einer Unbekannten, Ludwig
II., Hanussen 55* (also co-dir. with Georg
Marischka), *Ich suche Dich 56* (also dir. and
scripted with Martin Morlock, Menzel and
Claus Hardt); *Mein Vater, der Schauspieler;
Herrscher ohne Krone, Skandal in Ischl, El
Hakim, Don Vesuvio und das Haus der
Strolche, ... und nichts als die Wahrheit,
Helden; Peter Voss, der Millionendieb, Men-
schen im Hotel, Und das am Montagmor-
gen, Abschied von den Wolken; Peter Voss,
der Held des Tages; Scheidungsgrund Liebe,
Mit Himbeergeist geht alles besser, Das Rie-
senrad, Es muss nicht immer Kaviar sein,
Diesmal muss es Kavia sein, Axel Munthe,
der Arzt von San Michele, Frühstück im
Doppelbett, Das Geheimnis der schwarzen
Witwe, Onkel Toms Hütte, Liebesvögel.*

101 FLICKENSCHILDT, ELISABETH
(1905-   ). B: Hamburg-Blankenese. Ac-

tress. Stage training in Hamburg under Robert Nhil. Stage *début:* Deutsches Schauspielhaus Hamburg. 1933-1936: Kammerspiele Munich. 1936-1941: Staatstheater
Berlin. 1941-1945: Tübingen. 1947-1955:
Theatres in Reutlingen, Munich and Schauspielhaus Düsseldorf. Since 1955: mainly
Deutsches Schauspielhaus Hamburg. Writes
for the stage and directs plays as well. Important theatre actress, especially in her
work with Gustaf Gründgens (q.v.). Often
roughly treated as the female villain in
thrillers.

Films: *Grossreinemachen, Du kannst
nicht treu sein, Der ahnungslose Engel,
Streit um den Knaben Jo, Der zerbrochene
Krug, Tango Notturno, Starke Herzen, Hei-
ratsschwindler, Der Maulkorb, Jugend, Ein
Mädchen geht an Land, Der Schritt vom
Wege, Robert Koch, Die barmherzige Lüge,
Die unheimlichen Wünsche, Der Fuchs von
Glenarvon, Ohm Krüger; Treck, der Pan-*

49

dur; Der grosse König, Zwischen Himmel und Erde, Rembrandt, Altes Herz wird wieder jung, Liebesgeschichten, Romanze in Moll, Die beiden Schwestern, Philharmoniker, Familie Buchholz, Neigungsehe, Seinerzeit zu meiner Zeit, Meine Herren Söhne; Der Mann, dem man den Namen stahl; Ein toller Tag, Shiva und die Galgenblume, Eine grosse Liebe, Madonna in Ketten, König für eine Nacht, Pikanterie, Toxi, Der Tag vor der Hochzeit, Hokuspokus, Die Nacht ohne Moral, Hochzeitsglocken, Das ideale Brautpaar, Rittmeister Wronski, Die spanische Fliege, Sohn ohne Heimat, Herrscher ohne Krone, Robinson soll nicht sterben, Stefanie, Auferstehung, Wir Wunderkinder, Labyrinth; Agatha, lass das Morden sein; Die Bande des Schreckens, Brücke des Schicksals; Faust, Eheinstitut Aurora, Frauenarzt Dr. Sibelius, Das Gasthaus an der Themse, Das schwarz-weiss-rote Himmelbett, Ferien vom Ich, Das indische Tuch, Das grosse Liebesspiel, DM-Killer, Einer frisst den andern, Lausbubengeschichten, Das Phantom von Soho, Diamantenbillard, Tante Frida – neue Lausbubengeschichten, Onkel Filser – Allerneueste Lausbubengeschichten, Der Lügner und die Nonne, Wenn Ludwig ins Manöver zieht, Dr. Fabian – Lachen ist die beste Medizin.

102 **FLORATH, ALBERT** (1888-1957). B: Bielefeld. D: Gaildorf/Würtemberg. Actor. 1908-1919: Hoftheater Munich, then to Berlin. Enters cinema in 1920, works for radio from 1925 onwards. 1920-1945: actor, dramaturg and director at Staatstheater Berlin. After 1945: Würtembergisches Staatstheater Stuttgart.

Films (incomplete): *Die letzte Droschke von Berlin, Gehetzte Frauen, Schinderhannes, Zwei unterm Himmelszelt, Napoleon auf St. Helena.* Then sound: *Man braucht kein Geld, Berlin-Alexanderplatz, Der Hauptmann von Köpenick* (31), *Goethe lebt . . .!, Die Herren vom Maxim, Das Meer ruft, Reifende Jugend; Ein Kind, ein Hund, ein Vagabund; Der schwarze Walfisch, Herz ist Trumpf; Liebe, Tod und Teufel; Kirschen aus Nachbars Garten, Das Mädchen Johanna, Der Gefangene des Königs, Donogoo Tonka, Eine Frau ohne Bedeutung, Glückskinder, Weisse Sklaven, Die grosse und die kleine Welt, Dahinten auf der Heide, Boc-*

caccio; *Donner, Blitz und Sonnenschein; Unter Ausschluss der Oeffentlichkeit, Capriolen, Fremdenheim Filoda, Die Austernlilli, Der Schimmelkrieg in der Holedau, Brillanten, Der Biberpelz, Ein Volksfeind, Spiel im Sommerwind, Fortsetzung folgt, Eine Nacht im Mai, Eine Frau kommt in die Tropen, Die Umwege des schönen Karl, Yvette, Steputat & Co., Skandal um den Hahn, Fünf Millionen suchen einen Erben, Frauen für Golden Hill, Irrtum des Herzens, Im Namen des Volkes, Hurra! Ich bin Papa!, Eine Frau wie Du, Alarm auf Station III, Die Stimme aus dem Aether, Drunter und drüber, Ein ganzer Kerl, Der Gouverneur, Schneider Wibbel, Das Paradies der Junggesellen, Roman eines Arztes, Wer küsst Madeleine?, Die Reise nach Tilsit, Die unvollkommene Liebe, Die Rothschilds, Der Fuchs von Glenarvon, Angelika, Der dunkle Punkt, Zwischen Hamburg und Haiti, Lauter Liebe, Jud Süss, Friedrich Schiller, Wunschkonzert, Männerwirtschaft, Jakko, Der Weg ins Freie, Friedemann Bach, Ich klage an, Clarissa, Am Abend auf der Heide, Der Seniorchef, Das grosse Spiel, Diesel, Himmelhunde, So ein Früchtchen, Symphonie eines Lebens, Weisse Wäsche, Die Erbin vom Rosenhof, Stimme des Herzens, Immensee, Die beiden Schwestern, Ein Walzer mit Dir, Wenn die Sonne wieder scheint, Um 9 kommt Harald, Nora, Seinerzeit zu meiner Zeit, Junge Adler, Junge Herzen, Zwischen Nacht und Morgen, Moselfahrt mit Monika, Am Abend nach der Oper, Die Feuerzangenbowle, Sag' die Wahrheit, Via Mala, Tierarzt Dr. Vlimmen* (45), *Shiva und die Galgenblume, Dr. med. Döderlein, Das kleine Hofkonzert, Die Schenke zur ewigen Liebe, Der Puppenspieler, Die kupferne Hochzeit, Der Herr vom andern Stern, Schuld allein ist der Wein, Verführte Hände, Liebe* (47), *Diese Nacht vergess' ich nie, Nichts als Zufälle, Die Freunde meiner Frau, Derby, Der Bagnosträfling, Zukunft aus zweiter Hand, Kätchen für alles, Gefährliche Gäste, Frauenarzt Dr. Prätorius, Schatten der Nacht, Absender unbekannt, Dieser Mann gehört, mir, Gabriela, Die wunderschöne Galathee, Export in Blond, Das Mädchen aus der Südsee, Hochzeitsnacht im Paradies, Insel ohne Moral, Tobias Knopp, Abenteuer einer Junggesellen* (speaker), *Das gestohlene Jahr, Professor Nachtfalter, Was* das Herz befiehlt, Das Haus in Montevideo, Der eingebildete Kranke, Toxi, Einmal am Rhein; Oh, du lieber Fridolin; Heimatglocken, Rosen blühen auf dem Heidegrab, Wenn abends die Heide träumt, Keine Angst vor grossen Tieren, Südliche Nächte, Die Mühle im Schwarzwäldertal, Moselfahrt aus Liebeskummer, Wenn der weisse Flieder wieder blüht, Dein Herz ist meine Heimat, Hochzeitsglocken, Sanatorium total verrückt, Aennchen von Tharau, Columbus entdeckt Krähwinkel, Die schöne Müllerin, Der schweigende Engel, Die spanische Fliege Der dunkle Stern, Zwei blaue Augen, Das Forsthaus im Tirol, Die Herrin vom Sölderhof, Das Erbe vom Puggerhof, Unternehmen Schlafsack, Kirschen in Nachbars Garten, Drei Birken auf der Heide, Ein Herz kehrt heim, Wenn wir alle Engel wären, Mädchen mit schwachem Gedächtnis, Tierarzt Dr. Vlimmen (56).

103 **FÖRNBACHER, HELMUT** (1936-). B: Basle. Actor and director. Theatrical training. Appears on stage in Zurich, Basle and Munich (also directs). 1956: makes *début* on television, over seventy TV-plays in Germany, then moves to filmmaking in Switzerland. Starts his career as director with the "Bonnie and Clyde" style *Sommersprossen*.

Acted in: *Lampenfieber, Schüsse aus dem Geigenkasten, Schonzeit für Füchse, Der Mörderklub von Brooklyn, St. Pauli zwischen Nacht und Morgen*. Films as director: *Sommersprossen* 68 (also acted), *Fiestas* 69 (short), *... Köpfchen in das Wasser, Schwänzchen in die Höh* 69 (co-prod., also acted and co-scripted with Martin Roda-Becher).

104 **FORST, WILLI** (1903-). B: Vienna. Actor and director. RN: Willi Frohs. Son of a porcelain manufacturer. At first makes stage appearances in the provinces. Later Karlstheater Vienna, Metropoltheater Berlin, mainly in light entertainment. 1928-1933: Apollotheater Vienna and Deutsches Theater Berlin. Enters films in 1922. Famous "Beau."

Films (incomplete): *Der Wegweiser; Oh, du lieber Augustin; Strandgut, Café Electric, Drei Niemandskinder, Die elf Teufel, Amor auf Ski, Ein besserer Herr, Die blaue Maus,*

Liebfraumilch, Die lustigen Vagabunden, Unfug der Liebe, Fräulein Fähnrich; Die Frau, die jeder liebt, bist Du!; Katherina Knie, Gefahren der Brautzeit, Der Sträfling aus Stambul, Die weissen Rosen von Ravensburg. Then sound: *Atlantik, Ein Tango für Dich, Der Herr auf Bestellung, Das Lied ist aus, Zwei Herzen im 3/4-Takt, Ein Burschenlied aus Heidelberg, Die lustigen Weiber von Wien, Der Raub der Mona Lisa; Peter Voss, der Millionendieb; So ein Mädel vergisst man nicht, Der Prinz von Arkadien, Ein blonder Traum; Ihre Durchlaucht, die Verkäuferin; Brennendes Geheimnis, Leise flehen meine Lieder* 33 (only dir. and script), *Maskerade* 34 (only dir. and script), *So endete eine Liebe, Ich kenn' Dich nicht und Liebe Dich, Mazurka* 35 (only dir.), *Königswalzer, Burgtheater* 36 (only dir. and scripted with Jochen Huth), *Allotria* 36 (only dir. and scripted with Huth), *Serenade* 37 (only dir. and co-scripted), *Capriolen* 37 (only scripted with Huth), *Ich bin Sebastian Otto* 39 (also co-dir. with Viktor Becker), *Bel ami* 39 (also dir. and co-scripted), *Operette* 40 (also dir. and co-scripted), *Wiener Blut* 42 (also dir.), *Frauen sind keine Engel* 43 (only dir.), *Wiener Mädeln* 45 (also dir. and scripted with Franz Gribitz), *Die Sünderin* 50 (only dir. and scripted with Menzel and Georg Marischka), *Es geschehen noch Wunder* 51 (also dir. and scripted with Johannes Mario Simmel), *Alle kann ich nicht heiraten* (only idea), *Bei Dir war es immer so schön, Ein Mann vergisst die Liebe, Weg in die Vergangenheit, Dieses Lied bleibt bei Dir* 54 (only dir.), *Die Drei von der Tankstelle* 55 (only supervision), *Kaiserjäger* 56 (only dir.), *Die unentschuldigte Stunde* 57 (only dir.), *Wien, du Stadt meiner Träume* 57 (only dir. and scripted with Kurt Nachmann).

105 **FORSTER, RUDOLF** (1884-1968). B: Gröbming. D: Attersee. Actor. Stage training at the Konservatorium Vienna. Theatres: Vienna, Munich, St. Petersburg, Bucharest. 1910: goes to Berlin to work with Jessner and Reinhardt (both q.v.). Early silent period partner of Ossi Oswalda (q.v.) and Eva May. 1937-1940: plays on Broadway and in American films. After 1945: makes many guest appearances, mainly in Austrian and German theatres,

and at the Burgtheater Vienna.

Films (incomplete): *Fahrt ins Blaue, Das Geheimnis der Gladiatorenwerke, Glanz und Elend der Kurtisanen, Die Jagd nach der Wahrheit, Kurfürstendamm, Manolescus Memoiren, Der Schädel der Pharaonentochter, Zehn Milliarden Volt, Der Abenteuer, Die rote Hexe, Frau Sünde, Das Licht um Mitternacht, Die Mausefalle, Die Schuhe einer schönen Frau, Der stärkste Trieb, Adam und Eva, Auferstehung, Das Erbe, Erdgeist, Die Marionetten der Fürstin, SOS,*

Die Insel der Tränen, Ssasin, Tragödie der Liebe, Horrido, Zur Chronik von Grieshuus, Sein grosser Fall, Fame, Die Hose, Pique Dame. Then sound: *Die Dreigroschenoper, Yorck, Ariane, Die Gräfin von Monte Christo, Der träumende Mund, Morgenrot, Hohe Schule, ... nur ein Komödiant, Die ganz grossen Torheiten, Wien 1910, Ein Blick zurück, Der gebieterische Ruf, Fahrt ins Glück; Der Mann, der zweimal leben wollte; Liebestraum, Unvergängliches Licht, Im weissen Rössl, Viktoria und ihr Husar, Rittmeister Wronski, Eine Frau genügt nicht?, Der letzte Mann (55), Regine, Spionage, Waldwinter, Kaiserjäger; Liane, das Mädchen aus dem Urwald; Und führe uns nicht in Versuchung, Skandal in Ischl, Spielbank-*

affäre, Die unentschuldigte Stunde, Die Halbzarte, Man müsste nochmal zwanzig sein, Der Rest ist Schweigen, Lass mich am Sonntag nicht allein, Der liebe Augustin, Morgen wirst Du um mich weinen, Das Glas Wasser, Im Stahlnetz des Dr. Mabuse, Das Riesenrad, Der Teufel spielte Balaleika, Er kann's nicht lassen, Lulu, Der Henker von London, Die Gruft mit dem Rätselschloss, Tonio Kröger, Wälsungenblut, Der Turm der verbotenen Liebe.

106 **FRANK, HORST** (1929-   ). B: Lübeck. Actor. Trained at the State High School in Hamburg (Eduard Marks). Theatres: Lübeck, Bonn, Basle, Baden-Baden. Guest appearances. Enters cinema in 1957, usually cast as a villain. International career.

Films: *Haie und kleine Fische, Der Stern von Afrika, Der Greifer, Blitzmädels an die Front, Das Mädchen Rosemarie, Das Mädchen vom Moorhof, Meine 99 Bräute, Schwarze Nylons – heisse Nächte, Die Nackte und der Satan, Hunde wollt ihr ewig leben, Abschied von den Wolken, Bumerang, Fabrik der Offoziere, Kein Engel ist so rein, Die zornigen jungen Männer, Treibjagd auf ein Leben, Unser Haus in Kamerun, Hass ohne Gnade, Zwischen Shanghai und St. Pauli, Die Flusspiraten vom Mississippi; Mein Onkel, der Gangster; Der schwarze Panther von Ratana, Die weisse Spinne, Die Diamantenhölle am Mekong, Das Geheimnis der chinesischen Nelke, Die Goldsucher von Arkansas, Die letzten Zwei vom Rio Bravo, Die Tote von Beverly Hills, Weisse Fracht für Hongkong, Der Fluch des schwarzen Rubins, Das Geheimnis der drei Dschunken, Die letzten Drei der Albatros, Die schwarzen Adler von Santa Fé; Der Spion, der in die Hölle ging; Fünf vor zwölf in Caracas, Für eine Handvoll Diamanten, Um null Uhr schnappt die Falle zu, Fünf gegen Casablanca, Geheimnisse in goldenen Nylons, Die letzte Kompanie, Die Rache des Dr. Fu Man Chu, Django – die Totengräber warten schon, Django – Ein Sarg voll Blut, Marquis de Sade: Justine, Cosi dolce ... cosi perversa, Cathérine – Ein Leben für die Liebe.*

107 **FREUND, KARL** (1890-1969). B: Königinhof. D: Hollywood. Director of photography. Enters cinema in 1906, at

first (1908) cameraman for newsreels. Later achieves international fame and importance through his work for Murnau, Dupont and Lang (all q.v.). 1930: to U.S.A. From 1950: work confined mainly to American television.

Films (incomplete): *Venetianische Nacht, Satanas, Brandherd, Der Bucklige und die Tänzerin; Der Golem, wie er in die Welt kam; Der Januskopf* (co-phot.), *Die Spinnen II* (co-phot.); *Marizza, genannt die Schmugglermadonna; Der Roman der Christine von Herre, Der verlorene Schatten, Der brennende Acker* (co-phot.), *Lukrezia Borgia* (co-phot. with Drews and Karl Voss), *Tiefland, Die Finanzen des Grossherzogs* (co-phot.), *Der letzte Mann, Michael, Tartüff, Varieté, Metropolis* (co-phot.), *Berlin – Die Symphonie einer Grosstadt* (only co-scripted), *Dona Juana* (co-phot. with Baberske and Adolf Schlasy), *Eine Nacht in London* (co-phot.), *Fräulein Else* (co-phot. with Schlasy and Baberske).

108 **FRITSCH, WILLY** (1901-   ). B: Kattowitz. Actor. Born of a miner's family. Trained as engineer. Then studies under Reinhardt (q.v.) and at Grosses Schauspielhaus Berlin. Enters cinema in 1921 thanks to Erich Pommer (q.v.). Formed the perfect partnership with Lilian Harvey, and later with Käthe von Nagy (both q.v.).

Films (incomplete): *Razzia, Die Fahrt ins Glück; Seine Frau, die Unbekannte, Guillotine, Mutter und Kind, Blitzzug der Liebe, Der Farmer aus Texas, Das Mädchen mit der Protektion, Der Tänzer meiner Frau, Ein Walzertraum, Die Boxerbraut, Die Fahrt ins Abenteuer, Die keusche Susanne, Der Prinz und die Tänzerin, Die Frau im Schrank, Der letzte Walzer, Schuldig, Die selige Exzellenz, Die sieben Töchter der Frau Guyrkovics, Die Carmen von St. Pauli, Ihr dunkler Punkt, Spione, Der Tanzstudent, Ungarische Rhapsodie, Die Frau im Mond.* Then sound: *Melodie des Herzens, Die Drei von der Tankstelle, Liebeswalzer, Einbrecher, Hokuspokus, Ronny, Im Geheimdienst, Ihre Hoheit befielt, Der Kongress tanzt, Ich bei Tag und Du bei Nacht, Ein blonder Traum, Frechdachs, Ein toller Einfall, Saison in Kairo, Des jungen Dessauers grosse Liebe, Walzerkrieg, Prinzessin Tourandot, Die Töchter Ihrer Exzellenz,*

Die Insel, Schwarze Rosen, Amphitryon, Boccaccio, Glückskinder, Streit um den Knaben Jo, Menschen ohne Vaterland, Gewitterflug zu Claudia, Sieben Ohrfeigen, Preussische Liebesgeschichte, Am seidenen Faden, Zwischen den Eltern, Das Mädchen von gestern Nacht, Frau am Steuer, Die Geliebte, Die keusche Geliebte, Die unvollkommene Liebe, Das leichte Mädchen, Leichte Muse, Dreimal Hochzeit, Frauen sind doch bessere Diplomaten, Wiener Blut, Anschlag auf Baku, Geliebte Welt, Die Gattin, Der kleine Grenzverkehr, Liebesgeschichten, Junge Adler, Die tolle Susanne, Die Fledermaus, Finale, Film ohne Titel, Hallo – Sie haben Ihre Frau vergessen, Derby, Kätchen für alles, Zwölf Herzen für Charly, König für eine Nacht, Die wunderschöne Galathee, Herrliche Zeiten, Schatten der Nacht, Mädchen mit Beziehungen, Schön muss man sein, Die verschleierte Maja, Grün ist die Heide, Die Dubarry, Mikosch rückt ein, Ferien vom Ich, Am Brunnen vor dem Tore, Von Liebe reden wir später, Damenwahl, Wenn der weisse Flieder wieder blüht, Ungarische Rhapsodie, Weg in die Vergangenheit, Maxie, Stern von Rio, Drei Tage Mittelarrest, Der fröhliche Wanderer, Liebe ist ja nur ein Märchen,

Die Drei von der Tankstelle (55), *Solange noch die Rosen blühn, Das Donkosakenlied, Schwarzwaldmelodie, Wo die alten Wälder rauschen, Der schräge Otto, Die Beine von Dolores, Zwei Herzen im Mai, Schwarzwälder Kirsch, Mit Eva fing die Sünde an, Hubertusjagd, Liebling der Götter, Was macht Papa denn in Italien?, Das hab' ich von Papa gelernt, Verliebt in Heidelberg.*

109 **FROEBE, GERT** (1913-   ). B: Planitz. Actor. At first stage designer in Dresden, then stage training under Erich Ponto (q.v.). Theatres: Wuppertal, Frankfurt, Burgtheater Vienna, Kammerspiele Munich; also cabaret appearances. Has worked increasingly abroad. International career, at first as a "heavy," in films like *Goldfinger* and *Is Paris Burning?*

Films: *Berliner Ballade, Nach dem Regen scheint Sonne, Der Tag vor der Hochzeit, Salto mortale, Die vertagte Hochzeitsnacht, Ein Herz spielt falsch, Arlette erobert Paris, Hochzeit auf Reisen, Die kleine Stadt will schlafen gehen, Morgengrauen, Das Kreuz am Jägersteig, Mannequins für Rio, Das zweite Leben, Ewiger Walzer, Vom Himmel gefallen, Der dunkle Stern; Ich weiss, wofur ich lebe; Das Forsthaus in Tirol, Ein Mäd-*

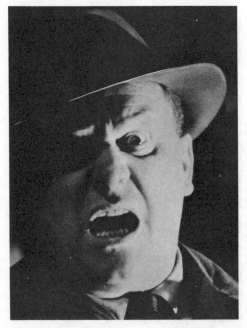

chen aus Flandern, Ein Herz schlägt für Erika, Waldwinter, Robinson soll nicht sterben, Der tolle Bomberg, Das Herz von St. Pauli, Nasser Asphalt, Es geschah am hellichten Tag, Der Pauker, Das Mädchen Rosemarie, Grabenplatz 17, Das Mädchen mit den Katzenaugen, Nick Knattertons Abenteuer, Menschen im Hotel, Und ewig singen die Wälder, Jons und Erdme, Alt-Heidelberg; Am Tag, als der Regen kam; Das kunstseidene Mädchen, Schüsse im Morgengrauen, Bis das Geld euch scheidet, Der grüne Bogenschütze, Der Gauner und der Liebe Gott, Soldatensender Calais, Die 1000 Augen des Dr. Mabuse, 12 Stunden Angst, Via Mala, Auf Wiedersehn, Heute kündigt mir mein Mann, Die Rote, Das Testament des Dr. Mabuse, Die Dreigroschenoper, Der Mörder Tonio Kröger, Das Liebeskarussell (i), Ganovenehre, Rififi in Paris, Caroline Chérie.

110 **FROELICH, CARL** (1875-1953). B and D: Berlin. Director. Enters cinema in 1902 as one of the first directors and production managers, working together with Oskar Messter (q.v.). A pioneer in producing newsreels (1918), and founds his own production company (1920). Many of his films featured Henny Porten (q.v.). Produced most of his own films between 1922 and 1941, together with the films of other directors.

Films (incomplete): *Das gefährliche Alter* (only camerawork), *Zu spät* 11, *Richard Wagner* 13, *Tirol in Waffen* (only acted), *Der Schirm mit dem Schwan* 15, *Der Liebesroman der Käthe Keller* 19, *Die Verführten* 19, *Die Brüder Karamasaff* 20 (co-dir.), *Die Toteninsel* 20 (also script in collab. with Walter Supper), *Irrende Seelen* 21 (also script in collab. with Supper), *Don Correa* 22, *Josef und seine Brüder* 22 (also script), *Luise Millerin* 22, *Der Taugenichts* 22 (also co-scripted with Pabst and Supper), *Der Wetterwart* 23, *Mutter und Kind* 24, *Das Abenteuer der Sybille Brandt* 25, *Im Banne der Kralle* 25, *Kammermusik* 25, *Tragödie* 25, *Die Flammen lügen* 26, *Rosen aus dem Süden* 26, *Wehe, wenn sie losgelassen* 26 (also co-scripted with Wilhelm Stücklen), *Die grosse Pause* 27, *Meine Tante – Deine Tante* 27, *Violantha* 27, *Liebe im Kuhstall* 28, *Liebe und Diebe* 28, *Liebfrau-*

milch 28, *Lotte* 28, *Zuflucht* 28, *Die Frau, die jeder liebt, bist Du!* 29. Then sound: *Die Nacht gehört uns* 29, *Brand in der Oper* 30, *Hans in allen Gassen* 30, *Mitternachtsliebe* 31 (co-dir. with Augusto Genina), *Luise, Königin von Preussen* 31, *Mieter Schulze gegen alle* 32, *Die – oder keine* 32, *Liebe auf den ersten Ton* 32, *Gitta entdeckt ihr Herz* 32, *Volldampf voraus* 33 (also scripted with E. Freiherr von Spiegel), *Reifende Jugend* 33, *Der Choral von Leuthen* 33, *Ich für Dich – Du für mich* 34, *Krach um Jolanthe* 34, *Frühlingsmärchen* 34, *Liselotte von der Pfalz* 35 (also scripted with Peter Gillmann and Wolfgang Hoffmann-Harnisch), *Oberwachtmeister Schwenke* 35, *Ich war Jack Mortimer* 35, *Wenn wir alle Engel wären* 36, *Traumulus* 36, *Das Schönheitsfleckchen* (only script and supervision), *Wenn der Hahn kräht* 36, *Die ganz grossen Torheiten* 37, *Heimat* 38, *Die 4 Gesellen* 38, *Die Umwege des schönen Karl*, 38, *Es war eine rauschende Ballnacht* 39, *Das Herz einer Königin* 40, *Der Gasmann* 41, *Hochzeit auf Bärenhof* 42, *Familie Buchholz* 44, *Neigungsehe* 44, *Komplott auf Erlenhof* 50, *Stips* 51 (also idea).

111 **FRÖHLICH, GUSTAV** (1902-   ). B: Hannover. Actor and director. Spent his early childhood in Wiesbaden and Würzburg. Began his career as a journalist and editor of a provincial paper, then moves to local theatres (e.g. the "Schwäbische Wanderbühnen"), and then to Frankfurt and the Volksbühne Berlin. Enters cinema thanks to Fritz Lang (q.v.).

Films: *Die Frau mit dem schlechten Ruf, Friesenblut, Schiff in Not; Die Frau, die nicht "nein" sagen kann; Metropolis, Die elf Teufel, Gehetzte Frauen, Ich heirate meine Frau, Jahrmarkt des Lebens, Jugendrausch, Die leichte Isabell, Der Meister von Nürnberg, Die Pflicht zu schweigen, Schwere Jungens – leichte Mädchen, Angst, Heimkehr; Hurrah! Ich lebe!; Die Rothausgasse, Wenn die Schwalben heimwärts ziehn, Asphalt, Das brennende Herz, Hochverrat.* Then sound: *Der unsterbliche Lump, Brand in der Oper, Zwei Menschen, Voruntersuchung, Die heilige Flamme, Kismet, Gloria, Liebeslied, Mein Leopold, So lang noch ein Walzer von Strauss erklingt, Liebeskommando, Unter falscher Flagge, Kaiserwalzer,*

Gitta entdeckt ihr Herz, Ein Mann mit Herz; Ein Lied, ein Kuss, ein Mädel; Die verliebte Firma Sonnenstrahl, Die Nacht der grossen Liebe, Rund um eine Million, Was Frauen träumen, Rakoczy-Marsch 33 (also co-dir. with Stefan Szekely), *Abenteuer eines jungen Herrn in Polen* 34 (also dir.), *Der Flüchtling aus Chikago, Stradivari, Barcarole, Liebesleute, Oberwachtmeister Schwenke, Ein Teufelskerl, Es flüstert die Liebe, Nacht der Verwandlung, Die Stunde der Versuchung, Die Entführung, Stadt Anatol, Gleisdreieck, Inkognito, Die unmögliche Frau; Gabriele ein, zwei, drei; Alarm in Peking, Frau Sixta, Die kleine und die grosse Liebe, In geheimer Mission, Renate im Quartett, Alarm auf Station III, Herz modern möbliert, Ihr Privatsekretär, Herz geht vor Anker, Alles Schwindel, Sechs Tage Heimaturlaub, Clarissa, Der grosse König, Mit den Augen einer Frau, Tolle Nacht, Das Konzert, Familie Buchholz, Neigungsehe, Der grosse Preis, Eine alltägliche Geschichte, Der grosse Fall, Leb' wohl Christina* 45 (only dir. and scripted with Bastian Müller), *Sag' die Wahrheit, Wege im Zwielicht* 48 (also dir.), *Das verlorene Gesicht, Diese Nacht vergess' ich nie, Der Bagnosträfling* 49 (only dir. and scripted), *Dieser Mann gehört mir, Die Sünderin, Die Lüge* 50 (only dir. and scripted), *Stips, Torreani* 51 (also dir.), *Gefährliches Abenteuer, Haus des Lebens, Ehe für eine Nacht, Von der Liebe reden wir später, Die kleine Stadt will schlafen gehen, Rosen aus dem Süden, Ball der Nationen, Seine Tochter ist der Peter* 55 (only dir.), *Der erste Frühlingstag; Vergiss, wenn Du kannst, ... und keiner schämte sich.*

112 **FUCHSBERGER, JOACHIM** (1927-   ). B: Stuttgart. Actor. At first miner, then printing technician and technical business manager with a big publisher. Involved with the German "Building Exhibition" (Bauausstellung). 1949: radio announcer, then newsreel reporter. Writes song lyrics and later enters films.

Films: *08/15 I, Wenn ich einmal der Herrgott wär', Das Lied von Kaprun, 08/15 II, Der letzte Mann (55), 08/15 in der Heimat, Symphonie in Gold, Lumpazivagabundus, Wenn Poldi ins Manöver zieht, Vater macht Karriere, Eva küsst nur Direktoren, Keine Zeit für schwache Stunden, Kleiner*

Mann – ganz gross, Die Zwillinge vom Zillertal, Die grünen Teufel von Monte Cassino, Liebe kann wie Gift sein, U 47 – Kapitänleutnant Prien, Mein Schatz ist aus Tirol, Das Mädchen mit den Katzenaugen, Die feuerrote Baronesse, Zwischen Glück und Krone, Der Frosch mit der Maske; Mein Schatz, komm mit ans blaue Meer; Die Bande des Schreckens, Endstation "Rote Laterne", Die toten Augen von London, Die zornigen jungen Männer, Das Geheimnis der gelben Narzissen, Die seltsame Gräfin, Auf Wiedersehn, Das Gasthaus an der Themse, Teppich des Grauens, Der Fluch der gelben Schlange, Der schwarze Abt, Die weisse Spinne, Der Hexer, Zimmer 13, Hotel der toten Gäste, Der letzte Mohikaner, Bel Ami 2000 oder: Wie verführt man einen Playboy?, 5000 Dollar für den Kopf von Jonny R., Ich habe sie gut gekannt; Lange Beine, lange Finger; Siebzehn Jahr, blondes Haar; Feuer frei auf Frankie, Der Mönch mit der Peitsche, Im Banne des Unheimlichen, Schreie in der Nacht, Sieben Tage Frist.

113 **GALEEN, HENRIK** (18 -19). Actor, scriptwriter and director. Starts career as actor in various theatres, later also directing. Works for Reinhardt (q.v.) for one year, also in Switzerland, and then back to Germany. Enters cinema circa 1910, first as actor, then also as scriptwriter. His most valuable work consists of scripts for expressionist films. Also director and co-director of some distinctive films. 1933: to U.S.A.

Films (incomplete): Der Golem 14 (co-dir., scripted, and acted), Peter Schlemihl (co-scripted and acted), Die rollende Kugel 19, Judith Trachtenberg 20, Die Geliebte Roswolskys (co-scripted with Hans Janowitz), Nosferatu – Eine Symphonie des Grauens (only scripted), Das Haus ohne Lachen (acted), Stadt in Sicht 23 (also script), Auf gefährlichen Spuren (co-scripted with Adolf Lentz, and acted), Die Liebesbriefe der Baronin von S . . . 24 (also co-scripted with Paul Reno), Das Wachsfigurenkabinett (only scripted), Das Fräulein vom Amt (co-scripted with Lantz), Zigano, der Brigant vom Monte Diavolo (scripted and acted), Der Student von Prag 26 (also co-scripted with Hanns Heinz Ewers), Al-

raune 27 (also scripted), Sein grösster Bluff 27 (co-dir.), Die Dame mit der Maske (co-scripted with Esway). Then sound: Schatten der Unterwelt (only scripted), Salon Dora Green 33.

114 **GEBÜHR, OTTO** (1877-1954). B: Kettwig. D: Wiesbaden. Actor. Theatres: Görlitz, Dresden, Hoftheater Berlin, Lessing-Theater, then to Reinhardt (q.v.). Well known for his numerous interpretations of Frederick the Great in both the silent and sound period.

Films (incomplete): Abend . . . Nacht . . . Morgen, Drei Nächte; Der Golem, wie er in die Welt kam; Das Floss der Toten, Mädchen aus der Ackerstrasse, Die Tänzerin Barberina, Flammende Völker, Sterbende Völker, Till Eulenspiegel, Fridericus Rex, Der Goldteufel, Gobsek; Mutter, Dein Kind ruft; Die Vergeltung, Wilhelm Tell, Ich hatt' einen Kameraden, Neuland, Die Perücke, Die eiserne Braut, Die Gesunkenen, Leidenschaft, . . . und es lockt ein Ruf aus sündiger Welt, In Treue stark, Die Mühle von Sanssouci, Die Sporckschen Jäger, Der alte Fritz, Die heilige Lüge, Waterloo, Die keusche Kokotte, Der Detektiv des Kaisers, Scapa Flow. Then sound: Das Flötenkonzert von

Sanssouci, Der Erlkönig, Die Tänzerin von Sanssouci, Der Choral von Leuthen, Fridericus, Nanon, Die barmherzige Lüge, Das schöne Fräulein Schragg, Bismarck, Casanova heiratet, Leidenschaft; Kopf hoch, Johannes; Viel Lärm um Nixi, Der grosse König, Immensee, Die goldene Spinne, Fritze Bollmann wollte angeln, Nacht ohne Abschied, Wenn der junge Wein blüht, Der Erbförster, Und über uns der Himmel, Anonyme Briefe, Der Bagnosträfling, Die Lüge; Tobias Knopp, Abenteuer eines Junggesellen (speaker); Melodie des Schicksals, Komplott auf Erlenhof, Unsterbliche Geliebte, Dr. Holl, Das ewige Spiel, Stips, Sensation in San Remo, Grün ist die Heide, Torreani, Wenn die Abendglocken läuten, Mein Herz darfst Du nicht fragen, Tausend rote Rosen blühn, Fritz und Friederike; Oh, du lieber Fridolin; Hab' Sonne im Herzen, Die blaue Stunde, Strassenserenade, Vati macht Dummheiten, Meines Vaters Pferde (ii), Die Gefangene des Maharadscha, Sauerbruch – Das war mein Leben, Rosen-Resli, Der Mann meines Lebens, Die blonde Frau des Maharadscha.

115 **GEORGE, HEINRICH** (1893-1946). B: Stettin. D: in a Soviet camp near Berlin. Actor. RN: Heinz Georg Schulz. 1912: plays in theatres in Kolberg, Bromberg, Dresden, Frankfurt, Vienna and Berlin (Deutsches Theater and Volksbühne). Director of the Schiller-Theater Berlin. Enters films in 1910. One of the greatest actors of his time in the German theatre and cinema.

Films (incomplete): *Der Andere, Kean, Der Roman der Christine von Herre, Das fränkische Lied, Der Graf im Pfluge, Lukrezia Borgia, Erdgeist, Der Mensch am Wege, Quarantäne, Steuerlos, Soll und Haben, Metropolis, Mirakel der Liebe, Das Panzergewölbe, Ueberflüssige Menschen, Die versunkene Flotte, Bigamie, Die Leibeigenen, Das Meer, Orientexpress, Die Dame mit der Maske, Kinder der Strasse, Das letzte Fort, Das letzte Souper, Der Mann mit dem Laubfrosch, Rutschbahn, Song, Manolescu, Sprengbagger 1010, Der Sträfling aus Stambul*. Then sound: *Der Andere, Dreyfus; Der Mann, der den Mord beging; 1914, die letzten Tage vor dem Weltbrand; Berlin – Alexanderplatz, Goethe lebt . . ., Reifende Jugend, Das Meer ruft, Schleppzug M 17* 33 (also directed), *Hitlerjunge*

Quex, Stützen der Gesellschaft, Das Mädchen Johanna, Das unsterbliche Herz, Die grosse und die kleine Welt, Stjenka Rasin, Wenn der Hahn kräht, Hermine und die sieben Aufrechten, Nacht der Verwandlung, Ball im Metropol, Der Biberpelz, Unternehmen Michael, Ein Volksfeind, Versprich mir nichts, Frau Sylvester, Heimat, Sensationsprozess Casilla, Der Postmeister, Friedrich Schiller, Jud Süss, Pedro soll hängen, Andreas Schlüter, Der grosse Schatten, Wien 1910, Schicksal, Hochzeit auf Bärenhof, Der Verteidiger hat das Wort, Die Degenhardts, Das Leben geht weiter, Frau über Bord, Dr. phil. Döderlein, Kolberg.*

116 **GERLACH, ARTHUR VON** (1860 or 1881-1925). Director. Worked mainly for the theatre. His two films belong to the genre of ghost stories, based on German legends of ghosts and spirits. One of the great unknown personalities of the German silent cinema.

Films: *Vanina oder die Galgenhochzeit* 22, *Zur Chronik von Grieshuus* 25.

117 **GERRON, KURT** (18 -1944). D: Auschwitz. Actor and director. RN: Kurt Gerson. Versatile comedian in many entertainment films. In early Thirties also directed. During Nazi period, Gerron was interned in the concentration camp Theresienstadt, where he directed under unknown circumstances a Nazi propaganda film *Der Führer schenkt den Juden eine Stadt*. When the film was completed, the entire crew and all the actors were sent to Auschwitz and killed. (A Czech film, *Transport z raje/Transport to Paradise* has been made of this incident by Zbynek Brynych.)

Films (incomplete): *Frau Sünde, Halbseide; O alte Burschenherrlichkeit, Varieté, Vorderhaus und Hinterhaus, Annemarie und ihr Ulan, Der Liebe Lust und Leid* 26 (also acted), *Die drei Mannequins, Der goldene Schmetterling, Die Kleine und ihr Kavalier, Mädchenhandel, Der Soldat der Marie, Eine tolle Nacht, Die Tragödie eines Verlorenen, Wien-Berlin, Benno Stehkragen, Die Dame mit dem Tigerfell, Dr. Bessels Verwandlung, Einbruch, Feme, Das Frauenhaus von Rio, Gefährdete Mädchen, Gehetzte Frauen, Glanz und Elend der Kurtisanen, Der grosse Unbekannte, Manege, Die Pflicht zu schwei-*

Kurt Gerron (right) being directed with Emil Jannings in DER BLAUE ENGEL, by Josef von Sternberg (at left)

gen; Ramper, der Tiermensch; Die schönsten Beine von Berlin, Ein schwerer Fall, Sein grösster Bluff, Ein Tag der Rosen im August . . . da hat die Garde fortgemusst, Das tanzende Wien, Der Ueberfall (short), Ueb' immer Treu und Redlichkeit, Die weisse Spinne, Wer wirft den ersten Stein, Casanovas Erbe, Heut tanzt Mariett, Die Jacht der sieben Sünden, Liebe und Diebe, Die Regimentstochter, Unmoral, Vom Täter fehlt jede Spur, Aufruhr im Junggesellenheim, Die Flucht vor der Liebe, Nachtgestalten, Tagebuch einer Verlorenen, Wir halten fest und treu zusammen. Then sound: Liebe im Ring, Der blaue Engel, Einbrecher, Die vom Rummelplatz, Die Drei von der Tankstelle, Die Marquise von Pompadour, Dolly macht Karriere, Vater geht auf Reisen, Salto Mortale, Bomben auf Monte Carlo, Man braucht kein Geld, Der Weg nach Rio, Ihre Majestät die Liebe, Eine Nacht im Grandhotel; Meine Frau, die Hochstaplerin 31 (only dir.), Zwei in einem Auto, Es wird schon wieder besser 32 (only dir.), Der weisse Dämon 32 (only dir.), Ein toller Einfall 32 (only dir.); Kind, ich freu' mich auf Dein Kommen 33 (only dir.), Heut' kommt's drauf an 33 (only dir.), Der Führer schenkt den Juden eine Stadt 44 (only dir., feature in documentary style shot in concentration camp Theresienstadt).

118 **GERT, VALESKA** (1900-   ). B: Berlin. Actress and dancer. RN: Gertrud Anderson, born Samosch, Stage training under Maria Moissi, then Kammerspiele Munich, Reinhardt-Theatres Berlin (q.v.). Expressionistic dancer in Germany and abroad. Later leader of cabaret the "Kohlkopp" (Berlin), the "Beggar Bar" (New York), the "Valeska" (Zurich), the "Hexenküche" (Berlin) and the "Ziegenstall" (Kam-

pen). Wrote two books: *Mein Weg* (1930) and *Die Bettlerbar in New York* (1950).

Films: *Ein Sommernachtstraum, Die freudlose Gasse, Nana, So ist das Leben, Alraune, Tagebuch einer Verlorenen.* Then sound: *Die Dreigroschenoper.*

119 **GESCHONNECK, ERWIN** (1906-). B: Berlin. Actor. Around 1930 he was performing in "Agitprop" groups. 1933: to U.S.S.R. 1939-1945: in concentration camp, survived sinking of the prisoner ship "Cap Arcona." After 1945: Kammerspiele Hamburg, then brought to the Berliner Ensemble by Brecht. Many films for DEFA (q.v.).

Films: *In jenen Tagen, Finale, Die letzte Nacht, Liebe 47, Hafenmelodie, Der Biberpelz, Das kalte Herz, Das Beil von Wandsbek, Schatten über den Inseln, Die Unbesiegbaren, Alarm im Zirkus, Der Hauptmann von Köln, Schlösser und Katen, Die Abenteuer des Till Ulenspiegel, Der Lotterieschwede, Die Geschichte vom armen Hassan, Die Sonnensucher, SAS 181 antwortet nicht, Musterknaben, Leute mit Flügeln, Fünf Patronenhülsen; Ach, du fröhliche; Nackt unter Wölfen, Karbid und Sauer-*

ampfer, Tiefe Furchen, Die Fahne von Kriwoj Rog, Geschichten jener Nacht (iv), Ein Lord am Alexanderplatz.

120 **GILLER, WALTER** (1927-). B: Recklinghausen. Actor. Studied medicine, then worked as electrician. Enters theatre as lighting technician (Kammerspiele Hamburg). Stage training under Eduard Marks. Married to Nadja Tiller (q.v.).

Films: *Artistenblut, Kein Engel ist so rein* (50), *Das Mädchen aus der Südsee, Insel ohne Moral, Die Frauen des Herrn S., Sensation in San Remo, Wildwest in Oberbayern, Primanerinnen, Falschmünzer am Werk, Der bunte Traum, Die Diebin von Bagdad, Liebe im Finanzamt, Der Tag vor der Hochzeit, Skandal im Mädchenpensionat, Südliche Nächte; Heimlich, still und leise; Fräulein Casanova, Irene in Nöten; Schlagerparade, Die tolle Lola, An jedem Finger zehn, Sie; Musik, Musik – und nur Musik; Schwedenmädel, Charleys Tante, Die Drei von der Tankstelle, Das Bad auf der Tenne, Ich und meine Schwiegersöhne, Spion für Deutschland, Nichts als Aerger mit der Liebe, Was die Schwalbe sang, Der Hauptmann von Köpenick, Das Sonntagskind, Schwarzwald-Melodie, Drei Mann auf einem Pferd, Der schräge Otto, Das Glück liegt auf der Strasse, Blaue Jungs, Die grosse Chance, Frühling in Berlin, Italienreise – Liebe inbegriffen, Zwei Herzen im Mai; Peter Voss, der Millionendieb; Geliebte Bestie, So angelt man keinen Mann, Rosen für den Staatsanwalt, Liebe auf krummen Beinen, Bobby Todd greift ein; Peter Voss, der Held des Tages; Kein Engel ist so rein* (60), *Ingeborg, Heldinnen, Geliebte Hochstaplerin, Affäre Nina B., Drei Mann in einem Boot, Zwei unter Millionen; Liebling, ich muss Dich erschiessen; Schneewittchen und die sieben Gaukler, Die Dreigroschenoper* (63), *Schloss Gripsholm, Das grosse Liebesspiel, Der Würger von Schloss Blackmoor, Die Tote von Beverly Hills, Der letzte Ritt nach Santa Cruz, Begegnung in Salzburg, Tonio Kröger, Fanny Hill, Heiss weht der Wind, DM-Killer; Pfeifen, Betten, Turteltauben; Ich suche einen Mann, Vergiss nicht Deine Frau zu küssen, Klassenkeile, Grimms Märchen von lüsternen Pärchen.*

121 GLIESE, ROCHUS (1891-   ). B: Berlin. Set designer and director. Studied painting and architecture. First known as "Ausstattungsmann" (all-round designer) to the newly opened Deutsches Künstler-Theater in Berlin (among other productions *Wilhelm Tell* by Schiller and Hauptmann and *Der zerbrochene Krug* by Kleist). 1913: meets Paul Wegener (q.v.), works for him for some time; but already in the silent period Gliese was active in the theatre and films. 1945: temporary director of Landestheater Potsdam. Also produced plays and designed for television.

Films: *Richard Hutter* (des.), *Eventrude, die Geschichte eines Abenteurers* 14 (co-dir., des.), *Der Golem* (co-scripted with R. A. Dietrich), *Rübezahls Hochzeit* 16 (co-dir., des., acted), *Der Rattenfänger von Hameln* 16 (co-dir., des.), *Der Yoghi* 16 (co-dir., des.), *Der Golem und die Tänzerin* 17 (co-dir., des.), *Der fremde Fürst* 18 (co-dir., des.), *Der Galeerensträfling* 19 (also des.), *Malaria* 19 (also des.), *Der Golem, wie er in die Welt kam* (co-scripted), *Der verlorene Schatten* 21 (co-dir., des.), *Alexandra* (des.), *Der brennender Acker, Herzog Ferrantes Ende* 22 (co-dir., des.), *Der Kampf ums Ich, Das Liebesnest, Die Austreibung, Brüder* 23 (prod., dir., co-scripted with Emil Kühne, also des?), *Mutter, Dein Kind ruft* (also des. sketches), *Die Finanzen des Grossherzogs* (co-scripted with Erich Czerwonski), *Komödie des Herzens* 24 (also co-scripted), *Die gefundene Braut* 25, *Der rosa Diamant* 25. Then sound: *Die Jagd nach dem Glück* 30 (also co-scripted and co-dir. with Reiniger and Karl Koch), *Hanna Amon* (co-dir. with Hans Berthel), *Ein Polterabend, Fidelio.*

122 GNASS, FRIEDRICH (1892-1958). B: Bochum. D: Berlin. Actor. At first trained as a locksmith, then stage training at actors school in Hamburg (with Madeleine Lüders). Soldier. Since 1924: Kammerspiele Hamburg, then Landes-Theater Beuthen, Volksbühne and Piscator-Bühne Berlin. Since 1949: member of the Berliner Ensemble and work for DEFA (q.v.).

Films (incomplete): *Jenseits der Strasse, Mutter Krausens Fahrt ins Glück.* Then sound: *Troika, M. Fra Diavolo; Luise, Königin von Preussen; Danton, F.P. 1 antwortet nicht, Rasputin, Ich bei Tag und Du bei Nacht, Razzia in St. Pauli, Morgenrot, Flüchtlinge, Stern von Valencia, Achtung! Wer kennt diese Frau, Abenteuer eines jungen Herrn in Polen, Hundert Tage, Blutsbrüder, Pour le mérite, Nordlicht, Capriccio, Kautschuk, Sergeant Berry, Geheimzeichen LB 17, Fahrendes Volk, Legion Condor, Aufruhr in Damaskus, Wozzek, Der Biberpelz, Die Buntkarierten, Unser täglich Brot, Familie Benthin, Der Untertan, Roman einer jungen Ehe, Das verurteilte Dorf, Schatten über den Inseln, Frauenschicksale, Die Geschichte vom kleinen Muck, Anna Susanna, Leuchtfeuer, Einmal ist keinmal, Wer seine Frau lieb hat, Tinko, Gejagt bis zum Morgen, Madeleine und der Legionär.*

123 GOETZKE, BERNHARD (1884-1964). B: Danzig. D: Berlin. Actor. Acted for many years on the Berlin stage and was well known for his film work, especially in collaboration with Fritz Lang (q.v.) who probably ensured that Goetzke was offered the best roles. After 1945: acted at Schlosspark- and Schiller-Theater.

Films (incomplete): *Veritas vincit, Madame Dubarry, Die Brüder Karamasoff, Das Geheimnis von Bombay, Mord ohne Töter, Opfer der Keuschheit, Der Schädel der Pharaonentochter, Die Toteninsel, Tschetschensen-Rache, Aus dem Schwarzbuch eines Polizeikommissars (ii), Die Jagd nach dem Tode, Der müde Tod, Das indische Grabmal, Das Weib des Pharao, Dr. Mabuse der Spieler, Peter der Grosse, Vanina oder die Galgenhochzeit, Dekameron-Nächte, Die Nibelungen; Briefe, die ihn nicht erreichten; Die Prinzessin und der Geiger, Die Verrufenen, Zapfenstreich, Zwei und die Dame, Der Bergadler, Die Unehelichen, Die versunkene Flotte, Feme, Das gefährliche Alter, Der Gefangene von Shanghai, Schuldig, Die Sache mit Schorrsiegel, Der Schöpfer, Der Staatsanwalt klagt an, Die Tragödie im Zirkus Royal, Frühlings Erwachen, Die Todesfahrt im Weltrekord.* Then sound: *Dreyfus, Stürmisch die Nacht, Alraune, Zwischen Nacht und Morgen, Schachmatt, Arme kleine Eva; 1914, die letzten Tage vor dem Weltbrand; Die Koffer des Herrn O.F., Nachtkolonne; Luise, Königin von Preussen; Geheimnis des blauen Zimmers, Theodor Körner, Kampf um die Frau, Teilnehmer antwortet nicht, Rasputin, Der schwarze*

Husar, *Einmal möcht' ich keine Sorgen haben*, *Die elf Schill'schen Offiziere*, *Die Tänzerin von Sanssouci*, *Der tolle Bomberg*, *Der verliebte Blasekopp*, *Schüsse an der Grenze*, *K 1 greift ein*, *Moral und Liebe*, *Polizeiakte 909*, *Das alte Recht*, *Abenteuer eines jungen Herrn in Polen*, *Viktoria*, *Eskapade*, *Der Kurier des Zaren*, *Fridericus*, *Robert Koch*, *Ballhaus goldener Engel*, *Salonwagen E 417*, *Die gute Sieben*, *Die 3 Codonas*, *Zwischen Hamburg und Haiti*, *Jud Süss*, *Der Fuchs von Glenarvon*, *Bismarck*, *Ich klage an*, *Tanz mit dem Kaiser*, *Die schwedische Nachtigall*, *Der grosse König*, *Paracelsus*, *Münchhausen*, *Der Majoratsherr*, *Das war mein Leben*, *Das kalte Herz*.

124 GOTTSCHALK, JOACHIM (1904-1941). B: Calau/Niederlausitz. D: Berlin. Actor. At first seaman. Then trained as an actor under Professor Ferdinand Gregori in Berlin. Theatres: Württembergische Landesbühne Stuttgart, Zwickau, Kolberg, Leipzig, Frankfurt, Volksbühne Berlin. The story of the Gottschalks, and in particular his committing suicide with his Jewish wife during the Nazi period, is told in *Marriage in the Shadows*, which is loosely based on facts.

Films: *Du und Ich*, *Flucht ins Dunkel*, *Aufruhr in Damaskus*, *Eine Frau wie Du*, *Das Mädchen von Fanö*, *Ein Leben lang*, *Die schwedische Nachtigall*.

125 GRABBERT, GÜNTHER (1931-). B: Schwerin. Actor. Trained at the Theatre Institute of Weimar. Then performs on stage at Altenburg. 1957: to Leipzig. Winner of state award in 1966.

Films: *Der Teufelskreis*, *Im Sonderauftrag*, *Einer von uns*, *Der Fremde*, *Professor Mamlock*, *Aerzte*, *Beschreibung eines Sommers*, *Der geteilte Himmel*, *Das Mädchen auf dem Brett*.

126 GRAF, ROBERT (1923-1966). B: Witten. D: Munich. Actor. At first studied philosophy and theatre science. Stage training, then theatres in Straubing, Wiesbaden and Salzburg. Since 1951: Kammerspiele Munich. Very versatile actor, also worked for TV, radio and dubbed films.

Films: *Bekenntnisse des Hochstaplers Felix Krull*, *El Hakim*, *Jonas*, *Wir Wunderkinder*, *Das schöne Abenteuer*, . . . *und das*

am Montagmorgen, *Buddenbrooks*, *Lampenfieber*, *Eine Frau am dunklen Fenster*, *Gauner in Uniform*, *Liebling der Götter*, *Mein Schulfreund*, *Der Fälscher von London*, *Mörderspiel*, *Die glücklichen Jahre der Thorwalds*, *Wenn beide schuldig werden*, *Zwei Whisky und ein Sofa*, *Frühstück mit dem Tod*, *Verdammt zur Sünde*, *Vorsicht*, *Mister Dodd*, *2 mal 2 im Himmelbett*.

127 GRANACH, ALEXANDER (JESSAJA) (1890-1949). B: Werbowitz. D: New York (after an operation). Actor. Much used in films as well as on stage. A significant actor at the Volksbühne Berlin (under Piscator). 1933: to U.S.A.

Films (incomplete): *Lukrezia Borgia*, *Nosferatu – eine Symphonie des Grauens*, *Erdgeist*, *I.N.R.I.*, *Der Mensch am Wege*, *Paganini*, *Schatten*, *Ein Weib, ein Tier, ein Diamant*, *Die Radio-Heirat*, *Ein Sommernachtstraum*, *Qualen der Nacht*, *Die berühmte Frau*, *Ich hatte einst ein schönes Vaterland*, *Svengali*, *Das letzte Fort*, *Flucht in die Fremdenlegion*, *Grosstadtschmetterling*, *Kampf ums Leben*. Then sound: *Die letzte Kompanie*, *Kameradschaft*, *Danton*, *Der Raub der Mona Lisa*; *1914, die letzten Tage vor dem Weltbrand*; *Kämpfer*.

128 GROTHE, FRANZ (1908-). B: Berlin. Composer. Musical training at the Music High School in Berlin under Hermann Dies, Walter Gmeindl, Cl. Schalstich and others). Pianist. 1940-1945: conductor of the German dance orchestra for Berlin Radio. Prolific composer of film scores.

Films: *Tingel-Tangel* (in collab. with Austin Egen), *Boykott* (in collab. with Alexander Laszlo), *Komm' zu mir zum Rendezvous* (in collab. with Eduard Künneke and Artur Guttmann), *Der ungetreue Eckehart*, *Arme kleine Eva*, *Die grosse Attraktion* (in collab. with Franz Lehar, Dessau and Kaper), *Das Geheimnis der roten Katzte*, *Der grosse Bluff*, *Eine von uns*, *Die Herren vom Maxim* (in collab. with Oscar Straus), *Das Schloss im Süden*, *Und wer küsst mich?*, *Keine Angst vor Liebe*; *Sag' mir, wer Du bist*; *Salon Dora Green*, *Walzerkrieg* (in collab.), *Moral und Liebe* (in collab. with Alfred Strasser), *Zwei im Sonnenschein*, *Ihr grösster Erfolg*, *So endete eine Liebe*, *Aufforderung zum Tanz* (in collab. with Kurt

Stiebitz), *Zwischen zwei Herzen; Peter, Paul und Nanette; Es tut sich was um Mitternacht, Ich kenn' Dich nicht und liebe Dich, Fräulein Frau, Heinz im Mond, Verlieb' Dich nicht am Bodensee, Die lustigen Weiber* (in collab. with Ernst Fischer), *Der Ammenkönig, Winternachtstraum, Die blonde Carmen, Die Liebe des Maharadscha, Wo die Lerche singt* (in collab. with Franz Lehar and Paul Hühm), *Die Entführung, Pat und Patachon im Paradies* (in collab. with Paul Hühn), *Das Schloss in Flandern, Diskretion – Ehrensache, Rote Orchideen, Napoleon ist an allem schuld, Geheimzeichen LB 17, Die fromme Lüge, Immer wenn ich glücklich bin, Ehe in Dosen, Ins blaue Leben* (in collab. with C. D' Anzi and Alessandro Cicognini), *Alarm auf Station III, Der Vorhang fällt, Das Abenteuer geht weiter, Der singende Tor* (in collab. with Franco Casavola, Ernesto de Curtis and Riccardo Zandonai), *Rosen in Tirol, Achtung! Feind hört mit!, Rote Mühle, Illusion, Tanz mit dem Kaiser, Frauen sind dich bessere Diplomaten, Hab' mich lieb, Die schwedische Nachtigall, Der Strom, Liebespremiere, Der ewige Klang, Ein Walzer mit Dir, Jan und die Schwindlerin, Aufruhr der Herzen, Spiel, Rätsel der Nacht, Eines Tages; Leb' wohl, Christina; Derby, Hafenmelodie, Kätchen für alles, Man spielt nicht mit der Liebe, Nichts als Zufälle, Frauenarzt Dr. Prätorius, Geliebter Lügner, Absender unbekannt, Die wunderschöne Galathee, Seitensprünge im Schnee, Vom Teufel gejagt, Opfer des Herzens, Taxi-Kitty, Fanfaren der Liebe, Das Haus in Montevideo, Der blaue Stern des Südens* (in collab. with Hans Martin), *Vater braucht eine Frau, Skandal im Mädchenpensionat, Die blaue Stunde, Muss man sich gleich scheiden lassen?, Man nennt es Liebe, Musik bei Nacht, Hokuspokus, Ave Maria, Fanfaren der Ehe, Sterne über Colombo, Die Gefangene des Maharadscha, Hannerl* (in collab. with Josef Bayer, Schmidt-Gentner, Anton Profes, and Friedrich Schröder), *Bildnis einer Unbekannten, Feuerwerk* (adapt., cond.), *Begegnung in Rom* (in collab. with Luigi Malatesta), *Verrat an Deutschland, An der schönen blauen Donau, Rosen im Herbst, Drei Mädels vom Rhein, Ich denke oft an Piroschka, Mädchen ohne Grenzen, Die wilde Auguste, Wenn wir alle Engel wären, Die Trapp-Familie, Kleines*

Zelt und grosse Liebe, Franziska, Die Lindenwir – in vom Donaustrand, Salzburger Geschichten, Die Heilige und ihr Narr, Ein Stück vom Himmel, Königin Luise; Junger Mann, der alles kann; Bühne frei für Marika, Mein ganzes Herz ist voll Musik (in collab. with Josef Niessen), *Hoch klingt der Radetzky-Marsch, Wir Wunderkinder, Die Trapp-Familie in Amerika, Der schwarze Blitz, Helden, Rendezvous in Wien* (in collab. with Heinz Neubrand), *Liebe auf krummen Beinen, 12 Mädchen und ein Mann; Der Engel, der seine Harfe versetzte; Jacqueline, Die schöne Lügnerin, Das schöne Abenteuer, Alt-Heidelberg, Ein Mann geht durch die Wand; Ein Tag, der nie zu Ende geht; Lampenfieber; Mein ganzes Herz ist voll Musik* (in collab. with Josef Niessen), *Eine Frau fürs ganze Leben, Heldinnen, Der letzte Fussgänger, Liebling der Götter, Im 6. Stock; Die Stunde, die Du glücklich bist; Zwei unter Millionen, Die blonde Frau des Maharadscha, Meine Tochter und ich, Wochentags immer; Heirate mich, Chéri; Vorsicht; Mister Dodd; Dr. med. Hiob Praetorius, Heidi, Hokuspokus – oder wie lasse ich meinen Mann verschwinden, Liselotte von der Pfalz, Herrliche Zeiten im Spessart.*

129 **GRÜNDGENS, GUSTAF** (1899-1963). B: Düsseldorf. D: Manila. Actor and director. Trained at Actor's school Schauspielhaus Düsseldorf. Theatres: Halberstadt, Berlin (with Max Reinhardt, q.v.). 1931: Director and head of Staatliches Schauspielhaus Berlin. 1937-1945: General director of Preussisches Staatstheater Berlin. 1945: works at Deutsches Theater Berlin. 1947: General director at Schauspielhaus Düsseldorf. 1955: same post at Deutsches Schauspielhaus Hamburg. Outstanding figure of the German stage whose film roles were rather limited. Gründgens was married to Erika Mann (daughter of author Thomas Mann) and to actress Marianne Hoope.

Films: *Va banque, Brand in der Oper, Danton, M; Luise, Königin von Preussen; Yorck, Der Raub der Mona Lisa, Teilnehmer antwortet nicht, Die Gräfin von Monte Christo, Eine Stadt steht Kopf 32* (only dir.), *Liebelei, Ich glaub' nie mehr an eine Frau, Hokuspokus, Der Tunnel, Die schönen Tage von Aranjuez, Das Erbe von Pretoria, Schwarzer Jäger Johanna, So endete eine*

Liebe, Die Finanzen des Grossherzogs 34 (only dir.), *Pygmalion, Das Mädchen Johanna, Hundert Tage, Eine Frau ohne Bedeutung, Capriolen* 37 (also dir.), *Tanz auf dem Vulkan, Der Schritt vom Wege* 39 (only dir.), *Zwei Welten* 40 (only dir.), *Friedemann Bach, Ohm Krüger, Ein Glas Wasser, Faust* 60 (co-dir. with Peter Gorski, acted.).

130 **GRUNE, KARL** (1890-1962). B: Vienna. D: Bournemouth. Director. Trained as an actor in Vienna, and performs on stage there and later in Berlin, Director of the Residenttheater. 1918: enters cinema thanks to the producer Max Schach; usually co-producer of his own films during the silent period. 1931: to France. 1932: to England, where he became artistic director of "Capitol Film Corporation." Spent his last years in Bournemouth.

Films (incomplete):*Aus eines Mannes Mädchenjahren* (co-scripted with Beate Schoch), *Der Mädchenhirt* 19, *Menschen in Ketten* 19 (co-dir. with Friedrich Zelnik), *Die Jagd nach der Wahrheit* 20, *Nachtbesuch* 20, *Nacht ohne Morgen* 20, *Mann über Bord* 21, *Der Eroberer* 22, *Frauenopfer* 22, *Der Graf von Charolais* 22, *Die Nacht der Medici* 22 (?), *Der stärkste Trieb* 22, *Schlagende Wetter* 23, *Die Strasse* 23 (also co-scripted with Julius Urgiss), *Arabella* 24, *Komödianten* 24, *Eifersucht* 25, *Die Brüder Schellenberg* 26 (also co-scripted with Willy Haas), *Am Rande der Welt* 27 (also co-scripted with Hans Brennert), *Königin Luise* 27, *Marquis d'Eon, der Spion der Pompadour* 28, *Waterloo* 28, *Katherina Knie* 29. Then sound: *Das gelbe Haus des King-Fu* 31.

131 **HAACK, KÄTHE** (1892-   ). B: Berlin. Actress. 1908: already on stage in Frankfurt and Berlin (Lessing-Theater and Künstler-Theater). Enters cinema in 1918.

Films (incomplete): *Die Stricknadeln, Die Hochzeit im Excentricclub, Baccarat; Der Weg, der in die Verdammnis führt; Föhn, Die Spieler, Am Webstuhl der Zeit; Arme, kleine Eva; Die Diktatur der Liebe, Die Dame und der Landstreicher, Freund Ripp, Jugend, Das Liebesnest, Die Schuhe einer schönen Frau, Die brennende Kugel, Das Kind des Andern, Wilhelm Tell, Hedda Gabler, Lebende Buddhas, Mein Leopold, Heiratsschwindler; Kubinke, der Barbier, und die drei Dienstmädchen; Menschen untereinander, Schwester Veronika, Die Unehelichen, Die versunkene Flotte, Der alte Fritz, Bennos Stehkragen, Irrwege der Liebe, Unter der Laterne, Detektiv des Kaisers.* Then sound: *Skandal um Eva, Alraune, Der Hauptmann von Köpenick, Emil und die Detektive, Nachtkolonne, Dann schon lieber Lebertran, Berlin – Alexanderplatz, Quick, Das schöne Abenteuer, Tannenberg, Die Herren vom Maxim, Liebe muss verstanden sein, Der Traum vom Rhein, Zwei glückliche Tage, Hanneles Himmelfahrt, Wilhelm Tell, Konjunkturritter, Der Meisterboxer, Der schwarze Walfisch, Ich heirate meine Frau, Herz ist Trumpf, Die vier Musketiere, Der Polizeibericht meldet, Hermine und die sieben Aufrechten, Die törichte Jungfrau, Wunder des Fliegens, Ein falscher Fuffziger, Pygmalion, Familie Schimek, Hans im Glück; Donner, Blitz und Sonnenschein; Geheimnis eines alten Hauses, Fridericus, Eine Frau ohne Bedeutung, Familienparade, Schloss Vogelöd, Der Herrscher, Urlaub auf Ehrenwort, Krach und Glück bei Künnemann, Rätsel um Beate, Steputat & Co., Das Ehesanatorium; Kleiner Mann, ganz gross; Der Tag nach der Scheidung, Der Fall Deruga, Der Schritt vom Wege, Verdacht auf Ursula, Dein Leben gehört mir, Der Stammbaum des Dr. Pistorius, Die gute Sieben, Bismarck, Bal paré, Heimaterde, Sechs Tage Heimaturlaub, Das himmelblaue Abendkleid, Annelie, Zweiin einer grossen Stadt, Liebesbriefe, Wildvogel, Münchhausen, Sophienlund, Seinerzeit zu meiner Zeit, Das Konzert, Meine vier Jungens, Eine alltägliche Geschichte, Dr. phil. Döderlein, Ruf an das Gewissen, Und finden dereinst wir uns wieder, Der grosse Mandarin, Anonyme Briefe, Der Biberpelz, Nachtwache, Gefährliche Gäste, Absender unbekannt, Gabriela, Das Mädchen aus der Südsee, Opfer des Herzens, Die verschleierte Maja, Königin einer Nacht, Wenn die Abendglocken läuten, Mein Freund der Dieb, Herz der Welt, Das Bankett der Schmuggler, Der Fürst von Pappenheim, Heimweh nach Dir, Der Tag vor der Hochzeit, Lockende Sterne, Ich warte auf Dich, Von der Liebe reden wir später, Die vertagte Hochzeitsnacht, Alles für Papa, Die tolle Lola, Rosen-Resli, Heimweh nach*

Deutschland, Die 7 Kleider der Katrin, Feuerwerk, Die Mücke, Schützenliesl, Der letzte Sommer, Heideschulmeister Uwe Karsten, Der Himmel ist nie ausverkauft, Eine Frau genügt nicht? Das Schweigen im Walde, Studentin Helen Willfüer, Auf Wiedersehen am Bodensee, Die Stimme der Sehnsucht, . . . wie einst Lili Marlen, Jede Nacht in einem andern Bett, Die grosse Chance, Das Leben geht weiter, Schwarze Nylons – heisse Nächte; Liebe, Luft und lauter Lügen; Bezaubernde Arabella, Zarte Haut in schwarzer Seide.

132 HAAS, DOLLY (1911-   ). B: Hamburg. Actress. At the age of six attends ballet school in Hamburg. Thanks to Max Pallenberg (q.v.) brought to Erik Charell (q.v.) and appeared in the "Nelson Revue" and in "Larifari". Much revered actress in the early Thirties, who was later also given roles in English films.

Films: *Eine Stunde Glück, Dolly macht Karriere, Der Ball, Liebeskommando, Der brave Sünder; Scampolo, ein Kind der Strasse; So ein Mädel vergisst man nicht, Ein steinreicher Mann, Es wird schon wieder besser, Kleines Mädel – grosses Glück, Grosstadtnacht, Das hässliche Mädchen, Die kleine Schwindlerin, Der Page vom Dalmasse-Hotel, Es tut sich was um Mitternacht, Warum lügt Fräulein Käthe?*

133 HAID, LIANE (1895-   ). B: Vienna. Actress. At first dancer, then appears on stage in Vienna, Budapest and Berlin. A discovery for the "Erste Wiener Kunstfilmgesellschaft" where she played in eighteen films. Now living in Marly/Fribourg, Switzerland.

Films (incomplete): *Mit Herz und Hand fürs Vaterland, Auf der Höhe, Die Landstreicher, Mit Gott für Kaiser und Reich, Sommeridylle, Die Tragödie auf Schloss Rottersheim, Lebenswogen, Mir kommt keiner aus, Der Schandfleck, Der Verschwender, Der Doppelselbstmord, Der König amüsiert sich, So fallen die Lose des Lebens, Die Ahnfrau, Doktor Ruhland, Durch Wahrheit zum Narren, Eva, die Sünde, Freut euch des Lebens, Der Herr des Lebens. Der Laiermann, Lasset die Kleinen zu mir kommen. Die Stimme des Gewissens, Der tanzende Tod, Verschneit, Die Filme der Prinzessin*

Fantoche, Die Frau in Weiss, Das Geheimnis Lord Percivals, Der Roman eines Dienstmädchens, Sein Lebenslicht, Das Geld auf der Strasse, Lady Hamilton, Lukrezia Borgia, Der Pantoffelheld, Die Tochter des Brigadiers, Schlagende Wetter, Ich liebe Dich, Die Insel der Träume, Liebesfeuer, Als ich wiederkam, Die Brüder Schellenberg, Der fesche Erzherzog, Im weissen Rössl, Der Provinzonkel, Der Sohn des Hannibal, Die Czardasfürstin, Die Dollarprinzessin und ihre sechs Freier, Der goldene Abgrund, Der letzte Walzer, Die weisse Sklavin, Die Dame in Schwarz, Die Königin seines Herzens; Marquis d'Eon, der Spion der Pompadour; Schiff in Not SOS, Der Weiberkrieg, Zwei rote Rosen, Schwarzwaldmädel, Spiel um den Mann. Then sound: Die grosse Sehnsucht, Das Lied ist aus, Der unsterbliche Lump, Zweimal Hochzeit, Madame hat Ausgang, Die Männer um Lucie, Schatten der Manege, Meine Cousine aus Warschau, Grock, Kaiserliebchen, Opernredoute, Der Prinz von Arkadien, Kaiserwalzer, Der Diamant des Zaren; Ich will nicht wissen, wer Du bist; Stern von Valencia, Eine Frau wie Du; Sag' mir, wer Du bist; Ihre Durchlaucht, die Verkäuferin; Madame wünscht keine Kinder, Roman einer Nacht, Keine Angst vor Liebe, Das Schloss im Süden, Besuch am Abend, Polizeiakte 909, Bei der blonden Kathrein, Die Fahrt in die Jugend, Tanzmusik, Ungeküsst soll man nicht schlafen geh'n, Peter im Schnee, Die unvollkommene Liebe, Die fünf Karnickel.

134 HAMEISTER, WILLY (18 -193). Director of photography. A versatile cameraman of the silent period, recognised as a very good technician, but lacking creative ability.

Films (incomplete): *Der Flug zur Westgrenze, Titanic, Das Kabinett des Dr. Caligari, Die Pest in Florenz* (co-phot. with Emil Schünemann and Hoffmann), *Totentanz; Der Weg, der in die Verdammnis führt; Das Blut der Ahnen, Genuine, Die Beute der Erinnyen, Die Hintertreppe* (co-phot.), *Peter der Grosse* (co-phot.), *Der schwarze Montag, Tingel-Tangel, Im Schatten der Moschee* (co-phot. with Kurt Grosstück), *Der Mensch am Wege, Der Puppenmacher von Kiang-Ning, Armes kleines*

Mädchen, Die Kleine vom Bummel, Leidenschaft (co-phot. with Erich Grimmler), *Liebe und Trompetenblasen, Der tanzende Tod, Das Geheimnis von St. Pauli, Herbstmanöver* (co-phot. with Friedrich Weinmann), *Der lachende Ehemann, Prinzessin Tralala, Schützenliesl, Wie bleibe ich jung und schön, Der Bettler vom Kölner Dom, Die Dollarprinzessin und ihre sechs Freier, Faschingszauber, Leichte Kavallerie* (co-phot. with Schünemann and Werner Bohne), *Rinaldo Rinaldini* (co-phot. with Edoardo Lamberti), *Ein schwerer Fall, Charlott etwas verrückt, Die drei Frauen von Urban Hell, G'schichten aus dem Wienerwald, Das Karussell des Todes, Mikosch rückt ein, Aufruhr im Junggesellenheim, Die Frau ohne Nerven* (co-phot. with Nietzschmann), *Polizeispionin 77* (co-phot. with Nietzschmann), *Wir halten fest und treu zusammen, Wer hat Robby gesehen?* Then sound: *Nur Du, Susanne macht Ordnung* (co-phot. with Werner Bohne), *Aschermittwoch, Zu Befehl, Herr Unteroffizier, Zwei himmelblaue Augen, Der Schrecken der Garnison* (co-phot. with Hans Gottschalk), *Der schönste Mann im Staate* (co-phot. with Gottschalk), *Dienst ist Dienst* (co-phot. with Gottschalk), *Arme kleine Eva, Vater geht auf Reisen* (co-phot. with Gottschalk), *Schneider Wibbel, Keine Feier ohne Meyer* (co-phot. with Gottschalk), *Liebe in Uniform, Tod über Shanghai; Annemarie, die Braut der Kompanie; Der verliebte Blasekopp, Ballhaus goldener Engel, Aus einer kleinen Residenz, Das lustige Kleeblatt, Zimmermädchen ... dreimal klingeln, K 1 greift ein, Der Kampf um den Bär, Die Unschuld vom Lande, Höllentempo* (co-phot. with Hugo von Kaweczynski and Bohne), *Heimat am Rhein, Die kalte Mamsell, Gretel zieht das grosse Los, Krach im Forsthaus, In Sachen Timpe, Pipin der Kurze, Mädchen in Weiss, Fest der Schönheit, Fest der Völker.*

Der Leidensweg der Inge Krafft (only idea), *Das wandernde Bild, Die Frauen von Gnadenstein* (co-scripted), *Der müde Tod* (co-scripted), *Das indische Grabmal* (co-scripted), *Der brennende Acker* (co-scripted with Willy Haas and Arthur Rosen), *Dr. Mabuse der Spieler* (co-scripted), *König Artus Tafelrunde* (co-scripted), *Phantom* (co-scripted), *Die Austreibung, Die Prinzessin Suwarin, Der steinerne Reiter* (only idea), *Die Finanzen des Grossherzogs, Michael* (co-scripted with Carl Theodor Dreyer), *Die Nibelungen, Zur Chronik von Grieshuus, Metropolis, Spione, Die Frau im Mond.* Then sound: *M, Das erste Recht des Kindes, Der Läufer von Marathon, Das Testament des Dr. Mabuse, Elisabeth und der Narr 33* (only dir.), *Prinzessin Tourandot, Was bin ich ohne Dich* (co-scripted with Carl Echtermayer), *Hanneles Himmelfahrt 34* (also dir.), *Der alte und der junge König* (co-scripted with Rolf Lauckner), *Ein idealer Gatte, Ich war Jack Mortimer* (co-scripted), *Der Mann mit der Pranke, Eine Frau ohne Bedeutung* (co-scripted with Bernd Hofmann), *Eskapade* (co-scripted with Rolf Meyer and C. and T. Echtermeyer), *Die unmögliche Frau, Der Herrscher* (co-scripted), *Versprich mir nichts* (co-scripted with Hofmann), *Der zerbrochene Krug, Mutterlied* (co-scripted with Hofmann), *Jugend, Verwehte Spuren* (co-scripted with Felix Lützkendorf and Harlan), *Die Frau am Scheidewege, Hurra! Ich bin Papa!; Wie konntest Du, Veronika?; Lauter Liebe* (co-scripted with Egbert von Putten), *Annelie, Am Abend auf der Heide, Mit den Augen einer Frau* (co-scripted with Karl Georg Külb), *Gefährtin meines Sommers, Die Gattin, Eine Frau für 3 Tage, Fahrt ins Glück, Via mala, Erzieherin gesucht, Es kommt ein Tag* (co-scripted with Hans Abich, Thiele, Ernst Penzolt and Fritz Grashoff), *Dr. Holl, Dein Herz ist meine Heimat.*

135 HARBOU, THEA VON (1888-1954). B. and D: Berlin. Scriptwriter, writer and director. Well known for her scripts for Lang (q.v.) to whom she was married 1924-1933. Earlier married to Rudolf Klein-Rogge (q.v.). Nazi. Successful writer from 1914 onwards with several books to her credit. Also directed films.

Films (incomplete): *Die heilige Simplizia,*

136 HARELL, MARTE (1919 or 1907 or 1915-   ). B: Vienna. Actress. RN: Martha Schömig. Theatres: Theater in der Josefstadt Vienna, Munich, Breslau, Berlin. After 1945: stage work at the Innsbruck and Bregenz Festivals.

Films: *Opernball, Rosen in Tirol, Dreimal Hochzeit, Wiener G'schichten, Traummusik, Brüderlein fein, Die heimliche Grä-*

fin, *Tolle Nacht, Frauen sind keine Engel, Der dunkle Tag, Romantische Brautfahrt, Schrammeln, Die tolle Susanne, Die Fledermaus, Umwege zu Dir, Glaube an mich, Nach dem Sturm, Erzherzog Johanns grosse Liebe, Wiener Walzer, Du bist die Rose vom Wörthersee, Liebeskrieg nach Noten, Spionage, Der Kongress tanzt, Im Prater blühn wieder die Bäume, Otto ist auf Frauen scharf, Begegnung in Salzburg, Die grosse Kür.*

137 **HARLAN, VEIT** (1899-1964). B: Berlin. D: Capri. Director and actor. Son of writer and literary manager Walter Harlan. Theatrical work in Berlin (especially with Reinhardt, q.v.). Also sculptor and photographer. Married to Hilde Körber and Kristina Söderbaum (both q.v.), the latter he featured in most of his films. When he first entered cinema he acted in certain films, and then in 1934 he turned to direction. An ambivalent figure somewhat notorious for his anti-semitic and pro-Nazi films. Wrote *Im Schatten meiner Filme,* published in 1966.

Films: *Eins plus Eins gleich Drei, Die Hose, Das Mädchen mit den fünf Nullen, Der Meister von Nürnberg, Es flüstert die*

Nacht . . ., Revolte im Erziehungshaus Somnambul. Then sound: *Die unsichtbare Front, Friederike, Die elf Schill'schen Offiziere, Hilfe! Ueberfall!, Yorck, Gefahren der Liebe, Flüchtlinge, Der Choral von Leuthen, Polizeiakte 909; Nur nicht weich werden, Susanne!; Das Mädchen Johanna, Mein Leben für Maria Isabell, Der rote Reiter, Stradivari, Ein kleines Mädchen mit Prokura, Der Fall Brenken.* Films directed: *Krach im Hinterhaus* 35, *Die Pompadour* 35 (ass. dir. and dir. of dialogue, also co-scripted with H. W. Becker), *Der müde Theodor* 36, *Kater Lampe* 36, *Alles für Veronika, Maria, die Magd* 36 (also co-script), *Mein Sohn, der Herr Minister* 37, *Die Kreutzersonate* 37, *Der Herrscher* 37, *Jugend* 38, *Verwehte Spuren* 38 (also co-scripted with von Harbou and Felix Lützkendorf), *Dei Reise nach Tilsit* 39 (also co-script), *Das unsterbliche Herz* 39 (also co-scripted with Werner Eplinius), *Jud Süss* 40 (also co-scripted with Ludwig Metzger and Eberhard Wolfgang Möller), *Pedro soll hängen* 41 (also co-scripted with Ludwig Hynitzsch and Friedel Hartlaub), *Die goldene Stadt* 42 (also co-scripted with Alfred Braun), *Der grosse König* 42 (also script), *Immensee* 43 (also co-scripted with Alfred Braun), *Opfergang* 44 (also co-scripted with Alfred Braun), *Kolberg* 45 (also co-scripted with Alfred Braun), *Der Puppenspieler* (only co-script with Alfred Braun), *Zwischen Nacht und Morgen* (only co-scripted with Alfred Braun), *Unsterbliche Geliebte* 50 (also script), *Hanna Amon* 51 (also script), *Die blaue Stunde* 53 (also script), *Sterne über Colombo* 54, *Die Gefangene des Maharadscha,* 54, *Verrat an Deutschland* 55 (also co-scripted with Thomas Harlan), *Anders als Du und ich* 57, *Liebe kann wie Gift sein* 58, *Ich werde Dich auf Händen tragen* 58 (also co-scripted with Guido Fürst), *Die blonde Frau des Maharadscha* 62.

138 **HARTMANN, PAUL** (1889-   ). B: Nuremberg. Actor. Theatres: Berlin, Stettin, Zurich, Vienna, Staatliches Schauspielhaus Berlin. After 1945: makes many guest appearances in Germany and at the Burgtheater in Vienna.

Films (incomplete): *Richard Hutter, Das dreizehnte Kreuz, Die reine Sünderin, Der Galeerensträfling, Maria Magdalena, Monika Vogelsang, Anna Boleyn, Gefesselte*

Menschen, Hochstapler, Der Roman der Christine von Herre, Schloss Vogelöd, Die Tänzerin Barberina, Der falsche Dimitri, Der Fluch der Vergangenheit, Herzog Ferrantes Ende, Luise Millerin, Kinder der Zeit, Der Pantoffelheld, Vanina oder die Galgenhochzeit, Alt-Heidelberg, Der Evangelimann, Tatjana, Der verlorene Schuh, Götz von Berlichingen zubenannt mit der eisernen Hand, Des Lebens Würfelspiel, Unser täglich Bot, Zur Chronik von Grieshuus, Der Rosenkavalier, Tingel-Tangel. Then sound: *F.P. 1 antwortet nicht, Salon Dora Green, Unsichtbare Gegner, Der Tunnel, Der Läufer von Marathon, Grossfürstin Alexandra, Schwarzer Jäger Johanna, Das Erbe von Pretoria, Alles um eine Frau, Mazurka, Die klugen Frauen, Port Arthur, Stärker als Paragraphen, Das Schloss in Flandern, Togger, Die Warschauer Zitadelle, Revolutionshochzeit, Mit versiegelter Order, Dreiklang, Pour le mérite, Der Schritt vom Wege, Legion Condor, Irrtum des Herzens, Bismarck, Bal paré, Ich klage an, Ueber alles in der Welt, Gefährtin meines Sommers, Die Affäre Roedern, Die Dame in Schwarz, Das Tor zum Frieden; Mönche, Mädchen und Panduren; Der grosse Zapfenstreich, Cuba Cubana, Der Klosterjäger, Mit Siebzehn beginnt das Leben, Regine Amstetten, Conchita, Rittmeister Wronski, Rosen im Herbst, Die Barrings, Wilhelm Tell, Es wird alles wieder gut, Der Fuchs von Paris, Rivalen der Manege, Der blaue Nachtfalter, Rosen für den Staatsanwalt, Buddenbrooks, Waldrausch.*

stehlen, Ihr dunkler Punkt, Eine Nacht in London, Adieu Mascotte. Then sound: *Wenn Du einmal Dein Herz verschenkst, Hokuspokus, Einbrecher, Die Drei von der Tankstelle, Liebeswalzer, Nie wieder Liebe, Der Kongress tanzt, Quick, Zwei Herzen und ein Schlag, Ein blonder Traum, Ich und die Kaiserin, Schwarze Rosen, Glückskinder, Sieben Ohrfeigen, Fanny Elssler, Capriccio, Frau am Steuer, Ins blaue Leben.*

139 HARVEY, LILIAN (1907-1968). B: London. D: Antibes. Actress. RN: Lilian Muriel Helen Harvey. Dance training under Mary Zimmermann. Works in ballet and revue. Enters cinema thanks to Richard Eichberg (q.v.). 1933-1936: stars in American and French films. Spends war period in England. After 1945: makes temporary guest appearances on tour. 1948: in Denmark. 1953: retires to the French Riviera. Formed romantic partnership with Willy Fritsch (q.v.).
Films: *Der Fluch, Die Kleine vom Bummel, Leidenschaft, Liebe und Trompetenblasen, Die keusche Suzanne, Prinzessin Tralala, Vater werden ist nicht schwer . . ., Eheferien, Die tolle Lola, Du sollst nicht*

140 HASSE, HANNJO (1921-   ). B: Bonn. Actor. After the war acts in Nordhausen, then in Berlin, Burg, Schwerin and elsewhere. Has also appeared in Czech films.
Films: *Der Untertan, Ernst Thälmann – Sohn seiner Klasse, Gefährliche Fracht, Stärker als die Nacht, Ernst Thälmann – Führer seiner Klasse, Thomas Muntzer, Der Hauptmann von Köln, Die Millionen der Yvette, Wo du hingehst, Kapitäne bleiben an Bord, Sterne, Bevor der Blitz einschlägt, Weisses Blut, Kabale und Liebe, Das schwarze Bataillon, Einer von uns, Seilergasse 8, Die schöne Lurette, Leute mit Flügeln, Der Arzt von Bothenow, Der Fall Gleiwitz, Freispruch mangels Beweisen, An französischen Kaminen, Nebel, Reserviert für den Tod, Das Lied vom Trompeter,*

Die Söhne der grossen Bärin, Lebende Ware, Die gefrorenen Blitze, Schwarze Panther, Das Mädchen auf dem Brett; Der Mord, der nie verjährt; Spur des Falken, Mohr und die Raben von London.

141 **HASSE, OTTO EDUARD** (1903-). B: Obersitzka (Posen). Actor. Educated at high school and university (law) in Posen. Stage training under Reinhardt (q.v.). Theatres: Kammerspiele Munich 1933-1938: Deutsches Theater Berlin 1937-1939: Breslau, Munich, Prague, Berlin (with Jürgen Fehling). After 1946: Berlin, Salzburg Festival. Many guest appearances.

Films: *Peter Voss, der Millionendieb; Muss man sich gleich scheiden lassen?, Kreuzer Emden, Fräulein Hoffmanns Erzählungen, Die vertauschte Braut, Peer Gynt, Ein ganzer Kerl, Die Gefangene des Königs, Der schüchterne Casanova, Diener lassen bitten, Der ahnungslose Engel, Die grosse und die kleine Welt, So weit geht die Liebe nicht, Drei wunderschöne Tage, Illusion, Stukas, Alles für Gloria, Dr. Crippen an Bord, Die Entlassung, Rembrandt, Gefährtin meines Sommers, Geliebter Schatz, Der ewige Klang, Philharmoniker, Aufruhr der Herzen, Der Täter ist unter uns, Der grosse Preis, Komm zu mir zurück, Berliner Ballade, Anonyme Briefe, Epilog, Der grosse Zapfenstreich, Der letzte Walzer, Wenn am Sonntagabend die Dorfmusik spielt, Canaris, 08/15 II, Alibi, 08/15 in der Heimat, Kitty und die grosse Welt, Die Letzten werden die Ersten sein, Der gläserne Turm, Der Arzt von Stalingrad, Der Maulkorb, Solange das Herz schlägt, Frau Warrens Gewerbe, Affaire Nabob, Die Ehe des Herrn Mississippi, Das Leben beginnt um acht, Lulu, Die Todesstrahlen des Dr. Mabuse.*

142 **HASSELMANN, KARL** (18 -194). Director of photography. Interesting technician and collaborator of many masterpieces of the German "expressionist" cinema. Later works mainly on entertainment films.

Films (incomplete): *Gelübde der Keuschheit, Die weissen Rosen von Ravensburg, Die Jagd nach der Wahrheit, Der weisse Pfau, Die Hintertreppe* (co-phot.), *Whitechapel, Frou-Frou, Der Graf von Charolais, Der Graf von Essex* (co-phot. with Wagner and Franz Stein), *Hanneles Himmelfahrt, Schlagende Wetter, Die Strasse, Sylvester* (co-phot.), *Arabella, Carlos und Elisabeth* (co-phot. with Kurt Vass, Karl Puth and Sparkuhl), *Die Fahrt ins Verderben, Garragan* (co-phot.), *Komödianten, Eifersucht, Die eiserne Braut, Die Verrufenen, Die Brüder Schellenberg; Kubinke, der Barbier, und die drei Dienstmädchen; Menschen untereinander, Schwester Veronika, Die Unehelichen, Der alte Fritz; Anastasia, die falsche Zarentochter; Die Geliebte des Gouverneurs, Die heilige Lüge, Der Katzensteg, Eva in Seide, Kinder der Strasse, Lemkes sel. Witwe, Der Mann mit dem Laubfrosch, Ossi hat die Hosen an* (co-prod. with Gottschalk and Buhlmann), *Sensations-Prozess, Unter der Laterne, Alimente, Blutschande § 173 St.G.B., Geschminkte Jugend, Katherina Knie, Der Sträfling von Stambul.* Then sound: *Zweierlei Moral* (co-phot. with Albert Schattmann), *Zwischen Nacht und Morgen, Schachmatt, Lumpenkavaliers, Trenck* (co-phot.), *Die Nacht der Versuchung, Was wissen denn Männer, Die Nacht im Forsthaus, Wenn am Sonntagabend die Dorfmusik spielt, Volldampf voraus* (co-phot. with Emil Schünemann, Karl Vass and Paul Lieberenz), *Der Meisterboxer, Das Erbe von Pretoria, Der Fall Brenken, Stosstrupp 1917* (co-phot. with Ludwig Zahn, Josef Wirsching and Bartl Seyr), *Die Katz' im Sack, Die letzte Fahrt der Santa Margareta, Der Aussenseiter* (co-phot. with Ewald Daub), *Der Schlafwagenkontrolleur, Die Stunde der Versuchung, Ein seltsamer Gast, Donaumelodien, Ein Lied klagt an, Unter Ausschluss der Oeffentlichkeit, Madame Bovary; Tiere, Menschen, Sensationen* (co-phot. with Bruno Timm and Fritz von Friedl), *Dreizehn Mann und eine Kanone, Salonwagen E 417, Frau im Strom, Morgen werde ich verhaftet, Herzensfreud – Herzensleid, Mädchen im Vorzimmer, Donauschiffer, Clarissa, Stimme des Herzens, Wildvogel, Quartett zu Fünft.*

143 **HATHEYER, HEIDEMARIE** (1918-). B: Villach. Actress. Theatres: Vienna, Kammerspiele Munich, Deutsches Staatstheater Berlin. After 1945: Munich, Düsseldorf, Hamburg, Zurich.

Films: *Der Berg ruft, Frau Sixta, Zwischen Strom und Steppe, Die Schuld der*

Gabriele Rottweil, Ein ganzer Kerl, Die Geierwally, Ich klage an, Der grosse Schatten, Die Nacht in Venedig, Man rede mir nicht von Liebe, Die Jahre vergehen, Regimentsmusik, Ich glaube an Dich, Begegnung mit Werther, Wohin die Züge fahren, Dieser Mann gehört mir; Der Mann, der zweimal leben wollte; Vom Teufel gejagt, Dr. Holl, Das letzte Rezept, Mein Herz darfst Du nicht fragen, Pünktchen und Anton, Sauerbruch – Das war mein Leben, Liebe ohne Illusion, Die Ratten, Du darfst nicht länger schweigen, Die Ehe des Dr. med. Danwitz, Der Meineidbauer, Tierarzt Dr. Vlimmen, Glücksritter, ... und führe uns nicht in Versuchung, Solange das Herz schlägt, Der Ruf der Wildgänse, Heiss weht der Wind.

144 HEESTERS, JOHANNES (1902-   ). B: Amersfoort (Netherlands). Actor. Trained in Amsterdam. Theatres: Amsterdam, The Hague, Brussels, Antwerp, Vienna, and Berlin (Komische Oper). Star of operettas.

Films: *Der Bettelstudent, Die Leuchter des Königs, Das Hofkonzert, Gasparone, Wenn Frauen schweigen, Nanon, Meine Tante – Deine Tante, Das Abenteuer geht weiter; Hallo, Janine!, Liebesschule, Die lustigen Vagabunden, Illusion, Jenny und der Herr im Frack, Immer nur Du, Rosen im Tirol, Karneval der Liebe, Es fing so harmlos an, Glück bei Frauen, Es lebe die Liebe, Frech und verliebt, Die Fledermaus, Wiener Melodien, Zweimal verliebt, Wenn eine Frau liebt, Hochzeitsnacht im Paradies, Tanz ins Glück, Professor Nachtfalter, Die Csardasfürstin, Im weissen Rössl, Liebeskrieg nach Noten, Die geschiedene Frau, Schlagerparade, Ich hab' nur Deine Liebe, Bel ami; Gestatten, mein Name ist Cox; Stern von Rio, Heute heiratet mein Mann, Opernball, ... und wer küsst mich?, Viktor und Viktoria, Von allen geliebt, Bühne frei für Marika, Besuch aus heiterem Himmel, Frau im besten Mannesalter, Die unvollkommene Ehe, Junge Leute brauchen Liebe.*

145 HELD, MARTIN (1908-   ). B: Berlin. Actor. Stage training under Leopold Jessner (q.v.). Goes on tour first in the provinces, then appears in theatres in Dresden, Bremerhaven, Darmstadt and Frankfurt. Since 1951: Berlin (Schlosspark- and Schiller-Theater).

Films: *Schwarze Augen, Heimweh nach Dir, Canaris, Alibi, Vor Sonnenuntergang, Spion für Deutschland, Der Hauptmann von Köpenick, Friederike von Barring, Der Fuchs von Paris, Banktresor 713, Nasser Asphalt, Meine Tochter Patricia, Rosen für*

den Staatsanwalt, Bumerang, Der letzte Zeuge, Die Ehe des Herrn Mississippi, Frau Cheney's Ende, Der Traum von Lieschen Müller, 90 Minuten nach Mitternacht, Das schwarz-weiss-rote Himmelbett, Ein fast anständiges Mädchen, Das grosse Liebesspiel, Liebe will gelernt sein, Verdammt zur Sünde, Das älteste Gewerbe der Welt; Lange Beine, lange Finger; Fast ein Held, Dr. Fabian – Lachen ist die beste Medizin.

146 HELLBERG, MARTIN (1905-   ). B: Dresden. Director. Evening courses at Dresden Konservatorium. 1924-1933: actor at Staatstheater Dresden, then appears in Stuttgart and Freiburg. After 1945: director at Kammerspiele Munich and head of an acting school there. 1949-1951: General director of the Staatstheater Dresden. Professor for Film. Winner of state award in 1952, and international peace award in

1953. 1955: publishes book *Bühne und Film (Stage and Film)*. Mainly known for his film *versions of stage productions*.

Acted in: *Die blonde Carmen, Roman einer jungen Ehe*. Films directed: *Das verurteilte Dorf* 51, *Geheimakte Solvay* 52, *Das kleine und das grosse Glück* 53, *Der Ochse von Kulm* 54, *Der Richter von Zalamea* 56 (also script), *Thomas Müntzer* 56 (also script), *Die Millionen der Yvette* 57 (also script), *Wo Du hingehst* 58, *Emilia Galotti* 58 (also script), *Senta auf Abwegen* 58 (also script), *Kabale und Liebe* 59, *Kapitäne bleiben an Bord* 59, *Minna von Barnhelm* 62, *Die schwarze Galeere* 62, *Viel Lärm um nichts* 64 (also script), *Turlis Abenteuer* (only acted).

147 **HELLER OTTO** (1896-1970). B: Prague. Director of photography. At first projectionist in Prague, then enters film industry. Many Czech films with Karel Lamac (known later in Germany as Carl Lamac) and Anny Ondra (q.v.). 1935: to England. Was a remarkable colour specialist in productions like *The Ipcress File*.

Films: *Der erste Kuss, Evas Töchter, Saxophon-Susi, Die Kaviorprinzessin, Das Mädel mit der Peitsche, Sündig und süss, Das Mädchen aus USA*. Then sound: *Das Kabinett des Dr. Larifari* (co-phot. with Eduard Hoesch), *Wiener Herzen, Der falsche Feldmarschall; Eine Freundin, so goldig wie Du; Die vom Rummelplatz* (co-phot. with Erisch Giese), *Die Fledermaus, Mamsell Nitouche, Der Zinker, Er und seine Schwester, Die Privatsekretärin* (co-phot.); *Wehe, wenn er losgelassen; Der Hexer, Die grausame Freundin, Kiki, Baby, Eine Nacht im Paradies, Das verliebte Hotel* (co-phot. with Ludwig Zahn and Josef Wirsching), *Betragen ungenügend, Der Adjudant seiner Hoheit, Fräulein Hoffmanns Erzählungen* (co-phot. with Otto Martini), *Die Tochter des Regiments* (co-phot. with Kurt Neubert), *Annette im Paradies, Polenblut* (co-phot. with Martini), *Die vertauschte Braut* (co-phot. with Martini), *Klein Dorrit* (co-phot. with Ludwig Zahn), *Karneval und Liebe* (co-phot. with Carl Kurzmayer), *Grossreinemachen* (co-phot. with Martini), *Der junge Graf* (co-phot. with Martini), *Knock out* (co-phot. with Zahn and Gustl A.

Weiss), *An heiligen Wassern* (co-phot. with Bertl Höcht and Lothar Kern).

148 **HELM, BRIGITTE** (1908-   ). B: Berlin. Actress. RN: Gisele Eve Schittenhelm. Officer's daughter. Educated in Berlin, where she acted in a student production and was discovered there by Fritz Lang (q.v.) for his *Metropolis*. Later she also worked in France (with Pabst among others, and notably in L'Herbier's *L'Argent*) and England (Herbert Wilcox's *The Blue Danube*). Retired soon after the coming of sound.

Films: *Metropolis, Alraune, Am Rande der Welt, Die Liebe der Jeanne Ney, Abwege, Die Jacht der sieben Sünden, Skandal in Baden-Baden, Manolescu, Die wunderbare Lüge der Nina Petrowna*. Then sound: *Die singende Stadt, Alraune, Gloria, Im Geheimdienst, Die Herrin von Atlantis, Eine von uns, Die Gräfin von Monte Christo, Hochzeitsreise zu Dritt, Der Läufer von Marathon, Inge und die Millionen, Spione am Werk, Die schönen Tage von Aranjuez, Die Insel, Gold, Fürst Woronzeff, Ein idealer Gatte*.

149 HENCKELS, PAUL (1885-1967). B: Hürth. D: Castle Hugenpoet near Kettwich (Düsseldorf). Actor. Stage training in Düsseldorf (under Luise Dumont). Actor and associate chief director at the Düsseldorf theatre. Then director of the Schlosspark-Theater Berlin. Then acted in other Berlin theatres (e.g. the Volksbühne). After 1945 made many guest appearances.

Films: *Das Geheimnis von Brinkenhof, Das Haus der Lüge, Staatsanwalt Jordan, Wenn das Herz der Jugend spricht, Am Rüdesheimer Schloss steht eine Linde, Feme, Frühere Verhältnisse, Der Kampf des Donald Westhof, Ariadne in Hoppegarten, Der Biberpelz, Du sollst nicht ehebrechen, Geschlecht in Fesseln, Der Ladenprinz, Liebfraumilch, Polnische Wirtschaft, Revolutionshochzeit, Die seltsame Nacht der Helgs Wangen, Der Unüberwindliche, Blutschande § 173 St.G.B., Durchs Brandenburger Tor, Die Frau ohne Nerven, Furchtbarkeit, Frühlings Erwachen, Die Liebe der Brüder Rott, Meineid, Morgenröte, Mutterliebe, Das närrische Glück, Napoleon auf St. Helena, Sprengbagger 1010, Tagebuch einer Kokotte.* Then sound: *Flachsmann als Erzieher, Pension Schöller* (30), *Dreyfus, Skandal um Eva, Einbrecher, Der wahre Jakob, Das Ekel, Der Stolz der 3. Kompanie, Täter gesucht, Ihre Majestät die Liebe, Er und seine Diener, Der ungetreue Eckehart, Kadetten, Mein Leopold, Gloria, Man braucht kein Geld, Schneider Wibbel, Unheimliche Geschichten, Das Testament des Cornelius Gulden, Rasputine, Mieter Schulze gegen alle, Der Hexer, Die – oder keine, Eine Stadt steht Kopf, Geheimnis des blauen Zimmers, Der tolle Bomberg, Es wird schon wieder besser, Cyankali, Die zärtlichen Verwandten, Die letzte Kompanie, Die Lindenwirtin, Das lustige Kleeblatt, Der Jäger aus Kurpfalz, Heideschulmeister Uwe Karsten, Das Testament des Dr. Mabuse, Der Traum vom Rhein, Reifende Jugend, Mädels von heute, Die Nacht im Forsthaus, Das gestohlene Gesicht, Die grosse Sehnsucht, Die schönen Tage von Aranjuez, Glückliche Reise, Der unsterbliche Lump, Dolly macht Karriere, Kleiner Mann – was nun?, Zwischen zwei Herzen, Charleys Tante, Der Herr Senator, Ein Mädchen mit Prokura, Das Erbe von Pretoria, Die grosse Chance, Die Finanzen des Gross-herzogs, Der Meisterboxer; Peter, Paul und Nanette; Polizeiakte 909, Ferien vom Ich, Liebe dumme Mama, Jede Frau hat ein Geheimnis, Ich Sachen Timpe, Der verlorene Sohn, Der alte und der junge König, Ein idealer Gatte, Alle Tage ist kein Sonntag, Das Einmaleins der Liebe, Verlieb' Dich nicht am Bodensee; Eine Seefahrt, die lustig ist; Liebesträume, Hermine und die sieben Aufrechten, Schabernack, Das Hermännchen, Der Dschungel ruft, Paul und Pauline, Mädchenjahre einer Königin, Eine Frau ohne Bedeutung, Der lustige Witwenball, Die grosse und die kleine Welt, Ein Lied klagt an, Die unmögliche Frau, Die Nacht mit dem Kaiser, Drei tolle Tage, Ave Maria, Karussell, Capriolen, Die gläserne Kugel, Zwei mal zwei im Himmelbett, Fremdenheim Filoda, Der Maulkorb, Skandal um den Hahn, Diskretion – Ehrensache, Napoleon ist an allem schuld, Ein ganzer Kerl, 12 Minuten nach 12, Der Florentiner Hut, Das unsterbliche Herz, Herz modern möbliert, Friedrich Schiller, Weisser Flieder, Frau Luna, Männerwirtschaft, Immer nur Du, Was wird hier gespielt?, Ihr Privatsekretär, So ein Früchtchen, Der Strom, Der grosse König, Rembrandt, Hab' mich lieb, Die Nacht in Venedig, Zwischen Himmel und Erde, Wiener Blut, Zwei in einer grossen Stadt, Herr Sanders lebt gefährlich, Grosstadtmelodie, Das Bad auf der Tenne, Altes Herz wird wieder jung, Liebesgeschichten, Die Feuerzangenbowle, Die Zaubergeige, Träumerei, Junge Adler, Das Leben ruft, Das kleine Hofkonzert, Das Leben geht weiter, Kolberg, Das seltsamen Fräulein Sylvia, Frühlingsmelodie, Eine reizende Familie; Der Mann, dem man den Namen stahl; Dr. phil. Döderlein, Eine alltägliche Geschichte, Wozzeck, Die seltsamen Abenteuer des Herrn Fridolin B., Diese Nacht vergess' ich nie, Hafenmelodie, Gesucht wird Majora, Insel ohne Moral, Rausch einer Nacht, Glück aus Ohio, Herz der Welt, Drei Tage Angst, Klettermaxe, Pension Schöller 52, Glück am Rhein, Einmal am Rhein, Ferien vom Ich, Der fröhliche Weinberg, Hollandmädel, Fräulein Casanova, Die Stärkere, Fanfare der Ehe, Das tanzende Herz, Königliche Hoheit, Clivia, Der Zarewitsch, Columbus entdeckt Krähwinkel, Ball der Nationen, Staatsanwältin Corda, Maxie, Die spanische Fliege, Griff nach den Ster-*

nen, Die Mädels vom Immenhof, Du darfst nicht länger schweigen, Mamitschka, Drei Mädels vom Rhein, Ich und meine Schwiegersöhne, Kirschen in Nachbars Garten, Küss mich noch einmal, Tausend Melodien, Drei Birken auf der Heide, Der Fremdenführer von Lissabon, Hochzeit auf Immenhof, Bekenntnisse des Hochstaplers Felix Krull, Tolle Nacht, Der tolle Bomberg; Egon, der Frauenheld; Ferien auf Immenhof, Heute blau und morgen blau, Ein Stück vom Himmel, Liebe kann wie Gift sein; Hier bin ich, hier bleib' ich; Immer die Mädchen, Frau Irene Besser.

150 HERLTH, ROBERT (PAUL, FRITZ) (1893-1962). B: Wriezen a/O. D: Munich. Set designer. Son of a brewer. His brother Kurt (who was at first an architect) entered the cinema in 1932. 1912-1914: Hochschule für Bildende Künste, Berlin. 1914: soldier. 1916-1918: meets Hermann Warm (q.v.) and works as a result as set-designer for the army theatre in Wilma. 1919: studies at the Staatliche Kunstgewerbeschule Berlin. Collaborated with Walter Röhrig (q.v.) for many years and on several films *. One of the most important German set designers, whose ideas greatly influenced the "expressionism" movement (q.v.) and the "Kammerspiel" (q.v.). Also worked for the theatre in the Twenties and Thirties and in 1945-1946.

Films: *Das lachende Grauen *, Das Geheimnis von Bombay *, Die Toteninsel * (and others), Irrende Seelen *, Das Spiel mit dem Feuer *, Der Idiot *, Der müde Tod *, Satansketten *, Die Intriguen der Madame de la Pommeraye *, Pariserinnen *, Fräulein Julie *, Der Graf von Essex *, Luise Millerin *, Der Taugenichts, Der Schatz *, Komödie des Herzens *, Der letzte Mann 24 *, Zur Chronik von Grieshuus *, (in collab.), Tartüff *, Faust *, Luther *, Looping the Loop *, Rutschbahn (in collab. with Werner Schlichting), Die wunderbare Lüge der Nina Petrowna *.* Then sound: *Manolescu *, Der unsterbliche Lump *, Hokuspokus *, Ein Burschenlied aus Heidelberg *, Rosenmontag *, Das Flötenkonzert von Sanssouci *, Der Mann, der seinen Mörder sucht *, Der falsche Ehemann *, Nie wieder Liebe *, Der kleine Seitensprung *, Im Geheimdienst *, Der Kongress tanzt *, Yorck *, Die Gräfin von Monte Christo *, Mensch ohne Namen *, Der schwarze Husar *, Morgenrot *, Ich und die Kaiserin *, Saison in Kairo *, Walzerkrieg *, Flüchtlinge *, Die Csardasfürstin *, Der junge Baron Neuhaus *, Prinzessin Tourandot *, Barcarole *, Das Mädchen Johanna *, Amphytrion *, Königswalzer *, Unterheissem Himmel *, Savoy-Hotel 217 *, Hans im Glück 36 (also script and dir. *), Der Herrscher, Der zerbrochene Krug, Der Maulkorb, Der Spieler, Fest der Völker* and *Fest der Schönheit* (film-technical designs), *Morgen werde ich verhaftet, Maria Ilona, Opernball, Kleider machen Leute, Rosen in Tirol, Die schwedische Nachtigall, Andreas Schlüter, Wenn die Sonne wieder scheint, Liebespremiere, Ein Mann mit Grundsätzen, Melusine, Die Fledermaus, Zwischen gestern und morgen, Film ohne Titel, Einmaleins der Liebe, Verspieltes Leben, Geliebter Lügner, Dämonische Liebe, Das doppelte Lottchen, Kein Engel ist so rein, Dr. Holl, Herz der Welt* (in collab. with Warm and Bruno Monden), *Das weisse Abenteuer, Hinter Klostermauern, Alraune, Die Försterchristl, Der grosse Zapfenstreich, Im weissen Rössl, Der Kaplan von San Lorenzo, Dorf unterm Himmel, Die geschiedene Frau, Musik bei Nacht, Hochzeitsglocken, Sauerbruch – Das war mein Leben* (in collab. with Gottfried Will), *Das fliegende Klassenzimmer* (in collab. with Wolf Englert), *Der letzte Sommer* (in collab. with Kurt Herlth), *Geliebte Feindin, Hanussen* (in collab.), *Der letzte Mann* (55) (in collab. with Kurt Herlth), *Solang' es hübsche Mädchen gibt* (in collab. with Walter Joseph Blokesch and Herlth), *Teufel in Seide, Regine* (in collab. with Herlth), *Heute heiratet mein Mann* (in collab. with Herlth), *Die Trapp-Familie* (in collab. with Will), *Heisse Ernte* (in collab with Alexander Indrak and Herlth), *Bekenntnisse des Hochstaplers Felix Krull, ... und führe uns nicht in Versuchung* (in collab. with Herlth), *Das Wirtshaus im Spessart, Taiga* (in collab. with Will), *Die Trapp-Familie in Amerika* (in collab. with Will), *Auferstehung* (in collab. with Will), *Dorothea Angerman* (in collab. with Robert Stratil and Herlth), *Das schöne Abenteuer* (in collab. with Otto Jaindl), *Ein Tag, der nie zu Ende geht* (in collab. with Jaindl), *Buddenbrooks* (in collab. with Arno Richter and Herlth), *Eine*

Frau fürs ganze Leben (in collab. with Stratil), *Auf Engel schiesst man nicht* (in collab with Stratil), *Gustav Adolfs Page* collab. with Leo Metzenbauer). Sketches * for *Der falsche Ehemann* and *Nie wieder Liebe*, (executed by Werner Schlichting).

151 **HESTERBERG, TRUDE** (1897-1967). B: Berlin. D: Munich. Actress. Trained at the Stern'sches Konservatorium in Berlin. Acted at various Berlin theatres from 1912 onwards (Scala, Deutsches Theater, Admiralspalast/Haller Revue), also in revue and in her own literary cabaret "Wilde Bühne." Many guest appearances. 1949-1950: Kammerspiele Munich.

Films (incomplete): *Der Roman eines Dienstmädchens, Fridericus Rex, Die Frau mit dem Etwas, Vorderhaus und Hinterhaus, Der dumme August des Zirkus Romanelli, Der Juxbaron, Liebeshandel, Madame wünscht keine Kinder, Mädchenhandel, Manon Lescaut, Wie einst im Mai, Flucht vor blond, Das gefährliche Alter, Laster der Menschheit, Die letzte Nacht, Die Lorelei. Zwei unterm Himmelzelt, Die grosse Abenteurerin, Heut' spielt der Strauss, Die kleine Sklavin, Wenn die Mutter und die Tochter . . ., Zwei rote Rosen, Aufruhr im Junggesellenheim, Der Sträfling aus Stambul.* Then sound: *In Wien hab' ich einmal ein Mädel geliebt, Die Männer um Lucie, Arm wie eine Kirchenmaus, Die nackte Wahrheit, Stürme der Leidenschaft, Die Nacht der Entscheidung, Ein blonder Traum, Mieter Schulze gegen alle, Ich will Dich Liebe lehren, Ist mein Mann nicht fabelhaft?, Der Page vom Dalmasse-Hotel, Der Fall Brenken, Mein Herz ruft nach Dir, Die grosse Chance, Alles weg'n dem Hund, Der grüne Domino, Drei tolle Tage, Paul und Pauline, Befehl ist Befehl, Der Raub der Sabinerinnen, Mädchenräuber, Sein bester Freund, Der Unwiderstehliche, Golowin geht durch die Stadt, Tip auf Amalia, Jakko, Der Hochtourist, Am Ende der Welt, Das Geheimnis der roten Katze, Der blaue Strohhut, Um eine Nasenlänge, Inkognito im Paradies, Die Nacht ohne Sünde, Corinna Schmidt, Schatten über Neapel, Alraune, Die geschiedene Frau, Briefträger Müller, Jonny rettet Nebrador, Die Geschichte vom kleinen Muck, Unter den Sternen von Capri, Der Zigeunerbaron, Oh – diese "Lieben" Ver-*wandten, *Der fröhliche Wanderer, Parole Heimat, Abenteuer aus 1001 Nacht; Weil du arm bist, musst Du früher sterben; Das alte Försterhaus, Holiday am Wörthersee, Sonnenschein und Wolkenbruch, Nachts im grünen Kakadu, Frauenarzt Dr. Bertram, Es wird alles wieder gut, Skandal um Dodo.*

152 **HEYNOWSKI, WALTER** (1927-   ). B: Ingolstadt. Director and scriptwriter. At first journalist, then for many years editor-in-chief of a satirical newspaper, and later programme director of East German television (Deutscher Fernsehfunk). Since *Der lachende Mann* works with Gerhard Scheumann (q.v.); the result of the fusion of ideas of these two men of varied abilities is regarded as a new step forwards in documentary filmmaking. Heynowski is a member extraordinary of the Akademie der Künste in Berlin. State award.

Films (all doc.): *o.k.* 65 (Scheumann as interviewer), *Der lachende Mann* 66, *PS zum lachenden Mann* 66, *Ehrenmänner* 66, *400 cm³* 66, *Heimweh nach der Zukunft* 67, *Geisterstunde* 67, *Der Fall Bernd K.* 67, *Mit vorzüglicher Hochachtung* 67, *Der Zeuge* 67, *Piloten im Pyjama* 68 (released in four parts), *Der Präsident im Exil* 69.

153 **HILDEBRANDT, HILDE** (1897-   ). B: Hannover. Actress. RN: Emma Minna Hildebrand. 1924-1942: comedienne mainly in Berlin (Barnowsky Theatres, Renaissance-Theater, Theater am Kurfürstendamm, Tribüne). 1947-1950: Kleine Komödie, Munich, then returns to Berlin. Many guest appearances.

Films: *Der Trödler von Amsterdam, Der fesche Husar, Rasputins Liebesabenteuer, Sechs Mädchen suchen Nachtquartier.* Then sound: *Zweierlei Moral, Arme kleine Eva, Panik in Chikago, Mein Leopold, Bobby geht los, Madame hat Ausgang, Der unbekannte Gast, Das Schicksal der Renate Langen, Der kleine Seitensprung, Strafsache van Geldern, Uumögliche Liebe, Wenn die Liebe Mode macht, Ballhaus goldener Engel, Das schöne Abenteuer, Liebe, Scherz und Ernst, Der Frauendiplomat, Drei von der Kavallerie, K 1 greift ein, Keine Angst vor Liebe! Gruss und Kuss, Veronika!; Gretel zieht das grosse Los, Wege zur guten Ehe, Viktor und Viktoria, Liebe muss verstanden sein; Ma-*

nolescu, der Fürst der Diebe; Sprung in den Abgrund, Moral und Liebe, Pipin der Kurze, Polenblut, Die englische Heirat; Peter, Paul und Nanette; Klein Dorrit, Mein Herz ruft nach Dir, Artisten, Der Gefangene des Königs, Barcarole, Amphytrion, Liselotte von der Pfalz, Ich war Jack Mortimer, Die letzte Fahrt der Santa Margareta, Ein falscher Fuffziger, Die selige Exzellenz, Maria, die Magd, Der Kurier des Zaren, Allotria, Alles für Veronika, Mutterlied, Das Mädchen von gestern Nacht, Tanz auf dem Vulkan, Der Tag nach der Scheidung, Bel ami, Parkstrasse 13, Silvesternacht am Alexanderplatz, Das Glück wohnt nebenan, Ehe in Dosen, Frau nach Mass, Der Kleinstadtpoet, Meine Tochter tut das nicht, Alarm, Jenny und der Herr im Frack, Die schwache Stunde, Reise in die Vergangenheit, Grosse Freiheit Nr. 7, Ich bitte um Vollmacht, Spiel, Schuss um Mitternacht, Shiva und die Galgenblume, Das Gesetz der Liebe, Glück muss man haben, Spuk im Schloss, Verlobte Leute, Ruf an das Gewissen, Der Herr vom andern Stern, Kätchen für alles, Kleiner Wagen – grosse Liebe, Epilog, Unvergängliches Licht, Der Tiger Akabar, Die Schuld des Dr. Homma, Sie, Die Drei von der Tankstelle, Bezaubernde Arabella, Die Fastnachtsbeichte, Die Dreigroschenoper.

154 **HINZ, WERNER** (1903-   ). B: Berlin. Actor. Trained at the actors' school of the Deutsches Theater in Berlin. Theatres: Frankfurt, Berlin, Hamburg, Oldenburg, Darmstadt, Zurich, Munich, etc.
Films: *Der alte und der junge König, Weisse Sklaven, Die Warschauer Zitadelle, Jugend, Der Vierte kommt nicht, Bismarck, Traummusik, Der Fuchs von Glenarvon, Ohm Krüger, Mein Leben für Irland, Schicksal, Die Entlassung, Grosstadtmelodie, Das Herz muss schweigen, Meine Herren Söhne, Ruf an das Gewissen, Wildvogel, Der Fall Molander, In jenen Tagen, Der Biberpelz, Die Buntkarierten, Martina, Die Schuld des Dr. Homma, Herz der Welt, Geständnis unter vier Augen, Feuerwerk, Der letzte Sommer, Geliebte Feindin, Der 20. Juli, Hotel Adlon, Du darfst nicht länger schweigen, Nina, Bekenntnisse des Hochstaplers Felix Krull, Made in Germany, Herz ohne Gnade, Das Mädchen vom Moorhof, Unruhige Nacht, Der blaue Nachtfalter, Geheimaktion Schwarze Kapelle, Buddenbrooks, Der letzte Zeuge, Der Lügner, Morgen beginnt das Leben, Die Stunde, die Du glücklich bist, Toller Hecht auf krummen Touren, . . . und so was nennt sich Leben, Tonio Kröger, Dr. med. Hiob Prätorius, Rheinsberg, Morgens um sieben ist die Welt noch in Ordnung, Wenn süss das Mondlicht auf den Hügeln schläft.*

155 **HISTORY OF GERMAN CINEMA:** Siegfried Kracauer does not consider the early period of German cinema (1905-1918) as being very important, and the real development of the German film began after the First World War.

(i) *Producers from 1895 to 1933:* But on November 1, 1895, almost two months before Lumière, the Skladanowsky brothers (q.v.) presented the first moving pictures to a paying audience in the Berlin Wintergarten. One year later, Oskar Messter opened his first "movement theatre" with artificial light, on Friedrichstrasse (for details *see* Messter). As the Danish star Asta Nielsen (q.v.) began her series of Danish-German co-productions with her husband-director Urban Gad and then moved to Germany,

Ernst Lubitsch playing the shop assistant, Moritz, in one of a series of comedies

the industry became more established, and several production companies sprang up. 1912: Paul Davidson, head of Produktions A.G., and Max Reinhardt, founded an association to improve the situation for both producers and artists. Writers took more and more interest in films (*cf. Kinobuch*, edited by Kurt Pinthus in 1914). 1914: first big film studios in Berlin. Directors of importance in the prewar and war period included: Paul Wegener, Stellan Rye, Otto Rippert, and Joe May (all q.v.). Popular *genres* were frothy comedies, farce (Kintopp), and serials (q.v.), most of them detective thrillers. Major production companies: see entry devoted to their work, and especially Ufa (the key company as far as the economy of the industry was concerned). After 1919, the most prolific producer was Erich Pommer, who attracted many talented figures to his side just as Reinhardt did in the theatre. Other producers included men who were also directors and exhibitors like Oswald (q.v. and *see* "sex education" films), Eichberg, Froelich, May, Mack (all q.v.), Mutz, Greenbaum; and players like Henny Porten, Harry Piel, Fern Andra, Ellen Richter, etc.

(ii) *Entertainment Films:* Ernst Lubitsch (q.v.) was undoubtedly the greatest "entertainer" of German Cinema during the silent period; he directed historical and costume films which were not only great commercial successes but also of considerable artistic value. The entertainment films of the German silent screen consisted mainly of adventure stories (featuring stars like Harry Piel, Hans Albers [all q.v.], Ellen Richter, etc.) although vaudeville and genteel comedies (with Georg Alexander, Jacob Tiedtke,

Alfred Abel, Ossi Oswalda, Mia May, Kurt Gerron, all q.v., etc.) were also very much in vogue.

The sound period began with an immediate wave of musical films and films based on operettas. Their stars included Willy Fritsch, Lilian Harvey, Adele Sandrock, Heinz Rühmann, Fritz Kampers, Paul Kemp, Theo Lingen (all q.v.) and Hans Moser. The influence of Austrian composers was very marked, especially through the work of Lehar, the Strauss family, Zierer, Robert Stolz, etc.

The best films of this *genre* were: *Melodie des Herzens, Drei von der Tankstelle, Der Kongress tanzt, Amphitryon*. Directors like Willi Forst (q.v.) and Geza von Bolvary continued to make their musical comedies during the Nazi period, and enchanted a public depressed by war. Films with music or about music were in particular demand at that juncture so as to let the people appreciate the significance of party politics and war; main productions of this type were: *Operette, Wunschkonzert, Friedemann Bach, Träumerei, Philharmoniker, Opernball, Wiener G'schichten, Bel Ami, Mazurka, Premiere, Es war eine rauschende Ballnacht, Capriccio*, etc.

The twenty-fifth anniversary of Ufa (q.v.) was celebrated in 1943 with the lavishly designed, all-star-cast comedy *Münchhausen*, written by the banned novelist Erich Kästner (pen name Berthold Bürger).

After 1945 the German entertainment film never regained its former heights although the industry survived mainly on "entertainment." Among the very few ac-

Germany in the Twenties: below, DAS WACHSFIGURENKABINETT

ceptable comedies have been *Herrliche Zeiten, Berliner Ballade, Wir Wunderkinder, Das Wirtshaus im Spessart* – and, much later, *Zur Sache, Schätzchen;* musicals, operettas and dance films have proved very poor in general. Other directors of this genre: Eduard von Borsody, E. W. Emo, Eric Ode, Franz Hubert, Georg and Ernst Marischka, Jürgen Roland, Geza von Cziffra, Harald Philipp, Hans Deppe, Rudolf Schündler, Paul May, etc.

(iii) *Nazi period:* Between 1930 and 1932 German cinema once again rose to a notably high level at a time of social and economic insecurity. The style was one of *Neue Sachlichkeit* (q.v.), and film themes showed an aversion to war and violence.

Key figures: Fritz Lang, Pabst, Sagan and Jutzi (all q.v.). Dudow made his first feature and Josef von Sternberg his only German film, using elements of "expressionism" and *"Kammerspiel"* (q.v.).

The Reichsfilmkammer, established on September 22, 1933, was probably the most important factor in Dr. Joseph Goebbels's programme as Minister of Propaganda for the Nazi Reich (deliberately imitating the U.S.S.R. and the Lenin slogans). Goebbels increasingly brought all production companies under his control until in 1942 he finally declared Ufa (q.v.) as the chief organisation (a State company), which was also to be responsible for all film distribution.

There were several types of films that Goebbels thought suitable for his purposes: Entertainment (q.v.); "Blut und Boden" (blood and earth) represented among others by *Schimmelreiter* (probably the best of them), *Mädchen vom Moorhof, Fährmann Maria, Peer Gynt, Ein Volksfeind, Viktoria, Pan, Die goldene Stadt, Immensee, Opfergang* – also *"mountain" films* by Trenker (q.v.); films about the greatness of the Führer like *Der Herrscher, Kadetten, Bismarck* and the *Frederikus* film (*see* Gebühr); films about the power of the army like *Kampfgeschwader Lützow* and *U-Boote westwärts;* films about the sense of duty towards the Fatherland, such as *Hans Westmar, Hitlerjunge Quex, Unternehmen Michael, Urlaub auf Ehrenwort, D III 88, Stukas;* films about the "one and only" Nazi party, like *Hitlerjunge Quex, Friesennot,*

Flüchtlinge, G.P.U.; films about "the final victory" like *Sieg im Westen* (doc. 1941, dir. Svend Noldau) and about the will to fight to the end like *Kopf hoch, Johannes!; Besatzung Dora, Heimkehr, Ueber alles in der Welt, Kolberg;* films about great German figures like Friedrich Schiller, Ohm Krüger, Carl Peters, Andreas Schlüter, Robert Koch, Paracelsus, films against the Jews and non-Aryans, like *Jud Süss, Robert und Bertram, Leinen aus Irland, Die Rothschilds* (also against England), *Ich klage an, Opfer der Vergangheit* (doc., 1937, dir. Gernot Bock Stieber), *Der ewige Jude* (doc., 1940, dir. Fritz Hippler); and documentaries about the splendours of the Nazi Reich by Leni Riefenstahl (q.v.).

Between 1933 and 1945 approximately 1,150 films were made. Only about a sixth of these featured direct propaganda; but the rest all had some kind of political motive.

Key directors of the period: Veit Harlan, Wolfgang Liebeneiner, Karl Ritter, Herbert Maisch, Hans Steinhoff, Gustav Ucicky, Luis Trenker, Leni Riefenstahl, Carl Froelich, Willi Forst, Helmut Käutner (poetic dramas, outside the party line).

Documentaries on the Nazi period were made among others by Paul Rotha and Erwin Leiser (*Mein Kampf, Eichmann und das Dritte Reich; Deutschland, erwache!*).

(iv) *Producers from 1945 onwards:* The loss of the Neubabelsberg studios in Berlin as well as the loss of Berlin's unity as a city and therefore of its central power in the German film world made it very difficult to build up a new industry after the war and licenses were only rarely dispensed by the responsible authorities in the American, British and French zones. There was also heavy competition from abroad, and the liquidation of Ufa at the end of the Forties made the situation even more complex. But with new companies like Real, Junge Film-Union, Comedia, camera, CCC (*see* Brauner), Cordial, NDF (Neue Deutsche Filmproduktion, *see* Harald Braun), Freie Film-Produktion GmbH (*see* Harald Braun), Filmaufbau Göttingen (*see* Rolf Thiele), Gloria (*see* Kubaschewski), Deutsche Film Hansa, Berolina, Bavaria, Carlton (see Ostermayr), Divina (later becomes Gloria), Roxy and Rialto the film industry slowly

Postwar German cinema: Peter Lorre with Renate Mannhardt in his own DER
VERLORENEN

gained ground, tailoring its production programme to public tastes. By 1950 over two
hundred producers or production companies
and eighty-five distributors were in existence. Obviously several of these firms could
not survive for long.

With the crisis mounting around 1960,
many companies disappeared and renters/
producers or producers/distributors as Ex-
portfilm Bischoff and Constantin became
important; independent producers and distributors like Atlas, Seitz (q.v.), Neue Filmkunst Walters Kirchner, and neue filmform
Heiner Braun brought new ideas in the
market and were also responsible for the
movement known as *Junger deutscher Film*
(q.v.).

(v) *Postwar Cinema:* Although *The Murderers Are among Us* marked a new depar-
ture in German film-making, i.e. the attempt to banish Nazi guilt feelings from
the people's minds ("unbewältigte Vergangenheit"), there were very few films that
avoided the convention for portraying the
small man as the symbol of purity in an
evil world. Two directors, Käutner and
Staudte, made the most valuable contribution to postwar cinema. Their's was a
critical analysis of the social, intellectual,
and economic situation in the years 1946-
1950. Film-making was subject to enormous
pressures in West Germany, but some
seminal works came from the newly formed
DEFA (q.v.), where the view of the past was
entirely different. It was tragic that in
these circumstances the directors (with very
few exceptions) increasingly ignored the real
issues of the period and concentrated instead
on purely entertainment films. In 1949 the
separation of the two Germanies was a fact.
The East veered towards propaganda pictures, and the West towards unimaginative
commercial productions. Only in 1962, with
the signing by twenty-six film personalities
of the Oberhausen Manifesto (q.v.), did the
situation improve and the *Junger deutscher*

Film (q.v.) get under way.

(vi) *Junger deutscher Film* (Young German Cinema) must be understood more as a definition of a period than as the characterisation of a group. *JdF* stemmed from group "DOC 59" which was engaged in film culture and founded by Haro Senft (q.v.) and Ferdinand Khittl (b. 1924 Frantiskovy Lazne, dir. *Die Parallelstrasse,* 1961). Other members of the group were: Wolf Wirth (q.v.), Hans Posegga (composer), Raimund Ruehl (1932-1965, director), and Franz Josef Spieker (b. 1933 Paderborn, dir. *Wilder Reiter GmbH* 1966, *Mit Eienlaub und Feigenblatt* 1967).

First significant statement of *JdF:* Oberhausen Manifesto (q.v.) then a half-hearted attempt at producing the episode-film *Hütet eure Töchter* (dir. Michael Blackwood), Wolf Hart, Rob Houwer, q.v., Walter Krüttner, Eberhard K. Hauff, Franz Josef Spieker and Karl Schedereit). The most important film of that period was *Das Brot der frühen Jahre,* directed by Vesely (q.v.). In February 1965 the "Kuratorium Junger deutscher Film" was founded to help to finance first films of young directors on a percentage-risk basis. 1969: the existence of the "Kuratorium" is officially secure as the State provides it with 750,000 marks annually, but is has lost its important place in German film culture.

The wave of *début* films started in 1966: *Schonzeit für Füchse, Der junge Törless, Abschied von gestern, Wilder Reiter GmbH.* In 1967 followed *Mahlzeiten, Der sanfte Lauf, Tätowierung.* Other significant works include: *Mädchen, Mädchen; Kopfstand, Madame!* by Christian Rischert, *Jet Generation* by Eckhart Schmidt, *Detektive* by Rolf Thomé, *Katz und Maus, Lebenszeichen* by Werner Herzog.

Junger deutscher Film: Alexandra Kluge in her husband's ABSCHIED VON GESTERN

Some fringe members of *JdF* are well known: Vlado Kristl, Herbert Vesely and Jean-Marie Straub (all. q.v., the latter emigrated to Italy), and George Moorse and Klaus Lemke.

Representatives of the young commercial cinema are Horst Manfred Adloff *(Die goldene Pille)*, Marran Gosov *(Engelchen, Bengelchen, Mit Zuckerbrot und Peitsche)*, Ulrich Schamoni *(Quartett im Bett)*, and Michel Verhoeven *(Engelchen macht weiter)*, etc.

156 **HOFFMANN, CARL (KARL)** (1881-1947). B: Neisse an der Wobert (Silesia). D: Berlin. Director of Photography Works in photo laboratory in Freiburg at first, then enters the cinema industry (1908) and works on about 150 films until 1912. Internationally acknowledged as one of the most important German cameramen, he also worked closely with Fritz Lang (q.v.). Father of the director Kurt Hoffmann (q.v.).

Films (incomplete): *Das Buch des Lebens* (date for that film unobtainable, but is was certainly made prior to 1923), *Fiesco, Homunculus, Hilde Warren und der Tod* (co-phot.), *Die Hochzeit im Excentricclub, Königskinder von Travankore, Klaus Störtebecker, Die Frau mit den Orchideen, Halbblut, Harakiri, Der Herr der Liebe* (co-phot. with Emil Schünemann), *Der Knabe in Blau, Die Pest in Florenz* (co-phot. with Hameister and Schünemann), *Prinz Kuckuck, Die Spinnen I* (co-phot. with Schünemann), *Unheimliche Geschichten, Der Graf von Cagliostro* (co-phot. with Kurt Lande), *Haus zum Mond* (co-phot. with Gotthard Wolf), *Der Hirt von Maria Schnee, Der Januskopf* (co-phot.), *Patience, Sehnsucht, Die Spinnen II* (co-phot.), *Die Verschwörung zu Genua, Von morgens bis Mitternacht, Uriel Acosta, Dr. Mabuse der Spieler, Das Geld auf der Strasse, Die Intrigen der Madame de la Pommeraye, Lady Hamilton, Der steinerne Reiter* (co-phot.), *Die Andere, Die Nibelungen* (co-phot.), *Blitzzug der Liebe, Die Frau mit den schlechten Ruf, Faust, Die Frauengasse von Algier, Der geheimnisvolle Spiegel 27* (co-dir. with Prof. Teschner, also phot.), *Jugendrausch* (co-phot. with Sparkuhl and Ladislaw Starewitsch), *Die sieben Töchter der Frau Guyrkovics, Looping the Loop, Ungarische Rhap-*

sodie, *Hochverrat* (co-phot. with Friedrich Weinmann), *Manolescu, Die wunderbare Lüge der Nina Petrowna.* Then sound: *Ein Burschenlied aus Heidelberg, Der unsterbliche Lump, Hokuspokus, Der Tiger, Das Flöterkonzert von Sanssouci, Im Geheimdienst, Der falsche Ehemann, Yorck, Der Kongress tanzt, Mensch ohne Namen, Der weisse Dämon, Zwei Herzen und ein Schlag, Wie sag' ich's meinem Mann, Inge und die Millionen, Der Tunnel, Morgenrot, Saison in Kairo, Walzerkrieg, Peer Gynt, Die Csardasfürstin *, Das Einmaleins der Liebe 35* (only dir.), *Viktoria 35* (only dir.), *Die lustigen Weiber 35* (only dir.), *Die Leute mit dem Sonnenstich 36* (only dir.), *Ab Mitternacht 38* (only dir.). *Befreite Hände* (co-phot. with Heinz Schnackertz), *Der Florentiner Hut* (co-phot.), *Ich bin Sebastian Ott* (co-phot.), *Gold in New Frisco* (co-phot. with Otto Baecker), *Golowin geht durch die Stadt* (co-phot. with Schnakkertz), *Das Mädchen von Fanö* (co-phot. with Schnakkertz), *Alarmstufe V* (co-phot. with Schnackertz), *Zwei in einer grossen Stadt* (co-phot. with Erich Nietzschmann), *Symphonie eines Lebens* (co-phot. with Nietzschmann), *Ein toller Tag, Shiva und die Galgenblume, Via Mala *.

157 **HOFFMANN, KURT** (1910-   ). B: Freiburg. Director. Son of Carl Hoffmann (q.v.). Enters industry as assistant to Reinhold Schünzel, Liebeneiner, Ucicky and Steinhoff (all q.v.). Well known for his light comedies.

Films: *Paradies der Junggesellen 39, Hurra, ich bin Papa 39, Quax der Bruchpilot 41, Kohlhiesels Töchter 43, Ich vertraue Dir meine Frau an 43, Ich werde Dich auf Händen tragen 43, Das verlorene Gesicht 48, Heimliches Rendezvous 49, Fünf unter Verdacht 50, Der Fall Rabanser 50, Taxi-Kitty 50, Fanfaren der Liebe 51, Königin einer Nacht 51, Klettermaxe 52, Liebe im Finanzamt 52, Musik bei Nacht 53, Hokuspokus 53, Moselfahrt aus Liebeskummer 53, Der Raub der Sabinerinnen 54, Drei Männer im Schnee 54, Das fliegende Klassenzimmer 54, Feuerwerk 54, Ich denke oft an Piroschka 55, Heute heirate ich mein Mann 56, Bekenntnisse des Hochstaplers Felix Krull 57, Salzburger Geschichten 57, Wir Wunderkinder 58, Das Wirtshaus im Spessart 58, Der En-*

gel, der seine Harfe versetzte 59; *Das schöne Abenteuer* 59, *Lampenfieber* 59, *Das Spukschloss im Spessart* 60, *Die Ehe des Herrn Mississippi* 61, *Liebe wil gelernt sein* 62, *Schneewittchen und die sieben Gaukler* 63, *Schloss Gripsholm* 64, *Das Haus in der Karpfengasse* 64, *Dr. med. Hiob Prätorius* 65. *Hokuspokus – oder wie lasse ich meinen Mann verschwinden* 66, *Liselotte von der Pfalz* 66, *Herrliche Zeiten im Spessart* 67, *Rheinsberg* 67, *Morgens um sieben ist die Welt noch in Ordnung* 68, *Ein Tag ist schöner als der andere* 69 (co-script).

158 HÖFLICH, LUCIE (1883-1956). B: Hannover. D: Berlin: Actress. RN: Helene Lucie von Holwede. Plays comic roles on stage while still only sixteen. Theatres: Bromberg, Prague, Nuremberg, Vienna, Berlin. Part-time head of state actors' school in Berlin. After 1945: performs on stage in Schwerin and Berlin. Was married to Emil Jannings (q.v.).

Films (incomplete): *Freie Liebe, Maria Magdalena, Der langsame Tod, Die Bestie im Menschen, Die Erbin von Toris, Die Ratten, Ein Puppenheim, Das Spiel der Königin, Nora, Die Strasse, Der verlorene Schuh, Der geheime Agent, Kaddisch, Götz von Berlichingen zubenannt mit der eisernen Hand, Das Haus der Lüge, Tartüff, Ein Walzertraum, Nur eine Tänzerin, Das gefährliche Alter, Manege, Der Biberpelz.* Then sound: *Zum goldenen Anker; 1914, die letzten Tage vor dem Weltbrand; Kampf, Strafsache van Geldern, Der weisse Dämon, Brennendes Geheimnis, Peer Gynt, Der Raub der Sabinerinnen, Friedericus, Der Kurier des Zaren, Familienparade, Schatten der Vergangenheit, Der Berg ruft, Manege, Starke Herzen, Die Warschauer Zitadelle, War es der im 3. Stock?, Wir tanzen um die Welt, Robert Koch, Der Fuchs von Glenarvon, Ohm Krüger, Weiss Wäsche, Das grosse Spiel, Altes Herz wird wieder jung, Lache Bajazzo, Himmel ohne Sterne; Anastasia, die letzte Zarentochter.*

159 HOLLÄNDER, FRIEDRICH (1896-). B: London. Composer. Studied at the Musikakademie in Berlin. Composer for Reinhardt (q.v.); many operattas, revues, songs and *chansons*. Famous songs for Marlene Dietrich (q.v.). Son of Victor Hollän-

der. 1935: to U.S.A.; after the war returning to Germany.

Films: *Einbrecher, Der blaue Engel, Pension Schöller* (in collab. with Jim Cowler and Werner Schmidt-Boelcke), *Der Andere* (in collab. with Will Meisel and Artur Guttmann), *Die grosse Sehnsucht* (in collab. with Rudolf Eisner, Dessau and Karl Brüll), *Das Lied vom Leben* (in collab. with H. Adams and Wachsmann), *Das gelbe Haus des King-Fu* (in collab. with Schmidt-Boelcke and Rolf Marbot), *Stürme der Leidenschaft* (in collab. with Gérard Jacobson), *Drei Tage Liebe, Das Schicksal der Renate Langen* (in collab. with Felix Günther and Rudolf Nelson), *Der Weg nach Rio* (in collab. with Guttmann and Stefan Rényi), *Der Mann, der seinen Mörder sucht* (in collab.), *Ich und die Kaiserin 33* (in collab., also dir.), *Das Spukschloss im Spessart* (in collab. with Olaf Bienert and Alfred Strasser).

160 HÖLLERING, GEORG (GEORGE HOELLERING) (1900-). B: Baden near Vienna. Producer and cinema owner, also scriptwriter and director. Producer in Austria and Hungary, later in Germany, then to England. Specialist as a distributor, later head of Academy Cinemas in London. Founded production company for *Murder in the Cathedral*, which he directed and co-scripted with T. S. Eliot in 1951. Produced *Kuhle Wampe.*

161 HOMOLKA, OSKAR (1901-). B: Vienna. Actor. Trained at actor's academy in Vienna. Theatres: Vienna and Berlin. Went to London in 1934, and to U.S.A. in 1936. His supporting roles in recent years have featured him as the jovial "Mitteleuropean."

Films: *Die Abenteuer eines Zehnmarkscheines, Brennende Grenze, Dirnentragödie, Fürst oder Clown, Die heilige Lüge, Der Kampf des Donald Westhof, Die Leibeigenen, Petronella, Regine, die Tragödie einer Frau, Schinderhannes, Die Rothausgasse, Masken, Revolte im Erziehungshaus.* Then sound: *Dreyfus, Hokuspokus, Nachtkolonne, Zwischen Nacht und Morgen; 1914, die letzten Tage vor dem Weltbrand; Der Weg nach Rio, Im Geheimdienst, Die Nächte von Port Said, Unsichtbare Gegner, Spione am Werk, Der schweigende Mund.*

162 HOPPE, MARIANNE (1911-   ).
B: Rostock. Actress. Stage training under
Lucie Höflich (q.v.). Theatres: Frankfurt,
Berlin (with Reinhardt, q.v.), Kammerspiele
Munich, Neues Theater Frankfurt, Staat-
liches Schauspielhaus Berlin (with Gründ-
gens, q.v.), Deutsches Schauspielhaus Ham-
burg (also with Gründgens to whom she
was married).
Films: *Heideschulmeister Uwe Karsten,
Der Judas von Tirol, Der Schimmelreiter,
Krach um Jolanthe, Schwarzer Jäger Jo-
hanna, Alles hört auf mein Kommando,
Oberwachtmeister Schwenke, Anschlag auf
Schweda, Die Werft zum grauen Hecht,
Wenn der Hahn kräht, Eine Frau ohne
Bedeutung; Gabriele eins, zwei, drei; Capriolen, Der Herrscher, Der Schritt vom Wege,
Kongo-Express, Auf Wiedersehen, Franziska, Stimme des Herzens, Romanze in
Moll, Ich brauche Dich, Das Leben geht
weiter, Das verlorene Gesicht, Schicksal aus
zweiter Hand, Nur eine Nacht, Der Mann
meines Lebens, 13 Kleine Esel und der Sonnenhof, Die seltsame Gräfin, Der Schatz im
Silbersee, Die Goldsucher von Arkansas.*

163 HÖRBIGER, ATTILA (1896-   ).
B: Budapest. Actor. 1914: soldier. Theatres:
Czernowitz and Wiener Neustadt. Then
stage training at Deutsches Theater in Berlin. Theatres: Stuttgart, Bozen, Raimund-
Theater (Vienna) 1921-1922. Reichenberg,
Lustspieltheater Vienna 1923-1925. Brünn,
Prague, Theater in der Josefstadt Vienna
1928-1950. Deutsches Theater Berlin 1934-
1944. Since 1950 has appeared at the Burgtheater in Vienna. Brother of Paul Hörbiger
(q.v.). Married to Paula Wessely (q.v.);
their daughter Christiane Hörbiger is also
well known as a stage actress.
Films: *Nachtlokal, Die Tat des Andreas
Harmer.* Then sound: *Das Flötenkonzert
von Sanssouci, Das Wolgamädchen, Kaiserliebchen, Ihre Hoheit befiehlt, Sehnsucht
202, Die grosse Liebe, Lumpenkavaliere,
Der Tunnel, Zwischen Himmel und Erde,
Punks kommt aus Amerika, Blutsbrüder,
Varieté (35), Die Liebe des Maharadscha,
Mädchenpensionat, Die Julika, Revolutionshochzeit, Premiere, Manege, Fracht von
Baltimore, Zwischen Strom und Steppe,
Das Mädchen mit dem guten Ruf, Spiegel
des Lebens, Grenzfeuer, Frau im Strom,*

*Menschen vom Varieté, Renate im Quartett,
Donauschiffer, Im Schatten des Berges, Die
letzte Runde, Heimkehr, Wetterleuchten um
Barbara, Freunde, Späte Liebe, Am Ende
der Welt, Die kluge Marianne, Die goldene
Fessel, Ulli und Marei, Das unsterbliche
Antlitz, Der Engel mit der Posaune, Gottes
Engel sind überall, Das vierte Gebot, Ma-
resi, Vagabunden der Liebe, Cordula, Ge-
fangene Seele, Maria Theresia, Der Ver-
schwender, Ich und meine Frau, Die Hexe,
Weg in die Vergangenheit, Spionage, Der
Major und die Stiere, Das Mädchen vom
Pfarrhof, Kaiserjäger, Der Meineidbauer;
Liebe, die den Kopf verliert; Kronprinz
Rudolfs letzte Liebe, Der Edelweisskönig,
Mann nent es Amore, Der Alpenkönig und
der Menschenfeind, An der schönen blauen
Donau.*

164 HÖRBIGER, PAUL (1894-   ). B.
Budapest. Actor. Studies at Technical High
School Vienna, then stage training. 1914-
1918: soldier. Theatres: Reichenberg (1919),
German Theatre in Prague, Vienna, Berlin,
Düsseldorf etc. Very busy actor with typical
Viennese humour. 1940-1946: member of
the Burgtheater Vienna. Brother of Attila
Hörbiger (q.v.). His son Thomas is also an
actor.
Films: *Die Dame mit der Maske, Der
fesche Husar, Die grosse Abenteurerin,
G'schichten aus dem Wienerwald, Heut'
spielt der Strauss, Das letzte Souper, Die
Räuberbande, Sechs Mädchen suchen
Nachtquartier, Song, Spione, Die tolle
Komptesse, Die Wochenendbraut, Asphalt,
Die Drei um Edith; Die Frau, die jeder
liebt, bist Du!, Frauen am Abgrund, Das
grüne Monokel, Ein kleiner Vorschuss auf
die Seligkeit, Möbelierte Zimmer, Der Sträfling aus Stambul.* Then sound: *Wer wird
denn weinen, wenn man auseinandergeht;
Wie werde ich reich und glücklich?, Der unsterbliche Lump, Ich glaub' nie mehr an
eine Frau, Nur Du, Delikatesse, Das alte
Lied, Der Herr auf Bestellung, Zwei Herzen
im 3/4-Takt, Drei Tage Mittelarrest, Das
lockende Ziel* (only script with Walter Forster), *Der Kongress tanzt, Die lustigen Weiber von Wien, Die Försterchristl, Der Zinker, Arm wie eine Kirchenmaus, Der ungetreue Eckehart, Reserve hat Ruh, Walzerparadies, Der verjüngte Adolar, Lügen auf*

Rügen, Grock, Mein Herz sehnt sich nach Liebe, Sein Scheidungsgrund, Ihre Hoheit befielt, Kyritz – Pyritz, Zwei glückliche Tage, So ein Mädel vergisst man nicht, Quick; Annemarie, die Braut der Kompanie; Das Geheimnis um Johann Orth, Es war einmal ein Walzer, Trenck; Scampolo, ein Kind der Strasse; Peter Voss, der Millionendieb; Der grosse Bluff, Die unsichtbare Front, Ein toller Einfall, Ein steinreicher Mann, Friederike; Johann Strauss, k. und k. Hofballmusikdirektor; Kaiserwalzer, Zwei gute Kameraden, Ein Lied für Dich, Skandal in Budapest, Liebelei, Des jungen Dessauers grosse Liebe, Keinen Tag ohne Dich, Heimkehr ins Glück; Gruss und Kuss, Veronika!, Spiel mit dem Feuer, Besuch am Abend, Der Herr ohne Wohnung, Die Csardasfürstin, Rosen aus dem Süden, Petersburger Nächte, Fräulein Frau, ... heute Abend bei mir, Mein Herz ruft nach Dir, Herz ist Trumpf, Ich heirate meine Frau, Wenn die Musik nicht wär', Das Einmaleins der Liebe, Frühjahrsparade, Frischer Wind aus Kanada, Liebeslied, Königswalzer, Endstation, Seine Tochter ist der Peter, Kinderarzt Dr. Engel, Schabernack, Fiakerlied, Die Puppenfee, Drei Mäderl um Schubert, Peter im Schnee, Der Scheidungsgrund, Florentine, Die Landstreicher, Lumpazivagabundus, Einmal werd' ich Dir gefallen; Immer, wenn ich glücklich bin; Prinzessin Sissy, Der Blaufuchs, Heiraten – aber wen?, Liebelei und Liebe, Heimat, Hochzeitsreise zu Dritt, Drunter und drüber, Unsterblicher Walzer, Ich bin Sebastian Ott, Männer müssen so sein, Opernball, Kitty und die Weltkonferenz, Salonwagen E 417, Mutterliebe, Maria Ilona, Wunschkonzert, Wiener G'schichten, Der liebe Augustin, Operette, Falstaff in Wien, Herzensfreud – Herzensleid, Oh diese Männer, Wir bitten zum Tanz, Die grosse Liebe, So ein Früchtchen, Wen die Götter lieben, Brüderlein fein, Die heimliche Gräfin, Schwarz auf Weiss, Lache Bajazzo, Schrammeln, Die Zaubergeige, Romantische Brautfahrt, Glück muss man haben, Der Hofrat Geiger, Die seltsame Geschichte des Brandner Kaspar, Der Bagnosträfling, Der Engel mit der Posaune, Kleine Melodie aus Wien, Der Seelenbräu, Eine Nacht im Separée, Epilog, Schwarzwaldmädel, Dämonische Liebe, Frühlingsstimmen, Der alte Sünder, Die Frauen des Herrn S., Verklungenes Wien, Wenn die Abendglocken läuten, Der fidele Bauer, Hallo Dienstmann (also idea), Was das Herz befiehlt, Ich heisse Niki, Mein Herz darfst Du nicht fragen, Mikosch rückt ein, Ich hab' mein Herz in Heidelberg verloren, Man lebt nur einmal, Das Land des Lächelns, Hannerl, Die Fiakermilli, Von der Liebe reden wir später, Die Rose von Stambul, Junges Herz voll Liebe, Das tanzende Herz, Mit 17 beginnt das Leben, Die Privatsekretärin, Der Raub der Sabinerinnen, Der Feldherrnhügel, Der treue Husar, Meine Schwester und ich, Der Zigeunerbaron, Die schöne Müllerin, Schützenliesel, Begegnung in Rom, Die Stadt ist voller Geheimnisse, Mädchenjahre einer Königin, Eine Frau genügt nicht?, Banditen der Autobahn, Der fröhliche Wanderer, Ein Herz bleibt allein, Du mein stilles Tal, Die Försterbuben; Ja, ja, die Liebe in Tirol; Ich lass mich nicht verführen, Hilfe – sie liebt mich!, An der schönen blauen Donau, Die Deutschmeister, Ehesanatorium, Die Christel von der Post, Das Donkosakenlied, Manöverball, Was die Schwalbe sang, Ihr Korporal, Charleys Tante, Bademeister Spargel, ...und wer küsst mich?, Lumpazivagabundus, Lügen haben hübsche Beine, Der schräge Otto, Heimweh ... dort wo die Blumen blüh'n; Ober, zahlen!, Der schönste Tag meines Lebens; Wien, Du Stadt meiner Träume; Die Winzerin von Langenlois, Hoch droben auf dem Berg, Lemkessel, Witwe, Hallo Taxi, Heiratskandidaten, Hoch klingt der Radetzkymarsch, Sebastian Kneipp, ... und die Liebe lacht dazu, Heimat – deine Lieder, Sabine und die 100 Männer, Kauf dir einen bunten Luftballon, Der Orgelbauer von St. Marien; ... und Du, mein Schatz, bleibst hier; Drei Liebesbriefe aus Tirol, Tanze mit mir in den Morgen, ... und ewig knallen die Räuber, Ferien vom Ich, Im singenden Hotel am Königssee, Die lustigen Vagabunden; Sing, aber spiel nicht mit mir; Unsere tollen Nichten, Das hab' ich von Papa gelernt, Die ganze Welt ist himmelblau, Die grosse Kür, Happy-end am Wörthersee, Der Alpenkönig und der Menschfeind, Das ist mein Wien.

165 **HORN, CAMILLA** (1906-   ). B: Frankfurt. Actress. At first dancer, then attends art school and also dance school. Appears in the Nelson revue, then works as

an extra. Discovered by Murnau (q.v.), playing Gretchen in his *Faust*. Works in Hollywood. 1929: to England, later also plays in Italian films.

Films: *Faust, die Frauengasse von Algier, Der fröhliche Weinberg, Jugendrausch, Die Drei um Edith, Mein Herz gehört Dir . . ., Fundvogel, Moral um Mitternacht.* Then sound: *Die Königsloge, Hans in allen Gassen, Sonntag des Lebens, Die grosse Sehnsucht, Die Nacht ohne Pause, Ich geh' aus und Du bleibst da, ·Leichtsinnige Jugend, Das Lied der Nationen, Der Frechdachs, Die fünf verfluchten Gentlemen, Moral und Liebe, Rakoczy-Marsch, Rund um eine Million, Der letzte Walzer, Die grosse Chance, Der Doppelgänger, Wenn ich König wär!, Ein Walzer für Dich, Ich sehne mich nach Dir, Der rote Reiter, Weisse Sklaven, Gauner im Frack, Sein letztes Modell, Fahrendes Volk, Rote Orchideen, Roman eines Arztes, Zentrale Rio, Die letzte Runde, Polterabend, Die keusche Geliebte, Herz ohne Heimat, Friedemann Bach, In geheimer Mission, Tragödie einer Liebe, Seine beste Rolle, Intimitäten, Gesucht wird Majora, Königin der Arena, Vati macht Dummheiten, Heisses Spiel für harte Männer.*

166 HORNEY, BRIGITTE (1911-   ). B: Berlin. Actress. Stage training at actors' school in the Deutsches Theater Berlin. Theatres: Würzburg and Berlin. 1946-1949: Schauspielhaus Zurich. 1953: Deutsches Theater Göttingen etc.

Films: *Abschied, Fra Diavolo, Rasputin, Heideschulmeister Uwe Karsten, Der ewige Traum, Liebe, Tod und Teufel, Ein Mann will nach Deutschland, Der grüne Domino, Blutsbrüder, Stadt Anatol, Savoy-Hotel 217, Der Katzensteg, Revolutionshochzeit, Verklungene Melodie, Du und Ich, Anna Favetti, Ziel in den Wolken, Der Gouverneur, Das Mädchen von Fanö, Illusion, Geliebte Welt, Am Ende der Welt, Münchhausen, Die Frau am Wege, Verspieltes Leben, Melodie des Schicksals, Solange Du da bist, Gefangene der Liebe, Der letzte Sommer, Der gläserne Turm, Nacht fiel über Gotenhafen, Das Erbe von Björndal, Der Ruf der Wildgänse, Neues vom Hexer, Ich suche einen Mann.*

167 HOUWER, ROB (1937-   ). B: Groningen (Netherlands). Producer and director. 1956: studies theatrical science and attends the German Institute for film and TV, both in Munich. At first film critic, asst. director and asst. cameraman, later finances himself as producer, cameraman and director. 1959: founds "Rob Houwer Film" in Munich, which issues several sponsored and short films directed by Houwer. Feature films since 1967. The most successful producer of the young German film movement. See also *Junger deutscher Film.* Producer of shorts and documentaries, some * of which he directed:

Hundstage * 59, *Das Begräbnis* * 60 (also phot.), *Gebt euch nicht der Trauer hin* * (also phot., co-scripted with Baasch), *Leitzach* 61 (also scr.), *Ein Nachmittag für uns* 61 (*Mississippi-Illusion*, dir. and scr. with Peter Schamoni, q.v.), *Der Schlüssel* * 61, *Ferien* * 61 (*Lydia*, episode from *Hütet Eure Töchter*, also scr. with Franz-Josef Spieker), *Der gelbe Wagen* * 62 (episode from *Hütet eure Töchter*), *Doppelkonzert* 63 (dir. Franz-Josef Spieker), *Madeleine-Madeleine* 63 (dir. Vlado Kristl), *Autorennen* (dir. Vlado Kristl), *Anmeldung* * 64, *Konferenz-Dolmetscher* * 64, *Das Malschiff* (dir. Franz-Josef Spieker), *Vierundzwanzig*

Bilder * 65, *Foul* 65 (dir. Raimund Ruehl), *Kinder im Fragealter* 65 (dir. Dieter Lemmel), *Verständigung* 65, *Das fünfte Element* 66 (dir. Volker Vogeler, q.v.), *Romy – Porträt eines Gesichts* 66 (dir. Hans-Jürgen Syderberg, for TV), *Meisjes* * 66, *Der Zirkus kommt* * 66, *Zweikampf* 66 (dir. Uwe Brandner), *Das Nest* 67 (dir. Friedrich Mayrhofer), *Mijnheer hat lauter Töchter* 67 (dir. Vogeler, Lebeck, Schaaf, for TV). Collaborated on: *Stunde X* 59 (dir. Dörries, Houwer asst. dir.), *Alles für den Hund* 60 (dir. Peter Schamoni, q.v., Houwer co-phot.), *Folkwangschule* 60 (dir. Herbert Vesely, q.v., Houwer co-phot.). Features produced: *Hütet eure Tächter* (see above, two of five episodes), *Mord und Totschlag*, *Tätowierung*, *Professor Columbus*, *Engelchen oder die Jungfrau von Bamberg*, *Zuckerbrot und Peitsche*, *Bübchen*, *Jagdszenen aus Niederbayern*, *Bengelchen*; *Engelchen macht weiter, hoppe hoppe Reiter; Michael Kohlhaas – Der Rebell* (co-prod. with Oceanic), *... Köpfchen in das Wasser, Schwänzchen in die Höh* (co-prod.), *Der Bettenstudent oder: Was mach' ich mit den Mädchen, O.K.*

168 HUBSCHMID, PAUL (1917-   ). B: Schönenwerd near Aarau (Switzerland). Actor. Stage training at Vienna-Schönbrunn. Appears at the Deutsches Volkstheater and the Theater in der Josefstadt, both in Vienna; also at the DeutschesTheater in Berlin. Enters cinema with role in *Füsilier Wipf* (in Switzerland). Quite a number of Swiss films, then (1949-1950) also in U.S.A., under the name of Paul Christian. After his success as Professor Higgins in the stage production of *My Fair Lady* in Berlin, he starts a new international career in films like *Funeral in Berlin*.

Films: *Maria Ilona, Der Fall Rainer, Meine Freundin Josefine, Wilder Urlaub, Altes Herz wird wieder jung, Liebesbriefe, Der gebieterische Ruf, Das seltsame Fräulein Sylvia, Das Gesetz der Liebe, Der himmlische Walzer, Gottes Engel sind überall, Arlberg-Express, Geheimnisvolle Tiefe, Maske in Blau, Musik bei Nacht, Mit siebzehn beginnt das Leben, Zwiespalt des Herzens, Ungarische Rhapsodie, Schule für Eheglück, Glückliche Reise, Ingrid – Geschichte eines Fotomodells, Die Frau des Botschaf*

ters, Die goldene Brücke, Die Zürcher Verlobung, Glücksritter, Du bist Musik, Heute heiratet mein Mann; Liebe, die den Kopf verliert; Salzburger Geschichten, Italienreise – Liebe inbegriffen, Scampolo, Meine schöne Mama, Ihr 106. Geburtstag, Der Tiger von Eschnapur, Das indische Grabmal, Alle Tage ist kein Sonntag; Liebe, Luft und lauter Lügen; Marili, Heldinnen, Die rote Hand, Die junge Sünderin, Ich bin auch nur eine Frau, Schwarze Rose, Rosemarie, Elf Jahre und ein Tag, Das grosse Liebesspiel, Die Diamantenhölle am Mekong, Heirate mich, Chéri, Die Lady, Die Unmoralischen, Die Herren, Playgirl, Ruf der Wälder, Die schwedische Jungfrau, Caroline und die Männer über vierzig, Ich suche einen Mann, Karriere, Der Mann mit den 1000 Masken, Hemmungslose Manon, Negresco ****.

169 HUNTE, OTTO (1883-194). Set designer. Belonged to the group of expressionist painters (*see* "Expressionism"), later worked in close collaboration with Lang, Pabst (both q.v.) and Josef von Sternberg (*Der blaue Engel*). His best work is probably the archaic sets for *Die Nibelungen*. Later Hunte worked on the Nazi propaganda film *Jud Süss*, as well as the anti-Nazi film *Die Mörder sind unter uns*.

Films (incomplete): *Spinnen I and II* (in collab. with Warm and Carl Kirmse), *Die Herrin der Welt* (in collab. with Martin Jacob-Boy), *Der Leidensweg der Inge Krafft, Das wandernde Bild, Die Frauen von Gnadenstein, Das indische Grabmal* (in collab. with Jacoby and Erich Kettelhut), *Dr. Mabuse der Spieler* (in collab. with Stahl-Urach), *Die Nibelungen* (in collab. with Kettelhut and Karl Vollbrecht), *Die Liebe der Jeanne Ney* (in collab.), *Die Frau im Mond* (in collab. with Emil Hasler and Vollbrecht), Then sound: *Der blaue Engel* (in collab. with Emil Hasler), *Die englische Heirat, Gold, Herr Kobin geht auf Abenteuer; Liebe, Tod und Teufel; Der Mann, der Sherlock Holmes war; Die Kreutzersonate* (in collab. with Willy Schiller), *Fräulein, Das Lied der Wüste, Jud Süss* (in collab. with Karl Vollbrecht), *Altes Herz wird wieder jung, Die Mörder sind unter uns* (in collab. with Bruno Monden), *Razzia*.

IRMEN-TSCHET, KONSTANTIN *see* TSCHET, KONSTANTIN.

170 JANNINGS, EMIL (1884-1950). B: Rorschach (Switzerland). D: Stroblhof/ Wolfgangsee. Actor. RN: Theodor Friedrich Emil Janenz. Stage training in Zurich and Görlitz. Trip around the world for recitals in various theatres. Joins Reinhardt (q.v.) and the Deutsches Theater Berlin thanks to Werner Krauss (q.v.) in 1914, and enters cinema in the same year. In 1916 he becomes Lubitsch's (q.v.) favourite actor. 1926-1929: to Hollywood, where he wins the Academy Award for his performance in *The Last Command*. One of the finest actors of German stage and film. Retires after 1945.

Films: *Keimendes Leben, Schützengraben* (dates for these films unobtainable, but all were made certainly prior to 1923).

Films (incomplete): *Arme Eva, Im Banne der Leidenschaften, Passionels Tagebuch, Stein unter Steinen, Die Ehe der Luise Rohrbach, Nacht des Grauens, Ein fideles Gefängnis, Klingendes Leben, Lulu, Die Seeschlacht, Der Mann der Tat, Rose Bernd, Madame Dubarry, Vendetta, Algol, Anna Boleyn, Die Brüder Karamasoff, Das grosse*

Licht, Kohlhiesels Töchter, Der Schädel der Pharaonentochter, Die Bergkatze, Danton, Die Ratten, Der Stier von Olivera, Das Weib des Pharao, August der Starke, Fuhrmann Henschel, Die Gräfin von Paris, Othello, Peter der Grosse, Alles für Geld (also prod.), *Tragödie der Liebe, Der letzte Mann, Nju, Das Wachsfigurenkabinett, Liebe macht blind, Tartüff, Varieté, Faust.* Then sound: *Der blaue Engel, Liebling der Götter, Stürme der Leidenschaft, Die Abenteuer des Königs Pausole, Der schwarze Walfisch, Der alte und der junge König, Traumulus, Der Herrscher, Der zerbrochene Krug, Robert Koch, Ohm Krüger, Die Entlassung, Altes Herz wird wieder jung, Wo ist Herr Belling?*

171 JESSNER, LEOPOLD (1878-1945). B: Königsberg. D: Hollywood. Director. Actor and stage director in Hamburg and Königsberg, then general director at the Staatstheater in Berlin. One of the most influential stage directors of his period (together with Reinhardt, q.v., and Jürgen Fehling). His few films show the influence of his theatre experience, of "expressionism" (q.v.), and "*Kammerspiel*" (q.v,). Leaves Germany for U.S.A. during the Nazi *régime*.

Films: *Die Hintertreppe* 21 (co-dir.), *Erdgeist* 23 (also prod.), *Maria Stuart* (supervision, also co-scripted with Friedrich Feher and Anton Kuh).

172 JOHN, KARL (19 -   ). B: Cologne. Actor. Studied architecture in Danzig. Stage training under Jessner (q.v.). Theatres: Bunzlau, Dessau, Kassel, Königsberg and Deutsches Theater, Berlin. After 1945: many guest appearances, also mainly in Berlin.

Films: *Der weisse Dämon; Kind, ich freu' mich auf Dein Kommen; Wenn der Hahn kräht, Weisse Sklaven, Der Lachdoktor, Unternehmen Michael, Legion Condor, Die unvollkommene Liebe, Bal paré, Fahrt ins Leben, Kora Terry, Stukas, U-Boote westwärts, Der Weg ins Freie, Mein Leben für Irland, Ueber alles in der Welt, Zwei in einer grossen Stadt, Andreas Schlüter, Grossstadtmelodie, In jenen Tagen, Unser Mittwochabend, Liebe 47, Die letzte Nacht, Der Verlorene, Das Bankett der Schmuggler, Weg ohne Umkehr, Des Teufels Gene-*

ral, Hotel Adlon, Urlaub auf Ehrenwort, 2 x Adam – 1 x Eva, Hunde wollt ihr ewig leben, Fabrik der Offiziere, Der Hexer.

173 JUGO, JENNY (1905-   ). B: Mürzzuschlag/Steiermark. Actress. RN: Jenny Walter. Studies in Vienna, and at the age of sixteen marries actor Emo Jugo (later divorced). Enters cinema in 1924, and acts in a good many films before making her reputation as a comedienne in *Pygmalion*. Her greatest years of popularity were between 1935 and 1939.

Films: *Die Puppe vom Lunapark, Blitzzug der Liebe, Friedenblut, Die gefundene Braut, Liebe macht blind, Schiff in Not, Wenn die Liebe nicht wär'!, Ledige Töchter, Die Hose, Die indiskrete Frau, Pique Dame, Prinz Louis Ferdinand, Die blaue Maus, Die Carmen von St. Pauli, Looping the Loop, Sechs Mädchen suchen Nachtquartier, Der Bund der Drei, Die Flucht vor der Liebe, Die Schmugglerbraut von Malorca.* Then sound: *Heute Nacht – eventuell, Ich bleib' bei Dir, Kopfüber ins Glück, Die nackte Wahrheit, Wer nimmt die Liebe ernst, Fünf von der Jazzband, Eine Stadt steht Kopf, Zigeuner der Nacht, Es gibt nur eine Liebe, Ein Lied für Dich, Herz ist Trumpf, Pechmarie, Fräulein Frau, Heute Abend bei mir, Pygmalion, Die Nacht mit dem Kaiser, Mädchenjahre einer Königin, Allotria, Gefährliches Spiel, Die kleine und die grosse Liebe, Ein hoffnungsloser Fall, Nanette, Unser Fräulein Doktor, Viel Lärm um Nixi, Die Gattin, Sag' endlich ja; Träum' nicht, Annette; Königskinder.*

174 JUNKERMANN, HANS (1872 or 1876-1943). B: Stuttgart. D: Berlin. Actor. Son of the Reuter performer August Junkermann. Instead of becoming an officer he undergoes stage training from his father. First discovered as a comic. Early work at the Thalia Theater in Hamburg. 1896: to Trianon-Theater in Berlin. 1912: enters cinema.

Films (incomplete): *Wo ist Coletti?, Gelöste Ketten, Marie d'amour und ihre Liebhaber, Hamlet, Lachte man gerne, C.d.E., Die Dame und ihr Friseur, Dr. Mabuse der Spieler, Der Film ohne Name, Maciste und die Tochter des Silberkönigs, Das Mädel mit der Maske, Sodoms Ende, Der Taugenichts,*

Wem nie durch Liebe Leid geschah, Die Fledermaus, Der Mann ohne Herz, Das Milliardensouper, Nanon, Colibri, Der gestohlene Professor, Die grosse Unbekannte, Königsliebchen, Die Radio-Heirat, Ein Traum vom Glück, Das alte Ballhaus, Blitzzug der Liebe, Der Farmer aus Texas, Herrn Filip Collins Abenteuer, Die Kleine aus der Konfektion, Die Kleine vom Bummel, Liebe und Trompetenblasen, Luxusweibchen, Das Mädchen mit der Protektion, Der Tänzer meiner Frau, Der tanzende Tod, Die unberührte Frau, An der schönen blauen Donau, Annemarie und ihr Ulan, Durchlaucht Radieschen, Der Feldherrenhügel, Die Fürstin der Riviera, Die keusche Suzanne, Menschen untereinander, Prinzessin Tralala, Der Bettelstudent, Es zogen drei Burschen, Der Fürst von Pappenheim, Die Geliebte, Das Heiratsnest, Der Orlow, Das Schicksal einer Nacht, Die selige Exzellenz, Der Sprung ins Glück, Die tolle Lola, Die beiden Seehunde, Dragonerliebchen, Der Faschingsprinz, Die Geliebte seiner Hoheit, Heiratsfieber, Liebe im Mai, Liebeskarneval, Das Mädchen von der Strasse, Majestät schneidet Bubiköpfe, Der Mann mit dem Laubfrosch, Mikosch rückt ein, Serenissimus und die letzte Jungfrau, Die Zirkusprinzessin, Meine Schwester und ich, Das närrische Glück, Der schwarze Domino, Sündig und süss, Das verschwundene Testament, Der Detektiv des Kaisers. Then sound: *Er oder Ich, Liebeswalzer, Anna Christie, Delikatessen, Aschermittwoch, Der Korvettenkapitän, Zapfenstreich am Rhein, In Wien hab' ich einmal ein Mädel geliebt, Olympia, Der Storch streikt, Die Schlacht von Bademünde, Liebe auf Befehl, Das Geheimnis der roten Katz, Man braucht kein Geld, Die Fledermaus, Solang noch ein Walzer von Strauss erklingt, Mamsell Nitouche, Schatten der Unterwelt, Die Vier vom Bob 13, Durchlaucht amüsiert sich, Die Gräfin von Monte Christo, Die Tänzerin von Sanssouci, Traum von Schönbrunn, Liebe in Uniform, Glück über Nacht, Volldampf voraus, Ist mein Mann nicht fabelhaft?, Hochzeit am Wolfgangsee, Heimat am Rhein, Ein Lied für Dich, Die kleine Schwindlerin, Der Page vom Dalmasse-Hotel, Die Blume von Hawaii, Regine, Rosen aus dem Süden, Musik im Blut, Der letzte Walzer, Der Meisterboxer, Eine Frau, die weiss, was sie will; Die Csardasfürstin; Peter, Paul und Nanette; Pipin der Kurze, Aristen, Der junge Graf, Der Aussenseiter, Königstiger, Der Gefangene des Königs, Mein Leben für Maria Isabell, Lärm um Weidemann, Der verkannte Lebemann, Drei Mäderl um Schubert, Der lustige Witwenball, Ein Hochzeitstraum, Eine Frau ohne Bedeutung, Ein kleiner goldener Ring, Mädchen in Weiss, Serenade; Der Mann, der Sherlock Holmes war; Die göttliche Jette, Ziel in den Wolken, Verliebtes Abenteuer, Der unmögliche Herr Pitt, Fortsetzung folgt, Schüsse in Kabine 7, Unsere kleine Frau, Das Ekel, Verdacht auf Ursula, Frau am Steuer, Salonwagen E 417, Der Herr im Haus, Das Herz der Königin, Leidenschaft, Der Kleinstadtpoet, Liebesschule, Akrobat schö-ö-ön, Altes Herz wird wieder jung, Münchhausen.*

175 **JÜRGENS, CURD** (1915-   ). B: Munich. Actor and director. Stage training with Walter Janssen. Theatres: Metropol-Theater Berlin (1936), Theater am Kurfürstendamm and Komödie Berlin. 1938-1941: Deutsches Volkstheater Vienna. 1941-1953: Burgtheater Vienna and appearances at Salzburg Festival. International career since 1955. Former wives include actresses Judith Holzmeister and Eva Bartok. Also directed films *.

Films: *Königswalzer, Die Unbekannte, Familienparade, Zu neuen Ufern, Liebe kann lügen, Salonwagen E 417, Weltrekord im Seitensprung, Herz ohne Heimat, Operette, Wen die Götter lieben, Stimme des Herzens, Frauen sind keine Engel, Ein glücklicher Mensch, Eine kleine Sommermelodie, Ein Blick zurück, Wiener Mädeln, Der himmlische Walzer, Hexen, An klingenden Ufern, Das singende Haus, Hin und her, Der Engel mit der Posaune, Das Kuckucksei, Küssen ist keine Sünd, Die gestörte Hochzeitsnacht, Verlorenes Rennen, Lambert fühlt sich bedroht, Prämien auf den Tod 50* (also * and script with Kurt Heuser), *Schuss durchs Fenster, Pikanterie, Das Geheimnis einer Ehe, Küssen ist keine Sünd, Gangsterpremiere 51* (also * and script with Franz Gribitz), *Der schweigende Mund, Du bist die Rose vom Wörthersee, Knall und Fall als Hochstapler, Haus des Lebens, 1. April 2000, Man nennt es Liebe,*

Musik bei Nacht, Der letzte Walzer, Alles für Papa, Meines Vaters Pferde (i), *Rummelplatz der Liebe, Praterherzen, Eine Frau von heute, Gefangene der Liebe, Das Bekenntnis der Ina Kahr, Du bist die Richtige, Des Teufels General, Liebe ohne Illusion, Orient-Express* (also dir. of dialogue on German version), *Du mein stilles Tal, Die Ratten. Teufel in Seide, Die goldene Brücke, Ohne Dich wird es Nacht 56* (also *), *Der Schinderhannes, Schachnovelle, Gustav Adolfs Page, Bankraub in der rue Latour 61* (also dir.), *Die Dreigroschenoper, Begegnung in Salzburg, DM-Killer, Das Liebeskarussell* (ii), *Blüten, Gauner und die Nacht von Nizza, Das Geheimnis der gelben Mönche, Der Kongress amüsiert sich, Zwei Girls vom roten Stern, Der Lügner und die Nonne, . . . und morgen fahrt ihr alle zur Hölle, Der Arzt von St. Pauli, Auf der Reeperbahn nachts um halb eins, Ohrfeigen.*

176 **JUTZI, PHIL (PIEL)** (1894-19   ). B: Rheinpfalz. Director of photography and director. Although he directed a few films during the silent period, he gained his reputation with realistic films of the late Twenties such as *Mutter Krausens Fahrt ins Glück* and *Berlin Alexanderplatz*, in the former

destroying the old operetta-type image of the Berlin "backyards," and in the latter adapting Alfred Döblin's important novel for the screen.

Films (incomplete): *Der maskierte Schrecken* 20 (also script), *Die grosse Gelegenhei* (co-phot. with Schlesinger von Günz), *Klass und Datsch, die Pechvögel* 26 (also script and phot.), *Kindertragödie* 27, *Die Machnower Schleusen* 27 (also script and phot., short), *Der lebende Leichnam* (co-phot. with Golownia), *Klippen der Ehe* (co-phot. with Harry Meerson), *Mutter Krausens Fahrt ins Glück* 29 (also phot.). Then sound: *Berlin — Alexanderplatz* 31, *Der Kosak und die Nachtigall* 35, *Lockspitzel Asew, Das Gewehr über, So ein Früchtchen.*

177 KAISER, WOLF (1916-   ). B. Frankfurt. Actor. At first studies chemistry and psychology. 1942: to Volksbühne Berlin. 1945: Schauspielhaus Leipzig. 1950: Deutsches Theater and Berlin Ensemble, Berlin. 1965: State award.

Films: *Das Leben ruft, Die Kreuzlschreiber, Die Buntkarierten, Der letzte Heuer, Das verurteilte Dorf, Die Unbesiegbaren, Die Geschichte vom kleinen Muck, Ernst Thälmann — Sohn seiner Klasse, Der Fall Dr. Wagner, Ernst Thälmann — Führer seiner Klasse, Der Ochse von Kulm, Die Millionen der Yvette, Thomas Müntzer, Das tapfere Schneiderlein, Senta auf Abwegen, Kabale und Liebe, Mutter Courage und ihre Kinder, Italienisches Capriccio, Der Dieb von San Marengo, Jetzt und in der Stunde meines Todes, Alaskafüchse, Die Abenteuer des Werner Holt.*

178 "KAMMERSPIEL": Term deriving from theatre, made famous through the work of Max Reinhardt. Therefore films with a concise and intimate psychological content, a minimum of characters and sparse *décors* can be classified as *"Kammerspiel."* As in "expressionism," Carl Mayer is again a key figure. The style of narration is naturalistic and spare, created primarily through the words in the script and secondarily by director and set designer. The themes dealt with in *"Kammerspiel"* appear to be much lighter than expressionist subjects and almost bourgeois. A strict unity of action, time and place distinguishes all films of this type. *"Kammerspiel"* films carry an air of finality and Destiny. Characters are nameless, appearing merely as figures the Mother, the Woman, etc. – and the goal is towards the "filmic film," the self-explanatory film free of captions *(Scherben*, 1921, was the first picture without these).

Key films: *The Joyless Street, Dirnentragödie, Sylvester, Scherben, The Last Laugh* (n.b. subjective camerawork). In *Nju*, Paul Czinner transcended the style, thanks to the performance of his wife Elisabeth Bergner.

"Kammerspiel" led to the so-called "street" films (e.g. Karl Grune's *The Street*, with the home as a place of refuge from the dangerous street), although this *genre* was later distorted by the wave of "social" films with their descriptions of urban squalor.

179 KAMPERS, FRITZ (1891-1950). B and D: Garmisch-Partenkirchen. Actor. Stage training under Franz von Possart. Theatres: Karlsruhe, Düsseldorf, Munich, Berlin etc. 1939: declared "Actor of the State."

Films (incomplete): *Else die Räuberbraut, Prinzessin Else, Ich hatt' einen Kameraden, Flametti, Die Apotheke des Teufels, Das offene Grab, Söhne der Hölle, Der grosse Preis, Jeanette Bussier, Monna Vanna, Passagier in der Zwangsjacke, Schamlose Seelen, Der Todesreigen, Lord Reginalds Derbyritt, Der Mensch am Wege, Nachtstürme, Nanon, Schlagende Wetter, Der steinerne Reiter, Der Weg zu Gott, Wilhelm Tell, Arabella, Aufstieg der kleinen Lilian, In den Krallen der Schuld, Komödianten, Die Liebesbriefe einer Verlassenen, Die Stimme des Herzens, Ein Traum vom Glück, Die vom Niederrhein, Götz von Berlichingen zubenannt mit der eisernen Hand, Grüsse mir das blonde Kind am Rhein, Halbseide, Heiratsannoncen, Menschen am Meer; Reveille, das grosse Wecken; Unser täglich Brot, Wallenstein, Zapfenstreich, Die Flucht in den Zirkus, Fünfuhrtee in der Ackerstrasse, Der Hauptmann von Köpenick, Ich hatt' einen Kameraden; In der Heimat, da gibt's ein Wiedersehn!, Der Jäger von Fall, Der Juxbaron, Die Kleine und ihr Kavalier; Kubinke, der Barbier, und die drei Dienstmäd-*

chen; *Der Mann ohne Schlaf, Nanette macht alles, Die Perle des Regiments, Der Pfarrer von Kirchfeld, Die Piraten der Ostseebäder, Der Prinz und die Tänzerin, Der Provinzonkel, Das rosa Pantöffelchen, Ueberflüssige Menschen, Wir sind vom k. und k. Infanterie-Regiment, Almenrausch und Edelweiss, Der Bettler vom Kölner Dom, Da hält die Welt den Atem an, Es zogen drei Burschen, Der Fluch der Vererbung, Frühere Verhältnisse, Funkzauber, Gustav Mond . . ., Du gehst so stille, Ich habe im Mai von der Liebe geträumt, Leichte Kavallerie, Ein Mädel aus dem Volke, Der Meister der Welt, Petronella, Schwere Jungens – leichte Mädchen, Ein schwerer Fall, Verbotene Liebe, Wenn Menschen reif zur Liebe werden, Wochenendzauber, Ein besserer Herr, Die Dame mit der Maske, Die Dame und ihr Chauffeur, Deutsche Frauen – deutsche Treue, Dragonerliebchen, Fräulein Chauffeur, Das Haus ohne Männer, Heiratsfieber, Herbstzeit am Rhein, Lamkes sel. Witwe, Mary Lou, Ossi hat die Hosen an, Der Piccolo vom Goldenen Löwen, Robert und Bertram, Der Staatsanwalt klagt an, Vom Täter fehlt jede Spur, Der Weiberkrieg, Die Zirkusprinzessin, Autobus Nr. 2, Drei Tage auf Leben und Tod, Durchs Brandenburger Tor, Ehe in Not, Die fidele Herrenpartie, Fräulein Fähnrich, Die Frau, die jeder liebt, bist Du!, Die Herrin und ihr Knecht, Jugendtragödie, Katherina Knie, Das Recht der Ungeborenen, Somnambul, Tempo! Tempo!, Der Witwenball, Wem gehört meine Frau?, Wenn Du noch eine Heimat hast, O Mädchen, mein Mädchen, wie lieb' ich Dich!.* Then sound: *Das Donkosakenlied, Zwei Welten, Der Korvettenkapitän, Lumpenball, Pension Schöller, Dreyfus, Die lustigen Musikanten, Die Drei von der Tankstelle, Kohlhiesels Töchter, ·Tingel-Tangel, Westfront 1918, Die Bräutigamswitwe, Gloria, Strohwitwer, Schützenfest in Schilda, Reserve hat Ruh, Der Stolz der 3. Kompanie, Kameradschaft, Ballhaus goldener Engel, Eine Stadt steht Kopf, Drei von der Stempelstelle, Drei von der Kavallerie, Der Rebell, Das Blaue vom Himmel, Strich durch die Rechnung, Frau Lehmanns Töchter, Liebe in Uniform, Strafsache van Geldern, Grün ist die Heide, Skandal in der Parkstrasse, Die vom Niederrhein, Die Fahrt ins Grüne, Der Jäger aus*

Kurpfalz, Der Judas von Tirol, Der Meisterdetektiv, Zwei gute Kameraden, Schüsse an der Grenze; Schön ist jeder Tag, den Du mir schenkst, Marie Luise, Drei blaue Jungs – ein blondes Mädel, Drei Kaiserjäger, Ein Lied geht um die Welt, Eine Frau wie Du, Manolescu, der Fürst der Diebe, Kleiner Mann – was nun?, Ganovenehre, Grosstadtnacht, La Paloma, Der Doppelbräutigam, Die vier Musketiere, Der Herr Senator, Die Liebe und die erste Eisenbahn, Zigeunerbaron, Leichte Kavallerie, Martha, Die Drei um Christine, Das Veilchen vom Potsdamer Platz, Der Bettelstudent, Weisse Sklaven, Stadt Anatol, Urlaub auf Ehrenwort, Meiseken, Spiel auf der Tenne, pour le mérite, Konzert in Tirol, Nordlicht, Spassvögel, Im Namen des Volkes, Das Ekel, Die goldene Maske, Verdacht auf Ursula, Robert und Bertram, Legion Condor, Weltrekord im Seitensprung, Bal paré, Stern von Rio, Das Fräulein von Barnhelm, Links der Isar – rechts der Spree, Der Feuerteufel, Ueber alles in der Welt, Der laufende Berg, Immer nur Du, Anschlag auf Baku, Der Ochsenkrieg, Die Entlassung, Kollege kommt gleich, Gabriele Dambrone, Der zweite Schuss, Akrobat Schö-ö-ön, Kohlhiesels Töchter; Freitag, der 13.; Das Konzert, Die Zaubergeige, Der Meisterdetektiv, In flagranti, Neigungsehe, Jugendliebe, Wir beide liebten Katharina, Der Scheiterhaufen, Die Kreuzlschreiben; Peter Voss, der Millionendieb; Morgen ist alles besser, Nichts als Zufälle, Ich mach' Dich glücklich, Das Geheimnis des Hohen Falken, Des Lebens Ueberfluss, Schwarzwaldmädel, Sensation im Savoy, Die Sterne lügen nicht, Die Nacht ohne Sünde.

180 **KAPER, BRONISLAV** (1902-   ). B: Warsaw. Composer. Worked for films in Germany with the Austrian composer Walter Jurman immediately after the coming of sound. Successful composer for, amongst others, Jan Kiepura (q.v.). 1935: to France, and later to Hollywood.

Films: *Die lustigen Musikanten, Der Korvettenkapitän* (in collab. with Ben Berlin), *Alraune, Ehe m.b.H.* (in collab. with Walter Jurmann), *Die grosse Attraktion* (in collab. with Dessau, Grothe and Franz Lehar), *Skandal in der Parkstrasse* (in collab. with Jurmann), *Die Zwei vom Südexpress* (in collab. with Jurmann, Friedrich Jung and Hans Wenning), *Ein toller Einfall* (in collab. with Jurmann and Hans-Otto Borgman), *Melodie der Liebe* (in collab. with Dessau and Jurmann), *Es wird schon wieder besser* (in collab. with Jurmann), *Hochzeitsreise zu Dritt* (in collab. with Jurmann) *Ich will Dich Liebe lehren* (in collab. with Jurman), *Ein Lied für Dich* (in collab. with Jurmann and Schmidt-Gentner), *Heut' kommt's drauf an* (in collab. with Jurmann, Helmuth Wolfes, Stephan Weiss and Paul Mann), *Madame wünscht keine Kinder* (in collab. with Jurmann and Hans J. Salter), *Kind, ich freu' mich auf Dein Kommen* (in collab. with Jurmann and Borgmann).

181 **KAUFMANN, CHRISTINE** (1945-   ). B: Lengdorf/Steiermark. Actress. Ballet training, children's parts at first, then appearances in Italian and Spanish films. Thanks to *Stadt ohne Mitleid* began a not very successful career in American films. Formerly married to Tony Curtis. Now back in Germany.

Films: *Im weissen Rössl, Salto mortale, Der Klosterjäger, Staatsanwältin Corda, Rosen-Resli, Der schweigende Engel, Wenn die Alpenrosen blüh'n, Ein Herz schlägt für*

Erika, Die Stimme der Sehnsucht, Witwer mit 5 Töchtern, Die Winzerin von Langenlois, Mädchen in Uniform, Der veruntreute Himmel, Alle lieben Peter, Ein Thron für Christine, Der letzte Fussgänger, Die letzten Tage von Pompei, Toller Hecht auf krummen Touren, Via Mala, 90 Minuten nach Mitternacht, Tunnel 28, Liebesvögel.

182 **KÄUTNER, HELMUT** (1908-   ). B: Düsseldorf. Director, actor and scriptwriter. Studied history of art, theatrical science and philology. Writes for cabaret and directs stage productions (e.g. in Leipzig, Munich, Berlin [also acts] between 1936 and 1938). One of the principal German directors during the last two years of the war and immediately after 1945. In recent years he has confined his directing mainly to the stage and TV.

Acted in: *Kreuzer Emden, Romanze in Moll, Grosse Freiheit Nr. 7, Der Apfel ist ab, Königskinder, Epilog.* Films: *Schneider Wibbel* (only script with B. E. Lüthge), *Salonwagen E 417* (only script with Lüthge), *Die Stimme aus dem Aether* (only script with Lüthge and Edgar Kahn), *Marguerite 3* (only co-scripted), *Kitty und die Weltkonferenz 39* (and script), *Kleider machen Leute 40* (and script), *Frau nach Mass 40* (and script), *Auf Wiedersehen, Franziska 41* (and co-scripted), *Wir machen Musik 42* (and script), *Anuschka 42* (and co-scripted), *Romanze in Moll 43* (and script with Willy Clever), *Grosse Freiheit Nr. 7 44* (and script with Richard Nicolas), *Unter den Brücken 45* (and script with Walter Ulbrich), *In jenen Tagen 47* (and script with Ernst Schnabel), *Der Apfel ist ab 48* (and script with Bobby Todd), *Film ohne Titel* (only script with Rudolf Jugert and Ellen Fechner), *Königskinder 49* (and script with Emil Burri and Herbert Witt), *Epilog 50* (and co-scripted), *Nachts auf den Strassen* (only script with Fritz Rotter), *Weisse Schatten 51* (also script with Maria Osten-Sacken), *Käpt'n Bay-Bay 52* (also script with Heinz Pauck and Per Schwenzen), *Die letzte Brücke 54* (also script with Norbert Kunze), *Bildnis einer Unbekannten 54* (also script with Hans Jacoby), *Des Teufels General 55* (also script with Georg Hurdalek), *Ludwig II. 55, Himmel ohne Sterne 55* (also script from his own play), *Ein Mädchen aus Flandern 55* (also script with Heinz Pauck), *Griff nach den Sternen* (only script with Osten-Sacken), *Der Hauptmann von Köpenick* 56 (also script with Carl Zuckmayer), *Die Zürcher Verlobung* 56, *Monpti* 56 (also script), *Franziska* (only script with C. J. Braun and Georg Hurdalek), *Der Schinderhannes* 58, *Der Rest ist Schweigen* 59 (also script), *Die Gans von Sedan* 59 (also script with Jean L'Hote), *Das Glas Wasser* 60 (also script), *Schwarzer Kies* 60 (also script with Ulbrich), *Der Traum von Lieschen Müller* 61, *Zu jung für die Liebe* (supervision, also acted), *Die Rote* 62, *Das Haus in Montevideo* 63, *Lausbubengeschichten* 64.

183 KAYSSLER, FRIEDRICH (1874-1945). B: Neurode/Grafschaft Glatz. D: Kleinmachnow, near Berlin. Actor. 1896: to Berlin for stage training. Theatres: Görlitz, Breslau, Berlin (1933-1944 Staatstheater). 1928-1933: director of the Volksbühne in Berlin. One of the most famous actors on the German stage prior to 1933. Declared an "Actor of the State." Father of actor Christian Kayssler (1898-1944).

Films: *Die Liebe einer Königin, Gräfin Donelli, Mutter und Kind, Schicksal, Tragödie im Hause Habsburg, Ein Lebenskünstler, Eine Dubarry von heute, Feme, Das brennende Herz.* Then sound: *Zwei Welten, Das Flötenkonzert von Sanssouci, Zwei Menschen, Stürme über dem Montblanc, Der Hauptmann von Köpenick, Yorck; Der Mann, der den Mord beging; 24 Stunden im Leben einer Frau; Luise, Königin von Preussen; Im Geheimdienst, Täter gesucht, Kadetten, Das Schiff ohne Hafen, Marschall Vorwärts, Strafsache van Geldern, Goethe lebt . . .!, Unter falscher Flagge, Die elf Schill-schen Offiziere, Gold, Der ewige Traum, Peer Gynt, Der höhere Befehl, Der alte und der junge König, Das Mädchen vom Moorhof, Mazurka, Friesennot, Der Hund von Baskerville, Eine Frau ohne Bedeutung, Der zerbrochene Krug, Dreizehn Mann und eine Kanone, Anna Favetti, Verwehte Spuren, Zwischen den Eltern, Der singende Tor, Friedrich Schiller, Der Fuchs von Glenarvon, Angelika, Bismarck, Der Strom, Träumerei, Das Leben geht weiter.*

184 KEMP, PAUL (1899-1953). B and D: Bad Godesberg. Actor. Studies architecture. Soldier. Stage training under Luise Dumont. Theatres: Düsseldorf, Remscheid, Hamburg, Berlin. Enters films through Alfred Zeisler.

Films (incomplete): *Cyankali, Seitensprünge, Dann schon lieber Lebertran, Die grosse Sehnsucht, Die blonde Nachtigall, Der Schuss im Tonfilmatelier, Der König von Paris, Lumpenball, Dolly macht Karriere, Um eine Nasenlänge, Meine Cousine aus Warschau, M, Der Raub der Mona Lisa, Die Dreigroschenoper, Ein Auto und kein Geld, Die schwebende Jungfrau, Sehnsucht 202, Zigeuner der Nacht, Die verkaufte Braut, Drei von der Stempelstelle, Gitta entdeckt ihr Herz, Ein Mann mit Herz, Mieter Schulze gegen alle, Das Lied vom Glück, Unsichtbare Gegner, Das Schloss im Süden; Ihre Durchlaucht, die Verkäuferin; Roman einer Nacht, Ein Lied für Dich, Mein Herz ruft nach Dir, Prinzessin Turandot, Mit Dir durch dick und dünn, Der Flüchtling von Chikago, Die Csardasfürstin, Der Gefangene des Königs, Amphitryon, Der mutige Seefahrer, Heisses Blut, Blumen aus Nizza Boccaccio, Glückskinder, Der schüchterne Casanova, Die verschwundene Frau, Musik für Dich, Zauber der Bohème, Ihr Leibhusar, Unsere kleine Frau, Capriccio, Dir gehör mein Herz, Premiere der Butterfly, Das Abenteuer geht weiter, Kornblumenblau Der Kleinstadtpoet, Das leichte Mädchen, Was wird hier gespielt?, Frau Luna, Jenny und der Herr im Frack, Immer nur Du Die grosse Nummer, Ein Windstoss, Fahr ins Abenteuer, Das Lied der Nachtigall Glück unterwegs, Dir zuliebe, Sieben Briefe Frech und verliebt, Liebe nach Noten, Spul im Schloss, Leuchtende Schatten, Der himmlische Walzer, Das singende Haus, Gefährliche Gäste, Triumph der Liebe, Absende unbekannt, Lambert fühlt sich bedroht, Die Nacht ohne Sünde; Der Mann, der sich selber sucht; Kein Engel ist so rein, Die Dritte von rechts, Mädchen mit Beziehungen, Die Mitternachtsvenus, Engel im Abendkleid, . . . Mutter sein dagegen sehr In München steht ein Hofbräuhaus, Fräulein Bimbi, Die Diebin von Bagdad, Königin der Arena, Salto mortale, Liebeskrie nach Noten, Glück muss man haben.*

185 **KIEPURA, JAN** (1902-1966). B: Sosnowice (Poland). D: Harrison, New York. Singer and actor. Studies in Warsaw, and voice training there. *Début* at Opera in Lemberg, then to Warsaw and Poznan. From 1926: guest appearances in Vienna, Milan, Paris, Berlin, Buenos Aires and Chicago. With the coming of sound, he entered films. Emigrated with his wife, soprano Martha Eggerth (q.v.), to America and made several films in Hollywood. Guest appearances in operas and operettas at many American theatres.

Films: *Die singende Stadt, Das Lied einer Nacht, Ein Lied für Dich, Mein Herz ruft nach Dir, Ich liebe alle Frauen, Im Sonnenschein, Zauber der Bohème, Das Land des Lächelns.*

186 **KIESLER, HEDWIG** (1914 or 1918-). B: Vienna of Czech origin. Actress. Stage training under Professor Arndt in Vienna. Theatres: Raimund-Theater and Theater in der Josefstadt, both Vienna. Became famous thanks to her lavish playing in Gustav Machaty's *Ekstase* (1932). In her

Hedwig Kiesler in EKSTASE

first two film appearances (small parts) she also worked as a script girl. 1937: to U.S.A., where she adopts a new name HEDY LAMARR. Autobiography: *Ecstasy and Me* (1965).

Films: *Das Geld liegt auf der Strasse, Die Blumenfrau von Lindenau, Die Koffer des Herrn O.F., Man braucht kein Geld, Symphonie der Liebe.*

187 **KINSKI, KLAUS** (1926-). B: Zoppot. Actor. RN: Claus Günther Nakszynski. Stage *début* at Theater in der Kaiserallee Berlin, then guest appearances in Munich and Berlin. Many tours and recitals. 1957: starts international career. Usually portrays villainous roles in German films.

Films: *Morituri, Ludwig II.; Kinder, Mütter und ein General; Hanussen, Sarajevo, Waldwinter, Geliebte Corinna, Der Rächer, Die toten Augen von London, Bankraub in der rue Latour, Das Geheimnis der gelben Narzissen, Das Rätsel der roten Orchideen, Die seltsame Gräfin, Das Gasthaus an der Themse, Der rote Rausch, Die Türe mit den sieben Schlössern, Das Geheimnis der schwarzen Witwe, Das indische Tuch; Piccadilly, null Uhr zwölf; Der schwarze Abt, Die schwarze Kobra, Scotland Yard jagt Dr. Mabuse, Der Zinker, Das Geheimnis der chinesischen Nelke, Die Gruft mit dem Rätselschloss, Kali Yug I & II, Der letzte Ritt nach Santa Cruz, Winnetou II, Für ein paar Dollar mehr, Das Geheimnis der gelben Mönche, Gern hab' ich die Frauen gekillt, Die blaue Hand, Der Bastard, Marquis de Sade: Justine, Mister zehn Prozent – Miezen und Moneten; Das Gesicht im Dunkeln, E Dio disse a Caino, How did a nice girl like you get into a business like this?*

188 **KLAGEMANN, EUGEN** (19 -). Director of photography. Enters cinema in the early Forties and works on some of the most important films made in East Germany after the Second World War. Joins DEFA.

Films: *Ich werde Dich auf Händen tragen* (co-phot.), *Herr Sanders lebt gefährlich* (co-phot.), *Das Konzert, Glück muss man haben, Der Mann im Sattel, Die Mörder sind unter uns* (co-phot.), *Razzia* (co-phot.), *Ehe im Schatten* (co-phot.), *Arche Nora, Finale, Das Mädchen Christine, Figaros Hochzeit* (co-phot. with Karl Plintzner), *Wir bummeln um die Welt* (only additional camerawork), *Die lustigen Weiber von Windsor* (co-phot. with Plintzner), *Corinna Schmidt* (co-phot. with Rudi Radünz), *Schatten über den Inseln, Geheimakte Solvay, Der Fall Dr. Wagner, Der Ochse von Kulm, Das Fräulein von Scudery, Heimliche Ehen, Damals in Paris, Alter Kahn und junge Liebe, Meine Frau macht Musik, Ware für Katalonien, Tilman Riemenschneider, Sie kannten sich alle, Bevor der Blitz einschlägt Trübe Wasser, Seilergasse 8, Die Liebe und der Co-Pilot, Die aus der 12 b.*

189 KLAREN, GEORG C. (1900-   ). B: Vienna. Scriptwriter, writer and director. RN: Georg Eugen Moritz Alexander Klaric. Studied philology at Vienna University. At first journalist, then writer and literary manager for Vita-Film Vienna. Scriptwriter of many silent and sound films (sometimes with Herbert Juttke), also in G.D.R. (where after 1945 he is main literary manager for DEFA, q.v.). His most successful artistic work is *Wozzeck*. * indicates work with Herbert Juttke.

Films: *Gern hab' ich die Frauen geküsst* *, *Das graue Haus* *, *Die Kleine und ihr Kavalier* *, *Nanette macht alles, Die Warenhausprinzessin* *, *Dr. Bessels Verwandlung* *, *Feme* *, *Gehetzte Frauen* *, *Der grosse Unbekannte* *, *Kleinstadtsünder* *, *Liebelei* *, *Mein Leben für das Deine* * (and Morat), *Casanovas Erbe, Die Dame und ihr Chauffeur* *, *Freiwild* *, *Geschlecht in Fesseln* *, *Der Herr vom Finanzamt* *, *Im Werder blühen die Bäume* *, *Eine Nacht in London* *, *Blutschande § 173 St.G.B.* *, *Ehe in Not* *, *Der Hund von Baskerville* *, *Kolonne X* *, *Peter, der Matrose* (co-scripted with Heinz Gordon), *Das Recht der Ungeborenen* *, *Sensation im Wintergarten* (co-scripted with Hans Jacoby), *Somnambul* *, *Das Weib am Kreuze, Gehetzte Mädchen* *, Then sound: *Zärtlichkeit* *, *O alte Burschenherrlichkeit* (co-scripted with Marcel Lion), *Tänzerinnen für Südamerika gesucht* (co-scripted with Leopold Thoma), *Mitternachtsliebe* (co-scripted with Maurice Kroll and Carl Behr), *Chauffeur Antoinette* (co-scripted with Robert Blum and Heinz Goldberg), *Gloria* (only idea with Hans Szekely), *Kinder vor Gericht 31* (also dir.), *Elisabeth von Oesterreich* (co-scripted with Adolf Lantz

and Alfred Schirokauer), *Mary* (co-scripted with Alma Reville and *), *Drei von der Stempelstelle* (co-scripted with F. A. Reisch), *Ballhaus goldener Engel 32* (co-scripted with Fritz Falkenstein, also dir.),*Eine Frau wie Du, Spione am Werk* *, *Es gibt nur eine Liebe, Höllentempo, Moral und Liebe, Johannisnacht; Manolescu, der Fürst der Diebe* (co-scripted with Hans Rameau), *Jede Frau hat ein Geheimnis* (co-scripted with Friedrich Walther), *Frasquita, Stützen der Gesellschaft* (co-scripted with Peter Gillmann), *Der Kosak und die Nachtigall, Ave Maria, Schatten der Vergangenheit* (treatment only), *Die Liebe des Maharadscha* (co-scripted with Corrado Alvaso), *Heimweh, Der Biberpelz, Die Kronzeugin* (co-scripted with Hofmann and Karl Lerbs), *Mit versiegelter Order* (co-scripted with Felix von Eckart), *Mordsache Holm* (co-scripted with Ilse Paul-Czech), *Der Schritt vom Wege* (co-scripted with Eckart von Naso), *Traummusik* (co-scripted with Richard Billinger and J. B. Malina), *Achtung! Feind hört mit!* (only idea), *Clarissa* (co-scripted with Ele Elborg), *Mutter* (co-scripted with Elborg and Guido Cantini), *Dr. Crippen an Bord* (co-scripted with Engels and Kurt E. Walter), *Das alte Lied* (only treatment of two Fontane novels), *Wozzek 47* (also dir.), *Semmelweis – Retter der Mütter 50* (only dir.), *Die Sonnenbrucks 51* (co-scripted with Maetzig, also dir.), *Karriere in Paris 51* (only co-dir. with Hans-Georg Rudolph), *Ruf aus dem Aether 51, Die Regimentsoochter 53* (only co-directed with Günther Haenel) *Rosenmontag* (co-scripted with Heinz-Werner John).

190 KLEIN-ROGGE, RUDOLF (1888-1955). B: Cologne. D: Graz. Actor. Studied history of art and literature. Private stage training, comes to theatre thanks to actor Sieber (Burgtheater Vienna), first in the provinces, then theatres in Halberstadt, Kiel, Nurenberg and (1918) Berlin (with Barnowsky). 1919: enters cinema, splendid character actor in Fritz Lang's films (q.v.). Was married for a time to Thea von Harbou (q.v.).

Films (incomplete): *Morphium, Das wandernde Bild, Kämpfende Herzen, Perlen bedeuten Tränen, Zirkus des Lebens, Dr. Mabuse der Spieler, Die Prinzessin Sswarin, Der steinerne Reiter, Die Nibelungen (ii),*

Pietro, der Korsar, Der Mann seiner Frau, Der rosa Diamant, Der Herr der Nacht, Die lachende Grille, Mädchenhandel, Metropolis, Die letzte Nacht, Das Mädchen aus Frisco, Die raffinierteste Frau Berlins, Die Sandgräfin, Tingel-Tangel, Der Zigeunerbaron, Mädchenschicksale, Die schönste Frau von Paris, Spione, Wolga-Wolga, Meineid. Then sound: Der weisse Gott, Der Judas von Tirol, Das Testament des Dr. Mabuse, Elisabeth und der Narr, Zwischen Himmel und Erde, Hanneles Himmelfahrt, Der Fall Brenken, Die Welt ohne Maske, Grenzfeuer, Gern hab' ich die Frau'n geküsst, Die Frauen vom Tannhof, Der alte und der junge König, Das Einmaleins der Liebe, Der Kosak und die Nachtigall, Der Ammenkönig, Ein seltsamer Gast, Moral, Truxa, Das Hofkonzert, Der Kaiser von Kalifornien, Intermezzo, Die un-erhörte Frau, Madame Bovary, Die göttliche Jette, Der Herrscher, Die gelbe Flagge, Streit um den Knaben Jo, Der Katzensteg, Zwei Frauen, Ab Mitternacht, Abenteuer in Marokko, Kennwort Machin, Parkstrasse 13, Robert Koch, Schneider Wibbel, Rheinische Brautfahrt, Menschen vom Varieté, Die unvollkommene Liebe, Das Herz einer Königin, Hochzeit auf Bärenhof.

191 KLÖPFER, EUGEN (1886-1950). B: Thalheim. D: Wiesbaden. Actor. Stage *début* in provincial theatres. Then: Colmar, Erfurt, Bonn, Frankfurt. Thanks to Barnowsky comes to Berlin, where he also studies under Reinhardt (q.v.). 1918: enters cinema through Dr. Guter and Carl Froelich (q.v.). Important actor of stage and film. 1936: General director of the Volksbühne Berlin. Declared an "Actor of the State."

Films (incomplete): *Cagliostros Totenhemd, Maria Magdalena, Brandherd, Jugend, Die lebende Fackel, Die letzten Menschen, Sehnsucht, Torgus, Um der Liebe willen, Die Ratten, Der brennende Acker, Der falsche Dimitri, Das Geld auf der Strasse, Der Graf von Charolais, Der Graf von Essex, Macbeth, Menschenopfer, Die Austreibung, Der Puppenmacher von Kiang-Ning, Schlagende Wetter, Die Strasse, Sylvester, Carlos und Elisabeth, Komödianten, Elegantes Pack, Der erste Stand, Götz von Berlichingen zubenannt mit der eisernen Hand, O alte Burschenherrlichkeit, Der tanzende Tod, Die lachende Grille, Ueberflüssige Menschen, Luther, Die Vorbestraften, Katherina Knie.* Then sound: *Die Pranke; 1914, die letzten Tage vor dem Weltbrand; Der Herzog von Reichstadt, Gehetzte Menschen, Unheimliche Geschichten, Flüchtlinge, Wilhelm Tell, Liselotte von der Pfalz, Pygmalion, Ich war Jack Mortimer, Liebeserwachen, Anschlag auf Schweda, Jugend, Die Spieler, Umwege zum Glück, Die fremde Frau, Der ewige Quell, Jud Süss, Friedrich Schiller, Mein Leben für Irland, Friedemann Bach, Stimme des Herzens, Die goldene Stadt, Der unendliche Weg, Gabriele Dambrone, Solistin Anna Alt, Der Erbförster, Philharmoniker, Die Zaubergeige, Der Puppenspieler, Shiva und die Galgenblume, Die Brüder Noltenius.*

192 KLUGE, ALEXANDER (1932-   ). B: Halberstadt/Harz. Writer and director. Studied law, history and clerical science in Berlin. Practised law. As writer, published *Lebensläufe* and *Schlachtbeschreibung.*

At left: Rudolf Klein-Rogge as Rotwang in METROPOLIS

Member of "Gruppe 47." 1958-1959: assistant to Fritz Lang (q.v.). Short films from 1960 onwards. Feature films from 1966, in close collaboration with actors and technicians. Kluge's complex style has both literary and visual significance, certainly makes him one of the most important representatives of the *Junger deutscher Film* (q.v.).

Collaborated on *Protokoll einer Revolution* 63 (short, dir. G. Lemmer; co-scripted), *Arena 61* 65 (short, dir. P. Perling; Kluge wrote the text), *Unendliche Fahrt – aber begrenzt* 65 (short, dir. Edgar Reitz; Kluge wrote the commentary), *Pokerspiel* 66 (a new German version of a 1923 Mack Sennett film), *Mahlzeiten* 67 (adviser). Kluge's own films (all also scripted): *Brutalität in Stein* 60 (short, scr. and dir. with Peter Schamoni, q.v.), *Thema Amore* 61 (short), *Rennen* 61 (short, script: Hans von Neuffer, co-dir. with Paul Kruntorad), *Rennfahrer* 61 (short, script: Paul Kruntorad), *Lehrer (im Wandel)* 63 (short, co-scripted with Karen Kluge), *Porträt einer Bewährung* 65 (short), *Abschied von gestern* 66, *Frau Blackburn wird gefilmt* 67 (short), *Feuerlöscher E. A. Winterstein* 67 (short), *Die Artisten in der Zirkuskuppel: ratlos* 68. (also prod.).

193 **KNEF, HILDEGARD** (1925-   ). B: Ulm. After 1945: appears at the Tribüne Theatre and the Schlosspark-Theater, both in Berlin, Film *début* as a newcomer at Ufa in 1945. Main part in *The Murderers Are among Us* starts her career. But she failed to make a real impact on German cinema, and so went to England in 1953 and to U.S.A. in 1957 (Broadway, and films like *The Snows of Kilimanjaro)*, where she was known under the name of Hildegarde Neff. Back to Europe, films in France and Germany. New career as singer.

Films: *Träumerei* (scenes cut out later), *Fahrt ins Glück, Unter den Brücken, Die Mörder sind unter uns, Zwischen Gestern und Morgen, Film ohne Titel, Die Sünderin, Es geschehen noch Wunder, Alraune, Illusion in Moll, Nachts auf den Strassen, Eine Liebesgeschichte, Geständnis unter vier Augen, Madeleine und der Legionär; Der Mann, der sich verkaufte; Lulu, Die Dreigroschenoper, Das grosse Liebesspiel, Wartezimmer zum Jenseits, Verdammt zur Sünde.*

194 KNUTH, GUSTAV (1901-   ). B: Brunswick. Actor. Stage training in Brunswick. Theatres; Hildesheim, Basle, Altona, Hamburg, Berlin (Volksbühne and Staatstheater). 1945: Deutsches Schauspielhaus Hamburg. Since 1949: lives in Switzerland and acts at Schauspielhaus Zurich. Favourite TV actor, especially serials.

Films: *Der Ammenkönig, Heimweh, Schatten über St. Pauli, Das Lied der Wüste, Mann für Mann, Der Vorhang fällt, Zwischen Hamburg und Haiti, Das Mädchen von Fano, Friedemann Bach, Pedro soll hängen, Das grosse Spiel, Schule des Lebens, Gefährtin meines Sommers, Ein glücklicher Mensch, Grosse Freiheit Nr. 7, Fahrt ins Glück, Tierarzt Dr. Vlimmen, Das Leben geht weiter, Unter den Brücken, Der blaue Strohut, Das Geheimnis der roten Katze, Einmaleins der Ehe, Tromba, Der Theodor im Fussballtor, Geliebter Lügner, Es kommt ein Tag, Eine Frau mit Herz, Das seltsame Leben des Herrn Bruggs, Das kann jedem passieren, Der blaue Stern des Südens, Der fröhliche Weinberg, Keine Angst vor grossen Tieren, Die Nacht ohne Moral, Muss man sich gleich scheiden lassen?, Der Raub der Sabinerinen, Die Mücke, Auf der Reeperbahn nachts um halb eins, Geliebte Feindin, Die Ratten, Griff nach den Sternen, Himmel ohne Sterne, Ich denke oft an Piroschka, Sissi, 08/15 in der Heimat, Regine, Der Bettelstudent, Heute heiratet mein Mann, Wenn wir alle Engel wären, Heidemarie, Hengst Maestoso Austria; Sissi, die junge Kaiserin; Spion für Deutschland, Robinson soll nicht sterben, Das Schloss in Tirol, Ein Stück vom Himmel, Der Graf von Luxemburg, Sissi – Schicksaljahre einer Kaiserin, Der schwarze Blitz, Man ist nur zweimal jung, Ihr 106. Geburtstag, Hoch klingt der Radetzkymarsch, Das Dreimäderlhaus, Geliebte Bestie, Kleine Leute – mal ganz gross, Alle lieben Peter, Buddenbrooks, 2 x Adam – 1 x Eva, Das kunstseidene Mädchen, Freddy unter fremden Sternen, Lampenfieber, Kein Engel ist so rein, Ich heirate Herrn Direktor, Conny und Peter machen Musik, Eine Frau fürs ganze Leben, Auf Engel schiesst man nicht, Eine hübscher als die andere, Der Lügner, ... nur der Wind, Meine Tochter und ich, Die Nylonschlinge, Das hab ich von Papa gelernt, Die ganze Welt ist himmelblau, Heiss weht der Wind, Jetzt dreht die Welt sich nur um Dich, Heidi, Schüsse im 3/4-Takt, Tante Frieda – neue Lausbubengeschichten, Onkel Filser – Allerneueste Lausbubengeschichten, Die tolldreisten Geschichten – nach Honoré de Balzac, Charley's Onkel, Die Lümmel von der ersten Bank III, Frau Wirtin hat auch einen Grafen.*

195 KOCH, MARIANNE (1931-   ). B: Munich. Actress. Studied medicine, but enters films in 1950 thanks to Victor Tourjansky (q.v.). Also acted in French, Italian and American films (using name Marianne Cook). Also works for TV (family programmes).

Films: *Der Mann, der zweimal leben wollte; Dr. Holl, Csardas der Herzen, Das Geheimnis einer Ehe; Mein Freund, der Dieb; Der keusche Lebemann, Wetterleuchten am Dachstein, Skandal im Mädchenpensionat, Der Klosterjäger, Die grosse Schuld, Liebe und Trompetenblasen, Geh' mach dein Fensterl auf, Schloss Hubertus, Ludwig II., Des Teufels General, Der Schmid von St. Bartholomä, Königswalzer, Solange Du lebst, Zwei blaue Augen, Und der Himmel lacht dazu, Die Ehe des Dr. med. Danwitz, Wenn wir alle Engel wären, Salzburger Geschichten, Vater sein dagegen sehr, Der Stern von Afrika, Der Fuchs von Paris, ... und nichts als die Wahrheit, Die Landärztin, Frau im besten Mannesalter, Die Frau am dunklen Fenster, Heldinnen, Mit Himbeergeist geht alles besser, Unter Ausschluss der Oeffentlichkeit, Die Fledermaus, Heisser Hafen Hongkong, Im Namen des Teufels; Liebling, ich muss Dich erschiessen; Der schwarze Panther von Ratana, Für eine Handvoll Dollars, Der letzte Ritt nach Santa Cruz, Das Ungeheuer von London City, Die Hölle von Manitosa, Vergeltung in Catano, 5000 Dollar für den Kopf von Jonny R., Schreie in der Nacht.*

196 KOCZIAN, JOHANNA VON (1933-   ). B: Berlin. Actress. RN: Johanna von Koczian-Miskolczy. Stage training at the Mozarteum in Salzburg 1950-1952. Theatres: Salzburg, Tübingen, Wuppertal, Berlin, Munich. Many guest appearances. Became popular with her performance in *Wir Wunderkinder.*

Films: *Viktor und Viktoria, Petersburger*

Nächte, Serenade einer grossen Liebe, Wir Wunderkinder, Menschen im Netz, Bezaubernde Arabella, Jacqueline, Lampenfieber, Heldinnen; Agatha, lass das Morden sein; Die Ehe des Herrn Mississippi, Unser Haus in Kamerun, Strasse der Verheissung, Das Liebeskarussell (iii).

197 **KÖRBER, HILDE** (1906-1969). B: Vienna. D: Berlin. Actress and writer. Stage training at the State Academy in Vienna. At first in children's roles at Volkstheater and Burgtheater Vienna. Then theatres: Oldenburg, Stuttgart, Magdeburg, Zurich, and several in Berlin. Head of the Max Reinhardt-school in Berlin. Lyric poet. Enters cinema in 1936. First wife of Veit Harlan (q.v.).

Films: *Fridericus; Maria, die Magd; Der Herrscher, Patrioten; Mein Sohn, der Herr Minister; Heiratsschwindler, Die Kreutzersonate, Brillanten, Der Spieler, Maja zwischen zwei Ehen, Eine Frau kommt in die Tropen, Grossalarm, Fasching, Der singende Tor, Salonwagen E 417, Robert Koch, Leidenschaft, Der Sündenbock, Der Fuchs von Glenarvon, Ohm Krüger, Jakko, Der grosse König, Damals, Ein Blick zurück, Das Leben geht weiter, Wie sagen wir es unseren Kindern?, Via Mala, Morituri, Verführte Jugend, Wenn die Abendglocken läuten, Das letzte Rezept, Mein Herz darfst Du nicht fragen, Rosen blühen auf dem Heidegrab, Ave Maria, Mit Siebzehn beginnt das Leben, Sauerbruch – Das war mein Leben, Das Bekenntnis der Ina Kahr, Rittmeister Wronski, Die Toteninsel; Mein Vater, der Schauspieler; Teufel in Seide, Heisse Ernte, Anders als Du und ich, Das Mädchen vom Moorhof, Ich werde Dich auf Händen tragen.*

198 **KORTNER, FRITZ** (1892-1970). B: Vienna. Actor and director. RN: Fritz Nathan Kohn. Studied at Academie für Musik und darstellende Kunst in Vienna. Theatres: Vienna, Berlin, Mannheim, Dresden. 1911: Deutsches Theater Berlin. 1919: Staatstheater Berlin under Leopold Jessner (q.v.). 1919-1933: frequent guest appearances throughout Europe. 1938: to U.S.A. 1948: back to German theatre – Kammerspiele and Bayerisches Staatstheater Munich, Hebbeltheater Berlin etc. More guest appearances. Enters cinema in 1916. Before 1933 Kortner was a very interesting actor on stage and screen, and since 1948 he has proved a significant theatre (and occasionally film) director.

Films (incomplete) * indicates those directed by Kortner: *Sonnwendfeuer, Police 1111, Das zweite Leben, Der Brief eines Toten, Das andere Ich, Frauenehre, Gregor Marold 18 *, Märtyrer seines Herzens* (also co-scripted with Emil Justitz and Emil Kolberg), *Sonnwendhof, Der Stärkere, Das Auge des Buddha, Else von Erlenhof 19 * (also acted), Gerechtigkeit, Ohne Zeugen, Prinz Kuckuck, Satanas, Die Brüder Karamasoff, Das Haus zum Mond, Die Jagd nach der Wahrheit, Katherina die Grosse, Die Lieblingsfrau des Maharadscha, Die Nacht der Königin Isabeau, Der Schädel der Pharaonentochter, Va banque, Die Verschwörung zu Genua, Weltbrand, Am roten Kliff, Christian Wahnschaffe, Danton, Der Eisenbahnkönig, Die Hintertreppe, Die Finsternis ist ihr Eigentum, Flammende Völker, Der Graf von Essex, Das Haus der Qualen, Luise Millerin, Landstrasse und Grosstadt, Die Mausefalle, Peter der Grosse, Ein Puppenheim, Ruf des Schicksals, Der stärkste Trieb, Sterbende Völker, Arme Sünderin, Nora, Schatten; Ein Weib, ein Tier,* *ein Diamant; Armes kleines Mädchen, Dr. Wislizenus, Moderne Ehe, Orleans Hände, Dürfen wir schweigen?*, *Alpentragödie, Die Ausgestossenen, Beethoven, Die Geliebte des Gouverneurs* (also co-scripted with Friedrich Feher), *Maria Stuart, Mata Hari, Mein Leben für das Deine, Primanerliebe, Frau Sorge, Marquis d'Eon, der Spion der Pompadour, Revolutionshochzeit, Die Büchse der Pandora, Die Frau im Talar, Die Frau nach der man sich sehnt, Giftgas, Die stärkere Macht, Das Schiff der verlorenen Menschen, Somnambul*. Then sound: *Atlantic, Dreyfus, Menschen im Käfig, Der Andere, Die grosse Sehnsucht, Der Mörder Dimitri Karamasoff, Danton, Der brave Sünder* 31 * only (also script with Alfred Polgar), *So ein Mädel vergisst man nicht* 32 * only (and script with Hans Wilhelm), *Der Ruf* 49 * (also acted and script), *Die Stimme des Andern* (only script with Stemmle, Engel and Horst Budjuhn), *Epilog, Blaubart, Die Stadt ist voller Geheimnisse* 54 * only (and co-scripted), *Sarajevo* 55 * only, *Die Sendung der Lysistrata* 61 (TV-film, * only).

199 **KOSTERLITZ, HERMANN** (1905-　). B: Berlin. Scriptwriter, later director. Studied at the Akademie der Schönen Künste in Berlin. At first painter and caricaturist. Enters cinema as scriptwriter, writing about fifty scripts for Ufa (q.v.), Universal and Terra. Becomes director for German Universal. 1936: via France and Italy to U.S.A. where he takes name of Henry Koster.

Films: *Die Dame aus Berlin, Die grosse Gelegenheit* (in collab. with Lorand von Kabdebo), *Die Waise von Lowood, Wenn Menschen irren* (in collab. with Otz Toller), *Eins plus Eins gleich Drei* (in collab.), *Kinderseelen klagen an* (in collab. with Luitpold Nusser), *Prinz Louis Ferdinand* (in collab. with Toller), *Sündig und süss* (in collab. with Hans Wilhelm), *Tagebuch einer Kokotte* (in collab. with Wilhelm). Then sound: *Seine Freundin Annette* (co-scripted with John Meehan), *Die letzte Kompanie* (idea with Hans Wilhelm), *Weib im Dschungel* (co-scripted with Garret Fort, Jean de Limur and Monta Bell), *Ich bleib' bei Dir* (co-scripted with Wolfgang Wilhelm), *Der Mann, der den Mord beging* (co-scripted with Heinz Goldberg and Harry Kahn), *Wer*

nimmt die Liebe ernst? (co-scripted with Curt Alexander), *Leichtsinnige Jugend* (co-scripted with Benno Vigny), *Zigeuner der Nacht, Fünf von der Jazzband* (co-scripted with Alexander), *Das Abenteuer der Thea Roland* 32 (only dir.), *Das hässliche Mädchen* 33 (dir. and script with Felix Joachimson).

200 **KOWA, VIKTOR DE** (1904-　). B: Hochkirch near Görlitz. Actor and director. RN: Viktor Kowalczyk. At first studied painting at Dresden art school, then stage training at Staatstheater Dresden. Theatres: Dresden, Lübeck, Frankfurt, Hamburg, Berlin. General director of Theater am Kurfürstendamm Berlin in 1943-1944, and then in charge of the Tribüne Berlin 1945-1946. Many guest appearances. Declared an "Actor of the State." During the Nazi period de Kowa was mainly in optimistic propaganda films.

Films: *Katherina Knie*. Then sound: *Pension Schöller; 1914, die letzten Tage vor dem Weltbrand; Die andere Seite, Der wahre Jakob, Der Stolz der 3. Kompanie, Die Faschingsfee, Tannenberg, Der Diamant des Zaren, Unheimliche Geschichten, Zwei im Sonnenschein, Das Schloss im Süden, Sag' mir, wer Du bist, Kleiner Mann – was nun?, Ein Lied geht um die Welt, Mädels von heute, Der Läufer von Marathon, Es war einmal ein Musikus, Wenn ich König wär', Was bin ich ohne Dich, Da stimmt was nicht, Polizeiakte 909, Lockvogel, Pappi, Der junge Baron Neuhaus; Ein Kind, ein Hund, ein Vagabund; Die Finanzen des Grossherzogs, Mein Leben für Maria Isabell, Lärm um Weidemann, Spiel an Bord, Skandal um die Fledermaus, Die grosse und die kleine Welt, Versprich mir nichts, Die göttliche Jette, Der Optimist, Scheidungsreise, Kleiner Mann, ganz gross, Ich liebe Dich* (also script with Felix von Eckardt), *Mit versiegelter Order, Schneider Wibbel* 39 (only dir.), *Casanova heiratet* 40 (only dir.); *Kopf hoch, Johannes* 41 (only dir.), *Die Sache mit Styx, Wir machen Musik, Ein glücklicher Mensch, Altes Herz wird wieder jung, Intimitäten; Peter Vos, der Millionendieb; Das Leben geht weiter, Zwischen Gestern und Morgen, Anonyme Briefe, Melodie des Schicksals, Die wunderschöne Galathee, Skandal in der Botschaft, Der blaue Stern des Südens, Der Fürst von Pappenheim, Eine Liebesgeschichte, Hochstaplerin der Liebe, Des Teufels General, Der Himmel ist nie ausverkauft, Vor Gott und den Menschen, Musik im Blut, Ein Mädchen aus Flandern, Kein Platz für wilde Tiere* (speaker), *Nichts als Aerger mit der Liebe, Der veruntreute Himmel, Scampolo, Bomben auf Monte Carlo, Schlussakkord, Es muss nicht immer Kaviar sein, Der Fälscher von London, Das Haus in Montevideo, Begegnung in Salzburg, Winnetou und sein Freund Old Firehand.*

201 **KRAHL, HILDE** (1915 or 1917-   ). B: Brod on the Save (Yugoslavia). Actress. RN: Hildegard Kolachy. Studied piano in Vienna; stage training at the Theater an der Wien (Vienna). Theatres: Kleinkunstbühne, Theater in der Josefstadt Vienna 1936-1955; Kammerspiele Hamburg 1945-1952. Cinema *début* in Austrian production *Mädchenpensionat*, then films in Germany, Austria and Switzerland. Married to Wolfgang Liebeneiner (q.v.).

Films: *Die Puppenfee, Mädchenpensionat, Lumpazivagabundus, Serenade, Der Hampelmann, Gastspiel im Paradies, Die barmherzige Lüge, Der Weg zu Isabell, Herz modern möbliert, Donauschiffer, Der Postmeister, Komödianten, Das andere Ich, Meine Freundin Josefine, Anuschka, Grossstadtmelodie, Träumerei, Das Leben geht weiter, Das Gesetz der Liebe, Liebe 47, Wenn eine Frau liebt, Meine Nichte Susanne, Schatten der Nacht, Weisse Schatten, Herz der Welt, Der Weibsteufel, Das Tor zum Frieden, 1. April 2000, Die Mükke, Hochstaplerin der Liebe, Ewiger Walzer; Kinder, Mütter und ein General; Eine Frau genügt nicht?, Geheimnis einer Aerztin; Mein Vater, der Schauspieler; Nacht der Entscheidung, Das Glas Wasser, Heute kündigt mir mein Mann, 90 Minuten nach Mitternacht.*

202 **KRÄHLY, HANNS** (1885-1950). B: in Germany. D: Los Angeles. Actor and scriptwriter. Until 1915 mostly actor, then became scriptwriter, especially for Ernst Lubitsch (q.v.), with whom he left Germany for the U.S.A. in 1923. Wrote various parts for Henny Porten, Asta Nielsen and Pola Negri (all q.v.) etc. His work in

America for Lewis Milestone, William Wyler and Henry Koster and others is unimportant compared with the scripts of his German period.

Films (incomplete): *Der fesche Tiroler* (only acted), *Die Kinder des Generals, Das Mädchen ohne Vaterland, Engelein* (co-scripted with Urban Gad, also acted), *Engeleins Hochzeit* (co-scripted with Urban Gad, also acted), *Die Filmprimadonna* (also acted), *Aschenbrödel, Elena Fontana, Die ewige Nacht, Das Feuer, Das Kind ruft, Standrechtlich erschossen, Weisse Rosen, Schuhpalast Pinkus* (co-scripted with Erich Schönfelder), *Komptesse Doddy* (co-scripted with Georg Jacoby), *Die Augen der Mumie Ma, Carmen, Fuhrmann Henschel, Der gelbe Schein* (co-scripted with Hans Brennert), *Meine Frau, die Filmschauspielerin* (co-scripted), *Die Austernprinzessin* (co-scripted), *Fahrt ins Blaue* (co-scripted with H. Fredall), *Madame Dubarry* (co-scripted with Fred Orbing), *Monika Vogelsang, Die Puppe* (co-scripted), *Rausch, Die verlorenen Töchter, Anna Boleyn* (co-scripted with Orbing), *Arme Violetta, Kohlhiesels Töchter (co-scripted), Medea* (co-scripted with Orbing), *Romeo und Julia im Schnee* (co-scripted), *Sumurun* (co-scripted), *Die Bergkatze* (co-scripted), *Das Weib des Pharao* (co-scripted with Norbert Falk), *Die Flamme, Alles für Gold* (co-scripted with Rudolf Stratz), *Bohème* (co-scripted with Gennaro Righetti), *Das Paradies im Schnee, Komödianten des Lebens* (co-scripted with Robert Liebmann).

203 **KRAUSE, GEORG** (19 -   ). Director of photography. Enters cinema as assistant cameraman, then becomes director of photography at then end of the silent period. His work varies from a serious and creative style to a straightforward technical expertise. Collaborated with Elia Kazan on *The Man on a Tightrope* and with Stanley Kubrick on *Paths of Glory.*

Films: *Kopf hoch, Charly!* (co-phot. with. Axel Graatkjaer). Then sound: *Im Kampf mit der Unterwelt* (co-phot. with Ewald Sudrow), *Das Kind und die Welt* (co-phot. with Günther Krampf, Viktor Trinkler and Erich Aurich), *Kavaliere vom Kurfürstendam* (co-phot. with Edgar Ziesemer), *Die Vier vom Bob 13* (co-phot. with Sudrow), *Das Lied vom Glück, Wege zur guten Ehe; Schön ist es, verliebt zu sein; Die beiden Seehunde, Das alte Recht; Eine Seefahrt, das ist lustig* (co-phot. with Frederik Fuglsang), *Die selige Exzellenz, Alles weg'n dem Hund, Moral, Arzt aus Leidenschaft, Mädchenräuber, Die un-erhörte Frau, Diener lassen bitten, Port Arthur, Abenteuer in Warschau, Der Katzensteg, Revolutionshochzeit, Der Biberpelz, Liebe geht seltsame Wege, Es leuchten die Sterne, Zwei Frauen, Verliebtes Abenteuer, Geheimzeichen LB 17, Verwandte sind auch Menschen, D III 88* (co-phot. with Heinz von Jaworsky), *Die letzte Runde, Der Sündenbock, Kampfgeschwader Lützow* (co-phot. with Jaworsky and Walter Rosskopf), *Krach im Vorderhaus, Diesel, Vom Schicksal verweht, Der verzauberte Tag, Der grüne Salon, Musik in Salzburg, Tierarzt Dr. Vlimmen, Berliner Ballade, Unser Mittwoch Abend 48* (also co-dir. with Werner Illing), *Schicksal am Berg, Die Sterne lügen nicht, Kronjuwelen, Das ewige Spiel, Herzen im Sturm* (co-phot.), *Wenn die Abendglocken läuten, Primanerinnen, Mönche, Mädchen und Panduren, Von Liebe reden wir später, Die Nacht ohne Moral, Hochzeitsglocken, Glück muss man haben, Phantom des grossen Zeltes, 08/15 II, 08/15 in der Heimat, Auf Wiedersehen am Bodensee, Vater macht Karriere, Nachts wenn der Teufel kam, Der Arzt von Stalingrad, Taiga, Dorothea Angermann, Kriegsgericht, Die Nackte und der Satan, Die Wahrheit über Rosemarie, Ein Toter hing im Netz, Geheimaktion Schwarze Kapelle, Der Satan lockt mit Liebe, Kirmes, Flitterwochen in der Hölle, Treibjagd auf ein Leben, Hass ohne Gnade, Tunnel 28, Wenn beide schuldig werden, Begegnung in Salzburg.*

204 **KRAUSS, WERNER** (1884-1959). B: Gestungshausen near Koburg. D: Vienna. Actor. First stage experience with theatres in the provinces. Then theatres: Gruben (1908), Berlin with Reinhardt (q.v.) 1913, Nuremberg, Burgtheater Vienna (after 1948), Schiller- and Schlosspark-Theater Berlin (1954), Schauspielhaus Düsseldorf. One of the most striking actors on the German stage during the Twenties and Thirties, especially when "Expressionism" was at its height in the theatre. Played some very

vicious parts in purely Fascist films. Enters cinema in 1916 thanks to Richard Oswald (q.v.).

Films (incomplete): *Die Pagode, Hoffmanns Erzählungen, Nacht des Grauens, Zirkusblut, Die Rache der Toten, Die Seeschlacht, Wenn Frauen lieben und hassen, Es werde Licht (iii), Opium, Die Frau mit den Orchideen, Das Kabinett des Dr. Caligari, Rose Bernd, Totentanz, Die Beichte einer Toten, Die Brüder Karamasoff, Der Bucklige und die Tänzerin, Hölle und Verfall, Johannes Goth, Das lachende Grauen, Die Beute der Erinnyen, Christian Wahnschaffe, Danton, Die Frau ohne Seele, Grausige Nächte, Der Mann ohne Namen, Das Medium, Der Roman der Christine von Herre, Scherben, Der Tanz um Liebe und Glück, Sappho, Zirkus des Lebens, Der brennende Acker, Der Graf von Essex, Josef und seine Brüder, Luise Millerin, Lady Hamilton, Die Marquise von Pompadour, Die Nacht der Medici, Nathan der Weise, Othello, Tragikomödie, Adam und Eva, Das alte Gesetz, Alt-Heidelberg, Fräulein Raffke, Fridericus Rex, I.N.R.I., Der Kaufmann von Venedig, Der Menschenfeind, Der Puppenmacher von Kiang-Ning, Der Schatz, Das unbekannte Morgen, Zwischen Abend*

und Morgen, Dekameron-Nächte, Ein Sommernachtstraum, Das Wachsfigurenkabinett, Die Dame aus Berlin, Eifersucht, Die freudlose Gasse; Das Haus der Lüge, Die Moral der Gasse, Reveille, das grosse Wecken; Tartüff, Der Trödler von Amsterdam, Geheimnisse einer Seele, Das graue Haus, Kreuzzug des Weibes, Man spielt nicht mit der Liebe!, Nana, Der Student von Prag, Ueberflüssige Menschen, Da hält die Welt den Atem an, Der fidele Bauer, Funkzauber, Die Hölle der Jungfrauen, Die Hose, Laster der Menschheit, Unter Ausschluss der Oeffentlichkeit, Looping the Loop, Napoleon auf St. Helena. Then sound: *Yorck, Mensch ohne Namen, Hundert Tage, Burgtheater, Robert Koch, Jud Süss, Annelie, Die Entlassung, Zwischen Himmel und Erde, Paracelsus, Prämien auf den Tod, Der fallende Stern, Sohn ohne Heimat.*

205 **KREUDER, PETER** (1905-   ). B: Aachen. Composer. Studied music in Munich and Hamburg. 1923: musical director at the Deutsches Theater Munich. 1926-1932: Reinhardt-Bühnen (q.v.) Berlin. Then worked mainly on music for films (exclusive contracts with Ufa, Tobis, Terra). 1947-1950: to Brazil, where he wrote scores for eight films. Prolific composer.

Films: *Kadetten; Peter Voss, der Millionendieb; Der goldene Gletscher, Wenn dem Esel zu wohl ist, Die Nacht der Versuchung* (in collab. with Friedrich Jung), *Die weisse Majestät* (in collab. with Hilmar Georgi), *Henker, Frauen und Soldaten, Das Stahltier, Das Mädchen Johanna, Mazurka, Burgtheater, Ein Hochzeitstraum, Glückskinder, Allotria, Weisse Sklaven* (in collab. with Friedrich Schröder),) *Gasparone, Capriolen, Serenade, Frauenliebe – Frauenleid, Rätsel um Beate, Der Maulkorb, Eine Nacht im Mai* (in collab. with Schröder), *Dreizehn Mann und eine Kanone, In geheimer Mission* (in collab. with Anton Profes), *Nanette, Opernball, Wasser für Canitoga; Hallo, Janine!; Die 3 Codonas, Traummusik* (in collab. with Riccardo Zandonai and Frank Fux), *Kora Terry* (in collab. with Fux), *Mein Mann darf es nicht wissen, Liebesgeschichten, Es lebe die Liebe, In flagranti, Es fing so harmlos an, Frühlingsmelodie, Frech und verliebt, Das singende Haus, Alle kann ich nicht heiraten* (in collab. with Bert

Grund), *So ein Affentheater* (in collab. wit Heinrich Riethmüller), *Arlette erobert Pari Liebeskrieg nach Noten, Der erste Kus Die Mücke, Ein Mädchen aus Paris, I erstes Rendezvous* (in collab. with Ren Sylvano), *An jedem Finger zehn* (in colla with Werner Müller, Hans Carste, Micha Jary etc.), *Herrn Josefs letzte Liebe* (in co lab. with Kurt Werner), *Frauen in Teufe Hand.*

206 **KRISTL, VLADO** (1923-   ). B Zagreb. Actor, scriptwriter and directo Educated in Yugoslavia and Vienna. 194 1949: studied at Academy in Zagreb, inter rupted by war service. At first painter an poet. 1953-1959: various jobs throughou Europe and South America. Back to Yugo slavia, makes some cartoons that are late destroyed. 1963: to Munich. Most persi tent and individual *cinéaste* of the *Junge deutscher Film* movement (q.v.). Acts i all his live-action films and played a part i short film *Friedliche Zeiten* (1965, di Christian Rischert). 1967-1968: mini-film for Bavarian TV studio programmes.

Films (cartoons *): *Jewel Robbery* * 5 (in Yugosl.), *Peau de Chagrin* * 60 (co-dir. in Yugosl.), *Don Quixote* * 61 (in Yugosl.) *The General* 62 (in Yugosl., destroyed *Arme Leute* 63 (short), *Madeleine-Made leine* 63 (short), *Autorennen* ` 64 (short *Maulwürfe* 64 (destroyed after first scree ning), *Der Damm* 64 (feature), *Prometheu * 65, *Der Brief* 66 (feature), *Utopen* * 67 *Hundert Blatt Schreibblock* 68 (short Scripted all his own films.

207 **KRÜGER, HARDY** (1928-   ). B Berlin. Actor. Theatres: Schauspielhau Hamburg (1945-1946), Hannover (1947 Junge Bühne Hamburg (1947-1949). Gues appearances in Berlin, Munich, Hamburg and Stuttgart. Introduced to cinema by Al fred Weidenmann (q.v.). Later internationa career. Director of short films and documen taries for TV. Father of actress Christian Krüger.

Films: *Junge Adler, Das Fräulein und de Vagabund, Diese Nacht vergess' ich ni Kätchen für alles, Das Mädchen aus de Südsee, Insel ohne Moral, Schön muss ma sein; Mein Freund, der Dieb; Ich heiss Niki, Alle kann ich nicht heiraten, Illusio*

Moll, Solange Du da bist, Muss man sich gleich scheiden lassen?, Ich und Du, Der letzte Sommer, Der Himmel ist nie ausverkauft, Alibi; Liane, das Mädchen aus dem Urwald; Die Christel von der Post, Der Fuchs von Paris, Banktresor 713, Gestehen Sie, Dr. Corda, Der Rest is Schweigen, Bumerang, Die Gans von Sedan, Zwei unter Millionen, Lautlose Waffen, Ein Mädchen wie das Meer.

208 KUBASCHEWSKI, ILSE (19 -). B: Berlin. Woman producer and distributor. N: Ilse Kramp. Married to Hans Werner Kubaschewski, film marketeer. 1931-1943: programme organiser at Siegel-Monopol-Film Company. 1949: founds "Gloria Film." Under her management Gloria distributes as well as produces films. "Divina-Film" is linked to Gloria. One of the most powerful producers of film in Germany during the fifties.

Films (including Gloria and Divina):*Sterne über Colombo, Die Gefangene des Maharadscha, 08/15 I, 08/15 II, 08/15 in der Heimat, Rosen im Herbst, Verrat an Deutschland, Die goldene Brücke, Kirschen in Nachbars Garten, Die Trapp-Familie; Weil du arm bist, musst du früher sterben;*

Wo die alten Wälder rauschen, Der Arzt von Stalingrad, Königin Luise; Nachts, wenn der Teufel kam, Eine verrückte Familie, Weisser Holunder, Heimatlos, Die Landärztin, Die Trappfamilie in Amerika, Alle lieben Peter (co-prod. with Melodie), *Arzt ohne Gewissen, Ein Tag der nie zu Ende geht, Der Gauner und der liebe Gott, Dorothea Angermann* (co-prod.), *Der Haustyrann, Heimat – Deine Lieder* (co-prod. with Paul May), *Auf Engel schiesst man nicht* (co-prod. with Utermann), *Faust, Mein Schulfreund* (co-prod. with Utermann), *Weit ist der Weg, Freddy und der Millionär, Vertauschtes Leben, Die blonde Frau des Maharadschas, Der Vogelhändler, Meine Tochter und ich; Piccadilly, null Uhr zwölf; Angélique I & II* (co-prod. with Francos Film & CICC Paris, Liber Film Rome); *Vorsicht, Mr. Dodd, Herr auf Schloss Brassac* (co-prod. with Copernic Paris & Fides Rome), *Angélique und der König* (co-prod. with Francos Film & CICC Paris, Fono Rome), *Das war Buffalo Bill* (co-prod. with Corona Paris & Rome), *Rififi in Paris* (co-prod. with Copernic Paris & Fida Rome), *Unbezähmbare Angélique, Angélique und der Sultan* (both Franco Film & CICC & Cinéphonic Paris & Fono Rome), *. . . und morgen fahrt ihr zur Hölle* (co-prod. with Italy and France), *Cathérine – Eine leben für die Liebe* (co.).

Lisa-Film productions (founded 1965): *Das Mädel aus dem Böhmerwald, Das Rasthaus der grausamen Puppen* (co-prod. with Bruno Ceria Trieste), *Sartana* (co-prod. with Metheus Rome), *Heisses Pflaster Köln, Heubodengeflüster, Mittsommernacht, Paradies der flotten Sünder, Engel der Sünde, Peter und Sabine, Immer Aerger mit den Paukern, Komm liebe Maid und mache . . ., Unser Doktor ist der beste, Django – Die Geier stehen Schlange* (co-prod. with Metheus Rome), *Hilfe, ich liebe Zwillinge.*

209 KUNERT, JOACHIM (1929-). B: Berlin. Director. Assistant to Kurt Maetzig (q.v.) for seven years, and a stage director in many East German theatres. Thanks to documentaries like *Ein Strom fliesst durch Deutschland* (53) and *Dresdner Philharmoniker* (54) he moves to features. State award in 1965.

Films: *Ein Strom fliesst durch Deutsch-*

land 54 (doc.), *Dresdner Philharmoniker 55* (doc.), *Besondere Kennzeichen: keine 56, Tatort Berlin 58* (also script with Jens Gerlach), *Der Lotterieschwede 58* (also script with Gerlach), *Ehesache Lorenz 59, Seilergasse 8 60* (also script with Günther Kunert), *Das zweite Gleis 62* (also script with Günter Kunert), *Die Abenteuer des Werner Holt 65* (also script with Claus Küchenmeister), *Die Toten bleiben jung 68* (also co-scripted with Christa Wolf and Gerhard Helwig).

210 KUNTZE, REIMAR (1902-1949). B: Berlin. D: Munich. Director of photography. At first photographer and cameraman for newsreels. In collaboration with Freund, Baberske (both q.v.) and others, he shot some of the most important German films at the end of the Twenties and beginning of the Thirties.

Films: *Adam und Eva* (co-phot.), *I.N.R.I.* (co-phot. with Axel Graatkjaer and Ludwig Lippert), *Garragan* (co-phot.), *Klabautermann* (co-phot.), *Lebende Buddhas* (co-phot. with Seeber and J. Rona), *Nju* (co-phot. with Graatkjaer), *Ein Sommernachtstraum* (co-phot.), *Frauen und Banknoten, Die Frau ohne Geld, Heiratsannoncen, Weil Du es bist* (co-phot. with Ernst Lüttgens), *Der Hauptmann von Köpenick* (26), *Berlin – Symphonie einer Grosstadt* (co-phot. with Baberske and Laszlo Schäffer), *Einer gegen alle* (co-phot. with Mois Saffra), *Der Kampf um den Mann, Liebe geht seltsame Wege, Der Mann ohne Kopf* (co-phot. with Edoardo Lamberti and Hans Karl Gottschalk), *Herr Meister und Frau Meisterin* (co-phot. with Willy Grosstück), *Morgenröte* (co-phot.). Then sound: *Die Nacht gehört uns* (co-phot. with Charles Metain), *Melodie der Welt* (co-phot. with Rudolph Rathmann, Wilhelm Lehne and Paul Holzki), *Das Land des Lächelns, Wie werde ich reich und glücklich?, Ich glaub' nie mehr an eine Frau* (co-phot. with Metain), *Das lockende Ziel, Mädchen in Uniform* (co-phot.), *Die schwebende Jungfrau, Die Kopper des Herrn O.F.* (co-phot. with Heinrich Balasch), *Die Privatsekretärin* (co-phot.), *Walzerparadies* (co-phot.), *Viktoria und ihr Husar, Ein steinreicher Mann, Hallo! Hallo! Hier spricht Berlin!, Der Rebell* (co-phot. with Benitz, Allgeier and Willy Goldberger), *Drei von der Kavallerie, Spione im Savoy-Hotel, Kaiserwalzer, Fünf von der Jazzband, Paprika, Die verkaufte Braut* (co-phot. with Franz Koch, Herbert Illig and Otto Wirsching), *Moral und Liebe, Hochzeit am Wolfgangsee, Ich will Dich Liebe lehren* (co-phot.), *Eine Frau wie Du* (co-phot. with Koch), *Die Blume von Hawaii, Ein Lied geht um die Welt; Sag' mir, wer Du bist* (co-phot. with Ewald Daub), *Reifende Jugend, Krach um Jolanthe, Frühlingsmärchen, Ihr grösster Erfolg, Der verlorene Sohn* (co-phot.), *Abenteuer eines jungen Herrn in Polen* (co-phot.), *Ich war Jack Mortimer, Wenn die Musik nicht wär', Die blonde Carmen, Liselotte von der Pfalz, Warum lügt Fräulein Käthe?, Wenn der Hahn kräht, Es geht um mein Leben, Traumulus, Das Schönheitsfleckchen, Wenn wir alle Engel wären, Der Raub der Sabinerinnen, Zwei mal zwei im Himmelbett, Die Austernlitti; Gabriele eins, zwei, drei; Der Weg des Herzens, Togger, Die 4 Gesellen, Der Maulkorb, Das Leben kann so schön sein, Andalusische Nächte, Die Umwege des schönen Karl, Die Geliebte; Sommer, Sonne, Erika, Nanette, Herz modern möbliert, Der liebe Augustin; Wie konntest Du, Veronika; Der Gasmann, Tanz mit dem Kaiser, Viel Lärm um Nixi, Hab' mich lieb, Ein Mann mit Grundsätzen?, Nacht ohne Abschied, Der Majoratsherr, Zwischen Nacht und Morgen, Sag' endlich ja, Sag' die Wahrheit, Die Brüder Noltenius; Träum' nicht, Annette* (co-phot. with Ernst Kunstmann), *Artistenblut* (co-phot. with Kurt Hasse), *Königskinder.*

211 LA JANA (1905-1940). B and D: Berlin. Actress and dancer. RN: Henriette Margarethe Hiebel. Assumed name means "Flower-like." Ballet training at the Opera in Frankfurt, where she continues as a child dancer. Revues in Paris, Stockholm and London. Berlin (Haller-Revues, Charell, q.v.). Also acted in Swedish films. In Germany she had her greatest triumph in *Das indische Grabmal* (37). Her sudden death established a tremendous cult around her personality.

Films: *Die weisse Geisha, Gaunerliebchen, Der Biberpelz, Du sollst nicht ehebrechen, Der Herzensphotograph, Der Ladenprinz, Ritter der Nacht, Zwei rote Rosen,*

Der lustige Witwer, Meineid. Then sound: *Die Warschauer Zitadelle, Der Schlemihl, Truxa, Der Tiger von Eschnapur, Das indische Grabmal, Es leuchten die Sterne, Menschen vom Varieté, Stern von Rio.*

LAMARR, HEDY *see* KIESLER, HEDWIG.

212 LAMPRECHT, GERHARD (1897-). B: Berlin. Director. Studied at Berlin University. At first scriptwriter. 1923: director. Proved himself an interesting film maker with social studies like *Die Unehelichen,* but his most famous film is *Emil and the Detectives.* Also very important film historian *(Deutsche Stummfilme 1923-1931,* plus a catalogue of even earlier films in preparation). A great collector of material about German cinema, mainly the silent period.

Films (incomplete): *Seelenverkäufer* (only co-scripted with F. Carlsen), *Niemand weiss es* (only co-scripted with John Gottowt), *Tötet nicht mehr* (co-scripted), *Der Friedhof der Lebenden* 21 (also co-scripted with Louise Heilborn-Körbitz/=LHK), *Fliehende Schatten* 22 (also co-scripted), *Die Buddenbrooks* 23 (also co-scripted with Alfred Fekete and LHK), *Das Haus ohne Lachen* 23 (also co-scripted with LHK), *Und dennoch kam das Glück* 23 (also script), *Die Andere,* 24, *Hanseaten* 25 (also co-scripted with LHK), *Die Verrufenen* 25 (also co-scripted with LHK), *Menschen untereinander* 26 (prod., also co-scripted with LHK and Rothauser), *Schwester Veronika* 26 (also co-scripted with LHK), *Die Unehelichen* 26 (prod., also co-scripted with LHK), *Der alte Fritz* 27 (prod., also co-scripted with LHK), *Der Katzensteg* 27 (prod., also co-scripted with LHK), *Der Mann mit dem Laubfrosch* 28 (prod., also co-scripted with LHK), *Unter der Laterne* 28 (prod., also co-scripted with LHK). Then sound: *Zweierlei Moral* 30 (also script), *Zwischen Nacht und Morgen* 31, *Emil und die Detektive* 31, *Der schwarze Husar* 32, *Was wissen denn Männer* 33, *Spione am Werk* 33, *Ein gewisser Herr Gran* 33, *Prinzessin Turandot* 34, *Einmal eine grosse Dame sein* 34, *Einer zuviel an Bord* 35, *Der höhere Befehl* 35, *Barcarole* 35, *Ein seltsamer Gast* 36, *Die gelbe Flagge* 37,

Madame Bovary 37, *Der Spieler* 38, *Die Geliebte* 39, *Frau im Strom* 39, *Mädchen im Vorzimmer* 40, *Clarissa* 41, *Diesel* 42 (also co-scripted), *Du gehörst mir* 43, *Kamerad Hedwig* 45, *Die Brüder Noltenius* 45, *Irgendwo in Berlin* 46 (also script), *Madonna in Ketten* 49, *Quartett zu Fünft* 49, *Meines Vaters Pferde* 54 I/II, *Der Engel mit dem Flammenschwert* 54, *Oberwachtmeister Borck* 55, *Menschen im Werk* 58 (short).

213 LANG, FRITZ (1890-). B: Vienna. Scriptwriter, director and producer. Son of an architect. Studied at the Polytechnikum Vienna and Akademie der Schönen Künste Munich. Enters cinema in 1916 as scriptwriter thanks to Erich Pommer (q.v.). Early collaboration with Thea von Harbou (q.v.) whom he marries in 1924 after her divorce from actor Rudolf Klein-Rogge (q.v.). One of the most important filmmakers of German silent cinema (in his strictly decorative manner); in films with social implications his approach was rather naïve. Makes some major and portentious (e.g. approach of the Nazi period) films at the beginning of the sound era. 1933: via France to U.S.A., where he makes some excellent Westerns and thrillers. His come-

back in Germany with re-makes of three silent classics was unsuccessful. Now lives in Hollywood. Acted in *Le Mépris*.

Films: *Hilde Warren und der Tod* (only script), *Die Hochzeit im Excentricclub* (only script), *Die Frau mit den Orchideen* (only script), *Halbblut* 19 (also script), *Harakiri* 19, *Der Herr der Liebe* 19 (also acted), *Lilith und Ly* (only script), *Die Pest in Florenz* (only script), *Die Spinnen I* 19 & *II* 20 (also script), *Totentanz* (only script), *Das wandernde Bild* 20, *Carola Hauser* (only script), *Das indische Grabmal* (co-scripted only), *Kämpfende Herzen* 21, *Der müde Tod* 21 (also co-scripted), *Dr. Mabuse der Spieler* 22 (also co-scripted), *König Artus Tafelrunde* (only co-scripted), *Die Nibelungen I & II* 24, *Metropolis* 26, *Spione* 28, *Die Frau im Mond* 29. Then sound: *M* 31, *Das Testament des Dr. Mabuse* 33, *Der Tiger von Eschnapur*, 58, *Das indische Grabmal* 58, *Die tausend Augen des Dr. Mabuse* 60 (co-scripted, with Heinz Oskar Wuttig).

214 **LEANDER, ZARAH** (1900 or 1902-). B: Karlstadt (Sweden). Actress and singer. RN: Zarah Hedberg. At the age of seventeen marries singer Leander, takes dance and vocal training, makes her *début* in operettas in Riga. At first in Swedish films, and later enters German cinema thanks to Carl Froelich (q.v.), but mainly in musicals and "Heimat" *(schmalz)* films.

Films: *Premiere, Zu neuen Ufern, La Habanera, Der Blaufuchs, Es war eine rauschende Ballnacht, Heimat, Das Lied der Wüste, Das Herz einer Königin, Der Weg ins Freie, Die grosse Liebe, Damals, Cuba Cubana, Ave Maria, Bei Dir war es immer so schön, Der blaue Nachtfalter.*

215 **LEIPNITZ, HARALD** (1926-). B: Wuppertal. Actor. At first assistant in Air Force, imprisoned, studies chemistry. Comes to the stage through Hans Caninenburg (from the Wuppertal artists group "Der Turm"), and takes his stage training at the actors' studio in the Städtische Bühnen Wuppertal. For twelve years performs in theatre in Wuppertal. Then to TV in Munich. Enters films thanks to Will Tremper (q.v.). Also plays in Italian, French and British films.

Films: *Die endlose Nacht, Und der Ama-*

zonas schweigt, Die Gruft mit dem Rätselschloss, Die Banditen vom Rio Grande, Der Oelprinz, Mädchen hinter Gittern, De unheimliche Mönch, Sperrbezirk, Playgirl Ich suche einen Mann, Winnetou und sei Freund Old Firehand, Liselotte von de Pfalz, Agent 505 – Todesfalle Beirut, Fün vor zwölf in Caracas, Die blaue Hand, Herr liche Zeiten im Spessart, Die Wirtin vor der Lahn I, Zuckerbrot und Peitsche, Bern gelchen liebt kreuz und quer, Frau Wirti hat auch einen Grafen, Frau Wirtin hat auch eine Nichte, Die Zeit der Kirschen ist vor bei, Lady Hamilton, Der Kerl liebt mich - und das soll ich glauben?

216 **LENI, PAUL A.** (1885-1929). B Stuttgart. D: Hollywood. Director, art direc tor and set designer. He worked with Rein hardt and Jessner (both q.v.) on their famou stage productions. All his work shows the influence of "Expressionism" (q.v.), al though his few American films also con tain horrific elements. He made two of the most important German films of the silen period: *Hintertreppe* (with Jessner), a mas terpiece of the "Kammerspielfilm" (q.v.) and *Waxworks* (supervised by Robert Wiene q.v.) where he studied three tyrants in a trio of linked stories. Set designer for all his own films, and many sets for other films *.

Films (incomplete): *Das Rätsel von Bangalore* 17, *Dornröschen* 18 (and *), *Veritas vincit *, *Die platonische Ehe* 19 (and *) *Prinz Kuckuck* 19 (also script), *Patience* 20, *Die Verschwörung zu Genua* 20 (and *), *Der weisse Pfau* (co-scripted and *), *Das Gespensterschiff* 21, *Die Hintertreppe* 21 (co-dir and *), *Komödie der Leidenschaften* 21, *Manon Lescaut *, *Das Tagebuch des Dr. Hartl* 21, *Frauenopfer *, *Kinder der Finsternis *, *Lady Hamilton * (in collab. with Hans Dreier), *Das Wachsfigurenkabinett* 24 (and *), *Die Frau in vierzig Jahren *, *Der Tänzer meiner Frau *, *Fiaker Nr. 13 *, *Der goldene Schmetterling *, *Manon Lescaut *.

217 **LEUWERIK, RUTH** (1926-). B: Essen. Actress. RN: Ruth Leeuwerik. Private stage training. Theatres: Münster, Bremen, Lübeck, Deutsches Schauspielhaus Hamburg. She is a symbol of "the mature woman" in several films of the Fifties.

Ruth Leuwerik with Hansjörg Felmy in
EIN TAG DER NIE ZU ENDE GEHT

Films: *13 unter einem Hut, Vater braucht eine Frau, Die grosse Versuchung, Ein Herz spielt falsch, Muss man sich gleich scheiden lassen?, Geliebtes Leben, Königliche Hoheit, Bildnis einer Unbekannten, Ludwig II., Geliebte Feindin, Rosen im Herbst, Die goldene Brücke, Die Trapp-Familie, Königin Luise, Franziska, Immer wenn der Tag beginnt, Taiga, Die Trapp-Familie in Amerika, Dorothea Angermann, Die ideale Frau; Ein Tag, der nie zu Ende geht; Liebling der Götter, Eine Frau fürs ganze Leben, Auf Engel schiesst man nicht; Die Stunde, die Du glücklich bist; Die Rote, Ein Alibi zerbricht, Elf Jahr und ein Tag, Das Haus in Montevideo.*

218 LIEBENEINER, WOLFGANG (1905–   ). B: Liebau. Scriptwriter, actor and director. Stage training in Munich (under Otto Falckenberg). Theatres: Munich, Berlin, Hamburg, Vienna (acting as well as directing). 1938-1945: artistic director of film Babelsberg Academy. 1942-1945: head of production at Ufa. 1938-1945: artistic director of German film academy in Berlin.

1945-1954: Kammerspiele Hamburg. Later Theater in der Josefstadt Vienna. His films of the Nazi period are much discussed especially *Ich klage an*, where a very subtle case was put forward for the extermination of sick, mentally ill and politically undesirable people. After the war Liebeneiner made mainly entertainment films for family audiences.

Acted in: *Die andere Seite, Wenn dem Esel zu wohl ist, Liebelei, Die schönen Tage von Aranjuez, Musik im Blut, Abschiedswalzer, Rivalen der Luft, Alles hört auf mein Kommando, Was bin ich ohne Dich, Freut Euch des Lebens, Alle Tage ist kein Sonntag, Die selige Exzellenz, Lockspitzel Asew, Künstlerliebe, Die blonde Carmen, Eine Nacht an der Donau, Donaumelodien, Das Schönheitsfleckchen, Die un-erhörte Frau, Friedemann Bach; Tobias Knopp, Abenteuer eines Junggesellen* (speaker), *Herz der Welt*. Films: *Versprich mir nichts* 37, *Ziel in den Wolken*, 38, *Yvette* 38, *Du und Ich* 38, *Der Florentiner Hut* 39, *Die gute Sieben* 40, *Bismarck* 40 (also co-scripted), *Das andere Ich* 41, *Ich klage an* 41, *Die Entlassung* 42, *Grosstadtmelodie* 43 (also script), *Das Leben geht weiter* 45 (also co-scripted), *Liebe 47* 49 (also script), *Des*

Lebens Ueberfluss 50, *Meine Nichte Suzanne* 50 (also script), *Wenn eine Frau liebt* 50, *Tobias Knopp, Abenteuer eines Junggesellen* 50 (dir. of dial.), *Der blaue Stern des Südens* 51, *Der Weibsteufel* 51, *Das Tor zum Frieden* 51, *1. April 2000* 52, *Die Stärkere* 53, *Das tanzende Herz* 53 (also co-scripted with Walter F. Fichelseher), *... und ewig bleibt die Liebe* 54, *Die schöne Müllerin* 54, *Auf der Reeperbahn nachts um halb eins* 54, *Die heilige Lüge* 55, *Ich war ein hässliches Mädchen* 55, *Urlaub auf Ehrenwort* 55 (also co-scripted with Felix Lützkendorf), *Waldwinter* 56, *Die Trapp-Familie* 56, *Königin Luise* 57, *Franziska* 57, *Immer wenn der Tag beginnt* 58 (also co-scripted with Utz Utermann), *Taiga* 58, *Die Trapp-Familie in Amerika* 58, *Sebastian Kneipp* 58, *Jacqueline* 59, *Meine Tochter Patricia* 59, *Eine Frau fürs ganze Leben* 60, *Ich heirate Herrn Direktor* 60 (also co-scripted with Heinrich Krackhardt), *Ingeborg* 60, *Schlussakkord* 60, *Das letzte Kapitel* 61, *Jetzt dreht die Welt sich nur um dich* 64, *Schwejks Flegeljahre* 64, *Wenn süss das Mondlicht auf den Hügeln schläft* 69.

219 **LIEDTKE, HARRY** (1881-1945). B: Königsberg. D: Bad Saarow-Pieskow (suicide with his third wife Christa Tordy). Actor. At first businessman, then tours with theatres in the provinces and finally wins a place in the Deutsches Theater Berlin. Enters cinema in 1911 thanks to Oskar Messter (q.v.). After First World War he became one of Lubitsch's favourite players, and also performed part-time in a "Joe Dobbs" serial (q.v.). Adventurous type, and an immensely popular actor in his day.

Films: *Rebellenliebe, Der Verschollene* (dates for these films unobtainable, but both were made certainly prior to 1923). Films (incomplete): *Die Rache ist mein, Zu spät, Eva, Schuldig, Die leere Wasserflasche, Das Bild der Ahnfrau, Ein fideles Gefängnis, Die Hochzeit im Excentricclub, Die Kameliendame, Komptesse Doddy, Lulu, Das Rätsel von Bangalore, Die Augen der Mumie Ma, Die blaue Mauritius, Carmen, Der gelbe Schein, Das Mädel vom Ballett, Der Rodelkavalier, Die Austerprinzessin, Das Karussell des Lebens, Kreuziget sie, Madame Dubarry, Tropenblut, Vendetta, Der Mann ohne Namen, Medea, Sumurun, Indische Rache, Die Tänzerin Barberina, Das Weib des Pharao; Peter Voss, der Millionendieb; So sind die Männer, Die Fledermaus, Der Kaufmann von Venedig, Die Liebe eines Königin, Der Seeteufel, Nanon, Die Finanzen des Grossherzogs, Die Hermannsschlacht, Orient, Paragraph 144, Die Puppenkönigin, Ein Traum vom Glück, Der Abenteurer, Die Frau für 24 Stunden, Gräfin Mariza, Die Insel der Träume, Liebe und Trompetenblasen, Um Recht und Ehre, Der Feldherrenhügel, An der Schönen blauen Donau, Die Försterchristl, Kreuzzug des Weibes, Die lachende Grille, Madame wünscht keine Kinder, Das Mädchen auf der Schaukel, Der Mann ohne Schlaf, Nixchen, Der Soldat der Marie, Eine tolle Nacht, Der Veilchenfresser, Die Welt will belogen sein, Die Wiskottens, Der Bettelstudent, Faschingzauber, Das Fürstenkind, Die Geliebte, Das Heiratsnest, Die letzte Nacht, Ein Mädel aus dem Volke, Mein Freund Harry; Regine, die Tragödie einer Frau; Die rollende Kugel, Das Schicksal einer Nacht, Die Spielerin, Wochenendzauber, Amor auf Ski, Dragonerliebchen, Der Faschingsprinz, Grosstadtjugend, Der Herzensphotograph, Der moderne Casanova, Robert und Bertram, Das Spiel mit der*

Liebe, Die Zirkusprinzessin, Der Erzieher meiner Tochter, Der Held aller Mädchen-träume, Die Konkurrenz platzt, Der lustige Witwer, Der schwarze Domino, Vater und Sohn, Donauwalzer; O Mädchen, mein Mäd-chen, wie lieb' ich Dich!. Then sound: *Ich küsse Ihre Hand, Madame; Der Korvetten-kapitän, Die grosse Sehnsucht, Delikates-sen, Der keusche Joseph, ... und das ist die Hauptsache, Nie wieder Liebe, Der Liebesarzt, Liebe in Uniform, Wenn am Sonntagabend die Dorfmusik spielt, Der Page vom Dalmasse-Hotel, Zwischen zwei Herzen, Liebesleute, Stadt Anatol, Gefähr-liches Spiel, Preussische Liebesgeschichte; Quax, der Bruchpilot; Sophienlund, Das Konzert, Der Majoratsherr.*

220 **LIEVEN, ALBERT** (1906-   ). B: Hohenstein. Actor. RN: Albert Fritz Liévin. 1928-1929: Schauspielhaus Königsberg, then Schauspielhaus Berlin. 1932-1933: acts in German films as well as in French ones. 1936: to England (theatre work and films). After 1945: partly in Germany, partly in international productions.

Films: *Ich bei Tag und Du bei Nacht, Annemarie, die Braut der Kompanie, Kampf um Blond, Reifende Jugend, Die vom Nie-derrhein, Eine. Siebzehnjährige, Charleys Tante, Glückspilze, Es tut sich was um Mit-ternacht, Fräulein Liselott, Krach um Jolan-the, Die klugen Frauen, Mach' mich glück-lich, Hermine und die sieben Aufrechten, Kater Lampe, Eine Frau ohne Bedeutung, Die Dubarry, Fritz und Friederike, Klet-termaxe, Die Rose von Stambul, Geliebtes Leben, Heimweh nach Deutschland, Das Bekenntnis der Ina Kahr, Frühlingslied, Das Lied von Kaprun, Des Teufels General, Der Fischer vom Heiligensee, Reifende Ju-gend (55), Nacht der Entscheidung, Alle Sünden dieser Erde, ... und abends in die Scala, Schachnovelle, Frau Irene Besser, Das Geheimnis der gelben Narzissen, Fred-dy und das Lied der Südsee, Im Namen des Teufels, Der Gorilla von Soho.*

221 **LINGEN, THEO** (1903-   ). B: Hannover. Writer, actor and director. RN: Franz Theodor Schmitz. Stage training and *début* in Hannover. Then acted in, and directed at several theatres in Germany and Austria, also plays written by him. Popular comic in German language films, his real talent shines only in very few films, e.g. *M* and *Opernball.*

Acted in: *Dolly macht Karriere, Das Flö-tenkonzert von Sanssouci, Zwei Krawatten, Nie wieder Liebe, M, Zwei himmelblaue Augen; Meine Frau, die Hochstaplerin; Der grosse Bluff, Eine Stadt steht Kopf, Frie-derike, Die Gräfin von Monte Christo, Das Testament des Cornelius Gulden, Der Frau-endiplomat, Der Diamant des Zaren, Zi-geuner der Nacht, So ein Mädel vergisst man nicht, Moderne Mitgift; Marion, das gehört sich nicht, Im Banne des Eulenspie-gels, Flucht nach Nizza, Ein toller Einfall, Gipfelstürmer, Ein Unsichtbarer geht durch die Stadt, Die kleine Schwindlerin, Der Jäger aus Kurpfalz, Das Lied vom Glück, Das Testament des Dr. Mabuse, Zwei im Sonnenschein, Kleines Mädel – grosses Glück, Liebe muss verstanden sein, Höllen-tempo; Ihre Durchlaucht, die Verkäuferin; Walzerkrieg, Und wer küsst mich?, Kleiner Mann – was nun?, Keine Angst vor Liebe; Schön ist es, verliebt zu sein; Ihr grösster Erfolg, Mein Herz ruft nach Dir, Peters-burger Nächte, Kunjunkturritter, Liebe dumme Mama, Das Blumenmädchen vom Grand-Hotel, Die Finanzen des Grossher-zogs, Der Doppelgänger, Ich sehne mich nach Dir, Ich kenn' Dich nicht und liebe Dich, Ich heirate meine Frau, ... heute Abend bei mir, Ein Mädel wirbelt durch die Welt, Ein Walzer für Dich, Früchtchen, Gern hab' ich die Frau'n geküsst, Einmal-eins der Liebe, Winternachtstraum, Im weis-sem Rössl, Der Ammenkönig, Der Himmel auf Erden, Der Schlafwagenkontrolleur, Ich liebe alle Frauen, Held einer Nacht, Früh-jahrsparade, Ein falscher Fuffziger, Die Katz' im Sack, Ungeküsst soll man nicht schlafen geh'n, Im Sonnenschein, Es geht um mein Leben, Ein Hochzeitstraum, Der verkannte Lebemann, Die Leute mit dem Sonnenstich, Alles für Veronika, Der Ku-rier des Zaren, Die Entführung; Der Mann, von dem man spricht; Premiere, Fremden-heim Filoda, Gefährliches Spiel, Heirats-institut Ida & Co., Die unentschuldigte Stun-de, Die Austernlilli, Die verschwundene Frau, Zauber der Bohème, Der Optimist, Die unruhigen Mädchen, Das indische Grab-mal, Der Tiger von Eschnapur, Tanz auf dem Vulkan, Dir gehört mein Herz; Immer,* wenn ich glücklich bin; Diskretion – Ehrensache, Das Abenteuer geht weiter, Opernball, Marguerite: 3, Drunter und drüber, Hochzeitsreise zu Dritt, Was wird hier gespielt?, Das Fräulein von Barnhelm, Rosen aus Tirol, 7 Jahre Pech, Ihr Privatsekretär, Der ungetreue Eckehart, Rote Mühle, Herz modern möbliert, Dreimal Hochzeit, Sonntagskinder, Was geschah in dieser Nacht, Frau Luna, Wiener Blut, Liebeskomödie, Sieben Jahre Glück, Das Lied der Nachtigall, Johann, Tolle Nacht, Schuss um Mitternacht, Es fing so harmlos an, Philine, Liebesheirat, Glück muss man haben, Nichts als Zufälle, Um eine Nasenlänge, Der Theodor im Fussballtor, Jetzt schlägt's 13, Hin und her, Die Mitternachts-Venus; Hilfe, ich bin unsichtbar; Durch Dick und Dünn, Man lebt nur einmal, Die Diebin von Bagdad, Wir werden das Kind schon schaukeln, Heute Nacht passiert's, Hurra – ein Junge!, Die Tochter der Kompanie, Die vertagte Hochzeitsnacht; Heimlich, still und leise; Die Wirtin zur Goldenen Krone, Wenn die Alpenrosen blüh'n, Wie werde ich Filmstar?, Meine Tante, Deine Tante, Das Liebesleben des schönen Franz, Opernball (56), Ein tolles Hotel, Wo die Lerche singt, Der Mustergatte, . . . und wer küsst mich?, Vater macht Karriere, August der Halbstarke, Familie Schimek, Die Unschuld vom Lande, Drei Mann auf einem Pferd, Mit Rosen fängt die Liebe an, Egon der Frauenheld, Almenrausch und Edelweiss, Die Beine von Dolores, Im Prater blüh'n wieder die Bäume, Die Sklavenkarawane, Eine Reise ins Glück, Ein Lied geht um die Welt, Die Nacht vor der Premiere, Der Löwe von Babylon, Die Gans von Sedan, Pension Schöller, Eine Frau fürs ganze Leben, Bei Pichler stimmt die Kasse nicht, Der Musterknabe; Hilfe, meine Braut klaut; Tonio Kröger, Die fromme Helene, Das grosse Glück, Die Heiden von Kummerov und ihre lustigen Streiche, Die Lümmel von der ersten Bank I & II & III & IV & V.

Films as director: Marguerite: 3 39, Herz modern möbliert 40, Was wird hier gespielt 40, Hauptsache glücklich 41, Was geschah in dieser Nacht 41, Frau Luna 41, Liebeskomödie 42, Das Lied der Nachtigall 43 (also co-scripted), Tolle Nacht 43, Es fing so harmlos an 44 (also co-scripted), Glück muss man haben 45 (also co-scripted),

Liebesheirat 45 (also co-scripted), Philine 45, Wiener Melodien 48 (co-dir. with Hubert Marischka), Hin und her 50 (also co-scripted), Durch Dick und Dünn 51 (also co-scripted), Wie werde ich Filmstar? 55, Die Wirtin zur Goldenen Krone 55.

222 LITERARY ADAPTATIONS: The works of the various authors are listed, followed by the dates of the film versions and any changes from the original titles are noted in brackets.

GOETZ, CURT (1888-1960). 'Dr. med. Hiob Prätorius' 1934: 1950 (Frauenarzt Dr. Prätorius), 1965. 'Das Haus in Montevideo' 1953: 1951, 1963. 'Hokuspokus' 1928: 1930, 1953, 1966. 'Ingeborg' 1921: 1960. 'Die Tote von Beverly Hills' 1951: 1964. Scripted: Napoleon ist an allem schuld 38 (also dir. and acted), Glückskinder (co-scripted with Stemmle and Paul Martin), Sieben Ohrfeigen (co-scripted with B. E. Lüthge and Paul Martin).

HAUPTMANN, GERHART (1862-1946). 'Der Biberpelz': 1928, 1937, 1949. 'Fuhrmann Henschel': 1918, 1922, 1956. 'Hanneles Himmelfahrt': 1922, 1934. 'Die Jungfern vom Bischofsberg': 1943. 'Phantom': 1922. 'Die Ratten': 1921, 1955. 'Rose Bernd': 1919, 1957. 'Vor Sonnenuntergang': 1937 (Der Herrscher), 1956. 'Die Weber': 1927.

SCHNITZLER, ARTHUR (1862-1931). 'Fräulein Else': 1929. 'Freiwild': 1928. 'Der junge Medardus': 1924. 'Liebelei': 1911 (in Austria, dir. Jacob and Luise Fleck), 1927, 1933, 1958 (Christine, G/I, dir. Pierre Gaspard-Huit). 'Der Reigen': 1920.

ZUCKMAYER, CARL (1896-   ). 'Das Engele von Löwen': 1956 (Ein Mädchen aus Flandern). 'Der fröhliche Weinberg': 1927, 1952. 'Der Hauptmann von Köpenick': 1926 (dir. Siegfried Dessauer, based on original facts, not Zuckmayer's play), 1931, 1956. 'Herr über Leben und Tod': 1955. 'Katherina Knie': 1929, 1942 (in Switzerland, Menschen, die vorüberziehn, dir. Max Haufler). 'Eine Liebesgeschichte': 1954. 'Die Fastnachtsbeichte': 1960. 'Der Schinderhannes': 1927, 1958. 'Der Seelenbräu': 1950. 'Des Teufels General': 1955.

WALLACE, EDGAR (1875-1932). 'The Squeaker' 1927: 1931 (Der Zinker), 1963 (Der Zinker). 'The Ringer' 1926: 1932 (Der

Hexer), 1964 *(Der Hexer).* 'The Double' 1928: 1934 *(Der Doppelgänger).* 'The Fellowship of the Frog': 1959 *(Der Frosch mit der Maske).* 'The Crimson Circle' 1922: 1960 *(Der rote Kreis).* 'The Terrible People' 1926: 1960 *(Die Bande des Schreckens).* 'The Avenger' 1925: 1960 *(Der Rächer).* 'The Green Archer' 1923: 1961 *(Der grüne Bogenschütze).* 'The Dark Eyes of London' 1926: 1961 *(Die toten Augen von London).* 'The Daffodil Mystery' 1920: 1961 *(Das Geheimnis der gelben Narzissen).* 'The Forger' 1928: 1961 *(Der Fälscher von London).* 'The Strange Countess' 1926: 1961 *(Die seltsame Gräfin).* 'When the Gangs Came to London' 1932: 1962 *(Das Rätsel der roten Orchidee).* 'The Door with Seven Locks' 1926: 1962 *(Die Tür mit den sieben Schlössern).* 'The India Rubber Man' 1930: 1962 *(Das Gasthaus an der Themse).* 'The Yellow Snake': 1963 *(Der Fluch der gelben Schlange).* 'The Black Abbott' 1927: 1963 *(Der schwarze Abt).* 'The Frightened Lady' 1932: 1963 *(Das indische Tuch).* 'Room 13': 1964 *(Zimmer 13).* 'The Curse of the Hidden Vault': 1964 *(Die Gruft mit dem Rätselschloss).* 'Traitor's Gate' 1927: 1965 *(Das Verrätertor).* 'Again the Ringer' 1929: 1965 *(Neues vom Hexer).* 'The Man without a Face': 1966 *(Das Rätsel des silbernen Dreiecks).* Other films adapted from Wallace novels include: *Der Bucklige von Soho* 1966, *Das Geheimnis der weissen Nonne* 1966, *Die Blaue Hand* 1967, *Der Mönch mit der Peitsche* 1967, *Der Hund von Blackwood Castle* 1967, *Im Banne des Unheimlichen* 1968, *Der Gorilla von Soho* 1968, *Der Mann mit dem Glasauge* 1968, *Das Gesicht im Dunkeln* 1969.

223 LÖB, KARL (19 -   ). Director of photography. Enters cinema in early Thirties working at first mainly in collaboration with Willy Winterstein (q.v.) and others. Works mostly on commercial films, including adaptations from the works of Edgar Wallace and Karl May (in collaboration with Harald Reinl, q.v.).

Films: *Die spanische Fliege* (co-phot.), *Der Judas von Tirol* (co-phot.), *Die Leute mit dem Sonnenstich, Signal in der Nacht, Ab Mitternacht, Ich bin Sebastian Ott* (co-phot.), *Der Florentiner Hut* (co-phot.), *Krambambuli* (co-phot. with Sepp Ketterer), *Seiten-*

sprünge, Torreani (co-phot.), *Mein Herz darfst Du nicht fragen* (co-phot.), *Der Fürst von Pappenheim* (co-phot.), *Ein ganz grosses Kind* (co-phot.), *Die Rose von Stambul* (co-phot.), *Fräulein Casanova* (co-phot.), *Der Vetter aus Dingsda* (co-phot.), *Die tolle Lola* (co-phot.), *Aus eigener Kraft* (co-phot. with Wagner, Wolf Göthe and Fritz Brill), *Der treue Husar* (co-phot.),*Konsul Strotthoff* (co-phot.), *Schützenliesel, Clivia* (co-phot),*Ball im Savoy, Der 20. Juli, Der Hauptmann und sein Held* (co-phot), *Musik im Blut; Liebe, Tanz und 1000 Schlager; Die schöne Meisterin, Der erste Frühlingstag, Die Rosel vom Schwarzwald, Einmal eine grosse Dame sein, Die Frühreifen, Europas neue Musikparade 1958, Münchhausen in Afrika, Der Stern von Santa Clara, Scalatotal verrückt, Was eine Frau im Frühling träumt, Aus dem Tagebuch eines Frauenarztes, . . . und das am Montagmorgen, Melodie und Rhythmus, Am Tag als der Regen kam, Kein Engel ist so rein, Die 1000 Augen des Dr. Mabuse, Geschminkte Jugend, Sabine und die 100 Männer, Die toten Augen von London, Der Fälscher von London, Im Stahlnetz des Dr. Mabuse, Unser Haus in Kamerun, Das Gasthaus an der Themse, Ich kann nicht länger schweigen* (co-phot. Ekkehard Kyrath), *Die Tür mit den sieben Schlössern, Hochzeit am Neusiedlersee, Das indische Tuch, Die Nacht am See* (co-phot. Ted Kornowicz), *Unsere tollen Nichten, Der Zinker, Der letzte Ritt nach Santa Cruz, Unsere tollen Tanten in der Südsee, Unter Geiern, Neues vom Hexer, Old Surehand I, Schüsse im 3/4-Takt, Der Bucklige von Soho, In Frankfurt sind die Nächte heiss; Lange Beine, lange Finger; Spukschloss im Salzkammergut, Winnetou und sein Freund Old Firehand, Der Hund von Blackwood Castle, Der Mönch mit der Peitsche, Das Rasthaus der grausamen Puppen, Der Gorilla von Soho, Im Banne des Unheimlichen, Der Mann mit dem Glasauge, Sieben Tage Frist, Dr. Fabian — Lachen ist die beste Medizin.*

224 LOOS, THEODOR (1883 or 1892-1954). B: Zwingenburg an der Bergstrasse. D: Stuttgart. Actor. Students' theatre Leipzig. Later theatres in Danzig and Berlin, where he acted in the Hauptmann production of *Wilhelm Tell* (see entry for Rochus

Gleise). 1914-1924: Barnowsky theatres Berlin. 1911-1945: appears at all important theatres in Berlin. 1945: Tübingen. 1949-1954: Stuttgart. 1933: declared an "Actor of the State." Enters cinema in 1912, at first as partner of Erna Morena, Henny Porten (q.v.) and Maria Carmi.

Films: *Die Eisbraut* (date for that film unobtainable, but it was made certainly prior to 1923). Films (incomplete): *Das goldene Bett, Arme Eva, Das Haus ohne Fenster und Türen, Friedrich Werders Sendung, Homunculus, Es werde Licht (iii), Nach dem Gesetz, Die verbote Frucht, Geschwister Barelli, Im Banne der Suggestion, Der Reigen, Sehende Liebe, Die Spielerin, Steuermann Holck, Der zeugende Tod, Christian Wahnschaffe, Das blinde Glück, Hanneles Himmelfahrt, Jugend, Der Kampf ums Ich, Lady Hamilton, Malmaison, Schuld und Sühne, Friedrich Schiller, Aufstieg der kleinen Lilian, Claire, Die Nibelungen, Soll und Haben, Der erste Stand, Götz von Berlichingen zubenannt mit der eisernen Hand, Der tanzende Tod, Was Steine erzählen, Wunder der Schöpfung, Frauen der Leidenschaft, Der Herr der Nacht, Das Lebenslied, Liebeshandel, Manon Lescaut, Metropolis, Der Veilchenfresser, Zopf und Schwert; Anastasia, die falsche Zarentochter; Bigamie, Die Hochstaplerin, Luther, Petronella, Prinz Louis Ferdinand, Die Weber, Heimkehr, Königin Luise, Die Sache mit Schorrsiegel, Sensationsprozess, Blutschande § 173 St.G.B., Diane; Ludwig der Zweite, König von Bayern; Die stärkere Macht, Napoleon auf St. Helena, Vertauschte Gesichter.* Then sound: *Atlantik, Zwei Menschen, Die grosse Sehnsucht, Das Flötenkonzert von Sanssouci, Ich geh' aus und Du bleibst da, Die andere Seite, M, Im Geheimdienst, Yorck; 1914, die letzten Tage vor dem Weltbrand; Der Fall des Generalstabs-Oberst Redl, Ariane, Unter falscher Flagge, Tod über Shanghai, Die elf Schill'schen Offiziere, Grün ist die Heide, Holzapfel weiss alles, 8 Mädels im Boot, Schuss im Morgengrauen, Trenck, Ikarus (Speaker), Rasputin, Marschall Vorwärts, An heiligen Wassern, Die unsichtbare Front, Geheimnis des blauen Zimmers, Goethe, Der Judas von Tirol, Das Testament des Dr. Mabuse, Wege zur guten Ehe, Spione am Werk, Was wissen denn Männer, Höllentempo, Filisabeth und ihr Narr, Die blonde Christel, Ein gewisser Herr Gran, Gipfelstürmer, Wilhelm Tell, Die Freundin eines grossen Mannes, Ein Mädchen mit Prokura, Hanneles Himmelfahrt, Die Sporck'schen Jäger, Stradivari, Das Mädchen vom Moorhof, Das Mädchen Johanna, Viktoria, Der höhere Befehl, Der grüne Domino, Der alte und der junge König, Der Student von Prag (35), Der Abenteurer von Paris, Verräter, Schlussakkord, Die Stunde der Versuchung, Weisse Sklaven, Monika, Die gläserne Kugel, Das Geheimnis um Betty Bonn, Der Herrscher, Kameraden auf See, Geheimzeichen LB 17, Der Maulkorb, Schatten über St. Pauli, Robert Koch, Roman eines Arztes, Parkstrasse 13, Falschmünzer, Jud Süss, Kora Terry, Heimaterde, Alarm, Andreas Schlüter, Rembrandt, Die Entlassung, Die Sache mit Styx, Reise in die Vergangenheit, Titanic, Gabriele Dambrone, Philharmoniker, Geld ins Haus, Shiva und die Galgenblume, Der Fall Molander, Mordprozess Dr. Jordan, Sterne über Colombo, Die Gefangene des Maharadscha, Rosen aus dem Süden.*

225 **LORRE, PETER** (1904-1964). B: Rosenberg (Hungary). D: Hollywood. Actor

and director. Stage training in Vienna. At first bank clerk, then extra. Until 1932 Lorre acted on stage in Zurich, Vienna and Theater am Schiffbauerdamm Berlin. 1933: via France and England (1935) to Hollywood. Made one remarkable film as director in Germany after the war – *Der Verlorene*. The ingratiating, faintly vulnerable look of his childmurderer in *M* made him the most unusual actor of his generation.

Acted in: *Die Koffer des Herrn O. F., M, Bomben auf Monte Carlo, F.P. 1 antwortet nicht, Schuss im Morgengrauen, Fünf von der Jazzband, Der weisse Dämon, Was Frauen träumen, Unsichtbare Gegner, Der Verlorene*. Directed *Der Verlorene* 51 (also co-scripted).

226 LOTHAR, HANNS (1929-1967). B: Hannover. D: Hamburg. Actor. RN: Hanns Neutze. 1945-1951: Landestheater Hannover. 1952-1953: Städtische Bühnen and Kleines Theater im Zoo Frankfurt. 1954-1955: Landestheater Hannover, then Thalia-Theater Hamburg. One of the most talented and prolific actors of the German theatre in the Fifties, although he was rarely seen at his best in films. Lothar was married to Ingrid Andree (q.v.).

Films: *Buddenbrooks, Menschen im Netz, Sturm im Wasserglas, Der letzte Zeuge, Bis zum Ende aller Tage, Wenn beide schuldig werden; Piccadilly, null Uhr zwölf; Schloss Gripsholm, Wochentags immer, Seelenwanderung, Vier Schlüssel, Lange Beine, lange Finger.*

227 LUBITSCH, ERNST (1892-1947). B: Berlin. D: Hollywood. Actor and director. Studied at the Sophien Gymnasium, where he acted in amateur performances (mainly as an old man!). Evening stage training under Victor Arnold, a famous comic of the Reinhardt-ensemble (q.v.), for which he was soon under contract. Enters cinema in 1913, first as actor, later as director. 1923: to Hollywood. A director of major importance in the German silent cinema on account of his historical films, with their astonishing crowd scenes, at the same time he was also a meticulous director of "Kammerspiel" (q.v.). In Hollywood Lubitsch gained a reputation as a director of brilliant comedies (with their famed "Lubitsch-touch").,

Acted in: *Eine Venezianische Nacht, Bedingung: kein Anhang, Die Firma heiratet, Meyer auf der Alm, Anne Marie, Fräulein Piccolo, Die ideale Gattin, Serenissimus lernt Tango, Der Stolz der Firma*. Directed: *Blinde Kuh* 14 (also acted), *Fräulein Seifenschaum* 14 (also script and acted), *Meyer als Soldat* 14 (also acted), *Aufs Eis geführt* 15 (also acted), *Robert und Bertram* (only acted), *Zucker und Zimt* 15 (also script and acted), *Als ich tot war* 16, *Dr. Satansohn* (only acted), *Der gemischte Frauenchor* 16 (also acted), *Der erste Patient* 16 (also acted), *Der GmbH-Tenor* 16 (also acted), *Leutnant auf Befehl* 16 (also acted), *Schuhpalast Pinkus* 16 (also acted), *Der schwarze Moritz* 16 (also acted), *Wo ist mein Schatz?* 16 (also acted), *Der Blusenkönig* 17 (also acted), *Ein fideles Gefängnis* 17, *Hans Trutz im Schlaraffenland* (only acted), *Der Kraftmeyer* 17 (also acted), *Ossis Tagebuch* 17 (also co-scripted with Erich Schönfelder, and acted), *Prinz Sami* 17 (also acted), *Der letzte Anzug* 17 (also acted), *Wenn vier dasselbe tun* 17 (also co-scripted with Schönfelder, and acted), *Die Augen der Mumie Ma* 18, *Carmen* 18, *Der Fall Rosentopf* 18 (also script and acted), *Fuhrmann Henschel* 18, *Das Mädel*

vom *Ballett* 18 (also script), *Meine Frau, die Filmschauspielerin* 18 (also co-scripted), *Der Rodelkavalier* 18 (also acted), *Die Austernprinzessin* 19 (also co-scripted), *Ich möchte kein Mann sein* 19 (also script), *Der lustige Ehemann* (only script), *Madame Dubarry* 19, *Meyer aus Berlin* 19 (also acted), *Die Puppe* 19 (also co-scripted), *Rausch* 19, *Schwabemädle* 19, *Anna Boleyn* 20, *Kohlhiesels Töchter* 20 (also co-scripted and acted), *Medea* 20, *Romeo und Julia im Schnee* 20 (also co-scripted), *Sumurun* 20 (also co-scripted), *Die tolle Rikscha* 20, *Die Bergkatze* 21 (also co-scripted), *Venedetta* 21, *Das Weib des Pharao* 21, *Die Flamme* 22.

228 LÜDDECKE, WERNER JÖRG (1912-   ). B: Hannover. Scriptwriter. At first author, journalist and editor in Kassel and Dresden. Soldier, imprisoned, then enters cinema. Writer of scenarios for various types of films. Solid reputation.
Films: *Das Beil von Wandsbek* (in collab. with Staudte, Hans R. Bortfeldt and Falk Harnack), *Jonny rettet Nebrador* (in collab. with Heinz Pauck and Per Schwenzen), *Geständnis unter vier Augen* (in collab. with Hugo Maria Kritz and Answald Krüger), *Leuchtfeuer* (in collab.), *Ein Mann vergisst die Liebe* (in collab. with Madeleine Paul), *Der 20. Juli* (in collab. with Günther Weisenborn), *Nacht der Entscheidung; Nachts wenn der Teufel kam; Madeleine und der Legionär* (in collab. with Johannes Mario Simmel and Emil Burri), *Der Tiger von Eschnapur, Das indische Grabmal, Das Totenschiff* (in collab. with Hans Jacoby and Tressler), *Herrenpartie.*

229 LÜDERS, GÜNTHER (1915-   ). B: Lübeck. Actor and director. 1924: stage training and *début* in Lübeck. Theatres: Dessau, Frankfurt, Berlin (Lessing-Theater, Komödie, "Katakombe" and "Tingeltangel" cabarets). 1946-1947: Flensburg, Hamburg, Lübeck, 1947-1954: General director and actor in Düsseldorf (Städtische Bühnen, Schauspielhaus), same position Wuppertal (1957-1958). 1959-1960: Bayerisches Staatsschauspiel Munich, Renaissance-Theater and Komödie Berlin. 1961-1964: General director of the Würtembergische Staatstheater Stuttgart. Solid reputation as stage director.

In films often featured as a servant or joker Directed certain films *.
Films: *Die Insel, Herz ist Trumpf, Fürst Woronzeff; Ein Kind, ein Hund, ein Vagabund; Fräulein Liselott, Lärm um Weidemann, Die törichte Jungfrau, Spiel an Bord, Autobus S, Alarm in Peking, Meine Frau, die Perle, Florentine, Der Etappenhase, Die Kreutzersonate, Schwarzfahrt ins Glück, Das Ehesanatorium, Musketier Meier III, Ein Mädchen geht an Land; Nanu, Sie kennen Korff noch nicht?, Männer müssen so sein, Hochzeitsreise zu Dritt, In letzter Minute, Schneider Wibbel, Mein Mann darf es nicht wissen, Rote Mühle, Alles Schwindel, Casanova heiratet, Wunschkonzert, Herzensfreud – Herzensleid, Sechs Tage Heimaturlaub, Am Abend auf der Heide, Frau Luna, Ehe man Ehemann wird, Hab' mich lieb, Geheimakte WB 1, Weisse Wäsche, Ein Mann für meine Frau, Ein Walzer mit Dir, Leichtes Blut, Floh im Ohr, Ein schöner Tag, Fritze Bollmann wollte angeln, Neigungsehe, Grosse Freiheit Nr. 7, Meine Herren Söhne, Verlobte Leute, Wir seh'n uns wieder, Tierarzt Dr. Vlimmen, Die Schenke zur ewigen Liebe, Frau über Bord, Die Zeit mit Dir; Tobias Knopp, Abenteuer eines Junggesellen* (speaker), *Kommen Sie am Ersten, Der Tag vor der Hochzeit, Der Mann in der Wanne, Vater braucht eine Frau, Skandal im Mädchenpensionat, Ein Herz spielt falsch, Keine Angst vor grossen Tieren, Musik bei Nacht, Muss man sich gleich scheiden lassen?, Der Vogelhändler, Königliche Hoheit, Das ideale Brautpaar, ... und ewig bleibt die Liebe, Heideschulmeister Uwe Karsten, Das sündige Dorf, Der falsche Adam, Vatertag, Drei Männer im Schnee, Das fröhliche Dorf, Rosen im Herbst, Der Frontgockel, Hilfe – sie liebt mich, Lumpazivagabundus, Das Sonntagskind, Manöverball, Ciske – Ein Kind braucht Liebe, Wenn wir alle Engel wären* * 56, *Rot ist die Liebe, Robinson soll nicht sterben, Alle Wege führen heim, Das Wirtshaus im Spessart, Kein Auskommen mit dem Einkommen, Vater unser bestes Stück* * 57, *Lilli – Ein Mädchen aus der Grosstadt, Hoppla – jetzt kommt Eddie, 13 kleine Esel und der Sonnenhof, Auferstehung, Ihr 106, Geburtstag* * 58, *Buddenbrooks, Liebe auf krummen Beinen, Bobby Todd greift*

ein, Kriminaltango, Mal drunter – mal drüber, Tonio Kröger, Ich bin ein Elefant, Madame.

230 **MACK, MAX** (1884-   ). B: Halberstadt. Director. Started in 1906 as an actor in provincial theatres, then began to write film scripts for film companies in Berlin. Thanks to Julius Greenbaum he was engaged at the Vitascop. He said, "I wrote, arranged and acted the main parts in several short films." At the same time, he was also his own production manager. He claims to have introduced close-ups into German films. In *Wo ist Coletti?*, he is one of the first to use a hidden camera. Founder of the *auteur* film in Germany with *Der Andere* by Lindau, for which he engaged Albert Bassermann (q.v.). Max Mack, one of the forgotten pioneers of the German cinema, had to emigrate to London after the seizure of power by the Nazis. There he shot two more films, *Be Careful, Mr. Smith* and *Mack's Comedies.* In 1916 he wrote (among others with E. A. Dupont, q.v.) the film book, *Die zappelnde Leinwand*, published in London in 1943 as *With a Sigh and a Smile.*

Films: *Der Mutter Augen* (also script and acted), *Der Diener ihres Freundes* (also script and acted), *Die Falle* (also script and acted), *Die Frau des Abgeordneten* (also script and acted), *Launen des Schicksals* (also script and acted), *Mahira, Opfer um Opfer, Wenn die Toten erwachen* (also script and acted) – (dates for these films unobtainable, but all were made certainly prior to 1923). Films (in complete): *Die blaue Maus* 12 (also script), *Der Andere* 13, *Der König* 13, *Der letzte Tag* 13, *Wo ist Coletti?* 13, *Anne Marie* 14, *Der Katzensteg* 15, *Robert und Bertram* 15, *Othello* 18, *Sein Weib* 18, *Freie Liebe* 19 (prod., also scripted with Adolf Lantz), *Leben die Toten?* 19 (also prod.), *Figaros Hochzeit* 20 (also script), *Die Lieblingsfrau des Maharadschas* 20, *Geheimnisse von Berlin* 21, *Das Frauenparadies* 22, *O du mein Vaterland* 22 (also scripted with Overway), *Das schöne Mädel* 22, *Die Tragödie im Hause Bang* 22, *Die Fledermaus* 23, *Quarantäne* 23, *Das Mädchen mit der Protektion* 25, *Der ungebetene Gast* 25, *Vater Voss* 25, *Die Fahrt ins Abenteuer* 26, *Ich hatte einst*

ein schönes Vaterland 27, *Steh' ich in finsterer Mitternacht* 27, *Ein Tag der Rosen im August . . . da hat die Garde fortgemusst* 27, *Der Kampf der Tertia* 28 (also co-scripted), *Autobus Nr. 2* 29. Then sound: *Nur am Rhein* 30 (also co-scripted with Jacques Bacherach), *Tausend für eine Nacht* 32.

231 **MACKEBEN, THEO** (1897-1953). B: Preussich-Stargard. D: Berlin. Composer. Private music training. Appeared as pianist at the age of fifteen. Composed mainly for light entertainments and operettas. With the coming of sound he started to write for films, and he was appreciated for his effective songs and even symphonic scores. He adapted several musical works for the cinema with great charm.

Films: *Die Jagd nach dem Glück, Ich geh' aus und Du bleibst da* (in collab.), *Die Dreigroschenoper* (in collab. with Kurt Weill), *Die verkaufte Braut, Wie sag ich's meinem Mann, Das Abenteuer der Thea Roland, Fünf von der Jazzband, Ein steinreicher Mann, Liebelei, Pechmarie, Die Finanzen des Grossherzogs; Liebe, Tod und Teufel; Pygmalion, Viktoria, Das Einmaleins der Liebe, Mach' mich glücklich, Der Student von Prag* (35), *Mädchen in*

115

Weiss, Die Leute mit dem Sonnenstich, Unter heissem Himmel, Intermezzo, Das grosse Abenteuer, Daphne und der Diplomat, Patrioten, Ein Mädchen geht an Land, Tanz auf dem Vulkan, Heimat, Bel ami, Ich bin Sebastian Ott, Es war eine rauschende Ballnacht, Die Hochzeitsreise, Das Herz der Königin, Bal paré, Der Weg ins Freie, Ohm Krüger, Hochzeit auf Bärenhof, Abenteuer im Grandhotel, Die Gattin, Frauen sind keine Engel, Germanin, Altes Herz wird wieder jung, Das Konzert, Sag' endlich ja, Das seltsame Fräulein Sylvia, Und über uns der Himmel, Chemie und Liebe, Anonyme Briefe, Die Reise nach Marrakesch; Träum' nicht, Annette; Wer bist Du, den ich liebe?, Die Sünderin, Die Dubarry (ad. from Carl Millöcker), *Gefangene Seele, Es geschehen noch Wunder, Der grosse Zapfenstreich, Rivalen der Manege* (ad. by Klaus Ogermann 58).

232 MAERTENS, WILLY (1893-1967). B: Brunswick. D: Hamburg. Actor. Stage training in Berlin (under Höppner), *début* at the Intimes Theater in Nuremberg, then stage work in Elbing and Bromberg. From 1927: Thalia Theater Hamburg. From 1945: General director there. Many stage productions.

Films:*Anschlag auf Baku, In jenen Tagen, Arche Nora, Der Apfel ist ab, Absender unbekannt, Der Schatten des Herrn Monitor, Nur eine Nacht, Schön muss man sein, Engel im Abendkleid, Die Stimme des Andern, Toxi; Oh, du lieber Fridolin; Ich warte auf Dich, Keine Angst vor grossen Tieren, Bei Dir war es immer so schön, Konsul Strotthoff, Geständnis unter vier Augen, Drei vom Varieté; Musik, Musik und nur Musik; Wie werde ich Filmstar?, Die Ehe des Dr. med. Danwitz, Der Hauptmann von Köpenick* (56), *Mädchen mit schwachem Gedächtnis, Wenn wir alle Engel wären, Tierarzt Dr. Vlimmen, Nachts im grünen Kakadu, Das haut einen Seemann doch nicht um; Der Mann, der nicht nein sagen konnte; Frau im besten Mannesalter, Die Nacht vor der Premiere, Die schöne Lügnerin, Nacht fiel über Gotenhafen, Das Wunder des Malachias.*

233 MAETZIG, KURT (1911-   ). B: Berlin. Director. Technical High School Munich. Studied at University of Paris. Enters cinema as asst. director in 1933. Co-founder (1945) of DEFA. Many documentaries in first months after the war. Profesor of film direction at German High School for film art in Potsdam. One of the most important directors in G.D.R. cinema. State award 1949, 1950, 1954, 1959.

Films: *Ehe im Schatten* 47 (also script), *Die Buntkarierten* 49, *Der Rat der Götter* 50, *Familie Benthin* 50 (co-dir.), *Roman einer Ehe* 51 (also script with Bodo Uhse), *Ernst Thälmann – Sohn seiner Klasse* 53, *Ernst Thälmann – Führer seiner Klasse* 55, *Schlösser und Katen* 57, *Vergesst mir meine Traudel nicht* 57 (also script with Kuba), *Das Lied der Matrosen* 58 (co-dir. with Günter Reisch), *Der schweigende Stern* 60, *Septemberliebe* 61, *Der Traum des Hauptman Loy* 61, *An französischen Kaminen* 63, *Preludio 11* 64, *Die Fahne von Kriwoj Rog* 67, *Das Mädchen auf dem Brett* 67.

234 MAJEWSKI, HANS-MARTIN (1911-   ). B: Schlawe/Pomerania. Composer. Studied medicine and music at Königsberg university 1931-1932, then Konservatorium Leipzig 1932-1935. 1933-1938: conductor at Theater des Volkes Berlin. Soldier. Wrote operettas and composed for cabaret ("Bonbonnière," "Kaleidoskop," "Kabarett der Zeit NWDR Hamburg") after 1945. Worked for Ufa, Terra, Tobis, also radio. One of the busiest musicians of the German film industry after 1945 whose ideas and unusual instrumentation are surprisingly effective.

Films: *Flucht ins Dunkel, Fronttheater* (in collab. with Werner Bochmann), *Blokkierte Signale, Amico, Liebe 47, Meine Nichte Susanne* (in collab. with Alexander Steinbrecher), *Wenn eine Frau liebt; 0 Uhr 15, Zimmer 9, Tobias Knopp, Abenteuer eines Junggesellen; Der blaue Stern des Südens, Primanerinnen, Klettermaxe, Postlagernd Turteltaube, Liebe im Finanzamt, Der Weg zu Dir* (in collab. with Lotar Olias), *Das Nachtgespenst, Weg ohne Umkehr, Männer im gefährlichen Alter, Das fliegende Klassenzimmer, Sie, Das zweite Leben, Drei vom Varieté, Die verschwundene Miniatur, Die goldene Pest, Herr über Leben und Tod; Gestatten, mein Name ist Cox; Ingrid – Geschichte eines Fotomodells, Hanussen, Alibi, Heldentum nach Ladenschluss* (in collab.), *Ich suche Dich, Parole Heimat* (in collab. with Herbert Jarczyk), *Urlaub auf Ehrenwort, Heute heiratet mein Mann, Nacht der Entscheidung, Ohne Dich wird es Nacht, Hochzeit auf Immenhof, Kitty und die grosse Welt, Liebe, Der tolle Bomberg, Der Stern von Afrika, Ferien auf Immenhof, Bekenntnisse des Hochstaplers Felix Krull, Haie und kleine Fische, Der Fuchs von Paris, El Hakim, Der Greifer; Scampolo, Prelude* (episode from *Maya*), *Nasser Asphalt, Die Halbzarte, Der Maulkorb, Unruhige Nacht; Peter Voss, der Millionendieb; Warum sind sie gegen uns?, Solange das Herz schlägt, Menschen im Hotel, Nacht fiel über Gotenhafen, Bumerang, Labyrinth, Und das am Montagmorgen, Die Brücke, Ich schwöre und gelobe, Bezaubernde Arabella, Schachnovelle, Division Brandenburg, Fabrik der Offiziere, Das Wunder des Malachias, Agatha, lass das Morden sein, Die Diktatoren, Die Ehe des Herrn Mississippi, Frage sieben, Frau Cheneys Ende, Das Riesenrad, Heute kündigt mir mein Mann; Liebling, ich muss Dich erschiessen; Der rote Rausch, Tunnel 28, Elf Jahre und ein Tag, Liebe will gelernt sein,* *Schloss Gripsholm, Der Besuch, Was Männer nicht wissen müssen, Ganovenehre, Rheinsberg, Sieben Tage Frist.*

235 MAJOR PRODUCTION COMPANIES. Silent period: Messter-Film (becomes Projektions GmbH in 1900), Deutsche Bioscop (from 1905, *see* Decla), Allgemeine kinematographische Theatergesellschaft (from 1906, later becomes Projektions-AG Union), Deutsche Lichtbildgesellschaft e.V. (from 1916, founded by Klitzsch – *see* Ufa), Deutsche Mutoscop, Duskes, Venus-Film, International-Kino, Ernemann, Welt-Film (established by Fanck, q.v.), Aafa, Decla (1920 becomes Decla-Bioscop AG with Deutsche Bioscop), Phoebus, Orbis, Promo, Terra, National, Ring, Nivo, Demos, Hansa, Münchner Lichtspielkunst AG (known as Emelka), Tobis, Union (founded as Pagu), Berliner Porzellanmanufaktur, Ufa (q.v.).

Sound period: *see* Ufa and Nazi period. Many of the above mentioned companies had to cease production during the difficult years 1925-1927, but already in the silent period actresses, actors and directors started to produce their own films, and people like the Greenbaums were involved with producing and film-making (cameraman Mutz Greenbaum) until 1933.

Tonbild-Syndikat AG (Tobis) and Klangfilm GmbH shared the rights of the sound equipment, developed already prior to 1923, although patents were sold to Switzerland and America, because of lack of interest in Germany itself. The German Tri-Ergon-System was invented by Engl, Vogt and Masolle. *Ich küsse Ihre Hand, Madame* included a song mimed by Harry Liedtke, sung by Richard Tauber. Germany's first entirely sound films were *Melodie der Welt* (feature doc.), *Dich hab ich geliebt* and *Die Königsloge* (made in U.S.A. with German actors).

After 1945: *see* History of German Cinema (iv).

236 MANNHEIM, LUCIE (1899-   ). B: Berlin. Actress. Stage training Reichersche Hochschule Berlin. 1916: on stage, at first in Hannover and Libau, then Königsberg and Berlin (under Friedrich Kayssler, q.v.). 1933: to England, acted on stage and in films, worked for B.B.C. From 1945: guest appearances in German theatres. Married to Marius Goring.

Films: *Die Austreibung, Die Prinzessin Suwarin, Der Puppenmacher von Kiang-Ning, Der Schatz, Der steinerne Reiter.* Then sound: *Atlantik, Der Ball, Danton, Madame wünscht keine Kinder, Nachts auf den Strassen, Ich und Du, Das ideale Brautpaar, Die Stadt ist voller Geheimnisse, Du darfst nicht länger schweigen, Frauenarzt Dr. Bertram; Gestehen Sie, Dr. Corda; Ihr 106. Geburtstag, Der eiserne Gustav, Arzt aus Leidenschaft, Der letzte Zeuge, Erste Liebe.*

237 MARIAN, FERDINAND (1902-1946). B: Vienna. D: near Dürneck (car accident). Actor. RN: Ferdinand Haschkowitz. His father was a singer at Vienna Hofoper and taught singing. Marian studied at Vienna Politechnikum, also stage training. Pupil of Graz theatre. Then theatres: Trier, Staatstheater Munich, Hamburg, Deutsches Theater Berlin. Played the elegant villain in several films and earned overnight fame in the title role of *Jud Süss.*

Films: *Der Tunnel, Ein Hochzeitstraum, Madame Bovary, Die Stimme des Herzens, La Habanera, Nordlicht, Morgen werde ich verhaftet, Der Vierte kommt nicht, Dein Leben gehört mir, Der Fuchs von Glenarvon, Aus erster Ehe, Jud Süss, Ohm Krüger, Ein Zug fährt ab, Die Reise in die Vergangenheit, Tonelli, Romanze in Moll, Münchhausen, Freunde, In flagranti, Dreimal Komödie, Das Gesetz der Liebe, Die Nacht der Zwölf.*

238 MARKUS, WINNIE (1921-   ). B: Prague. Actress. Ballet training in Prague, stage training at the Vienna Reinhardt-Seminar. At the age of eight appears as dancer at the Prague Deutsches Theater, and thanks to director Heinz Hilpert she graduated to the Theater in der Josefstadt Vienna 1939-1945. After 1945: theatres in Munich and Berlin (Komödie, Renaissance-Theater, Schlosspark-Theater), where in 1946 with Viktor de Kowa (q.v.) she founds the production firm "Filmstudio 1945."

Films: *Mutterliebe, Brand im Ozean, Herz geht vor Anker, Im Schatten des Berges, Die Geierwally, Die Kellnerin Anna,* *Wen die Götter lieben, Brüderlein fein, Kleine Residenz, Sommerliebe, Der verkaufte Grossvater, Gefährlicher Frühling, Tonelli, Fahrt ins Abenteuer, Dir zuliebe, Der verzauberte Tag, Das alte Lied, Mit meinen Augen, Das fremde Leben, Philine, In jenen Tagen, Zwischen Gestern und Morgen, Morituri, Der Bagnosträfling, Die Nacht vergess' ich nie, Dieser Mann gehört mir, Es begann um Mitternacht, Begierde, Tausend rote Rosen blüh'n, Man nennt es Liebe, Kaiserwalzer, Komm zurück . . ., Liebeserwachen, Die Sonne von St. Moritz, Kaisermanöver, Grosse Starparade, Roman eines Frauenarztes, Du mein stilles Tal, Das Mädchen Marion, Kronprinz Rudolfs letzte Liebe; Liebe, die den Kopf verliert; Teufel in Seide; Vergiss, wenn Du kannst; Nichts als Aerger mit der Liebe, Made in Germany, Frauenarzt Dr. Bertram, Man ist nur zweimal jung, Hoch klingt der Radetzky-Marsch, Was eine Frau im Frühling träumt.*

239 MATÉ, RUDOLF (Rudolph, Rudy) (1898-1964). B: Cracow. D: Hollywood. Director of photography and director. RN: Rudolf Mathéh. Educated Vienna and Budapest; soldier. Enters cinema in 1921 as asst. director to Alexander Korda in Hungary. 1925: to Germany and asst. cameraman to Karl Freund (q.v.). 1928: to France, where he worked for Carl Dreyer (*La passion de Jeanne d'Arc,* 1928 and *Vampyr,* 1931). 1935: to U.S.A., first film as director 1947. Later made films in Germany and Italy.

Films as director of photography: *Der Kaufmann von Venedig* (co-phot. with Axel Graatkjaer), *Pietro, der Korsar* (co-phot. with Wagner and George Schneevoigt), *Mitgiftjäger, Die Hochstaplerin, Unter Ausschluss der Oeffentlichkeit.* Then sound: *Vampyr, Die Abenteuer des Königs Pausole.* Film as director: *Serenade einer grossen Liebe* 58.

240 MATZ, JOHANNA (HANNERL) (1932-   ). B: Vienna. Actress. Ballet training at Vienna Academy. At age of sixteen has stage training under Helen Thimig and Alfred Neugebauer. 1950: to Burgtheater Vienna thanks to Berthold Viertel. After early successes in cinema returns to the stage. Acts in Austrian and German films, but only occasionally because she considers herself primarily as a theatre actress.

Films: *Der alte Sünder, Asphalt, Maria Theresia, Du bist die Schönste für mich!, Zwei in einem Auto, Die Försterchristl, Saison in Salzburg, Der grosse Zapfenstreich, Im weissen Rössl, Hannerl, Arlette erobert Paris, Alles für Papa, Die Perle von Tokay, Mannequins für Rio, Ingrid – Die Geschichte eines Fotomodells, Der Kongress tanzt; Reich mir die Hand, mein Leben; Regine, . . . und führe uns nicht in Versuchung, Es wird alles wieder gut, Im Prater blüh'n wieder die Bäume, Hoch klingt der Radetzkymarsch, Man müsste nochmal zwanzig sein, Das Dreimäderlhaus, Die unvollkommene Ehe, Frau Warrens Gewerbe, Die glücklichen Jahre der Thorwalds, Das Leben beginnt um acht, Die ganze Welt ist himmelblau, Ruf der Wälder, Gern hab' ich die Frauen gekillt.*

241 **MAURUS, GERDA** (1903-1968). B: Vienna. D: Dusseldorf. Actress. RN: Gertrud Maria Pfeil. Stage *début* in Vienna, then Volkstheater Munich, Scala Vienna and Stadttheater Graz. From 1932: Staatstheater and Deutsches Theater Berlin, Kleine Komödie Munich. 1947: Schauspielhaus Düsseldorf. Was married to R. A. Stemmle.

Films: *Spione, Die Frau im Mond, Hochverrat.* Then sound: *Seitensprünge, Der Schuss im Tonfilmatelier, Täter gesucht, Hilfe! Ueberfall!, Schachmatt, Die Fremde, Der Draufgänger, Tod über Shanghai, Der weisse Dämon, Unsichtbare Gegner, Der Doppelgänger, Ein Mädchen mit Prokura, Der Kosak und die Nachtigall, Der Dschungel ruft, Arzt aus Leidenschaft, Daphne und der Diplomat, Prinzessin Sissy, Grenzfeuer, Die gute Sieben, Schicksal aus zweiter Hand, Die Freunde meiner Frau, Die kleine Stadt will schlafen gehen.*

242 **MAY, JOE** (1880-1954). B: Vienna. D: Hollywood. Director and producer. RN: Joseph Mandel. Studied at Berlin University. At first owner of a textile firm in Trieste, then car salesman and racing owner. 1909: director of operettas in Hamburg. 1911: director for Continental Film Company. 1914: founds own company, "Joe May Gesellschaft" (allied to Ufa). Launched the first serials (q.v.) in Germany, e.g. "Joe Debbs" and "Stuart Webbs," inspired by American ideas. Built "film town," Woltersdorf, near Berlin. 1926: as director to Ufa. 1933: to France. 1934: to Hollywood, thanks to Erich Pommer (q.v.). Was married to actress Mia May (q.v.). Prolific director, especially between 1918 and 1926.

Films: *Er muss sie haben, Ein Filmabenteuer, In der Tiefe des Schachts, Sami der Seefahrer* (dates for these films unobtainable, but all were made certainly prior to 1923). Films (not complete): *Die geheimnisvolle Villa* 14 (also prod.), *Graue Elster* 14, *Die Pagode* 14 (also prod.), *Das Panzergewölbe* 15, *Charly, der Wunderaffe* 15 (also script), *Der Schuss im Traum* 15, *Das Gesetz der Mine* 16 (also prod. and script), *Nebel und Sonne* 16 (also prod.), *Die Sünde der Helga Arndt* 16 (also prod.), *Hilde Warren und der Tod* 17 (also prod.), *Die Hochzeit im Excentricclub* 17 (also prod.), *Veritas vincit* 18 (also prod.), *Amönenhof* (only prod.), *Die Gräfin von Monte Christi* 19 (also prod.), *Die platonische Ehe* (only prod. and co-scripted with Richard Hutter), *Die wahre Liebe* 19 (also prod. and co-scripted with Rudolf Baron), *Die heilige Simplizia* 20 (also prod.), *Die Herrin der Welt* 20 (also prod.), *Der Leidensweg der Inge Krafft*

(only prod. and scripted), *Sodom und Gomorra* 20 (also prod.), *Das wandernde Bild* (only prod.), *Die Frauen von Gnadenstein* (only prod. and co-scripted), *Der Henker von Sankt Marien* 21 (also prod.), *Das indische Grabmal I & II* 21 (also prod.), *Die Schuld der Lavinia Morland* 21 (also prod.), *Tobias Buntschuh* 21 (co-dir. with Holger-Madsen, also prod.), *Der Hof des Schweigens* (only prod.), *Die Jüdin* (only prod.), *Monna Beatrice* (only prod.), *Scheine des Todes* (only prod.), *Tragödie der Liebe* 23 (also prod.), *Der geheime Agent* (only prod.), *Die Liebesbriefe der Baronin S...* (only prod.), *Der Farmer aus Texas* 25 (also prod. and co-scripted with Rolf E. Vanloo), *Dagfin* 26 (also co-prod. with Phoebus, and co-scripted with Adolf Lantz, Jane Bess & Hans Szekely), *Staatsanwalt Jordan* (only prod.), *Heimkehr* 28 (also prod.), *Asphalt* 29 (also prod.), Then sound: *Ihre Majestät die Liebe* 31, *... und das ist die Hauptsache* 31, *Hochzeitsreise zu Dritt* 32 (art. supervision), *Ein Lied für Dich* 33.

243 MAY, MIA (1884-   ). B: Vienna. Actress. RN: Maria Pfleger. Ballet training in Vienna. Played children's parts at the Jantsch Theater and the Apollo Theater Vienna. Then theatres: Hamburg, Friedrich Wilhelmstädter Theater Berlin. Was married to Joe May (q.v.) who featured her in his main films. Mother of actress Eva May who died very young. 1934: to Hollywood, where she was manageress of a restaurant.
Films: In der Tiefe des Schachts (her first film; date unobatainable, but probably before 1915). Films (incomplete): *Ketten der Vergangenheit, Charly der Wunderaffe, Nebel und Sonne, Die Sünde der Helga Arndt, Hilde Warren und der Tod, Veritas vincit, Amönenhof, Die Gräfin von Monte Christo, Die platonische Ehe, Die wahre Liebe, Fräulein Zahnarzt, Die Herrin der Welt, Der Leidensweg der Inge Krafft, Ninon, Sodom und Gomorra, Das wandernde Bild, Das indische Grabmal, Die Schuld der Lavinia Morland, Tragödie der Liebe, Die Liebesbriefe der Baronin S...*

244 MAYER, CARL (1894-1944). B: Graz. D: London. Scriptwriter. At first actor and painter, then literary manager (Theater Graz). Wrote for the cinema from 1919

onwards. 1927: to U.S.A. (with Murnau, q.v.). 1932: to England, where he worked with documentarist Paul Rotha and Gabriel Pascal; adviser to production company "Two Cities."The scripts he wrote in England were never filmed. Most important *auteur* of expressionist and post-expressionist film, an absolute master of *"Kammerspiel."* His work for Murnau, Wiene, Czinner and Ruttman (all q.v.) was very important and stimulating for the directors and cameramen involved. Already in 1920 his script for *Das Cabinet des Dr. Caligari* (written with the former officer Hans Janowitz) was considered as pure literary expression.
Films: *Das Kabinett des Dr. Caligari* (co-scripted with Hans Janowitz), *Brandherd, Der Bucklige und die Tänzerin, Der Gang in die Nacht, Genuine, Johannes Goth, Das lachende Grauen, Grausige Nächte, Die Hintertreppe, Scherben, Schloss Vogelöd, Phantom* (co-scripted), *Tragikomödie, Vanina oder die Galgenhochzeit, Erdgeist, Der Puppenmacher von Kiang-Ning, Die Strasse* (idea), *Sylvester, Der letzte Mann, Tartüff, Berlin – Die Symphonie einer Grosstadt* (idea). Then sound: *Ariane* (co-scripted), *Der träumende Mund* (co-scripted), *Der träumende Mund* 53 (script by Czinner and Johanna Sibelius based on the 32 version, re-make).

245 MEISEL, KURT (1912-   ). B: Vienna. Actor and director. Studied law at Vienna University. Theatres: Volkstheater Vienna, Kammerspiele Munich (1933-1934), Leipzig, various theatres in Berlin (1936-1949), Kleine Komödie Munich (1950-1951), Schiller- and Schlosspark-Theater Berlin (1952-1953), Kammerspiele Munich, Salzburg Festival. Actor and managing director of the Bayerische Staatstheater Munich (1961-1964), Burgtheater Vienna. Important stage productions and performances. For a short period Meisel also worked for DEFA (q.v.). Directed certain films *.
Films: *Ehestreik, Schlussakkord, Das Hofkonzert, Spiel auf der Tenne, Liebe kann lügen, Die göttliche Jette, Andere Welt, Die ganz grossen Torheiten, Der Schimmelkrieg in der Holledau, Nanon, Frau Sylvelin, Eine Frau wie Du, Das Ekel, Eine kleine Nachtmusik, Der Feuerteufel, Die keusche Geliebte, Menschen im Sturm, Der Weg ins*

Emil Jannings in DER LETZTE MANN, scripted by Carl Mayer

Freie, Der Fall Rainer, Die goldene Stadt, Der grosse König, Klein-Dorrit, Ein toller Tag, Kolberg, Wozzeck, Verspieltes Leben 49 (also *), *Tragödie einer Leidenschaft* 49 (only *), *Liebe auf Eis* 50 (also *), *Dämonische Liebe* 51 (also *), *Die Spur führt nach Berlin, Bis wir uns wiederseh'n, Emil und die Detektive, Die Todesarena* 53 (only *), *Mannequins für Rio; Gestatten, mein Name ist Cox; Es geschah am 20. Juli, Unternehmen Schlafsack, Zwei blaue Augen, Das Sonntagskind* 56 (only *), *Vater sein dagegen sehr* 57 (also *), *Drei Mann auf einem Pferd* 57 (also *), *Der veruntreute Himmel; Romarei, das Mädchen mit den grünen Augen; Dorothea Angermann, Madeleine – Tel. 13 61 11* 58 (only *), *Kriegsgericht* 59 (only *), *Liebe verboten – heiraten erlaubt* 59 (also *), *Die rote Hand* 60 (also *), *Der Verschwender* 64 (only *), *Zwei Girls vom roten Stern, Michael Kohlhaas – Der Rebell.*

246 **MELICHAR, ALOIS** (1896-   ). B: Vienna. Composer and conductor. Conductor's son. Studied at the Staatsakademie für Musik in Vienna (under Joseph Marx) and Hochschule für Musik in Berlin (under Franz Schrecker). 1923-1926: conductor in U.S.S.R. (South Caucasus). 1927-1933: musical director for Deutsche Grammophon AG. Music critic and conductor of the Berlin Philharmonic. 1933-1935: freelance composer. 1945-1949: conductor of the Vienna Symphony Orchestra. 1946-1949: head of department for modern music at "Rot-Weiss-Rot" radio station. Wrote music for stage, radio and film, also choral and orchestral music. Author of the books: *Die unteilbare Musik* (1952), *Ueberwindung des Modernismus* (1954), *Musik in der Zwangsjacke* (1958) and *Schönberg und die Folgen* (1960), in which he states his arguments against modern music.

Films: *Walzerkrieg* (in collab.), *Der junge*

121

Baron Neuhaus, Abschiedswalzer, Stradivari, Zigeunerbaron, Wenn die Musik nicht
wär', Liselotte von der Pfalz, Vergiss mein
nicht, Der Bettelstudent, Ave Maria, Das
Mädchen Irene, Liebeserwachen, Drei Mä-
derl um Schubert, Die Fledermaus, Mutter-
lied, Land der Liebe, Capriccio, Nanon,
Dir gehört mein Herz (in collab. with C. A.
Bixio), Das unsterbliche Herz, Unsterblicher
Walzer, Maria Ilona, Eine kleine Nachtmu-
sik, Das Fräulein von Barnhelm, Michel-
angelo, Das Mädchen von Fanö, Falstaff in
Wien, Mein Leben für Irland, . . . reitet für
Deutschland, Kameraden, Anschlag auf
Baku, Rembrandt, Geheimnis, Tibet, Die
Zaubergeige, Philharmoniker (in collab. with
Friedl Heinz Heddenhausen), Freunde, Mu-
sik in Salzburg, Glück muss man haben,
Die Fledermaus (45), Ulli und Marei, Anni
(in collab. with Robert Stolz), Der himm-
lische Walzer (in collab. with Ludwig
Schmidseder), Der Prozess, Die seltsame
Geschichte des Brandner Kaspar, Das un-
sterbliche Antlitz, Der blaue Strohut,
Triumph der Liebe, Eroica, Küssen ist keine
Sünd, Angela, Das doppelte Lottchen, Das
Haus des Schweigens, Geheimnis einer Ehe,
Maria Theresia, Das Land des Lächelns, 1.
April 2000, Der träumende Mund, Vergiss
die Liebe nicht, Tagebuch einer Verliebten,
Aus eigener Kraft, . . . und ewig bleibt die
Liebe, Ewiger Walzer (adap.), Fledermaus
1955, Sohn ohne Heimat, Dunja, Fuhrmann
Henschel.

247 MENZEL, GERHARD (1894-   ).
B: Waldenburg/Silesia. Writer and script-
writer. At first bank clerk and jeweller in
Waldenburg. 1925: cinema owner in Gottes-
berg near Waldenburg. 1928: freelance writ-
er in Berlin, later in Vienna. 1946: lives in
Bad Reichenhall. 1952: in Vienna again.
Realistic author of dramas and novels with
contemporary themes. Successful scriptwrit-
er, especially during the Nazi period.
Films: Flüchtlinge, Morgenrot, Das Mäd-
chen Johanna, Barcarole, La Habanera.
Savoy-Hotel 217, Unter heissem Himmel.
Frau im Strom, Mutterliebe, Robert Koch
(only idea with Paul Josef Cremers), Der
Postmeister, Ein Leben lang, Dreimal Hoch-
zeit (only idea), Heimkehr, Wien 1910,
Schicksal, Späte Liebe, Am Ende der Welt.
Freunde, Das Herz muss schweigen, Ein

Blick zurück, Verspieltes Leben, Die Sünderin (co-scripted with Forst and Georg
Marischka), Wenn Du noch eine Mutter
hast . . ., Hanussen, Dunja, Ich suche Dich
(co-scripted with Fischer, Martin Morlock
and Claus Hardt), Herrscher ohne Krone
(co-scripted with Odo Krohmann), Der Edelweisskönig.

248 MESSEMER, HANNES (1924-   ).
B: Dillingen. Actor. At first waiter and book
keeper, then writer. Début in 1945 without
training on open air stages, then appears
at the municipal theatre in Tübingen. 1950-
1956: Bochum, since then Kammerspiele
Munich. Prominent stage actor and also in
the cinema, but up to now he has only
had a few interesting screen parts.
Films: Rose Bernd, Nachts wenn der Teufel kam, Der gläserne Turm, Madeleine und
der Legionär, Taiga, Der Arzt von Stalingrad, Menschen im Netz, Das kunstseidene
Mädchen; Ein Tag, der nie zu Ende geht;
Lampenfieber, Die rote Hand, Brücke des
Schicksals, Auf Engel schiesst man nicht, 12
Stunden Angst, Der Transport, Mord am
Canale Grande, Grieche sucht Griechin, Der
Kongress amüsiert sich, Lautlose Waffen.

249 MESSTER, OSKAR (1866-1943). B: Berlin. D: Tegernsee. Inventor, pioneer and producer. After taking over his father's optical laboratory in 1895-1896 he formed his own "Kinematograph" system for transporting film through the camera free of any "jerking" effect. 1896: launches his own film production. October 1897: places eighty-four of his own films on the market. First close-ups in *Vom Ernst zum Lachen: Die Mimik des Gesangskomikers Franz Amon* (No. 4 in the Messter catalogue). First animation effects in *Schnellmaler Clown Jigg* (No. 5 in the catalogue). First speeded-up motion effect in *Flower Arrangement*. 1901: establishes "Projektion GmbH," changed in the following year to "Messter's Projektion GmbH" (until 1930). Produced all his own films until 1913. 1910: founds the "Kosmograph Compagnie GmbH" for the manufacture of film equipment, and in 1913 this was developed into an actual production company known as "Messter-Film GmbH." On October 1, 1914: first newsreel screened under the title of "Messter-Woche" (absorbed by "Deulig-Woche" on January 1, 1920). 1917: all Messter's companies come under control of Ufa. Messter himself had a share in founding the Tonbild-Syndikat AG (Tobis) in 1927. Messter had already experimented with sound images as early as 1903, in order to combine songs with film by means of records etc. Several directors *(see* Froelich) and players (Henny Porten, q.v., among others) began under his aegis. Many stars of opera and operetta sung for his "Tonbilder" and many dancers and composers worked for him. The following actors and actresses (who later became stars of German cinema) made their *début* under Messter: Lil Dagover, Ossi Oswalda, Adele Sandrock, Emil Jannings, Hans Junkermann, Harry Liedtke, Harry Piel, Reinhold Schünzel, Conrad Veidt (all q.v.), Leopoldine Konstantin, Erna Morena, Olga Limburg, Frieda Richard, Wanda Treumann, Richard Alexander, Karl Becker-Sachs, Erich Kaiser-Titz, Max Landa, Viggo Larsen, Hans Mierendorff, Paul Otto, Albert Paulig, Ernst Reicher, etc. Author of memoirs, *Mein Weg mit dem Film* (36).

Films (incomplete): *Rapunzel, Die Sonne* (co-prod. with Union), *Gestörtes Rendezvous* 97 (also dir.), *Gemütlich beim Kaffee*

98 (also dir.), *Rückkehr der Truppen von der Frühjahrsparade* 1900 (also dir.), *Salome* 02 (also dir.), *Auf der Radrennbahn* 03 (also dir.), *Apachentanz* 06 (also dir.), *Fra Diavolo, Lohengrin, Meissner Porzellan, Desdemona, Tief im Böhmerwald, Wiegenlied, Andreas Hofer, Der Kinderarzt, Liebesglück einer Blinden; Mütter, verzaget nicht; Verkannt* 10 (also dir.), *Adressatin verstorben, Die Blinde, Der Eindringling, Das gefährliche Alter, Die Magd, Maskierte Liebe, Die Rache ist mein, Ein schweres Opfer, Zwei Frauen, Zu spät, Des Pfarrers Töchterlein, Eva, Feenhände, Gefangene Seelen, Kuss des Fürsten, Die Nacht des Grauens, Richard Wagner, Schatten des Meeres, Gräfin Küchenfee, Die grosse Sünderin, Heroismus eines Französin, Schuldig, Das Tal des Lebens, Um Haaresbreite, Ungarische Rhapsodie, Abseits vom Glück, Alexandra, Arme Eva, Das Ende vom Lied, Nordlandlore, Tirol in Waffen, Auf der Alm da gibt's ka Sünd, Claudi vom Geisterhof, Der Schirm mit dem Schwan, Ein Ueberfall in Feindesland, Die Ehe der Luise Rohrbach, Der Liebesbrief der Königin, Der Mann im Spiegel, Problematische Naturen, Der Sekretär der Königin, Das wandernde Licht; Die Dame, der Teufel und die Probiermamsell; Die*

Faust des Riesen, Die blaue Laterne, Maskenfest der Liebe, Odysseus' Heimkehr, Die rollende Kugel, Anna Boleyn (co-prod. with Ufa and Union), Die goldene Krone, Die Tarantel, Die Kunst zu heiraten, Der Mann mit den sieben Masken, Der Stier von Olivera, Tatjana, Gehetzte Menschen (co-prod.). – A very few copies of the catalogue of practically all (?) Messter productions exists.

250 **METZNER, ERNÖ** (1892-   ). B: in Hungary. Set designer and director. Studied at Akademie der Schönen Künste in Budapest. Enters cinema in 1920 as set designer. Important work for Pabst (p.v.), and his film Ueberfall is a major contribution to the avant-garde (q.v.). Leaves Germany in 1933.

Films (incomplete): Sumurun (in collab. with Kurt Richter and ? Ernst Stein), Das Weib des Pharao (in collab. with Ernst Stein and Max Gronau), Don Juan (in collab. with Michl Fingesten and Georg Meyer), Fra Diavolo (costumes?), Salome 22 (co-dir. with Ludwig Kozma), Alt-Heidelberg, Fridericus Rex (in collab. with Hans Dreier), Arabella, Ein Sommernachtstraum, Gemeimnisse einer Seele, Man steigt nach 27 (also co-scripted with Emil Waldmann, des.), Hotelgeheimnisse (in collab. with Ernst Meiwers), Mikosch rückt ein (in collab. with Meiwers), Der Ueberfall 28 (also co-scripted with Grace Chiang), Tagebuch einer Verlorenen (in collab. with Emil Hasler), Die weisse Hölle von Piz Palü. Then sound: Rivalen im Weltrekord (also co-scripted with Bob Stoll and dir.), Westfront 1918, Kameradschaft, Die Herrin von Atlantis.

251 **MINETTI, HANS-PETER** (1926-   ). B: Berlin. Actor. Studied history of art and philosophy in Kiel, Hamburg and Berlin. Then trained at the theatre institute in Weimar, later Maxim Gorki Theater and Deutsches Theater Berlin. 1958: member of the Central Committee of the G.D.R. Socialist Party. State award in 1966.

Films: Ernst Thälmann – Sohn seiner Klasse, Ernst Thälmann – Führer seiner Klasse, Der Teufel vom Mühlenberg, Spur in der Nacht, Tinko, Polonia-Express, Lissy, Tatort Berlin, Im Sonderauftrag, Eine alte Liebe, Zu jeder Stunde, Wo der Zug nicht

lange hält, Kuttel, Die schwarze Galeere, Geheimarchiv an der Elbe, Reserviert für den Tod, Alaskafüchse, Die Suche nach dem wunderbunten Vögelchen.

252 **MOISSI, BETTINA** (1923-   ). B: Berlin. Actress. Stage training in Berlin (under Otto Falckenberg), then in theatres under Gustaf Gründgens (q.v.) in Berlin and Munich. A prominent actress of stage and screen with a subtle personality, even though she only acted in a few films (notably with Käutner, q.v.). After 1950: leaves the film business and settles in Paris. Daughter of the actor Alexander Moissi.

Films: In jenen Tagen, Der Apfel ist ab, Lang ist der Weg, Epilog.

253 **MONDI, BRUNO** (1903-   ). B: Schwetz. Director of photography. Trained at Lehranstalt für Kinetechnik in Berlin. 1921: School of Photography in Berlin. 1924: asst. cameraman to Richard Eichberg (q.v.). Since 1927: freelance cameraman. After 1945: part time for DEFA (q.v.). An expert in the field of colour photography.

Films: Die Frau mit dem Etwas (co-phot. with Heinrich Gärtner), Durchlaucht Radieschen (co-phot. with Gärtner), Die Leibeigenen (co-phot. with Gärtner), Die tolle Lola (co-phot. with Gärtner), Das Girl von der Revue (co-phot. with Gärtner), Song (co-phot. with Gärtner), Die tolle Komptesse (co-phot. with Hugo von Kaweczynski), Jennys Bummel durch die Männer, Ein kleiner Vorschuss auf die Seeligkeit (co-phot. with Kaweczynski). Then sound: Wer wird denn weinen, wenn man auseinandergeht (co-phot. with Heinrich Gärtner), Zärtlichkeit, Hai-Tang (co-phot. with Heinrich Gärtner), Der Greifer (co-phot. with Gärtner), Tingel-Tangel, Die Bräutigamswitwe (co-phot. with Gärtner), Trara um Liebe (co-phot. with Gärtner), Das Geheimnis der roten Katze, Der Draufgänger (co-phot. with Gärtner), Die unsichtbare Front, Unmögliche Liebe, Kriminalreporter Holm, Das Millionentestament, Holzapfel weiss alles (co-phot. with Gärtner), Salon Dora Green, Heimkehr ins Glück, Drei Kaiserjäger, Heut' kommt's drauf an; Gruss und Kuss, Veronika!; Der Vetter aus Dingsda, Da stimmt was nicht, Zigeunerblut (co-phot. with. E. W. Fiedler), Jungfrau gegen

Mönch, Ich kenn' Dich nicht und liebe Dich, Hohe Schule, Pygmalion, Der Student von Prag (35), *Nacht der Verwandlung, Frischer Wind aus Kanada, ... nur ein Komödiant* (co-phot. with E. W. Fiedler), *Krach im Hinterhaus, Schabernack, Fridericus, Ave Maria, Mädchenjahre einer Königin* (co-phot. with Otto Baecker), *Die Nacht mit dem Kaiser, Gefährliches Spiel, Die Fledermaus, Die Warschauer Zitadelle, Einmal werd' ich Dir gefallen* (co-phot. with Hugo von Kaweczynski), *Jugend, Du und ich, Verwehte Spuren, Das unsterbliche Herz, Die Reise nacht Tilsit, Falstaff in Wien, Jud Süss, Stern von Rio, Bismarck, Pedro soll hängen, Die goldene Stadt, Der grosse König, Immensee, Opfergang, Kolberg, Wozzeck, Chemie und Liebe, Und wieder 48!, Der Biberpelz, Rotation, Das kalte Herz* (co-phot. with Ernst Kunstmann); *0 Uhr 15, Zimmer 9; Sensation in San Remo, Pension Schöller, Die Czardasfürstin, Maske in Blau, Südliche Nächte, Hab' ich nur deine Liebe, Mädchen mit Zukunft, Gefangene der Liebe, Das sündige Dorf* (co-phot. with Heinz-Gönisch), *Mädchenjahre einer Königin, Die Deutschmeister, Das fröhliche Dorf, Sissi, Liebe ist ja nur ein Märchen, Waldwinter, Opernball* (56); *Sissi, die junge Kaiserin; Das Schloss in Tirol, Sissi – Schicksalsjahre einer Kaiserin, Scampolo, Der veruntreute Himmel, Das Dreimäderlhaus, Unser Wunderland bei Nacht, Ein Mann geht durch die Wand, Alt-Heidelberg, Der wahre Jakob; Willy, der Privatdetektiv; Davon träumen alle Mädchen.*

254 "MOUNTAIN" FILMS (Bergfilm):
A particular *genre* of nature and landscape film, in which the strength and magnificence of the mountain world are given dramatic stature. They are therefore ideally suited to purely cinematic effects. Tension in these films is often heightened by the presence of individual climbers or parties. The main examples of the *genre*, apart from certain Italian and Scandinavian productions, are the films of Arnold Fanck, Leni Riefenstahl, and Luis Trenker (all q.v.).

255 MÜLLER, RENATE (1907-1937). B: Munich. D. Berlin (suicide). Actress. Daughter of an editor of *Münchner Zeitung*. Trained at the actors' school set up by Max Rein-

hardt (q.v.), starts her film career as a gay, blonde beauty in 1928. One of the most popular actresses of her time.

Films: *Peter, der Matrose; Revolte im Erziehungshaus, Drei machen ihr Glück.* Then sound: *Liebe im Ring, Liebling der Götter, Der Sohn der weissen Berge, Das Flötenkonzert von Sanssouci, Die Blumenfrau von Lindenau, Liebeslied, Die Privatsekretärin, Der kleine Seitensprung, Mädchen zum Heiraten, Wie sag ich's meinem Mann, Wenn die Liebe Mode macht, Walzerkrieg, Viktor und Viktoria, Die englische Heirat, Liselotte von der Pfalz, Liebesleute, Allotria, Eskapade, Togger.*

256 MÜNCH, RICHARD (1916-   ). B: Giessen. Actor. Stage training and theatres in Frankfurt. 1952-1954: Kammerspiele Hamburg and Schauspielhaus Düsseldorf. Since 1945: Schauspielhaus Hamburg.

Films: *Es geschehen noch Wunder, Der Verlorene, Zwei blaue Augen, Dr. Crippen lebt, Nasser Asphalt, Unruhige Nacht, Der Schinderhannes, Frau im besten Mannesalter, Verbrechen nach Schulschluss, Hunde wollt ihr ewig leben; Himmel, Amor und Zwirn; Das Wunder des Malachias, Das Gasthaus an der Themse, Die Rote, Der Besuch, Wartezimmer zum Jenseits, Das Lie-*

Above, a typical "mountain" film: STÜRME ÜBER DEM MONTBLANC, directed by Arnold Fanck. Portrait below: Friedrich Wilhelm Murnau

beskarussell (iii), Mordnacht in Manhattan, Schüsse aus dem Geigenkasten, Hokuspoku – oder wie lasse ich meinen Mann ver schwinden, In Frankfurt sind die Nächte heiss; Pfeifen, Betten, Turteltauben; Um null Uhr schnappt die Fall zu, Rechnung - eiskalt serviert, Heisses Pflaster Köln, De Mörderclub von Brooklyn.

257 **MURNAU, FRIEDRICH WILHELM** (1888-1931). B. Bielefeld. D: California (car accident). Director. RN: Friedrich Wil helm Plumpe. Studied history of art and literature in Heidelberg. Pilot during war Pupil to Reinhardt (q.v.), asst. director and stage director in Berlin. Directed folk play *Marignano* in Berne (Switzerland), also some propaganda films for the German embassy in Berne. Ernst Hoffmann produced hi first films, then Murnau moved to Ufa where Erich Pommer (q.v.) proved an un derstanding and helpful friend. 1926: to U.S.A. Murnau created a remarkable serie of dramatic, fantastic, literary and documen

tary films. He was a master of *"Kammerspiel"* (q.v.) for which Carl Mayer wrote his ingenious scripts. "Peter Murglie" was the pseudonym for the scriptwriting team of Murnau and Rochus Gliese (q.v.).

Films: *Der Knabe in Blau* 19, *Satanas* 19, *Abend . . . Nacht . . . Morgen* 20, *Der Bucklige und die Tänzerin* 20, *Der Gang in die Nacht*, 20, *Der Januskopf* 20, *Sehnsucht* 20, *Marizza, genannt die Schmugglermadonna* 21, *Schloss Vogelöd* 21, *Der brennende Acker* 22, *Nosferatu – Eine Symphonie des Grauens* 22, *Phantom* 22, *Die Austreibung* 23, *Die Finanzen des Grossherzogs* 23, *Komödie des Herzens* (only co-scripted), *Der letzte Mann* 24, *Tartüff* 25, *Faust* 26.

258 NAGY, KÄTHE VON (1909-   ). B: Subotica near Budapest. Actress. RN: Kato Nagy. Appears at an early age in Budapest theatres. 1926: to Berlin, where director Constantin David (her husband) introduces her to films. 1929: acts in Italy, in Mario Camerini's *Rotaie*. 1935: to France and a handful of films in Nazi Germany. Lives in France.

Films: *Das brennende Schiff, Gustav Mond . . . Du gehst so stille, Männer vor der Ehe, Die Sandgräfin, Die Durchgängerin, Die Königin seines Herzens, Die Republik der Backfische, Aufruhr im Junggesellenheim, Mascottchen, Unschuld, Der Weg durch die Nacht, Gaukler.* Then sound: *Der Andere, Ihre Majestät die Liebe; Meine Frau, die Hochstaplerin; Ronny, Ihre Hoheit befielt, Das schöne Abenteuer, Ich bei Tag und Du bei Nacht, Der Sieger, Die Töchter Ihrer Exzellenz, Einmal eine grosse Dame sein; Liebe, Tod und Teufel; Prinzesin Turandot, Der junge Baron Neuhaus, Die Freundin eines grossen Mannes, Die Pompadour, Ave Maria, Unsere kleine Frau, Die unruhigen Mädchen, Am seidenen Faden, Salonwagen E 417, Renate im Quartett, Die Försterchristel.*

259 NAUMANN, GÜNTER (1925-   ). B: Chemnitz. Actor. Prisoner of war, then at first painter. Stage training in Leipzig. Appears at the Karl-Marx-Stadt Theatre. 1957: joins Berliner Ensemble.

Films: *Fünf Patronenhülsen, Steinzeitballade, Professor Mamlock, Der Fall Gleiwitz, Die Jagd nach dem Stiefel, Geheim-*

nis der 17, Auf der Sonnenseite, Königskinder, Sonntagsfahrer, Jetzt und in der Stunde meines Todes, Die Abenteuer des Werner Holt.

260 NEBENZAL, SEYMOUR (NEBENZAHL) (1899-   ). B: New York. Producer. Started his career in Berlin as producer for Nero Film Company. Guiding light behind *Menschen am Sonntag*, on which Moritz Seeler was associated producer. Nebenzal produced films by Lang and Pabst (both q.v.), went to France, where he produced *Mayerling* and *Werther*. 1940: to U.S.A. Since 1945: president of Nero Film Inc.

Films (incomplete): *Abenteuer einer Nacht* (co-prod.). Then sound: *Menschen am Sonntag, Westfront 1918, Ariane, M, Die Herrin von Atlantis, Das Testament des Dr. Mabuse.*

NEFF, HILDEGARDE *see* KNEF, HILDEGARDE

261 NEGRI, POLA (1894-   ). B: Janowa (Poland). Actress. RN: Barbara Appolonia Chapulek. Daughter of a gipsy violinist. After her father was deported (during the revolution of 1905), she went to Warsaw with her mother. Educated at the boarding school of Countess Platen, later ballet training at Imperial Ballet School St. Petersburg (dismissed because of a week heart). Stage training at Warsaw Konservatorium. Starts career in 1913 at Maly Theatre Warsaw and assumes name Pola Negri (because of her adoration for Italian poetess Ada Negri). Then Teatr Wielki. She made her first film appearances because of the closure of the Polish theatres, then invited to come to Berlin by Reinhardt (q.v.). 1917: to Berlin, where she is very successful, especially in films by Lubitsch (q.v.). 1923: to U.S.A. 1929-1930: in England, then back to Hollywood. 1935: to Austria and Germany. 1940: finally back to Hollywood. Star of the Polish, German, Austrian, Englisch, French and American cinema (1914-1940).

Films: *Der Tanz des Todes* (date unobtainable, but certainly made prior to 1923). Films (incomplete): *Komptesse Doddy, Nicht lange täuschte mich das Glück; Rosen, die der Sturm entblättert; Die toten Augen,*

Pola Negri and Harry Liedtke in
MADAME DUBARRY

Die Augen der Mumie Ma, Carmen, Der gelbe Schein; Küsse, die man im Dunkeln stiehlt; Manja, Wenn das Herz in Hass erglüht, Das Karussell des Lebens, Kreuziget sie, Madame Dubarry, Vendetta, Arme Violetta, Geschlossene Kette, Das Marthyrium, Medea, Der Bergkatze, Marchesa d'Armiani, Sappho, Die Dame im Glashaus, Die Flamme. Then sound: *Mazurka, Moskau – Shanghai, Madame Bovary, Tango Notturno, Die fromme Lüge, Die Nacht der Entscheidung.*

262   NEUE SACHLICHKEIT: Kracauer sees in the so-called "Querschnitts-Filme" (an expression coined by Béla Bálazs and illustrated in a film he wrote, *Die Abenteuer eines Zehnmarkscheins)* the purest expression of *Neue Sachlichkeit* ("new objectivity"). Kracauer wrote, "this picture of Berlin during the inflation consists of a number of episodes which record the capricious travels of a ten-mark note continually changing hands. Guided by it, the film meanders through the maze of those years, picking up otherwise unrelated characters, and glancing over such locales as a factory, a night café, a pawnshop, the music room of a profiteer, an employment agency, a ragpicker's den and a hospital. According to Bálazs, it is as if the plot 'followed a thread that, connecting the dramatic junctions of the ways of Fate, leads across the texture of life.' "

One of the most important representatives of the movement is the documentarist Walter Ruttmann, but the vital films are: *Markt am Wittenbergplatz* (directed by Wilfried Basse in 1929), *Deutschland von gestern und heute* (1934), and *People on Sunday* ("one of the first films to point out the misery of the 'small man' ").

263   NEUMANN, GÜNTHER (1913-   ). B: Berlin. Scriptwriter and composer. Trained at Hochschule für Musik in Berlin. Founded "Die Insulaner" cabaret in Berlin, for which he wrote and composed many tunes, and where his wife Tatjana Sais (she also acts in German films) played important parts for many years. Well known for his script for *Berliner Ballade* and texts for the period comedy. *Herrliche Zeiten* (1950, co-dir. Eric Ode). Later often worked with director Kurt Hoffmann (their best work together being *Wir Wunderkinder*). Also author.

Music for: *Einmal werd' ich Dir gefallen* (in collab.), *Der dunkle Punkt* (in collab. with Willy Richartz), *Berliner Ballade* (in collab.), *Herrliche Zeiten* (in collab.). Scripts for: *Paradies der Jungegesellen* (co-scripted with Karl Peter Gillmann), *Sommer, Sonne, Erika* (co-scripted with Kurt R. Neubert), *Himmel, wir erben ein Schloss* (co-scripted with Otto Ernst Hesse and Eberhard Keindorff), *Berliner Ballade, Herrliche Zeiten* (co-scripted with Fritz Aeckerle, Hans Vietzke and Erik Ode, also co-dir. with Ode, 50), *Feuerwerk* (co-scripted with Felix Lützkendorff and Herbert Witt), *Das Wirtshaus im Spessart, Wir Wunderkinder* (co-scripted with Heinz Pauck), *Das schöne Abenteuer* (co-scripted with Heinz Pauck), *Das Spukschloss im Spessart* (co-scripted with Heinz Pauck), *Herrliche Zeiten im Spessart.*

264   NEUSS, WOLFGANG (1923-   ) B: Breslau. Actor. After 1945: acted in "Simplizissimus" cabaret, Munich. Later Hebbel Theater Berlin and "Rauchfang" cabaret Berlin. 1955: Komödie Berlin. Worked for radio, and created his own cabaret programme in Berlin. Formed comic partnership with Wolfgang Müller (1922-1960) in films such as *Wir Wunderkinder* and *Das Wirtshaus im Spessart*.

Films: *Wer fuhr den grauen Ford?, Schön muss man sein, Pension Schöller, Ich hab' mein Herz in Heidelberg verloren, Die Spur führt nach Berlin, Man lebt nur zweimal, Mikosch rückt ein, Von der Liebe reden wir später, Keine Angst vor grossen Tieren, Holandmädel, Die Kaiserin von China, Weg ohne Umkehr, Die schöne Müllerin, Die goldene Pest, Auf der Reeperbahn nachts um halb eins, Des Teufels General, Ein Mann vergisst die Liebe, Die heilige Lüge, Oberwachtmeister Borck, Ich war ein hässliches Mädchen, Ein Herz bleibt allein, Banditen der Autobahn* (also collab. on script), *Unternehmen Schlafsack, Himmel ohne Sterne, Der fröhliche Wanderer, Die Drei von der Tankstelle* (55), *Urlaub auf Ehrenwort, Küss mich noch einmal, Charley's Tante* (56), *Mädchen mit schwachem Gedächtnis; Zu Befehl, Frau Feldwebel; Der Hauptmann von Köpenick* (56), *Die Christel von der Post, Ein Mann muss nicht immer schön sein, Frühling in Berlin, Der müde Theodor, Ferien auf Immenhof, Die grünen Teufel von Monte Cassino, Schwarzwälder Kirsch, Der Maulkorb, Nick Knattertons Abenteuer, Das Wirtshaus im Spessart, Der Stern von Santa Clara, Wir Wunderkinder, Die Nacht vor der Premiere, Rosen für den Staatsanwalt, Liebe verboten – heiraten erlaubt, Der lustige Krieg des Hauptmann Pedro, Als geheilt entlassen, Zwei Engel im Pullover, Wir Kellerkinder, Genosse Münchhausen 62* (also acted), *Die Tote von Beverly Hills, Katz und Maus.*

265 **NIELSEN, ASTA** (1881-). B: Copenhagen, Actress. Stage training at Royal Stage School Copenhagen. 1901-1910: various theatres in Denmark. Introduced to the cinema by her second husband Urban Gad, and became world famous after her first film *Afgrunden*. 1911: to Germany with Gad, where her natural expressiveness was ideally suited to the silent film. The sound film, however, did not really suit her talents. 1936: to Denmark, where she made some stage appearances after 1938. 1946:

author of *Die schweigende Muse*. One of the most important personalities of the German and Danish silent cinema.

Films (incomplete): *Der fremde Vogel, Im grossen Augenblick, Der schwarze Traum, Die Sünden der Väter, Die Verräterin, Zigeunerblut, Die arme Jenny, Jugend und Tollheit, Die Kinder des Generals, Die Macht des Goldes, Das Mädchen ohne Vaterland, Der Totentanz, Wenn die Maske fällt, Zu Tode gehetzt, Der brennende Acker, Engelein, Engeleins Hochzeit, Die Filmprimadonna, S. 1, Die Suffragetten, Der Tod in Sevilla, Aschenbrödel, Elena Fontana, Die ewige Nacht, Das Feuer, Das Kind ruft, Standrechtlich erschossen, Die Tochter der Landstrasse, Vorderhaus und Hinterhaus, Weisse Rosen, Zapatas Bande, Das Liebes-ABC, Die Börsenkönigin, Die Brüder, Der Meeres und der Liebe Wellen, Das Eskimo-Baby, Die Rose der Wildnis, Der verlorene Sohn, Das Waisenhauskind, Der Fackelträger, Das Ende vom Lied, Graf Sylvains Rache, Nach dem Gesetz, Rausch, Das Geheimnis von S.I., Hamlet, Kurfürstendamm, Der Reigen, Die Spielerin, Steuermann Holck, Amarant; Cleopatra, die Herrin des Nils; Faust, Die Geliebte Ros-*

wolskys, *Irrende Seelen, Die Spionin, Absturz, Brigantenrache, Die Büchse der Pandora, Der Widerspenstigen Zähmung, Fräulein Julie, Das Haus am Meer, Die Tänzerin Novarro, Vanina oder die Galgenhochzeit, Erdgeist, I.N.R.I., Die Frau im Feuer, Hedda Gabler, Lebende Buddhas, Die Schmetterlingsschlacht, Athleten, Die freudlose Gasse, Die Gesunkenen, Dirnentragödie, Das gefährliche Alter, Gehetzte Frauen, Kleinstadtsünden, Laster der Menscheit.* Then sound: *Unmögliche Liebe.*

266 **NIELSEN, HANS** (1911-1967). B: Hamburg. D: Berlin. Actor. At first trained as a businessman. 1932-1933: stage training at Kammerspiele Hamburg. 1933-1945: theatres in Augsburg, Kiel, Leipzig, Berlin. Since 1945: Düsseldorf, Berlin (Komödie, Renaissance-Theater, Freie Volksbühne). A prolific actor of stage and film, often wasted in insignificant roles.

Films: *Tango Notturno, Das Geheimnis der Betty Bonn, Daphne und der Diplomat, Rote Orchideen, Heimat, Preussische Liebesgeschichte, Dein Leben gehört mir, Fracht von Baltimore, Kautschuk, Fasching, Alarm auf Station III, Aufruhr in Damaskus, Falstaff in Wien; Trenck, der Pandur; Mein Mann darf es nicht wissen, Friedrich Schiller, Ich klage an, Der grosse König, Die Nacht in Venedig, Um 9 kommt Harald, Ich werde Dich auf Händen tragen, Titanic, Leichtes Blut, Musik in Salzburg, Der Engel mit dem Saitenspiel, Das kleine Hofkonzert, Dr. med. Döderlein, Der Scheiterhaufen, Herzkönig, In jenen Tagen, Die kupferne Hochzeit, Chemie und Liebe, Unser Mittwoch Abend, Heimliches Rendezvous, Nachtwache, Fünf unter Verdacht, Kronjuwelen, Die Tat des Anderen, Das späte Mädchen, Die Spur führt nach Berlin, Die blaue Stunde, Des Feuers Macht (speaker), Hokuspokus; Heimlich, still und leise; Die geschiedene Frau, Aus eigener Kraft (speaker), Der erste Kuss, Geliebtes Fräulein Doktor, Zwischenlandung in Paris, Die heilige Lüge, Hochstaplerin der Liebe, Meine Kinder und ich, Roman einer Siebzehnjährigen, Vor Sonnenuntergang, Der Bauer vom Brucknerhof, Kleines Zelt und grosse Liebe, Teufel in Seide; Vergiss, wenn Du kannst; Hochzeit auf Immenhof, Ein Herz kehrt heim, Made in Germany, Kein Aus-*

kommen mit dem Einkommen, Glücksritter, Königin Luise, Die liebe Familie, Tolle Nacht, Von allen geliebt, Nachts im grünen Kakadu, Anders als Du und ich, Zwei Herzen im Mai, Zwei Matrosen auf der Alm, Gestehen Sie, Dr. Corda; Schmutziger Engel, Mann im Strom, Der lachende Vagabund, Das Mädchen vom Moorhof, Das haut eine Seemann doch nicht um, Ich werde Dich auf Händen tragen, Herz ohne Gnade, Die feuerrote Baronesse, Kriegsgericht, Verbrechen nach Schulschluss, La Paloma, Die Wahrheit über Rosemarie, Bei der blonden Kathrein, Das blaue Meer und Du, Heimat − Deine Lieder, Bezaubernde Arabella, Der Jugendrichter, Herrin der Welt, Die zornigen jungen Männer, Freddy und die Melodie der Nacht, Das Erbe von Björndal, Mal drunter − mal drüber, Ich träume von der Liebe, Gustav Adolfs Page, Frau im besten Mannesalter, Gaunerserenade, Barbara, Ich bin auch nur eine Frau, Ich kann nicht länger schweigen; Liebling, ich muss Dich erschiessen; Sein bester Freund, Sherlock Holmes und das Halsband des Todes, So toll wie anno dazumal, Ein Toter sucht seinen Mörder, Die Türe mit den sieben Schlössern, Das indische Tuch, Die Nacht am See, Scotland Yard jagt Dr. Mabuse, Das Todesauge von Ceylon, Der Würger von Schloss Black-moor, Herrenpartie, Das siebente Opfer, Das Ungeheuer von London City, Hotel der toten Gäste, Die Pyramide des Sonnengottes, Der Schatz der Azteken.

267 **OBERBERG, IGOR** (1907-). B: Jekaterinburg (Russia). Director of photography. Educated in Berlin, trained as a still photographer. 1927: enters cinema as assistant to Wagner, Courant (both q.v.) and others. 1938: freelance cameraman. Best work in *Unter den Brücken* and *In jenen Tagen* in collaboration with Käutner (q.v.).

Films: *Kongo-Express, Die unvollkommene Liebe, Das leichte Mädchen, U-Boot westwärts, Der Meineidbauer* (co-phot.), *G.P.U., Um 9 kommt Harald, Liebesgeschichten, Man rede mir nicht von Liebe, Das Leben ruft, Unter den Brücken, In jenen Tagen, Film ohne Titel, Der Apfel ist ab, Der Bagonsträfling, Es kommt ein Tag (co-phot. with Walter Hrich), Dieser Mann gehört mir, Die wunderschöne Galathee, Sündige Grenze, Toxi, Heimweh nach Dir, Kö-*

nigin der Arena (co-phot. with Walter Hrich), *Die Stärkere, Das tanzende Herz, Das ideale Brautpaar, Aennchen von Tharau, Rittmeister Wronski* (co-phot. with Hugo Schott & Günther Knuth), *Du mein stilles Tal, Ferien in Tirol, Das Mädchen Marion, Made in Germany, Ist Mama nicht fabelhaft?, Solange das Herz schlägt, Der Rest ist Schweigen, Freddy und die Melodie der Nacht, Schlagerraketen, Zu jung für die Liebe, Eine hübscher als die andere, Lebensborn.*

268 **OBERHAUSEN MANIFESTO:** "The collaps of the conventional German film removes the economic basis for an attitude of mind towards cinema that we reject. Thus the new film has a chance to come to life again.

German short films by young authors, directors and producers have received a great number of prizes at international festivals during recent years and have been appreciated by foreign critics. These works and their success show that the future of the German film lies with those who have proved that they are speaking a new film language.

As in other countries, in Germany too the short film has become a school and experimental field for the feature film.

We announce our claim to create the new German feature film.

This new film needs freedom. Freedom from the conventions of the industry and from commercial interference from the establishment.

We have definite intellectual, formal and economic ideas about the production of a new type of German film. We are all prepared to undertake financial risks.

The old film is dead. We believe in the new one."

The Manifesto was issued by the following twenty-six young filmmakers at the Oberhausen Festival on February 28, 1962: Bodo Blüthner, Boris v. Borresholm, Christian Doermer, Bernhard Dörries, Heinz Furchner, Rob Houwer, Ferdinand Khittl, Alexander Kluge, Pitt Koch, Walter Krüttner, Dieter Lemmel, Hans Loeper, Ronald Martini, Hans-Jürgen Pohland, Raimond Ruehl, Edgar Reitz, Peter Schamoni, Detten Schleiermacher, Fritz Schwennicke, Haro Senft, Franz-Josef Spieker, Hans Rolf Strobel, Heinz Tichawsky, Wolfgang Urchs, Herbert Vesely, Wolf Wirth.

269 **OERTEL, CURT** (1890-1960). B: Osterfeld. D: Wiesbaden. Director, scriptwriter, director of photography and producer. Trained at Staatliche Lehr- und Versuchsanstalt Munich. Prolific documentarist. At first cameraman, worked for *Geheimnisse einer Seele* by Pabst. Own studios in Berlin, also stage producer *(Volksbühne* by Erwin Piscator). 1945: founds "Curt-Oertel-Film-GmbH Wiesbaden." 1947-1948: president of the Producers Association of the American Zone in Germany. 1949: installs "Freiwillige Selbstkontrolle der deutschen Filmwirtschaft" (German censorship). 1950: head of the German UNESCO group for films. Well known abroad for his documentary *Michelangelo.*

Films: *Die Abenteurer* (in collab. with Emil Schünemann), *Die vom Niederrhein* (in collab.), *Die freudlose Gasse* (in collab. with Seeber and Robert Lach), *Geheimnisse einer Seele* (in collab. with Seeber and Lach), *Man spielt nicht mit der Liebe!* (in collab. with Seeber and Lach), *Revolte im Erziehungshaus* (in collab. with Alexander von Lagorio), *Das Donkosakenlied* (in collab. with von Lagorio). Films as director in sound period: *Der Schimmelreiter* 34 (dir. and script with Hans Deppe), *Michelangelo* 40 (phot. with Harry Ringger, dir. and script), *Es war ein Mensch* 50 (doc.), *Der gehorsame Rebell* 52 (doc.), *Neue Welt* 54 (doc., also phot.).

270 **ONDRA, ANNY** (1903-). B: Tarnow (Poland). Actress. RN: Anna Sophie Ondrakowa. Stage training in Prague, then enters cinema thanks to director J. S. Solar. Karel Lamac (later known in Germany as director Karl/Carl Lamac) made her a star. Most of her Czech film were made by Lamac, scriptwriter Vaclav Wassermann and cameraman Heller (q.v.). 1926: to Vienna and Berlin. 1929: to England (in Hitchcock's *Blackmail,* etc.). 1930: back to Germany, where she founded "Ondra-Lamac-Film" with Lamac, remaining on the company board until 1936 (produced or coproduced all of her films from *Eine Freundin so goldig wie Du* up to *Ein Mädel vom*

Ballett). Natural successor to Ossi Oswalda (q.v.).

Films (incomplete): *Führe uns nicht in Versuchung, Hütet eure Töchter, Zigeunerliebe, Der Mann ohne Herz, Ich liebe Dich; Treude, die Sechzehnjährige; Pratermizzi; Seine Hoheit, der Eintänzer; Der erste Kuss, Evas Töchter, Saxophon-Susi, Die Kaviarprinzessin, Das Mädel mit der Peitsche, Sündig und süss, Das Mädel aus USA.* Then sound: *Die grosse Sehnsucht, Eine Freundin so goldig wie Du, Die vom Rummelplatz, Er und seine Schwester, Mamsell Nitouche, Die Fledermaus, Baby, Kiki, Die grausame Freundin, Eine Nacht im Paradies, Die Tochter des Regiments, Betragen ungenügend, Das verliebte Hotel, Fräulein Hoffmanns Erzählungen, Klein Dorrit, Polenblut, Die vertauschte Braut, Grossreinemachen, Der junge Graf, Knock out, Flitterwochen, Ein Mädel vom Ballett, Donogoo Tonka, Vor Liebe wird gewarnt, Der Unwiderstehliche, Der Scheidungsgrund, Narren im Schnee, Der Gasmann; Himmel, wir erben ein Schloss; Schön muss man sein.*

271 **OPHÜLS, MAX** (1902-1957). B: Saarbrücken. D: Hamburg. Director. RN: Max Oppenheimer. Studied at Hamburg University. At first actor. Over 150 stage productions and parts in various theatres in Austria, Germany and Switzerland; and since 1930 also productions of operas by Mozart and Verdi and operettas by Offenbach. Enters cinema as assistant and dialogue director to Anatole Litwak (for his only German film *Dolly macht Karriere).* First film in 1930. His best works in Germany are *Liebelei* and the underrated *Die verkaufte Braut* (based on Smetana's opera). 1933: leaves Germany for U.S.A. via Italy, France and England. 1950: returns to France, where he was to make his best films. Important adaptations of works by Arthur Schnitzler. Wrote book *Spiel im Dasein* (published in 1950). Died during his first stage production (since 1933) for the Deutsches Schauspielhaus Hamburg. With his subtle, impressionistic style, Ophüls was a master at studying human relationships.

Films: *Dann schon lieber Lebertran* 30, (medium-length feature, also co-scripted), *Die lachenden Erben* 31, *Die verliebte Firma* 31, *Die verkaufte Braut* 32, *Liebelei* 33, *Lola Montès* 55 (also script with Franz Geiger and Annette Wadement).

272 **OSTERMAYR, PETER** (1882-1967). B: Mühldorf. D: Munich. Producer, director and scriptwriter. One of the first producers in the history of the German film industry. Very successful with his popular bucolic films. 1907: tours with portable cinema and founds "Münchner Kunstfilm AG," producing scenic documentaries 1909: own studio at Karlsplatz in Munich where he makes the first surrealistic paper "cut-out" films. 1918: founds "Münchner Lichtspielkunst GmbH" and "Emelka." 1919: founds Geiselgasteig studios near Munich (first film shot there being *Der Ochsenkrieg* 1919, dir. Franz Osten, brother of Ostermayr, photographed by Franz Planer, q.v.). 1923: leaves Munich, joins Oskar Messter (q.v.) and founds the "Lucy-Dorraine-Filmgesellschaft" in Berlin with him and Karl Hofer. Produced about 425 films

273 **OSWALD, RICHARD** (1880-1963) B: Vienna. D: Düsseldorf. Director. RN Richard Ornstein. Trained at Dramatische Hochschule Vienna. 1898: stage producer (e.g. at Jarno theatres in Vienna). 1914

production manager and director at Union Film in Berlin. 1916: founds his own company "Oswald-Film" and opens an important first-run cinema. During Twenties very famous as producer and director of "Aufklärungsfilme" (q.v.). A profilic director with a talent for spectaculars and story adaptations. Discovered Conrad Veidt, Lya de Putti, Wilhelm Dieterle (all q.v.). amongst others. 1938: to U.S.A. (his remake of *Der Hauptmann von Köpenick* in 1941 is of some importance). * indicates produced.

Films: *Der ewige Zweifel* *, *Der Schlossherr von Hohenstein* *, *Das unheimliche Haus* * (dates for these films unobtainable, but they were all made certainly prior to 1923). Films (incomplete): *Das eiserne Kreuz* 14 *, *Die Geschichte der stillen Mühle* 15 * (also script), *Hampels Abenteuer* 16, *Hoffmanns Erzählungen* 16 (also co-scripted with Fritz Friedmann-Friedrich), *Seine letzte Maske* 16 *, *Zirkusblut* 16 *, *Das Bildnis des Dorian Gray* 17 *, *Des Goldes Fluch* 17 *, *Die Rache der Toten* 17 * (also script), *Die Seeschlacht* 17 *, *Die Sintflut* 17 *, *Dida Ibsens Geschichte* 18 *, *Das Dreimäderlhaus* 18 *, *Es werde Licht* 18 * (also co-scripted), *Der lebende Leichnam* 18 *, *Das Tagebuch einer Verlorenen* 18 *, *Anders als die andern* 19 *, *Lache Bajazzo* 19 *, *Das Laster* 19 * (also script), *Prostitution I & II* 19 * (also co-scripted with Magnus Hirschfeld), *Die Reise um die Erde in 80 Tagen* 19 *, *Die schwarze Katze* 19 *, *Sündige Eltern* 19 *, (also co-scripted), *Der Tod des Andern* 19 * *Unheimliche Geschichten* 19 * (also script), *Algol* 20 *, *Antisemiten* 20 *, *Das Geheimnis von London* 20, *Der grosse Krach* 20 *, *Kurfürstendamm* 20 * *Die letzten Menschen* *, *Manolescus Memoiren* 20 *, *Nachtgestalten* *, *Der Reigen* 20 * (also script), *Der Selbstmörderklub* 20 *, *Die Spielerin* 20 *, *Das System des Doktor Ther und Professor Feder* 20 *, *Die Tragödie eines Kindes* 20 *, *Das vierte Gebot* 20 *, *Das Leben des Menschen* 21 *, *Macbeth* 21 *, *Rückblick aus dem Jahre 3000* 21 *, *Engelchen* 21 *, *Die Dame und ihre Friseur* (* with Bioscop), *König Richard III.* (co *), *Lady Hamilton* 22 *, *Lord Byron* (co *), *Lukrezia Borgia* 22 * (also script), *Carlos und Elisabeth* 24 * (also script), *Lumpen und Seide* 24 *, *Die Frau in vier-*

zig Jahren 25 * (also script), *Halbseide* 25 (also script), *Vorderhaus und Hinterhaus* 25 * (also script), *Als ich wiederkam* 26 *, *Dürfen wir schweigen?* 26 (also script), *Im weissen Rössl* 26 *, *Eine tolle Nacht* 26 * (also script), *Wir sind vom k. und k. Infanterie-Regiment* 26 * (also script), *Dr. Bessels Verwandlung* 27 *, *Feme* 27 *, *Funkzauber* 27 *, *Gehetzte Frauen* 27 *, *Lützows wilde verwegene Jagd* 27 *, *Die Rothausgasse* 28 *, *Villa Falconieri* 28 *, *Ehe in Not* 29, *Frühlings Erwachen* 29 *, *Die Herrin und ihr Knecht* 29, *Der Hund von Baskerville* 29. Then sound: *Die zärtlichen Verwandten* 30 (and *), *Alraune* 30, *Dreyfuss* 30 (and *), *Wien, Du Stadt der Lieder* 30 (and *), *1914, die letzten Tage vor dem Weltbrand* 31 (and *), *Arm wie eine Kirchenmaus* 31 (and *), *Der Hauptmann von Köpenick* 31, *Viktoria und ihr Husar* 31 *Schubert's Frühlingstraum* 31 (and *), *Unheimliche Geschichten* 32, *Gräfin Mariza* 32, *Ein Lied geht um die Welt* 33, *Die Blume von Hawaii* 33, *Ganovenehre* 33.

274 **OSWALDA, OSSI** (1899-1948). B: Berlin. D: Prague. Actress. RN: Oswalda Stäglich. At first model and extra for the stage. Enters cinema thanks to Lubitsch (q.v.), who also gives her a new name. With Lubitsch she very soon becomes "the German Mary Pickford." After 1916: mainly in films directed by Victor Janson (a pupil of Lubitsch). Germany's most popular film star in the mid-Twenties, but soon forgotten. Her last film in 1933 was a French version of *Stern von Valencia*. Died in utter poverty.

Films (incomplete): *Der GmbH-Tenor, Nacht des Grauens, Schuhpalast Pinkus, Ein fideles Gefängnis, Ossis Tagebuch, Prinz Sami, Wenn vier dasselbe tun, Der Fall Rosentopf, Das Mädchen vom Ballett, Meine Frau, die Filmschauspielerin, Der Rodelkavalier, Die Austernprinzessin, Die Puppe, Schwabemädle, Die Millionenerbschaft, Der blinde Passagier, Das Mädel mit der Maske, Das Milliardensouper, Colibri* (also prod.), *Niniche, Blitzzug der Liebe, Herrn Filip Collins Abenteuer, Das Mädchen mit Protektion, Die Fahrt ins Abenteuer, Gräfin Plättmamsell, Die Kleine vom Varieté, Das Mädchen auf der Schaukel, Schatz, mach' Kasse; Eine tolle Nacht, Es zogen drei Burschen, Frühere Verhältnissen, Ein schwerer*

Fall, Wochenendbraut, Eddy Polo mit Pferd und Lasso, Das Haus ohne Männer, Ossi hat die Hosen an, Die Vierte von rechts, Der Dieb im Schlafcoupé. Then sound: *Der keusche Joseph, Stern von Valencia.*

275 **PABST, GEORG WILHELM** (1885-1967). B: Raudnitz. D: Vienna. Director. At first actor in Zurich and St. Gall. 1907: in Salzburg, then Berlin. 1910: Deutsches Theater New York. During First World War imprisoned in France. 1920: director at experimental "Neue Wiener Bühne" Vienna, where he tries to feature new dramatists. Enters cinema in 1921 thanks to Carl Froelich (q.v.), at first as an actor, later as asst. director and scriptwriter. 1932-1933: in France. 1934-1936: to Hollywood. 1936-1940: in France again. 1940: returns to Germany. After 1945: works in Germany and Austria, but only on rather commercial films. In his best years Pabst was the leading figure of the German cinema during both the silent and sound periods with his realistic films which were at first marked by a contemporary pessimism and interest in psychology.

Films: *Luise Millerin* (only co-scripted with Walter Supper, also acted), *Der Taugenichts* (co-scripted with Froelich and Walter

Supper, ass. dir.), *Der Schatz* 23 (also co-scripted with Willy Hennings), *Gräfin Donelli* 24, *Die freudlose Gasse* 25, *Geheimnisse einer Seele* 26, *Man spielt nicht mit der Liebe!* 26, *Die Liebe der Jeanne Ney* 27, *Abwege* 28, *Die Büchse der Pandora* 29, *Tagebuch einer Verlorenen* 29 (also prod.). Then sound: *Westfront 1918* 30, *Skandal um Eva* 30, *Die Dreigroschenoper* 31, *Kameradschaft* 31, *Die Herrin von Atlantis* 32, *Die weisse Hölle vom Piz Palü* 35 (codir.), *Komödianten* 41 (also co-scripted with Eggebrecht and Walther von Hollander), *Paracelsus* 43, *Der Fall Molander* 45, *Der Prozess* 48, *Duell mit dem Tod* 50 (co-scripted with Paul May, supervisor), *Geheimnisvolle Tiefe* 51, *Ruf aus dem Aether* 51 (supervisor), *Das Bekenntnis der Ina Kahr* 54, *Es geschah am 20. Juli* 55, *Der letzte Akt* 55, *Rosen für Bettina* 56, *Durch die Wälder, durch die Auen* ... 56.

276 **PALLENBERG, MAX** (1877-1934). B: Vienna. D: near Karlovy Vary ('plane crash). Actor. Theatres: Jagerndorf and Jarno theatres Vienna (from 1904), Munich (1911), Deutsches Theater Berlin (1914). Many guest appearances in Germany after 1918. Leading actor of his time in both dramatic and comedy roles. Was married to operetta star Fritzy Massary (1887-1969).

Films (incomplete): *Pampulik als Affe, Pampulik kriegt ein Kind, Pampulik hat Hunger, Die Nacht und der Leichnam.* Then sound: *Der brave Sünder.*

277 **PALMER, LILLI** (1914-). B: Posen. Actress. RN: Lillie Marie Peiser. Daughter of the Austrian actress Rosa Lissmann. Stage training in Berlin (under Ilka Grüning and Lucie Höflich, q.v.). 1932: Landestheater Darmstadt. 1933: to France with appearances as a dancer in Paris night clubs (Moulin Rouge and Monte Cristo). 1934: to London as a singer and soubrette, where she makes her first film. 1945: to U.S.A. with her first husband Rex Harrison, appearing on stage and in films. 1953: returns to Germany. Now married to actor Carlos Thompson. Star of international cinema.

Films: *Feuerwerk, Teufel in Seide; Anastasia, die letzte Zarentochter; Zwischen Zeit und Ewigkeit, Wie ein Sturmwind, Der*

g!äserne Turm; Eine Frau, die weiss was sie will; Mädchen in Uniform, Frau Warrens Gewerbe, Frau Cheney's Ende, Finden Sie, dass Constanze sich richtig verhält?; Julia, Du bist zauberhaft; Erotica, Das grosse Liebesspiel, Ein Frauenarzt klagt an, Die letzten Zwei vom Rio Bravo, Die Unmoralischen, Herr auf Schloss Brassac, Der Kongress amüsiert sich, Zwei Girls vom roten Stern, Paarungen.

278 **PARLO, DITA** (1907-   ). B: Stettin. Actress. RN: Grethe Gerda Kornstadt. Ballet training at Laban-Bode-School, and stage training at actors school of the Ufa, both in Berlin. Enters cinema in 1928 thanks to Erich Pommer (q.v.). 1932: to Hollywood. 1934: to France, where she acts in Vigo's L'Atalante (1934), Pabst's Mademoiselle Docteur (1937) and Renoir's La Grande Illusion (1937). 1934: to Switzerland for Dimitri Kirsanoff's Rapt. 1940: retires, but makes a brief return to films in 1950 with André Cayatte's Justice est faite.
Films: Die Dame mit der Maske, Geheimnisse des Orients, Heimkehr, Ungarische Rhapsodie, Manolescu. Then sound: Melodie des Herzens, Menschen hinter Gittern, Kismet, Tropennächte, Wir schalten um auf Hollywood, Die heilige Flamme, Tänzerinnen für Süd-Amerika gesucht.

279 **PETERS, WERNER** (1918-   ). B: Werlitzsch. Actor. Stage training at Altes Theater Leipzig. Soldier. Then theatres: Gera, Kammerspiele Munich, Deutsches Theater and Theater am Luxemburgplatz in Berlin, Schauspielhaus Düsseldorf. Until 1955: busy actor for DEFA (q.v.), especially in films directed by Staudte (q.v.). Now owner of a dubbing firm in Berlin. International career.
Films: Affäre Blum, Der Biberpelz, Die Buntkarierten, Rotation, Der Kahn der fröhlichen Leute, Karriere in Paris, Modell Bianka, Der Untertan, Anna Susanna, Die Unbesiegbaren, Die Geschichte vom kleinen Muck, Ernst Thälmann – Sohn seiner Klasse, Der 20. Juli, Sommerliebe, Der Teufel vom Mühlenberg, Ernst Thälmann – Führer seiner Klasse, Ein Polterabend, Star mit fremden Federn, Hotel Adlon, Vor Gott und den Menschen; Anastasia, die letzte Zarentochter; Das Sonntagskind, Die Stimme der Sehnsucht, Spion für Deutschland, Ein Abenteuer aus 1001 Nacht, Nachts wenn der Teufel kam, Das Herz von St. Pauli, Madeleine und der Legionär, Der Greifer, Lilli – Ein Mädchen aus der Grosstadt, Schmutziger Engel, Grabenplatz 17, Liebe kann wie Gift sein, Blitzmädels aus der Front, Das Mädchen Rosemarie, Unruhige Nacht, 13 kleine Esel und der Sonnenhof, Meine 99 Bräute, Romarei – Das Mädchen mit den grünen Augen, Die feuerrote Baronesse, Kriegsgericht, Jons und Erdme, Bobby Todd greift ein, Geheimaktion Schwarze Kapelle, Rosen für den Staatsanwalt, Der Schatz vom Toplitzsee, Strafbataillon 999, Die 1000 Augen des Dr. Mabuse, Gauner in Uniform, Schüsse im Morgengrauen, Endstation "Rote Laterne", Denn das Weib ist schwach, Es muss nicht immer Kaviar sein, Diesmal muss es Kaviar sein, Im Stahlnetz des Dr. Mabuse, Unter Ausschluss der Oeffentlichkeit, Auf Wiedersehn, Teppich des Grauens, Die Türe mit den sieben Schlössern, Die unsichtbaren Krallen des Dr. Mabuse, Die endlose Nacht, Das Feuerschiff, Der Flucht der gelben Schlange, Das Geheimnis der schwarzen Witwe, Der schwarze Abt, Scotland Yard jagt Dr. Mabuse, Die weisse Spinne, Einer frisst den andern, Die

135

Gruft mit dem Rätselschloss, Das Phantom von Soho, Durchs wilde Kurdistan, Die schwarzen Adler von Santa Fé, Die Hölle von Macao, Lotosblüten für Miss Quon, Die Zeugin aus der Hölle, Geheimnisse in goldenen Nylons, Zucker für den Mörder.

280 **PETROVICH, IVAN** (1894 or 1896-19). B: Novi Sad (Serbia). Actor. RN: Szvetiszlav Petrovics. Studied at Budapest Polytechnic. 1916-1918: soldier. 1918: enters cinema in Vienna. Part time actor in Hungary. 1920: to Berlin and Munich. 1923-1929: also in Paris and Nice (in American films for director Rex Ingram, playing opposite Alice Terry). 1930-1931: in U.S.A. 1931-1940: in Germany. 1940: to Hungary. After 1948: in German and Austrian films again, also international career (e.g. Louis Malle's *L'ascenseur pour l'échafaud*). Gentlemanly type.

Films (incomplete): *Der Unmensch, Die Dame mit den Sonnenblumen, Der Stern von Damaskus, Drei Scheine des Todes, Ein Walzer von Strauss, Alraune, Fürst oder Clown, Der Orlow, Frauenarzt Dr. Schäfer, Geheimnisse des Orients, Quartier Latin, Der Zarewitsch, Der Leutnant ihrer Majestät, Liebe und Champagner.* Then sound: *Der Günstling von Schönbrunn; Es gibt eine Frau, die Dich niemals vergisst; Der König von Paris, Opernredoute, Viktoria und ihr Husar, Die Fledermaus, Holzapfel weiss alles, Der Feldherrenhügel, Muss man sich gleich scheiden lassen?, Der Diamant des Zaren, Die Blume von Hawaii; Manolescu, der Fürst der Diebe; Gern hab' ich die Frauen geküsst, Polenblut, Der letzte Walzer, Der Kosak und die Nachtigall, Der rote Reiter, Königstiger, Das Frauenparadies, Ungeküsst soll man nicht schlafen geh'n, Drei Mäderl um Schubert, Mädchen in Weiss, Die Korallenprinzessin, Die Kronzeugin, Monika, Unter Ausschluss der Oeffentlichkeit, Frauenliebe – Frauenleid, Stärker als die Liebe, Die Nacht der Entscheidung, Zentrale Rio, Parkstrasse 13, Dein Leben gehört mir, Feinde, Einmal der liebe Herrgott sein, Macht im Dunkeln, Der Prozess; Wer bist Du, den ich liebe?; Arlberg-Express, Eroica, Maharadscha wider Willen, Csardas des Herzens, Verlorenes Rennen, Verklungenes Wien, Das letzte Rezept, Die Försterchristl, Fritz und Frederike, Man*

nennt es Liebe, Der Feldherrenhügel, Dalmatinische Hochzeit, Der Zarewitsch; Sissi, die junge Kaiserin; Witwer mit 5 Töchtern, Frühling in Berlin.

281 **PFLEGHAR, MICHAEL** (1933-). B: Stuttgart. Director. 1950: enters cinema as editor for Wolfgang Liebeneiner and Willi Forst (both q.v.), and works on special effects in Munich. 1954: as assistant director and editor to TV in Stuttgart. At end of 1968, he had directed more than sixty light entertainment shows on TV.

Films: *Die Tote von Beverly Hills* 64 (also script with Pohland and Peter Laregh), *Serenade für zwei Spione* 65 (also script), *Bel Ami 2000 oder wie verführt man einen Playboy* 66 (also script with Klaus Munro), *Fräulein Nini um 1900* 67 (episode from *Das älteste Gewerbe der Welt/Le plus vieux métier du monde*) (co-dir. Franco Indovina, Mauro Bolognini, Philippe de Broca, Claude Autant-Lara and Jean-Luc Godard.)

282 **PICK, LUPU** (1886-1931). B: Jassy (Romania). D: Berlin. Actor and director. Actor in Hamburg theatres and Deutsches Theater Berlin. Enters cinema in 1915, at first as an actor, then directs his first film in

1919. 1917: founds his own company, "Rex-Filmgesellschaft." 1930: elected president of DACHO (leading actors' union in Germany). Master of the *"Kammerspiel"* (q.v.). Films (incomplete): *Die Pagode* (only acted), *Nacht des Grauens* (only acted), *Höheluft* (acted), *Es werde Licht* (acted, ii), *Kitsch* 19, *Misericordia* 19, *Seelenverkäufer* 19, *Der Dummkopf* 20 (also acted), *Das lachende Grauen* 20, *Mister Wu* (only acted),*Niemand weiss es* 20 (also acted), *Oliver Twist* 20, *Tötet nicht mehr* 20 (also acted and co-scripted), *Grausige Nächte* 21, *Scherben* 21 (also prod.), *Irrende Seelen* (only acted), *Fliehende Schatten* (only acted and co-scripted), *Zum Paradies der Damen* 22, *Sylvester* 23, *Weltspiegel* 23, *Das Haus der Lüge* 25 (also co-scripted with Fanny Carlsen), *Die letzte Droschke von Berlin* (only acted), *Das Panzergewölbe* 26 (also co-scripted), *Eine Nacht in London* 28 (also prod.), *Spione* (only acted), *Napoleon auf St. Helena* 29 (also prod. and co-scripted with Willy Haas). Then sound: *Gassenhauer* 31.

283 **PIEL, HARRY** (1892-1963). B: Düsseldorf. D: Munich. Actor and director. First enters film industry in Paris. 1914: settles in Germany. Acted in many film serials (q.v.). Piel has appeared in well over a hundred films, and his acting style was much in vogue. 1923: makes a series of German-French co-productions. Married to actress Dary Holm (Anna Maria Dorothea Meyer), who was his partner in many films. * indicates directed and acted. Films: *Das amerikanische Duell* *, *Die grosse Wette* (acted), *Die Rache der Gräfin Barnetti* (dir.), *Sein Todfeind* (dir.), *Der stumme Zeuge* (dir.), *Zur Strecke gebracht* (dir.) – (dates for these films unobtainable, but they were all made certainly prior to 1923). Films (incomplete): *Ben Ali Bey* 13 *, *Police 1111* 16 *, *Unter heisser Sonne* 16 *, *Das Auge des Götzen* 19 *, *Das Geheimnis des Zirkus Barré* 20 *, *Der grosse Coup* 19 *, *Ueber den Wolken* 19 *, *Das geheimnisvolle Telephon*, *Luftpiraten*, *Der brennende Berg* 21 *, *Das fliegende Auto* 21 *, *Der Fürst der Berge* 21 * (also prod.), *Das Gefängnis auf dem Meeresgrunde* 21 *, *Das Geheimnis der Katakomben* 21 *, *Das lebende Rätsel*, *Panik* 21 *, *Der Ritt unter*

Wasser 21 *, *Die Todesfalle* 21 *; *Unus, der Weg in die Welt* 21, *Der Verächter des Todes* 21 *, *Das schwarze Kouvert* 22 *, *Das verschwundene Haus* 22 * (also prod.), *Abenteuer einer Nacht* 23 * (also co-prod.), *Der letzte Kampf* 23 *, *Menschen und Masken* 23 *, *Rivalen* 23 *, *Auf gefährlichen Spuren* 24 *, *Der Mann ohne Nerven* 24 * (also prod.), *Abenteuer im Nachtexpress* 25 *, *Schneller als der Tod* 25 *; *Zigaro, der Brigant von Monte Diavolo* 25 * (also prod.), *Achtung Harry! Augen auf!* 26 *, *Der schwarze Pierro* 26 * (also co-scripted with Edmund Heuberger), *Was ist los im Zirkus Beely* 26 *, *Rätsel einer Nacht* 27 *, *Sein grösster Bluff* 27 (co-dir. and acted), *Mann gegen Mann* 28 *, *Panik* 28 *, *Seine stärkste Waffe*, *Männer ohne Beruf* 29 *, *Die Mitternachts-Taxe* 29 *, *Sein bester Freund* 29 *, *Achtung! Auto-Diebe!* 30 *, *Menschen im Feuer* 30 *. Then sound: *Er oder ich* 30 *, *Bobby geht los* 31 *, *Schatten der Unterwelt* 31 *, *Der Geheimagent* 32 *, *Jonny stiehlt Europa* 32 *, *Das Schiff ohne Hafen* 32 *, *Sprung in den Abgrund* 33 *, *Ein Unsichtbarer geht durch die Stadt* 33 *, *Der Herr der Welt* 34 (dir.), *Die Welt ohne Maske* 34 *, *Artisten* 35 *, *90 Minuten Aufenthalt* 36 *, *Der Dschungel ruft* 36 *,

Sein bester Freund 37 *; *Menschen, Tiere, Sensationen 38* *, *Der unmögliche Herr Pitt 38* *, *Gesprengte Gitter 40* * (released 53), *Panik 40/43* *, *Der Mann im Sattel 45* *, *Der Tiger Akbar 50* *.

284 **PLANER, FRANZ (FRANK)** (1894-1964). B: Karlovy Vary. D: Hollywood. Director of photography. At first photographer. 1919: enters film industry in Berlin (shoots first film at Geiselgasteig Studios near Munich, *see* Ostermayr). 1934: to Sascha Company Vienna, and later in the same year to France and England. 1935: to Italy. 1936: to France and England (works several time for Ophüls, q.v.). 1937: to Hollywood (contract with Columbia). Academy Award in 1952 for *Death of a Salesman.*   ,

Films (incomplete):*Der Todesritt am Riesenrad, Der Ochsenkrieg, Der Arm Gottes* (co-phot. with Franz Koch), *Der Favorit der Königin, Mariett-Aktien, Schattenkinder des Glücks* (co-phot. with Koch), *Das schwarze Gesicht, Um Thron und Liebe* (co-phot. with Koch), *Die Finanzen des Grossherzogs* (co-phot.), *Gehetzte Menschen* (co-phot. with Josef Blasi),*Schicksal* (co-phot. with Blasi), *Finale der Liebe, Der Mann seiner Frau, Fünfuhrtee in der Ackerstrasse, Nur eine Tänzerin* (co-phot. with Hugo Edlund); *Schatz, mach' Kasse; Der Sohn des Hannibal, Die Achtzehnjährigen, Alraune, Die Ausgestossenen, Einbruch, Das Frauenhaus von Rio, Glanz und Elend der Kurtisanen, Der grosse Unbekannte, Die Pflicht zu schweigen, Wie heirate ich meinen Chef, Heut' spielt der Strauss, Die Rothausgasse, Weib in Flammen, Wolga-Wolga* (co-phot. with Akos Farkas), *Die Flucht vor der Liebe, Frauen am Abgrund, Die Liebe der Brüder Rott, Der Narr seiner Liebe, stud. chem. Helene Willfüer.* Then sound: *Die Drei von der Tankstelle, Heute Nacht – eventuell, Hans in allen Gassen, Der Sohne der weissen Berge* (co-phot. with Kurt Neubert and Benitz), *Zapfenstreich am Rhein* (co-phot.), *Sein Scheidungsgrund* (co-phot. with Bernhard Wentzel), *Nie wieder Liebe* (co-phot.), *Der Herr Bürovorsteher, Der Herzog von Reichstadt, Der Storch streikt, Eine Stadt steht Kopf, Die Gräfin von Monte Christo, Teilnehmer antwortet nicht, Der Prinz von Arkadien, Der schwarze Husar, Das erste Recht des Kindes, Leise flehen meine Lieder, Liebelei; Ihre Durchlaucht, die Verkäuferin; Der Choral von Leuthen* (co-phot. with W. Blum and Hugo von Kaweczynski), *Maskerade, So endete eine Liebe, Die Julika, Blumen aus Nizza, Im Sonnenschein, Premiere, Capriolen* (co-phot. with Neubert), *Die ganz grossen Torheiten, Zauber der Bohème.*

285 **POELZIG, HANS** (1869-1936). B and D: Berlin. Architect and set designer. His ideas exerted considerable influence on German architecture when he was a professor at the Technical High School in Charlottenburg (Berlin). Significant designs in several German towns. 1919: constructed Grosses Schauspielhaus Berlin for Reinhardt (q.v.) in the form of a "cavern" with stalactite-like pillars. His plan for a new Festspielhaus in Salzburg was never used. In later years his designs grew more monumental. Few but very impressive sets for films.

Films (incomplete): *Der Golem, wie er in die Welt kam* (in collab.), *Lebende Buddhas* (in collab. with Betho Höfer), *Zur Chronik von Grieshuus* (in collab.).

286 **POHLAND, HANSJÜRGEN** (1934-). B: Berlin. Producer and director. Technical training at Mosaik-Film in Berlin. 1955: founds "Hansjürgen Pohland Filmproduktion" and buys "modern art film gmbh." At first mainly producer of short films. 1961: first feature film.

Films: (short productions as director): *Freizeit und Erholung 56, Pferde – heute, gestern und morgen 56, Hunde – mit Liebe erzogen 56, Früh übt sich . . . 56, Ein Blick in die Max-Reinhardt-Schule 56, Kleine Welt in grosser Stadt 56, Was du ererbt von deinen Vätern 56, Strom über Berge 58, Kinderkrippe 58, Blech 59, Strandfreuden für Erwachsene 59, Knigge im Walde 59, Menschen beim Baden 59, Ein Gesetz will helfen 60, Nicht vergessen 60, Mit 18 nach 18 60, Schatten 60, Autos von morgen, Strassen von heute, Menschen von gestern 61, Brücke zur Sonne 61, Helfende Hände 61, Bürger Grass 65.* Collaboration: *Das war Königsberg. Mutter Ostpreussen. Das deutsche Danzig 54* (dir. J. Häussler, editor), *Graue Boote, Die von der Sonne leben 58* (dir. Hans Totter, prod. and photog. work),

Nicht vergessen I and II 58 (dir. Hans Totter, prod.), *Fechten* 59 (dir. Hans Totter, prod. and photog. work), *Um acht Uhr kommen die ... wieder* 59 (dir. Hans Totter, prod., script and photography), *Vom Rasten und Rosten* 61 (dir. Lutz Lehmann, Prod.), *Probeaufnahmen* 63 (dir. Michael Klier, prod. for TV), *Verletzung* 63 (dir. Josef Janos Kristof, prod.), *Fastfrühling* 66 (dir. Christa Pohland and Eva Häussler, prod.), *Die glücklichen Sonntage der Eheleute Plinsch* 66 (dir. Christa Pohland and Eva Häussler, prod.), *Verständigung* 66 (dir. Peter Gehrig, prod.). Feature films as producer: *Das Brot der frühen Jahre* 62, *Stück für Stück* 62 (dir. Peter Lilienthal for TV), *Die Tote von Beverly Hills* 64 (also script with Pfleghar and Peter Laregh), *Serenade für zwei Spione* 65. Produced and directed: *Tobby* 62 (also script), *Wenn ich Chef wäre* 62, *Katz und Maus* 66 (also co-scripted with Günther Grass, co-prod. with Film Polski), *Dieser Mann und Deutschland* 67 (co-dir. with Heinz von Cramer, who also scripted, for TV), *Tamara* 68 (also script).

287 **POMMER, ERICH** (1889-1966). B: Hildesheim. D: Hollywood. Producer. With Oskar Messter (q.v.) a key figure in German cinema. 1907-1914: works for Gaumont in Paris and later as their director for Central Europe. Then European director for Eclair. 1915: founds Decla (e.g. Deutsche Eclair) in Berlin which is later united with Bioscop to become Decla-Bioscop (a combination which was taken over by Ufa in 1923). 1922: he persuades Fritz Lang (q.v.) to make his Mabuse films. 1926: to U.S.A. 1927: returns to Berlin. 1933: as director of Fox-Europe to Paris (produces, amongst others, Lang's *Lilliom* 1934 and Ophüls's *On a volé un homme* 1933). 1934: to Hollywood. 1937: to England as producer of "Pendennis Pictures Corporation," and founds "Mayflower Pictures Corporation" with Charles Laughton. 1940: to U.S.A. for Paramount and RKO. 1946: returns to Germany as "Film Officer." 1950: founds "Intercontinental GmbH" and produces films like *Kinder, Mütter und ein General*. 1956: back to Hollywood. One of the greatest talent scouts in the history of the German cinema.

Films: *Dr. Mabuse der Spieler, Die Nibelungen I & II, Varieté, Metropolis, Die wunderbare Lüge der Nina Petrowna, Der verlorene Schuh, Der letzte Mann, Walzertraum, Heimkehr*. Then sound: *Melodie des Herzens, Ungarische Rhapsodie, Bomben auf Monte Carlo, Ich bei Tag und Du bei Nacht, F.P. 1 antwortet nicht, Der blaue Engel, Die Drei von der Tankstelle, Der Kongress tanzt, Nachts auf den Strassen, Illusion in Moll, Eine Liebesgeschichte; Kinder, Mütter und ein General*.

288 **PONTO, ERICH** (1884-1957). B: Lübeck. D: Stuttgart. Actor. At first studied chemistry and pharmacy in Munich. Private stage training. Theatres: Passau (1908), Reichenberg, Düsseldorf, Sächsisches Landestheater Dresden (1914-1917), Berlin. 1945-1946: General director Dresden. First film appearance in 1915, but did not appear regularly in films until 1934. Since 1947: theatres in Stuttgart, Göttingen, Munich and Wuppertal.

Films (incomplete): *Hampelmanns Glückstag, Der Geiger von Meissen*. Then sound: *Weib im Dschungel; Der Mann, der den Mord beging; Liebe, Tod und Teufel, Der Gefangene des Königs, Das Mädchen Johanna, Der Hund von Baskerville, Wei-*

berregiment, Die letzten Vier von Santa Cruz, Das Geheimnis um Betty Bonn, Tango Notturno, Die 4 Gesellen, Dreizehn Mann und eine Kanone, Am seidenen Faden; Hallo, Janine!; In letzter Minute, Schneider Wibbel, Kleider machen Leute, Achtung! Feind hört mit!, Aus erster Ehe; Wie konntest Du, Veronika; Das Fräulein von Barnhelm, Das Herz der Königin, Die Rothschilds, Der Feuerteufel, Blutsbrüderschaft, Leichte Muse, Das andere Ich, Ich klage an, Anschlag auf Baku, Der Fall Rainer, Die Nacht in Venedig, Der grosse Schatten, Diesel, Ein glücklicher Mensch, Die beiden Schestern, Am Abend nach der Oper, Der Engel mit dem Saitenspiel, Philharmoniker, Der Meisterdetektiv, Die Feuerzangenbowle, Das fremde Leben, Das kleine Hofkonzert, Der Scheiterhaufen, Das Fall Molander, Zwischen Gestern und Morgen, Das verlorene Gesicht, Die kupferne Hochzeit, Film ohne Titel, Liebe 47, Verspieltes Leben, Hans im Glück, Zukunft aus zweiter Hand, Frauenarzt Dr. Prätorius; Tobias Knopp, Abenteuer eines Junggesellen (speaker), *Geliebter Lügner, Was das Herz befiehlt, Primanerinnen, Herz der Welt, Liebe im Finanzamt, Haus des Lebens; Mönche, Mädchen und Panduren; Der weissblaue Löwe, Die grosse Versuchung, Keine Angst vor grossen Tieren, Hokuspokus, Sauberbruch – Das war mein Leben, Das fliegende Klassenzimmer, Die goldene Pest, Himmel ohne Sterne, Rosen für Bettina, Wenn wir alle Engel wären, Made in Germany, Der Stern von Afrika, Robinson soll nicht sterben.*

289 PORTEN, HENNY (1890-1960). B: Magdeburg. D: Berlin. Actress. Daughter of opera singer and film director Franz Porten *(see* Ostermayr *and* Messter). No formal stage training. Theatres: Kurfürstendamm and on tour. 1903-1907: in Sweden. 1910: exclusive contract with her discoverer Oskar Messter (q.v.), who makes her the leading star of the German cinema. Founded her own film company, which in 1924 becomes "Henny-Porten-Carl-Froelich-Filmgesellschaft." First married to director Kurt Stark (died 1916), who played opposite her in many films. Because of her later marriage to Dr. Wilhelm von Kaufmann, a Jew, she did not work during the Nazi period. After 1945: only a very few appearances, including two films for DEFA.

Film: *Die Sieger* (prod. and ? acted – date for this film unobtainable, but made certainly prior to 1923). Films (not complete): *Apachentanz, Lohengrin, Meissner Porzellan, Desdemona, Tief im Böhmerwald, Wiegenlied, Der Kinderarzt, Liebesglück einer Blinden; Mütter, verzaget nicht; Verkannt, Adressatin verstorben, Die Blinde, Der Eindringling, Das gefährliche Alter, Die Magd, Maskierte Liebe, Ein schweres Opfer, Zwei Frauen, Des Pfarrers Töchterlein, Eva, Feenhände, Gefangene Seelen, Kuss des Fürsten, Die Nacht des Grauens, Schatten des Meeres, Gräfin Küchenfee, Die grosse Sünderin, Heroismus einer Französin, Das Tal des Lebens, Um Haaresbreite, Ungarische Rhapsodie, Abseits vom Glück, Das Adoptivkind* (also prod.) *Alexandra, Das Ende vom Lied; Hans, Hein und Henny* (also prod.), *Nordlandlose, Tirol in Waffen, Auf der Alm da gibt's ka Sünd, Claudi vom Geisterhof, Gelöste Ketten* (also prod.), *Das Geschlecht deren von Ringwall* (also prod.), *Der Schirm mit dem Schwan, Ein Ueberfall in Feindesland, Die Ehe der Luise Rohrbach, Der Liebesbrief der Königin, Die Räuberbraut, Das wandernde Licht; Die Dame, der Teufel und die Probiermamsell; Die Faust des Riesen, Das goldene Kalb* (also prod.), *Höheluft, Die Schuld* (also prod.), *Die blaue Laterne, Irrungen* (also prod.), *Maskenfest der Liebe, Odysseus' Heimkehr, Rose Bernd* (also prod.), *Fahrt ins Blaue, Ihr Sport* (also prod.), *Die lebende Tote* (also co-prod. with Union), *Monika Vogelsang* (also prod.), *Anna Boleyn, Auf der Alm, Die blinden Gatten der Frau Ruth, Die eingebildete Kranke, Die goldene Krone, Kohlhiesels Töchter, Liebe auf den ersten Blick, Die Geierwally, Die Hintertreppe* (also prod.), *Cathérina Gräfin von Armagnac* (also prod.), *Frauenopfer* (also prod.), *Gespenster, Das grosse Schweigen, Minna von Barnhelm* (also prod.), *Mona Lisa* (also prod.), *Sie und die Drei, Das alte Gesetz, Das Geheimnis von Brinkenhof, Inge Larsen* (also prod.), *I.N.R.I., Der Kaufmann von Venedig, Die Liebe einer Königin, Das goldene Kalb, Gräfin Donelli, Mutter und Kind, Prater, Das Abenteuer der Sybille Brandt* (also co-prod.), *Kammermusik* (also co-prod.), *Tragödie* (also prod.), *Die Flam-*

men lügen (also prod.), *Rosen aus dem Süden* (also prod.), *Wehe, wenn sie losgelassen* (also prod.), *Die grosse Pause* (also prod.), *Meine Tante – Deine Tante* (also prod.), *Violanta* (also prod.), *Liebe im Kuhstall* (also prod.), *Liebe und Diebe* (also prod.), *Liebfraumilch* (also prod.), *Lotte* (also prod.), *Zuflucht* (also prod.), *Die Frau, die jeder liebt, bist Du!* (also co-prod.), *Die Herrin und ihr Knecht* (also prod.), *Mutterliebe* (also prod.). Then sound: *Skandal um Eva, Kohlhiesels Töchter; Luise, Königin von Preussen; 24 Stunden im Leben einer Frau, Mutter und Kind, Krach im Hinterhaus, Der Optimist, War es der im 3. Stock?, Komödianten, Symphonie des Lebens, Wenn der junge Wein blüht, Familie Buchholz, Neigungsehe, Absender unbekannt, Das Fräulein von Scüderi, Carola Lamberti.*

290 **PRESSBURGER, EMERICH** (1902-). B: Miskolc (Hungary). Scriptwriter and director. Studied at Universities in Prague and Stuttgart. At first journalist, then becomes scriptwriter on German and Austrian films. 1934: to France. 1936: to England, where in 1939 he forms partnership with Michael Powell. 1943: founds "The Archers" company with Powell, at first

within the Rank Organisation, later with Alexander Korda.

Films (incomplete): *Abschied* (co-scripted with Irma von Cube), *Der kleine Seitensprung* (co-scripted), *Ronny* (co-scripted), *Sehnsucht 202* (co-scripted with Irma von Cube and Karl Farkas), *Das schöne Abenteuer* (co-scripted), *... und es leuchtet die Puszta, Fledermaus 1955* 55 (co-dir. and scripted with Michael Powell).

291 **PULVER, LISELOTTE** (1929-). B: Berne (Switzerland). Actress. Stage training in Berne and with the Viennese director Paul Kahlbeck. 1949-1951: Theatre at Schauspielhaus Zurich. Enters films thanks to director Leopold Lindtberg, who directs her first film *Swiss Tour* in 1949. Later mainly in German films (two more Swiss films *Uli der Knecht* and *Uli der Pächter*). International career. Her best acting was in films for Kurt Hoffmann (q.v.).

Films: *Föhn, Heidelberger Romanze, Klettermaxe, Fritz und Frederike, Hab' Sonne im Herzen, Von der Liebe reden wir später, Das Nachtgespenst, Ich und Du, Männer im gefährlichen Alter, Schule für Eheglück, Der letzte Sommer, Griff nach den Sternen, Hanussen, Ich denke oft an Piroschka, Heute heiratet mein Mann, Die Zürcher Verlobung, Bekenntnisse des Hochstaplers Felix Krull, Das Wirtshaus im Spessart, Helden, Das schöne Abenteuer, Das Glas Wasser, Buddenbrooks, Das Spukschloss im Spessart, Gustav Adolfs Page, Kohlhiesels Töchter, Ein fast anständiges Mädchen, Frühstück im Doppelbett, Monsieur, Dr. med. Hiob Prätorius; Blüten, Gauner und die Nacht von Nizza; Hokuspokus – oder wie lasse ich meinen Mann verschwinden, Herrliche Zeiten im Spessart, Pistol Jenny, Hochzeitsreise.*

292 **PUTTI, LYA DE** (1900-1932). B: Budapest. D: New York. Actress. At first dancer. Enters cinema thanks to Richard Oswald and Joe May (both q.v.). Her best part was in *Variété*. 1926: to U.S.A. An actress who was endowed with a certain vamp-like mystique.

Films (incomplete): *Das indische Grabmal, Der brennende Acker, Ilona, Othello, Phantom, Die Fledermaus, Die Schlucht des Todes, SOS. Die Insel der Tränen; Thamar, das Kind der Berge; Claire, Komödianten, Malva, Eifersucht, Im Namen des Kaisers, Varieté, Junges Blut, Manon Lescaut, Charlott etwas verrückt.*

293 RABENALT, ARTHUR MARIA (1905-   ). B: Vienna. Director. *Début as stage director in Darmstadt, then at Krolloper and Volksbühne Berlin. After 1945: in Baden-Baden. 1947-1949: General director of Metropol-Theater Berlin. Worked for Jacques Feyder as dialogue director on the German versions of La Kermesse héroique (1936) and Les gens du voyage (1938).*

Films: *Pappi 34 (also script with Sybille Pietzsch), Eine Siebzehnjährige 34, Was bin ich ohne Dich 34, Ein Kind, ein Hund, ein Vagabund 34, Das Frauenparadies 36, Die Liebe des Maharadscha 36, Millionenerbschaft 37, Liebelei und Liebe 38, Männer müssen so sein 39, Johannisfeuer 39, Flucht ins Dunkel 39, Weisser Flieder 40, Achtung! Feind hört mit! 40, Die 3 Codonas 40, Leichte Muse 41, . . . reiet für Deutschland 41, Fronttheater 42, Meine Frau Teresa 42, Liebespremiere 43, Zirkus Renz 43, Die Schuld der Gabriele Rottweil 44, Am Abend nach der Oper 44, Regimentsmusik 45, Wir beide liebten Katharina 45, Chemie und Liebe 48, Morgen ist alles besser 48, Anonyme Briefe 49, Das Mädchen Christine 49, Martina 49, Nächte am Nil 49, Die Frau von gestern Nacht 50; 0 Uhr 15, Zimmer 9 50, Hochzeit im Heu 51, Unvergängliches Licht 51, Die Försterchristl 52, Das weisse Abenteuer 52, Alraune 52, Wir tanzen auf dem Regenbogen 52 (co-dir. with Carmine Gallone), Die Fiakermilli 53, Lavendel 53 (also script with Fritz Böttger), Der letzte Walzer 53, Der Vogelhändler 53, Der unsterbliche Lump 53, Die Sonne von St. Moritz 54, Der Zigeunerbaron 54, Der Zarewitsch 54, Solang' es hübsche Mädchen gibt 55, Unternehmen Schlafsack 55, Liebe ist ja nur ein Märchen 55, Die Ehe des Dr. med. Danwitz 56, Tierarzt Dr. Vlimmen 56, Zwischen Zeit und Ewigkeit 56, Glücksritter 57, Frühling in Berlin 57, Für zwei Groschen Zärtlichkeit 57; Eine Frau, die weiss, was sie' will 58 (also script with Herbert Witt, Per Schwenzen and Fritz Eckhardt), Das haut einen Seemann doch nicht um 58, Vergiss mein nicht 58, Geliebte Bestie 58, Lass mich am Sonntag nicht allein 59, Das grosse*

Wunschkonzert 60, Der Held meiner Träume 60, Mann im Schatten 61.

294 RADDATZ, CARL (1912-   ). B: Mannheim. Actor. *Private stage training with Herbert Maisch. Theatres: Mannheim, Aachen, Darmstadt, Worms, Bremen, Berlin. After 1945: in Göttingen, later to Berlin (Schlosspark and Schiller-Theater). Enters cinema in 1937. Well-known "voice" for dubbed films.*

Films: *Urlaub auf Ehrenwort, Verklungene Melodie, Liebelei und Liebe, Silvesternacht am Alexanderplatz, 12 Minuten nach 12, Wir tanzen um die Welt, Zwielicht, Wunschkonzert, Golowin geht durch die Stadt, Befreite Hände, Ueber alles in der Welt, Stukas, Heimkehr, Der 5. Juni, Immensee, Das war mein Leben, Opfergang, Eine Frau für 3 Tage, Unter den Brücken, Die Schenke der ewigen Liebe, In jenen Tagen, Und finden dereinst wir uns wieder, Zugvögel, Wohin die Züge fahren, Der Schatten des Herrn Monitor, Epilog, Gabriela, Schatten der Nacht, Taxi-Kitty, Gift im Zoo, Türme des Schweigens, Geliebtes Leben, Regina Amstetten, Geständnis unter vier Augen, Oase, Rosen im Herbst, Nacht der Entscheidung, Friederike von Barring, Das Mädchen Marion, Made in Germany, Das Mädchen Rosemarie, Jons und Erdme.*

295 RASP, FRITZ (HEINRICH) (1891-   ). B: Bayreuth. Stage training in Munich. Theatres: Tilsit, Detmold, Speyer, Deutsches Theater Berlin (with Reinhardt, q.v.). Enters cinema in 1920. Pabst (q.v.) gave him many intelligent roles. Now appears mainly in films adapted from the works of Edgar Wallace.

Films (incomplete): *Schuhpalast Pinkus, Lachte man gerne, Der Mensch am Wege, Schatten, Time is money, Zwischen Abend und Morgen, Arabella, Komödianten, Die Puppe vom Lunapark, Ein Sommernachtstraum, Götz von Berlichingen zubenannt mit der eisernen Hand, Das Haus der Lüge, Menschen am Meer, Der Liebe Lust und Leid, Metropolis, Qualen der Nacht, Ueberflüssige Menschen, Die Waise von Lowood, Der geheimnisvolle Spiegel, Kinderseelen klagen an, Der letzte Walzer, Die Liebe der Jeanne Ney, Schinderhannes, Die Carmen von St. Pauli, Spione, Die Drei um Edith,*

Die Frau im Mond, Frühlings Erwachen, Der Hund von Baskerville, Tagebuch einer Verlorenen. Then sound: *Die grosse Sehnsucht, Dreyfus, Der Zinker, Tropennächte, Emil und die Detektive, Die Dreigroschenoper, Die Pranke, Der Mörder Dimitri Karamasoff, Die Vier vom Bob 13, Der Hexer, Die grausame Freundin, Der Schuss am Nebelhorn, Der sündige Hof, Der Judas von Tirol, Grenzfeuer, Charleys Tante, Lockvogel, Klein Dorrit, Lockspitzel Asew, Die Teuchter des Kaisers, Onkel Bräsig, Der Hund von Baskerville, Togger, Einmal werd' ich Dir gefallen; Nanu, Sie kennen Korf noch nicht?; Frau im Strom, Es war eine rauschende Ballnacht, Leidenschaft, Alarm, Paracelsus, Irgendwo in Berlin, Skandal in der Botschaft, Haus des Lebens, Hokuspokus, Die Mühle im Schwarzwäldertal, Der Cornet, Der Frosch mit der Maske, Der rote Kreis, Die Bande des Schreckens, Das schwarze Schaf, Das Rätsel der roten Orchidee, Die seltsame Gräfin.*

296 RAUTENFELD, KLAUS VON (1909 -). B: Dorpat-Birkenruh. Director of photography. Studied law. At first sportsman, then trained at Ufa. Worked as a colour specialist for Ufa, Terra and Tobis before 1945. Rautenfeld has worked for both Harry Piel and Luis Trenker (both q.v.). His technical skill with the camera is seen at its best in some of the films of Rolf Thiele (q.v.).

Films: *Der Berg ruft* (co-phot.), *Condottieri* (co-phot. with Benitz and Walter Hege), *Liebesbriefe aus dem Engadin* (co-phot. with Hans Ertl, Walter Riml and Karl Puth), *Grenzfeuer* (co-phot. with Bruno Timm and Bertl Höcht), *Im Schatten des Berges* (co-phot. with Oskar Schnirch), *Der Feuerteufel, Immer nur Du* (co-phot. with Herbert Körner), *Anschlag auf Baku* (co-phot. with Baberske, Körner and H. O. Schulze), *Panik* (co-phot. with Puth and E. W. Fiedler), *Junge Adler, Die Schenke zur ewige Liebe, Und finden dereinst wir uns wieder, Zugvögel* (co-phot.), *Wohin die Züge fahren, Nach Regen scheint Sonne, Der Tiger Akbar* (co-phot. with Timm), *Weg ohne Umkehr, Sterne über Colombo* (co-phot.), *Die Gefangene des Maharadscha* (co-phot.), *Der rote Prinz* (co-phot. with Schnirch), *Heimweh nach Deutschland* (co-phot. with Helmuth Nath), *Frühlingslied, Die goldene Pest, Der Schmied von St. Bartholomä, Zwei Herzen und ein Thron, Mädchen ohne Grenzen, Viele kamen vorbei, Holiday am Wörthersee, Kleines Zelt und grosse Liebe, Rose Bernd, Zwei Bayern im Urwald, Blaue Jungs, Skandal in Ischl, El Hakim, Das Mädchen Rosemarie, Der schwarze Blitz* (co-phot. with Ernst W. Kalinke), *Peter Voss, der Millionendieb* (co-phot. with Günther Senftleben), *Helden, Die Halbzarte, Labyrinth, Abschied von den Wolken; Peter Voss, der Held des Tages; Scheidungsgrund Liebe, Stefanie in Rio, Das Wunder des Malachias, Bis zum Ende aller Tage, Barbara, Die blonde Frau des Maharadscha* (co-phot), *Heisser Hafen Hongkong, 90 Minuten nach Mitternacht, Strasse der Verheissung, Zwischen Shanghai und St. Pauli, Elf Jahre und ein Tag, Es war mir ein Vergnügen, Der schwarze Panther von Ratana, Wochentags immer, Die Lady, Ein Sarg aus Hongkong, Weisse Fracht für Hongkong, Kommissar X: Drei gelbe Katzen, Der nächste Herr − diesselbe Dame, Radhapura − Endstation der Verdammten, Heidi kehrt heim; Hugo, der Weiberschreck; Pudelnackt in Oberbayern; Zieh' dich aus, Puppe.*

297 REALISM. In literary circles, circa 1924, a formula was very familiar. "Reality is the only basis of art. Without reality the roots of everything are non-existent. Let us be modest and turn to small things. Observe a man, a soul, a fool!" German film realism as a movement runs counter to "Expressionism" (q.v.). Instead of eluding reality and in place of ideals, principles of characterisation are strictly defined, and objectivity constitutes the foundation of the cineaste's vision, which leads to *Neue Sachlichkeit* (q.v.).

The most significant personality in the movement was Pabst: "What is so good about romanticism; real life is romantic, even cruel enough." Kracauer mainly emphasises that in realistic films no questions were asked and no arguments set out, for him the mass of facts offered no deep meaning. These realistic films, although important documents of their time, lacked all critical analysis.

Varieté is a good example of a film midway between "*Kammerspiel*" and "Realism," in which Dupont compels the camera to perform realistically.

"Realism" had a considerable influence on "*mountain*" *films* (q.v.) and documentaries (Ruttmann and his work, q.v.).

298 REIMANN, WALTER (18 -   ). Set designer and painter. Enters cinema through Hermann Warm (q.v.), whom he met during the First World War working in an army theatre. Later to Berlin, where he painted sets, then gains reputation after commencing his film career with *Das Kabinett des Dr. Caligari (see* Warm and Röhrig). Distinctive personality of the silent cinema in the early Twenties, working in collaboration with Rippert, Wiene, Gerlach, Galeen and Berger (all q.v.). Also co-scripted *Elisabeth und der Narr* with Thea von Harbou (q.v.).

Films: *Das Kabinett des Dr. Caligari* (in collab.), *Die Pest in Florenz* (in collab. with Röhrig, Warm and Jaffé), *Algol, Genuine* (in collab. with César Klein), *Die Grüne Manuela* (in collab. with Alfred Junge), *Der falsche Dimitri, Ein Puppenheim, Vanina oder die Galgenhochzeit, Die Perücke, Der Hahn im Korb, Ich liebe Dich, Liebesfeuer, Wunder der Schöpfung, Ein Walzertraum, Die Aben-* *teuer eines Zehnmarkscheines* (in collab. with Robert Basilici), *Der Ritt in die Sonne, Alraune, Der letzte Walzer* (in collab. with Hans Minzloff), *Schuldig.* Then sound: *Zapfenstreich am Rhein, Rasputin, Unheimliche Geschichten, Geheimnis des blauen Zimmers, Theodor Körner, Die Herren vom Maxim, Elisabeth und der Narr,* (also co-scripted), *Hanneles Himmelfahrt, Was bin ich ohne Dich, Alte Kameraden, Das Mädchen Irene.*

299 REINECKER, HERBERT (1914-   ). B: Hagen. Writer and scriptwriter. At first journalist. After 1945: freelance writer and prolific author for the stage. A scriptwriter with a sharp eye for commercial subjects. Now working mainly for TV. Pen name: Dührkopp.

Films: *Junge Adler* (co-scripted), *Vater braucht eine Frau* (co-scripted with Herbert Witt and Christian Bock), *Ich und Du* (co-scripted), *Dalmatinische Hochzeit* (idea only), *Canaris; Kinder, Mütter und ein General* (co-scripted with Laszlo Benedek); *Verliebte Leute, Der Himmel ist nie ausverkauft* (co-scripted), *Alibi; Anastasia – die letzte Zarentochter; Spion für Deutschland, Kitty und die grosse Welt, Der Stern von Afrika, Banktresor 713, El Hakim, Scampolo* (co-scripted with Ilse Lotz-Dupont and Frank Höllering), *Taiga, Dorothea Angermann, Solange das Herz schlägt, Bumerang, Liebe auf krummen Beinen* (co-scripted with Utz Utermann), *Menschen im Netz, Schachnovelle, Eine Frau fürs ganze Leben* (co-scripted with Georg Hurdalek and Oliver Hassenkamp), *Ein Alibi zerbricht* (co-scripted with Werner P. Zibaso and Stefan Gammermann), *Das grosse Liebesspiel, Schloss Gripsholm, Der Hexer, Kennwort: Reiher, Das Liebeskarussell* (co-scripted with Kurt Nachmann and Paul Hengge), *Neues vom Hexer, Schüsse im 3/4-Takt, Der Bucklige von Soho, Ich suche einen Mann, Maigret und sein grösster Fall, Rheinsberg.*

300 REINHARDT, MAX (1873-1943). B: Baden near Vienna. D: New York. Director. RN: Maximilian Goldmann. One of the most important directors of the German theatre. Stage training with Professor Emil Burde. Theatres (as actor): Rudolfsheim and Salzburg. Otto Brahm took him to Berlin to his Deutsches Theater. Guest appearances in Reichenberg, Prague, Raimund Theater Vienna, Budapest and Salzburg. Opens cabaret houses, "Brille" and "Schall und Rauch," later becoming the official theatre Unter den Linden, and (in 1902) the Kleines Theater Berlin. 1903: Reinhardt breaks contract with Brahm and becomes director of Kleines Theater and Neues Theater on the Schiffbauerdamm. 1905: director of Deutsches Theater Berlin (which he purchased in 1906). 1906: introduces *"Kammerspiel"* to the Deutsches Theater. 1909-1911: Künstlertheater Munich. 1910: Exhibition Hall in Munich. 1915-1918: director of Berliner Volksbühne. 1919: opens the Grosse Schauspielhaus Berlin as General Director (*see* Poelzig). 1920: co-founder of Salzburg Festival (main productions over the years include *Jedermann* and *Das Grosse Salzburger Welttheater*, both by Hugo von Hofmannsthal, and *Faust* by Goethe). From 1920: mainly in Austria. 1924: general director of Theater in der Josefstadt Vienna. 1929: returns to Berlin in charge of the theatres there. Toured Europe with his companies presenting various guest productions. At the end of 1932 Reinhardt lost his theatres, and travelled to France, England, Italy and Salzburg as a guest director. 1935: to U.S.A., where he filmed with Wilhelm Dieterle (q.v.) his famous production of *A Midsummer Night's Dream* featuring American actors. 1937: emigrates to U.S.A. Reinhardt's influence through his work, his actors and his pupils has been enormous. 1913: contract with Union-Film. 1913-1914: film director with ensemble of Deutsches Theater Berlin. Directors trained by Reinhardt: Murnau, Leni (both q.v.), Riszard Ordynski, Lothar Mendes. Director/actors trained by Reinhardt: Lubitsch, Dieterle, Wegener, Hermann Thimig (q.v.) and Otto (Ludwig) Preminger (who was general director of Theater in der Josefstadt Vienna from 1923-1935, one film in Austria *Die grosse Liebe* 1932). Actors trained by Reinhardt include Veidt, Krauss, Jannings, Sokoloff, Bergner, Dietrich, Christians, Wessely (all q.v.), Joseph Schildkraut, Luise Rainer, Leopoldine Konstantin, Olivia de Havilland. His son Gottfried Reinhardt is also a director of mainly American and German films.

Films: *Sumurun* 08, *Das Mirakel* 12, *Die* *Insel der Seligen* 13 (artistic adviser: Paul von Schlippenbach), *Venezianische Nacht* 14.

301 **REINIGER, LOTTE** (1899-   ). B: Berlin. Director. 1916-1917: studies under Max Reinhardt (q.v.). Creator of silhoutte films, of which she and Dr. Hans Cuerlis are often cited as the inventors. 1918: enters film industry through Paul Wegener (q.v.) for whose *Pied Piper of Hamelin* she cuts the title vignettes. 1919: Wegener introduces her to the Institute of Cultural Reseach, for whom she begins a major series of silhouette films. 1926: after a number of shorts, she completes the first full-length animated film

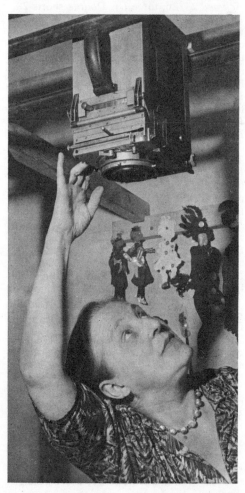

in the history of the cinema, which had its *première* in the Berliner Volksbühne. Her husband, Carl Koch, was her production supervisor and director, and Arthur Neher, Walter Ruttmann (q.v.) and Bertold Bartosch were her close collaborators on this and other films. 1937: contributes a shadow-play to Renoir's *La Marseillaise*. 1936-1939: in England. 1940: to Rome. 1944-1949: in Berlin. 1949: to London.

Films: *Das Ornament des verliebten Herzens* 19/20 (short), *Der Amor und das standhafte Liebespaar* 20/22 (short), *Der fliegende Koffer* 20/22 (short), *Der Stern von Bethlehem* 20/22 (short), *Aschenputtel* 20/22 (short), *Die Abenteuer des Prinzen Achmed* 23/26, three *Dr. Dolittle* shorts 28, *Die Jagd nach dem Glück* 30 (silhouette film within a feature film with actors in collab. with Gliese, Wagner (q.v.) and Berthold Bartosch), *Zehn Minuten Mozart* 30 (short), *Harlekin* 31 (short), *Sissy* 32 (interlude film), *Carmen* 33 (short), *Das rollende Rad* 34 (short), *Das gestohlene Herz* 34 (short), *Der Graf von Carabas* 34 (short), *Papagono* 35 (short), *Galathea* 35 (short), *Der kleine Schornsteinfeger* 35 (short).

302 **REINL, HARALD** (1908-   ). B: Bad Ischl. Director. Studied and practised law. Enters film industry as assistant to Arnold Fanck (q.v.) and Leni Riefenstahl (q.v.) for her *Tiefland*. 1949: sports films for Josef Plesner. Then directs films usually against a background of the Austrian and Bavarian Alps. Later works on action films, and now mainly specialises in films adapted from the works of Karl May, Edgar Wallace, Jerry Cotton and "Dr. Mabuse."

Films: *Bergkristall* 49 (also script with Hubert and Rose Schonger), *Gesetz ohne Gnade* 50, *Fegefeuer der Liebe* 51 (also script), *Der Herrgrottschnitzer von Ammergau* 52, *Hinter Klostermauern* 52 (also script), *Der Klosterjäger* 53, *Rosen-Resli* 54 (also script with Maria Osten-Sacken), *Der schweigende Engel* 54 (also script with Osten-Sacken), *Ein Herz schlägt für Erika* 55, *Solange Du lebst* 55 (also script with J. Joachim Bartsch), *Die Fischerin vom Bodensee* 56 (also script with Karl Heinz Busse), *Johannisnacht* 56, *Die Prinzessin von St. Wolfgang* 57 (also script with Bartsch), *Almenrausch und Edelweiss* 57, *Die Zwillinge*

vom Zillertal 57 (also script with Busse), *Die grünen Teufel von Monte Cassino* 58, *Romarei, das Mädchen mit den grünen Augen* 58, *U 47 – Kapitänleutnant Prien* 58, *Der Frosch mit der Maske* 59, *Paradies der Matrosen* 59, *Die Bande des Schreckens* 60, *Wir wollen niemals auseinandergehn* 60, *Der Fälscher von London* 61, *Im Stahlnetz des Dr. Mabuse* 61, *Der Schatz im Silbersee* 62, *Teppich des Grauens* 62, *Die unsichtbaren Krallen des Dr. Mabuse* 62, *Die weisse Spinne* 63, *Winnetou I* 63, *Der Würger von Schloss Blackmoor* 63, *Winnetou II* 64, *Zimmer 13* 64, *Der letzte Mohikaner* 65, *Der unheimliche Mönch* 65, *Winnetou III* 65, *Die Nibelungen I & II* 67 (also co-scripted with Harald G. Petersen and Ladislaus Fodor), *Die Schlangengrube und das Pendel* 67, *Dynamit in grüner Seide* 68, *Todesschüsse am Broadway* 68, *Der Tod im roten Jaguar* 68, *Winnetou und Shatterhand im Tal der Toten* 68 (also co-scripted with Alex Burg), *Die Lümmel von der ersten Bank III* 69, *Erinnerungen aus der Zukunft* 69.

303 **REISCH, WALTER** (1903-   ). B: Vienna. Scriptwriter and director. At first journalist, then scenarist (asst. to Alexander Korda), working in Germany and Austria. Also directed some films. 1938: to U.S.A. as scriptwriter (for Billy Wilder, among others) and director. Since 1955: president of the committee supervising Academy Awards for foreign films. 1953: Academy Award for his script of *Titanic*, directed by Jean Negulesco. In 1954 and 1955 he scripts and directs two features in Germany.

Films (incomplete): *Miss Hobbs, Der Fluch, Frauen aus der Wiener Vorstadt, Ein Walzer von Strauss* (co-scripted with Max Neufeld), *Küssen ist keine Sünd'* (co-scripted with Hans Otto), *Schützenliesl, Der Bettelstudent, Die Dollarprinzessin und ihre sechs Freier, Die elf Teufel, Faschingzauber, Das Heiratsnest, Die indiskrete Frau, Ein Mädel aus dem Volke, Pratermizzi (see* Ucicky), *Ein rheinisches Mädchen beim rheinischen Wein; Seine Hoheit, der Eintänzer; Tingel-Tangel, Dragonerliebchen, Der Faschingsprinz, Fräulein Fähnrich* (co-scripted with Alfred Schirokauer), *Die Frau, die jeder liebt, bist Du!; Der Held aller Mädchenträume, Der lustige Witwer* (co-scripted with Schulz), *Der schwarze Domino*

146

(co-scripted with Robert Liebmann), *Schwarzwaldmädel* (co-scripted with Max Jungk), *Donauwalzer.* Then sound: *Die Nacht gehört uns* (co-scripted with Walter Supper), *Dich hab' ich geliebt, Brand in der Oper* (co-scripted with Supper), *Das Flöten-konzert von Sanssouci, Mach' mir die Welt zum Paradies* (co-scripted with Franz Schulz), *Das Lied ist aus, Der Herr auf Bestellung, Hokuspokus* (co-scripted with Karl Hartl), *Wie werde ich reich und glück-lich?, Ein Tango für Dich, Va banque* (only idea), *Im Geheimdienst, Die lustigen Weiber von Wien, Der Raub der Mona Lisa, Ein blonder Traum* (co-scripted), *Der Prinz von Arkadien, F.P. 1 antwortet nicht, Die Grä-fin von Monte Christo, Ich und die Kaiserin* (co-scripted with Robert Liebmann), *Leise flehen meine Lieder* (only idea), *Saison in Kairo, Episode* 35 (also dir.), *Die Mücke* 54 (also dir.), *Der Cornet* 55 (also dir.).

304 **RICHTER, HANS** (1888-   ). B: Berlin. Director and theoretician on ab-stract film. Apprenticeship as carpenter. Studied at University and Hochschule für Bildende Kunst Berlin. 1909: Academy in Weimar. 1912: frequents the "Café des Wes-terns" with many artists of the period. Sol-dier in First World War, but released as an invalid in 1916 and enters Dada movement in Zurich. 1918: begins his friendship with Danish painter Viking Eggeling (1881-1925). 1919: first "Rollenbild" *Praeludium.* 1921: first film. 1926-1927: founds "Gesellschaft Neuer Film" with Guido Bagier and Karl Freund (q.v.). 1929: publishes his book *Filmgegner von heute – Filmfreunde von morgen* and participates in the first congress of independent film at the castle of Mme. de Mandrot in La Sarraz (Vaud, Switzer-land), where with Eisenstein, Tissé and Jean-Georges Auriol, he shoots the short film *Kampf des unabhängigen gegen den kom-merziellen Film* (also known as *Sturm über La Sarraz).* 1933: to France, Netherlands and Switzerland. 1941: to U.S.A. 1942: director, and in 1948 Professor at Film Institute of City College New York. 1952: returns to Europe, lives in Switzerland. Works also as a painter, several exhibitions around the world since 1946. 1967: publishes memoirs (on years 1915-1933) *Köpfe und Hinterköpfe.*

Films:*Rhythmus 21* 21, *Rhythmus 25* 25, *Filmstudie* 25, *Inflation* 26-27, *Vormittags-spuk* 27-28 *(photog:* Reimar Kuntze, q.v., *music:* Paul Hindemith, *actors:* Hindemith, Richter, Darius and Madeleine Milhaud, Jean Oser), *Rennsymphonie* 28-29 *(photog:* Tax Tober, short to *Ariadne in Hoppegar-ten* 29, dir. Robert Dinesen), *Zwischen-groschenzauber* 28-29, *Alles dreht sich, alles bewegt sich* 29 *(photog:* Kuntze), *Everyday* 29 (in London, Eisenstein as policeman), *Neues Leben* 29-30 (Switzerland), *Europa Radio* 31 (Netherlands), *Hallo Everybody* 33 (Netherlands), *Metall* 31-33 (for Prometheus in Berlin, shot in Berlin, Moscow and Odessa, unfinished), *Vom Blitz zum Fern-sehbild* 35-36 (Netherlands), *Eine kleine Welt im Dunkeln* 36-38 (Switzerland), *Die Entstehung der Farbe* 36-38 (Switzerland), *Die Eroberung des Himmels* 36-38 (Switzer-land, *music:* Milhaud), *Hans im Glück* 36-38 (Switzerland), *Die Börse* 39 (Switzer-land), 39-41 other commercials and docu-mentaries for Central Film in Zurich, *The Movies Take a Holiday* 44 (New York, compilation), *Dreams That Money Can Buy* 45-47 (assisted by Léger, Duchamp, Calder, Ernst, Man Ray, Milhaud, Cage, etc.), *Forty Years of Experiment* Parts One and Two 51-61 (excerpts from his experimental films), *Dadascope I and II* 56-67 (documentaries set to Dada poems 16-24), *Passionate Pas-time/Chesscetera* 56-57 (with Milhaud, Duchamp), *8 mal 8* 56-57 (with Arp, Jac-queline Matisse, Huelsenbeck, Calder, Ernst, Cocteau), *Alexander Calder: From the Cir-cus to the Moon* 63 (three episodes from *Dreams* and *8 mal 8).*

305 **RICHTER, PAUL** (1895-1965). B and D: Vienna. Actor. Stage training at Ar-nau and Konservatorium Vienna. Theatres: Trappau, Hoftheater Mannheim, Jarno-The-atres Vienna. 1914-1918: soldier. Appears at Stadttheater Vienna. 1919: first film ap-pearance. 1920: to Berlin. 1943-1944: guest appearances at Theater in der Josefstadt Vienna. Was first married to Aud Egede Nissen, a star of the silent period. Played his most important part in *Die Nibelungen* (Part One), later mainly in outdoor, folklore-type films.

Films (incomplete): *Sterbewalzer, Gefes-selt, Jagd nach dem Glück, Mord ohne Täter,*

Der Henker von Sankt Marien, Das indische Grabmal, Die Nacht des Einbrechers, Das Opfer der Ellen Larsen, Zirkus des Lebens, Dr. Mabuse der Spieler, Herzen im Sturm, Die Nibelungen I; Pietro, der Korsar; Die rote Maus, Dagfin, In Treue stark, Kampf der Geschlechter, Schwester Veronika, Tragödie einer Ehe, Der König der Mittelstürmer, Die letzte Nacht, Die Stadt der tausend Freunden, Die Geliebte seiner Hoheit, Lockendes Gift, Schneeschuhbanditen, Die Frau im Talar, Sensation im Wintergarten. Then sound: Der weisse Gott, Die Nacht ohne Pause, Die Försterchristl, Der Hexer, Das Geheimnis um Johann Orth, Marschall Vorwärts, Strafsache van Geldern, Drei Kaiserjäger, Der Choral von Leuthen, In Sachen Timpe, Jungfrau gegen Mönch, Schloss Hubertus, Was bin ich ohne Dich, Krach im Forsthaus, Das unsterbliche Lied, Die Frauen von Tannhof, Der Klosterjäger, Ehestreik, Der Jäger von Fall (36); Gordian, der Tyrann; Das Schweigen im Walde (37), Der Edelweisskönig, Frau Sylvelin, Narren im Schnee, Stärker als die Liebe, Waldrausch, Der laufende Berg, Der Ochsenkrieg, Kohlhiesels Töchter, Die schwache Stunde, Warum lügst Du, Elisabeth?, Ein Mann gehört ins Haus, Der Geigenmacher von Mittenwald, Die Alm an der Grenze, Die Martinsklause, Die schöne Tölzerin, Der Herrgottsschnitzer von Ammergau, Mikosch rückt ein, Der Klosterjäger, Schloss Hubertus, Das Schweigen im Walde (55), Der Jäger von Fall (57), Wetterleuchten um Maria, Der Schäfer von Trutzberg, Die singenden Engel von Tirol.

306 **RIEFENSTAHL, LENI (HELENE, BERTHA AMALIE).** (1902-   ). Actress and director. B: Berlin. At first studied painting at art school in Berlin, ballet training at State dance school Berlin (Eduardowa, Jutte Klamt and Mary Wigman). Arranges dance programmes in Deutsches Theater Berlin, Schauspielhaus Zurich and Deutsches Theater Prague. Enters cinema through Arnold Fanck (q.v.); acts in his *"mountain" films* (q.v.), and later becomes director in the same *genre*. Since 1931: head of "Leni Riefenstahl-Produktion." By order of Hitler she made two massive documentaries, both remarkably edited, with considerable aesthetic pretensions, although they were obviously designed to emphasise Nazi power. Worked for thirteen years on *Tiefland,* based on Eugène d'Albert's opera, which is her most recent film (apart from an unifinished documentary).

Films: *Der heilige Berg, Der grosse Sprung.* Then sound:*Der weisse Rausch, Das blaue Licht, S.O.S. Eisberg, Tiefland.* Directed films: *Das blaue Licht* 32 (also idea), *Der Sieg des Glaubens* 33 (doc.), *Triumph des Willens* 34 (doc.), *Tag der Freiheit – unsere Wehrmacht* 35 (doc.), *Fest der Völker and Fest der Schönheit* 36 (doc. on Olympic Games Berlin, *premièred* 38, also script), *Tiefland* 45 (also script and acted), *Schwarze Fracht* 56 (doc., unfinished).

307 **RIEMANN, JOHANNES** (1888-1959). B: Berlin. D: Konstanz. Actor and director. Private stage training under Alexander Strakosch. Theatres: Töplitz, Marienbad, Meran, Weimar, then to Reinhardt (q.v.) at the Deutsches Theater Berlin. Entered the cinema in 1916 as a light entertainer, especially as a gallant lover. His first success stemmed from a film with Henny Porten (q.v.). In 1943 Riemann fell seriously ill and made only a few more films before his death.

Films (incomplete): *Ein Opfer der Leidenschaft, Ahasver, Die Faust des Riesen, Das goldene Kalb, Veritas vincit, Kitsch, Die verbotene Frucht, Die drei Tanten, Die Herren vom Maxim, Lacht man gerne, Niemand weiss es, Sehnsucht Nr. 13, Tötet nicht mehr, Die im Schatten gehen, Fasching, Sappho, Der Herzog von Algerien, Das hohe Lied der Liebe* (also script), *Keimende Saat, Der Liebesroman des Cesare Ubaldi, Der Todesreigen, Wem nie durch Liebe Leid geschah, Graf Cohn, Der Herzog von Aleria, Der Schatz der Gesine Jakobsen, Die Sonne von St. Moritz, Wilhelm Tell, Gehetzte Menschen, Das goldene Kalb, Lumpen und Seide, Prater, Die Stadt ohne Juden, Elegantes Pack, Heiratsannoncen, Der Liebeskäfig, Die Moral der Gasse; In der Heimat, da gibt's ein Wiedersehn!; Der Jünglich aus der Konfektion, Das Panzergewölbe, Die Wiskottens, Die Tochter des Kunstreiters, Valencia, Fräulein Chauffeur, Die Frau auf der Folter.* Then sound: *Heute nacht – eventuell, Der falsche Ehemann, Kadetten, Die Liebesfiliale, Mein Herz sehnt*

A typical aerial shot from Leni Riefenstahl's TRIUMPH DES WILLENS

sich nach Liebe, So'n Windhund, Sein Scheidungsgrund, Liebe auf Befehl 31 (also co-dir. with Ernst L. Franck, script with Benjamin Glazer, Tom Reed and E. Redlich), Liebe auf den ersten Ton, Das Millionentestament, Fräulein – falsch verbunden, Die Herren vom Maxim, Hasenklein kann nichts dafür, Moral und Liebe, Grossfürstin Alexandra, Der Polizeibericht meldet, Zwei im Sonnenschein (only script), Ich heirate meine Frau (only script with Joe Stöckel), Ich sehne mich nach Dir 34 (only dir.), Der Mann mit der Pranke, Eva 35 (only dir.), Die un-erhörte Frau (and dir. of dialogue), Kinderarzt Dr. Engel 36 (only dir. and script with S. S. von Varady and Harald Röbbeling), Die grosse und die kleine Welt 36 (only dir. and script with Varady and Gritz and M. Rau), Gauner im Frack 37 (only dir. and script with F. D. Andam and

Walther von Hollander), Einmal werd' ich Dir gefallen 37 (only dir. and script with Hans Schweikart and W. E. von Gordon), Der Tag nach der Scheidung, Yvette, Lauter Lügen, Drunter und drüber, Ehe in Dosen, Hochzeitsreise zu Dritt, Bel ami, Renate im Quartett, Ihr erstes Erlebnis, Die gute Sieben, Alles für Gloria (also script with Boese, Fritz and M. Rau), Oh diese Männer, Friedemann Bach, Sonntagskinder, Liebeskomödie, Kleine Residenz, Drei tolle Mädels, Das Lied der Nachtigall, Geliebter Schatz, Ein Mann für meine Frau, Was die Schwalbe sang, Jede Nacht in einem andern Bett, Der schräge Otto, Zwei Bayern im Harem.

308 **RIPPERT, OTTO** (18 -19). Director. Mainly remembered for his costume films after the First World War and for the Homunculus serial, produced in 1916 in

149

six parts and re-issued in three parts in 1920. Olaf Föns portrays the creature made by Professor Hansen in the serial.

Films (incomplete): *Friedrich Werders Sendung* 16, *Homunculus* 16, *Königskinder von Travankore* 17, *Die Frau mit den Orchideen* 19, *Gräfin Walewska* 19, *Die Pest in Florenz* 19, *Der Schatten der Stunde* 19, *Totentanz* 19, *Der Weg, der in die Verdammnis führt* 19, *Aschermittwoch* 20, *Die Beute der Erinnyen* 21, *Das Geheimnis einer Schuld* 21, *Wie Satan starb* 21 (co-dir. with Heinz Hanus), *Frou-Frou* 22, *Tingel-Tangel* 22, *Die brennende Kugel,* 23, *So ist das Leben* 24, *Winterstürme* 24.

309 **RITTAU, GÜNTHER** (1893-   ). B: Königshütte. Director of photography. Studied at technical high school Berlin, worked in a factory making optical instruments. Decla commissions him to develop special techniques for documentary and scientific films. Enters the industry through Erich Pommer (q.v.) and, after a few scientific films, becomes assistant to Carl Hoffmann (q.v.) on *Die Nibelungen.* Further collaboration with Freund and Schneeberger (both q.v.). Only returns to the studios after 1945. 1948: founds production company "Stella Film" which soon disappeared. Also directed some mediocre films.

Films (incomplete): *Der Eisenbahnkönig* (co-phot. with Friedrich Paulmann), *Der steinerne Reiter* (co-phot.), *Die Nibelungen* (co-phot.), *Der Turm des Schweigens, Metropolis* (co-phot.), *Fürst oder Clown, Der Kampf des Donald Westhof* (co-phot.), *Heimkehr, Was ist los mit Nanette* (co-phot. with Gottschalk), *Asphalt.* Then sound: *Melodie des Herzens* (co-phot.), *Einbrecher* (co-phot.), *Der blaue Engel* (co-phot.), *Liebling der Götter* (co-phot.), *Ihre Hoheit befielt* (co-phot.), *Bomben auf Monte Carlo* (co-phot.), *Stürme der Leidenschaft, Der Sieger* (co-phot. with Otto Baecker), *F.P. 1 antwortet nicht* (co-phot. with Baecker and Tschet), *Quick* (co-phot. with Beacker), *Ein blonder Traum* (co-phot. with Baecker and Tschet), *Abel mit der Mundharmonika* (co-phot. with Baecker), *Kind, ich freu' mich auf Dein Kommen* (co-phot. with Baecker), *Gold* (co-phot. with Baecker and Werner Bohne), *Fürst Woronzeff* (co-phot. with Baecker), *Der grüne Domino* (co-phot. with

Baecker), *Liebeslied* (co-phot. with Baecker), *Zigeunerbaron* (co-phot. with Baecker), *Waldwinter* (co-phot. with Baecker), *Ritt in die Freiheit* (co-phot. with Baecker), *Starke Herzen, Nordlicht* (co-phot. with Ekkehard Kyrath), *Verklungene Melodie* (co-phot with Kyrath), *Der Vorhang fällt* (co-phot with Kyrath), *Brand im Ozean* 39 (only dir.),*U-Boote westwärts* 41 (only dir.), *Der Strom* 42 (only dir.), *Der ewige Klang* 43 (only dir. and script with Arthur A. Kuhnert), *Die Jahre vergehen* 44 (only dir.), *Meine vier Jungens* 44 (only dir.), *Eine alltägliche Geschichte* 45 (only dir.), *Der Scheiterhaufen* 45 (only dir.), *Vor uns liegt das Leben* 48 (only dir. and script with H A. von der Heyde), *Das Kreuz am Jägersteig* (co-phot. with Erich Küchler); *Kinder, Mütter und ein General; Der Fischer vom Heiligensee* (co-phot. with Küchler), *Das Forsthaus in Tirol, Das Erbe vom Pruggerhof, Wenn wir alle Engel wären, Die fröhliche Wallfahrt, Die fidelen Detektive, Hände weg von Frauen.*

310 **RITTER, KARL** (1888-   ). B: Würzburg. Director and scriptwriter. Up to 1919: officer, then painter and designer. 1925: enters films as public relations man for Südfilm and Emelka. From 1932: director and production manager for Ufa; a post he held until 1945. Nazi. From 1948: in Argentina, head of Eos-Film Mendoza and director of films there. 1954: returns to Germany. One of the most vaunted directors during the Nazi period who managed to introduce a certain artistic sense into films of purely political and propaganda interest.

Films: *Das Spreewaldmädel* (only co-scripted with Victor Abel). Then sound: *Weiberregiment* 36, *Verräter* 36, *Unternehmen Michael* 37 (also script with Wieman and Fred Hildenbrand), *Urlaub auf Ehrenwort* 37, *Patrioten* 37 (also script with Felix Lützkendorf and Philip Lothar Mayring), *Pour le mérite* 38 (also script with Hildenbrand), *Legion Condor* 39 (also script with Lützkendorf), *Capriccio* 39, *Die Hochzeitsreise* 39 (also script with Lützkendorf), *Bal paré* 40 (also script with Lützkendorf), *Kadetten* 41 (also script with Lützkendorf), *Ueber alles in der Welt* 41 (also script with Lützkendorf), *Stukas* 41 (also script with Lützkendorf), *G.P.U.* 42 (also script with

Lützkendorf and Andrews Engelmann), *Besatzung Dora* 43 (also script with Hildenbrand), *Sommernächte* 44, *Das Leben geht weiter* (only co-scripted), *Ball der Nationen* 54, *Staatsanwältin Corda* 54.

311 **ROBERTS, RALPH ARTHUR** (1884 -1940). B: Meerane (Saxony). D: Berlin. Actor, scriptwriter and director. RN: Robert Arthur Schönherr. Stage and musical training in Dresden, Theatres: Residenz-Theater Wiesbaden, Breslau, Thalia-Theater Hamburg. 1914-1918: soldier (officer), then to Berlin in various theatres. 1928: owner of Theater in der Behrenstrasse. Author of comedies and scripts for vaudeville. Plays comic roles in many films. A very popular actor and singer. Also scripted and directed films. Composer of famous song "Auf der Reeperbahn nachts um halb eins . . ."

Films (incomplete): *Erniedrigte und Beleidigte, Sodoms Ende, Die Buddenbrooks, Der Frauenkönig, Lord Reginalds Derbyritt, Die Blumenfrau vom Potsdamer Platz, Elegantes Pack, Die dritte Eskadron, Die Tragödie eines Verlorenen, Einbruch, Fürst oder Clown, Meine Tante − Deine Tante, Ein rheinisches Mädchen beim rheinischen Wein, Ein schwerer Fall, Der Biberpelz, Heut tanzt Mariett, Der Ladenprinz, Lotte, Marys grosses Geheimnis, Moral, Der Raub der Sabinerinnen, Die tolle Komptesse, Anschluss um Mitternacht, Polizeispionin 77.* Then sound: *Einbrecher, Zwei Krawatten, Zweimal Hochzeit, Die zärtlichen Verwandten, Komm' zu mir zum Rendezvous, Der schönste Mann im Staate, Dienst ist Dienst, Die spanische Fliege, Die Firma heiratet, Der ungetreue Eckehart, Der wahre Jakob, Jeder fragt nach Erika, Gesangverein Sorgenfrei; Zu Befehl, Herr Unteroffizier; Lügen auf Rügen, So'n Windhund, Keine Feier ohne Meyer, Hurra − ein Junge!, Ihre Majestät die Liebe, Eine Nacht im Paradies, Der Frechdachs, Die Unschuld vom Lande, Keine Angst vor Liebe, Es war einmal ein Musikus, Es gibt nur eine Liebe, Ein Lied für Dich, Spiel mit dem Feuer* 34 (also dir. and script with Herbert B. Fredersdorf), *Zigeunerblut, Abenteuer im Südexpress, Alte Kameraden; Schön ist es, verliebt zu sein; Meine Frau, die Schützenkönigin; Da stimmt was nicht, Der kühne Schwimmer, Es tut sich was um Mitternacht, Der Schrecken vom Heidekrug, Punks kommt aus Amerika, Hilde Petersen postlagernd, Mach' mich glücklich, Der geheimnisvolle Mister X, Soldaten − Kameraden, Engel mit kleinen Fehlern, Der verkannte Lebensmann; Husaren, heraus; Wenn Du eine Schwiegermutter hast; Meine Frau, die Perle; Heiratsinstitut Ida & Co., Mädchen für alles, Tanz auf dem Vulkan, Der Maulkorb, Diskretion − Ehrensache, Ehe in Dosen, Das Glück wohnt nebenan, Meine Tante − Deine Tante* (also script with Kurt Bortfeldt), *Wie konntest Du, Veronika* (also idea with Erich Ebermayer), *Meine Tochter tut das nicht.*

312 **ROBISON, ARTHUR (ROBINSON)** (1888-1935). B: Chicago. D: Berlin? Director. German parents of Israelite descent. Studied at Munich University. Doctor of Medicine. Actor in theatres in Switzerland and Germany. Enters cinema in 1914 as literary manager, scriptwriter and director. 1922: directs *Schatten*, one of the most important films of the "expressionism" (q.v.) genre, and also one of the first films without captions.

Films (incomplete): *Nacht des Grauens* 16, *Schatten* 23 (also co-scripted with Rudolf Schneider), *Zwischen Abend und Morgen* 23 (also script), *Pietro, der Korsar* 24 (also script), *Manon Lescaut* 26 (also script), *Der letzte Walzer* 27 (also co-scripted with Alice Miller), *Looping the Loop* 28 (also co-scripted with Robert Liebmann). Then sound: *Mordprozess Mary Dugan* 31, *Des jungen Dessauers grosse Liebe* 33, *Fürst Woronzeff* 34, *Mach' mich glücklich* 35, *Der Student von Prag* 35.

313 **RÖHRIG, WALTER** (18 -19). Set designer. At first painter for theatre sets in Zurich. Enters cinema circa 1918 with Warm (q.v.). Gains reputation after his work on *Das Kabinett des Dr. Caligari* with Warm and Reimann (both q.v.). *See also* "Expressionism," Lang and Murnau. Works for a long time with Robert Herlth (q.v.). From 1936 onwards: mainly entertainment films under the Nazi regime.

Films: *Das Kabinett des Dr. Caligari* (in collab.), *Die Pest in Florenz* (in collab. with Jaffé. Reimann and Warm); *Der Golem, wie er in die Welt kam* (in collab.). Films from 1920 to 1936 *see* Robert Herlth. Then: *Urlaub auf Ehrenwort, Patrioten, Unternehmen Michael, Capriccio, Pour le mérite, Die Hochzeitsreise, Bal paré, Das Herz einer Königin, Ueber alles in der Welt, Heimkehr, Rembrandt*.

314 **RÖKK, MARIKA** (1913-). B: Cairo. Actress. Ballet training in Budapest, and appears at the age of nine in variety shows. As a member of a revue troupe she visits the U.S.A. and tours Europe. Later acts and sings in operetta. Speech training and then in theatres in Budapest, where she is discovered for films. Many of her films were made under the direction of her first husband Georg Jacoby (1890-1965), one of the busiest directors in the German cinema.

Films: *Leichte Kavallerie, Heisses Blut; Und Du, mein Schatz, fährst mit; Der Bettelstudent, Gasparone, Karussell, Eine Nacht im Mai; Hallo, Janine; Es war eine rauschende Ballnacht, Kora Terry, Wunschkonzert, Tanz mit dem Kaiser, Frauen sind doch besser Diplomaten, Hab' mich lieb, Die Frau meiner Träume, Fregola, Das Kind der Donau, Sensation in San Remo, Die Csardasfürstin, Maske in Blau, Die geschiedene Frau, Nachts im grünen Kakadu, Bühne frei für Marika, Die Nacht vor der Premiere; Mein Mann, das Wirtschaftswunder; Die Fledermaus, Hochzeitsnacht im Paradies*.

315 **RÜHMANN, HEINZ** (1902-). B: Essen. Actor and director. Stage training in Munich. Theatres: Breslau, Hannover, Bremen, Schauspielhaus Munich (1923-1925). 1926-1932: Deutsches Theater Berlin under Reinhardt (q.v.) where he was first spotted for films. 1938-1945: Staatstheater Berlin. After 1945: guest appearances and tours. 1955: Renaissance-Theater Berlin, and since 1960 also with Burgtheater Vienna. In his early films he appeared as a comic, playing the innocent little man, but later he developed into a considerable character actor (chiefly after 1950). One of the busiest actors in the German industry and a major box-office draw. Has also produced and directed films.

Films: *Das deutsche Mutterherz, Das Mädchen mit den fünf Nullen*. Then sound: *Die Drei von der Tankstelle, Einbrecher, Der brave Sünder, Bomben auf Monte Carlo; Meine Frau, die Hochstaplerin; Man braucht kein Geld; Der Mann, der seinen Mörder sucht; Der Stolz der 3. Kompanie, Es wird schon wieder besser, Strich durch die Rechnung, Drei blaue Jungs – ein blondes Mädel, Lachende Erben, Ich und die Kaiserin, Es gibt nur eine Liebe, Heimkehr ins Glück, Die Finanzen des Grossherzogs, So ein Flegel, Pipin der Kurze, Heinz im Mond, Ein Walzer für Dich, Frasquita, Der Himmel auf Erden, Der Aussenseiter, Eva, Wer wagt – gewinnt!, Ungeküsst soll man nicht schlafen geh'n, Wenn wir alle Engel wären, Allotria, Der Mustergatte; Der Mann, von dem man spricht; Der Mann, der Sherlock Holmes war; Lumpazivagabundus; Nanu, Sie kennen Korff noch nicht?, Die Umwege des schönen Karl, Lauter Lügen* 38 (only dir.), *Fünf Millionen suchen einen Erben, Paradies der Junggesellen, Hurra! Ich bin Papa; Der Florentiner Hut, 13 Stühle, Kleider machen Leute, Lauter Liebe* 40 (only dir.), *Wunschkonzert, Der Gasmann, Hauptsache glücklich; Quax, der Bruchpilot; Ich vertraue Dir meine Frau an, Sophienlund* 43 (only dir.), *Die Feuerzangenbowle, Der Engel mit dem Saitenspiel* 44 (only dir.), *Quax in Fahrt, Sag' die Wahrheit, Der Herr vom andern Stern, Die kupferne Hochzeit* 48 (only dir.), *Das Geheimnis der roten Katze, Ich mach' Dich glücklich, Das kann jedem passieren, Wir werden das Kind schon schaukeln, Keine Angst vor grossen Tieren,*

Briefträger Müller 53 (also dir. co John Reinhardt), *Auf der Reeperbahn nachts um halb eins, Zwischenlandung in Paris, Wenn der Vater mit dem Sohne, Charley's Tante, Der Hauptmann von Köpenick, Das Sonntagskind, Vater sein dagegen sehr, Es geschah am hellichten Tage, Der eiserne Gustav, Der Pauker, Ein Mann geht durch die Wand, Menschen im Hotel, Der Jugendrichter, Mein Schulfreund, Der brave Soldat Schwejk, Das schwarze Schaf, Der Lügner, Er kann's nicht lassen; Max, der Taschendieb; Das Haus in Montevideo, Meine Tochter und ich; Vorsicht, Mister Dodd; Dr. med. Hiob Prätorius, Geld oder Leben, Das Liebeskarussell (iii), Grieche sucht Griechin, Hokuspokus — oder wie lasse ich meinen Mann verschwinden, Maigret und sein grösster Fall, Die Abenteuer des Kardinal Braun, Die Ente klingelt um ½ 8.*

316 RUNKEHL, KARLA (1930-   ). B: Stettin. Actress. Stage training in Berlin. Since 1952: short periods with Deutsches Theater East Berlin. Acted for TV and radio.

Films: *Saure Wochen — frohe Feste, Corinna Schmidt, Frauenschicksale, Hexen, Ernst Thälmann — Sohn seiner Klasse, Ernst Thälmann — Führer seiner Klasse, Genesung, Schlösser und Katen, Nur eine Frau,* *Maibowle, Einer von uns, Aerzte, Urlaub ohne Dich, Die Entdeckungen des Julian Böll, Die aus der 12 b, Mord ohne Sühne; Ach, du fröhliche; Daniel und der Weltmeister, Igelfreundschaft.*

317 RUTTMANN,   WALTER (1887-1941). B: Frankfurt. D: Berlin. Director, director of photography, also photographer. Precocious musical talent. Lieutenant in First Word War on Eastern Front. Studied architecture in Zurich and Munich, trained as a painter under Angelo Jank. Successful poster designer. 1918: turns to abstract films. From 1927: documentarist. Adviser to Leni Riefenstahl (q.v.) on *Olympia* and collaborated with Lotte Reiniger on *Die Abenteuer des Prinzen Achmed.* Worked with Piscator.

Films: *Die tönende Welle* 21 (experimental sound film), *Opus I, II, III* and *IV* 21-24 *(avantgarde* experiments, q.v.), *Der Falkentraum* 24 (insert for *Die Nibelungen), Berlin — Die Symphonie einer Grosstadt* 27 (feature documentary), *Deutscher Rundfunk* 28, *Feind im Blut* 31 (for Praesens-Film in Berlin in collab. with Vsevolod Pudovkin), *Arbeit macht frei* 33 (also called Stahl), *Altgermanische Bauernkultur* 34, *Metall des Himmels* 34, *Kleiner Film einer grossen Stadt: Düsseldorf* 35, *Stuttgart, Grosstadt zwischen Wald und Reben* 35, *Schiff in Not* 36, *Mannesmann* 37, *Acciaio* 38 (feature film in Italy), *Hamburg — Weltstrasse, Welthafen* 38, *Im Zeichen des Vertrauens* 38, *Im Dienste der Menschlichkeit* 38, *Henkel, ein deutsches Werk in seiner Arbeit* 38, *Die deutsche Waffenschmiede* 40, *Deutsche Panzer* 40, *Aberglaube* 40.

318 RYE, STELLAN (1880-1914). B: Randers or Copenhagen. D: in a French war hospital. Director and scriptwriter. 1912: stage director in Copenhagen. Enters films as a scriptwriter, and then to Berlin. Scripts and directs many important films (especially with Paul Wegener, q.v.).

Films: *Bedingung: kein Anhang* 13, *Sommernachtstraum* 13, *Der Student von Prag* 13, *Die Verführte* 13 (artistic collab. Carl Ludwig Schleich), *Die Augen des Ole Brandes* 14 (co-dir.), *Erlenkönigs Tochter* 14, *Evintrude, die Geschichte eines Abenteurers* 14 (co-dir., co-scripted), *Das Haus ohne*

A frame reproduction from Ruttmann's BERLIN – DIE SYMPHONIE EINER GROSSTADT

Fenster und Türen 14, *Serenissimus lernt Tango* 14, *Peter Schlemihl* 15.

319 **SAGAN, LEONTINE** (1889-   ). B: Austria. Director. RN: Leontine Schlesinger. 1910: to Johannesburg, married to Dr. Victor Fleischer. To Berlin as a pupil of Reinhardt (q.v.). Actress and director at theatres in Dresden, Vienna, Frankfurt and Berlin. Became stage director thanks to Richard Weichert. Directed one film in Germany (supervised by Carl Froelich, q.v.). 1932: to England, where she directs another film *Men of Tomorrow*. Part time activity at the Korda studios, and then returns to the theatre. 1939-1945: intensive theatre work in South Africa. Co-founder of the National Theatre in Johannesburg.

Film: *Mädchen in Uniform* 31.

320 **SALMONOVA, LYDA** (1889-1968). B and D: Prague. Actress. Dancer at first, and then prominent partnership with Paul Wegener (q.v.) to whom she was married for many years.

Films (incomplete): *Die Löwenbraut, Sumurun, Der Student von Praag, Die Verführte; Evintrude, die Geschichte eines Abenteurers; Der Golem, Die ideale Gattin, Rübezahls Hochzeit, Der Rattenfänger von Hameln, Der Yoghi, Der Golem und die Tänzerin, Hans Trutz im Schlaraffenland, Der fremde Fürst, Der Galeerensträfling; Der Golem, wie er in die Welt kam; Steuermann Holck, Irrende Seelen, Die Tänzerin Barberina, Der verlorene Schatten, Das Weib des Pharao, Herzog Ferrantes Ende, Lukrezia Borgia, Monna Vanna.*

321 SANDROCK, ADELE (1864-1937).
B: Rotterdam. D: Berlin. Actress. Stage
training with her mother. Theatres: Berlin
(first appearance in 1878),Meiningen, Riga,
Budapest, Moscow, Volkstheater Vienna
(1895-1898), Deutsches Theater Berlin
(1905-1910). Many guest appearances. Well
known for her portrayal of grumbling old
ladies in films of the Twenties and Thirties.
Famous stage actress, who entered films
relatively late in her career.

Films (incomplete): *Marianne, ein Weib
aus dem Volke; Der Galeerensträfling, Gebannt und erlöst, Malaria, Brandherd, Das
goldene Netz, Patience, Grausige Nächte;
Marriza, genannt die Schmugglermadonna;
Der Roman der Christine von Herre, Die
Tänzerin Barberina, Absturz, Dr. Mabuse
der Spieler, Kinder der Finsternis, Lukrezia
Borgia, Die Tänzerin Novarro, Der Hof
ohne Lachen, Die Liebe einer Königin, Die
Magyarenfürstin, Die Fahrt ins Verderben,
Helena, Die Radio-Heirat, Die Schmetter-
lingsschlacht, Aschermittwoch, Das Mäd-
chen mit der Protektion, Deutsche Herzen
am deutschen Rhein, Nixchen; Trude, die
Sechzehnjährige; Die Waise von Lowood,
Arme kleine Sif, Drei Niemandskinder,
Feme, Frühere Verhältnisse, Die Geliebte,
Der Himmel auf Erden, Im Luxuszug, Kö-
nigin Luise, Die leichte Isabell, Das Mäd-
chen mit den fünf Nullen, Ein rheinisches
Mädchen beim rheinischen Wein, Die rol-
lende Kugel, Das Schicksal einer Nacht, Die
Stadt der tausend Freuden, Deutsche Frauen
– Deutsche Treue, Kaczmarek, Der Ladenprinz, Leontines Ehemänner, Lotte, Mary
Lou, Sechs Mädchen suchen Nachtquartier,
Serenissimus und die letzte Jungfrau, Die
Zirkusprinzessin, Aufruhr im Junggesellenheim, Die Drei um Edith, Der Erzieher meiner Tochter, Fräulein Else, Katherina Knie,
Verirrte Jugend, Donauwalzer, Der Nächste,
bitte.* Then sound: *Die grosse Sehnsucht, Seitensprünge, 1000 Worte deutsch, Die zärtlichen Verwandten, Skandal um Eva, Ein
Walzer im Schlafcoupé, Eine Freundin so goldig wie Du, Strohwitwer, Walzerparadies,
Der Kongress tanzt, Keine Feier ohne Meyer,
Ihre Majestät die Liebe, Jeder fragt nach Erika, Die schwebende Jungfrau, Der Schrecken
der Garnison, Die Schlacht von Bademünde, Der verjüngte Adolar, Die Försterchristl,
Die Königin einer Nacht, Ballhaus goldener*

*Engel; Liebe, Scherz und Ernst; Liebe auf
den ersten Ton, Das schöne Abenteuer, Der
Sieger, Ein steinreicher Mann; Goldblondes
Mädchen, ich schenk Dir mein Herz; Der
grosse Bluff, Der tolle Bomberg, Der verliebte Blasekopp, Ein toller Einfall, Kaiserwalzer, Friederike, Einmal möcht' ich keine
Sorgen haben, Eine Frau wie Du, Die Tochter des Regiments, Morgenrot, Kleines Mädel – grosses Glück, Glückliche Reise, Zigeunerblut, Petersburger Nächte, Ich sehne
mich nach Dir, Alles hört auf mein Kommando, Da stimmt was nicht, Der Fall
Brenken, Der Flüchtling aus Chikago, Ich
sing' mich in Dein Herz hinein, Gern hab'
ich die Frau'n geküsst, Ein Walzer für Dich,
Die Töchter Ihrer Exzellenz, Der Herr ohne
Wohnun, Der Herr Senator, Der letzte Walzer, Die englische Heirat, Mach' mich glücklich, Knox und die lustigen Vagabunden,
Kirschen in Nachbars Garten, Es waren
zwei Junggesellen, Eva, Ich liebe alle Frau-
en, Frühjahrsparade, Alle Tage ist kein
Sonntag, Amphitryon, Der blaue Diamant,
Ein Teufelskerl, Ein falscher Fuffziger, Der
Kampf mit dem Drachen, Der Gefangene
des Königs, Der Himmel auf Erden, Der
Favorit der Kaiserin, Der schüchterne Ca-
sanova, Die grosse und die kleine Welt,
Skandal um die Fledermaus, Engel mit klei-*

nen Fehlern, Die Puppenfee, Flitterwochen, Rendezvous in Wien.

322 SCHAAF, JOHANNES (1933-   ). B: Stuttgart. Director. Spent his early life in Königsberg (Kalingrad) and Stuttgart, studied medicine in Tübingen and Berlin.

Asst. director at theatres in Stuttgart, Ulm, Bremen and Hamburg. Since 1963: freelance director for stage and TV. First film in 1967. *See also* Junger deutscher Film, Films for TV include: *Ein ungebetener Gast 63, Hotel Iphigenie 64, Im Schatten einer Grosstadt 65, Die Gegenprobe 65, Grosse Liebe 66, Der Mann aus dem Bootshaus 67, Lebeck 67.* Acted in *Alle Jahre wieder, Erste Liebe.* Feature film: *Tätowierung 67.*

323 SCHAMONI, PETER (1934-   ). B: Berlin. Producer and director. Second son of director Victor Schamoni; his elder brother Victor (b. 1932) works as a cameraman for TV, his younger brothers are Thomas (b. 1936, director for TV) and Ulrich (b. 1939), who started with shorts (*Hollywood in Deblatschka Pescara 65, Lockenköpfchen oder Wie manipuliert man die Wirklichkeit 67, Geist und ein wenig Glück 65* for TV and *Der Kahle Sänger 67* for TV

as a longer version of *Lockenköpfchen*) and then made feature films *Es 65, Alle Jahre wieder 67* and *Quartett im Bett 68.* Peter Schamoni studied the history of art, theatre and literature in Münster and Munich, stage training in Munich, asst. director at Bayerisches Staatstheater. Since 1957 he has directed and produced short films, 1966: feature film *début.* Mainly known as a producer of some successful films. *See also* Junger deutscher Film.

Work in collaboration: *Tote Saison 61* (co-scripted), *Die Gartenzwerge 61* (dir. Wolfgang Urchs, co-scripted), *Der Brief* (actor). Short films: *Moskau 1957 57, Jazz Kreml 57, Osterspaziergang 59, Brutalität in Stein 59* (with Kluge, q.v.), *Alles für den Hund 59, Moskau ruft 59* (compilation material from *Moskau 1957* and *Jazz im Kreml*), *Missbraucht 59, Mississippi-Illusion 60, Ein Nachmittag für uns 61* (new version of earlier short), *Jugend photographiert 61* (also called *Jugend sieht sich selbst*), *Schach dem Zufall 61, Bodega Bohemia 62, Die Teutonen kommen 62, Die Ewigkeit von gestern 63* (new version of *Brutalität in Stein*), *Der Topf 63* (produced and edited by Schamoni, directed by Kristl, q.v.), *Max Ernst – Entdeckungsfahrten ins Unbewusste 64, So zwitschern die Jungen 64, Im Zwinger 64, Die widerrechtliche Ausübung der Astronomie 67* (some of these films were also produced and scripted or co-scripted by Schamoni – *see* entries for Houwer and Wirth). Feature film as director and producer: *Schonzeit für Füchse 66.* Feature films as producer: *Alle Jahre wieder 67, Zur Sache, Schätzchen 67, Quartett im Bett 68, Deine Zärtlichkeiten 69* (co-prod. and dir.).

324 SCHELL, MARIA (GRIT) (1926-   ). B: Vienna. Actress. RN: Margarete Schell. Daughter of Swiss author Hermann Ferdinand Schell and Viennese actress Margarete von Noé, sister of Maximilian Schell (q.v.) and Carl H. Schell (b. 1928) and Immaculata (Immy) Schell. At first secretary. Stage training in Zurich. *Début* in Swiss films in 1942 with *Steibruch* and in 1943 with *Maturareise* (both directed by Sigfrit Steiner). Acted at theatres in Zurich and Basle. 1945: Theater in der Josefstadt Vienna. The second phase of her film career began in Austria in 1948, and launched her international reputation. Theatres: Berlin, Kammerspiele Munich, Salzburg Festival. Since 1963: theatre tours. Films in Austria, Germany, England, France, Italy and U.S.A. Well known for her gay, sincere and forthright performances.

Films: *Die letzte Nacht, Der Engel mit der Posaune, Maresi, Es kommt ein Tag, Dr. Holl, Bis wir uns wiederseh'n, Der träumende Mund, Solange Du da bist, Tagebuch einer Verliebten, Die letzte Brücke, Herr über Leben und Tod, Die Ratten, Liebe, Rose Bernd, Der Schinderhannes, Raubfischer in Hellas, Das Riesenrad, Ich bin auch nur eine Frau, Zwei Whisky und ein Sofa.*

325 **SCHELL, MAXIMILIAN** (1930-   ). B: Vienna. Actor. Brother of Maria Schell (q.v.). Studied languages and theatrical science in Zurich and Munich (where he also studied music). Theatres: Basle (1952-1953), Essen (1953-1954), Bonn (1954-1955), Lübeck, Kammerspiele Munich, Berlin. Many tours. Enters film thanks to director Laszlo Benedek with *Kinder, Mütter und ein General.* From 1957: international career. Wins Academy Award in 1961 for his performance in *Judgement at Nuremburg.* Al-

ways faithful to the stage, and has acted in and directed many controversial productions.

Films: *Kinder, Mütter und ein General; Der 20. Juli, Reifende Jugend, Ein Mädchen aus Flandern, Die Ehe des Dr. med. Danwitz, Ein Herz kehrt heim, Die Letzten werden die Ersten sein, Heidi kehrt heim, Das Schloss* (also co-prod. with Rudolf Noelte and Alfa), *Erste Liebe 69* (prod. with Barry Levinson), dir., co-script and acted).

326 **SCHEUMANN, GERHARD** (1930-   ). B: Ortelsburg. Scriptwriter and director. At first journalist, then commentator and editor at East German Radio. Works in close collaboration with Walter Haynowski (q.v.). Member extraordinary of the Akademie der Künste in Berlin. State Award. For films *see* Heynowski.

327 **SCHLETTOW, HANS ADALBERT (VON)** (1888-1945). B: Frankfurt. D: Berlin. Actor. RN: Droescher. 1908: stage *début.* Theatres include Frankfurt, Stuttgart, Mannheim and Berlin. 1919: to films with some roles in films for Fritz Lang (q.v.). A precise and very persuasive talent who developed into a fine character actor during the sound period. 1923: acted in D. W. Griffith's *Isn't Life Wonderful.*

Films: *Schatten des Glücks* (date unobtainable but certainly made prior to 1923), *Wenn das Herz in Hass erglüht, Der breite Weg, Komptesse Doddy, Der Tod aus dem Osten, Die weissen Rosen von Ravensburg, Algol, Föhn, Maria Tudor, Am roten Kliff, Am Webstuhl der Zeit, Die Frauen vom Gnadenstein, Tobias Buntschuh, Don Juan, Dr. Mabuse der Spieler, Die Finsternis ist ihr Eigentum, Gespenster, Das Liebesnest, Die Schatten jener Nacht, Der Todesreigen, Die Fahrt ins Verderben, Malva, Die Nibelungen, So ist das Leben, Winterstürme, Friesenblut, Im Namen des Kaisers, Schiff in Not, Wenn die Liebe nicht wär'!, Brennende Grenze, Deutsche Herzen am deutschen Rhein, Die Eule, Die Flammen lügen, In Treu stark, Die letzte Droschke von Berlin, Sein grosser Fall, Spitzen, Die Frauengasse von Algier, Die Frau mit dem Weltrekord, Das gefährliche Alter, Kleinstadtsünder, Klettermaxe, Königin Luise, Der letzte Walzer; Mein Heidelberg, ich kann*

Dich nicht vergessen; Schuldig, Die Sieb-
zehnjährigen, Song, Wenn die Mutter und
die Tochter ..., Wolga-Wolga, Asphalt,
Diane, Heilige oder Dirne, Das Recht der
Ungeborenen, Das Weib am Kreuze, Es
kommt alle Tage vor ... Then sound: *Das*
Donkosakenlied, Troika, Der unsterbliche
Lump, Die grosse Sehnsucht, Ein Mädel auf
der Reeperbahn, Bockbierfest, Der Schle-
mihl, Chauffeur Antoinette, Mitternachts-
liebe, Die nackte Wahrheit, Kennst Du das
Land, Gefahren der Liebe, An heiligen Was-
sern, Marschall Vorwärts, Der tolle Bom-
berg; Ja, toll ist die Soldatenliebe; Geheim-
nis des blauen Zimmers; Du bist entzückend,
Rosmarie!; Ein gewisser Herr Gran, Der
Choral von Leuthen, Eine Nacht im Forst-
haus, Der Jäger aus Kurpfalz, Flüchtlinge,
Der Page vom Dalmasse-Hottel, Zimmer-
mädchen ... dreimal klingeln, Ferien vom
Ich, Konjunkturritter, Schloss Hubertus,
Ich sing' mich in Dein Herz hinein, Ein
Mädchen mit Prokura, Regine, Alte Kame-
raden; Nur nicht weich werden, Susanne!;
Liebesleute, Familie Schimek, Hundert Tage,
Liselotte von der Pfalz, Leichte Kavallerie,
Der Jäger von Fall, Schloss Vogelöd, Der
Favorit der Kaiserin, Stjenka Rasin, Kater
Lampe, Die gelbe Flagge, Das schöne Fräu-
lein Schragg, Das Schweigen im Walde,
Gastspiel im Paradies, Mit versiegelter Or-
der; Kleiner Mann, ganz gross; Andalusi-
sche Nächte, Yvette, War es der im 3.
Stock?, Scheidungsreise, Frauen für Golden
Hill, Schneider Wibbel, Anton der Letzte,
Grenzfeuer, Kongo-Express, Menschen vom
Varieté, Waldrausch, Die Rothschilds, Zwi-
schen Hamburg und Haiti, Tiergarten Süd-
amerika (speaker), *Die Geierwally, Links*
der Isar – rechts der Spree; Kinder, wie die
Zeit vergeht; Wunschkonzert, Ohm Krüger,
Heimaterde, Die grosse Nummer, Viel Lärm
um Nixi, Gefährtin meines Sommers; War-
um lügst Du, Elisabeth?, Melusine, Jugend-
liebe, Ein Mann gehört ins Haus, Die
Kreuzlschreiber.

328 SCHLÖNDORFF, VOLKER (1939-

). B: Wiesbaden. Director. Studied
mostly in Paris, entered IDHEC. Asst. director to Louis Malle, Alain Resnais and Jean-
Pierre Melville. Reports for TV on Algeria
and Vietnam. His first short on exiled
French people in Frankfurt was refused a

release. Important figure of *Junger deut-*
scher Film (q.v.).

Films: *Wen kümmert's* 60 (short), *Der*
junge Törless 66 (also script), *Mord und*
Totschlag 67 (also script with Gregor von
Rezzori and Niklas Frank), *Michael Kohl-*
haas – Der Rebell 69 (also co-script).

329 SCHMIDT-GENTNER, WILLY

(1894-1964). B: Neustadt/Thüringen. D:
Vienna. Composer. Studied music with Max
Reger. From 1918: conductor at many of
the great cinemas in Berlin (including Ufa-
Palast am Zoo, Alhambra and Capitol).
Composed music for many silent films.
Head of the music departments of Tobis and
Ufa during the silent period. 1933: German
head of Mondial-Film Vienna. Also direct-
ed films during this period.

Films: *Wenn Du einmal Dein Herz ver-*
schenkst (in collab. with Willi Rosen), *Cyan-*
kali, Aschermittwoch, Die heiligen drei
Brunnen, Rosenmontag, Dolly macht Kar-
riere (in collab. with Rudolf Nelson and
Alfred Strasser), *Die blonde Nachtigall* (in
collab. with Willi Kollo and Hans J. Salter),
Das Flötenkonzert von Sanssouci, Der weis-
se Teufel, Liebling der Götter (in collab.
with Karl M. May), *Hokuspokus* (in collab.

with Robert Stolz), *Die Jugendgeliebte, Ein Walzer im Schlafcoupé, Jeder fragt nach Erika* (in collab. with Grete Walter, Michael Eisemann and Paul Hühn), *... und das ist die Hauptsache* (in collab. with Walter Jurmann), *Schneider Wibbel, Ihre Majestät die Liebe* (in collab. with Jurmann), *Das Lied einer Nacht* (in collab. with Mischa Spoliansky), *Eine Stadt steht Kopf* (in collab. with Spoliansky), *Marschall Vorwärts, Zwei in einem Auto* (with Bruno Granichstaedten), *Tausend für eine Nacht* (in collab. with Otto Stransky), *Sehnsucht 202* (in collab. with Richard Fall), *Leise flehen meine Lieder, Das hässliche Mädchen, Die kalte Mamsell* (in collab. with Gustav Althoff), *Ihre Durchlaucht, die Verkäuferin* (in collab. with Ralph Benatzky), *Ein Lied für Dich* (in collab. with Kaper and Jurmann), *Maskerade, Frasquita* (in collab. with Franz Lehar), *G'schichten aus dem Wienerwald, Hohe Schule, Lockspitzel Asew* (in collab. with Gerd von Stetten), *... nur ein Komödiant, Der Kosak und die Nachtigall, Die ganze Welt dreht sich um Liebe* (in collab with Lehar), *Episode, Ein Teufelskerl, Die Pompadour 35* (co-dir.), *Die Leuchter des Kaisers, Eva* (in collab. with Lehar), *Blutsbrüder, Meine Tochter ist der Peter, Blumen aus Nizza* (in collab. with Denes von Buday), *In Sonnenschein* (in collab. with Buday), *Rendenzvous in Wien, Peter im Schnee, Liebling der Matrosen, Der Weg des Herzens 37* (also dir.), *Premiere* (in collab. with Buday and Fenyes Szabolcs), *Konzert in Tirol, Prinzessin Sissy, Hotel Sacher, Mutterliebe, Aufruhr in Damaskus, Der Postmeister, Operette, Krambambuli, Ein Leben lang, Der liebe Augustin, Dreimal Hochzeit, Heimkehr, Brüderlein fein* (in collab. with Alexander Steinbrecher), *Wiener Blut, Wien 1910, Am Rande der Welt, Späte Liebe, Lache Bajazzo, Der gebieterische Ruf, Schrammeln, Das Herz muss schweigen, Ein Blick zurück, Wie ein Dieb in der Nacht, Wiener Mädeln* (in collab. with Karl von Pauspertl), *Die Frau am Wege, Praterbuben, Die Welt dreht sich verkehrt, Wintermelodien, Erde, Singende Engel, Zyankali, Alles Lüge, Der Engel mit der Posaune, Fregola* (in collab. with Theo Nordhaus), *Hexen, Es lebe das Leben, Wiener Mädel, Um eine Nasenlänge, Der Seelenbräu, Schuss durchs Fenster, Prämien auf den Tod, Cordula* (in collab. with Joseph Marx and Heinz Sandauer), *Erzherzog Johanns grosse Liebe, Gruss und Kuss aus der Wachau, Wiener Walzer, Der Verlorene, Wenn die Abendglocken läuten, Verlorene Melodie, Mein Herz darfst Du nicht fragen, Der fröhliche Weinberg, Am Brunnen vor dem Tore, Von der Liebe reden wir später, Rose von Stambul* (arr.), *Wenn am Sonntagabend die Dorfmusik spielt, Saison in Salzburg, Hannerl* (in collab. with Grothe, Joseph Beyer, Anton Profes and Friedrich Schröder), *Rummelplatz der Liebe, Dieses kleine Lied bleibt bei Dir, Der treue Husar, Wenn Du noch eine Mutter hast...*, *Emil und die Detektive, Der Weg in die Vergangenheit, Spionage, Heimatland* (in collab. with Nico Dostal), *Kronprinz Rudolfs letzte Liebe.*

330 **SCHMITZ, SYBILLE** (1909-1955). B: Düren. D: Munich (suicide). Actress. After her stage training in Cologne, she went immediately to Berlin, where she worked with Reinhardt (q.v.) and his Deutsches Theater. 1929: first films. Her best part was probably in 1931 for Dreyer's *Vampyr*. Often in films not worthy of her talent, and extraordinary powers of expression. Gradually she became more and more depressed by her career and the lack of inspiring scripts and committed suicide in Munich.

Films: *Der Ueberfall, Tagebuch einer Verlorenen.* Then sound: *Vampyr, F.P. 1 antwortet nicht, Rivalen der Luft, Musik im Blut, Abschiedswalzer, Der Herr der Welt, Stradivari, Ein idealer Gatte, Punks kommt aus Amerika, Oberwachtmeister Schwenke, Ich war Jack Mortimer, Wenn die Musik nicht wär', Die Leuchter des Kaisers, Die Unbekannte, Fährmann Maria, Die Kronzeugin, Signal in der Nacht, Tanz auf dem Vulkan, Die Umwege des schönen Karl, Hotel Sacher, Die Frau ohne Vergangenheit; Trenck, der Pandur; Wetterleuchten um Barbara, Clarissa, Vom Schicksal verweht, Titanic, Die Hochstaplerin, Das Leben ruft, Zwischen Gestern . und Morgen, Die letzte Nacht, Die Lüge, Der Fall Rabanser, Kronjuwelen, Sensation im Savoy, Illusion in Moll.*

331 **SCHNEEBERGER, HANS** (1895-). B: Brandberg im Zillertal (Tyrol). Director of photography. Studied architec-

ture. With Allgeier and Angst (both q.v.) important cameraman from Arnold Fanck's "Freiburger Kameraschule." He shot several of Fanck's mountain and sports films. Also worked for Leni Riefenstahl (q.v.). Since 1922: cameraman on over 120 films in Austria, Germany, Switzerland, Italy and for Alexander Korda in England.

Films (incomplete): *Das Wunder des Schneeschuhs* (only acted), *Der Berg des Schicksals* (co-phot. with Allgeier, Eugen Hamm, Fanck and Herbert Oettel), *Der heilige Berg* (co-phot. with Benitz, Allgeier, Kurt Neubert and Helmar Lerski), *Der grosse Sprung* (co-phot. with Allgeier, Benitz, Angst, Karl Neubert and Charles Métain, also acted). Then sound: *Melodie des Herzens* (co-phot.), *Der blaue Engel* (co-phot.), *Stürme über dem Montblanc* (co-phot.), *Abenteuer im Engadin* (co-phot. with Angst and Heinrich Gärtner), *Das blaue Licht*, *S.O.S. Eisberg* (co-phot. with Angst, Ernst Udet and Franz Schrieck), *Das unsterbliche Lied*, *Rivalen der Luft*, *Wunder des Fliegens* (co-phot. with Heinz von Jaworsky), *Die weisse Hölle vom Piz Palü* (co-phot.), *Die Wildnis stirbt* (co-phot. with Paul Lieberenz). *Das indische Grabmal* and *Der Tiger von Eschnapur* (co-phot. with Ewald Daub and H. O. Schulze), *Frau Sixta*, *Kameraden auf See*, *Narren im Schnee*, *Ziel in den Wolken*, *Leinen aus Irland*, *Unsterblicher Walzer*, *Marguerite: 3*, *Mutterliebe*, *Das Abenteuer geht weiter*, *Der Postmeister*, *Operette*, *Ein Leben lang*, *Brüderlein fein*, *Wien 1910*, *Schicksal*, *Später Liebe*, *Der weisse Traum*, *Die kluge Marianne*, *Die goldene Fessel*, *Freunde*, *Liebe nach Noten*, *Ein Mann gehört ins Haus*, *Glaube an mich*, *Gottes Engel sind überall*, *Königin der Landstrasse*, *Die seltsame Geschichte des Brandner Kaspar*, *Der Seelenbräu* (co-phot. with Sepp Ketterer), *Die Lüge*, *Cordula*, *Gruss und Kuss aus der Wachau*, *Geheimnisvolle Tiefe* (co-phot.), *Das vierte Gebot* (co-phot. with Ketterer), *Verklungenes Wien* (co-phot. with Ketterer); *Hilfe, ich bin unsichtbar*; *Der fidele Bauer*, *Gangsterpremiere*, *Die schöne Tölzerin* (co-phot. with Franz Hofer), *Der Mann aus der Wanne*, *Der fröhliche Weinberg* (co-phot. with Hofer), *Liebeskrieg nach Noten*, *König der Manege*, *Jonny rettet Nebrador*, *Eine Liebesgeschichte*, *Pepi Columbus* (doc.), *Bei Dir war es

immer so schön, *Die Hexe* (co-phot. with Hofer), *Glückliche Reise* (co-phot. with Hofer), *Oberarzt Dr. Solm* (co-phot. with Hofer), *Die Försterbuben*, *San Salvatore*, *Frucht ohne Liebe*, *Heidemelodie*, *Uns gefällt die Welt*, *Jede Nacht in einem andern Bett*, *Romarei – das Mädchen mit den grünen Augen*, *La Paloma*; *Adieu, lebwohl, good bye*; *Der Satan mit den roten Haaren*.

332 SCHNEIDER, MAGDA (1909-   ). B: Augsburg. Actress. Trained as a singer at Konservatorium Augsburg. Dance lessons. *Début* in operetta in Ingolstadt. Enters films thanks to Joe May (q.v.) in 1931. Theatres: Augsburg, Munich, Vienna. First married to actor Wolf Albach-Retty, mother of Romy Schneider.

Films: *Zwei in einem Auto*, *Das Lied einer Nacht*, *Ein bisschen Liebe für Dich*, *Glück über Nacht*, *Sehnsucht 202*, *Das Testament des Cornelius Gulden*, *Fräulein – falsch verbunden*; *Marion, das gehört sich nicht*; *Kind, ich freu' mich auf Dein Kommen*; *Glückliche Reisse*, *Liebelei*, *Fräulein Liselott*, *Ein Mädel wirbelt durch die Welt*, *Ich kenn' Dich nicht und ich liebe Dich*, *G'schichten aus dem Wienerwald*, *Vergissmeinnicht*, *Die Katz im Sack*, *Winternachtstraum*, *Eva*, *Die lustigen Weiber*, *Geheimnis eines alten Hauses*, *Die Puppenfee*, *Rendezvous in Wien*, *Der Weg des Herzens*, *Frauenliebe – Frauenleid*, *Musik für Dich*, *Ihr Leibhusar*, *Die Frau am Scheidewege*, *Frühlingsluft*, *Wer küsst Madeleine?*, *Das Recht auf Liebe*, *Mädchen im Vorzimmer*, *Herzensfreud – Herzensleid*, *Am Abend auf der Heide*, *Liebeskmödie*, *Zwei glückliche Menschen*, *Ein Mann für meine Frau*, *Die himmlichen Bräute*, *Eines Tages*, *Ein Mann gehört ins Haus*, *Die Sterne lügen nicht*, *Wenn der weisse Flieder wieder blüht*, ... *und ewig bleibt die Liebe*, *Mädchenjahre einer Königin*, *Sissi*, *Die Deutschmeister*; *Sissi, die junge Kaiserin*; *Von allen geliebt*; *Sissi, Schicksalsjahre einer Kaiserin*; *Das Dreimäderlhaus*, *Robinson soll nicht sterben*, *Die Halbzarte*, *Morgen beginnt das Leben*.

333 SCHNEIDER, ROMY (1938-   ). B: Vienna. Actress. RN: Rosemarie Albach. Her mother Magda Schneider (q.v.) introduced her to films and she became well

teuer, *Man spricht über Jacqueline, Die Kreutzersonate, Tango Notturno, Die gläserne Kugel, Rote Orchideen, Rätsel um Beate, Maja zwischen zwei Ehen, Der Spieler, Nanette, Ich verweigere die Aussage, Die Frau ohne Vergangenheit, Roman eines Arztes, Einer zuviel an Bord, Ihr grösster Erfolg, Angelika, Herz ohne Heimat, Traummusik; Kopf hoch, Johannes; Vom Schicksal verweht, Man spielt nicht mit der Liebe, Export in Blond, Komplott auf Erlenhof, Eva und der Frauenarzt, Die Schuld des Dr. Homma, Illusion in Moll, Bei Dir war es immer so schön, Bildnis einer Unbekannten, Das Forsthaus im Tirol, Scotland Yard jagt Dr. Mabuse.*

335 SCHRECK, MAX (1879-1936). B: Berlin. D: Munich. Actor. At first business apprenticeship, then stage training Staatstheater Berlin. *Début* in Messeritz, then Speyer. Tours for two years, then theatres in Zittau, Erfurt, Lucerne, Bremen, Gera, Berlin with Reinhardt (q.v.) and Frankfurt. 1919-1922: Kammerspiele Munich. 1922-1926: Staatstheater Berlin. 1926: until his death at Kammerspiele Munich. His best part, and the one for which he is most remembered, was that of the Vampire in *Nos-*

known thanks to the *Sissi* series (starting in 1955, dir. Ernst Marischka). She retired from the screen for a time after starring in a number of box-office failures, and then made a successful comeback in Visconti's episode of *Boccaccio '70.* Since then she has figured in several international productions.

Films: *Wenn der weisse Flieder wieder blüht, Feuerwerk, Mädchenjahre einer Königin, Die Deutschmeister, Der letzte Mann* (55), *Sissi, Kitty und die grosse Welt; Sissi, die junge Kaiserin; Robinson soll nicht sterben, Monpti; Sissi, Schicksalsjahre einer Kaiserin; Scampolo, Mädchen in Uniform, Die Halbzarte, Ein Engel auf Erden, Die schöne Lügnerin, Die Sendung der Lysistrata, Der Prozess, Schornstein Nr. 4.*

334 SCHOENHALS, ALBRECHT (1888-). B: Mannheim. Actor. Studied medicine. Doctor, and practises as such during First World War. 1918: stage training with Eduard von Winterstein (q.v.). Theatres: Freiburg, Halberstadt, Frankfurt, Dortmund, Hamburg, Enters cinema in 1934.

Films: *Fürst Woronzeff, Mazurka, April, April, Stradivari, Warum lügt Fräulein Käthe?, Stützen der Gesellschaft, Boccaccio, Hannerl und ihre Liebhaber, Intermezzo, Arzt aus Leidenschaft, Das grosse Aben-*

feratu. Schreck was married to actress Fanny Normann.

Films (incomplete): *Am Narrenseil, Der Favorit der Königin, Nosferatu – Eine Symphonie des Grauens, Pique Ass, Der Kaufmann von Venedig, Die Strasse; Dudu, ein Menschenschicksal; Die Finanzen des Grossherzogs, Die gefundene Braut, Krieg im Frieden, Der rosa Diamant, Der alte Fritz, Am Rande der Welt, Dona Juana, Luther, Der Sohn der Hagar, Der Kampf der Tertia, Das Mädchen von der Strasse, Moderne Piraten, Rasputins Liebesabenteuer, Die Republik der Backfische, Ritter der Nacht, Serenissimus und die letzte Jungfrau, Wolga-Wolga; Ludwig der Zweite, König von Bayern.* Then sound: *Das Land des Lächelns, Im Banne der Berge, Muss man sich gleich scheiden lassen?, Die Nacht der Versuchung, Ein Mann mit Herz, Die verkaufte Braut, Fürst Seppl; Peter Voss, der Millionendieb; Der Tunnel, Ein Kuss in der Sommernacht, Das verliebte Hotel, Roman einer Nacht, Eine Frau wie Du, Fräulein Hoffmanns Erzählungen, Der Schlafwagenkontrolleur, Donogoo Tonka, Die letzten Vier von Santa Cruz.*

336 **SCHÜFFTAN, EUGEN** (1893-   ). B: Wroclaw/Breslau. Director of photography. At first architect, painter, sculptor and designer. Enters cinema circa 1920 and at first devotes himself to optical effects. Developed the so-called "Schüfftan process" (q.v.), used for the first time in *Metropolis.* 1932: to France. 1935-1936: part time in England, back to France. 1939: to U.S.A., where at first he, is unable to work, later only with great difficulty. 1947: American citizen. 1949: to France for some time, and since 1954 international activity. Famous for his extraordinary lighting effects (e.g. in Pabst's *L'Atlantide,* Feher's *The Robber Symphony* and Carné's *Drôle de Drame* and *Quai des Brumes*). Professional name in France and U.S.A. is Eugene (Eugène) Shuftan. Also director and technical supervisor.

Films (incomplete): *Menschen am Sonntag.* Then sound: *Das gestohlene Gesicht* co-phot. with Werner Bohne), *Dann schon lieber Lebertran, Das Ekel* 31 (co-phot. with Bernhard Wentzel, also dir. with Franz Wenzler), *Gassenhauer* (co-phot.), *Meine Frau, die Hochstaplerin* (co-phot. with Karl Puth), *Zigeuner der Nacht, Die Herrin von Atlantis* (co-phot. with Ernst Koerner), *Der Läufer von Marathon, Unsichtbare Gegner* (co-phot.), *Das Bankett der Schmuggler* (co-phot. with Raymond Picon-Borel), *Begegnung in Rom, Der Arzt stellt fest.*

337 **SCHÜFFTAN PROCESS.** A trick shot named after its inventor Eugen Schüfftan (q.v.), who patented the idea of building sets in miniature and reflecting them onto a glass with a mirrored surface, the glass being placed at an angle of 45 degrees in front of the camera. From those areas where action was to take place the mirrored surface was scraped away, and behind the holes thus created actual pieces of set were built, these pieces of set being lighted to coincide with the reflected model. First used in *Metropolis* and *Die Nibelungen.*

338 **SCHÜNZEL, REINHOLD** (1888-1954). B: Hamburg. D: Munich. Actor and director. At first businessman and journalist, then becomes actor for stage and film. Gradually develops into character actor and founds his own production company. 1938: to Hollywood, at first contracted to M-G-M as a director, but later returns to acting. 1949: returns to Germany. 1953: Kammerspiele Munich.

Films (incomplete): *Die Stricknadeln, Es werde Licht (iv), Das Tagebuch einer Verlorenen, Anders als die andern, Baccarat, Das Karussell des Lebens, Der Liebesroman der Käthe Keller, Madame Dubarry, Das Mädchen und die Männer, Maria Magdalena 19* (also acted), *Prostitution, Die Reise um die Welt in 80 Tagen, Seine Beichte, Sündige Eltern, Unheimliche Geschichten, Die Banditen von Asnières, Das Chamäleon, Drei Nächte, Der Graf von Cagliostro 20* (also acted), *Katherina die Grosse 20, Die letzte Stunde, Marquis d'or 20* (also prod. and acted), *Moriturus, Weltbrand, Mädchen aus der Ackerstrasse 21* (also acted), *Der Roman eines Dienstmädchens 21* (also acted), *Die Tänzerin Barberina, Bigamie, Don Juan und die drei Marien 22, Das Geld auf der Strasse 22* (also acted), *Luise Millerin, Lady Hamilton, Das Liebesnest, Der Pantoffelheld 22* (also acted), *Alles für Geld 23* (also acted), *Der Menschenfeind, Der Schatz der Gesine Jakobsen, Lumpen und Seide,*

A fine example of the Schüfftan process: METROPOLIS

Neuland, Die Schmetterlingsschlacht, Windstärke 9 24, Die Blumenfrau vom Potsdamer Platz, Der Flug um den Erdball, Die Frau für 24 Stunden 25 (also co-scripted with Alfred Schirokauer), Der Hahn im Korb (also co-scripted with Schirokauer), Heiratsschwindler, Die Kleine aus der Konfektion, Sündenbabel, Der dumme August des Zirkus Romanelli (also co-scrited with Schirokauer), Fünfuhrtee in der Ackerstrasse (also co-scripted with Schirokauer), Hallo Caesar! 26 (also co-scripted with Szöke Szakall and acted), In der Heimat, da gibt's ein Wiedersehn! 26 (co-dir. with Leo Mittler, also prod. and acted), Der Juxbaron, Die Perle des Regiments (also co-scripted with Schirokauer), Gustav Mond ... Du gehst so stille 27 (also acted), Herkules Maier (also prod. and co-scripted with Schirokauer), Himmel auf Erden (also prod. and co-scripted with Schirokauer), Ueb' immer Treu und Redlichkeit 27 (also prod. and acted and co-scripted with Schirokauer), Adam und Eva 28 (also prod. and acted and co-scripted with Schirokauer), Aus dem Tagebuch eines Junggesellen, Don Juan in der Mädchenschule 28 (also acted), Kolonne X 29 (also prod. and acted), Peter, der Matrose 29 (also prod. and acted). Then sound: Phantome des Glücks 29 (also dir. and script), Der Ball, Die Dreigroschenoper, Ihre Hoheit befielt; 1914, die letzten Tage vor dem Weltbrand; Liebe im Ring 30 (only dir.), Der kleine Seitensprung 31 (only dir. and co-script, Ronny 31 (only dir. and co-scripted), Das schöne Abenteuer 32 (only dir. and co-script), Wie sag' ich's meinem Mann 32 (only dir.), Viktor und Viktoria 33 (only dir. and script), Saison in Kairo 33 (only dir.), Die englische Heirat 34 (only dir.), Amphitryon 35 (only dir. and script), Das Mädchen Irene 36 (only dir. and script with Eva Leidmann), Donogoo Tonka 36 (only dir. and script), Land der Liebe 37 (only dir.

163

and script with Leidmann), *Liebe im Finanz-amt* (only script), *Meines Vaters Pferde II, Eine Liebesgeschichte.*

339 SEEBER, GUIDO (CONRAD-GUIDO) (1879-1940). B: Chemnitz. Director of photography. Son of photographer Clemens Seeber. After photographer's apprenticeship obtains chief post in the raw stock department of Dr. Schleussner's factory in Frankfurt. 1908-1914: technical head of "Deutsche Bioscop-Gesellschaft". With Wagner, Freund and Hoffmann (all q.v.) most important director of photography of German silent cinema. Well known for his work for Wegener, Pick, Pabst (all q.v.) and Bruno Rahn.

Films (incomplete): *Sumurun, Der frèmde Vogel, Im grossen Augenblick, Die Sünden der Väter, Die Verräterin, Zigeunerblur, Die arme Jenny, Jugend und Tollheit, Die Kinder des Generals, Komödianten, Die Macht des Goldes, Das Mädchen ohne Vaterland, Der Totentanz, Wenn die Maske fällt, Zu Tode gehetzt,* Engelein (co-phot. with Axel Graatkjaer), *Engeleins Hochzeit* (co-phot. with Graatkjaer), *Die Filmprimadonna* (co-phot. with Graatkjaer), *S. 1* (co-phot. with Graatkjaer), *Der Streichholzkünstler 13* (prod., script and phot.), *Der Student von Prag, Die Suffragetten* (co-phot. with Graatskjaer), *Der Tod in Sevilla, Elena Fontana, Das Feuer, Der Golem, Das Haus ohne Fenster und Türen, Das Kind ruft, Standrechtlich erschossen, Die Tochter der Landstrasse, Vorderhaus und Hinterhaus* (co-phot. with Graatkjaer), *Weisse Rosen, Zapatas Bande, Der Rattenfänger von Hameln* (co-phot. with Frederik Fuglsang), *Alraune und der Golem, Das wandernde Bild, Hochstapler, Adam und Eva* (co-phot.), *Alt-Heidelberg, Fridericus Rex* (co-phot. with Ernst Lüttgens), *Sylvester* (co-phot.), *Wilhelm Tell* (co-phot. with Toni Mülleneisen), *Garragan* (co-phot.), *Gräfin Donelli, Klabautermann* (co-phot.), *Lebende Buddhas* (co-phot. with Kuntze and J. Rona), *Ein Sommernachtstraum* (co-phot.), *Die vom Niederrhein* (co-phot.), *Die freudlose Gasse* (co-phot. with Oertel and Robert Lach), *Geheimnisse einer Seele* (co-phot. with Oertel and Lach), *Man spielt nicht mit der Liebe!* (co-phot. with Oertel and Lach), *Schenk mir das Leben* (co-phot. with Karl

Attenberger), *Der Bettelstudent* (co-phot. with Edoardo Lamberti), *Dirnentragödie,* *Ehekonflikte, Das Heiratsnest, Kleinstadt-sünde, Liebesreigen, Ein Mädel aus dem Volke, Mein Freund Harry* (co-phot. with Lamberti), *Ein rheinisches Mädchen beim rheinischen Wein, Wochenendzauber* (co-phot. with Lamberti), *Dragonerliebchen* (co-phot. with Lamberti), *Der Faschingsprinz* (co-phot. with Lamberti), *Grosstadtjugend* (co-phot. with Lamberti), *Liebe im Schnee* (co-phot. with Lamberti), *Der moderne Casanova* (co-phot. with Lamberti), *Robert und Bertram* (co-phot. with Victor Gluck), *Das Spiel mit der Liebe* (co-phot. with Lach), *Der Unüberwindliche* (co-phot. with Lamberti and Lach), *Die Zirkusprinzessin* (co-phot. with Lamberti), *Es flüstert die Nacht . . .* (co-phot. with Lamberti), *Die fidele Herrenpartie* (co-phot. with Lamberti), *Die Konkurrenz platzt, Das närrische Glück* (co-phot. with Lamberti), *Der schwarze Domino* (co-phot. with Lamberti), *Tempo! Tempo!* (co-phot. with Lamberti), *Donauwalzer,* *Fundvogel* (co-phot. with Karl Puth), *Grosstadtpiraten* (co-phot with Sophus Wangoe), *Die Jagd nach der Million* (co-phot. with Lamberti). Then sound: *Kasernenzauber,* *Die lustigen Musikanten, Der Bettelstudent,* *Reserve hat Ruh* (co-phot. with Hugo von Kaweczynski), *Mein Herz sehnt sich nach Liebe, Lügen auf Rügen, Die Blumenfrau von Lindenau* (co-phot. with Bruno Timm); *Die Frau, von der man spricht; Zwei glückliche Tage* (co-phot. with Kawczynski), *Drei von der Stempelstelle* (co-phot. with Kawczynski), *Die Fahrt ins Grüne, Zwei gute Kameraden, Das Tankmädel, Die vom Niederrhein, Ein Mädchen mit Prokura; Nur nicht weich werden, Susanne!; Ewiger Wald* (co-phot. with Allgeier etc.).

340 SEECK, ADELHEID (1899-). B: Berlin. Actress. At first dancer (e.g. at "Kabarett der Künstler" Berlin). Theatres (as actress): Bunzlau, Staatstheater Berlin (1940-1944), Heidelberg (1946), Hamburg (1947), Schauspielhaus Düsseldorf (1948-1955). Many guest appearances.

Films: *Leichte Muse, Tierarzt Dr. Vlimmen, Die Brüder Noltenius, Komplott auf Erlenhof, Der Tag vor der Hochzeit, Dalmatinische Hochzeit, Geliebte Feindin, Reifende Jugend, Teufel in Seide; Anastasia,* die letzte Zarentochter; Vater unser bestes Stück, Die Letzten werden die Ersten sein, Schmutziger Engel, Mädchen in Uniform, Ohne Mutter geht es nicht, Der Rest ist Schweigen; Mein Mann, das Wirtschaftswunder; Der letzte Zeuge, Zu jung für die Liebe, Wartezimmer zum Jenseits, Mädchen hinter Gitter.

341 **SEITZ, FRANZ** (1921-). B: Munich. Producer, director and scriptwriter. Son of Franz Seitz (a very versatile and busy director during both silent and sound periods). At first studies medicine, then soldier. After the War returns to his studies (including art). Enters cinema as designer for Richard Eichberg (q.v.). 1951: founds own production company. Scriptwriter using pen name of Georg Laforet. Manages to produce both commercial successes as well as films of artistic interest (including work of Schlöndorff and Straub).

Films: *Der letzte Schuss, Ehe für eine Nacht, Die vertagte Hochzeitsnacht, Heute nacht passiert's, Tante Jutta aus Kalkutta, Die süssesten Früchte, Moselfahrt aus Liebeskummer, Angst, Ein Mädchen aus Paris 54* (also dir.), *Morgengrauen, Es geschah am 20. Juli* (in collab. with Jochen Genzow), *Heldentum nach Ladenschluss 55* (co-dir. Wolfgang Schleif, Edic Odę and Wolfgang Becker), *Kleiner Mann ganz gross* (also script with Ilse Lotz-Dupont), *Die Zwillinge vom Zillertal, Die grünen Teufel von Monte Cassino, Mein Schatz ist aus Tirol, Die feuerrote Baronesse, Bei der blonden Kathrein; Ja, so ein Mädchen mit sechzehn, Mein Schatz, komm mit ans blaue Meer, Die zornigen jungen Männer, Schick deine Frau nicht nach Italien, Schön ist die Liebe am Königssee, Was macht Papa denn in Italien?, Der verkaufte Grossvater, Isola Bella, Muss i denn zum Städtele hinaus, Das schwarz-weiss-rote Himmelbett* (also script

A dream sequence composed by Guido Seeber in GEHEIMNISSE EINER SEELE

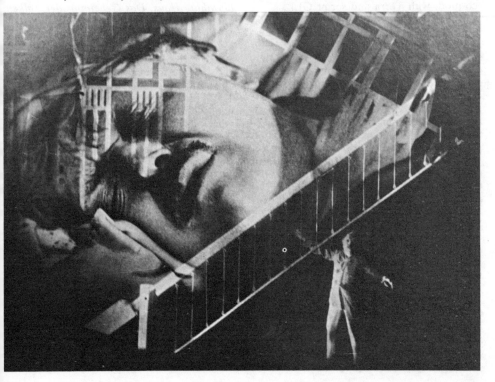

GL), *Venusberg, Moral 63, Ferien vom Ich, Kennwort Reiher* (co-prod. with Independant and Filmaufbau), *Tonio Kröger, Die schwedische Jungfrau* (only script GL), *Die Herren 65* (also dir. one episode, other script writers are Gregor von Rezzori, Paul Hengge, Kurt Heuser and Joe Lederer), *Lausbubengeschichten* (also script GL), *Wälsungenblut* (also script GL in collab. with Erika Mann); *An der Donau, wenn der Wein blüht; Die fromme Helene, Tante Frida – neue Lausbubengeschichten* (also script GL), *Ich suche einen Mann, Grieche sucht Griechin* (also script GL), *Der junge Törless* (co-prod. with Nouvelle Edition Paris), *Onkel Filser – Allerneueste Lausbubengeschichten* (also script GL), *Chronik der Anna Magdalena Bach* (co-prod. with Italy), *Fast ein Held* (co-prod. with Jadran), *Wenn Ludwig ins Manöver zieht* (also script GL), *Dr. van de Velde – Die vollkommene Ehe I* (co-prod. also script), *Dr. van de Velde – Das Leben zu zweit* (only script), *Die Lümmel von der ersten Bank I & II* (also script GL), *Die Lümmel von der ersten Bank III* etc. (co-prod. with Terra and script GL).

342 **SENFT, HARO** (1928-   ). B: Ceské Budejovice. Director and producer. 1949: studied at Wiesbaden film academy. Enters cinema as asst. production manager. 1954: starts his own short film production. 1959: co-founder of "DOC 59" group. 1961-1963: guest teacher at "Hochschule für Gestaltung" in Ulm. Important *avant-garde* director of young German cinema. *See also Junger deutscher Film.* Also produced *.
Films: *XY 54* *, *Die Brücke* 57 (third episode of feature *Maya*), *Autobahn 57* * (dir. Herbert Vesely, q.v.), *Von sechs bis sechs 59* *, *Patience 59* co-*, *Kahl 61, Atmokraftwerk Kahl 61, Plakate, Parolen, Signale 62* *, *Auto Auto 64* *, *Ein Anlass zum Sprechen 66* * (Lengthy documentary), *Die Prager Filmschule 66* * (from material of *Ein Anlass zum Sprechen,* for TV), *Der sanfte Lauf 67* * (feature).

343 **SERIALS.** Favourite *genre* of the German cinema between 1910 and 1920, mostly one or two-reelers, made by the same actors and directors. At first they were used as programmes for vaudeville-cinemas, later as fillers in the normal programme.

1918-1922: many big films, announced as serials, offered great names as Asta Nielsen, Fern Andra, Mia May (all. q.v.), Hedda Vernon, Leontine Kühnberg, Erna Morena, Aud Egede Nissen. The action and the characters were normally not conceived as part of a serial, but finally emerged in this way.
Detective Serials with adventures featuring the same people, mostly set in England. 1915-1922 with the following heroes:
Joe Debbs. Started by Joe May (q.v.) with Max Landa (*Das Gesetz der Mine*), later with Harry Liedtke (q.v.) (*Die leere Wasserflasche, Die Hochzeit im Excentricclub);* then with Ferdinand von Alten at Ufa, and with Carl Auen (*Der heulende Wolf, Tambourin und Kastagnetten,* etc.).
Stuart Webbs. With Ernst Reicher (circa 40 to 50 films, *Die geheimnisvolle Villa, Das Panzergewölbe),* later probably also with Harry Liedtke.
Harry Higgs. With Hans Mierendorff (*Die Fusspur; Hallo, Harry Higgs, wer dort?, Der Mann im Nebel,* etc.).
Harry Hill. With Valy Arnheim (*Das unbewohnte Haus, Das Geheimnis der Falken, Die Höllenmaschine, Das Detektivduell, Die Schmuggler von San Diego,* etc.).
Also well known was the *Homunculus* Serial, directed by Rippert (q.v.), which was very much influenced by films like *Der Golem* and *Der Student von Prag.*
The films by and with Harry Piel are in line with the trend of the serials but rely more heavily on sensational effects.
Joe May (q.v.) also started the real adventurer films in series (as in America) with *Die Herrin der Welt* (eight episodes, normally six reels each: *Die Freundin des gelben Mannes, Die Geschichte der Maud Gregaard, Der Rabbi von Kuan-Fu, König Makombe; Ophir, die Stadt der Vergangenheit; Die Frau mit den Milliarden, Die Wohltäterin der Menschheit, Die Tragödie der Rache).*
Today's Serials
Karl May: Films based on the novels by May (1842-1912), adventure stories among the American indians and in the Near East, produced by CCC Berlin (*see* Brauner) and Rialto in Hamburg (*see* Horst Wendlandt), mostly in co-production with Yugoslavia (*Der Schatz im Silbersee, Winnetou i-iii, Unter Geiern, Winnetou und das Halbblut*

Apanatschi, Winnetou und sein Freund Old Firehand, Winnetou und Shatterhand im Tal der Toten, etc.). Costume films in European "Western" style. Directors. Harald Reinl, Alfred Vohrer (both q.v.), Harald Philipp, Hugo Fregonese. Actors: Pierre Brice *(Winnetou)*, Lex Barker *(Old Shatterhand)*, Stewart Granger *(Old Surehand)*, etc.

Lümmel and *Pauker* (mostly produced by Seitz, Rialto and Constantin) featuring schoolboy pranks "idealising" them as during the Nazi period *(Die Lümmel von der ersten Bank, Zur Hölle mit den Paukern, Zum Teufel mit der Penne; Pepe, der Paukerschreck*, etc.). Directors: Werner Jacobs, Harald Reinl (q.v.).

Lausbub (produced by Seitz and Constantin), based on novels by Ludwig Thoma 1867-1926), located in Bavaria *(Lausbubengeschichten, Tante Frida – Neue Lausbubengeschichten, Onkel Filser – Allerneuste Lausbubengeschichten, Wenn Ludwig ins Manöver zieht*, etc.). Directors: Helmut Käutner (q.v.), Werner Jacobs.

For sex education films *see* separate entry, and for Edgar Wallace films *see* Literary Adaptations.

344 SEX EDUCATION FILMS. Films about sexual behaviour and sexual abnormalities, made for purely commercial purposes but mostly pretending to give scientific enlightenment. The big waves of sex education films were after the First World War and in the late Sixties, mainly as a reaction to a period of political and social discontent.

Films. (a) 1918-1922: *Es werde Licht* (part i-iv), *Prostitution* (part i-iv), *Anders als die andern, Moral und Sinnlichkeit, Keimendes Leben*, etc.

(b) Early Thirties: *Gefahren der Liebe, Wege zur guten Ehe, Liebe – ein Naturgesetz*, etc.

(c) Late Forties: *Vom Mädchen zur Frau*, etc.

(d) Late Sixties: *Wunder der Liebe* (Oswalt Kolle, part i-vi), *Die vollkommene Ehe* (Van de Velde, part i and ii), *Du – Zwischenzeichen der Sexualität, Helga, Helga und Michael, Helga und die sexuelle Revolution*, etc.

Directors: *see* Richard Oswald, Dupont.

The recent films were made mainly by dilettante directors.

Films des moeurs (Sittenfilme) following the wave of sex education films from 1918-1922 where sexual themes were used in thrillers *(Die Verführten, Die Geschichte einer Gefallenen, Prinz Kuckuck, Polygamie, Freie Liebe, Paradies der Dirnen*, etc.)

The same wave also included films tending to "illuminate other vices" (also made from 1918-1922), but they were unbelievable as well *(Alkohol, Der gelbe Tod, Opium, Morphium, Nerven*, etc.).

345 SIERCK, DETLEF HANS (1900-). B: Skagen (Denmark). Actor and director. Educated in Copenhagen, Hamburg and Munich. Since 1923: journalist, actor and stage director. 1929: scriptwriter for Ufa, then becomes film actor. 1935: directs his first film. Emigrates via South Africa and Australia to U.S.A. 1943: in Hollywood, where the first film that he directs is the anti-Nazi *Hitler's Madman*. In U.S.A. known as Douglas Sirk.

Films: *April, April* 35, *Stützen der Gesellschaft* 35, *Das Mädchen vom Moorhof* 35, *Das Hofkonzert* 36 (also script with Franz Wallner-Basté), *Schlussakkord* 36 (also script with Kurt Heuser), *La Habanera* 37, *Liebling der Matrosen* 37 (also script with Karl Peter Gillmann), *Zu neuen Ufern* 37 (also script with Heuser), *Dreiklang* (only idea).

346 SIMON, GÜNTHER (1925-). B: Berlin. Actor. Stage training, prisoner of war, then finished studies and to theatre in Köthen. Worked with Lucie Höflich (q.v.) in Schwerin. His most important part is in *Ernst Thälmann (Parts One and Two)*, for which he received the State Award in 1954.

Films: *Das verurteilte Dorf, Anna Susanna, Jacke wie Hose, Ernst Thälmann – Sohn seiner Klasse, Ernst Thälman – Führer seiner Klasse, Das Traumschiff, Treffpunkt Aimée, Damals in Paris, Tinko, Vergesst mir meine Traudel nicht, Sheriff Teddy, Meine Frau macht Musik, Das Lied der Matrosen, Geschwader Fledermaus, Der Lotterieschwede, Senta auf Abwegen, Das schwarze Bataillon, Eine alte Liebe, Einer von uns, Die heute über 40 sind, Die Sonnensucher, Der schweigende Stern, Der Moorhund, Die Liebe und der Co-Pilot, Der Fremde, Eine Handvoll Noten, Der Traum*

des Hauptman Loy, Mord ohne Sühne, Aerzte, Der Tod hat ein Gesicht, An französischen Kaminen, Nebel, Geheimarchiv an der Elbe, Schwarzer Samt, Preludio 11, Das Lied vom Trompeter, Der Reserveheld, Alfons Zitterbacke, Lots Weib, Reise ins Ehebett, Brot und Rosen, Heroin.

347 **SIODMA(R)K, ROBERT** (1900-   ). B: Memphis (U.S.A.). Director. 1910: to Leipzig, studied at University of Marburg. At first bank clerk, then actor and director for the stage. 1929: to Ufa as actor, scriptwriter and editor. Experimental films. Worked with Edgar G. Ulmer (co-director), Billy Wilder (q.v.), Fred Zinnemann (co-script), Eugen Schüfftan (q.v.) and Moritz Seeler (production manager) for feature documentary *Menschen am Sonntag (see also* Nebenzal). 1933: to Paris, mainly directing adaptations of plays. 1940: to Hollywood. 1952: returns to Europe, first to France, and then to Germany. For some of his films, the scripts were written by his brother Kurt (Curt) Siodmark (b. 1902 in Dresden).

Films: *Menschen am Sonntag* 29 (co-dir. with Edgar G. Ulmer). Then sound: *Abschied* 30, *Der Mann, der seinen Mörder sucht* 31, *Voruntersuchung* 31, *Stürme der*

Leidenschaft 31, Quick 32, Brennendes Geheimnis 33, Die Ratten 55, Mein Vater, der Schauspieler 56, Nachts, wenn der Teufel kam 57, Dorothea Angermann 59, Mein Schulfreund 60, Tunnel 28 62, Der Schut 64, Der Schatz der Azteken 65, Die Pyramide des Sonnengottes 65, Kampf um Rom I & II 68.

348 **SKLADANOWSKY, MAX** (1863-1939). B and D: Berlin. Pioneer of cinematography and producer. His father, Carl, was a magic lanternist, and Max was apprenticed to a firm of lantern manufacturers. He gave his first public performance of moving pictures at the Berlin Wintergarten as part of a variety programme on February 1, 1895. His system of projection was somewhat involved as it entailed projecting two strips of films simultaneously through two objectives which were alternatively covered by a shutter to allow alternate frames on the two strips to follow each other in logical sequence. Both rolls were projected at eight frames per second, producing when combined a frequency of sixteen frames per second. Skladanowsky's system was far too complicated to receive anything but momentary success, although a few performances were

given outside of Germany. He worked in close collaboration with his brother Emil (1859-1945).

349   SLEZAK, LEO (1873-1946). B: Mährisch-Schünberg. D: Rottach-Egern. Actor and singer. At first locksmith. Then stage and voice training in Brünn (Brno). *Début* in Brünn as *Lohengrin*, then Hofoper Berlin in 1898. Since 1910: member of the Hofoper Vienna, e.g. the Staatsoper, where featured as one of the most prominent singer of his day. Many guest appearances (including London and New York), Author of *Meine gesammelten Werke, Der Wortbruch, Wann fährt der nächste Schwan?* After retiring from the opera he became one of the best known comedians in German and Austrian films. Father of Walter Slezak (q.v.)

Films: *Der Frauendiplomat, Skandal in der Parkstrasse, Die Herren vom Maxim, Moderne Mitgift, Ein toller Einfall, Grossfürstin Alexandra, Mein Liebster ist ein Jägersmann, Der Herr ohne Wohnung, Musik im Blut, Ihr grösster Erfolg, Freut Euch des Lebens, La Paloma, G'schichten aus dem Wienerwald, Die blonde Carmen, Tanzmusik, Knox und die lustigen Vagabunden, Eine Nacht an der Donau, Die Fahrt in die Jugend, Die ganze Welt dreht sich um Liebe, Die lustigen Weiber, Herbstmanöver, Ein Walzer um den Stephansturm, Die Pompadour, Unsterbliche Melodien, Konfetti, Das Frauenparadies, Der Postillon von Lonjumeau, Rendezvous in Wien, Liebe im Drievierteltakt, Die glücklichste Ehe der Welt, Gasparone; Husaren, heraus; Der Mann, der nicht nein sagen konnte; Heimat, Die 4 Gesellen, Frau am Steuer, Es war eine rauschende Ballnacht, Operette, Golowin geht durch die Stadt, Rosen in Tirol, Der Herr im Haus, Alles für Gloria, Geliebter Schatz, Münchhausen.*

350   SLEZAK, WALTER (1902-   ). B: Vienna. Actor. Son of Leo Slezak (q.v.). Speech training. At first bank clerk in Vienna. Enters films thanks to Michael Kertesz (Curtis). Theatre work in Berlin. 1930: to U.S.A. (with several successes on Broadway). 1932: returns to Berlin for one film, and then finally back to America.

Films (incomplete): *Sodom und Gomorra, Mein Leopold, Michael, Die gefundene Braut, Grüss mir das blonde Kind am Rhein, O alte Burschenherrlichkeit, Sumpf und Noral, Das wir in Heidelberg in blauer Sommernacht, Junges Blut, Marcos tollste Wette, Der Seekadett, Die Wacht am Rhein, Wie bleibe ich jung und schön, Almenrausch und Edelweiss, Der Fahnenträger von Sedan, Die grosse Pause, Ledige Mütter, Liebe geht seltsame Wege, Die Lorelei, Das Recht zu leben, Das Hannerl vom Rolandsbogen, Einen Jux will er sich machen, Eros in Ketten.* Then sound: *Spione im Savoy-Hotel, Der Kongress amüsiert sich, Heidi kehrt heim.*

351   SÖDERBAUM, KRISTINA (1912-   ). B: Djursholm near Stockholm. Actress. At the age of sixteen to Germany, stage training with Rudolf Klein-Rogge (q.v.). 1936: first German film, and two years later is launched as a star by her husband Veit Harlan (q.v.). Short break from films after 1945. 1951-1955: appears in Harlan's films again. Now working as freelance photographer in Munich.

Films: *Onkel Bräsig, Jugend, Verwehte Spuren, Die Reise nach Tilsit, Das unsterbliche Herz, Jud Süss, Der grosse König, Die goldene Stadt, Immensee, Opfergang, Kolberg, Unsterbliche Geliebte, Hanna Amon,*

Die blaue Stunde, Sterne über Colombo, Die Gefangene des Maharadscha, Verrat an Deutschland, Zwei Herzen im Mai, Ich werde Dich auf Händen tragen, Die blonde Frau des Maharadscha.

352 **SÖHNKER, HANS** (1903-   ). B: Kiel. Actor. At first bank clerk, then thanks to Gustaf Gründgens (q.v.) decides to become an actor. Stage training in Kiel. Theatres: Frankfurt, Danzig, Baden-Baden, Chemnitz, Bremen, and since 1933 has appeared in various theatres (Renaissance, Hebbel, Schlosspark, etc.). After 1945: in various theatres. Guest appearances.

Films: *Der Zarewitsch, Schwarzwaldmädel, Annette im Paradies, Jede Frau hat ein Geheimnis, Die Czardasfürstin, Die grosse Chance, Ich sing' mich in Dein Herz hinein, Sie und die Drei, Der junge Graf, Eva, Herbstmanöver, Liebesträume, Wo die Lerche singt, Arzt aus Leidenschaft, Flitterwochen, Truxa, Die Drei um Christine, Diener lassen bitten; Und Du, mein Schatz, fährst mit; Musik für Dich, Der Unwiderstehliche, Die Fledermaus, Der Mustergatte, Geld fällt vom Himmel, Der Tag nach der Scheidung, Die Frau am Scheidewege, Die 4 Gesellen, Irrtum des Herzens, Brand im*

Ozean, Gold in New Frisco, Nanette, Männer müssen so sein, Blutbrüderschaft, Frau nach Mass; Auf Wiedersehen, Franziska; Der Strom, Meine Frau Teresa, Liebespremiere, Ein Mann mit Grundsätzen?, Nacht ohne Abschied, Der Engel mit dem Saitenspiel, Grosse Freiheit Nr. 7, Tierarzt Dr Vlimmen, Film ohne Titel; Hallo, Fräulein! Einmaleins der Ehe, Geliebter Lügner, Nur eine Nacht, Der Fall Rabanser, Schatten über Neapel, Weisse Schatten; Mein Freund der Dieb; Königin der Arena, Das singende Hotel, Die Stärkere, Muss man sich gleich scheiden lassen?, Ein Leben für Do, Männer im gefährlichen Alter, Hoheit lasser bitten, Ihre grosse Prüfung, Oberarzt Dr Solm, Eine Frau genügt nicht?, Vor Gott und den Menschen, Studentin Helen Willfüer, Zärtliches Geheimnis, Ferien in Tirol Geliebte Corinna, Wenn wir alle Engel wären, Die Freundin meines Mannes, Immer wenn der Tag beginnt, Worüber man nicht spricht, Serenade einer grossen Liebe; Wie schön, das es Dich gibt; Die singenden Engel von Tirol, Jacqueline, Ich heirate Herrn Direktor, Die Fastnachtsbeichte, Schachnovelle, Immer will ich Dir gehören, Wegen Verführung Minderjähriger, Unser Haus in Kamerun, Sherlock Holmes und das Halsband des Todes, Jetzt dreht die Welt sich nur um dich, Das Phantom von Soho, Der Hund von Blackwood Castle.*

353 **SOKOLOFF, VLADIMIR** (1889-1962). B: Moscow. D: Hollywood. At first studied at Moscow University, then stage training at Academy of Dramatic Art in Moscow. Appeared in artists' theatre Moscow, first as actor, then also as asst. director and director. 1923: to Berlin as actor in theatres and films. 1932: to France. 1937: to Hollywood.

Films: *Die Abenteuer eines Zehnmarkscheines, Die Liebe der Jeanne Ney, Der Sohn der Hagar, Die weisse Sonate, Katherina Knie, Das Schiff der verlorenen Menschen, Sensation im Wintergarten, Moral um Mitternacht.* Then sound: *Liebling der Götter, Abschied, Das Flötenkonzert von Sanssouci, Die heilige Flamme, Kismet, Niemandsland, Die Dreigroschenoper, Strafsache van Geldern, Die Herrin von Atlantis, Teilnehmer antwortet nicht, Gehetzte Menschen.*

354 SOMMER, ELKE (1940-   ). B: Berlin. Actress. RN: Elke Schletz. Au pair in England, then modelling in Italy, also plays small parts in Italian films. International career as a sexy blonde, mainly in American films.

Films: *Das Totenschiff, Am Tag als der Regen kam, Lampenfieber, Himmel, Amor und Zwirn, . . . und sowas nennt sich Leben, Geliebte Hochstaplerin, Zarte Haut in schwarzer Seide, Auf Wiedersehn, Café Oriental, Das Mädchen und der Staatsanwalt, Nachts ging das Telephon, Verführung am Meer, Denn die Musik und die Liebe im Tirol, Unter Geiern, Hotel der toten Gäste, Die Hölle von Macao, An einem Freitag in Las Vegas.*

355 SPARKUHL, THEODOR (1894-   ). B: Hannover. Director of photography. Studied at university in Hannover. 1911: projectionist. 1918: cameraman, at first mainly for Lubitsch (q.v.). 1930: in England, later also to France (photographed Renoir's *La Chienne*). 1933: to Hollywood. 1946: retires. Worked in Germany on many adventure films, and should also be noted for his masterly handling of crowd scenes in Lubitsch's films.

Films (incomplete): *Die Augen der Mumie Ma* (co-phot. with Alfred Hansen), *Carmen, Fuhrmann Henschel, Das Mädchen vom Ballett, Die Austernprinzessin, Komptesse Doddy, Das Karussell des Lebens, Kreuziget sie, Madame Dubarry* (co-phot.), *Die Puppe, Rausch, Vendetta, Anna Boleyn, Kohlhiesels Töchter, Romeo und Julia im Schnee, Sumurun, Die Bergkatze, Grausige Nächte, Marchesa d'Armiani, Der Roman eines Dienstmädchens, Das Weib des Pharao* (co-phot. with Hansen), *Die Finsternis ist ihr Eigentum, Die Flamme* (co-phot. with Hansen), *Sein ist das Gericht, Das alte Gesetz, Die fünfte Strasse* (co-phot. with Emil Schünemann and Carl Hilbiber), *SOS. Die Insel der Tränen* (co-phot. with Brandes, Julius Balting and Karl Vass), *Carlos und Elisabeth* (co-phot. with Hasselmann, Karl Puth and Vass), *Dekameron-Nächte, Komödie des Herzens, Neuland* (co-phot. with Curt Heling, Erich Waschneck and Hyalmar Lerski), *Die Frau in vierzig Jahren* (co-phot. with J. Hermann), *Die Gesunkenen, Die Prinzessin und der Geiger, Die Boxerbraut, Fedora* (co-

phot. with Otto Tober and Willy Gaebel), *Die Flucht in den Zirkus* (co-phot. with Mutz Greenbaum), *Madame wünscht keine Kinder* (co-phot.), *Manon Lescaut, Der Soldat der Marie, Der Fluch der Vererbung* (co-phot. with Johannes Männling), *Ich hatte einst ein schönes Vaterland, Jugendrausch* (co-phot. with Hoffmann and Ladislaw Starewitsch),*Der letzte Walzer* (co-phot. with Joe Rive), *Der Sohn der Hagar* (co-phot. with Günther Krampf and Baberske), *Die Spielerin, Zwei unterm Himmelzelt, Abwege, Liebeskarneval* (co-phot. with Weinmann), *Der Staatsanwalt klagt an* 28 (co-dir. with Adolf Trotz, co-phot. with Männling). Then sound: *Moritz macht sein Glück* (co-phot. with Arthur von Schwertführer).

356 SPIRA, CAMILLA (1906-   ). B: Hamburg. Actress. Daughter of actor Fritz Spira (1881-1945). 1922: on stage and soon afterwards enters films. Although she has appeared in many films, she much prefers the theatre. 1922-1933: Wallner-Theater, Deutsches Theater and Volksbühne, all in Berlin. 1933: banned from any artistic activity. 1938: leaves Germany and travels to the Netherlands and U.S.A. 1947: returns to Germany, appearing at theatres in Berlin.

171

Works part time for DEFA (q.v.). Mainly character roles after 1945.

Films: *Mutter und Sohn, Das Herz am Rhein, Die dritte Eskadron, Brennende Grenze, Die Perle des Regiments, Die versunkene Flotte, Wie einst im Mai, An der Weser, Liebeskarneval, Sechzehn Töchter und kein Papa, Meine Schwester und ich.* Then sound: *Die Jugendgeliebte, Die lustigen Musikanten, Die Faschingsfee, Mein Leopold, Der schönste Mann im Staate, Gehetzte Menschen, Die elf Schill'schen Offiziere; Ja, treu ist die Soldatenliebe; Skandal in der Parkstrasse, Grün ist die Heide, Der Judas von Tirol, Das Testament des Dr. Mabuse, Sprung in den Abgrund, Morgenrot, Die Nacht im Forsthaus, Die Buntkarierten, Epilog, Semmelweis – Retter der Mütter, Die lustigen Weiber von Windsor, Stunde der Entscheidung, Drei Tage Angst, Pension Schöller, Der fröhliche Weinberg, Emil und die Detektive, Roman eines Frauenarztes, Des Teufels General, Vatertag, Der letzte Mann (55), Himmel ohne Sterne, Zwei blaue Augen, Liebe, Fuhrmann Henschel, Made in Germany, Der tolle Bomberg, Das Herz von St. Pauli, Nachtschwester Ingeborg, Der Csardaskönig; Vater, Mutter und neun Kinder; Freddy, die Gitarre und das Meer; Buddenbrooks, Rosen für den Staatsanwalt, Freddy unter fremden Sternen, Vertauschtes Leben; Piccadilly, null Uhr zwölf.*

357 **STAPENHORST, GÜNTHER** (1883-   ). B: Gebweiller (Elsass). Producer. 1909-1919: Naval officer, then employed in an export firm and works as a bank clerk. Enters cinema in 1926 as production manager, then joins Ufa and becomes one of their producers. 1935: to England (with "London Films"). 1938: to Switzerland, where he becomes co-owner of "Gloria-Film" in Zurich and producer. 1945: to Germany. 1949: starts to produce again when he founds "Carlton Film" in Munich. He produced some important films mainly at the beginning of the sound period.

Films: *Ich hatt' einen Kameraden* (for Ifco), *Kreuzzug des Weibes* (for Arthur Ziehm), All for Ufa: *Der Tanzstudent, Die Jacht der sieben Sünden, Die blaue Maus, Ihr dunkler Punkt, Adieu Mascotte, Der Sträfling aus Stambul, Wenn Du einmal Dein Herz verschenkst, Der unsterbliche Lump* (30), *Hokuspokus, Das Flötenkonzert von Sanssouci, Der kleine Seitensprung, Emil und die Detektive, Ronny, Morgenrot, Das schöne Abenteuer, Mensch ohne Namen, Walzerkrieg, Saison in Kairo, Flüchtlinge, Die Töchter Ihrer Exzellenz, Der junge Baron Neuhaus, Prinzessin Turandot, Barcarole, Amphitryon.* For Carlton in Munich: *So sind die Frauen, Das doppelte Lottchen, Das weisse Abenteuer, Die Försterchristl* (52) *Alraune, Im weissen Rössl* (52), *Einen Jux will er sich machen, Der letzte Walzer, Meines Vater Pferde, Der unsterbliche Lump* (53), *Lachkabinett, Dieses Lied bleibt Dir, Das fliegende Klassenzimmer, Die verschwundene Miniatur, Solang' es hübsche Mädchen gibt, Königswalzer, Rosen für Bettina, Der Bettelstudent, Manöverball, Ich war ihm hörig, Unruhige Nacht, Gräfin Mariza, Paprika, Bei der blonden Kathrein, Im weissen Rössl* (60), *Försterchristl* (62).

358 **STAUDTE, WOLFGANG (GEORG)** (1906-   ). B: Saarbrücken. Actor and director. Son of film and stage director Franz Staudte. Stage training with Reinhardt (q.v.) and Erwin Piscator. Until 1933 stagework, then into films as an actor. At first works as scriptwriter and director for advertisement films and shorts. First feature in 1943. Co-founder with Harald Braun and Käutner (both q.v.) of "Freie Film-Produktions-GmbH." After 1945: works for DEFA (q.v.) and makes *Die Mörder sind unter uns,* first postwar German film. Since 1953: permanently in West Germany. Important figure of the postwar cinema especially with his socially committed films for DEFA, where he was primarily engaged with the problem of de-Nazification.

Acted in: *Gassenhauer, Geheimnis des blauen Zimmers, Tannenberg, Der Choral von Leuthen, Heimkehr ins Glück, Pechmarie, Die Bande von Hoheneck, Schwarzer Jäger Johanna, Stärker als Paragraphen, Gleisdreieck, Susanne im Bade, Am seidenen Faden, Lauter Lügen, Pour le mérite, Mordsache Holm, Spiel im Sommerwind, Das Gewehr über, Die fremde Frau, Drei Unteroffiziere, Brand im Ozean, Legion Condor, Blutsbrüderschaft, Aus erster Ehe, Jud Süss, Jungens, Friedemann Bach, ... reitet für Deutschland, Das grosse Spiel.*

Directed films: *Akrobat schö-ö-ön* 43 (also script), *Ich hab' von Dir geträumt* 44, *Der Mann, dem man den Namen stahl* (only script with Josef Maria Frank), *Frau über Bord* 45, *Die Mörder sind unter uns* 46 (also script), *Die seltsamen Abenteuer des Herrn Fridolin B.* 48 (also script), *Rotation* 49 (also script with Erwin Klein and Fritz Staudte), *Schicksal aus zweiter Hand* 49 (also script), *Das Beil von Wandsbek* (only script with Lüddecke, Hans R. Bortfeld and Falk Harnack), *Der Untertan* 51 (also script with Fritz Staudte), *Die Geschichte des kleinen Muck* 53 (also script with Peter Podehl), *Leuchtfeuer* 54 (also co-scripted), *Ciske — Ein Kind braucht Liebe* 55 (also script), *Rose Bernd* 57, *Kanonen-Serenade* 58 (also script with Ennio de Concini and Duccio Tessari), *Madeleine und der Legionär* 58, *Der Maulkorb* 58, *Rosen für den Staatsanwalt* 59 (also idea), *Kirmes* 60 (also script), *Der letzte Zeuge* 60, *Die glücklichen Jahre der Thorwalds* 62 (co-dir. with John Olden), *Die Dreigroschenoper* 63, *Herrenpartie* 64, *Das Lamm* 64, *Ganovenehre* 66, *Heimlichkeiten* 68 (also co-scripted with Angel Wagenstein).

359 STECKEL, LEONARD (1901-   ). B: Kuihinin (Hungary). Actor and director. Interrupted his studies in chemistry and medicine in Berlin to join the theatre. 1921-1923: Neues Volkstheater Berlin. Various theatres in Berlin until 1932. 1933-1945: Schauspielhaus Zurich as actor and director. During this period he also directed some Swiss films. After 1945: many guest appearances as actor and director in Germany, Switzerland and Israel. Famous and important actor (e.g. Brecht), but often miscast in films.

Films: *Phantome des Glücks*, *Der Hauptmann von Köpenick* (31), *Die Abenteuerin in Tunis*, *M*, *Der Draufgänger*, *Gitta entdeckt ihr Herz*, *Der Geheimagent*, *Die verliebte Firma*, *Die Nächte von Port Said*, *Kampf um Blond*, *Spione im Savoy-Hotel*, *Mieter Schulze gegen alle*, *Salon Dora Green*, *Unsichtbare Gegner*, *Ein Lied für Dich*, *Hände aus dem Dunkel*, *Südliche Nächte*, *Meines Vaters Pferde* (ii), *Die 7 Kleider der Kathrin*, *Viktoria und ihr Husar*, *Der letzte Sommer*, *Frühlingslied*, *Ewiger Walzer*, *Liebe ohne Illusion*, *Du mein stilles Tal* 55 (also dir.), *Geliebte Feindin*, *Rosen für Bettina*, *Der Hauptmann von Köpenick* (56), *Ohne Dich wird es Nacht*, *Stresemann*, *Madeleine und der Legionär*, *Der Arzt von Stalingrad*, *Das Mädchen vom Moorhof*, *Majestät auf Abwegen*, *Romarei — das Mädchen mit den grünen Augen*, *Unser Wunderland bei Nacht*, *Marili*, *Ja, so ein Mädchen mit sechzehn*; *Liebling der Götter*, *Der Besuch*.

360 STEINHOFF, HANS (1882-1945). B: Pfaffenhofen. D: in 'plane crash near Luckenwalde. Scriptwriter and director. Interrupted his studies in medicine to join the theatre, first as actor, and later also as a director. Enters cinema in 1922. Very much in demand during the Nazi period, when he directs some State and propaganda films.

Films (incomplete): *Bräutigam auf Kredit* 21, *Der Bettelstudent* 22, *Biribi* 22 (also script), *Der falsche Dimitri* 22 (also scripted with Paul Beyer), *Kleider machen Leute* 22 (also co-scripted with Robert Weil), *Die Fledermaus* (only co-scripted with Robert Liebmann), *Inge Larsen* 23, *Mensch gegen Mensch* 24, *Gräfin Mariza* 25, *Der Mann, der sich verkauft* 25 (also co-scripted with

Max Glass), *Der Mann im Sattel* (only co-scripted with Margarete Maria Langen), *Der Herr des Todes* 26, *Die Tragödie eines Verlorenen* 26, *Wien-Berlin* 26, *Schwiegersöhne* 26 (also co-scripted with Ida Jenbach), *Familientag im Hause Prellstein* 27, *Das Frauenhaus von Rio* 27, *Die Sandgräfin* 27, *Ein Mädel und drei Clowns* 28, *Das Spreewaldmädel* 28, *Nachtgestalten* 29, *Fundvogel* (only script). Then sound: *Rosenmontag* 30, *Die Pranke* 31, *Kopfüber ins Glück* 31, *Die Faschingsfee* 31, *Mein Leopold* 31, *Der wahre Jakob* 31, *Scampolo, ein Kind der Strasse* 32, *Mutter und Kind* 33, *Liebe muss verstanden sein* 33, *Madame wünscht keine Kinder* 33, *Hitlerjunge Quex* 33, *Freut Euch des Lebens* 34, *Die Insel* 34, *Lockvogel* 34, *Der alte und der junge König* 35, *Der Ammenkönig* 35, *Eine Frau ohne Bedeutung* 36, *Ein Volksfreind* 37 (also script with Erich Ebermayer), *Tanz auf dem Vulkan* 38 (also script with Hans Rehberg and Peter Hagen), *Robert Koch* 39, *Die Geierwally* 40, *Ohm Krüger* 41, *Rembrandt* 42 (also script with Kurt Heuser), *Gabriele Dambrone* 43 (also script with Per Schwenzen), *Melusine* 44 (also script with Werner Eplinius), *Shiva und die Galgenblume* 45 (also script with Hans-Rudolf Berndorff).

361 **STEINRÜCK, ALBERT** (1872-1929). B: Wettenburg-Waldeck. D: Berlin. Actor. At first painter and decorator, then after the war he enters the cinema and acts in the films of many famous directors. It is a tragic state of affairs that after 1925 he failed to obtain parts commensurate with his acting talents. Only after his death was his true worth realised. But at least he had many possibilities on stage and the Theater am Gendarmenmarkt in Berlin payed a memorable homage to him with an all-star performance of *Der Marquis von Keith* by Wedekind, directed by Leopold Jessner (q.v.).

Films (incomplete): *Der Golem, Geschlossene Kette; Der Golem, wie er in die Welt kam; Der Leidensweg der Inge Krafft, Madame Recamier, Der Richter von Zalamea, Brennendes Land, Exzellenz Unterrock, Mädchen aus der Ackerstrasse, Perlen bedeuten Tränen, Sappho, Die Schuld der Lavinia Morland, Der Streik der Diebe, Monna Vanna, Die Nacht der Medici, Der Todes-*reigen, Der Kaufmann von Venedig, Der rote Reiter, Der Schatz, Der Wetterwart, Dekameron-Nächte, Das goldene Kalb, Das Haus am Meer, Hedda Gabler, Helena; Mädchen, die man nicht heiratet; Die Schuld, Sklaven der Liebe, Die Tragödie der Entehrten, Die vom Niederrhein, Der erste Stand, Götz von Berlichingen zubenannt mit der eisernen Hand, Das Haus der Lüge, Reveille, das grosse Wecken; Der tanzende Tod, Brennende Grenze, Die drei Kuckucksuhren, Die elf Schillerschen Offiziere, Liebeshandel, Mitgiftjäger, Die Sporckschen Jäger, Ueberflüssige Menschen, Zopf und Schwert, Am Rande der Welt, Einer gegen alle, Das Frauenhaus von Rio, Kinderseelen klagen an, Leichte Kavallerie, Lützows wilde verwegene Jagd, Das Mädchen aus der Fremde, § 182 Minderjährig; Regine, die Tragödie einer Frau; Die Sandgräfin, Schinderhannes, Venus im Frack, Die Vorbestraften, Angst, Die von der Scholle sind, Herbstzeit am Rhein, Das letzte Fort, Majestät schneidet Bubiköpfe, Der rote Kreis, Der Zarewitsch, Asphalt, Fräulein Else.*

362 **STEMMLE, ROBERT ADOLF (R.A.)** (1903-). B: Magdeburg. Scriptwriter, author and director. Studied at Hamburg

University. Read theatrical history at Wilhelm Humboldt University in Berlin. With the success of his play *Kampf um Kitsch* he decided to work entirely for the theatre. Literary Manager at Freie Volksbühne and Komödie in Berlin. 1930-1934: Head Literary Manager for Tobis. 1935-1939: director for Ufa. 1940-1945: for Bavaria. 1946-1948: teacher at actors' school of the Kammerspiele in Munich. 1949-1951: NWDR Berlin. Directed at theatres in Heidelberg, Munich, Konstanz, Vienna. After 1945: worked also for DEFA (q.v.). Author of many books which were partly adapted or directed for the screen by him. He is (together with Gerhart Hermann Mostar) editor of *Der neue Pitaval,* a collection of criminal cases, originally started by Friedrich von Schiller.

Films * indicates script: *Der Rebell* * (co-scripted with Walter Schmidkunz), *Die unsichtbare Front* * (co-scripted with Max Kimmich), *Mädels von heute* * (co-scripted with Charlie Roellinghoff), *Mutter und Kind* *, *Reifende Jugend* * (co-scripted with Walter Supper), *Charleys Tante* 34 (and *), *Glückspilze* 34 (and *), *Krach um Jolanthe* * (co-scripted with Supper), *Heinz im Mond* 34 (and *), *Es tut sich was um Mitternacht* 34 (and *), *Das Blumenmädchen vom Grand-Hotel* *, *So ein Flegel* 34, *Viktoria* *, *Oberwachtmeister Schwenke* * (co-scripted with E. Freiherr von Spiegel), *Die klugen Frauen* * (co-scripted with Bernhard Zimmer), *Ich war Jack Mortimer* * (co-scripted), *Der Raub der Sabinerinnen* 36 (and *), *Traumulus* * (co-scripted with Erich Ebermayer), *Gleisdreieck* 36 (and * co-scripted with Rolf E. Vanloo), *Glückskinder* * (co-scripted with Paul Martin and Curt Goetz), *Der Mann der Sherlock Holmes war* * (co-scripted with Karl Hartl), *Das Geheimnis um Betty Bonn* 37 (and * co-scripted with Ernst Hasselbach), *Daphne und der Diplomat* 37 (and * co-scripted with O. B. Wendler), *Kleiner Mann, ganz gross* 38 (and * co-scripted with A. Zeltner and H. F. Beckman), *Am seidenen Faden* 38 (and * co-scripted with Eberhard Frowein), *Mann für Mann* 39 (and * co-scripted with Hans Schmodde and Wendler), *Golowin geht durch die Stadt* 40 (and * co-scripted with Emil Burri and Peter Francke), *Donauschiffer* 40, *Jungens* 41 (and * co-scripted with

Wendler and Horst Kerutt), *Quax, der Bruchpilot* *, *Das grosse Spiel* 42 (and * co-scripted with Richard Kirn), *Herr Sanders lebt gefährlich* 43 (and * co-scripted with Jacob Geis), *Johann* 43 (and * co-scripted with Ernst von Salomon and Franz Gribitz), *Geld ins Haus* 45, *Meine Herren Söhne* 45, *Affaire Blum* *, *Berliner Ballade* 48, *Wege im Zwielicht* 48 (and *), *Der Biberpelz* 49, *Die Kuckucks* * (co-scripted with Martha Moyland), *Epilog* *, *Sündige Grenze* 51 (and * co-scripted with Gerda Corbett and Moyland), *Toxi* 52 (and * co-scripted with Maria Osten-Sacken), *Heimweh nach Dir* 52 (and * co-scripted with Aldo Pinelli), *Die Stimme des Andern* * (co-scripted), *Südliche Nächte* 53 (and * co-scripted with Pinelli), *Das ideale Brautpaar* 53 (and *), *Wenn Du noch eine Mutter hast* 54, *Emil und die Detektive* 54 (and *), *Ein Herz voll Musik* 55 (and *), *Du darfst länger schweigen* 55 (and *), *Die Försterbuben* 55 (and *), *Die ganze Welt singt nur Amore* 56 (and * co-scripted with Gérard Carlier), *Uns gefällt die Welt* 56 (and * co-scripted with Carlier), *Es wird alles wieder gut* *, *... und die Liebe lacht dazu* 57 (and *), *Gestehen Sie, Dr. Corda!* *, *Majestät auf Abwegen* 58 (and *), *Jons und Erdme* * (co-scripted with Victor Vicas), *Die unvollkommene Ehe* 59 (and * co-scripted with Juliane Kay), *Das kunstseidene Mädchen* * (co-scripted with Julien Duvivier and René Barjavel), *Mein Schulfreund* * (co-scripted with Johannes Mario Simmel), *Der letzte Zeuge* * (co-scripted with Thomas Keck), *Die seltsame Gräfin* *, *Der Henker von London* *, *Die Gruft mit dem Rätselschloss* *, *Old Shatterhand* * (in collab. with Ladislaus Fodor), *Das Ungeheuer von London City* *, *Die Pyramide des Sonnengottes* * (in collab. with Georg Marischka and Fodor), *Der Schatz der Azteken* * (in collab. with Fodor and Georg Marischka).

363 **STEPPAT, ILSE** (1917-1970). B: Elberfeld. Actress. Stage training and music school. Theatres: Gladbach-Rheydt, Düsseldorf, Osnabrück, Oldenburg. Since 1937: in Berlin. 1940: Altes Theater Leipzig. 1943: Deutsches Theater Berlin. 1945-1949: Hebbel-Theater Berlin. Plays best part as the wife of actor Joachim Gottschalk (q.v.) in *Ehe ohne Schatten.* Later she did not re-

ceive film parts commensurate with her talent.

Films: *Ehe im Schatten, Die blaue Schwerter, Die Brücke; Der Mann, der zweimal leben wollte; Der Fall Rabanser, Die Tat des Andern, Was das Herz befiehlt, Die Schuld des Dr. Homma, Hanna Amon, Lockende Sterne, Wenn abends die Heide träumt, Der Kaplan von San Lorenzo, Rittmeister Wronski, Waldwinter; Weil du arm bist, musst Du früher sterben; Der Adler vom Velsatal, Bekenntnisse des Hochstaplers Felix Krull, Madeleine – Tel. 13 62 11, Nachtschwester Ingeborg, Der achte Wochentag, Romarei – das Mädchen mit den grünen Augen, Sehnsucht hat mich verführt, Pension Schöller, Im Namen einer Mutter, Auf Engel schiesst man nicht, Der Unsichtbare, Der unheimliche Mönch, Karriere, Die blaue Hand.*

364 STRAUB, JEAN-MARIE (1933-   ). B: Metz (France). Director. Studied literature in Strasbourg and Nancy. 1954-1958: in Paris, meets Danièle Hullet, Abel Gance, Jean Renoir, Alexandre Astruc and Jacques Rivette. Since 1958: in Munich. Became internationally famous for *Nicht versöhnt* and *Chronik der Anna Magdelena Bach*. All films made in collaboration with his wife, Hullet. His spare, elliptical style is considered by some to mark a new approach to film-making. *See also Junger deutscher Film.*

Films: *Machorka-Muff* 63 (short), *Nicht versöhnt* 65 (medium length), *Chronik der Anna Magdelena Bach* 67 (feature), *Der Bräutigam, die Komödiantin und der Zühalter* 68 (short).

365 STROBEL, HANS RUDOLF (1929-   ). B: Falkenstein (Vogtland). Director. Started as film critic in Munich in 1948. 1950-1953: editor of *Korrespondenz für Filmkunst.* Collaborated on scripts (uncredited) and volunteered as production assistant. 1954-1955: reports for Bavarian TV. Teamed with Tichawsky (q.v.) since 1957. 1968: first feature film together.

Films: TV (alone): *Lopar* 54 (co-dir. Bodo Blüthner), *Ein Tag in Weissenburg* 55 (with Blüthner), *Bier für Paris* 55 (with Blüthner). Acted in *Der Brief.* Films (in collab. with Tichawsky). Shorts: *Alberobello* 57, *Der grosse Tag des Giovanni Farina* 58, *Orff-Schulwerk, rhythmisch-melodische Erziehung* 59, *Den Schlüssel um den Hals* 59, *Ivan Hellberg, Baggerführer in Kiruna* 60, *Eine Brücke für Europa* 60 (also called *Brücke der Hoffnung*), *Erzstadt Kiruna* 60, *Holz* 60, *Notizen aus dem Altmühtal* 61, *Süditalien* 61, *La Scampagnata* 62, *Ponte Vecchio* 62. Full-length documentaries: *Nur wer im Wohlstand lebt . . .* 59, *Notabene Mezzogiorno* 62, *Der Sountag der Tapatis* 65, *Die Wunder von Mailand* 66. Films for TV: *Die abenteuerliche Reise des Giovanni Farina* 56, *Ein Münchner erlebt Wien* 56, *Krippe Neapel* 57, *Bilder aus dem Mittagsland* 58, *Stockholm ohne Beispiel* 59, *Unruhe im stillen Tal* 60, *Autostrada del Sole* 60, *Neapel* 60, *Die Strassenhändler von Paris* 60, *Die kleinen Bälle von Paris* 60, *Zum Beispiel St. Tropez* 60, *Mediolanum* 60 (also called *Drei Mann und ein Zug*), *Die höchsten Deutschen* 60, *Notizen aus dem Vilstal* 61, *Notizen aus dem Wörnitztal* 61, *Protokoll auf Rhein-Main* 61, *Satellitenstädte* 61, *Trastevere* 61, *Battistas grosse Fische* 61, *Via Margitta* 61, *Morgen im Mittagsland* 61, *Hochzeit auf Ischia* 62, *Dalmatinische Inselreise* 62 (Part One: *Von Rijeka bis Split*, Part Two: *Von Split bis Dubrov-*

nik), Die Tarantel 62, Piemont à la carte 62, Die Rauschberger und die Miesenbacher 62, Sonntags ein Graf 62, Die verödete Stadt 62, Die Wohnstadt im Grünen 62, Die Zukunft wird schon verbaut 62, Zum Beispiel Ingolstadt 64, Ausflug auf italienisch 64, Musikproduktion 66, Bauen für morgen 66, Mädchen von Mailand (also called *Die kleinen Bälle von Mailand), Zwischen Boom und Krise – Norditalien 66, Siena 66,* Feature film: *Eine Ehe 67-68.*

366 STROH, HEIDI (1941-   ). B: Jena. Actress. Studied ballet and singing, but trained as dentist's assistant. Model in Italy, musical soubrette at Teatro Sistina in Rome. Enters cinema in Italy. Important actress in the productions of *Junger deutsche Film* (q.v.).

Films: *Mahlzeiten, Eine Ehe, Neun Leben hat die Katz, Die Söhne, Der Fall Lena Christ.*

367 THATE, HILMAR (1931-   ). B: Halle/Saale. Actor. 1947: trained at State actors' school in Halle, then at theatres in Cottbus and Berlin (Maxim Gorki theatre and Berliner Ensemble). State Award in 1966.

Films: *Leuchtfeuer, Einmal ist keinmal, Robert Mayer – Der Arzt aus Heilbronn, Jahrgang 21, Das Lied der Matrosen, Leute mit Flügeln, Mutter Courage und ihre Kinder, Professor Mamlock, Der Fall Gleiwitz, Der geteilte Himmel.*

368 THIELE, HERTHA (1912-   ). B: Leipzig. Actress. Stage *début* at Schauspielhaus Leipzig, then to Berlin (Theater am Kurfurstendamm and Theater Unter den Linden). Enters cinema thanks to Carl Froelich (q.v.) in *Mädchen in Uniform (see* Sagan). After 1933: emigrates to Switzerland. 1942: Stadttheater Berne. After 1945: to East Berlin, where she becomes the head of an *avant-garde* theatre. Now retired.

Films: *Mädchen in Uniform, Mensch ohne Namen, Das erste Recht des Kindes, Die elf Schill'schen Offiziere, Kuhle Wampe, Frau Lehmanns Töchter, Elisabeth und ihr Narr, Anna und Elisabeth, Kleiner Mann – was nun?, Reifende Jugend, Die weisse Majestät.*

369 THIELE, ROLF (1918-   ). B: Redlice (Czechoslovakia). Director. Studied in Berlin. Prague and Göttingen. 1945: own studio. 1946: obtains production licence and co-founds "Filmaufbau GmbH Göttingen" with Hans Abich. The company was responsible for some remarkable postwar films. First film as director in 1951, then films mainly with erotic themes (*Lulu, Wälsungenblut, Moral 63, Venusberg, Komm nur mein liebstes Vögelein*).

Films: *Liebe 47* (only prod.), *Nachtwache* (only prod.), *Es kommt ein Tag* (only prod. and script with Harbou, Hans Abich, Fritz Grashoff and Ernst Penzoldt), *Primanerinnen 51* (and script), *Der Tag vor der Hochzeit 52* (and script), *Königliche Hoheit* (only prod.), *Geliebtes Leben 53* (and script), *Sie 54* (and script), *Mamitschka 55* (and script), *Die Barrings 55* (and script with Felix Lützkendorf), *Friederike von Barring 56* (and script), *Skandal in Ischl 57, El Hakim 57, Der tolle Bomberg 57, Das Mädchen Rosemarie 58* (and script with Rolf Ulrich, Jo Herbst and Erich Kuby), *Die Halbzarte 59, Labyrinth 59* (also co-scripted with Gregor von Rezzori), *Die Botschafterin 60* (prod.

and co-scripted), *Auf Engel schiesst man nicht* 60 (also script), *Der liebe Augustin* 60, *Man nennt es Amore* 61 (also co-scripted), *Lulu* 62 (also script), *Das schwarz-weiss-rote Himmelbett* 62, *Moral 63* 63 (also script), *Venusberg* 63 (also script), *DM-Killer* (also co-scripted with Merz),*Tonio Kröger* 64, *Wälsungenblut* 64, *Die Herren* 65 (co-dir.), *Das Liebeskarussell (i & ii)* 65, *Grieche sucht Griechin* 66, *Der Tod eines Doppelgängers* 66 (also script), *Der Lügner und die Nonne* 67, *Die Ente klingelt um ½8* 68, *Komm nur, mein liebstes Vögelein ...* 68 (also co-scripted with Ernst Flüge), *Grimms Märchen von lüsternen Pärchen* 69, *Ohrfeigen* 69 (also script), *Komm nach Wien – ich zeig Dir was* 69.

370 **THIELE, WILHELM (WILLIAM)** (1890-   ). B: Vienna. Director. Studied at Konservatorium. 1909-1913: actor and director for the stage. Début in Austrian films in 1923 with *Märchen aus Alt-Wien*, then literary manager and author for Ufa. From 1926: films in Germany. 1933: to U.S.A., where he specialises in "Tarzan" films. After 1945: a few films in Germany.

Films (incomplete): *Carl Michael Ziehrer, der letzte Walzerkönig* (only co-scripted with Toni Gerlich and Gabriele Modl, also acted), *Götzendämmerung* (only co-scripted with Robert Heymann), *Carl Michael Ziehrers Märchen aus Alt-Wien* 23 (also co-scripted with Hans Torre), *Fiat Lux* 23, *Franz Lehar* 23 (co-dir. with Hans Torre), *Das Totenmahl auf Schloss Begalitza* 23 (also script), *Zwei Kinder* (only script), *Die Insel der Träume* (only co-scripted with Paul Rosenhayn), *Liebesfeuer* (only script), *Gräfin Plättmamsell* (only co-scripted with Robert Reinert), *Die Kleine vom Varieté* (only script), *Sein grosser Fall* (only co-scripted with Fritz Wendhausen), *Der Anwalt der Herzens* 27 (also co-scripted with Werner Scheff), *Die Czardasfürstin* (only co-scripted), *Jugendrausch* (only co-scripted with Reinert), *Orientexpress* 27 (also script), *Die selige Exzellenz* 27 (also co-scripted with Adolf Edgar Licho), *Die Dame mit der Maske* 28, *Adieu Mascotte* 29. Then sound: *Die Drei von der Tankstelle* 30, *Liebeswalzer* 30, *Die Privatsekretärin* 31, *Der Ball* 31, *Madame hat Ausgang* 31 (also script with Franz Schulz), *Zwei Herzen auf einen Schlag* 32, *Mädchen zum Heiraten* 32, *Grossfürstin Alexandra* 33, *Der letzte Fussgänger* 60 (also script with Eckart Hachfeld), *Sabine und die 100 Männer* 60.

371 **THIMIG, HERMANN** (1890-   ). B: Vienna. Actor. Son of actor and stage director Hugo Thimig (1854-1944). No stage training. 1910: *début* in Meiningen. 1914-1916: soldier. 1919-1924: theatres in Berlin with Reinhardt (q.v.). 1924-1932: Theater in the Josefstadt Vienna. Since 1934: Burgtheater Vienna. Enters cinema after First World War playing opposite Ossi Oswalda, Mia May, Henny Porten, Pola Negri (all q.v.) and others. Named "Kammerschauspieler" in 1937. Many guest appearances throughout Europe. Brother of Helene (b. 1889, first married to Max Reinhardt, q.v.) and Hans. Married to actress Vilma Degischer.

Films (incomplete): *Komptesse Doddy, Die Puppe, Rausch, Die Brüder Karamasoff, Die Bergkatze, Bräutigam auf Kredit, Die Flamme, Der Fluch des Schweigens, Kleider machen Leute, Die Küsse der Lea Foscari, Sie und die Drei, Der Strom, Alles für Geld, Der Kaufmann von Venedig, Der verlorene Schuh, Paragraph 144, Die Radio-*

Heirat, Mädels von heute, Der ungebetene Gast, Madame macht einen Seitensprung, Die Familie ohne Moral, Im Hotel "Zur süssen Nachtigall," Napoleon auf St. Helena. Then sound: *Der kleine Seitensprung, Die Dreigroschenoper, Ich bleib' bei Dir, Zwei himmelblaue Augen, Der Herr Bürovorsteher, Mein Leopold; Mein Freund, der Millionär, Wenn die Soldaten . . ., Die Privatsekretärin, Das Blaue vom Himmel; Marion, das gehört sich nicht, Ein bisschen Liebe für Dich, Mädchen zum Heiraten, Kiki, Glück über Nacht, Eine Stadt steht Kopf, Eine Nacht im Paradies, Traum von Schönbrunn, Kleiner Mann – was nun?, Die Fahrt ins Grüne, Viktor und Viktoria; Peter, Paul und Nanette; Liebe dumme Mama, Früchtchen, Der Herr ohne Wohnung, Karneval und Liebe, Im weissen Rössl, Tanzmusik, Der Himmel auf Erden, Die Fahrt in die Jugend, Der geheimnisvolle Mister X, Die Austerlilli, Marguerite: 3, Brüderlein fein, Johann, Die kluge Marianne, Liebesbriefe, Die goldene Fessel, Ein Blick zurück, Wie ein Dieb in der Nacht, Der Prozess, Praterbuben, Prämien auf den Tod, Geheimnisvolle Tiefe, Der Fünf-Minuten-Vater, Fräulein Bimbi, Ich hab' mich so an Dich gewöhnt, Eine Nacht in Venedig, Ewiger Walzer, Die Magd von Heiligenblut, Eine Reise ins Glück, Tausend Sterne leuchten, Wenn die Glocken hell erklingen, Frau Irene Besser, Die vergessenen Jahre.*

372 THORNDIKE, ANDREW (1909-   ). B: Frankfurt. Documentarist and director. Prior to 1939 he was the main representative for Ufa and their publicity shorts. 1942: soldier on the Eastern Front, prisoner of war. 1948: to G.D.R. Meets Annelie Thorndike (q.v.), marries her and works in close collaboration with her. *Das russische Wunder* is regarded as a significant film in the realistic style of postwar Communist cinema. State Awards in 1952, 1956 and 1963, patriotic order of merit in 1959, Lenin prize in 1963 (both Andrew and Annelie).

Films: *Der 13. Oktober* 49 (doc.), *Von Hamburg bis Stralsund* 49 (second episode from *Aus unseren Tagen*, also script), *Der Weg nach oben* 50 (doc., also phot.), *Wilhelm Pieck – das Leben unseres Präsidenten* 51 (doc., also script), *Freundschaft siegt* 51 (doc.), *Die Prüfung* 52 (doc., also script), *Sieben vom Rhein* 54 (doc., also script), *. . . Du und mancher Kamerad* 56 (doc., also script), *Urlaub auf Sylt* 57 (doc., also script), *Unternehmen Teutonenschwert* 58 (doc., also script), *Das russische Wunder I & II* 63 (doc., also script), *Tito in Deutschland* 65 (doc., also script), *Du bist min, ein deutsches Tagesbuch* 69 (doc., also script).

373 THORNDIKE, ANNELIE (1925-   ). B: Klützow. Documentarist and director. Meets Andrew Thorndike (q.v.) when making *Der Weg nach oben*. Literary manager and later works with her husband. First film together *Die Prüfung*. Films: see Andrew Thorndike.

374 TICHAWSKY, HEINZ (1924-   ). B: Teschen/Oberschlesen (in Polish Cieszyn). Director. Soldier, prisoner of war, then studies pharmacy. Head of the student film club in Munich. 1954: starts production of shorts and documentaries for TV. Since 1956 Tichawsky has worked in close collaboration with Hans Rolf Strobel (q.v.) as a successful TV production team. First feature film in 1968. Films: *Fern der grossen Strasse* 54, *Musik für Kinder* 55, *Die selige Insel* 57. For his other films see Strobel.

375 TIEDTKE, JAKOB (KARL) (1875-1960). B and D: Berlin: Actor. Stage training at Königliches Schauspielhaus Berlin, making his *début* in 1889. 1899-1915: plays in Berlin theatres (including Reinhardt's). 1915-1918: Burgtheater Vienna. Then several guest appearances. 1933-1945: Volksbühne Berlin. After 1945: Schiller-Theater Berlin and guest appearances. Entered the cinema in 1905. One of the best German film comedians in both the silent and sound period. Was often referred to as "Filmvater Tiedtke" (film father Tiedtke).

Films (incomplete): *Schuldig, Kulicks Gewissensbisse, Der Rattenfänger von Hameln, Fahrt ins Blaue, Die Puppe, Kohlhiesels Töchter, Sumurun, Der Mann ohne Namen, Die Flamme, Der Strom, Der Tiger des Zirkus Farini, Das alte Gesetz, Die Austreibung, Das Karussell des Lebens, Der Kaufmann von Venedig, Maciste und die chinesische Truhe, Nanon, Arabella, Auf Befehl der Pompadour, Dr. Wislizenus; Pietro, der*

Andrew and Annelie Thorndike at work

Korsar, Die Radio-Heirat, Das Spiel mit dem Schicksal, Tragödie im Hause Habsburg, Ein Traum vom Glück, Die Dame aus Berlin, Die drei Portiermädel, Husarenfieber, Kammermusik, Der gute Ruf; In der Heimat, da gibt's ein Wiedersehn!; Der Mann im Feuer, Die Mühle von Sanssouci, Nur eine Tänzerin, Das Panzergewölbe, Der Provinzonkel, Schenk mir das Leben, Die Apachen von Paris, Arme kleine Sif, Die Bräutigame der Babette Bomberling, Dr. Bessels Verwandlung, Die Frau ohne Namen, Gehetzte Frauen, Gustav Mond ... Du gehst so stille, Luther, Primanerliebe, Unter Ausschluss der Oeffentlichkeit, Was Kinder den Eltern verschweigen, Don Juan in der Mädchenschule, Ehre Deine Mutter, Heut' spielt der Strauss, Heut tanzt Mariett, Liebe im Schnee, Moral, Das Spreewaldmädel, Autobus Nr. 2, Die Liebe der Brüder Rott, Mascottchen, Meine Schwester und ich, Drei machen ihr Glück. Then sound: *Die Jugendgeliebte, Das Flötenkonzert von Sanssouci, Pension Schöller, Zum goldenen Anker, Yorck, Voruntersuchung, Berlin-Alexanderplatz, Ein Auto und kein Geld, Mein Freund, der Millionär, ... und das ist die Hauptsache, Zwei glückliche Tage, Das Blaue vom Himmel, Das Mädchen vom Montparnasse, Ein toller Einfall, Tausend für eine Nacht, Strich durch die Rechnung, Das Testament des Cornelius Gulden; Ja, treu ist die Soldatenliebe; Hasenklein kann nichts dafür, Fräulein − falsch verbunden, Wenn am Sonntagabend die Dorfmusik spielt; Schön ist jeder Tag, den Du mir schenkst; Marie-Louise, Saison in Kairo, Kleiner Mann − was nun?, Gretel zieht das grosse Los, Heimat am Rhein, Das Lied vom Glück, Der Kampf um den Bär, Die kalte Mamsell, Die schönen Tage von Aranjuez, Des jungen Dessauers grosse Liebe;*

Ihre Durchlaucht, die Verkäuferin, Schwarzer Jäger Johanna, So ein Flegel, Besuch am Abend, Schützenkönig wird der Felix; Schön ist es, verliebt zu sein; Petersburger Nächte, Peter, Paul und Nanette, Das Blumenmädchen vom Grand-Hotel, Der Doppelbräutigam, Der Döppelgänger, Der Vetter aus Dingsda, Lockvogel, Fürst Woronzeff, Frühlingsmärchen, Ein Mädel wirbelt durch die Welt, Die Liebe und die erste Eisenbahn, Die Liebe siegt, Die grosse Chance, Frischer Wind aus Kanada, Der junge Graf, Der Vogelhändler, Hilde Petersen postlagernd, Spiel an Bord, Onkel Bräsig, Savoy-Hotel 217, Gewitterflug zu Claudia, Zu neuen Ufern, Die göttliche Jette, Meine Freundin Barbara; Nanu, Sie kennen Korff noch nicht?; Das unsterbliche Herz, Verwehte Spuren, Die Reise nach Tilsit, Falschmünzer, Das leichte Mädchen, Jud Süss, Der Weg ins Freie, Die schwedische Nachtigall, Pedro soll hängen, Frau Luna, Leichte Muse, So ein Früchtchen, Der grosse König, Das schwarze Schaf, Jungfern vom Bischofsberg, Johann, Die Frau meiner Träume, Das war mein Leben, Familie Buchholz, Schicksal am Strom, Schuss um Mitternacht, Das alte Lied, Die tolle Susanne, Kolberg, Heidesommer, Ich glaube an Dich, Shiva und die Galgenblume, Wiener Mädeln, Morgen ist alles besser, Das Geheimnis der roten Katze, Hans im Glück, Kleiner Wagen – grosse Liebe, Einmaleins der Liebe, Nichts als Zufälle, Es begann um Mitternacht, Das seltsame Leben des Herrn Bruggs, Hanna Amon, Durch dick und dünn, Königin einer Nacht, Am Brunnen vor dem Tore, Unsterbliche Geliebte, Die blaue Stunde, Keine Angst vor grossen Tieren, Damenwahl, Der Raub der Sabinerinnen, . . . und ewig bleibt die Liebe, Emil und die Detektive, Urlaub auf Ehrenwort.

376 TILLER, NADJA (1929-   ). B: Vienna. Actress. Trained as a dancer and for the stage, then small parts at Theater an der Josefstadt Vienna. Model. 1949: Miss Austria, and makes *début* in Austrian films. Her German films were mainly with director Rolf Thiele (q.v.). International career. Married to actor Walter Giller (q.v.).

Films: *Eroica, Märchen vom Glück, Kleiner Schwindel am Wolfgangsee, Das Kind an der Donau, Wir werden das Kind schon schaukeln, Ich hab' mich so an Dich gewöhnt, Illusion in Moll, Einmal keine Sorgen haben, Die Kaiserin von China, Ein tolles Früchtchen, Schlagerparade, Liebe und Trompetenblasen, Mädchen mit Zukunft, Sie, Der letzte Sommer, Ball im Savoy, Gestatten, mein Name ist Cox, Griff nach den Sternen, Wie werde ich Filmstar?, Hotel Adlon, Die Barrings, Reich mir die Hand, mein Leben, Das Bad auf der Tenne, Ich suche Dich, Friederike von Barring, Fuhrmann Henschel, Spion für Deutschland, Banktresor 713, Drei Mann auf einem Pferd, El Hakim, Das Mädchen Rosemarie, Labyrinth, Buddenbrooks, An einem Freitag um half zwölf, Die Botschafterin, Geliebte Hochstaplerin, Lulu, Das grosse Liebesspiel, Moral 63, Schloss Gripsholm, Tonio Kröger, Erotica, Das Liebeskarussell (ii), Rendezvous der Killer, Das gewisse Etwas der Frauen, Rififi in Paris, Lady Hamilton. Ohrfeigen.*

377 TOURJANSKY, VICTOR (1891-). B: Kiev. Director. Studied sculpting, then attends Academy of Dramatic Art (with Stanislavsky). Acted in theatres in Moscow. 1912: enters cinema as actor. 1914: first film of Russian film industry. 1919: to

France and Hollywood, with occasional films in Germany and Czechoslovakia. Since 1958: mainly in Italy with costume dramas. Films: *Wolga-Wolga* 28, *Manolescu* 29. Then sound: *Der Herzog von Reichstadt* 31, *Die ganze Welt dreht sich um Liebe* 35, *Stadt Anatol* 36, *Der Blaufuchs* 38, *Geheimzeichen LB 17* 38, *Verklungene Melodie* 38, *Eine Frau wie Du* 39, *Der Gouverneur* 39, *Feinde* 40 (also script with Emil Burri and Arthur Luethy), *Die keusche Geliebte* 40, *Illusion* 41 (also script with Werner Eplinius), *Liebesgeschichten* 43, *Tonelli* 43 (also script with Burri), *Orient-Express* 44 (also script with Burri and Peter Groll), *Dreimal Komödie* 45 (also script with Burri), *Der blaue Strohut* 49 (also script with Burri), *Der Mann, der zweimal leben wollte* 50, *Vom Teufel gejagt* 50 (also script with Burri), *Mutter sein dagegen sehr* 51, *Ehe für eine Nacht* 52, *Salto mortale* 53, *Arlette erobert Paris* 54, *Morgengrauen* 54, *Die Toteninsel* 55 (also script with Juliane Kay Victor de Fast, Lore Stapenhorst and Erich Kröhnke), *Königswalzer* 55, *Beichtgeheimnis* 56, *Herz ohne Gnade* 58.

378 **TREBITSCH, GYULA** (1914-   ). B: Budapest. Producer. Commercial High School in Budapest. Training at Ufa. 1932-1938: at Ufa Budapest. 1939: co-owner of Objektiv-Film in Budapest. Then in concentration camp. 1945-1947: manager of a cinema in Itzehoe. 1947: as partner and head of production to Real-Film in Hamburg. Many shorts, documentaries and features. Later, when Real-Film was dissolved he becomes managing partner of Studio Hamburg Atelierbetriebsgesellschaft (company which runs studios in Hamburg). 1969: member of the Board of Polytel-Film Ltd. in London.
Films (assoc. prod.): *Arche Nora, Finale, Derby, Die Freundin meiner Frau, Die letzte Nacht, Gefährliche Gäste, Hafenmelodie, Kätchen für alles, Schicksal aus zweiter Hand, Absender unbekannt, Der Schatten des Herrn Monitor, Des Lebens Ueberfluss, Gabriela, Schatten der Nacht, Mädchen mit Beziehungen, Die Dritte von rechts, Schön muss man sein; Weh' dem, der liebt; Engel im Abendkleid, Lockende Gefahr, Kommen Sie am Ersten, Die Stimme des Andern, Keine Angst vor grossen Tieren,*

Columbus entdeckt Krähwinkel, Die Stadt ist voller Geheimnisse. (Producer): *Des Teufels General, Unternehmen Schlafsack, Zwei blaue Augen, Die Ehe des Dr. med. Danwitz, Ich und meine Schwiegersöhne, Der Hauptmann von Köpenick, Drei Birken auf der Heide, Tierarzt Dr. Vlimmen, Das Herz von St. Pauli, Dr. Crippen lebt, Herz ohne Gnade, Bühne frei für Marika, Die schöne Lügnerin, Salem aleikum, Zwei Engel im Pullover, Frau Warrens Gewerbe, Die Frau am dunklen Fenster, Pension Schöller, Gauner in Uniform, Geliebte Hochstaplerin.*

379 **TREMPER, WILL** (1928-   ). B: Braubach a/Rh. Scriptwriter and director. 1946: police correspondent in Berlin. Since 1947: author of novels and controversial serials for magazines and newspapers. 1956: enters cinema as scriptwriter (at first for Georg Tressler, q.v.). 1960: first feature film. All his films, excepting *Sperrbezirk* are based on his own scripts. Formed his own distribution organisation for *Playgirl*, which was still a failure. Tremper brings a journalistic style to his films, and is much concerned with social themes.
Films: *Die Halbstarken* (only co-scripted), *Endstation Liebe* (only script), *Nasser Asphalt* (only script), *Flucht nach Berlin* 61 (also script), *Verspätung in Barienborn* (only script), *Die endlose Nacht* 63 (also script), *Playgirl* 66 (also script), *Sperrbezirk* 66, *How Did a Nice Girl Like You Get into This Business* 69.

380 **TRENKER, LUIS** (1892 or 1903-   ). B: St. Ulrich/Südtirol (or Ortisei/Alto Adige, Italy). Actor and director. At first studied architecture, and for a time he was a mountain guide. Enters cinema through Arnold Fanck (q.v.), and so figured mostly in *"Mountain" films* (q.v.), often in collaboration with Fanck and Leni Riefenstahl (q.v.). Also a large number of documentaries, and after 1945 a few feature films in Germany. Forms his own production company in Munich. Also author of mountain books and actor in TV commercials.
Films: *Das Wunder des Schneeschuhs, Der Berg des Schicksals, Der heilige Berg, Der grosse Sprung, Der Kampf ums Matter-*

comes asst. director to Rabenalt (q.v.) and Geza von Bolvary. 1935-1939: actor and asst. director in Austrian film industry. After 1945: head of film department within the Marshall Plan for Austria, and later goes to Munich. 1956: first feature film *Die Halbstarken* (considered as one of the first films of the *Junger deutscher Film movement*, q.v.). Many short films and works for TV.

Acted in: *Episode, Männer müssen so sein. Der Angeklagte hat das Wort*. Films: *Die Halbstarken* 56 (also co-scripted), *Noch minderjährig* 57 (also script with Emil Burri and Johannes Mario Simmel), *Endstation Liebe* 58, *Das Totenschiff* 59 (also script with Hans Jacoby and Lüdekke), *Geständnis einer Sechzehnjährigen* 60, *Die lustigen Weiber von Windsor* 65, *Der Weibsteufel* 66 (also co-scripted with Adolf Oppel).

382 TRIVAS, VICTOR (1896-1970). B: in Russia. D: New York. Set designer, scriptwriter and director. Enters cinema as set designer for Pabst (q.v.) and collaborates with Warm and Hunte (both q.v.). Directed important pacifist film *Niemandsland*. Later worked as director in France and U.S.A. His return to the German cinema with *Die Nackte und der Satan* was unsuccessful. Later set designer for insignificant films.

Films: *Die Dame aus Berlin* (sets), *Die Liebe der Jeanne Ney* (in collab.), *Evas Töchter* (in collab. with W. Starke),*Majestät schneidet Bubiköpfe, Aufruhr des Blutes* 29 (also co-scripted with Paul Schiller). Then sound: *Niemandsland* 31 (dir. and script), *Der Mörder Dimitri Karamasoff* (script with Leonhard Frank and Fedor Ozep), *Das Lied vom Leben* (script with H. Lechner and Walter Mehring), *Grosstadtnacht* (script with Ozep and Hans H. Zerlett), *Die Nackte und der Satan* 59 (dir. and script with Jacques Magé).

383 TSCHECHOWA, OLGA (1896 or 1897-). B: Alexandropol. Actress. RN: Olga von Knipper-Dolling. Studied at Academy of Arts in Moscow. Sculptress. When sixteen, she married actor Michael Tschechow (later divorced). Stage training with Stanislavsky. 1921: to Germany, and enters cinema thanks to Murnau (q.v.). 1938: declared an "Actress of the State." Mother

horn, Der Ruf des Nordens. Then sound: *Die heiligen drei Brunnen, Die grosse Sehnsucht, Der Sohn der weissen Berge* (also treatment with Walter Schmidkunz), *Berge in Flammen* 31 (also script and dir. with Karl Hartl), *Der Rebell* 32 (also treatment and co-dir.), *Der verlorene Sohn* 34 (also script with Arnold Ulitz and Reinhart Steinbicker and dir.), *Polarstürme, Der Kampf ums Matterhorn, Der Kaiser von Kalifornien* 36 (also script and dir.), *Condottieri* 37 (also script with Kurt Heuser and Mirko Jelusich and dir.), *Der Berg ruft* 37 (also script with Hanns Sassmann and Richard Billinger and dir.), *Liebesbriefe aus dem Engadin* 38 (also script with Sassmann and dir. with Werner Klingler), *Der Feuerteufel* 40 (also script with Sassmann and dir.), *Germanin, Im Banne des Monte Miracolo* 45 (also script and dir.), *Flucht in die Dolomiten* 55 (only dir., and script with Giorgio Bassano and Pier Paolo Pasolini), *Von der Liebe besiegt* 56 (also dir.), *Wetterleuchten um Maria* 57 (only dir.), *Sein bester Freund* 62.

381 TRESSLER, GEORG (1917-). B: Vienna. Actor and director. Son of actor Otto Tressler. At first caricaturist, then be-of actress Ada Tschechowa (who was first married to cameraman Franz Weihmeyr, q.v.), grandmother of actress Vera Tschechowa (b. 1940, RN: Vera Rust).

Films: (incomplete): *Todesreigen, Hochstapler, Schloss Vogelöd, Das Haus der Unseligen* (also prod.),*Der Kampf ums Ich, Ein Puppenheim Die Fahrt ins Glück, Nora, Die Pagode* (also prod.), *Tatjana, Der verlorene Schuh, Die Bacchantin, Die Frau im Feuer, Soll und Haben, Das alte Ballhaus, Die Gesunkenen, Mädels von heute, Der Mann aus dem Jenseits, Die Millionenkompagnie, Soll man heiraten?, Die Stadt der Versuchung, Die Venus vom Montmartre, Der Feldherrenhügel, Brennende Grenze, Familie Schimeck, Der Mann im Feuer, Die Mühle von Sanssouci, Sein grosser Fall; Trude, die Sechzehnjährige; Das Meer, Der Meister der Welt, Die selige Exzellenz, Marter der Liebe, Weib in Flammen, Blutschande 173 St.G.B., Diane* (also prod.), *Die Liebe der Brüder Rott, Der Narr seiner Liebe 29* (also prod.), *stud. chem. Helene Willfüer, Der Detektiv des Kaisers.* Then sound: *Die grosse Sehnsucht, Die Drei von der Tankstelle, Troika, Zwei Krawatten, Liebe im Ring, Ein Mädel von der Reeperbahn, Liebling der Götter, Liebe auf Befehl, Die Nacht der Entscheidung, Das Konzert, Panik in Chikago, Nachtkolonne, Mary, Spione im Savoy-Hotel, Trenck, Wege zur guten Ehe, Heideschulmeister Uwe Karsten, Ein gewisser Herr Gran, Liebelei, Der Choral von Leuthen, Peer Gynt, Zwischen zwei Herzen, Was bin ich ohne Dich, Regine, Maskerade, Die Welt ohne Maske, Abenteuer eines jungen Herrn in Polen, Der Polizeibericht meldet, Die ewige Maske, Liebesträume, Lockspitzel Asew, Künstlerliebe, Ein Walzer um den Stephansturm, Hannerl und ihre Liebhaber, Der Favorit der Kaiserin, Manja Valewska, Seine Tochter ist der Peter, Burgtheater, Unter Ausschluss der Oeffentlichkeit, Gewitterflug zu Claudia, Liebe geht seltsame Wege, Die gelbe Flagge, Verliebtes Abenteuer, Rote Orchideen, Das Mädchen mit dem guten Ruf, Befreite Hände, Bel ami, Zwei Frauen, Ich verweigere die Aussage, Parkstrasse 13, Die unheimlichen Wünsche, Leidenschaft, Angelika, Der Fuchs von Glenarvon, Andreas Schlüter, Menschen im Sturm, Mit den Augen einer Frau, Reise in die Vergangenheit, Gefähr-*

licher Frühling, Der ewige Klang, Melusine, Mit meinen Augen; Der Mann, der zweimal leben wollte; Eine Nacht im Séparée, Kein Engel ist so rein, Zwei in einem Anzug, Maharadscha wider Willen, Aufruhr im Paradies, Die Perlenkette, Eine Frau mit Herz, Das Geheimnis einer Ehe; Mein Freund, der Dieb; Hinter Klostermauern, Heute nacht passiert's, Alles für Papa, Rosen-Resli, Rittmeister Wronski, Ich war ein hässliches Mädchen, Die Barrings, U-47 Kapitänleutnant Prien.

384 **TSCHESNO-HELL, MICHAEL** (1902-). B: Wilna. Scriptwriter. At first journalist. 1933: emigrates. Returns to East Germany after the War and in 1947 founds a publishing house, "Volk und Welt." famous for his script for the two films *Ernst Thälmann* (in collaboration with Willy Bredel). State Awards in 1954, 1957 and 1966.

Films: *Ernst Thälmann – Sohn seiner Klasse* (co-scripted with Willy Bredel), *Ernst Thälmann – Führer seiner Klasse* (co-scripted with Bredel), *Der Hauptmann von Köln* (co-scripted with Henryk Keisch and Dudow), *Solange Leben in mir ist.*

385 TSCHET, KONSTANTIN (19 -). Director of photography. RN: Konstantin Irmen-Tschetwerikoff (also known as Irmenschet). Enters cinema at the end of the silent period. At first well known for his special effects work (e.g. Lang's *Die Frau im Mond*). Then rather busy cameraman on entertainment films, also working in Switzerland.

Films: *Der Weltkrieg* (co-phot. with Ewald Daub, Hans Scholz, Swend Nolden and Wagner), *Die Frau im Mond* (co-phot. with Courant and Oskar Fischinger). Then sound: *Liebeswalzer* (co-phot.), *Einbrecher* (co-phot.) *Liebling der Götter* (co-phot.), *Der Mann, der seinen Mörder sucht; Bomben auf Monte Carlo* (co-phot.), *Voruntersuchung* (co-phot. with Otto Baecker), *Ihre Hoheit befiehlt* (co-phot.), *Der Hochtourist* (co-phot. with Bernhard Wentzel), *Ein blonder Traum* (co-phot. with Rittau and Baecker), *Ein toller Einfall* (co-phot. with Werner Bohne), *Der Frechdachs* (co-phot. with Bohne), *F.P. 1 antwortet nicht* (co-phot. with Rittau and Baecker), *Schuss im Morgengrauen* (co-phot. with Bohne),*Hitlerjunge Quex, Viktor und Viktoria, Liebe muss verstanden sein* (co-phot. with Baecker), *Die Insel, Lockvogel* (co-phot. with Erich Schmidtke), *Freut Euch des Lebens, Königswalzer, Mazurka, Glückskinder, Boccacio, Weiberregiment, Die letzten Vier von Santa Cruz, Fanny Eissler, Gasparone, Menschen ohne Vaterland, Sieben Ohrfeigen, Grossalarm, Fortsetzung folgt, Nanon; Hallo, Janine!; Der Gouverneur, Ins blaue Leben* (cophot. with Günther Anders), *Kora Terry, Männerwirtschaft, Frauen sind doch bessere Diplomaten* (co-phot. with Alexander von Lagorio), *Münchhausen* (co-phot. with Werner Krien), *Das Hochzeitshotel, Die Frau meiner Träume, Der Puppenspieler, Der Posaunist, Verspieltes Leben, Der blaue Strohut, Alles für die Firma; Der Mann, der zweimal leben wollte; Die fidele Tankstelle* (co-phot. with Gerhard F. Peters), *Unvergängliches Licht, Heidelberger Romanze, Das kann jedem passieren* (co-phot. with Pitt Peters), *Wir tanzen auf dem Regenbogen* (co-phot. with G. Peters and Giovanni Pucci), *Der träumende Mund, Salto mortale* (cophot.), *Die geschiedene Frau* (co-phot. with G. Peters, Herbert Müller and Hans Osterrieder), *Hoheit lassen bitten* (co-phot. with G. Peters), *Weg in die Vergangenheit, Vergiss, wenn Du kannst.*

386 TWARDOWSKI, HANS HEINRICH VON (1898-1958). D: New York. Actor and stage director. Acted in Berlin, mainly in the theatres of Reinhardt (q.v.). Since 1930: in American films. Later also directed stage productions in New York.

Films (incomplete): *Gerechtigkeit, Das Kabinett des Dr. Caligari, Genuine, Die Nacht der Königin Isabeau, Von morgens bis Mitternacht, Am Webstahl der Zeit; Marizza, genannt die Schmugglermadonna; Die Exiliere des Teufels, Lady Hamilton, Malmaison, Phantom* (also co-scripted), *Tingel-Tangel, I.N.R.I., Der Sprung ins Leben, Die Bacchantin, Gefährliche Freundschaft, Die Feuertänzerin, Herbstmanöver, Die lachende Grille, Arme kleine Sif, Der falsche Prinz, Die heilige Lüge, Die Hölle der Jungfrauen, Rätsel einer Nacht, Die Weber, Geschlecht in Fesseln, Ludwig der Zweite, König von Bayern; Peter, der Matrose.* Then sound: *Der König von Paris, Die singende Stadt, Die heilige Flamme, Der Herzog von Reichstadt, Menschen hinter Gittern.*

387 UCICKY, GUSTAV (1898-1961). B: Vienna. D: Hamburg. Director. At first public relations expert, then enters cinema as cameraman in Vienna, working with director Michael (Mihaly) Kertesz (Michael Curtis, 1888-1962). First film in Austria. 1928: to Germany. During the Nazi period Ucicky made several significant and obvious films such as *Flüchtlinge, Morgenrot, Heimkehr,* etc. After 1945: mainly films of local interest. His most famous films are *Der zerbrochene Krug* and *Der Postmeister,* a rather misleading adaptation of the Pushkin novel

Films (incomplete): *Sodom und Gomorra* (co-phot.),*Der junge Medardus* (co-phot. with Eduard von Borsody), *Die Lawine, Harun als Raschid, Die Sklavenkönigin* (in collab. with Neukut and Graf Alexander Kolowrat as technical supervisor), *Das Spielzeug von Paris* (in collab. with Neukut), *Die dritte Eskadron* (in collab. with Borsody), *Fiaker Nr. 13* (in collab. with Borsody), *Der goldene Schmetterling* (in collab. with Borsody), *Die Mühle von Sanssouci* (in collab. with

Borsody and Frederik Fuglsang), *Café Electric* 27, *Pratermizzi* 27 (co-dir. with Reisch, Graf Alexander Kolowrat, Arthur Berger, Karl Leiter, Karl Hartl, Borsody and Emil Stepanek, co-phot. with Borsody), *Tingel-Tangel* 27, *Ein besserer Herr* 28, *Herzen ohne Ziel* 28 (co-dir. with Benito Peroja), *Der Sträfling aus Stambul* 29, *Vererbte Triebe* 29. Then sound: *Das Flötenkonzert von Sanssouci* 30, *Hokuspokus* 30, *Der unsterbliche Lump* 30, *Yorck* 31, *Im Geheimdienst* 31, *Mensch ohne Namen* 32, *Morgenrot* 33, *Flüchtlinge* 33, *Der junge Baron Neuhaus* 34 (also script), *Das Mädchen Johanna* 35, *Unter heissem Himmel* 36, *Savoy-Hotel 217* 36, *Der zerbrochene Krug* 37, *Frau Sixta* 38, *Mutterliebe* 39, *Aufruhr in Damaskus* 39, *Der Postmeister* 40, *Ein Leben lang* 40, *Heimkehr* 41, *Späte Liebe* 43, *Am Ende der Welt* 43, *Der gebieterische Ruf* 44, *Das Herz muss schweigen* 44, *Singende Engel* 49 (also script with Rolf Olsen), *Der Seelenbräu* 50, *Cordula* 50 (also script with Max Mell), *Bis wir uns wiederseh'n* 52, *Der Kaplan von San Lorenzo* 52, *Ein Leben für Do* 53, *Die Hexe* 54 (also script with Emil Burri and Johannes Mario Simmel), *Zwei blaue Augen* 55, *Die Heilige und ihr Narr* 57, *Der Jäger von Fall* 57, *Der Edelweisskönig* 57, *Das Mädchen vom Moorhof* 58, *Der Priester und das Mädchen* 58, *Das Erbe von Björndal* 60.

388 UFA: Universum Film Aktien Gesellschaft, founded December 18, 1917. The name of Ufa is really synonymous with German cinema at its best. At first founded for nationalistic reasons, as propaganda for the moribund German empire (the central government donated twenty-five million Marks to launch the company, a further seven millions came from two private banks). Up to 1926 the following companies were absorbed by Ufa (partly to build up its importance, both commercially and artistically, and partly to attract directors and actors who were under contract elsewhere): Nordisk-Film, Messter-Film, Union, May-Film, Terra (co-productions 1924-1927), Decla-Bioscop. Gradually Ufa bought cinemas, went into distribution and developed the newsreel service.,

Owing to heavy financial losses and in order to avoid the competition of American film Ufa signed a contract with Famous Players Lasky (Paramount) and Metro-Goldwyn-Mayer in 1926 and became "Parufamet Distribution Company" (dissolved in 1932). Even so the economic situation grew worse and in 1927 Ufa was saved by the Scherl Trust, Dr. Alfred Hugenberg, a very important financier, became head of the board of governors and was mainly responsible for a new policy, e.g. Ufa as the national film company promoting nationalism etc. During the Nazi period (q.v.) Ufa G.m.b.H. was the top organisation in State film production and in the Reichsfilmkammer, which included Ufa, Tobis, Terra, Berlin-Film, Bavaria, Wien-Film and Prag-Film as production companies – but all these films were under state control (Ufa in 1937). In 1945 the organisation ceased to exist, and their studios at Neubabelsberg were taken over by DEFA (q.v.). The new Ufa was founded in 1956, but after various failures it changed to a sales company and producer for TV.

Key figure on the board from 1927 onwards: Ludwig Klitzsch, a superb organiser. Key producers: Erich Pommer (q.v.) and Ernst Hugo Carell (who took over when Pommer left). All important directors worked part-time or even full-time for Ufa. Commercial successes at the beginning were the historical and costume films *(see* Lubitsch, Buchowetzki and May); commercial failures included *Der letzte Mann, Metropolis* and *Faust.*

389 ULLRICH, LUISE (1909 or 1910-). B: Vienna. Actress. Stage training at Akademie für Musik und darstellende Kunst in Vienna. 1928: Volksbühne Kunst in Vienna. 1928: Volkstheater Vienna. 1932: Staatstheater Berlin. Enters cinema thanks to Luis Trenker (q.v.). She played her best parts during the Thirties; her acting after 1945 is of little importance compared to her earlier work.

Films: *Goethe lebt . . ., Der Rebell, Flucht ins Glück, Leise flehen meine Lieder, Liebelei, Glück im Schloss, Heimkehr ins Glück, Regine, Vorstadtvarieté, Zwischen zwei Herzen, Liebe dumme Mama, Der Flüchtling von Chikago, Das Einmaleins der Liebe, Viktoria, Schatten der Vergangenheit, Versprich mir nichts, Ich liebe Dich, Der Tag nach der Scheidung, Liebesschule, Annelie,*

From an Ufa film of the Twenties, DER MÜDE TOD. Note the familiar symbol at bottom right-hand corner of still

Der Fall Rainer, Nora, Kamerad Hedwig (also script with Toni Huppertz and Ulrich Erfurth), *Die Reise nach Marakesch, Nachtwache, Vergiss die Liebe nicht, Regina Amstetten, Eine· Frau von heute, Ihre grosse Prüfung; Ich weiss, wofür ich lebe; Sarajevo, Die liebe Familie, Der erste Frühlingstag, Alle Wege führen heim, Ist Mama nicht fabelhaft?, Ein Student geht vorbei, Bis dass das Geld Euch scheidet, Frau Irene Besser.*

390 ULMER, EDGAR G. (GEORG) (1900 or 1904-   ). B: Vienna. Set designer and director. Studied at Academy of Arts and Sciences in Vienna as a student of architecture. Actor and asst. set designer for the theatre (for conductor and opera director Arthur Nikisch and Max Reinhardt, q.v.). 1918-1920: set designer on films for Decla in Berlin, later working in Austria (e.g. with Alexander Korda). 1922: to Berlin, collaborates with Murnau (q.v.) and follows him to U.S.A. 1929: works on *Menschen am Sonntag (see* Nebenzal, Siodmark, etc.). 1930: finally to U.S.A. on various projects. 1950: some films in Italy. Claims to have made over a hundred films. His work is much praised by the French film critics.

Ass. set designer and ass. dir.: *Der letzte Mann, Tartüff, Faust.* Film as director: *Menschen am Sonntag* 29 (in collab.).

391 VAJDA, LADISLAUS (18 -1933). B and D: Budapest. Scriptwriter. RN: Laszlo Vajda. Father of Ladislao (Laszlo) Vajda (1905-1965). Director of a theatre in Budapest, and works for films (e.g. for Michael

Curtiz) in Hungary and Austria. Comes to Germany in the mid-Twenties mainly as a scriptwriter for Pabst.

Films (incomplete): *Sodom und Gomorra* (co-scripted with Michael Kertesz), *Der junge Medardus* (co-scripted with Arthur Schnitzler), *Die Lawine, Die Sklavenkönigin, Der fesche Erzherzog; Schatz, mach' Kasse* (co-scripted with Felix Basch), *Die Czardasfürstin* (co-scripted), *Die Liebe der Jeanne Ney* (co-scripted with Ilja Ehrenburg), *Venus im Frack, Abwege* (co-scripted with Adolf Lantz), *Die Dame in Schwarz; Guten Tag, Schwiegermama; Einen Jux will er sich machen, Rutschbahn* (co-scripted with Lantz and Helen Gosenich), *Unmoral* (co-scripted with Wolff), *Die Büchse der Pandora* (co-scripted with Joseph R. Fliesler); *Die Frau, nach der man sich sehnt; Der Leutnant ihrer Majestät, Polizeispionin 77, Diebe und Champagner* (co-scripted with André Zsoldos). Then sound: *Die weisse Hölle vom Piz Palü* (co-scripted), *Der Günstling von Schönbrunn, Das Land ohne Frauen, Nur Du* (co-scripted with Hans Rameau and Willi Wolff); *Es gibt eine Frau, die Dich niemals vergisst* (co-scripted with André Zsoldos), *Zwei Krawatten, Westfront 1918* (co-scripted with Peter Martin Lampel), *Die Dreigroschenoper* (co-scripted with Leo Lenia and Balázs), *Kameradschaft* (co-scripted with Karl Otten and Lampel), *Der Liebesexpress* (co-scripted with Zsoldos and Alexander Engel), *Die Herrin von Atlantis* (co-scripted with Hermann Oberländer). Posthumous: *Tarankowa* (co-scripted with André Lang, re-make).

392 VALETTI, ROSA (18 -19). B: Berlin. D: Vienna. Actress. RN: Rosa Vallentin. Well known comedienne of the Berlin theatres prior to 1933. Acted in many mediocre comedies of the silent period as well as in some classics *(Schloss Vogelöd, Haus zum Mond, Tartüff, Der blaue Engel).*

Films (incomplete): *Nicht lange täuschte mich das Glück, Das Laster, Ballhaus-Anna, Der Dummkopf, Die glühende Kammer, Haus zum Mond, Planetenschieber, Weltbrand, Die im Schatten gehen, Hannerl und ihr Liebhaber, Mädchen aus der Ackerstrasse, Madeleine, Schloss Vogelöd, Die Tänzerin Barberina, Die Finsternis ist ihr Eigentum, Das Frauenparadies, Gespenster, Der Graf von Essex, Die Küsse der Lea Foscari, Der Strom, Glanz gegen Glück, Das Karussell des Lebens, Steuerlos, Das goldene Kalb, Die Blumenfrau vom Potsdamer Platz, Die Feuertänzerin, Die Frau ohne Geld, Heiratsschwindler, Die Moral der Gasse, O alte Burschenherrlichkeit, Die Prinzessin und der Geiger, Tartüff, Die da unten. Fünfuhrtee in der Ackerstrasse, Gasthaus zur Ehe, Der Hauptmann von Köpenick; Schatz, mach' Kasse; Die Waise von Lowood, Dr. Bessels Verwandlung, Gaunerliebchen, Herkules Maier, Der Sprung ins Glück, Ueb' immer Treu und Redlichkeit, Wie heirate ich meinen Chef, Asphalt, Das brennende Herz, Der Held aller Mädchenträume.* Then sound: *Die blaue Engel, M, Täter gesucht, Das Ekel, Hirsekorn greift ein, Die Abenteuerin von Tunis, Ehe m.b.H., Das Geheimnis der roten Katze, Der Raub der Mona Lisa, Die unsichtbare Front, Skandal in der Parkstrasse, Zwei Herzen und ein Schlag, Die Tänzerin von Sanssouci, Moral und Liebe.*

393 VANDENBERG, GERARD (1932-). B: Amsterdam. Director of photography. At first painter, sculptor, photographer, cameraman. Various prizes and awards for his painting, and later for his camerawork. Worked mainly in Germany, but also in Australia, the Netherlands and Italy. Known for his natural lighting and mobile camerawork. An expert in colour cinematography. Together with Wolf Wirth (q.v.) the most important and influential cameraman of *Junger deutscher Film*. Works closely with George Moorse (especially on new camera techniques).

Films: *Der Damm, Es, Die Söhne, Kuckucksjahre, Der Findling, Der Griller, Liebe und so weiter; Ich bin ein Elefant, Madame; Robinson, Tanker.*

394 VEIDT, CONRAD (1893 or 1892-1943). B: Potsdam near Berlin. D: Hollywood. Actor. Stage training at Deutsches Theater with Reinhardt (q.v.). Actor at the Deutsches Theater Berlin. Enters cinema in 1917. Famous for his demoniac appearance in early "expressionist" films (q.v.). 1933: to England, France and Hollywood.

Films (incomplete): *Opfer der Gesell-*

schaft, Das Rätsel von Bangalore, Die See-schlacht, Dida Ibsens Geschichte, Es werde Licht (iv), Nocturno der Liebe, Opium, Das Tagebuch einer Verlorenen, Anders als die andern, Das Geheimnis von Bombay, Das Kabinett des Dr. Caligari, Nacht auf Gol-denhall, Prinz Kuckuck, Prostitution, Die Reise um die Erde in 80 Tagen, Satanas, Sündige Eltern, Unheimliche Geschichten, Abend ... Nacht ... Morgen, Die Augen der Nacht, Der Gang in die Nacht, Der Graf von Cagliostro, Der Januskopf, Kur-fürstendamm, Der Leidensweg der Inge Krafft, Manolescus Memoiren, Menschen im Rausch, Patience, Der Reigen, Sehn-sucht, Weltbrand, Christian Wahnschaffe, Die E-Saite, Das indische Grabmal, Liebes-taumel, König Richard III. (also co-prod.), Lady Hamilton, Landstrasse und Grosstadt, Lord Byron 22 (dir., also co-prod., acted and script), Lukrezia Borgia, Glanz gegen Glück, Paganini (also prod.), Wilhelm Tell, Carlos und Elisabeth, Nju, Schicksal, Das Wachs-figurenkabinett, Liebe macht blind, Orlacs Hände, Die Brüder Schellenberg, Dürfen wir schweigen?, Die Flucht in die Nacht, Der Geiger von Florenz, Kreuzzug des Weibes, Der Student von Prag. Then sound: Das Land ohne Frauen, Menschen im Käfig, Die grosse Sehnsucht, Die letzte Kompanie,

Der Kongress tanzt, Die Nacht der Ent-scheidung, Die andere Seite; Der Mann, der den Mord beging; Rasputin, Der schwarze Husar, Ich und die Kaiserin, Wilhelm Tell.

395 **VERHOEVEN, PAUL** (1901-   ). B: Unna/Westfalen. Actor and director. Stage training with Karl Wüstenhagen. Ac-tor and manager at theatres: Munich, Al-bert Theater Dresden, Kammerspiele Vien-na, Theater am Schiffbauerdamm Berlin (1943-1944). 1945-1949: general director Bayerische Staatsschauspiele Munich. Guest appearances as actor and director. In films, Verhoeven has mainly been the director of commercial films with a degree of artistic quality. Also acted in films *. Father of director Michael Verhoeven (see Senta Ber-ger).

Films: Der Kaiser von Kalifornien *, Die Fledermaus 37, Es leuchten die Sterne *, Unsere kleine Frau 38 (* and dir. and script with Otto Ernst Lubitz), Der Tag nach der Scheidung 38 (also script with Wolf Neumeister and Wilhelm Ehlers), Sa-lonwagen E 417 39, Gold in New Frisko 39, Renate im Quartett 39 (also script with Her-bert Tjadens), Was wird hier gespielt? *, Die 3 Codonas *, Aus erster Ehe 40, Jakko *, Die Nacht in Venedig 42 (also *), Der grosse Schatten 42 (also *), Der Fall Rainer 42 (also script with Jacob Gais and Wilhelm Krug), Herr Sanders lebt gefährlich *, Ein glücklicher Mensch 43 (also *), Das Kon-zert 44, Philharmoniker 44 (*, also script with Erich Ebermayer), Das kleine Hofkon-zert 45, Du bist nicht allein 49 (* and script), Das kalte Herz 50 (also script with Wolfgang Weyrauch and Wolf von Gordon), Dieser Mann gehört mir 50, Eva im Frack 50, Die Schuld des Dr. Homma 51 (also *), Heidelberger Romanze 51 (also *), Die leib-haftige Unschuld 52 (also *), Das kann je-dem passieren 52, Vergiss die Liebe nicht 53, Hochzeit auf Reisen 53 (*and script with Charlotte Diller and Erich Morawsky), Praterherzen 53 (also *), Eine Frau von heute 54 (* and script with Juliane Kay), Hoheit lassen bitten 54 (and script with Per Schwenzen), Ewiger Walzer (* and script with Alexander Lix and Friedrich Schrey-vogel), Ich weiss, wofür ich lebe 55, Roman einer Siebzehnjährigen 55 (* and script), Die goldene Brücke 56, ... wie einst Lili

Marleen 56 (also script with Ilse Lutz-Du-pont), *Von allen geliebt* 57 (also script with Hannelore Holtz), *Jede Nacht in einem andern Bett* 57, . . . *und nichts als die Wahrheit* *, *Menschen im Netz* *, *Der Jugendrichter* 60, *Ihr schönster Tag* 62, *An der schönen blauen Donau* *, *Paarungen* *.

396 VESELY, HERBERT (1931-   ). B: Vienna. Director. Studied history of art, theatre science and film in Vienna. Began as an extra. At first made experimental 16 mm productions, mostly shorts. 1961: first feature film *Das Brot der frühen Jahre* (adapted from Böll's novel). Important maker of experimental films in Germany after 1945, now working mainly for TV. See *Junger deutscher Film.*

Films (shorts): *Und die Kinder spielen so gern Soldaten* 51 (in Austria), *An diesen Abenden* 52 (in Austria), *Porträt einer Pause* 56 (also called *Prélude*, fourth episode for *Maya*), *Autobahn* 57, *Mode in der Stadt* 59, *Die Stadt* 60, *Folkwangschulen* 60, *Düsseldorf – modisch, heiter, im Wind verspielt* 61, *Die Paletten der Mode* 65, *Ich habe ein Kleid* 66 (short version of *Die Paletten der Mode).* Features: *Nicht mehr fliehen* 55, *Das Brot der frühen Jahre* 62 (also co-scripted with Leo Ti), *Sie fanden ihren Weg* 63, *Deine Zärtlichkeiten* 69 (idea and treatment, began as director but replaced by Peter Schamoni, q.v.).

397 VICH, VACLAV (1898-   ). B: Karlovy Vary. Director of photography. At first amateur photographer. During First World War photo-reporter. Returns to Prague after liberation of Czechoslovakia. At first assistant to director of photography Jan Stallich, and later becomes one of the leading cameramen in Czechoslovakia. 1929: worked on Gustav Machaty's *Erotikon.* 1936: to Italy, later also shoots Austrian, Italian and English films. Most of his German work was done around 1930 and after 1950.

Films: *Der Fall des Generalstabs-Oberst Redl* (co-phot. with Eduard Hoesch), *Der Doppelbräutigam, 7 Jahre Glück, Matthäus-Passion, Die Sünderin* (co-phot. with Klaus Schumann), *Es geschehen noch Wunder, Der Verlorene, Nachts auf den Strassen, Illusion in Moll, Pulverschnee nach Uebersee, Der tolle Bomberg, Der schönste Tag meines Lebens, Madeleine und der Legionär, Morgen beginnt das Leben, An einem Freitag um halb 'zwölf, Romanze in Venedig, Der Tod fährt mit.*

398 VIERTEL, BERTHOLD (1885-1953). B and D: Vienna. Scriptwriter and director. Studied philosophy at Vienna University. Then actor, literary manager and director for theatres in Dresden, Vienna, Munich and Berlin. 1923: founded *avant-garde* theatre group "Die Truppe." Poet and author, translated plays and worked for reviews such as "Die Fackel" and "Simplizissimus." 1928: to Hollywood (Fox). 1933: to London (Gaumont British). 1937: to U.S.A. 1945 returns to Europe as director at the Burgtheater Vienna and guest producer in Berlin. 1923: first film (an adaptation of the Ibsen play *Nora).* His most important film is *Die Abenteuer eines Zehnmarkscheins* in collaboration with Bela Bálasz and Karl Freund (q.v.). First married to actress Salka Viertel-Steuermann (scriptwriter Peter Viertel is their son).

Films: *Ein Puppenheim* 22 (also co-scripted with Georg Fröschel), *Nora* 23 (also co-scripted with Fröschel), *Die Perücke* 24

(also script), *Die Abenteuer eines Zehnmarkscheines* 26. Then sound: *Die heilige Flamme* 31 (also script with Heinrich Fraenkel).

399 **VOGEL, RUDOLF** (1900-1967). B and D: Munich. Actor. Father of actor Peter Vogel (b. 1937). Stage training with Konstantin Delcroix in Munich. Theatres: Schauspielhaus Munich (1924-1925), Landesbühne Hof, Landesbühne Munich (1926-1929), Bayerisches Staatstheater Munich (1929-1945). Soldier and prisoner of war. Since 1948: at Kammerspiele Munich. 1941: enters cinema, mainly in comedy roles, also in vaudeville.

Films: *Venus vor Gericht, Kleine Residenz, Einmal der liebe Hergott sein, Zwischen Gestern und Morgen, Der Apfel ist ab, Das verlorene Gesicht, Der Herr vom andern Stern, Hans im Glück, Zwei in einem Anzug, Die gestörte Hochzeitsnacht, Csardas des Herzens, Fanfaren der Liebe, Der blaue Stern des Südens, Der letzte Schuss, Mönche, Mädchen und Panduren, Drei Kavaliere, Der Weibertausch, Vater braucht eine Frau, Ein Herz spielt falsch, Musik bei Nacht, Der Klosterjäger, Fanfaren der Ehe, Arlette erobert Paris, Der Vogelhändler* (53), *Muss man sich gleich scheiden lassen?, Jonny reitet Nebrador, Der Ehestreik, Sterne über Colombo, Die Gefangene des Maharadscha, Der erste Kuss, Sauerbruch – Das war mein Leben, Das fliegende Klassenzimmer, Feuerwerk, Mädchenjahre einer Königin, Ein Haus voll Liebe; Gestatten, mein Name ist Cox; Solang' es hübsche Mädchen gibt, Ein Herz voll Musik, Zwei Herzen und ein Thron, Ich denke oft an Piroschka, Hilfe sie liebt mich, Urlaub auf Ehrenwort, Die Drei von der Tankstelle, Die goldene Brücke, Bonjour Kathrin, Der Bettelstudent; Durch die Wälder, durch die Auen; Schwarzwaldmelodie, Der k. und k. Feldmarshall, Opernball, Sonnenschein und Wolkenbruch, Uns gefällt die Welt, Robinson soll nicht sterben, Die verpfuschte Hochzeitsnacht, Schön ist die Welt, Ein Stück vom Himmel, Das Wirtshaus im Spessart; Eine Frau, die weiss, was sie will; Der Kaiser und das Waschermädel, Casino de Paris, Wenn die Conny mit dem Peter, Die Landärztin, Vergiss mein nicht, Der veruntreute Himmel; Hula-hopp, Conny!, Du bist wunderbar, Ein Mann geht durch die Wand, Alt-Heidelberg, Marili, Frau Warrens Gewerbe, Ingeborg, Pension Schöler, Kriminaltango, Der Gauner und der liebe Gott, O diese Bayern, Ach Egon, Im 6. Stock, Eheinstitut Aurora, Die Försterchristl, Kohlhiesels Töchter, Der Vogelhändler* (62), *Charley's Tante, Heidi, ... und so was muss um acht ins Bett.*

400 **VOGELER, VOLKER** (1930-   ). B: Bad Polzin/Ostpommern. Studied at Humboldt University in East Berlin, then in Göttingen. 1956: four terms at DIFF (Deutsches Institut für Film und Fernsehen/German Institute for Film and TV) in Munich. Then to television, where he has made several full-length feature films, using a "cinematic" format, as it were, to reach a wide audience.

Films: shorts: *Tradition und Fortschritt* 61, *Ein Konto für jeden* 61, *Der Maschinenring* 62, *Mit Konflikten leben* 63, *Trommeln, Tanz ... und morgen* 63, *Unser aller Geld* 63, *Hörfunk ... Fernsehen oder Der Bayerische Rundfunk* 63, *Spargiro* 64, *Eigentum macht frei* 65, *Die Deutsche Bundesbahn zwischen heute und morgen* 65, *Was ein rechter Bauer ist* 65, *Mit dem Einkommen auskommen* 65, *Vom Brennen und Löschen I* 66. *Feuer! Es brennt!* 66 (also called *Vom Brennen und Löschen II*). Shorts for TV: *Gaudeamus Igitur* 58, *Der einfache Tag* 59, *Der sechste ... und der siebte Tag* 62, *Strassenmusikanten* 63, *Berlin ... woher ... wohin?* 65, *Das fünfte Element* 66, *Das Bild* 67, *Mijnheer hat lauter Töchter* 67. Films for TV: *Die Söhne* 68, *Tanker* 69, *Der Bettenstudent oder: Was mach' ich mit den Mädchen* 69 (script only), *Varna* 69.

401 **VOHRER, ALFRED** (1918-   ). B: Stuttgart. Director. Stage training. Because of war injuries he had to give up acting. Asst. director to Harald Braun. 1946-1948: director for Radio Stuttgart. Director on dubbed versions, with own dubbing company. 1958: first film, then specialises in adaptations (q.v.) of novels by Karl May and Edgar Wallave.

Films: *Schmutziger Engel* 58, *Meine 99, Bräute* 58, *Verbrechen nach Schulschluss* 59, *Mit 17 weint man nicht* 60, *Bis dass das Geld Euch scheidet* 60, *Unser Haus in Ka-*

191

merun 61, *Die toten Augen von London* 61, *Die Tür mit den sieben Schlössern* 61, *Das Gasthaus an der Themse* 62, *Ein Alibi zerbricht* 63, *Der Zinker* 63, *Das indische Tuch* 63, *Der Hexer* 64, *Unter Geiern* 64, *Wartezimmer zum Jenseits* 64, *Neues vom Hexer* 65, *Old Surehand I* 65, *Lange Beine – Lange Finger* 66, *Winnetou und sein Freund Old Firehand* 66, *Der Bucklige von Soho* 66, *Die blaue Hand* 66-67, *Der Mönch mit der Peitsche* 67, *Der Hund von Blackwood Castle* 67, *Im Banne des Unheimlichen* 68, *Der Gorilla von Soho* 68, *Der Mann mit dem Glasauge* 68, *Sieben Tage Frist* 69.

402 **WACHSMANN, FRANZ** (1906-1967). B: Königshütte. D: Los Angeles. Composer. At first bank clerk, studies at Konservatorium Dresden and Berlin. Musician in dance bands. Composed some scores for German films. 1934: to U.S.A. He had an unfailing flair for title themes and suspenseful background music, thanks to his wide control of orchestral means. Managed to strike a specifically American note in his scores and incorporated a little "psychology" into the best of them. Academy Awards for Billy Wilder's *Sunset Boulevard* in 1950 and George Stevens's *A Place in the Sun*, in 1951. Name in U.S.A.: Franz Waxman.

Films: *Das Kabinett des Dr. Larifari* (in collab. with Robert Stolz and Max Hansen), *Der Mann, der seinen Mörder sucht* (in collab.), *Das Lied vom Leben* (in collab. with Holländer and H. Adams), *Paprika, Das Mädel vom Montparnasse, Das erste Recht des Kindes; Scampolo, ein Kind der Strasse* (in collab. with Artur Guttmann), *Ich und die Kaiserin* (in collab.); *Gruss und Kuss, Veronika!* (in collab. with Helmut Wolfes).

403 **WAGNER, FRITZ ARNO** (1889 or 1891-1958). B: Schmiedefeld am Rennsteig. D: Göttingen. Director of photography. Technical school in Ilmenau, commercial training at Leipzig University, then Academy of Arts in Paris. Enters cinema in Paris working for Pathé Frères. As newsreel reporter goes to New York and Mexico. 1919: to Berlin and cameraman at Decla-Bioscop. Up to 1933: one of the most important cameramen of the German cinema, working with Murnau, Lang, Robison (all q.v.) and others. After 1933 his work was of little importance.

Films (incomplete): *Der Galeerensträfling* (co-phot. with Frederik Fuglsang), *Madame Dubarry* (co-phot.), *Das Skelett des Dr. Markulics, Arme Violetta, Geschlossene Kette, Das Marthyrium, Der müde Tod* (co-phot. with Erich Nietzschmann and Hermann Saalfrank), *Schloss Vogelöd* (co-phot. with Laszlo Schäffer), *Das Spiel mit dem Feuer, Der brennende Acker* (co-phot.), *Der Graf von Essex* (co-phot. with Hasselmann and Franz Stein), *Lebenshunger, Nosferatu – Eine Symphonie des Grauens* (co-phot. with Günther Krampf), *Pariserinnen, Wem nie durch Liebe Leid geschah, Der Grossindustrielle, Die Magyarenfürstin, Schatten, Der Sprung ins Leben, Zwischen Abend und Morgen; Pietro, der Korsar* (co-phot. with Maté and George Schneevoigt), *Das Fräulein vom Amt, Der rosa Diamant, Zur Chronik von Grieshuus* (co-phot. with Drews and Ernst Nietzschmann), *Die drei Kuckucksuhren, Eine Dubarry von heute, Liebeshandel, Vater werden ist nicht schwer . . .* (co-phot. with Walter Harvey-Pape), *Am Rande der Welt, Die Liebe der Jeanne Ney* (co-phot. with Walter Robert Lach), *Der Weltkrieg (see* Tschet), *Das letzte Fort* (co-phot. with Schwertführer), *Marquis d'Eon, der Spion der Pompadour; Spione, Waterloo* (co-phot. with Wirsching and Hugo von Kaweczynski), *Napoleon auf St. Helena* (co-phot. with Baberske, Lippert and Weinmann). Then sound: *Wenn Du einmal Dein Herz verschenkst, Skandal um Eva, Brand in der Oper, Die Jagd nach dem Glück* (co-phot.), *Westfront 1918* (co-phot. with Charles Metain), *Dolly macht Karriere* (co-phot.), *Ronny* (co-phot.),*Die Dreigroschenoper, M, Kameradschaft* (co-phot.), *Es wird schon wieder besser* (co-phot.), *Das schöne Abenteuer* (co-phot.), *Spione am Werk* (co-phot. with Baberske and Robert Weichel), *Das Schloss im Süden, Die Nacht der grossen Liebe, Flüchtlinge, Das Testament des Dr. Mabuse, Prinzessin Turandot; Liebe, Tod und Teufel; Ein Mann will nach Deutschland, Spiel mit dem Feuer, Amphitryon* (co-phot. with Werner Bohne), *Schwarze Rosen, Unter heissem Himmel, Savoy-Hotel 217, Tango Notturno; Der Mann, der Sherlock Holmes war; Der zerbrochene Krug, Schatten über St. Pauli, Das Mädchen mit dem guten Ruf, Robert Koch, Der Vierte kommt nicht, Ein hoffnungsloser Fall, Friedrich

Schiller, Aus erster Ehe, Feinde, Der Fuchs von Glenarvon, Ohm Krüger (co-phot. with Karl Puth and Behn-Grund), *Was geschah in dieser Nacht?, Die Entlassung, Der Fall Rainer, Ein glücklicher Mensch* (co-phot. with Erich Nietzschmann), *Lache Bajazzo* (co-phot. with Nietzschmann), *Altes Herz wird wieder jung, Herr Sanders lebt gefährlich* (co-phot.), *Ich werde Dich auf Hände tragen* (co-phot.), *Meine Herren Söhne* (co-phot. with Eduard Mayer), *Das kleine Hofkonzert, Mädchen hinter Gittern, Die Brücke, Du bist nicht allein, Das Mädchen aus der Südsee, Frauenarzt Dr. Prätorius, Herrliche Zeiten, Die Frauen des Herrn S.* (co-phot.), *Die Schuld des Dr. Homma* (co-phot.), *Torreani* (co-phot.), *Der Fürst von Pappenheim* (co-phot.), *Mein Herz darfst Du nicht fragen* (co-phot.), *1. April 2000* (co-phot. with Sepp Ketterer), *Die leibhaftige Unschuld* (co-phot.), *Die Rose von Stambul* (co-phot.), *Fräulein Casanova* (co-phot.), *Die tolle Lola* (co-phot.), *Der Vetter aus Dingsda* (co-phot.), *Der treue Husar* (co-phot.), *Konsul Strotthof* (co-phot.), *Clivia* (co-phot.), *Heideschulmeister Uwe Karsten, Kennen Sie Berlin?* (doc., co-phot. with Hans Minzloff and Horst Kaskeline), *Aus eigener Kraft* (doc., co-phot. with Löb, Wolf Göthe and Fritz Brill), *Die Frau des Botschafters, Hotel Adlon, Meine 16 Söhne* (co-phot. with Hrich), *Tausend Melodie* (co-phot. with Hrich), *Hochzeit auf Immenhof, Geliebte Corinna* (co-phot. with Hrich), *Ferien auf Immenhof, Das Mädchen ohne Pyjama, Kindermädchen für Papa gesucht; Liebe, Jazz und Uebermut; Der Csardaskönig, Ohne Mutter geht es nicht.*

404 WALDMÜLLER, LIZZI (1904-1945). B: Knitterfeld (Tyrol). D: Vienna (air raid). Actress. Voice and stage training in Vienna. Theatres: Graz, Vienna, Berlin, and Hamburg. Enters cinema in 1931, usually in musical films.

Films: *Die spanische Fliege, Strafsache van Geldern, Liebe auf den ersten Ton, Lachende Erben, Peer Gynt, Bel ami, Casanova heiratet, Traummusik, Alles für Gloria, Frau Luna, Liebeskomödie, Die Nacht in Venedig, Ein Walzer mit Dir, Ein Mann wie Maximilian, Es lebe die Liebe.*

405 WANGENHEIM, GUSTAV VON (ADOLF FREIHERR G.v.W.) (1895-   ). Actor and director. B: Wiesbaden. Son of Eduard von Winterstein (q.v.) and actress Hedwig Pauly. Training at Reinhardt School Vienna, then at Burgtheater Vienna and Landestheater Darmstadt. 1916: Deutsches Theater Berlin. 1931: founds "Truppe 31" revolutionary actors' group. 1933-1945: in U.S.S.R. After 1945: to G.D.R. as director and actor at Deutsches Theater in East Berlin. Also author for the stage. Winner of State Award.

Films (incomplete): *Kohlhiesels Töchter, Romeo und Julia im Schnee, Das Feuerschiff, Nosferatu – Eine Symphonie des Grauens, Schatten, Der steinerne Reiter, Die Frau im Mond.* Then sound: *Danton, Kämpfer* 35 (dir. and script), *Und wieder 48!* 48 (dir. and script), *Der Auftrag Höglers* 50 (dir. and script), *Gefährliche Fracht* 53 (dir.), *Heimliche Ehen* 55 (dir. and script).

406 WARM, HERMANN (1889-   ). B: Berlin. Set designer. Trained at Kunstgewerbeschule in Berlin, then at "Szenograph" in Berlin and Schauspielhaus Düsseldorf. Enters cinema in 1912 as set designer. One of the most important figures in "expressionism" (q.v.). 1924-1933: freelance architect and set designer in Hungary, France and England. His films during this period include Dreyer's *La Passion de Jeanne d'Arc* in 1928 and *Vampyr* in 1931. 1941-1944: in Switzerland. After 1947 returns to Germany.

Films (incomplete): *Die blaue Maus, Der Andere, Der König, Der Hund von Baskerville, Der Spion, Die Geschichte der stillen Mühle, Das Kabinett des Dr. Caligari* (in collab.), *Die Pest in Florenz* (in collab. with Röhrig, Jaffé, Reimann), *Die Spinnen I & II* (in collab. with Hunte & Carl Kirmse), *Totentanz, Der Tunnel, Das Blut der Ahnen, Die Toteninsel* (in collab.), *Die Jagd nach dem Tode, Kämpfende Herzen* (in collab. with Ernst Meivers), *Der müde Tod* (in collab.), *Schloss Vogelöd, Zirkus des Lebens, Phantom* (in collab. with Erich Czerwonski), *Das Spiel der Königin* (in collab. with Czerwonski & Rudolf Bamberger), *Der Kaufmann von Venedig, Quarantäne, Gräfin Donelli, Königsliebchen* (in collab. with Gustav Knauer), *Rosenmontag, Mädels von*

One of Hermann Warm's designs for DAS KABINETT DES DR. CALIGARI

heute, Die rote Maus, Soll man heiraten?,
Die Flucht in die Nacht, Fräulein Josette –
meine Frau, Die Frauen von Folies Ber-
gères, Die Insel der verbotenen Küsse (in
collab. with Franz Schroedter), *Liebe* (in
collab. with Ferdinand Ballan), *Parkettsessel*
47, Das süsse Mädel (in collab. with Knauer), *Der Student von Prag, Die Frau ohne*
Namen (in collab. with Schroedter), *Die*
Jagd nach der Braut (in collab. with
Schroedter), *Die Liebe der Jeanne Ney* (in
collab.), *Colonialskandal, Millionenraub im*
Rivieraexpress, Eine Nacht in London, Pris-
cillas Fahrt ins Glück, Das Erlebnis einer
Nacht, Freiheit in Fesseln, Masken, Ver-
tauschte Gesichter, Die weissen Rosen von
Ravensburg, Es kommt alle Tage vor . . .,
Fundvogel (in collab. with Mathieu Oster-
mann). Then sound: *Dreyfus; Der Mann,*
der den Mord beging; Vampyr, Friederike,
Hochzeit am Wolfgangsee, Wenn am Sonn-
tagabend die Dorfmusik spielt, Wenn ich
König wär!, Musik im Blut; Peter, Paul und
Nanette; Pappi, Zigeunerblut, Peer Gynt,
Ich liebe alle Frauen, Der Student von
Prag, Mazurka, Krach im Hinterhaus, Ein
Hochzeitstraum, Mädchenjahre einer Köni-
gin, Die Nacht mit dem Kaiser, Gefährliches
Spiel, Ein Volksfeind, Die Warschauer Zita-
delle, Jugend, Verwehte Spuren, Das un-
sterbliche Herz, Die Geierwally, Wozzeck
(in collab. with Bruno Monden), *Vor uns*
liegt das Leben (in collab. with Monden),
Morituri (in collab. with Monden), *Tragödie*
einer Leidenschaft (in collab. with Monden),
Königskinder (in collab. with Monden),
Frühlingsromanze (in collab. with Monden),
Sehnsucht des Herzens (in collab. with Monden), *Das ewige Spiel* (in collab. with Monden), *Herz der Welt* (in collab. with Herlth
and Monden), *Cuba Cubana* (in collab. with
Monden), *Hokuspokus* (in collab. with Kurt

Herlth), *Die Privatsekretärin* (in collab. with Alfons Windau), *Der Raub der Sabinerinnen* (in collab. with Erich Grave and Paul Markwitz), *Verrat an Deutschland* (in collab. with Windau), *Hanussen* (in collab. with Herlth), *Königswalzer* (in collab. with Windau), *Dany, bitte schreiben Sie!* (in collab. with Windau), *Helden* (in collab. with Monden), *Die Nackte und der Satan* (in collab. with Monden), *Die Wahrheit über Rosemarie, Die Botschafterin* (in collab. with Fritz Maurischat), *Männer sind zum Lieben da* (acted).

407 **WEGENER, PAUL** (1874-1948). B: Bischdorf (East Prussia). D: Berlin. Actor and director. High school in Königsberg, and then studied law in Freiburg and Leipzig. 1895: as actor to Rostock. After various jobs, and thanks to Rudolf Schildkraut, he joins Max Reinhardt (q.v.) at his Deutsches Theater in Berlin from 1906-1920. Shortly before the First World War, Wegener turned to films; his double role in the classic *Der Student von Prag (The Student of Prague)*, directed by Stellan Rye (q.v.), is one of the first great acting performances in the German cinema. Primarily interested in the mystic and fantastic *(Der Golem, Lebende Buddhas)*. An excellent actor, he loved acting great classic figures in the Reinhardt tradition. But during the Nazi era he allowed himself to make various propaganda films *(Der grosse König, Kolberg)*. In 1937, he was made state actor by the Hitler administration. Paul Wegener was married to Lyda Salmonova (q.v.), who acted in nearly all his early films.

Films (incomplete): *Der Student von Prag* (acted and co-scripted with Hanns Heinz Ewers), *Die Verführte, Die Augen des Ole Brandis* 14 (co-dir., acted), *Evintrude, die Geschichte eines Abenteurers* 14 (co-dir., co-scripted, acted), *Der Golem* 14 (co-dir., acted), *Die Rache des Blutes, Peter Schlemihl* (co-scripted, acted), *Rübezahls Hochzeit* 16 (co-dir., scripted, acted), *Der Rattenfänger von Hameln* 16 (co-dir., acted), *Der Yoghi* 16 (co-dir., acted), *Der Golem und die Tänzerin* 17 (co-dir., acted), *Hans Trutz im Schlaraffenland* 17 (also acted), *Dornröschen, Der fremde Fürst* 18 (co-dir., scripted, acted), *Welt ohne Waffen* 18 (doc.), *Der Galeerensträfling* (scripted and acted),

Nachtgestalten; Der Golem, wie er in die Welt kam 20 (co-dir., scripted and acted), *Medea, Steuermann Holck, Sumurun, Die Geliebte Roswolskys, Der verlorene Schatten* 21 (co-dir., scripted, acted), *Das Weib des Pharao, Flammende Völker, Herzog Ferrantes Ende* 22 (co-dir., acted), *Das Liebesnest, Lukrezia Borgia, Monna Vanna, Sterbende Völker, Vanina oder die Galgenhochzeit, Der Schatz der Gesine Jakobsen, SOS. Die Insel der Träen, Lebende Buddhas* 24 (prod., dir., co-scripted with Hans Sturm, acted), *Der Mann aus dem Jenseits, Dagfin, Alraune, Arme kleine Sif, Glanz und Elend der Kurtisanen; Ramper, der Tiermensch; Svengali, Die Weber, Fundvogel.* Then sound: *Marschall Vorwärts, Das Geheimnis um Johann Orth, Unheimliche Geschichten, Inge und die Millionen, Hans Westmar, Ein Mann will nach Deutschland* 34 (only dir.), *Die Freundin eines grossen Mannes* 34 (only dir.), *Der Mann mit der Pranke, . . . nur eine Komödiant, August der Starke* 36 (only dir.), *Moskau – Shanghai* 36 (only dir.), *Die Stunde der Versuchung* 36 (only dir.), *Unter Ausschluss der Oeffentlichkeit* 37 (only dir.), *Kracht und Glück um Künnemann* 37 (only dir.), *In geheimer Mission, Stärker als die Liebe, Das Recht auf*

Liebe, Das unsterbliche Herz, Zwielicht, Das Mädchen von Fanö, Mein Leben für Irland, Diesel, Der grosse König, Hochzeit auf Bärenhof, Wenn die Sonne wieder scheint, Zwischen Nacht und Morgen, Seinerzeit zu meiner Zeit, Der Fall Molander, Dr. phil. Döderlein, Tierarzt Dr. Vlimmen, Kolberg, Der grosse Mandarin.

408 WEIDENMANN, ALFRED (1916-   ). B: Stuttgart. Director. Studied painting, amateur *cinéaste*, then war correspondent for *Berliner Illustrierte*. Enters cinema in 1941 as scriptwriter, first films as director in 1942. Soldier and prisoner of war. After 1945: documentaries. His most interesting film is *Der Weg in die Freiheit*, apart from which he has directed well-made commercial films of no artistic importance

Films: *Hände hoch* 42 (also script), *Junge Adler* 44 (also co-scripted), *Die Schenke zur ewigen Liebe* 45 (also script with Heinz Kückelhaus), *Wir bummeln um die Welt* 49 (doc., dir. and and script with Paul Lieberenz), *Der Weg in die Freiheit* 52 (short.), *Ich und Du* 53 (also co-scripted), *Canaris* 54, *Der Himmel ist nie ausverkauft* 55 (also co-scripted), *Alibi* 55 (also co-idea), *Kitty und die grosse Welt* 56, *Der Stern von Afrika* 57, *Scampolo* 58, *Solange das Herz schlägt* 58, *Buddenbrooks* 59, *Bumerang* 59, *Ich bin auch nur eine Frau* 62, *Julia, du bist zauberhaft* 62, *Das grosse Liebesspiel* 63, *Verdammt zur Sünde* 64, *Die Herren* 65 (co-dir.), *Das Liebeskarussell (iii)* 65, *Schüsse im 3/4-Takt* 65, *Ich suche einen Mann* 66, *Maigret und sein grösster Fall* 66, *Pistol Jenny* 69.

409 WEIHMAYR, FRANZ (1903-1969). B and D: Munich. Director of photography. Trained as photographer at Staatliche Lehranstalt für Fotografie in Munich. Enters cinema in 1922 as asst. cameraman. Since 1923: cameraman, also worked in Paris, London (for Korda), Poland (for Aleksander Ford) and Italy. Very important cameraman in the German cinema of the Twenties and Thirties. First married to actress Ada Tschechowa (*see* Olga Tschechowa).

Films: *Dieter, der Mensch unter Sternen, Die Galgenbraut* (co-phot. with Benno Rauch), *Die Schuld, Die vertagte Hochzeitsnacht, Auf der Reeperbahn nachts um halb eins* (co-phot. with Akos Farkas), *Die nicht heiraten dürfen, Menschen zweiter Güte.* Then sound: *Mädchen in Uniform* (co-phot.), *Anna und Elisabeth, Hans Westmar, Elisabeth und ihr Narr, Wilhelm Tell* (co-phot.), *Das verlorene Tal, Die Werft zum grauen Hecht, Hermine und die sieben Aufrechten, Stjenka Rasin, Moskau – Shanghai, Das Hofkonzert, Fährmann Maria, La Habanera, Daphne und der Diplomat, Zu neuen Ufern, Yvette, Heimat, Der Blaufuchs, Am seidenen Faden, Meine Tante – Deine Tante, Es war eine rauschende Ballnacht, Das Lied der Wüste, Das Herz der Königin, Wunschkonzert* (co-phot.), *Der Kleinstadtpoet, Der Weg ins Freie, Geliebte Welt, Die grosse Liebe, Die Gattin, Damals, Jan und die Schwindlerin, Nora, Fahrt ins Glück, Erzieherin gesucht, Wege im Zwielicht, Liebe 47, Amico; Wer bist Du, den ich liebe; Meine Nichte Susanne, Melodie des Schicksals, Das doppelte Lottchen* (co-phot. with Walter Riml), *Dr. Holl, Das letzte Rezept, Zwei Menschen, Die grosse Versuchung* (co-phot.), *Vergiss die Liebe nicht, Pünktchen und Anton, Ich und Du, Männer im gefährlichen Alter, Eine Frau von heute, Conchita* (co-phot. with Edgar Eichhorn), *Unternehmen Edelweiss* (co-phot. with Karl Schröder), *Canaris, Teufel in Seide, Wo der Wildbach rauscht, Die Letzten werden die Ersten sein, Heiraten verboten!, . . . und führe uns nicht in Versuchung, Auferstehung; Nackt, wie Gott sie schuf; Tränen in Deinen Augen, Orientalische Nächte, . . . und keiner schämte sich, Vertauschtes Leben, Trompeten der Liebe, Paris oh là là* 64 (doc., dir. and co-phot. with Pierre Guenguen).

410 WENDLANDT, HORST (1922-   ). B: Criewem (near Angermünde). Producer. Enters film industry in 1939, to start with for two and a half years as film trader with Tobis. Afterwards until 1944 in Prague as film buyer. After French prison of war, becomes buyer with Carl Fröhlich. Then production assistant and production manager with Central Europa Film. 1956: executive producer with Arthur Brauner's (q.v.) CCC-Filmkunst. In 1960 joins up with Preben Philipsen in Berlin to form "Rialto Film Preben Philipsen." Produces mainly thrillers in the Edgar Wallace series (q.v.), making approximately thirty films up to 1969, more Karl May films (q.v.) and a few more ambitious films. Since 1969 co-productions with Britain and U.S.A.

Films: *Der Frosch mit der Maske* (co-prod.),*Der rote Kreis, Die Bande des Schreckens, Der grüne Bogenschütze* (co-prod. with Constantin), *Gehn Sie nicht allein nach Hause* (co-prod. with Constantin), *Die toten Augen von London, Das Geheimnis der gelben Narzissen, Der Fälscher von London, Die seltsame Gräfin, Unser Haus in Kamerun, Das Rätsel der roten Orchidee, Die Tür mit den sieben Schlössern, Ich bin auch nur eine Frau, Das Gasthaus an der Themse, Der Schatz im Silbersee* (co-prod.), *Der Zinker, Der schwarze Abt, Das indische Tuch, Zimmer 13, Winnetou I* (co-prod.), *Die Gruft mit dem Rätselschloss, Wartezimmer zum Jenseits, Der Hexer, Das Verrätertor* (co-prod.), *Winnetou II* (co-prod.), *Unter Geiern* (co-prod.), *Neues vom Hexer, Der unheimliche Mönch, Winnetou III* (co-prod.), *Der Oelprinz* (co-prod.), *Old Shurehand I* (co-prod.), *Der Bucklige von Soho, Das Geheimnis der weissen Nonne* (co-prod.), *Winnetou und sein Freund Old Firehand* (co-prod.), *Winnetou und das Halbblut Apanatschi* (co-prod.), *Die blaue Hand, Der Mönch mit der Peitsche, Der Hund von Blackwood Castle, Die Zeit der Kirschen ist vorbei* (co-prod.), *Das älteste Gewerbe der Welt* (co-prod.), *Im Banne des Unheimlichen, Der Gorilla von Soho, Der Mann mit dem Glasauge, Dr. van de Velde – Die vollkommene Ehe I* (co-prod.), *Das Gesicht im Dunkeln* (co-prod.), *Dr. van de Velde – Das Leben zu zweit II, How Did a Nice Girl Like You Get into This Business* (in U.S.A.), *Der Kerl liebt mich – und das soll ich glauben?*

411 **WERNER, ILSE** (1918 or 1921-   ). B: Batavia/Java. Actress. RN: Ilse Charlotte Still. Stage training at Reinhardt Seminary Vienna. Theatres: Theater in der Josefstadt Vienna, Salzburg, Kleine Komödie Munich, Frankfurt, Hamburg. Many guest appearances (also in U.S.A.). Enters cinema in 1938, especially popular during Second World War, but only a few films after 1945.

Films: *Frau Sixta, Das Leben kann so schön sein, Die unruhigen Mädchen, Fräulein, Bel ami, Drei Väter um Anna, Ihr erstes Erlebnis, Bal paré, Wunschkonzert, U-Boote westwärts, Die schwedische Nachtigall, Wir machen Musik, Hochzeit auf Bärenhof, Münchhausen, Grosse Freiheit Nr. 7; Das seltsame Fräulein Sylvia, Ein toller Tag, Die gestörte Hochzeitsnacht, Mutter sein dagegen sehr, Königin einer Nacht, Geheimnisvolle Tiefe, Der Vogelhändler, Aennchen von Tharau, Griff nach den Sternen, Die Herrin vom Sölderhof.*

412 **WERNICKE, OTTO** (1893-1965). B: Osterode/Harz. D: Munich. Actor. At first works in a bookshop. Theatres: Erfurt (1909-1913), then Eisenach. Soldier. 1919-1921: Stadttheater Bonn. 1921-1937: Staatstheater Munich. 1934-1935: Deutsches Theater and Staatstheater Berlin. After 1945: Bayerisches Staatsschauspiel Munich. Enters cinema in 1919, but his most important roles came during the sound period. Also part time teacher at Falckenberg School of Acting in Munich.

Films (incomplete): *Der Mädchenhändler von Kairo, Wo Menschen Frieden finden, Die suchende Seele, Das Parfüm der Mrs. Worrington, Die Hölle von Montmartre.* Then sound: *Stürme der Leidenschaft, M, Die nackte Wahrheit; Peter Voss, der Mil-*

lionendieb; *Die Zwei vom Südexpress, Die Nacht der Versuchung, SA-Mann Brand, Die blonde Christel, Das Testament des Dr. Mabuse, Der Tunnel, Der Flüchtling von Chikago, Zwischen Himmel und Erde, Achtung! Wer kennt diese Frau?, Der Herr der Welt, Die vertauschte Braut, Peer Gynt, Liebe dumme Mama, Knock out, Henker, Frauen und Soldaten, Der mutige Seefahrer, Die lustigen Weiber, Ein ganzer Kerl, Strassenmusik, Arzt aus Leidenschaft, Das Schloss in Flandern, Gleisdreieck, Onkel Bräsig, Autobus S, Heimweh, Wie einst im Mai, Wie der Hase läuft, Unternehmen Michael, Starke Herzen, Manege, Das grosse Abenteuer, Der Katzensteg, Nordlicht, Eine Frau kommt in die Tropen, Liebesbriefe aus dem Engadin, Rätsel um Beate, Geheimzeichen LB 17, Gold in New Frisco, D III 88, Silvesternacht am Alexanderplatz, Johannisfeuer, Maria, Ilona, Drei wunderschöne Tage, Der Stammbaum des Dr. Pistorius, Was wird hier gespielt?, Sein Sohn, Ohm Krüger, Heimkehr, Die Kellnerin Anna, Friedemann Bach, Der grosse König, Der Seniorchef, Titanic, Der grosse Preis, Das Leben ruft, Seinerzeit zu meiner Zeit, Kamerad Hedwig, Kolberg, Zwischen Gestern und Morgen, Lang ist der Weg, Der Herr vom andern Stern, Amico, Du bist nicht allein, Die fidele Tankstelle, Wer fuhr der grauen Ford?* 50 (also dir.), *Vom Teufel gejagt, Schatten über Neapel, Susanna Jakobäa Krafftin, Himmel ohne Sterne, Das Sonntagskind, Studentin Helen Willfüer, Die feuerrote Baronesse, Immer die Mädchen.*

413 WERY, CARL (1897-   ). B: Trostberg. Actor. Stage training with Friedrich Ulmer in Munich. At first businessman, then stage *début* in Bielefeld. Theatres: Münster, Schiller-Theater Berlin. To Kammerspiele in Munich, thanks to Otto Falckenberg. Enters cinema in 1933.

Films: *Drei Kaiserjäger, Keinen Tag ohne Dich, Anna und Elisabeth, Königswalzer, Fasching, Gold in New Frisco, Wasser für Canitoga, Der ewige Quell, Was will Brigitte?, Feinde, Venus vor Gericht, Kameraden, Kleine Residenz, Die See ruft, Der verkaufte Grossvater, Via Mala, Frau Holle Tromba, Die seltsamen Geschichte des Brandner Kaspar, Susanna Jakobäa Krafftin, Blaubart, Dr. Holl, In München steht*

ein *Hofbräuhaus, Das letzte Rezept, Die grosse Versuchung, Hab' Sonne im Herzen, Ein Herz spielt falsch, Ave Maria, Liebeserwachen, Hochzeitsglocken, Konsul Strotthoff, Columbus entdeckt Krähwinkel, Und der Himmel lacht dazu, Es geschah am 20. Juli, San Salvatore, Rosen für Bettina, Der Meineidbauer, Ohne Dich wird es Nacht, Schwarzwaldmelodie, Nina, Der Bauerndoktor von Bayrisch-Zell, Ein Amerikaner in Salzburg, Meine schöne Mama, Die grünen Teufel von Monte Cassino, Nackt wie Gott sie schuf, Sebastian Kniepp, Kriegsgericht, Arzt aus Leidenschaft, Tränen in Deinen Augen, Am Galgen hängt die Liebe, Frau Irene Besser, Kriegsgericht; Ein Sommer, den man nie vergisst; Mein Vaterhaus steht in den Bergen, Kohlhiesels Töchter, Trompeten der Liebe, Lausbubengeschichten.*

414 WESSELY, PAULA (1908-   ). B: Vienna. Actress. Music and stage training at Reinhardt School in Vienna. Theatres: Deutsches Volkstheater Vienna (*début*), Deutsches Theater Prague, back to Vienna (Volkstheater). 1929-1944: Theater in der Josefstadt Vienna and Deutsches Theater Berlin. Since 1953: Burgtheater Vienna. En-

ters cinema in 1934 thanks to Willi Forst (q.v.) with the leading role in *Maskerade*. 1949: founds her own production company "Paula Wessely Filmgesellschaft" which produces some films starring Miss Wessely. Married to Attila Hörbiger (q.v.).

Films:*Maskerade, So endete eine Liebe, Episode, Die Julika, Die ganz grossen Torheiten, Spiegel des Lebens, Maria Ilona, Ein Leben lang, Heimkehr, Die kluge Marianne, Späte Liebe, Das Herz muss schweigen, Der Engel mit der Posaune, Vagabunden der Liebe, Cordula, Maria Theresia, Ich und meine Frau, Wenn Du noch eine Mutter hast, Der Weg in die Vergangenheit, Die Wirtin zur goldenen Krone, Anders als Du und ich, Noch minderjährig, Die unvollkommene Ehe, Der Bauer als Millionär, Jedermann.*

415 WICKI, BERNHARD (1919-   ). B: St. Pölten. Actor and director. Trained at the State Actors' School Berlin and State Academy Vienna. Theatres: Schönbrunner *(début)*, Burgtheater Vienna, Bremen, Staatstheater Munich, Schauspielhaus Zurich, Stadttheater Basle (1945-1950), Staatstheater Munich and Salzburg Festival. Excellent photographer (in 1960 published book *Zwei*

Gramm Licht with a preface by Friedrich Dürrenmatt). Wicki's first film as director was the feature documentary *Warum sind sie gegen uns?* in 1958. Directed * films in Germany, U.S.A. (German episodes for *The Longest Day* in 1961 and *Morituri* in 1965), Italy *(The Visit* in 1964) and Switzerland *(Transit* in 1966, based on a script by Max Frisch, unfinished).

Films:*Der fallende Stern, Junges Herz voll Liebe, Rummelplatz der Liebe, Die letzte Brücke, Gefangene der Liebe, Die Mücke, Das zweite Leben, Ewiger Walzer; Kinder, Mütter und eine General; Es geschah am 20. Juli, Du mein stilles Tal, Rosen im Herbst, Frucht ohne Liebe; Weil Du arm bist, musst Du früher sterben; Tierarzt Dr. Vlimmen, Königin Luise, Die Zürcher Verlobung, Flucht in die Tropennacht, Es wird alles wieder gut, Madeleine und der Legionär, Frauensee, Unruhige Nacht, Frau im besten Mannesalter, Warum sind sie gegen uns?* 58 * (and script, feature doc.), *Lampenfieber, Die Brücke* 59 *, *Das Wunder des Malachias* 61 * (and script with Heinz Pauck),*Elf Jahre und ein Tag, Erotica, Der Besuch* 64 *, *Deine Zärtlichkeiten.*

416 WIECK, DOROTHEA (1905 or 1908-   ). B: Davos (Switzerland). Actress. Stage training with Maria Moissi-Urfuss. Theatres: Theater in der Josefstadt (under Reinhardt, q.v.), Kammerspiele Munich (with Otto Falckenburg), Volksbühne and Schillertheater in Berlin. After 1945: many guest appearances. Enters films with Emelka Production Company, her best performance being in *Mädchen in Uniform*. 1933-1934: two films in U.S.A. After 1945: mainly in supporting roles.

Films: *Heimliche Sünder, Ich hab' mein Herz in Heidelberg verloren, Die kleine Inge und ihre drei Väter, Hast Du geliebt am schönen Rhein, Klettermaxe; Mein Heidelberg, ich kann Dich nicht vergessen; Sturmflut, Valencia, Wenn die Schwalben heimwärts ziehen.* Then sound: *Mädchen in Uniform, Gräfin Mariza, Theodor Körner, Trenck, Teilnehmer antwortet nicht, Ein toller Einfall, Anna und Elisabeth, Liselotte von der Pfalz, Der Student von Prag, Der stählerne Strahl, Die unmögliche Frau, Die gelbe Flagge, Liebe kann lügen, Die Vierte kommt nicht, Dein Leben gehört mir, Ge-*

sprengte Gitter; Kopf hoch, Johannes; Andreas Schlüter, Panik, Der grüne Salon, Leb' wohl, Christina, Mordprozess Dr. Jordan, Fünf unter Verdacht, Herz der Welt, Das seltsame Leben des Herrn Bruggs, Hinter Klostermauern, Der Mann meines Lebens, Der Froschkönig, Unternehmen Schlafsack, Das Fräulein von Scuderi, Das Forsthaus im Tirol, Roman einer Siebzehnjährigen; Anastasia, die letzte Zarentochter; Aus dem Tagebuch eines Frauenarztes, Menschen im Hotel, Schachnovelle, Morgen wirst Du um mich weinen.

417 WIEMAN, MATHIAS (1902-1969). B: Osnabrück. D: Zurich. Actor. Studies literature and philosophy, painting and languages in Berlin. Extra at Deutsches Theater in Berlin. After touring, returns to Reinhardt (q.v.) and also appears at Theater in der Josefstadt Vienna. Enters cinema towards the end of the Twenties, played important parts in some films of the Nazi period. Declared "Actor of the State" in 1937. After 1945: many guest appearances.

Films: *Potsdam, das Schicksal einer Residenz; Feme, Der fidele Bauer, Königin Luise, Mata Hari, Der Sohn der Hagar, Die Durchgängerin, Unter der Laterne, Tagebuch einer Kokotte.* Then sound: *Das Land ohne Frauen, Stürme über dem Montblanc, Rosenmontag, Zum goldenen Anker, Die Herrin von Atlantis, Die Gräfin von Monte Christo, Das blaue Licht, Mensch ohne Namen, Anna und Elisabeth, Das verliebte Hotel, Fräulein Hoffmanns Erzählungen, Achtung! Wer kennt diese Frau?, Klein Dorrit, Das verlorene Tal, Vorstadtvarieté, Der Schimmelreiter, Die ewige Maske, Viktoria, Patrioten, Unternehmen Michael, Togger, Anna Favetti, Michelangelo* (doc., speaker), *Kadetten, Ich klage an, Das andere Ich, Paracelsus, Man rede mir nicht von Liebe, Das Herz muss schweigen, Träumerei, Wie sagen wir es unseren Kindern?, Melodie des Schicksals, Wenn eine Frau liebt, Herz der Welt, Solange Du da bist, Königliche Hoheit, Eine Liebesgeschichte, Der letzte Sommer, Angst, Reifende Jugend, Die Ehe des Dr. med. Danwitz, Robinson soll nicht sterben, Wetterleuchten um Maria.*

418 WIENE, ROBERT (1881-1938). B: Sasku (Sachsen). D: Paris. Actor and direc-

tor. Brother of director Conrad Wiene. At first actor in Dresden, then actor, literary manager and director in Berlin. Enters cinema in 1914 as a scriptwriter. Then becomes director and scriptwriter for Henny Porten and Emil Jannings (q.v.). His most important film is *Das Kabinett des Dr. Caligari* in 1919, after which he never again achieved the same international fame. His other "expressionistic" films (q.v.) such as *Genuine, Raskolnikow* and *Orlacs Hände* were too imitative of his earlier success.

Films (incomplete): *Arme Eva* 14 (co-dir. with A. Berger), *Der Stolz der Firma* (co-scripted with Carl Wilhelm), *Er rechts, sie links* 15, *Die Konservenbraut* 15, *Der Schirm mit dem Schwan* (script), *Der Liebesbrief der Königin* 16, *Der Mann im Spiegel* 16, *Die Räuberbraut* 16, *Der Sekretär der Königin* 16, *Das wandernde Licht* 16, *Am Tor des Lebens* (script), *Odysseus' Heimkehr* (script), *Ein gefährliches Spiel* 19 (also script), *Das Kabinett des Dr. Caligari* 19, *Satanas* (script and supervision), *Der Umweg zur Ehe* 19 (co.-dir. and script), *Das Blut der Ahnen* (co-scripted with Johannes Brandt), *Die drei Tänze der Mary Wilford* 20, *Genuine* 20, *Die Nacht der Königin Isabeau* 20 (also script), *Die Rache einer Frau* 20, *Höllische Nacht* 21, *Das Spiel mit dem Feuer* 21 (co-dir. with Georg Kroll), *Salome* 22 (artistic advisers: Metzner, Kozma), *Tragikomödie* 22 (also co-prod. with Lind and Lionardo), *I.N.R.I.* 23 (also script), *Die Nacht der Finsternis* (script), *Der Puppenmacher von Kiang-Ning* 23, *Raskolnikoff* 23 (also script), *Orlacs Hände* 25, *Pension Groonen* 25, *Der Gardeoffizier* 26, *Die Königin vom Moulin-Rouge* 26, *Der Rosenkavalier* 26 (also co-scripted with Louis Nerz and Hugo von Hofmannsthal), *Die berühmte Frau* 27, *Die Geliebte* 27, *Die Frau auf der Folter* 28, *Die grosse Abenteurerin* 28, *Heut' spielt der Strauss* (script), *Leontines Ehemänner* 28, *Unfug der Liebe* 28. Then sound: *Der Andere* 30, *Panik in Chikago* 31, *Der Liebesexpress* 31, *Polizeiakte 909* 34 (also script), *Eine Nacht in Venedig* 34 (also script).

419 WILDER, BILLIE (BILLY) (1906-   ). B: Vienna. Scriptwriter and director. At first journalist in Vienna, then studies in Berlin and becomes court correspondent for

Nachtausgabe. Enters cinema in 1923 as scriptwriter. His best work during the German period is his script for *Menschen am Sonntag (see* Nebenzal, Siodmark and Ulmer). 1933: to U.S.A., via France, where he first becomes a scriptwriter (e.g. with Walter Reisch, q.v., and Charles Brackett). 1942: first American film.

Films: *Menschen am Sonntag* (co-scripted with Fred Zinnemann), *Der Teufelsreporter.* Then sound: *Seitensprünge* (idea), *Der Mann, der seinen Mörder sucht* (co-scripted with Ludwig Hirschfeld and Curt Siodmak), *Emil und Detektive, Ihre Hoheit befiehlt* (co-scripted with Liebmann and Paul Franck), *Ein blonder Traum* (co-scripted) *Scampolo, ein Kind der Strasse* (co-scripted with Max Kolpe), *Es war einmal ein Walzer, Das Blaue vom Himmel* (co-scripted with Kolpe), *Was Frauen träumen* (co-scripted with Franz Schulz), *Madame wünscht keine Kinder* (co-scripted with Kolpe).

420 WINDT, HERBERT (1894-   ). B: Senftenberg/Niederlausitz. Composer. Studied in Berlin (with Franz Schreker). Some early significant works, including *Kammer-Symphonie* (1921), *Andromache* (1932, opera and *Der Flug zum Niederwald* (1935, cantata for radio). Later only light scores. Enters cinema in 1933, and becomes famous for his scores for Nazi and patriotic films. There is a strong resemblance between these scores and the music he wrote for anti-Nazi war films after 1945.

Films: *Flüchtlinge* (in collab. with Ernst Erich Buder), *Morgenrot, Du sollst nicht begehren, Wilhelm Tell, Die Reiter von Deutsch-Ostafrika, Die vier Musketiere, Rivalen der Luft* (in collab. with Franz Friedl), *Mein Leben für Isabell, Hermine und die sieben Aufrechten* (in collab. with A. Hörler), *Fährmann Maria, Standschütze Bruggler, Unternehmen Michael, Starke Herzen, Am seidenen Faden, Pour le mérite, Frau Sixta, Nordlicht, Fest der Völker* and *Fest der Schönheit* (Doc. on Olympics, in collab. with Walter Gronostay), *Roman eines Arztes, Johannisfeuer, Waldrausch, Angelika, Friedrich Schiller, Wetterleuchten um Barbara, Stukas, Kadetten, Ueber alles in der Welt, G.P.U., Die Entlassung, Paracelsus. Besatzung Dora, Die Degenhardts, Solistin Anna Alt, Menschen unter Haien, Die Frau von gestern Nacht, Stips, Der Kampf der Tertia, Wenn abends die Heide träumt, Christina, Leuchtfeuer, Heldentum nach Ladenschluss* (in collab.), *Rosen für Bettina; Durch die Wälder, durch die Auen* (in collab. with Erwin Halletz), *Rose Bernd, Herz ohne Gnade, Hunde wollt ihr ewig leben, Im Namen einer Mutter, Acht Mädels im Boot.*

421 WINTERSTEIN, EDUARD VON (1871-1961). B: Vienna. D: East Berlin. Actor. RN: Eduard Klemens Franz Anna Freiherr von Wangenheim. Father of Gustav von Wangenheim (q.v.). Stage training in Vienna, tours in the provinces. 1894: Schillertheater and Lessing Theatre Berlin. 1905-1938: Deutsches Theater Berlin. 1938-1944: Schillertheater Berlin. Although a very busy stage actor, he found time to play in both silent and sound films. After 1945: in G.D.R., with the Deutsches Theater East Berlin. A few films for DEFA (q.v.). State Award in 1950, 1952 and 1959. Memoirs *Meine Leben und meine Zeit* published in 1963.

Films (incomplete): *Sonnwendfeuer* (date for this film unobtainable, but certainly made prior to 1923), *Schuldig, Die Faust des Riesen, Opium, Madame Dubarry, Maria Magdalena, Das Frauenhaus von Brescia, Die glühende Kammer, Hamlet, Der langsame Tod, Das Marthyrium, Der Reigen, Aus dem Schwarzbuch eines Polizeikommissars II & III, Die Bestie im Menschen, Die Beute der Erinnyen, Danton, Madeleine, Der müde Tod, Schloss Vogelöd, Bigamie, Der brennende Acker, Das Diadem der Zarin, Die vom Zirkus, Der falsche Dimitri, Das Feuerschiff, Das fränkische Lied, Frau Sünde, Der Graf im Pfluge, Der Strom, Die Stumme von Portici, Die Tänzerin des Königs, Die weisse Wüste, Wer wirft den ersten Stein, Die Zirkusdiva, Der allmächtige Dollar, Dämon Zirkus, Die Frau mit den Millionen (ii), Frau Schlange, Fridericus Rex, Glanz gegen Glück, Der Menschenfeind, Der Schatz der Gesine Jakobsen, Der Weg zu Gott, Wilhelm Tell, Claire Garragan, Guillotine, In den Krallen der Schuld, Der kleine Herzog, Mutter und Sohn, Die Radio-Heirat, Schicksal, Der Abenteurer, Aschermittwoch, Der erste Stand, Die Gesunkenen, Götz von Berlichingen zubenannt* mit der eisernen Hand, Das Haus der Lüge, Der tanzende Tod, Volk in Not, Wallenstein, Was Steine erzählen, Das war in Heidelberg in blauer Sommernacht, Fedora, Die Försterchristl, Fräulein Josette – meine Frau, Frauen der Leidenschaft, Die Frau in Gold, Gern hab' ich die Frauen geküsst, Der gute Ruf, Der Herr des Todes, Die Kleine und ihr Kavalier, Des Königs Befehl, Der Meineidbauer, Die Mühle von Sanssouci, Das rosa Pantöffelchen, Tragödie einer Ehe, An der Weser, Da hält die Welt den Atem an, Elternlos, Der geheimnisvolle Spiegel, Ich war zu Heidelberg Student, Lützows wilde verwegene Jagd, Ein Mädel aus dem Volke, Prinz Louis Ferdinand, Stolzenfels am Rhein, Ein Tag der Rosen im August ... da hat die Garde fortgemusst, Vom Leben getötet, Die Siebzehnjährigen, Napoleon auf St. Helena. Then sound: Der blaue Engel, Der Andere, Rosenmontag, Liebling der Götter, Er oder Ich, Zwischen Nacht und Morgen, Kennst Du das Land, Arme kleine Eva, Der Weg nach Rio, Im Geheimdienst, Mensch ohne Namen, Der Geheimagent, Der weisse Dämon, Friederike, Trenck, Morgenrot, An heiligen Wassern, Das erste Recht des Kindes, Der Judas von Tirol, Die Nacht im Forsthaus, Der Läufer von Marathon, Hochzeit am Wolfgangsee, Spione am Werk, Regine, Der letzte Walzer, Zu Strassburg auf der Schanz, Der Schimmelreiter, Der ewige Traum, Hundert Tage, Krach im Hinterhaus, Das Mädchen vom Moorhof, Familie Schimek, Die selige Exzellenz, Der stählerne Stahl, Der höhere Befehl, Waldwinter, Martha, 90 Minuten Aufenthalt, Madame Bovary, Das schöne Fräulein Schragg, Der Etappenhase, Der Katzensteg, Unter Ausschluss der Oeffentlichkeit, Serenade; Der Mann, der Sherlock-Holmes war; Heiratsschwindler, Die Korallenprinzessin, Ballade, Steputat & Co.; Der Mann, der nicht nein sagen konnte; Napoleon ist an allem Schuld, Preussische Liebesgeschichte, Maja zwischen zwei Ehen, Befreite Hände, Robert Koch, Das unsterbliche Herz, Der grüne Kaiser, D III 88, Menschen vom Varieté, Im Namen des Volkes, Die goldene Maske, Die Reise nach Tilsit, Die barmherzige Lüge, Die Frau ohne Vergangenheit, Für die Katz, Bismarck, Das Herz der Königin, Das Fräulein von Barnhelm, Annelie, Stukas, Ohm Krü-

ger; Kopf hoch, Johannes; Rembrandt, Andreas Schlüter, Wenn der junge Wein blüht, Münchhausen, Gefährtin meines Sommers, Ein glücklicher Mensch, Philharmoniker, Der Verteidiger hat das Wort, Meine vier Jungens, Der Puppenspieler, Und wieder 48! Die Buntkarierten, Die Jungen vom Kranichsee, Der Auftrag Höglers, Semmelweis – Retter der Mütter, Die Sonnenbrucks, Der Untertan, Das verurteilte Dorf, Gefährliche Fracht, Heimliche Ehen, Friedrich Schiller, Genesung, Emilia Galotti.

422 **WINTERSTEIN, WILLY** (1895-   ). B: Schelkowitz/Leitmeritz. Director of photography. Studied at Graphische Lehr- und Versuchsanstalt Vienna. 1922: enters film industry in Austria. One of the busiest cameramen in the entire history of the German cinema, the quality of whose work has varied from the remarkable to the indifferent.

Films (incomplete): Hand des Schicksals, Casanovas erste und letztes Liebe, Der Dämon des "Grand Hotel Majestic" (co-phot. with Julius Jonak), Die "Huronen" (co-phot. with Hugo Eywo), Die Macht der Mary Murton, Der Marquis von Bolibar, Die Tochter des Brigadiers, Almenrausch und Edelweiss, Eine kleine Freundin braucht jeder Mann, Das Geheimnis von Genf, Die Hafenbraut, Die Rastelbinder, Die Waise vom Wedding, Der Hafenbaron, Der Kampf ums Matterhorn (co-phot.), Der Ruf des Nordens (co-phot. with Eduard von Borsody and Franz Eigner); Der Mann, der nicht liebt. Then sound: Zweimal Hochzeit, Pension Schöller (co-phot. with Georg Muschner), Die heiligen drei Brunnen (co-phot. with Angst and Viktor Gluck), Der keusche Joseph, Der Liebesarzt (co-phot. with Behn-Grund and Hermann Böttcher), Tänzerinnen für Süd-Amerika gesucht, Der Schlemihl, Der unbekannte Gast, Schön ist die Manöverzeit, Die spanische Fliege (co-phot.),Kaiserliebchen, Ein ausgekochter Junge, Goldblondes Mädchen, ich schenk' Dir mein Herz (co-phot. with Heinrich Balasch), Es gibt nur eine Liebe, Kampf, Das Meer ruft (co-phot. with Kurt Neubert), Der Judas von Tirol (co-phot.), Ich sehne mich nach Dir, Herz ist Trumpf, ... heute abend bei mir, Der Kampf ums Matterhorn (co-phot.), Fräulein Frau, Ein Walzer für Dich

Fräulein Liselott, Zu Strassburg auf der Schanz, Rosen aus dem Süden, Pechmarie, Polarstürme; April, April; Sie und die Drei, Familie Schimek, Eine Nacht an der Donau, Das Mädchen vom Moorhof, Der schüchterne Casanova, Der Hund von Baskerville, Ein Mädel vom Ballett, Wie einst im Mai, Vor Liebe wird gewarnt, Spiel auf der Tenne, Der Schimmelkrieg in der Holledau, Pat und Patachon im Paradies, Peter im Schnee (co-phot. with Hans Imber), Frühlingsluft, Kautschuk (co-phot. with Edgar Eichhorn), Der grüne Kaiser, Die Frau ohne Vergangenheit, Renate im Quartett, Opernball, Kitty und die Weltkonferenz, Johannisfeuer, Rosen in Tirol, Wiener G'schichten, Achtung! Feind hört mit!, Leichte Muse, Dreimal Hochzeit, Die heimliche Gräfin, Zirkus Renz, Ich vertraue Dir meine Frau an, Tolle Nacht (co-phot. with Erich Nietzschmann), Sophienlund, Aufruhr der Herzen (co-phot.), Seinerzeit zu meiner Zeit, Die Fledermaus, Die tolle Susanne, Die letzte Nacht, Hafenmelodie, Zukunft aus zweiter Hand, Schatten der Nacht, Kätchen für alles, Absender unbekannt, Gabriela; Der Mann, der sich selber sucht; Mädchen mit Beziehungen, Die Dritte von rechts, Schön muss man sein, Des Lebens Ueberfluss; Weh' dem, der liebt; Die Dubarry, Die Diebin von Bagdad, Alle kann ich nicht heiraten (co-phot.), Ferien vom Ich, Wenn abends die Heide träumt, Das singende Hotel, Der Vogelhändler, Blume von Hawaii, Staatsanwältin Corda, Dein Mund verspricht mir Liebe, Geld aus der Luft, ... und ewig bleibt die Liebe, Tanz in der Sonne, Drei vom Varieté, Die spanische Fliege 55, Stern von Rio, Der Pfarrer von Kirchfeld, Wenn die Alpenrosen blüh'n, Ihr Leibregiment, Die gestohlene Hose (co-phot. with Siegfried Hold), Drei Birken auf der Heide, Mädchen mit schwachem Gedächtnis; Zu Befehl, Frau Feldwebel!, Der Fremdenführer von Lissabon, Viktor und Viktoria, Der müde Theodor, Witwer mit 5 Töchtern, Die grosse Chance, Nachts im grünen Kakadu, Rivalen der Manege, Bühne frei für Marika, Besuch aus heiterem Himmel, Die Nacht vor der Premiere, Der blaue Nachtfalter, Der lustige Krieg des Hauptmann Pedro, Salem aleikum, Pension Schöler, Gauner in Uniform, Kauf Dir einen bunten Luftballon, Junge Leute brauchen Liebe, Ein Stern fiel vom Himmel, Orientali-sche Nächte, Die Fledermaus, Kohlhiesels Töchter, Nachts ging das Telefon, Das süsse Leben des Grafen Bobby, Der Vogelhändler, Charley's Tante.

423 **WIRTH, WOLF** (1928-   ). B: Nuremberg. Director of photography. 1954: becomes asst. cameraman. First film as cameraman in 1961, in which year he also signed the Oberhausen Manifesto. Wirth, with Gerard Vandenberg, is the most important cameraman of Junger deutscher Film (q.v.).

Films: Tobby (also script with Pohland, Hans Häussler and Siegfried Hofbauer), Kalamitäten, Das Brot der frühen Jahre, Moral 63, Venusberg, DM-Killer, Kennwort: Reiher, Tonio Kröger, Wälsungenblut, Die Herren, Das Liebeskarussell, Tante Frieda – neue Lausbubengeschichten, Grieche sucht Griechin, Ich suche einen Mann, Katz und Maus, Der Tod eines Doppelgängers, Der Lügner und die Nonne, Tätowierung, Wenn Ludwig ins Manöver zieht, Die Ente klingelt um $\frac{1}{2}$8, Heimlichkeiten.

424 **WISBAR, FRANK** (1899-1967). B: Tilsit. D: Mainz. Director. At first officer, then scriptwriter and literary manager for various film companies. 1930: technical training with Carl Boese and Carl Froelich (both q.v.). 1932: first film as director. 1938-1956: in U.S.A. as scriptwriter, director and producer (over 300 films for TV). 1956: returns to Germany. His last film Marcia o crepa was made in Italy.

Films: Im Banne des Eulenspiegels 32, Anna und Elisabeth 33 (also script with Gina Fink), Rivalen der Luft 34, Hermine und die sieben Aufrechten 35 (also script with H. F. Köllner), Die Werft zum grauen Hecht 35 (also script), Fährmann Maria 36 (also script with Hans Jürgen Nierentz), Die Unbekannte 36 (also script with Reinhold Conrad Muschler), Petermann ist dagegen 37 (also script with O. B. Wendler), Ball im Metropol 37 (also script with Wolf Neumeister and Ilse Maria Spath), Haie und kleine Fische 57, Nasser Asphalt 58, Hunde wollt ihr ewig leben 59 (also script with Frank Dimen and Heinz Schröter), Nacht fiel über Gotenhafen 60 (also script with Victor Schuller), Fabrik der Offiziere 60 (also script with Franz Hoellering), Bar-

bara 61, *Durchbruch Lok 234* 63, *Marschier und krepier* 63 (also co-scripted with Giuseppe Mangione, Mino Guerrino, Tofanelli and Krims).

425 WITT, GEORG (1899-   ). B: Moscow. Producer. 1922: works as journalist and publicity man for Decla-Bioscop in Berlin, then assistant to producer Erich Pommer (q.v.) at Ufa. Part-time in U.S.A. with Pommer. 1932: own production company in Germany, then own production company within Ufa. After 1945: own company again.

426 WOHLBRÜCK, ADOLF (1900-1967). B: Vienna. D: Starnberg. Actor. Stage training in Vienna. Theatres: Vienna, Munich, Berlin, Düsseldorf. Since 1936: in U.S.A., England and France (as Anton Walbrook). Film *début* as *Stuart Webbs* (*see* Serials).

Films (incomplete): *Mater Dolorosa, Das Geheimnis auf Schloss Elmshöh.* Then sound: *Der Stolz der 3. Kompanie, Salto mortale, Baby, Melodie der Liebe, Die fünf verfluchten Gentlemen, Drei von der Stempelstelle, Keine Angst vor Liebe, Walzerkrieg, Viktor und Viktoria, Regine, Maskerade, Die englische Heirat; Eine Frau, die weiss, was sie will; Die vertauschte Braut, Zigeunerbaron, Der Student von Prag, Ich war Jack Mortimer, Port Arthur, Allotria, Der Kurier des Zaren, Wiener Walzer, Fledermaus 1955, Lola Montès, König für eine Nacht.*

427 WOLF, KONRAD (1925-   ). B: Hechingen. Director. Son of dramatist Friedrich Wolf. 1933: to U.S.S.R. with his parents, soldier in the Red Army during the War. 1949: studied at VGIK in Moscow (with Sergej Gerassimov). Assistant to Kurt Maetzig (q.v.) for the first *Ernst Thälmann.* Wolf is considered one of the most distinguished directors in the G.D.R. Close collaboration with cameraman Werner Bergmann (q.v.). State Award in 1959.

Films: *Einmal ist keinmal* 55, *Genesung* 56, *Lissy* 57 (also script with Alex Wedding), *Sterne* 58, *Die Sonnensucher* 58, *Leute mit Flügeln* 60, *Professor Mamlock* 61 (also script with Karl-Georg Egel), *Der geteilte Himmel* 64 (also script with Christa and Gerhard Wolf, Willi Brückner and Kurt

Barthel), *Ich war neunzehn* 68 (also script with Wolfgang Kohlhaase).

428 YORK, EUGEN (1912-   ). B: Rybinsk (Russia). Director. Educated in Berlin. Assistant to Walter Ruttmann (q.v.). 1937-1943: supervising editor at documentary department of Ufa. 1945: first film *Heidesommer* (unfinished). After Second World War works at first as director for dubbed versions, then comes his most important film *Morituri.* 1955: works for DEFA (q.v.) *Das Fräulein von Scudery* (planned as a comeback for Henny Porten which failed). Since 1958: in West Germany again with routine thrillers. Acted in *Die letzte Nacht, Export in Blond.*

Films: *Heidesommer* 45, *Morituri* 48, *Die letzte Nacht* 49, *Schatten der Nacht* 50, *Die Schatten des Herrn Monitor* 50, *Export in Blond* 50, *Lockende Gefahr* 51, *Das Fräulein von Scuderi* 55, *Ein Herz kehrt heim* 56, *Das Herz von St. Pauli* 57, *Mann im Strom* 58, *Der Greifer* 58, *Das Mädchen mit den Katzenaugen* 58, *Nebelmörder* 64.

429 ZELLER, WOLFGANG (1893-1967). B: Biesenrode. D: Berlin. Composer. After

First World War finished his studies in music, and was sponsored by Friedrich Kayssler (q.v.) as a composer for the stage. 1926: original score for Lotte Reiniger's *Abenteuer des Prinzen Achmed* (q.v.). 1921-1929: conductor Volksbühne Berlin (succeeding his teacher, Heinz Tiessen), then freelance composer. Thanks to Walter Ruttmann (q.v.), for whom he writes the score for *Melodie der Welt*, becomes increasingly involved in German sound films. His best scores are for Dreyer's *Vampyr* and *Die Herrin von Atlantis*. With Windt (q.v.) one of the most important composers for Nazi films, despite which since 1945 he has been able to write scores for such anti-Nazi films as *Ehe im Schatten* and *Morituri*.

Films: *Das Land ohne Frauen, Melodie der Welt, Menschen im Busch; Himatschal, der Thron der Götter; Im Auto durch zwei Welten, Feind im Blut, Ikarus, An heiligen Wassern, Vampyr, Die Herrin von Atlantis, Unmögliche Liebe, Die Insel der Dämonen, Das alte Recht, Der Mann mit der Pranke, Der alte und der junge König, Der Gefangene des Königs, Ewiger Wald, Ritt in die Freiheit, Die Kopfjäger von Borneo, Pan, Petermann, Der Herrscher, Der zerbrochene Krug, Du und ich, Schatten über St. Pauli, Fahrendes Volk, Ziel in den Wolken, Spiel im Sommerwind, Der Gouverneur, Der Polizeifunk meldet, Robert Koch, Die unheimlichen Wünsche, Die fremde Frau, Jud Süss, Seitensprünge, Unser kleine Junge, Die Kellnerin Anna, Menschen im Sturm, Andreas Schlüter, Wenn die Sonne wieder scheint, Immensee, Der verzauberte Tag, Zwischen Nacht und Morgen, Meine vier Jungens, Die Jahre vergehen, Ein toller Tag, Der Puppenspieler, Das kleine Hofkonzert, Ehe im Schatten, Grube Morgenrot, Morituri, Die Brücke, Die letzte Nacht, Und wenn's nur einer wär', Wohin die Züge fahren, Zukunft aus zweiter Hand, Mordprozess Dr. Jordan, Schatten der Nacht, Export in Blond, Die Lüge, Die Schatten des Herrn Monitor, Unsterbliche Geliebte, Zwei Menschen; Rote Rosen, rote Lippen, roter Wein; Mit siebzehn beginnt das Leben, Aennchen von Tharau, Du darfst nicht länger schweigen, Meine 16 Söhne, Ein Herz kehrt heim, Kein Platz für wilde Tiere, Die Landärztin, Serengeti darf nicht sterben.*

430 **ZIEMANN, SONJA** (1925-   ). B: Eichwalde near Berlin. Actress. Dance training with Tatjana Gsovsky in Berlin. 1940-1942: soubrette and prima ballerina at Plaza Berlin. Later works for radio and films. First film appearances in musical and operetta films. Her best performances are in *Liebe ohne Illusion* and the German-Polish coproduction *Der achte Wochentag*. Some guest appearances in theatres after 1955.

Films: *Die Jungfern vom Bischofsberg, Beliebter Schatz, Ein Windstoss, Freunde, Eine kleine Sommermelodie, Hundstage, Eine reizende Familie, Spuk im Schloss, Liebe nach Noten, Sag' die Wahrheit, Herzkönig, Wege im Zwielicht, Die Freunde meiner Frau, Nach Regen scheint Sonne, Nichts als Zufälle, Nächte am Nil, Um eine Nasenlänge, Eine Nacht im Séparée, Maharadscha wider Willen, Schwarzwaldmädel, Die lustigen Weiber von Windsor, Schön muss man sein, Die Frauen des Herrn S., Johannes und die 13 Schönheitsköniginnen, Grün ist die Heide, Die Diebin von Bagdad, Alle kann ich nicht heiraten, Am Brunnen vor dem Tore, Hollandmädel, Mit siebzehn beginnt das Leben, Die Privatsekretärin, Bei Dir war es immer so schön, Meine Schwester und ich, Die 7 Kleider der Katrin, Das Zarewitsch, Liebe ohne Illusion, Grosse Star-*

Parade, Ich war ein hässliches Mädchen, Mädchen ohne Grenzen, Das Bad auf der Tenne; Dany, bitte schreiben Sie; Opernball, Kaiserball, Nichts als Aerger mit der Liebe, Die grosse Sünde, Frauenarzt Dr. Bertram, Frühling in Berlin, Die Zürcher Verlobung, Der achte Wochentag, Menschen im Hotel, Liebe auf krummen Beinen, Abschied von den Wolken, Nacht fiel über Gotenhafen, Strafbataillon 999, Denn das Weib ist schwach; Hunde, wollt ihr ewig leben, Affäre Nabob, Der Traum von Lieschen Müller; Axel Munthe, der Arzt von San Michele; Ihr schönster Tag, Der Tod fährt mit, Frühstück mit dem Tod, 2 mal 2 im Himmelbett.

431 **ZILLIG, WILFRIED** (1905-1963). B: Würzburg. D: Hamburg. Composer. Educated at Preussische Akademie der Künste as a pupil of Arnold Schönberg. Opera conductor in Oldenburg, Düsseldorf, Essen, Possen. 1947-1952: Radio Frankfurt, then freelance composer. 1959: head of music department of NDR Hamburg. Wrote symphonic scores, chamber music and significant operas. Comparitively few scores for films, but all of special merit (especially *Die Andere* and *Jonas* in collaboration with Duke Ellington). Author of the book *Variationen über neue Musik* in 1959.

Films: *Der Schimmelreiter, Schwarzer Jäger Johanna, Anschlag auf Schweda, Der Ochsenkrieg, Violanta, Die unheimliche Wandlung des Axel Roscher, Sommernächte, Finale, Die Andere, König für eine Nacht, Sarajevo, Wo der Wildbach rauscht, Jonas* (in collab. with Duke Ellington), *Heiraten verboten, Traumstrasse der Welt I & II, Bilderbuch Gottes, Gino.*

Index

429

Alter Kahn und junge Liebe (1957, Hans Heinrich, DE-FA) 78, 188

Altes Herz wird wieder jung (1943) **89,** 101, 149, 158, 168, 169, 170, 174, 200, 231, 403

Alte Sünder, Der (1951, Franz Antel) 164

Alte und der junge König, Der (The Young and the Old King, 1935) **360,** 5, 135, 149, 154, 170, 183, 190, 224, 429

Alt-Heidelberg (Student Prince, 1923, Hans Behrendt) 138, 204, 250, 339

Alt Heidelberg (1959, Ernst Marischka) 44, 109, 128, 253, 399

Am Abend auf der Heide (1941, Jürgen von Alten) 102, 135, 229, 332

Am Abend nach der Oper (1944) **293,** 26, 102, 288

Amarant (1921 ?) 265

Am Brunnen vor dem Tore (1952, Hans Wolff) 98, 108, 329, 375, 430

Am Ende der Welt (At the Edge of the World, 1943) **387,** 9, 151, 164, 166, 247, 329

Amerikaner in Salzburg, Ein (1958, Helmut Weiss) 413

Amerikanische Duell, Das (19 ?) **283**

Am Galgen hängt die Liebe (1960, Edwin Zbonek) 413

Amico (1949, Gerhard T. Buchholz) 70, 234, 409, 412

Ammenkönig, Der/Tal des Lebens, Das (1935) **360,** 26, 81, 128, 190, 194, 221

Am Narrenseil (1921, Josef Firmans, i & ii, i re-issue, re-edited 1923) 335

Amönenhof (1919, Uwe Jens Krafft) 243

Amor an der Leine (1933) see Kind, ich freu' mich auf Dein Kommen

Amor auf Ski (1928, Rolf Randolf) 104, 219

Amore difficile L' (1963) see Erotica

Amphitryon/Aus den Wolken komt das Glück (1935) **338,** 26, 108, 150, 153, 155 ii, 185, 313, 321, 357, 403

Am Rande der Welt (1927) **130,** 68, 148, 335, 361, 403

Am roten Kliff (1921, Hanna Henning) 198, 327

Am Rüdesheimer Schloss steht eine Linde (1927, Johannes Guter) 149

Am seidenen Faden (1938) **362,** 108, 258, 288, 358, 409, 420

Am Sonntag will mein Süsser mit mir Segeln gehn/Leben wie im Paradies, Ein (1961, Franz Marischka) 73

Am Tag als der Regen kam (1959, Gerd Oswald) 3, 109, 223, 354

Am Tor des Lebens/Am Tor des Todes (1918, Conrad Wiene, A) 418

Am Tor des Todes (1918) see Am Tor des Lebens

Am Vorabend (1944) see Blick zurück, Ein

Am Webstuhl der Zeit (1921, Holger-Madsen) 131, 327, 386

Anastasia, die falsche Zarentochter (1927, Arthur Bergen) 42, 142, 224

Anastasia – die letzte Zarentochter (Is Anna Anderson Anastasia?, 1956, Falk Harnack) 24, 63, 80, 158, 277, 279, 299, 340, 416

Ancient Law, The see Alte Gesetz, Das

Andalusische Nächte (1938, Herbert Maisch, G/Sp) 210, 327

An der blauen Adria (1937) see Korallenprinzessin, Die

An der Donau, wenn der Wein blüht (1965, Geza von Cziffra, G/A) 97, 341

Andere, Der (1913) **230,** 22, 115, 406

Andere, Der (1930) **418,** 95, 115, 159, 198, 258, 421

Andere, Die (The Other, 1924) **212,** 156

Andere, Die (The Other, 1949, Alfred E. Sistig) 431

Andere Ich, Das (1918, Fritz Freisler, A) 198

Andere Ich, Das (1941) **218,** 24, 201, 288, 417

Andere Seite, Die (1931, Heinz Paul) 200, 218, 224, 394

Andere Welt (1937, Marc Allégret, G/F) 66, 245

Anders als die andern/§ 175 (Different from the others, 1919) **273,** 338, 344, 394

Anders als Du und ich/Dritte Geschlecht, Das (The Third Sex, 1957) **137,** 59, 197, 266, 414

An der schönen blauen Donau (1926, Friedrich Zelnik) 4, 174, 219

An der schönen blauen Donau (1955, Hans Schweikart, A) 128, 164, 207

An der schönen blauen Donau (1965, John Olden, A) 163, 395

An der Weser (1926/27, Siegfried Philippi) 356, 421

...And Nobody Was Ashamed see ...Und keiner schämte sich

Andreas Hofer (1909, Rudolf Biebrach) 249

Andreas Hofer (1929, Hanns Prechtl) 61

Andreas Schlüter (1942, Herbert Maisch) 59, 115, 150, 172, 224, 383, 416, 421, 429

André und Ursula (1955, Werner Jacobs) 63

And So To Bed see Grosse Liebesspiel, Das

An einem Freitag in Las Vegas/They Came To Rob Las Vegas (1967/68, Antonio Isasi, G/Sp/I/F) 354

An einem Freitag um halb zwölf (1961, Alvin Rakoff, G/I/F) 93, 376, 397

An französischen Kaminen (1963, Defa) **233,** 72, 140, 346

Angel Baby see Engelchen oder die Jungfrau von Bamberg

Angeklagte hat das Wort, Der (1948) see Maresi

Angela/Bergwasser/Weisses Gold (1949, Eduard von Borsody, A) 246

Angelika (1940, Jürgen von Alten) 61, 102, 183, 334, 383, 420

Angélique I & II (1964, Bernard Borderie, G/F/I) 208

Angélique und der König (1966, Bernard Borderie, G/F/I) 208

Angélique und der Sultan (1967/68, Bernard Borderie, G/F/I) 208

Backstairs *see* Hintertreppe, Die

Bad auf der Tenne, Das (1943, Volker von Collande) 98, 149, 231

Bad auf der Tenne, Das (1956, Paul Martin, A) 44, 47, 120, 376, 430

Bademeister Spargel (1956, Alfred Lehner, A) 164

Bagnosträfling, Der (1949) **111,** 59, 74, 85, 102, 114, 164, 238, 267

Bajazzo (1920) *see* Sehnsucht

Ball, Der (1931, G/F) **370,** 95, 132, 236, 338

Ballade/Prinzessin kehrt heim, Die (1938, Peter Hagen = Willi Krause) 421

Ballad of Berlin, The *see* Berliner Ballade

Ball der Nationen (1954) **310,** 111, 149

Ballhaus-Anna (1920, ?) 392

Ballhaus goldener Engel (1932) **189,** 91, 123, 134, 153, 179, 321

Ball im Metropol (1937) **424,** 55, 115

Ball im Savoy (1955, Paul Martin) 223, 376

Ballnacht, Eine (1931) *see* . . . und das ist die Hauptsache

Bal paré/Münchner G'schichten (1940) **310,** 9, 131, 138, 172, 179, 231, 313, 411

Bande des Schreckens, Die (The Terrible People, 1960) **302,** 25, 73, 101, 112, 222, 295, 410

Bande von Hoheneck, Die (1934, Hans F. Wilhelm) 41, 358

Banditen der Autobahn (1955, Geza von Cziffra) 25, 34, 66, 164, 264

Banditen vom Rio Grande, Die (1965, Helmuth M. Backhaus) 215

Banditen von Asnières, Die (1920, ?) 338

Bankett der Schmuggler, Das (1952, Henri Storck, G/F) 131, 172, 336

Bankraub in der Rue Latour (1961) **175,** 187

Bankraub Unter den Linden, Der (1925, Paul Merzbach) 1, 4

Banktresor 713 (1957, Werner Klingler) 15, 85, 145, 207, 299, 376

Barbara (1961) **424,** 85, 266, 296

Barcarole (1930) *see* Brand in der Oper

Barcarole (1935) **212,** 24, 33, 111, 150, 153, 247, 313, 357

Bärenburger Schnurre (1957, Ralf Kirsten, Defa) 78

Barmherzige Lüge, Die (1939, Werner Klingler) 42, 59, 101, 114, 201, 421

Baronchen auf Urlaub (1917, M. Leckband) 4

Barrings, Die (1955) **369,** 9, 40, 58, 138, 376, 383

Bastard, Der/Bastard, The (1968, Duccio Tessari, G/I) 187

Bastard, The (1968) *see* Bastard, Der

Battle Inferno *see* Hunde wollt ihr ewig leben

Bauer als Millionär, Der (1961, Alfred Stöger, A) 414

Bauerndoktor von Bayrischzell (1957, H. Schott-Schöbinger) 47, 413

Bauer vom Brucknerhof, Der/ Mein Bruder Josua (1956, Hans Deppe) 12, 266

Beate (1948) **36**

Beates Flitterwochen (1940, Paul Ostermayr) 102, 305, 358

Beaver Coat, The *see* Biberpelz, Der (1928)

Bedingung: Kein Anhang (1913) **318,** 227

Beethoven (1927, Hans Otto Köwenstein, A) 198

Beethovens Lebensroman (1918) *see* Märtyrer seines Herzens

Befehl ist Befehl (1936, Alwin Elling) 151

Befreite Hände (1939, Hans Schweikart) 21, 59, 156, 166, 294, 383, 421

Begegnung in Rom (1954, Erich Kobler, G/I) 128, 164, 336

Begegnung in Salzburg (1964, Max Friedmann, G/F) 59, 120, 136, 175, 200, 203

Begegnung mit Werther (1949, Karl Heinz Stroux) 24, 59, 143

Beichte einer Toten, Die (1920, ?) 204

Beichtgeheimnis (1956) **377**

Beiden Gatten der Frau Ruth, Die (1919/20, ?) 289

Beiden Schwestern, Die (1943, Erich Waschneck) 5, 85, 100, 101, 102, 288

Beiden Seehunde, Die (1928, Max Neufeld, A) 174

Beiden Seehunde, Die/Seine Hoheit der Dienstmann (1934, Fred Sauer) 26, 203

Bei der blonden Kathrein (1934, Franz Seitz) 133

Bei der blonden Kathrein (1959, Hans Quest) 266, 341, 357

Bei Dir war es immer so schön (1954, Hans Wolff) 75, 104, 214, 231, 232, 331, 334, 430

Beil von Wandsbek, Das (1951, Falk Harnack, Defa) 18, 61, 119, 228, 358

Beine von Dolores, Die (1957, Geza von Cziffra) 47, 221

Bei Pichler stimmt die Kasse nicht (1961, Hans Quest) 25, 26, 73, 221

Bekenntnis der Ina Kahr, Das (Afraid To Love, 1954) **275,** 9, 175, 197, 220

Bekenntnisse des Hochstaplers Felix Krull, Die (1957) **157,** 12, 24, 48, 58, 126, 149, 150, 154, 234, 291, 363.

Bel ami/Liebling schöner Frauen, Der (1939) **104,** 81, 153, 155 ii, 231, 307, 383, 404

Bel ami (1955, Louis Daquin, A) 86, 144

Bel Ami 2000 oder: Wie verführt man einen Playboy? (1966, A/I) **281,** 10, 112

Ben Ali Bey (1913) **283**

Bengelchen liebt kreuz und quer . . . (1968, Marran Gosov) 155 vi, 167, 215

Benno Stehkragen (1927, Trude Santen) 117, 131

Bergadler, Der/Mountain Eagle, The/Fear O'God (1926, Alfred Hitchcock, G/GB) 123

Berg des Schicksals, Der (Peak of Destiny, 1924) **94,** 6, 331, 380

Berge in Flammen (Doomed Battalion, 1931) **380,** 6, 23, 25

Bergkatze, Die (The Mountain Cat, 1921) **227,** 92, 170,

Briefträger Müller (1953) **315,** 98, 151

Brigantenrache (1922, Reinhard Bruck) 265

Brillanten (1937, Eduard von Borsody) 9, 102, 197

Broken, Jug, The *see* Zerbrochene Krug, Der

Brot der frühen Jahre (1962) **396,** 155 vi, 286, 423

Brothers Karamazov, The *see* Brüder Karamasoff, Die

Brot und Rosen (1967, Heinz Thiel & Horst E. Brandt, Defa) 346

Brücke, Die (The Bridge, 1949, Arthur Pohl, Defa) 363, 403, 429

Brücke, Die (The Bridge, 1959) Brüder, Die (1917, ?) 265 Michael Kehlmann) 101, 248

Brücke des Schicksals (1960, Brüder (1922) **121**

Brüder Karamasoff, Die (The Brothers Karamazov, 1920) **49 & 110,** 123, 170, 198, 204, 371

Brüderlein fein (1942, Hans Thimig) 136, 164, 238, 329, 331, 371 **415,** 234

Bruder Martin (1954) *see* Und der Himmel lacht dazu

Brüder Noltenius, Die (1945) **212,** 33, 191, 210, 340

Brüder Schellenberg, Die (Two Brothers, 1925/26) **130,** 58, 133, 142, 394

Bübchen (1968, Roland Klick) 167

Buch des Lasters, Das (19 ?, ?) 156

Buchhalterin, Die (19 ?) **79**

Büchse der Pandora, Die (1922, Arsen von Czerepy) 265

Büchse der Pandora, Die (Pandora's Box, 1928/29) **275,** 46, 67, 198, 391

Bucklige und die Tänzerin, Der (1920) **257,** 107, 204, 244

Bucklige von Soho, Der (1966) **401,** 222, 223, 299, 410

Buddenbrooks, Die (1923) **212,** 1, 54, 311

Buddenbrooks, Die (1959) **408,** 24, 43, 58, 85, 97, 126, 138, 150, 154, 194, 226, 229, 291, 356, 376

Bühne frei für Marika (1958, Georg Jacoby) 128, 144, 314, 378, 422

Bumerang (1960) **408,** 3, 106, 145, 207, 234, 299

Bunbury (1932) *see* Liebe, Scherz und Ernst

Bund der Drei, Der (1929, Hans Behrendt) 1, 41, 173

Bunte Traum, Der (1952, Geza von Cziffra) 47, 120

Buntkarierten, Die (1949, Defa) **233,** 24, 122, 154, 279, 356

Bürgermeister Anna (1950, Hans Müller, Defa) 18

Burgtheater (1936, A) **104,** 204, 205, 383

Burning Soil *see* Brennende Acker, Der (1922)

Burschenlied aus Heidelberg, Ein (1930, Karl Hartl) 104, 150, 156, 313

C

Cadets (1941) *see* Kadetten

Cafe Electric/Wenn ein Weib den Weg verliert/Liebesbörse, Die (1927, A) **387, 69,** 104

Cafe Oriental (1962, Rudolf Schündler) 354

Cagliostros Totenhand (1919, Nils Chrisander) 191

Caligari (1919) *see* Kabinett des Dr. Caligari, Das

Call Girls *see* Für zwei Groschen Zärtlichkeit

Camorra (1951) *see* Schatten über Neapel

Canaris (1954) **408,** 141, 145, 299, 409

Cape Forlorn (1930) *see* Menschen im Käfig

Capriccio (1938) **310,** 9, 59, 122, 139, 155 ii, 185, 246

Capriolen (1937) **129,** 26, 102, 104, 149, 162, 205, 284

Captain of Köpenick, The *see* Hauptmann von Köpenick, Der

Cardillac (1969, Edgar Reitz) 34

Carl Michael Ziehrer, der letzte Walzerkönig (1922, ?, A) 370

Carl Michael Ziehrers Märchen aus Alt-Wien (1923, A) **370**

Carlos und Elisabeth (1924) **273,** 68, 142, 191, 355, 394

Carl Peters (1941, Herbert Selpin) 4

Carmen (Gipsy Love, 1918) **227,** 202, 219, 261, 355

Carola Hansen (1921, ?) 213

Carola Lamberti – Eine vom Zirkus (Woman of the Circus, 1954, Hans Müller, Defa) 289

Caroline Cherie/Schön wie die Sünde (1967, Denys de la Patelliere, G/I/F) 73, 109

Caroline und die Männer über Vierzig (1966, Jacques Pinoteau, G/I/F) 168

Casanova heiratat (1940) **200,** 24, 26, 114, 229, 404

Casanovas Erbe (1928, Manfred Noa) 61, 117, 189

Casanovas erste und letzte Liebe (1920, Julius Szöreghi, A) 422

Casino de Paris (1957, Andre Hunnebelle, G/I/F/) 399

Castle in Flanders, A *see* Schloss in Flandern, Das

Cathérine – Ein Leben für die Liebe/Cathérine (1968, Bernard Borderie, G/F/I) 106, 208

Catherine Gräfin von Armagnac (1922, Karl Vollmöller) **289**

C.d.E./Club der Entgleisten (1922, Rolf Petersen & ? Friedrich Zelnik) 174

Chamäleon, Das (1920, ?) 338

Charley's Onkel (1969, Werner Jacobs) 194

Charleys Tante (1934) **362,** 26, 76, 149, 185, 220, 295

Charley's Tante (1956, Hans Quest) 96, 120, 164, 264, 315

Charley's Tante (1963, Geza von Cziffra, A) 399, 422

Charlott etwas verrückt (1927/28, Adolf Edgar Licho) 134, 292

Charly, der Wunderaffe (1915, A) **242,** 243

Chauffeur Antoinette (1931, Herbert Selpin) 76, 189, 327

Chef schickt seinen besten Mann, Der (1966, Sergio Sollima, G/I/Sp) 93

Chemie und Liebe (1948, Defa) **293,** 20, 231, 253, 266

Children of No Importance *see* Unehelichen, Die

217

Downfall *see* Absturz
Dragonerliebchen (1927/28, Rudolf Walther-Fein) 174, 179, 219, 303, 339
Drama von Mayerling, Das (1924) *see* Tragödie im Hause Habsburg
Draufgänger, Der (1931) **83,** 4, 82, 241, 253, 359
Dr. Bessels Verwandlung (1927) **273,** 38, 117, 189, 375, 392
Dr. Crippen an Bord (1942) **90,** 59, 62, 84, 141, 189
Dr. Crippen lebt (1958) **90,** 25, 93, 256, 378
Dreaming Mouth, The *see* Träumende Mund, Der
Drei blaue Jungs – ein blondes Mädel (1933) **36,** 179, 315
Drei Birken auf der Heide (1956, Ulrich Erfurth) 102, 149, 422
3 Codonas, Die (1940) **293,** 24, 62, 123, 205, 395
Drei Dorfheiligen, Die (1949, Ferdinand Dörfler) 55
Drei Frauen von Urban Hell, Die (1928, Jaap Speyer) 134
Dreigroschenoper (The Threepenny Opera, 1931) **275,** 20, 51, 105, 118, 185, 231, 295, 338, 353, 371, 391, 403
Dreigroschenoper, Die (The Threepenny Opera, 1963, G/F) **358,** 120, 153, 175, 193
Drei Kaiserjäger (1933, Robert Land & Franz Hofer) 179, 253, 305, 413
Drei Kavaliere (1951, Joe Stöckel) 91, 399
Dreiklang (1938, Hans Hinrich) 58, 138
Dreiklang der Nacht (1924, Karl Berhardt) 76
Drei Kuckucksuhren, Die (1925/26, Lothar Mendes) 361, 403
Drei Liebesbriefe aus Tirol (1962, Werner Jacobs, A) 164
Drei machen ihr Glück (1929, Carl Wilhelm) 4, 90, 255, 375
Drei Mädels vom Rhein (1955, Georg Jacoby) 26, 149
Dreimäderlhaus, Das (1918) **273**
Dreimäderlhaus (1936) *see*

Drei Mäderl um Schubert
Dreimäderlhaus, Das (1958, Ernst Marischka, A) 21, 37, 194, 240, 253, 332
Drei Mäderl um Schubert/Dreimäderlhaus (1936, E. W. Emo) 8, 164, 174, 246, 280
Dreimal Hochzeit (1941, Geza von Bolvary) 35, 108, 136, 221, 247, 329, 422
Dreimal Komödie/Liebeswirbel (1945) **377,** 59, 237
Drei Mann auf einem Pferd (1957) **245,** 120, 221, 376
Drei Mannequins, Die (1926, Jaap Sepyer) 4, 117
Drei Männer im Schnee (1955) **157,** 13, 59, 229
Drei Mann in einem Boot (1961, Helmut Weiss, G/A) 120
Drei Minuten vor Zehn (1930) *see* Tat des Andreas Harmer, Die
Drei Nächte (1920) **36,** 114, 338
Drei Niemandskinder, Die (1927, Fritz Freisler) 104, 321
Drei Portiermädel, Die (1925) **36,** 61, 375
Drei Scheine des Todes (1921, Lothar Mendes) 280
Drei Seelen – ein Gedanke (1927, Fred Sauer) 4
Drei Tage Angst (1952, Erich Waschneck) 149, 356
Drei Tage auf Leben und Tod (1929, Heinz Paul) 179
Drei Tage Liebe (1931, Heinz Hilpert) 4, 74, 159
Drei Tage Mittelarrest (Three Days in the Guardhouse, 1930) **36,** 2, 45, 91, 164
Drei Tage Mittelarrest (Three Days in the Guardhouse, 1955, Georg Jacoby) 55, 108
Drei Tanten, Die (1920, Rudolf Biebrach) 307
Drei Tänze der Mary Wilford, Die (1920) **418**
Drei tolle Mädels (1934, Hubert Marischka, G/I) 91, 307
Drei tolle Tage (1936, Hans Deppe) 55, 149, 151
Drei um Christine, Die (1936, Hans Deppe) 8, 179, 352
Drei um Edith, Die (1929, Erich Waschneck) 24, 67,

164, 165, 295, 321
Drei Unteroffiziere (1939, Werner Hochbaum) 358
Drei Väter um Anna (1939) **36,** 411
Drei vom Varieté (1954, Kurt Neumann) 12, 59, 232, 234, 422
Drei von denen man spricht (1953) *see* Glück muss man haben
Drei von der Kavallerie (1932) **36,** 153, 164, 179, 210
Drei von der Stempelstelle (1932, Eugen Thiele) 179, 185, 189, 339, 426
Drei von der Tankstelle, Die (1930) **370,** 45, 108, 117, 139, 155 ii, 179, 284, 287, 315, 383
Drei von der Tankstelle, Die (1955, Hans Wolff) 104, 120, 153, 264, 399
Drei weisse Birken (1961, Hans Albin) 91
Drei wunderschöne Tage (1939, Fritz Kirchhoff) 42, 55, 141, 412
13 kleine Esel und der Sonnenhof (1958, Hans Deppe) 4, 73, 162, 229, 279
Dreizehn Mann und eine Kanone (1938, Johannes Meyer) 142, 183, 205, 288, 412
13 Stühle (1938, E. W. Emo) 35, 315
Dreizehnte Kreuz, Das (1918, Hubert Moest) 138
13 unter einem Hut (1950, Johannes Meyer) 26, 217
Dreyfus (1930) **273,** 22, 24, 115, 123, 149, 161, 179, 198, 295, 406
Dr. Fabian – Lachen ist die beste Medizin (1969) **302,** 101, 145
Dr. Holl (1951, Rolf Hansen) 40, 114, 135, 143, 150, 195, 324, 409, 413
Drillinge an Bord (1959, Hans Müller) 59
Dritte Eskadrone Die (1926, Carl Wilhelm, G/A) 311, 356, 387
Dritte Geschlecht, Das (1957) *see* Anders als Du und ich
Dritte von rechts, Der (1950, Geza von Cziffra) 93, 185, 422
Driven from Home *see* Aus-

treibung, Die

Dr. Mabuse der Spieler (Dr. Mabuse, the Gambler, Mabuse, 1922, i: Spieler aus Leidenschaft; ii: Inferno des Verbrechens) **213**, 1, 2, 58, 92, 123, 135, 156, 169, 174, 190, 287, 305, 321, 327

Dr. Mabuse, the Gambler *see* Dr. Mabuse der Spieler

Dr. med. Hiob Prätorius (1965) **157**, 13, 70, 128, 154, 222, 291, 315

Dr. phil. Döderlein (1945, Werner Klingler, unfinished) 24, 85, 115, 131, 149, 266, 407

Dr. Satansohn (1916, Edmund Edel) 227

Dr. Semmelweis (1950) *see* Semmelweis – Retter der Mütter

Drunter und drüber (1939, Hubert Marischka) 26, 102, 164, 221, 307

Dr. van der Velde – Die vollkommene Ehe I (1968, F. J. Gottlieb) 341, 410

Dr. Wislizenus (1924, Hanns Ch. Kobe) 198, 375

Dschungel ruft, Der (1936) **283**, 47, 149, 241

Dubarry, Die (1951, Georg Wildhagen) 108, 220, 231, 422

Dubarry von heute, Eine (1926, Alexander Korda) 1, 4, 69, 183, 403

Du bist die Richtige (1955, G/A) **89**, 175

Du bist die Rose vom Wörthersee (1952, Hubert Marischka) 136, 175

Du bist die Schönste für mich! (1951) *see* Zwei in einem blauen Auto

Du bist entzückend, Rosemarie/Rosl vom Traunsee, Die (1933, Hans von Wolzogen) 327

Du bist mein Glück (1936, Karl Heinz Martin) 23

Du bist Musik (1956, Paul Martin) 44, 47, 168

Du bist nicht allein (1949) **395**, 403, 412

Du bist wunderbar (1959, Paul Martin) 44, 399

Du darfst nicht länger schweigen (1955) **362**, 12, 15, 39, 143, 149, 154, 236, 429

Dudu, ein Menschenschicksal/Geschichte eines Clowns, Die (1924, Rudolf Meinert) 1, 61, 335

Duell mit dem Tod (1949, Paul May, A) 15, 275

Duell vor Sonnenuntergang (1965, Leopold Lahola, G/Yug) 93

Du gehörst mir (1959, Wilm ten Haaf) 93

Du gehörst zu mir (1943) **212**, 33

Du kannst nicht treu sein (1936, Franz Seitz) 91, 101

Du mein stilles Tal (1955) **359**, 44, 164, 175, 238, 267, 415

Dumme August des Zirkus Romanelli, Der (1926, Georg Jacoby) 151, 338

Dummkopf, Der (1920) **282**, 2, 244, 392

Dummy of Death *see* Nur tote Zeugen schweigen

Dunja (1955, A) **19**, 9, 37, 63, 246, 247

Dunkle Punkt, Der (1940, Georg Zoch) 102, 263

Dunkle Stern, Der (1955, Hermann Kugelstadt) 84, 102, 109, 363

Dunkle Tag, Der (1943, Geza von Bolvary) 21, 33, 55, 136

Durchbruch Lok 234 (1963) **424**,

Durch dick und dünn (1951) **221**, 26, 91, 375

Durch die Wälder, durch die Auen (1956) **275**, 399, 420

Durchgängerin, Die (1928), Hanns Schwarz) 41, 242, 258, 417

Durchlaucht amüsiert sich (1932, Conrad Wiene) 5, 76, 174

Durchlaucht Hypochonder (19 ?) **79**

Durchlaucht Radieschen (1926) **83**, 174, 253

Durchs Brandenburger Tor (1929, Max Knaacke) 149, 179

Durchs wilde Kurdistan (1965, F. J. Gottlieb, G/Sp) 40, 44, 279

Durch Wahrheit zum Narren (1920, Luise Kolm & Jacob Fleck, A) 133

Dürfen wir schweigen? (1926) **273**, 198, 387, 394

Du Rififi à Paname (1966) *see* Rififi in Paris

Du sollst nicht begehren (1933, Richard Schneider-Edenkoben) 420

Du sollst nicht ehebrechen!/Thérèse Raquin (1927/28, Jacques Feyder) 149, 211

Du sollst nicht stehlen (1927/28, Victor Janson) 83, 139

Du und ich (1938) **218**, 42, 124, 166, 429

Dyckerpotts Erben (1928, Hans Behrendt) 5

Dynamit in grüner Seide (1968, G/I) **302**

D-Zug 13 hat Verspätung (1931, Alfred Zeisler) 41

E

Earth Spirit *see* Erdgeist

Eddy Polo mit Pferd und Lasso (1927/28, Eddie Polo) 274

Edelweisskönig, Der (1938, Paul Ostermayr) 305

Edelweisskönig, Der (1957) **387**, 23, 163, 247

E Dio disse a Caino (1969, Anthony Dawson, G/I) 187

Edle Blut, Das (1927/28) 36

Effie Briest (1939) *see* Schritt vom Wege, Der

Effie Briest (1955) *see* Rosen im Herbst

Egon, der Frauenheld (1957, Hans Albin) 149, 221

Ehe, Die (1928/29, Eberhard Frowein) 58, 67

Ehe, Eine (1968) **365** & **374**, 366

Ehe der Luise Rohrbach (1916, Rudolf Biebrach) 170, 249, 289

Ehe des Dr. med. Danwitz, Die (1956) **293**, 25, 37, 59, 143, 195, 232, 325, 378, 417

Ehe des Herrn Mississippi, Die (1961, G/Switz) **157**, 44, 97, 141, 145, 196, 234

Eheferien (1927, Victor Janson) 139

Ehe für eine Nacht (1953) **377**, 111, 341

Ehe im Schatten (Marriage in the Shadow, 1947, Defa) **233**, 24, 80, 188, 363, 429

Ehe in Dosen (1939, Johannes Meyer) 128, 153, 307, 311

Ehe in Not (1929) **273**, 1, 24, 179, 189

Feldherrenhügel, Der (1926, Hans Otto Löwenstein, Erich Schönfelder, G/A/H) 174, 219, 383
Feldherrenhügel, Der (1932, Eugen Thiele) 280
Feldherrenhügel, Der (1953, Ernst Marischka, A) 164, 280
Feme (1927) **273,** 105, 117, 123, 149, 183, 189, 321, 417
Fenton (1923) *see* Geldteufel, Der
Ferdinand Lassalle (19 ?, ?) 79
Ferien auf Immenhof (1957, Hermann Leitner) 149, 234, 264, 403
Ferienbett mit 100 PS, Ein (1965, Wolfgang Becker) 47
Ferien in Tirol *see* Zärtliches Geheimnis
Ferienkind, Das (1943, Karl Leiter) 9
Ferien mit Piroschka (1965, Franz Josef Gottlieb, G/A/H) 13
Ferien vom Ich (1934, Hans Deppe) 99, 149, 327
Ferien vom Ich (1952, Hans Deppe) 108, 149, 422
Ferien vom Ich (1963, Hans Grimm) 101, 164, 341
Fesche Erzherzog, Der (1926, Robert Land) 56, 133, 391
Fesche Husar, Der (1928, Geza von Bolvary) 153, 164
Fesche Tiroler, Der (1910, ?) 202
Fest der Schönheit/Olympia II (1938) **306,** 134, 150, 420
Fest der Völker/Olympia I (1938) **306,** 134, 150, 420
Feuer, Das (1914, Urban Gad) 202, 265, 369
Feuer frei auf Frankie (1967, José Antonio de la Loma, G/I/Sp) 112
Feuerrote Baronesse, Die (1959, Rudolf Jugert) 59, 112, 266, 279, 341, 412
Feuerschiff, Das (1922, Richard Löwenbein) 405, 421
Feuerschiff, Das (1963, Ladislaus Vajda) 40, 279
Feuertänzerin, Die (1925, Robert Dinesen) 1, 392, 386
Feuerteufel, Der (1940) **380,** 23, 25, 179, 245, 288, 296
Feuerwerk (Oh! My Pa-pa, 1954) **157,** 9, 52, 128, 131,

154, 263, 277, 333, 399
Feuerzangenbowle, Die (1944, Helmut Weiss) 102, 149, 288, 315
Fiakerlied (1936, E. W. Emo) 164
Fiakermilli, Die (1953, A) **293,** 91, 164
Fiaker Nr. 13 (1925/26, Michael Kertesz = Michael Curtiz, A) 216, 387
Fiat Lux/Es ward Licht (1923, A) **370**
Fidele Bauer, Der (1927, Franz Seitz) 204, 417
Fidele Bauer, Der (1951, Georg Marischka, A) 164, 331
Fidele Herrenpartie, Die (1929, Rudolf Walther-Fein) 179, 339
Fidelen Detektive, Die (1957, Hermann Kugelstadt) 91, 309
Fideles Gefängnis, Ein (1917) **227,** 170, 219, 274
Fidele Tankstelle, Die, (1950, Ferdinand Dörfler) 385, 412
Fidelio (1956, Walter Felsenstein, A) 86, 121
Fiesco (1913, ?) 68, 156
Fiesco (1920) *see* Verschwörung zu Genua, Die
Figaros Hochzeit (The Marriage of Figaro, 1920) **230**
Figaros Hochzeit (The Marriage of Figaro, 1949, Georg Wildhagen, Defa) 188
Figlia del Regimente, La *see* Tochter der Kompanie, Die
Filme der Prinzessin Fantoche, Die (1921, Max Neufeld, A) 133
Filmabenteuer, Ein (19 ?, A) **242**
Film ohne Namen, Der (1922, Erich Schönfelder) 5, 174,
Film ohne Titel (Film Without Title, 1948, Rudolf Jugert) 84, 99, 108, 150, 182, 193, 267, 288, 352
Filmprimadonna, Die/Filmprimadonna, Den (1913, Urban Gad, G/D) 202, 265, 339
Film Without Title *see* Film ohne Titel
Finale (1948, Ulrich Erfurth) 108, 119, 188, 431
Finale der Liebe (1925, Felix Basch) 284
Finanzen des Grossherzogs,

Die (The Grand Duke's Fiances, 1923) **257,** 1, 54, 106, 121, 135, 219, 284, 335
Finanzen des Grossherzogs, Die (The Grand Duke's Fiances, 1934) **129,** 149, 200, 221, 231, 315
Finden Sie, dass Constanze sich richting verhält (1962, Tom Pevsner) 24, 93, 277
Findling, Der (1968, George Moorse) 393
Finsternis ist ihr Eigentum (1922, Martin Hartwig) 198, 355, 327, 392
Fire, The *see* Feuer, Das
Firma heiratet, Die (1913, Carl Wilhelm) 227
Firma heiratet, Die (1931, Carl Wilhelm) 95, 221, 311
First Love (1970) *see* Erste Liebe
First Spaceship on Venus *see* Schweigende Stern, Der
Fischerin vom Bodensee, Die (1956) **302**
Fischer vom Heiligensee, Der (1955, Hans H. König) 58, 220, 309
Fistful of Dollars, A *see* Für eine Handvoll Dollars
Flachsmann als Erzieher (1930, Carl Heinz Wolff) 149
Flame of Love (1930) *see* Hai-Tang
Flametti (1920, Bruno Eichgrün) 179
Flaming Frontier *see* Old Surehand I
Flamme, Die (Montmartre, 1922) **227,** 1, 2, 202, 261, 355, 371, 375
Flammende Völker (1922, Robert Reinert) 114, 198, 407
Flammen lügen, Die (1926) **110,** 289, 327
Fledermaus, Die (1923) **230,** 174, 219, 292, 360, 375
Fledermaus, Die (1931, Carl Lamac) 5, 147, 174, 270, 280
Fledermaus, Die (1937) **395,** 5, 246, 253, 352
Fledermaus, Die (1945, Geza von Bolvary) 108, 136, 144, 150, 246, 422
Fledermaus, Die (1962, Geza von Cziffra, A) 195, 314, 422
Fledermaus 1955/Fledermaus 55 (1955, G/GB) **290,** 246,

151, 236, 238, 430
Frauenarzt Dr. Prätorius (1950, Curt Goetz & Karl Peter Gillmann) 70, 102, 128, 222, 288, 403
Frauenarzt Dr. Schäfer (1928, Jacob & Luise Fleck) 4, 280
Frauenarzt Dr. Sibelius (1962, Rudolf Jugert) 28, 101
Frauenarzt klagt an, Ein (1964, Falk Harnack) 40, 44, 266
Frauen aus der Wiener Vorstadt/15 Jahre schweren Kerker (1925, Heinz Hanus, A) 303
Frauen der Leidenschaft (1926, Rolf Randolf, i-iii) 11, 224, 421
Frauen der Nacht (1924) see Tragödie der Entehrten, Die
Frauen des Herrn S., Die (1951, Paul Martin) 26, 99, 120, 164, 403, 430
Frauendiplomat, Der (1932, E. W. Emo) 42, 76, 82, 153, 221, 349
Frauenehre (1918, Georg Kundert, A) 198
Frauen für Golden Hill (1938, Erich Waschneck) 59, 85, 102, 114, 327
Frauengasse von Algier, Die (1927, Wolfgang Hoffmann-Harnisch) 156, 165, 327
Frauenhaus von Brescia, Das (1920, Hubert Moest) 65, 421
Frauenhaus von Rio, Das (1927) 360, 65, 117, 284, 361
Frauen in Teufels Hand (1960, Hermann Leitner, A) 205
Frauenkönig, Der (1923, Jaap Speyer) 5, 311
Frauenliebe – Frauenleid (1937, Augusto Genina) 205, 280, 332
Frauenopfer (1922) 130, 22, 68, 216, 289
Frauenparadies, Das (1922) 230, 392
Frauenparadies, Das (1939) 293, 5, 280, 349
Frauenschicksale (1952, Defa) 77, 18, 61, 86, 122, 316
Frauensee (1958, Rudolf Jugert, A) 63, 415
Frauen sind doch bessere Diplomaten (1941, Georg Jacoby) 5, 108, 128, 314, 385

Frauen sind keine Engel (1942) 104, 7, 35, 136, 175, 232
Frauen um den Sonnenkönig (1935) see Liselotte von der Pfalz
Frauen und Banknoten (1925, Fritz Kaufmann) 210
Frauen vom Gnadenstein, Die (1920/21, Robert Dinesen) 135, 169, 242, 327
Frauen vom Tannhof, Die (1934, Franz Seitz) 190, 305
Frauen von Folies Bergères, Die (1926, Max Obal) 406
Frau für Drei, Eine (1939) see Marguerite: 3
Frau für 3 Tage, Eine (1944, Fritz Kirchhoff) 135, 294
Frau fürs ganze Leben, Eine (1960) 218, 128, 150, 194, 217, 221, 299
Frau für 24 Stunden, Die (125) 338, 219
Frau im besten Mannesalter (1959) 7, 24, 144, 195, 232, 256, 415
Frau im Feuer, Die (1924) 36, 1, 265, 383
Frau im Mond (The Girl in the Moon; The Woman on the Moon; 1929) 213, 56, 80, 108, 135, 169, 241, 295, 385, 405
Frau im Schrank, Die (1927, Rudolf Biebrach) 41, 108
Frau im Strom (1939) 212, 23, 96, 142, 163, 247, 295
Frau im Talar, Die (1929, Adolf Trotz) 198, 305
Frau in Gold, Die (1926, Pierre Marodon) 421
Frau in Versuchung, Die (1924, ?) 1
Frau in vierzig Jahren, Die (1925) 273, 216, 355
Frau in Weiss, Die (1921, Max Neufeld, A) 133
Frau Irene Besser (1960, John Olden) 149, 220, 371, 389, 413
Frau kommt in die Tropen, Eine (1938, Harald Paulsen) 76, 102, 197, 412
Frau Lehmanns Töchter (1932, Carl Heinz Wolff) 179, 368
Fräulein (1939, Erich Waschneck) 18, 85, 169, 411
Fräulein Bimbi/Unmögliche Mädchen, Das (1951, Akos von Rathony, A) 25, 185, 371

Fräulein Casanova (1953, E. W. Emo, A) 120, 149, 223, 403
Fräulein Chauffeur (1928, Jaap Speyer) 42, 54, 179, 307
Fräulein Else (1928/29) 57, 18, 22, 30, 107, 321, 361
Fräulein Fähnrich (1929, Fred Sauer) 104, 179, 303
Fräulein – falsch verbunden (1932, E. W. Emo) 307, 332, 375
Fräulein Frau (1934) 36, 81, 128, 164, 173, 422
Fräulein Hoffmanns Erzählungen (1933, Carl Lamac) 141, 147, 270, 335, 417
Fräulein Josette – meine Frau (1926, Gaston Ravel) 406, 421
Fräulein Julie (Lady Julia, 1922, Felix Basch) 68, 74, 150, 265, 313
Fräulein Liselott (1934, Johannes Guter) 220, 229, 332, 422
Fräulein Piccolo (1914, Franz Hofer) 227
Fräulein Raffke (1923) 83, 4, 204
Fräulein Seifenschaum (1914) 227
Fräulein und der Vagabund, Das (1949) 25, 85, 207
Fräulein vom Amt, Das (1925, Hans Schwarz) 113, 403
Fräulein vom Amt (1954, Carl-Heinz Schroth) 26, 55
Fräulein von Barnhelm, Das (1940, Hans Schweikart) 21, 26, 59, 156, 179, 221, 234, 288, 421
Fräulein von Kasse 12, Das (1927, Erich Schönfelder) 83
Fräulein von Scüderi, Das (1955, Defa/Sw) 428, 188, 289, 416
Fräulein Zahnarzt (1920, ?) 243
Frau Luna (1941) 221, 5, 26, 149, 185, 229, 375, 404
Frau meiner Träume, Die (1944, Georg Jacoby) 5, 128, 314, 385
Frau mit dem Etwas, Die (1925, Erich Schönfelder) 83, 151, 253
Frau mit dem schlechten Ruf, Die (1925, Benjamin Christensen) 111, 156

(1916) **308**, 224

Friesenblut (1925, Fred Sauer) 111, 173, 327

Friesennot/Dorf im roten Sturm (1935, Peter Hagen) 6, 155 iii, 183

Frischer Wind aus Kanada (1935, Heinz Kenter & Erich Holder) 99, 164, 253, 375

Fritze Bollmann wollte angeln/Wer zuletzt lacht (1943, Volker von Collande) 24, 84, 114, 229

Fritz und Friederike (1952, Geza von Bolvary) 114, 220, 280, 291

Fröhliche Dorf, Das/Krach um Jolanthe (1955, Rudolf Schündler) 229, 253

Fröhliche Wallfahrt, Die (1956, Ferdinand Dörfler) 8, 309

Fröhliche Wanderer, Der (1955, Hans Quest) 108, 151, 164, 264

Fröhliche Weinberg, Der (The Gay Vineyard; The Happy Vineyard, 1927, Jacob & Luise Fleck) 165, 222

Fröhliche Weinberg, Der (The Gay Vineyard; The Happy Vineyard, 1952) **89**, 42, 149, 194, 222, 329, 356

Fromme Helene, Die (1965) **7**, 24, 221, 341

Fromme Lüge, Die (1938, Nunzio Malasomma) 128, 142, 261

From Morn to Midnight see Von morgens bis Mitternacht

Frön med masken (1959) see Frosch mit der Maske, Der

Frontgockel, Der (1955, Ferdinand Dörfler) 229

Fronttheater (1942) **293**, 62, 98, 234

Fröschkönig, Der (1954, Otto Meyer) 416

Frosch mit der Maske, Der/ Frön med masken (1959, G/D) **302**, 112, 222, 295, 410

Frou-Frou (1922) **308**, 142

Fruchtbarkeit (1929, Eberhard Frowein) 149

Früchtchen (1934, A) **83**, 47, 221, 371

Frucht ohne Liebe (1956, Ulrich Erfurth) 44, 59, 331, 415

Frühere Verhältnisse (1927, Arthur Bergen) 149, 179, 274, 321

Frühjahrsparade (1935, Geza von Bolvary, G/A) 164, 221, 321

Frühling in Berlin (1957) **293**, 42, 47, 82, 120, 264, 280, 430

Frühlings Erwachen (The Awakening of Spring, 1929) **273**, 123, 149, 295

Frühlingslied (1954, Hans Albin) 62, 220, 296, 359

Frühlingsluft (1938, Carl Lamac) 332, 422

Frühlingsmärchen/Verlieb' Dich nicht in Sizilien (1934) **110**, 210, 375

Frühlingsmelodie (1945, Hans Robert Bortfeldt, unfinished) 149, 205

Frühlingsrauschen (1929) **68**

Frühlingsromanze see Sehnsucht des Herzens

Frühlingsstimmen (1952, Hans Thimig, A) 164

Frühreifen, Die (1957) **19**, 44, 223

Frühstück im Doppelbett (1963) **7**, 13, 44, 100, 291

Frühstück mit dem Tod (1964, Franz Antel, G/A) 63, 126, 430

Fuchs von Glenarvon, Der (1940, M. W. Kimmich) 66, 101, 102, 123, 154, 158, 183, 237, 383, 403

Fuchs von Paris, Der (1957, Paul May) 47, 138, 145, 195, 207, 234

Führe uns nicht in Versuchung /Und führe uns nicht in Versuchung (1922, Sidney M. Goldin, A) 270

Fuhrmann Henschel (1918) **227**, 170, 202, 222, 355

Fuhrmann Henschel (1922, Lothar Mendes) 170, 222

Fuhrmann Henschel (1956, A) **19**, 9, 222, 246, 356, 376

Fundvogel (1930, Wolfgang Hoffmann-Harnisch) 165, 339, 360, 406, 407

Fünf gegen Casablanca (1967, Umberto Lenzi, G/I/F) 106

Fünf Kapitel aus einem alten Buch (1923) see Weib, ein Tier, ein Diamant, Ein

Fünf Karnickel, Die (1953, Kurt Steinwender, A) 91,

133

Fünf Millionen suchen einen Erben (1938) **36**, 102, 315

Fünf-Minuten-Vater, Der (1951, J. A. Hübler-Kahla, A) 371

Fünf Patronenhülsen 1960, Defa) **32**, 119, 259

Fünf Tage – fünf Nächte (1961, Lew Arnschtam. & Heinz Thiel & Anatoli Golowanow, Defa/USSR) 50

5000 Dollar für den Kopf von Jonny R. (1966, José Luis Madrid, G/Sp) 44, 112, 195

5000 Mark Belohnung (1942, Philipp Lothar Mayring) 59

5. Juni, Der/Einer unter Millionen (1942, Fritz Kirchhoff) 66, 294

Fünfte Stand, Der (1925) see Verrufenen, Die

Fünfte Strasse, Die/Spiel aus dem Leben der ersten Vierhundert, Ein (1923, Martin Hartwig) 355

Fünfuhrtee in der Ackerstrasse (1926, Paul Ludwig Stein) 179, 284, 338, 392

Fünf unter Verdacht/Stadt im Nebel (1950) **157**, 44, 266, 416

Fünf verfluchten Gentlemen, Die (1932, Julien Duvivier, G/F) 165, 426

Fünf vom Titan, Die (1948) see Vor uns liegt das Leben

Fünf von der Jazzband (1932) **89**, 173, 210, 225, 231

Fünf vor zwölf in Caracas (1966, Marcello Baldi) G/I/ F) 106, 215

15 Jahre schweren Kerker (1925) see Frauen aus der Wiener Vorstadt

50 Jahre – heiter betrachtet (1950) see Herrliche Zeiten

Funkzauber (1927) **273**, 11, 179, 204

Für die Katz (1940, Hermann Pfeiffer) 421

Für eine Handvoll Diamanten /Safari Diamants (1966, Michel Drach, G/F) 106

Für eine Handvoll Dollars/ Per und pugnio di dollari (A Fistful of Dollars, 1964, Sergio Leone) 195

Für ein paar Dollar mehr/Per qualque dollari in più (For a Few Dollars More, 1965,

341, 423

Ich tanze mit Dir in den Himmel hinein (1952) *see* Hannerl

Ich und die Kaiserin (1933) **159**, 24, 54, 139, 150, 303, 313, 315, 394, 402

Ich und Du (1953) **408**, 207, 236, 291, 299, 409

Ich und meine Frau (1953, Eduard von Borsody, A) 9, 163, 414

Ich und meine Schwiegersöhne (1956, Georg Jacoby) 55, 99, 120, 149, 378

Ich vertraue Dir meine Frau an (1943) **157**, 59, 315, 422

Ich verweigere die Aussage (1939, Otto Linnekogel) 47, 67, 334, 383

Ich war ein hässliches Mädchen (1955) **218**, 37, 40, 61, 264, 383, 430

Ich war ihm hörig (1958, Wolfgang Becker) 357

Ich war Jack Mortimer (1935) **110**, 135, 153, 191, 210, 330, 362, 426

Ich war neunzehn (1968, Defa) **427**, 29

Ich warte auf Dich (1952, Volker von Collande) 131, 232

Ich war zu Heidelberg Student (1927, Wolfgang Neff) 421

Ich weiss, wofür ich lebe (1955) **395**, 58, 109, 389

Ich werde Dich auf Händen tragen (1943) **157**, 98, 188, 266, 403

Ich werde Dich auf Händen tragen (1958) **137**, 85, 197, 266, 351

Ich will Dich Liebe lehren (1933, Heinz Hilpert) 56, 151, 180, 210

Ich will nicht wissen, wer Du bist (1932, Geza von Bolvary) 111, 133, 321, 359

Ideale Brautpaar, Das (1954) **362**, 101, 229, 236, 267

Ideale Frau, Die (1959) **19**, 217

Ideale Gattin, Die (1914, Hans Heinz Ewers) 227, 320

Idealer Gatte, Ein (1935, Herbert Selpin) 5, 66, 135, 148, 149, 330

Idiot, Der (1921) *see* Irrende Seelen

Igelfreundschaft (1962, Hermann Zschoche, Defa/Cz)

316

Ihr dunkler Punkt (1928, Johannes Guter) 76, 108, 139, 357

Ihre Durchlaucht, die Verkäuferin (1933, Karl Hartl) 104, 133, 185, 221, 284, 329, 375

Ihre grosse Prüfung (1954, Rudolf Jugert) 73, 352, 389

Ihre Hoheit befielt (1931, Hanns Schwarz) 108, 163, 164, 258, 309, 338, 385, 419

Ihre Hoheit, die Tänzerin (1922, ?) 83

Ihre Majestät die Liebe (1931) **242**, 117, 149, 258, 311, 329

Ihr erstes Erlebnis (1939) **19**, 18, 307, 411

Ihr erstes Rendezvous (1955, G/A) **7**, 59, 205

Ihr grösster Erfolg/Therese Krones (1934, Johannes Meyer) 82, 128, 210, 221, 334, 349

Ihr 106. Geburtstag (1958) **229**, 24, 44, 168, 194, 236

Ihr Junge/Wenn die Geigen klingen (1931, Friedrich Feher, G/A/Cz) 142

Ihr Korporal/Husarenmanöver (1956, E. W. Emo, G/A) 164

Ihr Leibhusar (1937, Hubert Marischka, G/A/H) 81, 91, 185, 332

Ihr Leibregiment (1955, Hans Deppe) 12, 422

Ihr Privatsekretär (1940, Charles Klein) 8, 26, 111, 149, 221

Ihr schönster Tag (1962) **395**, 430

Ihr Sport (1918/19, ?) 289

Ikarus/Gunther Plüschows Fliegerschicksal (1932, Gunther Plüschow) 224, 429

Illusion (1941) **377**, 128, 141, 144, 166

Illusion in Moll (1952, Rudolf Jugert) 193, 207, 287, 330, 334, 376, 397

Ilona (1921/22, Robert Dinesen) 242, 292

Im Auto durch zwei Welten (1931, Clärenore Stinnes & Carl Axel Söderström) 429

Im Banne der Berge/Almenrausch (1931, Franz Osten) 84, 335

Im Banne der Kralle (1925, A) **110**, 67

Im Banne der Leidenschaften (1914, Schmidt-Hässler) 170

Im Banne der Schuld (19 ?, ?) 83

Im Banne der Suggestion (1920, ?) 224

Im Banne des Eulenspiegels (1932) **424**, 221

Im Banne des Monte Miracolo (1944) **380**, 23, 25

Im Banne des Unheimlichen (1968) **401**, 112, 222, 223, 410

Im Geheimdienst (1931) **387**, 66, 108, 148, 150, 156, 161, 183, 224, 303, 313, 421

Im grossen Augenblick (1911, Urban Gad) 4, 261, 339

Im Hotel "Zur süssen Nachtigall"/Madame wagt einen Seitensprung (1928, Hans Otto Löwenstein, A) 371

Im Kampf mit der Unterwelt (1931, Carlo Aldini) 203

Im Krug zum grünen Kranze (1954) *see* Fünf Karnickel, Die

Im Luxuszug (1927, Erich Schönfelder) 6, 321

Immensee (1943) **137**, 102, 114, 155 iii, 253, 294, 351, 429

Immer Aerger mit dem Bett (1961, Rudolf Schündler) 28

Immer Aerger mit den Paukern (1968, Harald Vock) 208

Immer die Mädchen (1959, Fritz Remond, A) 26, 149, 412

Immer nur Du (1941, Karl Anton) 26, 144, 149, 179, 185, 296

Immer, wenn der Tag beginnt (1957) **218**, 128, 217, 352

Immer, wenn ich glücklich bin (1938, Carl Lamac, A) 82, 91, 128, 164, 221

Immer will ich Dir gehören (1960, Arno Assmann) 352

Im Namen des Kaisers (1925, Robert Dinesen) 292, 327

Im Namen des Teufels (1962, John Paddy Carstairs, G/GB) 93, 195, 220

In Namen des Volkes (1939) **90**, 102, 179, 421

Im Namen einer Mutter (1960) **90**, 363, 420

Im Prater blüh'n wieder die Bäume (1958, Hans Wolff,

A) 136, 221, 240
Im Rausche der Leidenschaft (1923, Guido Schamberg) 1
Im Reiche des silbernen Löwen (1965, Franz Josef Gottlieb, G/Sp) 44
Im Schatten der Moschee (1924, Walter Richard Hall) 134
Im Schatten des Berges (1940, Alois Johannes Lippl) 163, 238, 296
Im schwarzen Rössl (1961, Franz Antel, A) 73
Im 6. Stock (1961, John Olden) 128, 399
Im singenden Rössl am Königssee (1963, Franz Antel, A) 164
Im Sonderauftrag (1959, Heinz Thiel, Defa) 125, 251
Im Sonnenschein/Opernring (1936, Carmine Gallone, A) 184, 221, 284, 329
Im Stahlnetz des Dr. Mabuse (1961) **302**, 44, 105, 109, 223, 279
Im Trommelfeuer der Westfront (1936, Charles Willy Kaiser) 9
Im weissen Rössl (1926) **273**, 133
Im weissen Rössl (1935, Carl Lamac, A) 221, 371
Im weissen Rössl (1952) **104**, 9, 52, 85, 105, 144, 150, 181, 240, 357
Im weissen Rössl (1960, Werner Jacobs, G/A) 73, 99, 357
Im Werder blühen die Bäume (1928, Fred Sauer) 189
In den Krallen der Schuld/ Muttersorgen (1924, ?) 179, 421
In der Heimat, da gibt's ein Wiedersehn! (1926) **338**, 179, 307, 375
In der Tiefe des Schachts (19 ?) **242**, 243
Indian Tomb, The *see* Indische Grabmal, Das
Indische Grabmal, Das (The Indian Tomb, 1921, i Die Sendung des Yoghi & ii Der Tiger von Eschnapur) **242**, 41, 123, 135, 169, 213, 243, 292, 305, 394
Indische Grabmal, Das (The Indian Tomb, 1938, i Der Tiger von Eschnapur & ii)

83, 67, 211, 221, 331
Indische Grabmal, Das (The Tigress of Bengal, 1959) **213**, 13, 44, 62, 168, 228
Indische Rache (1921, ?) 219
Indische Tuch, Das (1963) **401**, 75, 101, 187, 222, 223, 266, 410
Indiskrete Frau, Die (1927) **36**, 5, 76, 173, 303
Inferno/Spiel mit dem Teufel, Das (1920, A) **57**
In flagranti (1944, Hans Schweikart) 179, 205, 237
In Frankfurt sind die Nächte heiss (Hot Nights in Frankfurt, 1966, Rolf Olsen, A) 223, 256
Ingeborg (1960) **218**, 26, 120, 222, 399
In geheimer Mission (1938, Jürgen von Alten) 111, 165, 205, 407
Inge Larsen (1923) **360**, 289
Inge und die Millionen (1933) **89**, 42, 148, 156, 407
Ingrid – die Geschichte eines Fotomodells (1955, Geza von Radvanyi) 13, 168, 234, 240
In jenen Tagen (1947) **182**, 84, 119, 154, 172, 232, 238, 252, 266, 267, 294
Inkognito (1936, Richard Schneider-Edenkoben) 18, 111
Inkognito im Paradies (1950, Joe Stöckel) 151, 383
In letzter Minute (1939, Friedrich Kirchhoff) 229, 288
In München steht ein Hofbräuhaus (1952, Siegfried Breuer) 26, 55, 185, 413
I.N.R.I. (1923) **418**, 127, 204, 210, 265, 289, 386
In Sachen Timpe (1934, Carl Heinz Wolff) 134, 149, 305
Ins blaue Leben (1939, Augusto Genina, G/I) 9, 128, 139, 385
Insel, Die (1934) **360**, 108, 148, 229, 385
Insel der Dämonen, Die (1933, Dr. Dalsheim) 429
Insel der Seligen, Die (1913) **300**
Insel der Tränen (1922, ?) 407
Insel der Träume, Die (1925, Paul Ludwig Stein) 56, 133, 219, 370
Insel der verbotenen Küsse,

Die (1926, Georg Jacoby) 5, 406
Insel ohne Moral (1950, Volker Collande) 102, 120, 149, 207
Intermezzo (1936) **19**, 190, 231, 334
Intermezzo einer Ehe in sieben Tagen (1925) *see* Soll man heiraten?
Intimitäten/Dreimal klingeln (1944, Paul Martin) 165, 200
In Treue stark (1926, Heinrich Brandt) 114, 305, 327
Intrigen der Madame de la Pommeraye, Die (1922, Fritz Wendhausen) 1, 150, 156, 313
In Wien hab' ich einmal ein Mädel geliebt (1930, Erich Schönfelder) 151, 174
Io la conosceva bene (1966) *see* Ich habe sie gut gekannt
Irene in Nöten (1953, E. W. Emo, A/Yug) 120
Irgendwo in Berlin (1946, Defa) **212**, 295
Irgendwo in Europa (1947) *see* Valahol Europaban
Irrende Seelen/Sklaven der Sinne/Idiot, Der (1921) **110**, 1, 150, 265, 282, 313, 320
Irrtum des Herzens (1939, Bernd Hoffmann) 47, 74, 102, 138, 352
Irrungen (1918, Rudolf Biebrach) 289
Irrwege der Liebe (1927, Heinrich Lisson) 131
Is Anna Anderson Anastasia? *see* Anastasia – die letzte Zarentochter
Isola Bella (1961, Hans Grimm) 341
Ist Geraldine kein Engel? (1963, Steve Previn, A) 47, 63
Ist Mama nicht fabelhaft (1958, Peter Beauvais) 26, 267, 389
Ist mein Mann nicht fabelhaft? (1933, Georg Jacoby) 5, 151, 174
Italienisches Capriccio (1961, Glauco Pellegrini, Defa) 53, 177
Italienreise – Liebe inbegriffen (1958, Wolfgang Becker) 44, 120, 168
It's a Great Life *see* Toller

Asagaroff) 111, 156, 165, 355, 370

Jugendrichter, Der (The Judge and the Sinner, 1960) **395,** 17, 266, 315

Jugendtragödie (1929, Adolf Trotz) 179

Jugend und Tollheit/Ungdom og Daarskab (1912, Urban Gad, G/D) 265, 339

Jugend von morgen (1918) see Kampf der Tertia, Der

Jungens (1941) **362,** 18, 358

Julia, du bist zauberhaft/Adorable Julie (1962, A/F) **408,** 277

Julia lebt (1963, Frank Vogel, Defa) 29, 72

Julika, Die/Ernte (1936, Geza von Bolvary, A) 163, 284, 414

Junge Adler (1944) **408,** 102, 108, 149, 207, 296, 299

Junge Baron Neuhaus, Der (1934) **387,** 24, 150, 200, 246, 258, 313, 357

Junge Engländer, Der (1958, Gottfried Kolditz, Defa) 53

Junge Graf, Der (1935, Carl Lamac) 147, 174, 270, 352

Junge Herzen (1944, Boleslav Barlog) 102

Junge Leute brauchen Liebe (1961, Geza von Cziffra, A) 28, 144, 422

Junge Medardus, Der (1923, Michael Kertesz = Michael Curtiz, A) 387, 391

Jungen vom Kranichsee, Die (1950, Arthur Pohl, Defa) 61, 421

Junger Mann, der alles kann (1957, Thomas Engel) 128

Junges Blut (1926, Manfred Noa) 292, 350

Junges Gemüse (1956, Günter Reisch, Defa) 53

Junges Herz voll Liebe (1953, Paul May) 23, 164, 415

Junges Mädchen – ein junger Mann, Ein (1935) see Knock out

Junge Sünderin, Die (1960, Rudolf Jugert) 17, 168

Junge Törless, Der (Young Torless, 1966, G/F) **328,** 155 vi, 341

Jungfern vom Bischofsberg, Die (1943, Peter Paul Brauer) 222, 430

Jungfrauenkrieg (1957, Her-

mann Kugelstadt, A) 91

Jungfrau gegen Mönch (1934, E. W. Emo) 99, 253, 305

Junggesellenfalle (1953, Fritz Böttger) 8, 55

Jünglich aus der Konfektion, Der (1926, Richard Löwenbein) 38, 307

Justine (1968) see Marquis de Sade: Justine

Juxbaron, Der (1926, Willi Wolff) 69, 151, 179, 338

K

Kabale und Liebe (1922) see Luise Millerin

Kabale und Liebe (1959, Defa) **146,** 177

Kabale und Liebe im Zirkus (1924) see Liebe ist der Frauen Macht, Die

Kabinett des Dr. Caligari, Das (1919) **418,** 58, 92, 134, 204, 244, 298, 313, 386, 394, 406

Kabinett des Dr. Larifari, Das (1930, Robert Wohlmuth) 147, 402

Kaczmarek (1928, Carl Wilhelm) 321

K – Das Haus des Schweigens (1951, Hans Hinrich) 65, 246

Kaddisch/Totengebet, Das (1924, Adolf Edgar Licho) 158

Kadetten/Hinter den roten Mauern von Lichterfelde (1931, Georg Jacoby) 22, 149, 183, 205, 307

Kadetten (1941) **310,** 9, 155 iii, 417, 420

Kahn der fröhlichen Leute, Der (1950, Hans Heinrich, Defa) 61, 279

Kaiserball (1956, Franz Antel, A) 8, 430

Kaiserin von China, Die (1953, Steve Sekely = Stefan Szekely) 44, 264, 376

Kaiserjäger (1956, A) **104,** 9, 105, 163

Kaiserliebchen (1931, Hans Tintner) 133, 163, 422

Kaisermanöver (1954, Franz Antel, A) 47, 238

Kaiser und das Wäschermädel, Der (1957, Ernst Neubach, A) 399

Kaiser von Kalifornien, Der (1936) **380,** 23, 25, 190, 395

Kaiserwalzer/Audienz in Ischl

/Heut' macht die Welt Sonntag für mich (1932, Friedrich Zelnik) 82, 164, 210

Kaiserwalzer (1932) see Johann Strauss, K. und K. Hofballmusikdirector

Kaiserwalzer (1953, Franz Antel, A) 238

Kalamitäten (1961, Alwin Woesthoff) 423

Kali Yug (1964, Mario Camerini, i Göttin der Rache, ii Das Geheimnis des indischen Tempels) 28, 187

Kalte Herz, Das (1950, Defa) **395,** 123, 253

Kalte Mamsell, Die (1933) **36,** 91, 134, 329, 375

Kameliendame, Die (1917, ?) 219

Kameraden (1919, Johannes Guter) 1

Kameraden (1935) see Alles um eine Frau

Kameraden (1941, Hans Schweikart) 33, 59, 246, 413

Kameraden auf See (1938, Heinz Paul) 224, 331

Kamerad Hedwig (1945, unfinished) **212,** 389, 413

Kameradschaft (1931) **275,** 18, 51, 127, 179, 250, 391, 403

Kammermusik (1925) **110,** 289, 375

Kampf (1932, Erich Schönfelder) 1, 158, 422

Kampf der Geschlechter (1926, Heinrich Brandt) 305

Kampf der Tertia, Der/Jugend von morgen (1928) **230,** 81, 335

Kampf der Tertia (1953, Erik Ode) 420

Kampf des Donald Westhof, Der (1927, Fritz Wendhausen) 56, 149, 161, 309

Kämpfende Herzen/Vier um die Frau (1921) **213,** 190, 406

Kämpfer (1935, USSR) **405,** 51, 127

Kampf gegen Berlin, Der (1925, Max Reichmann) 42

Kampfgeschwader Lützow (1941, Hans Bertram) 155 iii, 203

Kampf mit dem Drachen, Der (1935, Franz Seitz) 91, 321

Kampf um Blond/Mädchen, die spurlos verschwinden

245

246

tull ?) 261

Küsse, die man nicht vergisst (1928, Georg Jacoby) 95

Küssen ist keine Sünde/Letzte Einquartierung, Die (1926, Rudolf Walther-Fein) 4, 303

Küssen ist keine Sünd (1950, Hubert Marischka, A) 175, 246

Kuss in der Sommernacht, Ein (1933, Franz Seitz) 335

Küss' mich Casanova (1949) see Märchen vom Glück

Küss mich noch einmal (1956, Helmut Weiss) 149, 264

Kuss nach Ladenschluss, Ein (1934) see Annette im Paradies

Kuttel (1961, Siegfried Menzel, Defa) 251

Kyritz – Pyritz (1931, Carl Heinz Wolff) 2, 164

L

Labyrinth (1959) **369,** 80, 93, 99, 101, 234, 296, 376

Lachdoktor, Der (1937, Fred Sauer) 172

Lache Bajazzo (1919) **273,** 1

Lache Bajazzo (1943, Leopold Hainisch) 158, 164, 329, 403

Lachende Dritte, Der (1936, Georg Zoch) 91

Lachende Ehemann, Der (1926, Rudolf Walther-Fein) 4, 134

Lachende Erben (1933) **271,** 2, 315, 404

Lachende Grauen, Das (1920) **282,** 150, 204, 244, 313

Lachende Grille, Die (1926, Friedrich Zelnik) 1, 190, 191, 219, 386

Lachende Vagabund, Der (1958, Thomas Engel) 266

Lachkabinett (1953, Willem Holsboer) 141, 203, 357

Lachte man gerne (1920, ?) 174, 295, 307

Ladenprinz, Der (1928, Erich Schönfelder) 42, 149, 211, 311, 321

Lady, Die (1964, Hans Albin & Peter Berneis, G/F) 168, 296

Lady Hamilton (1922) **273,** 5, 131, 156, 204, 216, 224, 338, 386, 394

Lady Hamilton (1968, Christian Jaque, G/I/F) 40, 215, 376

Lady Julia see Fräulein Julie

Lady Windermeres Fächer (1935, Heinz Hilpert) 58, 59

Lady with the Mask, The see Dame mit der Maske

La Habanera (1937) **345,** 99, 214, 237, 247, 409

Laiermann, Der (1920, Luise Kolm & Jacob Fleck, A) 133

Lambert fühlt sich bedroht (1949, Geza von Cziffra, A) 175, 185

Lamm, Das (1964) **358**

Lampenfieber (1960) **157,** 103, 126, 128, 194, 196, 248, 354, 415

Landärztin, Die (1958, Paul May) 195, 208, 399, 429

Land der Liebe (1937) **338,** 246

Land des Lächelns, Das (1930, Max Reichmann) 42, 210, 335

Land des Lächelns, Das (1952, Hans Deppe) 81, 82, 164, 184, 246

Land of Fire (1965) see Vergeltung in Catano

Land ohne Frauen, Das (1929, Carmine Gallone) 391, 394, 417, 429

Landstrasse und Grosstadt (1922, ?) 198, 394

Landstreicher, Die (1916, Jacob Fleck & Luise Kolm, A) 133

Landstreicher, Die (1937, Carl Lamac) 91, 99, 164

Landstreicherin Courage (1922) **36**

Lange Beine, lange Finger (1966) **401,** 28, 44, 112, 145, 223, 226

Lang ist der Weg (Long Is the Road, 1948, Herbert B. Fredersdorf & Marek Goldstein) 59, 252, 412

Langsame Tod, Der (1920, Carl Wilhelm) 158, 421

La Paloma (1934, Karl Heinz Martin) 76, 179, 349

La Paloma (1944) see Grosse Freiheit Br. 7

La Paloma (1959, Paul Martin) 13, 37, 266, 331

Lärm um Weidemann (1935, J. A. Hübler-Kahla) 174, 200, 229

Lass die Sonne wieder scheinen (1955, Hubert Marisch-

ka) 96

Lasset die Kleinen zu mir kommen (1920, Max Neufeld, A) 133

Lass mich am Sonntag nicht allein (1959) **293,** 105

Last Bridge, The see Letzte Brücke, Die

Last Company, The see Letzte Kompanie, Die

Laster, Das (1919) **273,** 1, 392

Laster der Menschheit (Lusts of Mankind, 1926/27, Rudolf Meinert) 1, 151, 204, 265

Last Laugh, The see Letzte Mann, Der (1924)

Last of the Renegades see Winnetou II

Last Tomahawk, The see Letzte Mohikaner, Der

Last Will of Dr. Mabuse, The see Testament des Dr. Mabuse, Das (1962)

Laubenkolonie (1930) see Lustigen Musikanten, Die

Laufende Berg, Der (1941, Hans Deppe) 8, 179, 305

Läufer von Marathon, Der (1933) **79,** 23, 99, 135, 138, 148, 200, 336, 421

Launen des Schicksals (19 ?) **230**

Launen einer Weltdame (1914, ?) 80

Lausbubengeschichten (1964) **182,** 101, 341, 343, 413

Lauter Liebe (1940) **315,** 96, 102, 135

Lauter Lügen (1938) **315,** 26, 76, 96, 307, 358

Lautlose Waffen/Defector, The (1966, Raoul Levy, G/F) 207, 248

Lavendel (1953, G/A) **293**

Lawine, Die (1923, Michael Kertesz = Michael Curtiz, A) 387, 391

Leben beginnt um acht, Das (1962, Michael Kehlmann) 141, 240

Lebende Buddhas/Götter von Tibet (1924) **407,** 131, 210, 265, 285, 339

Lebende Fackel, Die (1920, Josef Delmont) 191

Lebende Leichnam, Der (1918) **273**

Lebende Leichnam, Der (1928, Fedor Ozep) 67, 176

Lebende Propeller, Der (1921)

Lümmel von der ersten Bank, Die II/Zum Teufel mit der Penne (1968, Werner Jacobs) 221, 341, 343

Lümmel von der ersten Bank, Die III/Pepe, der Paukerschreck (1969) **302**, 194, 221, 341, 343

Lumpazivagabundus (1937, Geza von Bolvary, A) 41, 164, 201, 315

Lumpazivagabundus (1956, Franz Antel) 99, 112, 164, 229

Lumpazivagabundus (1965, Edwin Zbonek, A) 9

Lumpenball (1930, Carl Heinz Wolff) 179, 185

Lumpenkavaliere/Wiener Lumpenkavaliere (1932, A) **36**, 142, 163

Lumpen und Seide (1924) **273**, 61, 307, 338

Lust for Love see Mahlzeiten

Lustige Ehemann, Der (1919, Leo Lasko) 227

Lustige Kleeblatt, Das/Gasthaus zur treuen Liebe (1933) **90**, 134, 149

Lustige Krieg des Hauptmann Pedro, Der (1959, Wolfgang Becker) 264, 422

Lustigen Musikanten, Die/Laubenkolonie (1930, Max Obal) 179, 180, 339, 356

Lustigen Vagabunden, Die (1928, Jacob & Luise Fleck) 5, 104

Lustigen Vagabunden, Die 1940, Jürgen von Alten) 144

Lustigen Vagabunden, Die/Das haben die Mädchen gern (1963, Kurt Nachmann, A) 164

Lustigen Weiber, Die (1935) **156**, 9, 128, 332, 349, 412

Lustigen Weiber von Tirol, Die (1964, Hans Billian) 98

Lustigen Weiber von Wien, Die (1931, Geza von Bolvary) 104, 164, 303

Lustigen Weiber von Windsor, Die (The Merry Wives of Windsor, 1950, Georg Wildhagen, Defa) 150, 188, 356, 430

Lustigen Weiber von Windsor, Die (The Merry Wives of Windsor, 1965, A/GB) **381**

Lustige Witwe, Die (1962, Werner Jacobs, A/F) 24

Lustige Witwenball, Der (1936, Alwin Elling) 149, 174

Lustige Witwer, Der (1929, Robert Land) 76, 211, 219, 303

Lusts of Mankind, see Laster der Menschheit

Luther (1927, Hans Kyser) 150, 191, 224, 313, 335, 375

Lützows wilde verwegene Jagd (1926/27) **273**, 361, 421

Luxusweibchen (1925, Erich Schönfelder) 4, 83, 174

Lydia Sanin (1923, Friedrich Zelnik) 4

M

M/Mörder unter uns (1931) **213**, 122, 129, 135, 185, 221, 224, 225, 260, 359, 392, 403, 412

Mabuse see Dr. Mabuse der Spieler

Macbeth (1920/21) **273**

Macbeth (1922, Heinz Schall) 191

Mach' mich glücklich (1935) **312**, 18, 220, 231, 311, 321

Mach' mir die Welt zum Paradies (1930, Paul Merzbach, D/Sw) 303

Machnower Schleusen, Die (1927, short) **176**

Macht der Finsternis, Die (The Power of Darkness, 1923, Conrad Wiene) 418

Macht der Mary Murton, Die (1921, Friedrich Porges, A) 422

Macht der Versuchung (1922, Paul Ludwig Stein) 58

Macht des Blutes, Die (1921, ?) 83

Macht des Goldes, Die/Gulden Magt (Golden Magt, 1912, Urban Gad, G/D) 4, 265, 339

Macht im Dunkeln (1947, Hermann Wallbrück, A) 280

Maciste und die chinesische Truhe (1923) **36**, 375

Maciste und die Tochter des Silberkönigs (1922, Romano Borgnotto) 174

Madame Blaubart (1932) see Schicksal einer schönen Frau, Das

Madame Bovary (1937) **212**, 23, 142, 190, 237, 261, 421

Madame Dubarry (Passion, 1919) **227**, 123, 170, 202, 219, 261, 338, 355, 403, 421

Madame hat Ausgang (1931, G/F) **370**, 95, 133, 153

Madame macht einen Seitensprung (1926, Hans Otto) 371

Madame Recamier (1920, Joseph Delmont) 11, 361

Madame wagt einen Seitensprung (1928) see Im Hotel "Zur süssen Nachtigall'

Madame wünscht keine Kinder (1926, Alexander Korda) 18, 20, 151, 219, 355

Madame wünscht keine Kinder (1933, G/A) **360**, 4, 133, 180, 236, 419

Mädchen am Kreuz (1929, Jacob & Luise Fleck) 95

Mädchen auf dem Brett, Das (1967, Defa) **233**, 53, 125, 140

Mädchen aus dem goldenen Westen, Das (1922, Hans Werckmeister) 5

Mädchen aus der Ackerstrasse (1921) **338**, 56, 114, 361, 392

Mädchen aus der Fremde, Das (1921, Georg Jacoby) 5

Mädchen aus der Fremde, Das (1926/27, Franz Eckstein) 76, 361

Mädchen aus der Konfektion, Das/Unschuld in Nöten (1951) **36**, 44

Mädchen aus der Südsee, Das (1950, Hans Müller) 120, 131, 207, 403

Mädchen aus Flandern, Ein (1956) **182**, 24, 84, 109, 200, 222, 325

Mädchen aus Frisco, Das (1927, Wolfgang Neff) 190

Mädchen aus Paris, Ein (1954) **341**, 205

Mädchen Christine, Das (1949, Defa) **293**, 188

Mädchen, die man nicht heiratet (1924, Geza von Bolvary) 361

Mädchen für alles (1937) **36**, 76, 311

Mädchen geht an Land, Ein (1938, Werner Hochbaum) 101, 229, 231

Mädchenhandel (1926, Jaap Speyer) 117, 151, 190

Mädchenhändler von Kairo, Der (1919, ?) 412

fred Hitchcock) 1, 189, 383

Mary Lou (1928, Friedrich Zelnik) 179, 321

Marys grosses Geheimnis (1927/28, Guido Brignone) 311

Marys Start in die Ehe (1931) *see* Ich bleib's bei Dir

Mascottchen (1929, Felix Basch) 4, 258, 375

Maske fällt, Die/Way of All Men (1930, G/USA, Frank Lloyd) 68

Maske in Blau (1953, Georg Jacoby) 168, 253, 314

Masken (1929, Rudolf Meinert) 66, 161, 406

Maskenfest des Lebens (1918, Rudolf Biebrach) 249, 289

Maskerade (1934, A) 104, 284, 329, 383, 414, 426

Maskierte Liebe (1912, Kurt Stark) 249, 289

Maskierte Schrecken, Der (1920) 176

Massacre at Marble City *see* Goldsucher von Arkansas, Die

Master of Nuremberg, The *see* Meister von Nürnberg, Der

Mata Hari (1921) *see* Spionin, Die

Mata Hari (1927, Friedrich Feher) 198, 417

Mater Dolorosa (1922, Geza von Bolvary) 426

Matthäus-Passion (1949, Ernst Marischka, A) 397

Maulkorb, Der (1938) 89, 99, 101, 149, 150, 205, 210, 224, 311

Maulkorb, Der (1958) 358, 47, 96, 97, 141, 234, 264

Mausefalle, Die (1922, Hanns Kobe) 105, 198

Max, der Taschendieb (1962, Imo Moszkowicz) 10, 25, 315

Maxie (1954, Eduard von Borsody, A) 26, 108, 149

Maya (1957, Franz Schömbs i, Wolf Schneider ii, H. C. Opfermann v, Walter Koch vi) 342 iii, 396 iv, 99, 234

Mazurka (1935) 104, 138, 155 ii, 183, 205, 261, 334, 385, 426

Mea Culpa (1953) *see* Kaplan von San Lorenzo, Der

Medea (1920) 227, 202, 219, 261, 407

Medium, Das (1920/21, Hermann Rosenfeld) 58, 204

Meer, Das (1926/27, Peter Paul Felner) 115, 383

Meer ruft, Das (1933, Hans Hinrich) 51, 102, 115, 422

Mein Bruder Josua (1956) *see* Bauer vom Brucknerhof, Der

Meine Cousine aus Warschau (1931) 36, 56, 133, 185

Meine Frau, die Filmschauspielerin (1918) 227, 202, 274

Meine Frau, die Hochstaplerin (1931) 117, 1, 61, 221, 258, 315, 336

Meine Frau, die Perle (1937, Alwin Elling) 229, 311

Meine Frau, die Schützenkönigin (1934) 36, 47, 91, 311

Meine Frau macht Musik (1958, Hans Heinrich, Defa) 61, 188, 346

Meine Frau Teresa (1942) 293, 352

Meine Freundin Barbara (1937, Fritz Kirchhoff) 47, 375

Meine Freundin Josefine (1942, Hans H. Zerlett) 26, 42, 168, 201

Meine Herren Söhne (1945) 362, 101, 154, 229, 403

Meineid (1929, Georg Jacoby) 149, 189, 211

Meineidbauer, Der (1926, Jacob & Luise Fleck) 421

Meineidbauer, Der (1941, Leopold Mainisch) 47, 100, 267

Meineidbauer, Der (1956, Rudolf Jugert) 143, 163, 413

Meine Kinder und ich (1955, Wolfgang Schleif) 55, 59, 266

Meine 99 Bräute (1958) 401, 106, 279

Meine Nichte Susanne (1950) 218, 99, 201, 234, 409

Meine schöne Mama (1958, Paul Martin, G/A) 13, 168, 413

Meine Schwester und ich (1929, Manfred Noa) 54, 174, 356, 375

Meine Schwester und ich (1954, Paul Martin) 25, 44, 164, 430

Meine 16 Söhne (1956) 70, 58, 66, 403, 429

Meines Vaters Pferde (1954, i

& ii) 212, 9, 13, 24, 114 ii, 175, 338 ii, 357, 359 ii

Meine Tante – Deine Tante (1926/27) 110, 289, 311

Meine Tante – Deine Tante (1939) 36, 144, 311, 409

Meine Tante, Deine Tante (1956) 36, 221

Meine Tochter lebt in Wien (1940, E. W. Emo) 35, 42, 47, 100

Meine Tochter Patricia (1959, A) 218, 145

Meine Tochter tut das nicht (1940, Hans H. Zerlett) 47, 153, 311

Meine Tochter und ich (1963, Thomas Engel) 55, 128, 194, 208, 315

Meine vier Jungen (1944) 309, 131, 421, 429

Mein Freund, der Chauffeur (1925, Erich Waschneck) 4, 24

Mein Freund, der Dieb (1951, Helmut Weiss) 55, 131, 195, 207, 352, 383

Mein Freund, der Millionär (1931, Hans Behrendt) 371, 375

Mein Freund Harry (1927, Max Obal) 219, 339

Mein Freund Shorty (1964) *see* Heiss weht der Wind

Mein ganzes Herz ist voll Musik (1959, Helmut Weiss) 128

Mein Heidelberg, ich kann Dich nicht vergessen (1927, James Bauer) 327, 416

Mein Herz darfst Du nicht fragen (1952, Paul Martin) 21, 33, 114, 143, 164, 197, 223, 329, 403

Mein Herz gehört Dir . . . (1929, Max Reichmann) 165

Mein Herz ist eine Jazzband (1928, Friedlich Zelnik) 1, 42

Mein Herz ruft nach Dir (1934, Carmine Gallone) 24, 82, 151, 153, 164, 184, 185, 221

Mein Herz sehnt sich nach Liebe/Hellseher, Der (1931, Eugen Thiele) 2, 164, 307, 339

Mein ist die Welt (1933) *see* Unsichtbarer geht durch die Stadt, Ein

Mein Leben für das Deine

Nur eine Tänzerin (1926, Olof Morel-Molander) 4, 58, 158, 284, 375

... nur ein Komödiant (1935, A) **89**, 105, 253, 329, 407

Nur nicht aufregen (1953, Harald Röbbeling) 234

Nur nicht weich werden, Susanne! (1934, Arsen von Cserepy) 61, 137, 327, 339

Nur tote Zeugen schweigen (Dummy of Death, 1963, Eugen Martin, G/I/Sp) 75

Nur um tausend Dollars (191?) **79**

Nylonschlinge, Die (1963, Rudolf Zehetgruber, D/Switz) 194

O

O alte Burschenherrlichkeit (1925, Helene Lackner & Eugen Rex) 117, 191, 350, 392

O alte Burschenherrlichkeit (1930, Rolf Randolf) 76, 189

Oase/Oasis (1955, Yves Allégret, G/F) 294

Oberarzt Dr. Solm (1955, Paul May) 331, 352, 363

Oberwachtmeister Borck (1955) **212**, 12, 264, 363

Oberwachtmeister Schwenke (1935) **110**, 111, 162, 330, 362

Ober, zahlen! (1957, E. W. Emo, A) 91, 164

Ochsenkrieg, Der (1919, Franz Osten) 284

Ochsenkrieg, Der (1942, Hans Deppe) 179, 305, 431

Ochse von Kulm, Der (1955, Defa) **146**, 188

O diese Bayern (1960, Arnulf Schröder) 399

O du mein Vaterland (1922) **230**

Odysseus' Heimkehr (1918, Rudolf Biebrach) 249, 289, 418

Oelprinz, Der 1965, Harald Philipp, G/Yug) 215, 410

Offene Grab, Das (1921, Bruno Eichgrün) 179

Offizierstragödie, Eine (1924) see Rosenmontag

Oh diese "lieben" Verwandten! (1955, Joe Stöckel, G/A) 91, 151

Oh diese Männer (1941, Hubert Marischka) 5, 85, 164, 307

Oh, du lieber Augustin (1922, H. K. Breslauer, A) 104

Oh, du lieber Fridolin (1952, Peter Hamel) 12, 102, 114, 232

Ohm Krüger (1941) **360**, 24, 101 129, 154, 158, 170, 197, 231, 237, 403, 412, 421

Oh! My Pa-pa see Feuerwerk

Ohne Datum (1962) **71**

Ohne Dich kann ich nicht leben (1958) see Vergiss mein nicht

Ohne Dich wird es Nacht (Without You It Is Night, 1956) **175**, 24, 62, 234, 359, 413

Ohne Krimi geht die Mini nie ins Bett (1962, Franz Antel, A) 73

Ohne Mutter geht es nicht (1958, Erik Ode) 21, 44, 340, 403

Ohne Pass in fremden Betten (1965, Vladimir Brebera, Defa) 53

Ohne Zeugen (1919, Erwin Baron or Georg Kunder, A) 198

Ohrfeigen (1969) **369**, 175, 376

O.K. (1970, Michael Verhoeven) 167

Old and the Young King, The see Alte und der junge König, Der

Oldest Profession, The see Aelteste Gewerbe der Welt, Das

Old Shatterhand (Apaches Last Battle, 1964, Hugo Fregonese, G/F/I/Yug) 362

Old Surehand I (Flaming Frontier, 1965, G/Yug) **401**, 223, 410

Oliver Twist (1920) **282**

Olympia/His Glorious Night (1930, Jacques Feyder/Lionel Barrymore, G/USA) 174

Olympia-Film I (1938) see Fest der Völker

Olympia-Film II (1938) see Fest der Schönheit

O Mädchen, mein Mädchen, wie lieb' ich Dich (1929/30) **36**, 24, 179, 219

Omicida, L' (1963) see Mörder, Der

One Arabian Night see Sumurun (1920)

Onkel aus Amerika, Der (1953) **36**, 25, 44

One Enchanted Evening see Es war eine rauschende Ballnacht

Onkel Bräsig (1936, Erich Waschneck) 47, 295, 351, 412

Onkel Filser – Allerneueste Lausbubengeschichten (1966, Werner Jacobs) 101, 194, 341, 343

Onkel Toms Hütte (Uncle Tom's Cabin, 1965, Geza von Radvanyi, G/I) 100

Onyxknopf, Der (191?) **79**

Operazione San Gennaro (1966) see Unser Boss ist eine Dame

Operette (1940) **104**, 81, 150 ii, 164, 175, 329, 331, 349

Opernball (1939, Geza von Bolvary) 26, 98, 136, 150, 155 ii, 164, 205, 221, 422

Opernball (1956, Ernst Marischka, A) 26, 96, 144, 221, 253, 399, 430

Opernredoute (1931, Max Neufeld) 5, 133, 280

Opernring (1936) see Im Sonnenschein

Opfer der Ellen Larsen (1921, ?) 305

Opfer der Gesellschaft (1917, ?) 394

Opfer der Keuschheit (1920, Manfred Noa) 123

Opfer der Leidenschaft, Ein (19 ?, ?) 307

Opfer des Herzens (1950, Johannes Meyer) 21, 93, 128, 131

Opfergang (1944) **137**, 155 iii, 253, 294, 351

Opfer um Opfer (19 ?) **230**

Opium (1918, Robert Reinert) 204, 344, 394, 421

Optimist, Der (1938, E. W. Emo) 200, 221, 289

Orgelbauer von St. Marien, Der (1961, August Rieger, A) 164

Orient/Tochter der Wüste, Die (1924, Gennaro Righelli) 219

Oriental Nights see Orientalische Nächte

Orientalische Nächte (Oriental Nights, 1960, Heinz Paul) 409, 422

Residenz (1926, Hans Behrendt) 417
Pour le Mérite (1938) **310**, 9, 59, 122, 138, 179, 313, 358, 420
Power of Darkness, The *see* Macht der Finsternis, Die
Prämien auf den Tod (1950, A) **175**, 9, 204, 329, 371
Pranke, Die (1931, G/I) **360**, 191, 295
Präsident Barrada (1920, Erik Lund) 56
Prater/Erlebnisse zweier Nähmädchen, Die (1924, Peter Paul Felner) 289, 307
Praterbuben (1947, Paul Martin, A) 329, 371
Praterherzen/Tingeltangel (1953, A) **395**, 175
Pratermizzi (1927, A) **303** & **387**, 270
Preis der Nationen (1956) *see* Mädchen Marion, Das
Preludio 11. (1964, Defa) **233**, 346
Premiere (1937, Geza von Bolvary, A) 155 ii, 163, 214, 221, 284, 329
Premiere der Butterfly (1939, Carmine Gallone, G/I) 91, 185
Preussische Liebesgeschichte/Liebeslegende (1938, Paul Martin) 18, 40, 108, 219, 266, 421
Priester und das Mädchen, Der (1958, A) **387**, 9, 21, 33, 128, 238
Primanerehre (1930) *see* Boykott
Primanerinnen (1951) **369**, 12, 120, 203, 234, 288
Primanerliebe (1927, Robert Land) 4, 198, 375
Prinzessin auf Urlaub (1929) *see* Dieb im Schlafcoupé, Der
Prinzessin Dagmar (1936) *see* Mädchenpensionat
Prinzessin Else (19 ?, ?) 179
Prinzessin kehrt heim, Die (1938) *see* Ballade
Prinzessin Olala, (1928, Robert Land) 4, 5, 69
Prinzessin Sissy (1938, Fritz Thiery) 47, 164, 241, 329
Prinzessin Suwarin, Die (1923, Johannes Guter) 1, 58, 135, 190, 236
Prinzessin Trulala (1926, Erich

Schönfelder) 83, 134, 139, 174
Prinzessin Turandot (1934) **212**, 108, 135, 150, 185, 258, 313, 357, 403
Prinzessin und der Geiger, Die (1925, Graham Cutts) 123, 355, 392
Prinzessin von St. Wolfgang, Die (1957) **302**
Prinz Karnival (1923, Fritz Freisler) 80
Prinz Kuckuck (– Leben und Höllenfahrt eines Wollüstlings) (1919) **216**, 156, 198, 344, 394
Prinz Louis Ferdinand (1926/27, Hans Behrendt) 76, 173, 199, 224, 421
Prinz Sami (1917) **227**, 274
Prinz und die Tänzerin, Der (1926) **83**, 4, 108, 179
Prinz von Arkalien, Der (1932, Karl Hartl, A) 35, 104, 133, 284, 303
Priscillas Fahrt ins Glück (1928, Anthony Asquith) 54, 406
Private Secretary *see* Privatsekretärin, Die
Privatsekretärin, Die (Private Secretary, 1931) **370**, 45, 147, 255, 371
Privatsekretärin, Die (Private Secretary, 1953, Paul Martin) 25, 44, 164, 406, 430
Problematische Naturen (1916, Hans Oberländer) 83, 249
Professor Columbus (1968, Rainer Erler) 167
Professor Mamlock (1961, Defa) **427**, 29, 125, 259, 367
Professor Nachtfalter (1951, Rolf Meyer) 47, 102, 144
Proletarpigen (1912) *see* Arme Jenny, Die
Prostitution (1918/19, i & ii) **273**, 338, 344, 394
Provinzonkel, Der (1926, Manfred Noa) 133, 179, 375
Prozess, Der (1948, A) **275**, 15, 21, 65, 67, 246, 280, 371
Prozess, Der/Trial, The (1963, Orson Welles, G/F/I) 333
Pudelnackt in Oberbayern (1968, Hans Albin) 296
Pulverschnee nach Uebersee (1956, Hermann Leitner) 397
Punks kommt aus Amerika (1935, Karl Heinz Martin)

76, 163, 311, 330
Pünktchen und Anton (1953, Thomas Engel, A) 96, 143, 409
Puppe, Die (The Doll, 1919) **227**, 202, 270, 355, 371, 375
Puppenfee, Die (1936, E. W. Emo, A) 164, 201, 321, 332
Puppenheim, Ein (1922) **398**, 158, 198, 298, 383
Puppenkönigin, Die (1924, Gennaro Righelli) 219
Puppenmacher von Kiang-Ning, Der (1923) **418**, 134, 191, 204, 235, 244
Puppenspieler, Der/Pole Poppenspäler (1945, unfinished) **137**, 102, 191, 385, 421, 429
Puppen vom Lunapark, Die (1924, Jaap Speyer) 173, 295
Pusztaliebe (1938) *see* Zwischen Strom und Steppe
Pygmalion (1935) **89**, 35, 129, 131, 173, 191, 231, 253
Pyramide des Sonnengottes, Die (1965, G/I/F/Yug) **347**, 44, 266, 362

Q

Qualen der Nacht (1925/26) **31**, 68, 127, 295
Quarantäne (1923) **230**, 115, 406
Quartett im Bett (1968, Ulrich Schamoni) 155 vi, 323
Quartett zu Fünft/Vier mal Liebe (1949, Defa) **212**, 142
Quartier Latin (1928, Augusto Genina) 42, 280
Quax, der Bruchpilot (1941) **157**, 219, 815, 362
Quax in Fahrt (1945, Helmut Weiss) 96, 315
Queen Luise *see* Königin Luise
Queen of the Night Clubs, The (1929) *see* Königsloge, Die
Querkopf, Der (1932) *see* Millionentestament; Das
Question seven (1961) *see* Fragesieben
Quick (1932) **347**, 4, 131, 139, 164, 309

R

Rache der Gräfin Barnetti, Die (19 ?) **283**
Rache der Pharaonen, Die (1925, Hans Theyer, A) 67, 95
Rache der Toten, Die (1917) **273**, 65, 204

Rache des Blutes, Die (1914, ?) 407

Rache des Dr. Fu Man Chu, Die (1967, Jeremy Summers, G/GB) 106

Rache einer Frau, Die (1920) **418**

Rache ist mein, Die (1914, ?) 219, 249

Rächer, Der (1960, Karl Anton) 75, 187, 222

Radhapura – Endstation der Verdammten (1967, Akos von Rathony) 296

Radio-Heirat, Die (1924, Wilhelm Prager) 127, 174, 321, 371, 375, 421

Raffinierteste Frau Berlins, Die (1927, Franz Osten) 190

Ragazza della Salina, La (1956) *see* Harte Männer – heisse Liebe

Rakoczy-Marsch (1933, G/H/A) **111,** 165

Ramona (1961, Paul Martin) 13, 28

Ramper, der Tiermensch (1927, Max Reichmann) 42, 117, 407

Rapunzel (19 ?, ?) 249

Raskolnikow/Schuld und Sühne (1923) **418,** 92

Rasputin/Dämon der Frauen, Der (1932, Adolf Trotz) 56, 66, 122, 123, 149, 166, 224, 298, 394

Rasputins Liebesabenteuer (1928, Martin Berger) 1, 4, 153, 335

Rastelbinder, Die (1927, Maurice Armand Mondet & Heinz Hanus & Arthur Göttlein, A) 422

Rasthaus der grausamen Puppen, Das/Locanda delle bambole crudeli, La (1967, Rolf Olsen, G/I) 10, 208, 223

Rat der Götter, Der (1950, Defa) **233,** 24, 86

Rätsel der roten Orchidee, Das (1961) **15,** 187, 222, 295, 410

Rätsel einer Nacht (1927) **283,** 386

Rätsel um Beate (1938, Johannes Meyer) 58, 131, 205, 334, 412

Rätsel von Bangalore, Das (1917) **216,** 219, 394

Ratten, Die (1921, Hanns Kobe) 158, 170, 191, 222

Ratten, Die (1955) **347,** 44, 85, 143, 175, 194, 222, 324

Rattenfänger von Hameln, Der (The Pied Piper of Hamelin, 1918) **121** & **407,** 68, 320, · 339 ?, 375

Raub der Mona Lisa, Der (1931, Geza von Bolvary) 104, 127, 129, 185, 303, 392

Raub der Sabinerinnen, Der (1928, Robert Land) 311

Raub der Sabinerinnen, Der (1936) **362,** 151, 158, 210

Raub der Sabinerinnen, Der (1954) **157,** 25, 26, 44, 164, 194, 375, 406

Räuberbande, Die (The Robber Band, 1928, Hans Behrendt) 164

Räuberbraut, Die (1916) **418,** 289

Raubfischer in Hellas (As the Sea Rages, 1959, Horst Hächler) 324

Raub in der Zentralbank (1925) *see* Grosse Gelegenheit, Die

Rausch (1919) **227,** 1, 202, 265, 355, 371

Rausch einer Nacht (1951, Eduard von Borsody) 24, 59, 149

Rauschgift (1932) *see* Weisse Dämon, Der

Razzia (1921, Wolfgang Neff) 108

Razzia (1947, Werner Klingler, Defa) 24, 85, 169, 188

Razzia in St. Pauli (1932, Werner Hochbaum) 23, 51, 122

Rebel, The *see* Rebell, Der

Rebel Flight to Cuba *see* Abschied von den Wolken

Rebell, Der (The Rebel, 1932) **31** & **380,** 23, 25, 179, 362, 389

Rebellenliebe (19 ?, Bruno Decarli ?) 219

Rechnung – eiskalt serviert, Die (1966, G/F) **15,** 256

Recht auf Liebe, Das (1929, Jacob & Luise Fleck) 5, 95

Recht auf Liebe, Das (1939, Joe Stöckel) 332, 407

Recht des Ungeborenen, Das (1928/29, Adolf Trotz) 42, 61, 179, 327

Recht zu leben, Das (1927, Robert Wohlmuth, A) 61, 350

Red Dawn *see* Morgenrot

Red Dragon *see* Geheimnis der drei Dschunken, Das

Refuge *see* Zuflucht

Refugees *see* Flüchtlinge

Regimentsmusik (1945) **293,** 143

Regimentstochter, Die (1928, Hans Behrendt) 117

Regimentstochter, Die (1933) *see* Tochter des Regiments, Die

Regimentstochter, Die (1953, A) **42**

Regina Amstetten (1954, Kurt Neumann) 138, 294, 389

Regine (1934, Erich Waschneck) 41, 174, 327, 383, 389, 421, 426

Regine (1956) **43,** 15, 48, 74, 105, 150, 194, 240

Regine, die Tragödie einer Frau (1927, Erich Waschneck) 24, 161, 219, 361

Reich mir die Hand, mein Leben/Mozart 1955, Karl Hartl, A) 240, 376

Reifende Jugend (1933) **110,** 102, 115, 149, 210, 220, 362, 368

Reifende Jugend (1955, Ulrich Erfurth) 220, 325, 340, 417

Reigen, Der (1920) **273,** 222, 224, 265, 394, 421

Reine Sünderin, Die (1918, Hubert Moest) 138

Reise in die Vergangenheit (1943, Hans H. Zerlett) 84, 153, 224, 237, 383

Reise ins Ehebett (1966, Joachim Hasler, Defa) 346

Reise ins Glück, Eine (1958, Wolfgang Schleif) 221, 371

Reise nach Marrakesch, Die (1949) **83,** 59, 66, 231, 389

Reise nach Tilsit, Die (1939) **137,** 102, 253, 351, 375, 421

Reise um die Erde in 80 Tagen, Die (1919) **273,** 338, 394

Reiter von Deutsch-Ostafrika, Die (1934, Herbert Selpin) 420

... reitet für Deutschland (1941) **293,** 33, 59, 246, 358

Reizende Familie, Eine/Danke, es geht mir gut (1945, Erich Waschneck) 85, 149, 430

Rembrandt (1942) **360,** 13, 21,

Rosel vom Schwarzwald, Die (1956, Rudolf Schündler) 223

Rose Monday see Rosenmontag

Rosen aus dem Süden (1925/26) **110,** 289

Rosen aus dem Süden (1934, Walter Janssen) 164, 174, 422

Rosen aus dem Süden (1934, Walter Janssen) 164, 174, 422

Rosen aus dem Süden (1954, Franz Antel) 111, 224

Rosen blühen auf dem Heidegrab (1952, Hans H. König) 102, 197

Rosen der Liebe (1949) see Liebling der Welt

Rosen, die der Sturm entblättert (1917, Curt Matull ?) 261

Rosen für Bettina (1956) **275,** 33, 63, 288, 357, 359, 413, 420

Rosen für den Staatsanwalt (1959) **358,** 12, 99, 120, 138, 145, 264, 279, 356

Rosen im Herbst/Effi Briest (1955, Rudolf Jugert) 58, 128, 138, 208, 217, 229, 294, 415

Rosen in Tirol (1940, Geza von Bolvary) 128, 136, 144, 150, 221, 349, 422

Rosenkavalier, Der (1926, A) **418,** 138

Rosenmontag/Offiziertragödie, Eine (Rose Monday, 1924, Rudolf Meinert) 406

Rosenmontag (Rose Monday, 1930) **360,** 41, 66, 150, 313, 329, 417, 421

Rosenmontag (Rose Monday, 1955) **33,** 47, 189

Rosen-Resli (1954) **302,** 73, 84, 114, 131, 181, 383

Roses for the Prosecutor see Rosen für den Staatsanwalt

Rose von Stambul, Die (1953, Karl Anton) 164, 220, 223, 329, 403

Rosl vom Traunsee, Die (1933) see Du bist entzückend, Rosemarie!

Rotation (1949, Defa) **358,** 253, 279

Rote, Die (1962 G/I) **182,** 109, 217, 256

Rote Hand, Die (1960) **245,** 168, 248

Rote Hexe, Die (1921, Friedrich Feher) 105

Rote Kreis, Der (1928, Friedrich Zelnik) 4, 361

Rote Kreis, Der (1959, Jürgen Roland) 222, 295, 410

Rote Lippen soll man küssen (1964) see Ganze Welt ist himmelblau, Die

Rote Maus, Die (1925, Rudolf Meinert) 305, 406

Rote Mühle, Die (1921) **36,** 1

Rote Mühle (1940, Jürgen von Alten) 128, 221, 229

Rote Mütze, Die (1937) see Heiratsschwindler

Rote Orchideen (1938, Nunzio Malasomma) 128, 165, 266, 334, 383

Rote Prinz, Der (1954, Hans Schott-Schöbinger, A) 296

Rote Rausch, Der (1962, Wolfgang Schleif) 40, 187, 234

Rote Reiter, Der (1923, Franz W. Koebner) 11, 361

Rote Reiter, Der (1935, Rolf Randolf) 137, 165, 280

Rote Rosen, rote Lippen, roter Wein (1953, Paul Martin) 25, 58, 429

Rothausgasse, Die (1927/28) **273,** 111, 161, 284

Rothschilds, Die (1940, Erich Waschneck) 18, 102, 155 iii, 288, 327

Rot ist die Liebe (1957, Karl Hartl) 40, 229

Royal Scandal see Hose, Die

Rübezahls Hochzeit (1916) **121** & **407,** 320

Rückblick aus dem Jahre 3000 (1920/21) **273** ?

Rückkehr der Truppen von der Frühjahrsparade, Die (1900) **249**

Ruf, Der (1949) **19,** 198

Ruf an das Gewissen/Ruf des Gewissens (1945, Karl Anton) 66, 67, 131, 153, 154

Ruf aus dem Aether (1951) **189** & **275**

Ruf der Berge (1954, Eduard Wieser, A/Switz. doc.) 23

Ruf der Wälder (1965, Franz Antel, A) 168, 240

Ruf der Wildgänse, Der (1961, Hans Heinrich, A) 21, 143, 166

Ruf des Gewissens (1945) see Ruf an das Gewissen

Ruf des Nordens (1929, Nunzio Malasomma; see also Polarstürme 1934) 42, 380, 422

Ruf des Schicksals, Der (1922, Johannes Guter) 198

Ruhiges Heim mit Küchenbenutzung (1929, Carl Wilhelm) 90, 91

Rummelplatz der Liebe (1954, Kurt Neumann) 175, 328, 415

Rund um eine Million (1933, Max Neufeld, G/F) 111, 165

Rutschbahn (1928) **83,** 115, 150, 391

S

Sabine und der Zufall (1940) see Mein Mann darf es nicht wissen

Sabine und die 100 Männer (1960) **370,** 40, 44, 164, 223

Sache August Schulze, Die (1931) see Kinder vor Gericht

Sache mit Schorrsiegel, Die (1927/28, Jaap Speyer) 95, 123, 224

Sache mit Styx, Die (1942, Karl Anton) 42, 47, 200, 224

Safari Diamants (1966) see Für eine Handvoll Diamanten

Sag' die Wahrheit (1945, Helmut Weiss, unfinished) 96, 102, 210, 315

Sag' die Wahrheit (1946, Helmut Weiss) 44, 85, 111, 430

Sag' endlich ja (1945, Helmut Weiss, unfinished) 100, 173, 210, 231

Sag ja, Mutti (1958) see Singenden Engel von Tirol, Die

Sag' mir, wer Du bist (1933, Georg Jacoby) 128, 133, 200, 210

Saison in Kairo (1933) **338,** 108, 150, 156, 255, 303, 313, 357, 375

Saison in Oberbayern (1956) see Hotel Allotria

Saison in Salzburg (1952, Ernst Marischka, A) 240, 329

Salem Aleikum (1959, Geza von Cziffra) 378, 422

Salome (1902) **249**

Salome (1922) **418,** 250

Schicksal (1942, Geza von Bolvary) 115, 154, 247, 331
Schicksal am Berg (1950, Ernst Hess) 203
Schicksal am Lenkrad (1953, Aldo Vergano, A) 86
Schicksal am Strom (1944, Heinz Paul) 375
Schicksal aus zweiter Hand (1949) **358**, 39, 102, 162, 288, 422, 429
Schicksal der Renate Langen, Das/Sein letzter Brief (1931, Rudolf Walther-Fein) 1, 54, 153, 159
Schicksal des Leutnant Thomas Glahn, Das (1937) *see* Pan
Schicksal einer Nacht, Das (1927, Erich Schönfelder) 174, 219, 321
Schicksal einer schönen Frau, Das/Madame Blaubart (1932, Conrad Wiene, G/A) 58, 189
Schicksal in Ketten (1946, Eduard Hoesch, A) 8
Schiff der verlorenen Menschen, Das (1929, Maurice Tourneur) 69, 95, 198, 353
Schiff in Not (1925, Fred Sauer) 111, 173, 327
Schiff in Not SOS (1928, Carmine Gallone) 24, 133
Schiff ohne Hafen, Das/Gespensterschiff, Das (1932) **283**, 183
Schimmelkrieg in der Holledau, Der (1937, Alois Johannes Lippl) 98, 102, 245, 422
Schimmelreiter, Der (1934) **269**, 155 ii, 162, 417, 421, 431
Schinderhannes (1927) **31**, 102, 161, 222, 295, 361
Schinderhannes, Der (1958), **182**, 84, 175, 222, 256, 324
Schirm mit dem Schwan, Der (1915) **110**, 2, 249, 289, 418
Schlacht von Bademünde, Die (1921, Philipp Lothar Mayring) 2, 174, 321
Schlafwagenkontrolleur, Der (1935) **83**, 5, 142, 221, 335
Schlag auf Schlag (1959, Geza von Cziffra) 12, 47
Schlagende Wetter (1923) **130**, 133, 142, 179, 191
Schlagerparade (1953, Erik Ode) 13, 120, 144, 376

Schlagerraketen 1960, Erik Ode) 267
Schlangengrube und das Pendel, Die (The Blood Demon, 1967) **302**, 73
Schleiertänzerin, Die (1929, M. C. Burguet) 47
Schlemihl, Der (1931, Max Nosseck) 38, 211, 327, 422
Schleppzug M 17 (1933) **115**
Schloss, Das (1968, Rudolf Nolte) 325
Schlösser und Katen (1957, Defa) **233**, 61, 78, 119, 316
Schloss Gripsholm (1963) **157**, 13, 120, 226, 229, 234, 376
Schlossherr von Hohenstein, Der (19 ?, ?) 273
Schloss Hubertus (1934, Hans Deppe) 305, 327
Schloss Hubertus (1954, Helmut Weiss) 58, 84, 195, 305
Schloss im Süden, Das (1933, Geza von Bolvary) 128, 133, 185, 200, 403
Schloss in Flandern, Das (1936, Geza von Bolvary) 5, 41, 42, 82, 128, 138, 412
Schloss in Tirol, Das (1957, Geza von Radvanyi) 8, 37, 194, 253
Schloss Vogelöd (Vögelod Castle, 1921) **257**, 138, 244, 383, 392, 403, 406, 421
Schloss Vogelöd (Vögelod Castle, 1936, Max Obal) 131, 327
Schlucht des Todes, Die/Pampasreiter (1923, Luciano Albertini & Francis A. Bertoni) 292
Schlussakkord (1936) **345**, 18, 33, 58, 224, 245, 288
Schlussakkord (1960) **218**, 200
Schmetterlingsschlacht, Die (1924, Franz Eckstein) 265, 321, 338
Schmied von St. Bartolomä, Der (1955, Max Michel) 195, 296
Schmugglerbraut von Malorca, Die (1929, Hans Behrendt) 1, 24, 173
Schmutziger Engel (1958) **401**, 93, 266, 279, 340
Schneeschuhbanditen (1928, Uwe Jens Krafft) 305
Schneewittchen und die sieben Gaukler (1962, G/Switz) **157**, 120
Schneider Wibbel (1931) **149**,

134, 329
Schneider Wibbel (1939) **200**, 24, 26, 102, 182, 190, 229, 288, 327
Schneller als der Tod (1925) **283**
Schöne Abenteuer, Das (1924, Manfred Noa) 4, 5,
Schöne Abenteuer, Das (1932) **338**, 1, 18, 131, 153, 258, 290, 321, 357, 403
Schöne Abenteuer, Das (1959) **157**, 9, 126, 128, 150, 263, 291
Schöne Fräulein Schragg, Das (1937, Hans Deppe) 114, 327, 420, 421
Schöne Lügnerin, Die (1959, G/F) **7**, 84, 128, 232, 333, 378
Schöne Lurette, Die (1960, Gottfried Kolditz, Defa) 140
Schöne Mädel, Das (1922) **230**
Schöne Meisterin, Die (1956, Rudolf Schündler) 223
Schöne Müllerin, Die (1954) **218**, 96, 102, 164, 264
Schönen Tage von Aranjuez, Die (1933, Johannes Meyer) 24, 129, 148, 149, 218, 375
Schöner Tag, Ein (1943, Philipp Lothar Mayring) 13, 229
Schöne Tölzerin, Die (1952, Richard Häussler) 85, 305, 331
Schönheitsfleckchen, Das (1936, Rolf Hansen) 58, 110, 210, 218
Schön ist die Liebe am Königssee (1960, Hans Albin) 341
Schön ist die Manöverzeit/Kartoffelsupp, Kartoffelsupp (1931, Erich Schönfelder) 422
Schön ist die Welt (1957, Geza von Bolvary) 399
Schön ist es, verliebt zu sein! (1934, Walter Janssen) 203, 221, 311, 375
Schön ist jeder Tag, den Du mir schenkst, Marie Louise/Sonne geht auf, Die (1933, Willy Reiber) 18, 179, 375
Schön muss man sein (1951, Akos von Rathony) 108. 207, 232, 264, 270, 422, 430
Schönste Frau der Welt, Die

berg (1923)
Student von Prag, Der (1913) **318,** 320, 339, 343, 407
Student von Prag, Der (1926) **113,** 204, 343, 394, 406
Student von Prag, Der (1935) **312,** 224, 231, 253, 406, 416, 426
Stukas (1941) **310,** 141, 172, 294, 420, 421
Stumme Gast, Der (1945) **43,** 18, 62, 85
Stumme von Portici, Die (1922, Arthur Günsberg) 421
Stumme Zeuge, Der (19 ?) **283**
Stunde der Entscheidung see Semmelweis – Retter der Mütter
Stunde der Versuchung, Die (1936) **407,** 23, 111, 142, 190, 224
Stunde, die Du glücklich bist, Die (1961, Rudolf Jugert) 93, 128, 154, 217
Stunde Glück, Eine (1930) **68,** 132
Sturm auf drei Herzen (1929, Wolfgang Neff) 47
Stürme der Leidenschaft (1931) **347,** 151, 159, 170, 309, 412
Stürme über dem Montblanc (Avalanche, 1930) **94,** 6, 13, 64, 183, 306, 331, 417
Sturmflut (1917, Willy Zeyn) 79
Sturmflut (1927, Willy Reiber) 416
Sturm im Wasserglas (1931) see Blumenfrau von Lindenau, Die
Sturm im Wasserglas (1960) **19,** 12, 85, 226
Stürmisch die Nacht (1930, Curt Blachnitzki, G/A) 123
Stützen der Gesellschaft (1935) **345,** 76, 115, 189, 334
Suche nach dem wunderbunten Vögelchen, Die (1964, Rolf Losansky, Defa) 251
Suchende Seele, Die (1923, Rudolf Biebrach) 412
Such Is Life see So ist das Leben (1924)
Suchkind 312 (1955, Gustav Machaty) 84, 98
Südliche Nächte (1953) **362,** 102, 120, 253, 359
Suffragetten, Die/Semmeretsdamen (1913, Urban Gad,

G/D) 265, 339
Sumpf und Moral (1925, Rudolf Walter-Fein) 68, 350
Sumurun (1908) **300,** 339
Sumurun (1912, ?) 320
Sumurun (One Arabian Night, 1920) **227,** 150, 202, 219, 261, 355, 375, 407
Sünde der Helga Arndt, Die (1916) **242,** 243
Sünde der Lissy Krafft, Die (1930, F. W. Andersen) 47, 61
Sündenbabel (1925, Constantin J. David) 61, 338
Sündenbock, Der (1940, Hans Deppe) 197, 203
Sünden der Eltern (1919) **83**
Sünden der Väter, Die/Faedrenes Synd (1911, Urban Gad, G/D) 4, 265, 339
Sünderin, Die (The Sinner, 1951) **104,** 111, 193, 231, 247, 397
Sündige Dorf, Das (1940, Joe Stöckel) 6
Sündige Dorf, Das (1954, Ferdinand Dörfler) 229, 253
Sündige Grenze (1951) **362,** 40, 44, 267
Sündige Haus, Das (1950) see Verführte Jugend
Sündige Hof, Der/Lona und ihr Knecht (1933, Franz Osten) 295
Sündige Mütter (1919) **273,** 1, 79, 338, 394
Sündig und süss (1929, Carl Lamac) 147, 174, 199, 270
Sunken, The see Gesunkenen, Die
Susanne Jakobäa Krafftin (1950, Heinz Galetzki) 399, 412, 413
Susanne im Bade (1936, Jürgen von Alten) 9, 358
Susanne macht Ordnung (1930, Eugen Thiele) 134
Süsse Leben des Grafen Bobby, Das (1962, Geza von Cziffra, A) 422
Süsse Mädel, Das (1926, Manfred Noa) 406
Süsses Geheimnis, Ein (1931, Friedrich Zelnik) 76
Süssesten Früchte, Die (1954, Franz Antel) 341
Svengali (1927, Gennaro Righelli) 127, 407
Swan Lake see Schwanensee
Sylvester (New Year's Eve,

1923) **282,** 142, 178, 191, 244, 339
Sylvia und ihr Chauffeur (1935) see Walzer um den Stephansturm, Ein
Symphonie der Berge (1930) see Heiligen drei Brunnen, Die
Symphonie der Liebe/Ekstase (1932/34, Gustav Machaty, A/Cz) 23, 186
Symphonie eines Lebens (1942, Hans Bertram) 102, 156, 289
Symphonie in Gold (1956, Franz Antel, A) 112
Symphonie Wien (1952, Albert Quendlinger, A) 65
System des Doktor Ther und Professor Feder, Das (1920) **273**

T
Tabula rasa – Fünf, die töten (1960) see An einem Freitag um halb zwölf
Tag, der nie zu Ende geht, Ein (1959, Franz Peter Wirth) 97, 128, 150, 208, 217, 248
Tag der Rosen im August... da hat die Garde fortgemusst, Ein (1927) **230,** 1, 117, 421
Tagebuch Colins, Das (19 ?, ?) 83
Tagebuch der Baronin W., Das (1935) see Selige Exzellenz, Die
Tagebuch des Dr. Hartl, Das (1921) **216**
Tagebuch einer Kokotte (1928 /29, Constantin J. David) 149, 199, 417
Tagebuch einer Verliebten (Diary of a Married Woman, 1953) **19,** 100, 246, 324
Tagebuch einer Verlorenen, Das (1918) **273,** 338, 394
Tagebuch einer Verlorenen (Diary of a Lost Girl, 1929) **275,** 6, 46, 117, 118, 250, 295, 330
Tagebuch eines Matrosen, Das (1940) see Robinson, Ein
Tagebuch meiner Frau, Das (1920, ?) 1
Tag ist schöner als der andere, Ein (1969) **157**
Tag nach der Scheidung, Der (1938) **395,** 24, 131, 153, 307, 352, 389

(1927)

Unmensch, Der (1919, A) **57,** 280 ,

Unmögliche Frau, Die (1936, Johannes Meyer) 111, 135, 149, 416

Unmögliche Herr Pitt, Der (1938) **283,** 174

Unmögliche Liebe/Vera Holgk und ihre Töchter (1932, Erich Waschneck) 153, 253, 265, 429

Unmögliche Mädchen, Das (1951) *see* Fräulein Bimbi

Unmoral (1928, Willi Wolff) 5, 117, 391

Unmoralischen, Die (1964, Pierre Kast, G/I/F) 168, 277

Unruhige Nacht (1958, Falk Harnack) 24, 97, 154, 234, 256, 279, 357, 415

Unruhigen Mädchen, Die (1938, Geza von Bolvary, A) 41, 91, 221, 258

Unschuld (1929, Robert Land) 61, 258

Unschuld in Nöten (1951) *see* Mädchen aus der Konfektion, Das

Unschuld vom Lande, Die (1933) **36,** 91, 134, 311

Unschuld vom Lande, Die (1957, Rudolf Schündler) 44, 221

Unser Boss ist eine Dame/ Operazione San Gennaro (1966, Dino Risi, G/I/F) 3, 28

Unser Doktor ist der beste (1969, Harald Vock) 10, 208

Unsere kleine Frau (1938) **395,** 5, 91, 174, 185, 258

Unsere tollen Nichten (1963, Rolf Olsen, A) 164, 223

Unsere tollen Tanten in der Südsee (1964, Rolf Olsen, A) 223

Unser Fräulein Doktor (1940) **89,** 173

Unser Haus in Kamerun (1961) **401,** 106, 196, 223, 352, 410

Unser kleine Junge (1941, Boleslav Barlog) 429

Unser Mittwoch Abend (1948) **203,** 172, 266

Unser täglich Brot (1925, Constantin J. David) 138, 179

Unser täglich Brot (1949, Defa) **77,** 18, 86, 122

Unser Wunderland bei Nacht (Mainly for Men, 1959, Jürgen Roland & Richard Elsner & Hans Heinrich) 253, 359

Uns gefällt die Welt (1956) **362,** 331, 399

Unsichtbare, Der (1963, Raphael Nussbaum) 63, 363

Unsichtbare Front, Die (1932) **83,** 66, 137, 164, 224, 253, 352, 392

Unsichtbare Gegner (1933, Rudolf Katscher, A) 47, 138, 161, 185, 225, 241, 336, 359

Unsichtbaren Krallen des Dr. Mabuse, Die (1962) **302,** 44, 73, 279

Unsichtbarer geht durch die Stadt, Ein/Mein ist die Welt (1933) **283,** 221

Unsterbliche Antlitz, Das (1947, Geza von Cziffra, A) 100, 163, 246

Unsterbliche Geliebte (1951) **137,** 70, 114, 375, 429

Unsterbliche Herz, Das (1939) **137,** 115, 149, 246, 253, 351, 375, 406, 407, 421

Unsterbliche Lump, Der (1930) **387,** 111, 133, 149, 150, 156, 164, 313, 327, 357

Unsterbliche Lump, Der (1953) **293,** 37, 42, 357

Unsterbliche Melodien (1935, Heinz Paul, A) 349

Unsterblicher Walzer (1939, E. W. Emo) 8, 164, 246, 331

Unsterbliches Lied, Das (1934, Hans Marr) 305, 331

Unter achzehn (1957) *see* Noch minderjährig

Unter Ausschluss der Oeffentlichkeit (1926/27, Conrad Wiene) 61, 68, 204, 239, 375

Unter Ausschluss der Oeffentlichkeit (1937) **407,** 1, 102, 142, 280, 383, 421

Unter Aufschluss der Oeffentlichkeit (1961, Harald Philipp) 24, 44, 84, 93, 195, 279

Unter den Brücken (1945) **182,** 84, 193, 194, 267, 294

Unter den Sternen von Capri (1953, Otto Linnekogel) 151

Unter den tausend Laternen (1952) **89,** 62, 232, 362

Unter der Laterne (1928) **212,** 131, 142, 417

Unter der schwarzen Sturmfahne (1933, Rolf von Sonjevski-Jamrowski) 76

Unter falscher Flagge (1932, Johannes Meyer) 23, 111, 183, 224

Unter Geiern (1964, G/I/F/ Yug) **401,** 223, 343, 354, 410

Unter Geschäftsaufsicht (1932) *see* Wehe, wenn er losgelassen

Unter heissem Himmel (1936) **387,** 4, 62, 150, 231, 247, 313, 403

Unter heisser Sonne (Under a Hot Sun, 1916) **283**

Unternehmen Edelweiss (1954, Heinz Paul) 409

Unternehmen Michael (1937) **310,** 9, 33, 115, 155 iii, 172, 313, 412, 417, 420

Unternehmen Schlafsack (1955) **293,** 25, 37, 102, 245, 264, 378, 416

Untertan, Der (The Underdog, 1951, Defa) **358,** 18, 80, 122, 279, 421

Until Hell Is Frozen *see* Teufel spielte Balalaika, Der

Unüberwindliche, Der (1928, Max Obal) 149, 339

Unus, der Weg in die Welt (1921) **283**

Unvergängliches Licht (1951) **293,** 105, 153, 385

Unverstandene Frau, Eine (1924) *see* Nju

Unvollkommene Ehe, Die (1959, A) **362,** 24, 144, 420, 414

Unvollkommene Liebe, Die (1940, Erich Waschneck) 102, 108, 131, 172, 190, 267

Unwelcome Children *see* Kreuzzug des Weibes

Unwiderstehliche, Der (1937, Geza von Bolvary) 41, 151, 270, 352

Uriel Acosta (1921, Ernst Wendt) 156

Urlaub auf Ehrenwort (1937) **310,** 9, 62, 131, 155 iii, 179, 294, 313

Urlaub auf Ehrenwort (1955) **218,** 172, 234, 264, 375,

287

407, 429

Wenn die Toten erwachen (19 ?) **230**

Wenn Du eine Schwiegermutter hast (1937, Joe Stöckel) 76, 311

Wenn Du eine Tante hast (1925) **36, 61**

Wenn Du einmal Dein Herz verschenkst (1929, Johannes Güter) 139, 329, 357, 403

Wenn Du noch eine Heimat hast (1929, Siegfried Philippi) 179

Wenn Du noch eine Mutter hast/Zirkus Brown (1924, Desider Kertesz, A) 95

Wenn Du noch eine Mutter hast..../Licht der Liebe, Das (1954) **362,** 15, 247, 329, 414

Wenn Du zu mir hälst... (1962, Hans-Erich Korbschmitt, Defa) 72

Wenn eine Frau liebt (1950) **218,** 47, 144, 201, 234, 417

Wenn ein Mädel Hochzeit macht (1934) **36,** 47, 85, 91

Wenn ein Weib den Weg verliert (1927) see Café Electric

Wenn Frauen lieben und hassen (1917, Jaap Speyer) 204

Wenn Frauen schweigen (1937, Fritz Kirchhoff) 26, 144

Wenn Frauen schwindeln/Europas neue Musikparade (1957, Paul Martin) 26, 223

Wenn ich Chef wäre (1962) **286**

Wenn ich einmal der Herrgott wär (1954, Anton Kutter, G/A) 112

Wenn ich König wär! (1934, J. A. Hübler-Kahla) 165, 200, 406

Wenn Ludwig ins Manöver zieht (1967, Werner Jacobs) 40, 101, 341, 343, 423

Wenn Männer schwindeln/Taxi-Gattin (1950) **36**

Wenn Männer verreisen (1939, Georg Zoch) 5

Wenn Menschen irren (1926, Otz Ollen) 199

Wenn Menschen reif zur Liebe werden (19 ?) **11**

Wenn Menschen reif zur Liebe werden (1927, Jacob & Luise Fleck) 179

Wenn Poldi ins Manöver zieht

/Manöverzwilling (1956, Hans Quest, A) 112

Wenn süss das Mondlicht auf den Hügeln schläft (1969) **218,** 154

Wenn vier dasselbe tun (1917) **227,** 170, 274

Wenn wir alle Engel wären (1936) **110,** 210, 315

Wenn wir alle Engel wären (1956) **229,** 26, 40, 102, 128, 194, 195, 232, 288, 309, 352

Wer bist Du den ich liebe? (1949, Geza von Bolvary) 231, 280, 409

Wer das Scheiden hat erfunden (1927/28, Wolfgang Neff) 1, 4

Wer die Heimat liebt (1957) see Heilige Erbe, Das

Werft zum grauen Hecht, Die (1935) **424,** 26, 162, 409

Wer fuhr den grauen Ford? (1950, Paul Pfeiffer) 264, 412

Wer hat Robby gesehen? (1929/30, Rolf Randolf) 134

Wer küsst Madeleine? (1939, Victor Janson) 59, 102, 332

Wer nimmt die Liebe ernst? (1931) **89,** 56, 173, 199

Wer wagt – gewinnt!/Bezauberndes Fräulein (1935, Walter Janssen) 315

Wer wird den weinen, wenn man auseinandergeht (1929) **83,** 164, 253

Wer wirft den ersten Stein? (1922, Arthur Günsburg) 421

Wer wirft den ersten Stein (1927, Erik Eriksen) 117

Westfront 1918/Vier von der Infanterie (1930) **275,** 67, 179, 250, 260, 391, 403

West-östliche Hochzeit (1950) see Auftrag Höglers, Der

Wetterleuchten (1924/25, Rudolf Walther-Fein) 68

Wetterleuchten am Dachstein/Herrin vom Salzerhof, Die (1953, Anton Kutter, A) 195

Wetterleuchten um Barbara (1941, Werner Klingler) 6, 163, 330, 420

Wetterleuchten um Maria (1957) **380,** 25, 305, 417

Wetterwart, Der (1923) **110,** 54, 361

When Strangers Meet see Einer frisst den andern

Whisky, Wodka, Wienerin (1959) see Redenz-vous in Wien

Whitechapel (1921) **79,** 142

White Frenzy, The see Weisse Rausch, Der

White Hell of Pitz Palü, The see Weisse Hölle von Piz Palü, Die

Whither Germany? see Kuhle Wampe

Wie bliebe ich jung und schön (1926, Wolfgang Neff) 68, 134, 350

Whom the Gods Wish To Destroy see Nibelungen, Die (1966/67)

Wie der Hase läuft (1937) **36,** 98, 412

Wie d'Warret würkt (1933, Lesch, Switz) 45

Who Wants To Sleep see Liebeskarussell, Das

Wie der Sturmwind (The Night of the Storm, 1957, Falk Harnack) 24, 44, 63, 277

Wie ein Dieb in der Nacht/Herzensdieb, Der (1945, Hans Thimig) 329, 371

Wie einst im Mai (1926, Willi Wolff) 151, 356

Wie einst im Mai (1937, Richard Schneider-Edenkoben) 40, 412, 422

...wie einst Lili Marlen (1956) **395,** 131

Wiegenlied (1908, Friedrich Porten) 249, 289

Wie heirate ich meinen Chef (1927, Erich Schönfelder) 284, 392

Wie kommt ein so reizendes Mädchen wie Sie zu diesem Gewerbe? (1969) see How Did A Nice Girl Like You Get into This Business?

Wie konntest Du, Veronika? (1940, Milo Habich) 85, 135, 210, 288, 311

Wien – Berlin (1926) **360,** 117

Wien, Du Stadt der Lieder (1930) **273,** 24

Wien, Du Stadt meiner Träume (1957, A) **104,** 9, 96, 164

Wiener Blut (1942) **104,** 35, 81, 108, 149, 221, 329

Wiener Fiakerlied (1937) see

Zwei Matrosen auf der Alm (1957, Peter Hamel) 266

Zwei Menschen (1930, Erich Waschneck) 13, 91, 111, 183, 224

Zwei Menschen (1952, Paul May) 409, 429

Zwei Mütter (1957, Defa) **32**

Zwei rote Rosen (1928, Robert Land) 131, 151, 211

Zweite Gleis, Das (1962, Defa) **209,** 50

Zweite Leben, Das (1916, ?, A) 198

Zweite Leben, Das (1954, Victor Vicas, G/F) 109, 234, 415

Zweite Schuss, Der (1923, Maurice Krol) 68

Zweite Schuss, Der (1943, Martin Fric) 179

Zwei und die Dame, Die (1925, Alwin Neuss) 123

Zwei unterm Himmelszelt (1927, Johannes Guter) 65, 102, 151, 355

Zwei unter Millionen (1961, Victor Vicas) 120, 128, 207

Zwei vom Südexpress, Die (1932, Robert Wohlmuth) 51, 180, 412

Zwei Welten/Two Worlds (1930, G/GB) **79,** 179, 183

Zwei Welten (1940) **129**

Zwei Whisky und ein Sofa (1963, Günter Gräwert) 126, 324

Zwielicht (1940, Rudolf van der Noss) 294, 407

Zwillinge vom Zillertal, Die (1957) **302,** 73, 99, 112, 341

Zwischen Abend und Morgen/Spuk einer Nacht, Der (1923) **312,** 204, 295, 403

Zwischen den Eltern (1938, Hans Hinrich) 108, 183

Zwischen Gestern und Morgen (1947) **43,** 9, 33, 85, 150, 193, 200, 238, 288, 330, 412

Zwischen Glück und Krone (1959, Rudolf Schündler) 112

Zwischen Hamburg und Haiti (1940, Erich Waschneck) 18, 85, 102, 123, 194, 327

Zwischen Himmel und Erde (1942) **43,** 18, 85, 101, 149, 204

Zwischen Himmel und Hölle/Liebe lässt sich nicht erzwingen (1934, Franz Seitz) 163, 190, 412

Zwischenlandung in Paris (1955, Jean Dréville, G/F) 15, 40, 266, 315

Zwischen Liebe und Pflicht

(1928) *see* Schöpfer, Der

Zwischen Nacht und Morgen/Dirnentragödie (1931) **212,** 23, 123, 142, 161, 421

Zwischen Nacht und Morgen/Augen der Liebe (1944, Alfred Braun)' 62, 102, 137, 210, 407, 429

Zwischen Shanghai und St. Pauli (1962, Wolfgang Schleif, G/I) 17, 106, 296

Zwischen Strom und Steppe/Pusztaliebe (1938, Geza von Bolvary) 41, 143, 163

Zwischen Zeit und Ewigkeit (Between Time and Eternity, 1956) **293,** 33, 47. 277

Zwischen zwei Herzen (1934, Herbert Selpin) 42, 128, 149, 219, 383, 389

Zwölf Herzen für Charly (1949, Fritz Andelfinger) 98, 108

12 Mädchen und ein Mann (1959, Hans Quest, A) 128

12 Minuten nach 12 (1939, Johannes Guter) 62, 149, 294

12 Stunden Angst (1960, Geza von Radvanyi, G/F) 109, 248

Zyankali (1948, Max Neufeld, A) 8, 329

Alexandra Kluge in ABSCHIED VON GESTERN